Look,
I Made a Hat

Stephen Sondheim

Look, I Made a Hat

Collected Lyrics (1981-2011)
with Attendant Comments,
Amplifications, Dogmas,
Harangues, Digressions,
Anecdotes and
Miscellany

Alfred A. Knopf ⚞ New York 2011

This Is a Borzoi Book
Published by Alfred A. Knopf

Copyright © 2011 by Stephen Sondheim

www.aaknopf.com

Knopf, Borzoi Books, and the colophon are registered trademarks
of Random House, Inc.

Library of Congress Cataloging-in-Publication Data
Sondheim, Stephen.
[Songs. Texts. Selections]
Look, I made a hat : collected lyrics (1981–2011) with attendant
comments, amplifications, dogmas, harangues, digressions, anecdotes
and miscellany / by Stephen Sondheim.—1st ed.
p.   cm.
Includes bibliographical references and index.
ISBN 978-0-307-59341-2
1. Musicals—Excerpts—Librettos.   2. Songs—Texts.   I. Title.
ML54.6.S69S66 2011
782.1'40268—dc22   2011014604

Jacket design by Carol Devine Carson

Manufactured in the United States of America
First Edition

Once, in China, the writer and director Anthony Minghella came upon a street artist working randomly on a pavement picture. "What are you doing?" Minghella asked. "Taking a line for a walk," the artist replied. He was quoting the Swiss painter Paul Klee.

This book is dedicated to everyone who has taken a line for a walk.

Contents

Note to the Reader

This is the second and final installment of a two-volume compendium of my lyrics, the first of which, called *Finishing the Hat*, is a collection of those I wrote between 1954 and 1981, and was published in 2010. If you haven't read it, it might be wise to do so before you read this one. In its Note to the Reader I explained the reason for certain elisions, omissions and discrepancies, all of which are relevant to this volume as well, and in its Introduction I laid down some personal ground rules about rhyme, content, form, economy, detail, simplicity and other basics that I will be treating herein as assumed truths.

Three other things to note: The cover of this book says *Collected Lyrics (1981–2011)*, but at the request of friends I'm throwing in a sprinkling of miscellany preceding those dates.

At times I'll refer to *Finishing the Hat* as "volume one," just for variety.

As in the previous volume, I'll be using "he" and "his" to signify both men and women, unless I'm referring to a particular person. Politically incorrect though it may be, it relieves some strenuousness for both the writer and the reader.

Cast of Characters

(In order of appearance)

Most of the lyricists and composers referred to in the following pages hail from musicals written before the 1980s. For those readers to whom some of these writers may be unfamiliar, let me offer this glossary of names and musical theater credits (a number of them were playwrights, poets and novelists as well), accompanied by some of their more well-known shows (in italics) and theater songs (in quotation marks), thus avoiding the bumpy intrusions of having to identify them as they pop up in the commentaries.

Oscar Hammerstein II (1895–1960)
lyricist, librettist
Show Boat; Oklahoma!; Carousel; The King and I
"Ol' Man River," "All the Things You Are," "Some Enchanted Evening"

Burt Shevelove (1915–1982)
lyricist, librettist
Small Wonder; A Funny Thing Happened on the Way to the Forum; The Frogs
"Looking for a Bluebird," "Think Beautiful Thoughts," "I'm in Trouble"

Leonard Bernstein (1918–1990)
composer, occasional lyricist
On the Town; West Side Story; Candide
"New York, New York," "Maria," "Make Our Garden Grow"

Lillian Hellman (1905–1984)
playwright, occasional librettist and lyricist
Candide
"Eldorado"

Frank Loesser (1910–1969)
lyricist, composer
Where's Charley?; Guys and Dolls; The Most Happy Fella
"Once in Love with Amy," "Luck, Be a Lady Tonight," "Standing on the Corner"

Alan Jay Lerner (1918–1986)
lyricist, librettist
Brigadoon; My Fair Lady; On a Clear Day You Can See Forever
"I Could Have Danced All Night," "On a Clear Day You Can See Forever," "If Ever I Would Leave You"

Richard Rodgers (1902–1979)
composer, occasional lyricist
On Your Toes; The Boys from Syracuse; South Pacific
"My Funny Valentine," "Bewitched, Bothered and Bewildered," "If I Loved You"

E. Y. Harburg (1896–1981)
lyricist, co-librettist
Walk a Little Faster; Life Begins at 8:40; Finian's Rainbow
"Fun to Be Fooled," "Down With Love," "How Are Things in Glocca Morra?"

Sheldon Harnick (b. 1924)
lyricist
Tenderloin; The Apple Tree; She Loves Me
"Politics and Poker," "Sunrise, Sunset," "Ice Cream"

Jerry Bock (1928–2010)
composer, lyricist
Fiorello!; Fiddler on the Roof; The Rothschilds
"If I Were a Rich Man," "When Did I Fall in Love?," "She Loves Me"

Manos Hadjidakis (1925–1994)
composer
Illya Darling
"Never on Sunday," "Piraeus, My Love"

Michael Flanders (1922–1975)
lyricist, librettist
At the Drop of a Hat; At the Drop of Another Hat
"Have Some Madeira, M'Dear," "The Gnu"

Donald Swann (1923–1994)
composer
At the Drop of a Hat; At the Drop of Another Hat
"The Youth of the Heart," "The Gas-Man Cometh"

Mary Rodgers (b. 1931)
composer
Once Upon a Mattress; The Mad Show; Working
"Happily Ever After," "The Boy From"

William Goldman (b. 1931)
novelist, playwright, screenwriter, occasional lyricist
A Family Affair; Butch Cassidy and the Sundance Kid; The Princess Bride
"There's a Room in My House," "Anything for You"

Cole Porter (1891–1964)
lyricist, composer
Anything Goes; DuBarry Was a Lady; Kiss Me, Kate
"Night and Day," "I Get a Kick Out of You," "Begin the Beguine"

Harold Arlen (1905–1986)
composer, occasional lyricist
Bloomer Girl; St. Louis Woman; House of Flowers
"The Eagle and Me," "Any Place I Hang My Hat Is Home," "Sleepin' Bee"

DuBose Heyward (1885–1940)
lyricist, librettist, playwright
Porgy and Bess
"Summertime," "My Man's Gone Now," "I Loves You, Porgy"

Richard Wilbur (b. 1921)
poet, lyricist
Candide
"Glitter and Be Gay," "Make Our Garden Grow"

Howard Dietz (1896–1983)
lyricist
The Little Show; At Home Abroad; The Band Wagon
"Dancing in the Dark," "You and the Night and the Music," "Haunted Heart"

P. G. Wodehouse (1881–1975)
novelist, playwright, librettist, lyricist
Rosalie; Oh, Boy; Leave it to Jane
"Bill," "Very Good Eddie," "Oh, Lady, Lady!"

Leo Robin (1900–1984)
lyricist
By the Way; Hello Yourself; Gentlemen Prefer Blondes
"Thanks for the Memory," "Louise," "Diamonds Are a Girl's Best Friend"

Johnny Mercer (1909–1976)
lyricist, composer
St. Louis Woman; Texas, Li'l Darlin'; Top Banana
"Jeepers Creepers," "Any Place I Hang My Hat is Home," "I Wonder What Became of Me"

John La Touche (1914–1956)
lyricist
Candide; The Golden Apple; Banjo Eyes
"Takin' a Chance on Love," "Cabin in the Sky," "Lazy Afternoon"

Hugh Martin (1914–2011)
lyricist, composer
Meet Me in St. Louis; Best Foot Forward; Look Ma, I'm Dancin'!
"The Trolley Song," "The Boy Next Door," "Gotta Dance"

Meredith Willson (1902–1984)
lyricist, composer
The Music Man; The Unsinkable Molly Brown; Here's Love

"Till There Was You," "Pick-a-Little, Talk-a-Little,"
"Seventy-Six Trombones"

Carolyn Leigh (1926–1983)
lyricist
Peter Pan; Little Me; How Now, Dow Jones
"I Won't Grow Up," "On the Other Side of the
Tracks," "Real Live Girl"

Jule Styne (1905–1994)
composer
High Button Shoes; Gypsy; Funny Girl
"I Still Get Jealous," "Everything's Coming Up Roses,"
"People"

Kurt Weill (1900–1950)
composer
*The Threepenny Opera; Lady in the Dark; One Touch of
Venus*
"Ballad of Mack the Knife," "Speak Low," "September
Song"

Ira Gershwin (1896–1983)
lyricist
Lady, Be Good; Funny Face; Lady in the Dark
"Embraceable You," "The Man I Love,"
"'S Wonderful"

At the piano

Preface

There are three principles for a lyric writer to follow, all of them familiar truisms. They were not immediately apparent to me when I started writing, but have come into clearer and clearer focus over the years through the combination of Oscar Hammerstein's tutoring, Strunk and White's huge little book *The Elements of Style* and my own practice of the craft. I have not always been skilled or diligent enough to follow them as faithfully as I would like, but they underlie everything I've ever written. In no particular order, and to be written in stone:

Less Is More

Content Dictates Form

God Is in the Details

all in the service of

Clarity

without which nothing else matters.

If a lyric writer observes this mantra rigorously, he can turn out a respectable lyric. If he also has a feeling for music and rhythm, a sense of theater and something to say, he can turn out an interesting one. If in addition he has such qualities as humor, style, imagination and the numerous other gifts every writer could use, he might even turn out a good one, and with an understanding composer and a stimulating book writer, the sky's the limit.

Reintroduction

Finishing the Hat was intended to to be a collection of all the lyrics I've written since I became a professional, together with things I wanted to say about lyric writing in general. Three-quarters of the way through assembling it, however, I realized it was going to be encyclopedic in length and cautioned the publisher that readers would be likely to remark, as the old joke has it, "I couldn't put it down—but then I couldn't pick it up." I suggested that the book be split into two volumes, published seriatim, the first spanning the years 1954 through 1981, the second 1981 to the present. As a result, during the year's interim since the first volume was published I've had the opportunity to consider reactions from readers, the complainers and nitpickers as well as the enthusiasts. Some nits were worth picking, and I wince with embarrassment at the omitted lyrics, the misquotations and the errors of attribution which I made—not many, but enough. Subsequent printings of volume one enabled me to rectify mistakes, some of which were typographical errors. Having spent decades of proofing both music and lyrics, I now surrender to the inevitability that no matter how many times you reread what you've written, you fail to spot all the typos and oversights. As do your editors. Most of the omissions I was castigated for concerned either incomplete or nonexistent lyrics, arising from misinformation all too available on the Internet and in old programs which list numbers never performed. This book allows me to supply the lyrics which I actually overlooked.

The omissions and the nits duly dispatched, some of the complaints are also worth addressing. The most common of them is that I didn't speak enough about my personal life, "personal" being the euphemism for "intimate," which is the euphemism for "sexual." I was as personal as I could be about my creative life:

my opinions, my prejudices, my enthusiasms, my grudges and heresies, as promised in the subtitle. But Finishing the Hat was not meant to be a memoir. If I'd wanted to write a memoir, I would have, but I don't, and I didn't. Caveat to the general: This book is going to be no more satisfying to the seriously prurient than the previous one.

Another complaint, and an expected one, concerns the sidebars sprinkled throughout, which expressed my feelings about musical theater's major lyricists. Some readers were outraged by my assessments; this was particularly and understandably the reaction of some British readers, due to my lack of generosity (by their lights) toward Noël Coward and W. S. Gilbert. Having had my say about the major figures, all but two of the sidebars in this book will deal with subjects other than particular writers; those two, however, should generate enough irritation to go around.

The only other complaint worth responding to is that Finishing the Hat pays too little attention to the musical aspects of songwriting. I agree. The trouble is that although I could be just as detailed about how and why I compose as I do and just as analytically opinionated about Richard Rodgers, Harold Arlen, Cole Porter and Irving Berlin as I was about Lorenz Hart, E. Y. Harburg, Cole Porter and Irving Berlin, the technique of composition is impossible to be precise and articulate about without using jargon. The inner workings of lyrics can be communicated easily without resorting to arcane terms; understanding what a perfect rhyme is requires no special knowledge. But understanding what a perfect cadence is requires knowing something about harmony and the diatonic scale. Music is a foreign language which everyone knows but only musicians can speak. The effect is describable in everyday language; how to achieve it is not.

None of these reactions to *Finishing the Hat,* however, is as important as my own. The hiatus between books has allowed me to reread what I wrote (partly to avoid repeating myself) and to reassess it in the light of the comments I received, both supportive and critical, as well as the distance from my original impulses, brief though it is. One of the reasons I embarked on these books is to answer the classic question "How do I know what I think till I hear what I say?" I want to know more, hence this Reintroduction. Stimulated by both readers and myself, I want to use it as a gallimaufry of miscellaneous subjects I haven't touched on, or haven't touched on enough—a repository of notions, big and small. Since they are random items disparate in size and subject, I've listed them in alphabetical order, because I can think of no better organizing principle.

Amplification In the days before I started earning serious money—that is, money serious enough to afford a $4.40 orchestra seat at a Broadway musical—I settled for standing room if the theater sold standing room, or second balcony if there was one: in other words, the cheapest seat available. These were the days before amplification,* about which I have mixed feelings. I'm not referring to the tinned sound that many people complain of—I've heard natural, unobtrusive sound in a lot of amplified shows. What bothers me is the softening effect it has on the audience's concentration. Hal Prince pointed out to me that sitting in those ceiling-scraping seats, hearing an orchestra hundreds of feet away, and squinting at Mary Martin's face, which was the size of a dime, we had to concentrate. Mary Martin had a small, coy voice, and in order to hear her, we had to lean vertiginously forward. None of the luxury of sitting back and letting the show come to us—*we* had to lean into *it.* The concentration required was so great that we had to shut out the real world, and in so doing we became participants in the experience, all of which made it easy to suspend disbelief and enter another world; and the more of that in the theater, the better. With the advent of amplification, ears became lazy and audiences now tend to visit rather than enter. The issue is not one of volume, but of concentration. Ethel Merman's voice was famously loud, but to lazy ears she wouldn't have sailed over the orchestra the way she did.

Audiences are not the only victims of amplification. In 1984, when we were checking the floor mi-

crophones at the Booth Theatre a few days before the first preview of *Sunday in the Park with George,* James Lapine and I and the sound department decided to try something daring: not to use them. For the first time in decades, we would present a musical in a Broadway theater with natural sound, without the aid and comfort of amplification. The Booth was a modest size, the band small, the orchestrations transparent and the acoustics excellent. Moreover, in Bernadette Peters and Mandy Patinkin we had two strong voices with clear diction, and we asked them to sing a bit on the empty stage so that we could test our plan. They sounded rich and luscious, and we were just about to tell them of our notion when they murmured that the theater sounded dead to them. We assured them that it was not, and they sang again, but once again complained of the deadness. As an experiment, the sound engineer switched the microphones on; the actors sang again and were visibly relieved, and grateful. And at their request, we gave them body mics.

What had happened, of course, was that over many years of amplified sound the ears of performers themselves had become lazy—or more accurately, dependent on the feedback from the loudspeaker system out front and the monitors backstage. That dependency takes a toll on young performers as well, whose voices expect microphones to amplify not only their volume but their emotions. On the other hand, there are shows where sitting back and not hearing too clearly is the best way to enjoy them.

Art is edited truth—edited to give it shape, rhythm, speed and punch. I've quoted the Communist dictum before: "If it isn't art, it isn't propaganda." Art is skill in the service of passion.

Art versus Craft Received wisdom has it that the sweat poured into the final product should never show. Someone once said in praise about Irving Berlin's lyrics that "he hides the creative sweat behind the art" and in criticism about Ira Gershwin's that "he makes you feel the sweat." It was me. Even patter songs, I thought, should hide the effort that went into making them and be admired only on analysis. Rereading what I'd set in cement ever since I started to think seriously about writing lyrics, I suddenly and with dismay thought of instances where that wasn't exactly true: the cathedral at Chartres, for example. *Ulysses,* for example. Glenn Gould, for example. There are experiences where the effort is part of the pleasure—craft demonstrating itself. Balance is what's necessary to make it artful: Sweat mustn't be the feature, or the work becomes boring, because the substance becomes subservient to the stunt. Novels written without the letter "e" are awesome but uninteresting. Nevertheless, although concealing the craft

---

* Although microphones were used on Broadway as early as 1938, they didn't become common practice until the late 1950s.

makes for better lyrics, in other fields there is room for showing off. E. B. White is one thing, James Joyce another; both are pleasures.

Blackwing Pencils In *Finishing the Hat* I sang a paean of praise to the Blackwing pencil, followed by a lament over its disappearance. Good news—it's been reissued, although with a few minor changes. It's now called the Palomino Blackwing, soon (as of this writing) to be issued in a new improved version as the Palomino Blackwing 602. If you're one of the dwindling few who still uses a pencil, get it before it disappears again. (This is not a paid announcement.)

Clarity As with *Finishing the Hat*, the three principles stated in my mantra are printed conveniently in the end papers of this book, the back set graphically depicting that they are all in the service of clarity on every level, from intention to diction. Let me be clear about clarity, however: of itself it is, in the end, not very nourishing. Narrative art must be clear, but it must also be mysterious. Something should remain unsaid, something just beyond our understanding, a secret. If it's only clear, it's kitsch; if it's only mysterious (a much easier path), it's condescending and pretentious and soon monotonous. Forster and Fitzgerald knew how to be both. So did Tennessee Williams.

Collaborators Because songs take up so much room in a musical, the book writer has to establish character as quickly as possible, sometimes in broader strokes than he might wish (see Arthur Laurents on the subject of *Gypsy* in the first volume). There's no time to dawdle, poking and pricking into the characters and revealing them gradually, the way Chekhov, O'Neill and Paddy Chayefsky did. There's no space for scenes of small talk which escalate into revelation or small incidents that illuminate character, all the things that enrich plays. Of course, music fills in (or should) some of the empty spaces, but the best book writers—and I've had the luck and taste to work with most of them—know how to establish character with vivid immediacy. They may have vastly different sensibilities and styles, but they have one thing in common: when you read their scenes, you immediately start thinking of whom to cast. Better yet, you know all you need to know in order to write the songs.

I've claimed many times that when I write a score, I inhabit the characters the way an actor would. Even if I'm writing no more than a birthday song for someone, I try to get into the character of the recipient—or target, as I like to think of it. Therefore, the character the book writer presents has to have some dimension or I don't want to accept the role. Sensibil-

ities and styles, however, are crucial. Book writers have to be cast just as carefully as actors in order to avoid misfitting them to the subject and tone, even though they usually cast themselves. I wouldn't ask John Weidman to collaborate on *A Little Night Music* or try to interest George Furth in *Pacific Overtures*. And despite the fact that they are the two most versatile book writers I've worked with (that is, they have the least definable personal style), I wouldn't want to work on Hugh Wheeler's version of *West Side Story* or Arthur Laurents's version of *Sunday in the Park with George*. Nor would they, I suspect.

Worse mismatches have happened. For real. On Broadway. At great expense.

Connecting with Your Subject The old saw that a playwright has to connect with all his characters, even the despicable ones, in order for them to be believable, is an old saw because it's true. Similarly, a songwriter has to find a way to connect to the project he's working on, no matter how distant he may feel from it. Connecting with your collaborators is the first step, of course, and can help in connecting to the subject, as it did me with *Pacific Overtures*. My faith in Hal Prince's judgment at the time overcame my inability to share in his and John Weidman's vision. Except for the shows that I initiated or helped initiate—ideas that made me want to go to work immediately—I have been able to connect in numerous ways.

In the case of *West Side Story*, with my upper-middle-class DNA, street gangs were no more my provenance than—well, that of Arthur Laurents, Leonard Bernstein and Jerome Robbins. Still, the idea had excited them for years. What excited me was the chance to work with Arthur Laurents, Leonard Bernstein and Jerome Robbins, and the theatrical style that might result. With *Gypsy*, strange as it may seem coming from someone who had a difficult mother, it was neither the relentless mother nor the parent-child relationship that got me; it was a chance to work with Arthur again, to write my first Broadway score and, failing that (as it did), to write for a star personality. With *Anyone Can Whistle* it was the chance to be theatrically freewheeling and flashy, both musically and lyrically; with *Do I Hear a Waltz?* it was a way to fulfill a promise and make a buck at the same time, or so I mistakenly thought; *Merrily We Roll Along* was a play I'd always loved because of its "sophisticated" show business milieu and its spectacularly crafted structure.

As for the shows that I initiated or helped to initiate, the attraction was always the style or the genre or the subject or the librettist: apart from love, those are the four best reasons to write a musical, especially when they all come in one package.

Dreams Daydreams may be the main source of creativity, but night dreams are the main source of solving the problems engendered by the daydreams, at least in my experience. The solutions aren't direct, of course: you rarely wake up in the middle of the night with the phrase of the lyric or the chord progression that you gave up on yesterday popping out full-grown and ready to inscribe on your night pad—although I've occasionally dreamt an entire musical number, usually an oratorio of sorts, knowing that I was dreaming and knowing that I had to remember it when I woke up, to no avail. But if you concentrate on the problem just before going to sleep, it happens more often than not that the minute you attack the yellow pad or the keyboard next morning, you suddenly come up with ideas that lead not just to the solutions you were searching for, but to improvements. My advice: if you feel like going to sleep while you're working, don't fight it.

Finding Your Voice At a Museum of Modern Art retrospective of the work of Piet Mondrian, I was walking along a small passageway, on the right hand wall of which was a series of small studies of a cow painted over a period of time, and as I passed through the hall I saw the cow start slowly to distort from painting to painting, then splinter. When I had turned the corner, it had lost its cowness altogether and become an abstract design. And a little farther into the gallery was Mondrian's iconic *Broadway Boogie Woogie*. In short, I had watched an artist, in increments, discover a style and find his voice. This may very well have been the curator at work, but I knew that what I was seeing was the truth, and I started to wonder if Mondrian knew what was happening to him.

Most artists begin by imitating and find their own voice incrementally, as Mondrian did. Certainly, that's what happened to me, and I'm arrogant enough to believe that my experience is not unique. Oscar Hammerstein had urged me to write from my own sensibility, but at that time I had no sensibility, no take on the world. My voice snuck up on me. I started to develop an attitude in *Saturday Night*, a laconic lyrical style in *Gypsy* and a structurally experimental musical one in *Anyone Can Whistle*. They all came together in full-throated fruition in *Company*. I heard it at the *sitzprobe,* the rehearsal where orchestra and singers go through a score together for the first time. "Oh," I thought at the end of the opening number, "that's who I am." From then on I could afford to try anything, because I knew I had a home base that was mine alone and that would inform everything I would write, good and bad.

Hits There is a tonic in the things men do not wish to hear, it's been said. But not much money. The biggest hit shows always tell you stories you want to hear. You can be true to your calling as a nun and marry the richest man in the county and still escape from the Nazis into a lucrative show business future. Who can't identify with that?

Irony is a form of subtext.

Memorable Moments When I get discouraged with what I'm writing, I don't play recordings of past triumphs; I think instead of startling or funny or powerful moments from shows I've worked on, to remind myself of what musical theater can be, such as John McMartin's breakdown during "Live, Laugh, Love" in *Follies;* David Burns as Senex in *A Funny Thing Happened on the Way to the Forum,* hiding on the top of a house, responding to Philia's "Take me!" with "Yes, my dear, but not on the roof"; the Zapruder film of the Kennedy assassination projected onto Neil Patrick Harris's T-shirt in *Assassins;* Julia McKenzie dumping buckets of blood in Declan Donnellan's Royal National Theatre production of *Sweeney Todd;* Bill Parry as the Boatman in *Sunday in the Park with George,* the last person George places in his painting, moving reluctantly into position; Daniel Evans as George in Sam Buntrock's production of the same show, drawing his first line as it was projected across the entire set; and a couple of moments that never got beyond workshops: Nathan Lane's reading of Sam Byck's monologues in *Assassins* and Mandy Patinkin's reading of George's monologue about his death in *Sunday in the Park with George,* one of the most beautiful pieces of writing I've ever heard, which was cut.

There are more—enough, anyway, to get me back to work.

Operetta My father's generation loved operetta as much as it loved musicals—grandiose, humorless, with sweepingly romantic music and stories which took place in long-ago times and faraway places, brimming with spectacle and recitative. Shows like *The Desert Song* and *The New Moon,* with scores by composers such as Sigmund Romberg and Rudolf Friml, were the staples of Broadway and perennial hits until they were displaced by the more colloquial musicals of Porter, the Gershwins, Rodgers and Hart and their successors. By the 1960s they had disappeared, along, it would seem, with their audiences. On the rare occasions when they were produced, usually by light opera companies, they were viewed as nothing more than relics of a quaint and dusty past.

In fact, operettas have been alive and well for many years now, but in another guise. Grandiosity, humorlessness, romantic sweep, melodramatic stories which take place in long-ago times and faraway places, brimming with spectacle and recitative—what

better description of the biggest hits of recent decades, shows like *The Phantom of the Opera* and *Les Misérables*? This is not a criticism, merely a description of the phenomenon, which in turn is now receding—it would seem. There will always be a public for the past. The problem is to attract one for the future.

Public Performance The songwriter Craig Carnelia asked me in an interview when the first moment was that I saw a song of my own performed in a theater. I replied that I couldn't really remember, although it was in *By George,* the show I wrote at George School when I was sixteen, but that I had a vivid memory of hearing music of my own played for the first time to the general public.

The song was a ballad in *All That Glitters,* the second of my Williams College shows, and it was called "I Must Be Dreaming." My father often went to the Barberry Room, a chic mid-Manhattan cocktail lounge/restaurant that no longer exists, to hear Cy Walters and Stan Freeman play two-piano arrangements of show tunes and popular songs. He knew Walters slightly and took a copy of my song to him, and a couple of weeks later the duo played it on WNEW, the most popular music-and-news radio station in New York City and environs. My father wanted me to listen to the broadcast with him, but I was too nervous and wanted to listen to it alone. The only place where I could be completely by myself was at the Hammersteins' townhouse, a five-story brownstone off Fifth Avenue. They were away for the weekend, the house was empty and I could listen in total solitude. I went into the living room, turned on the radio and sat under a table. I have no wish to go into the psychological implications of that, but when the program was over, I crawled out, stood up and felt enormously proud. Still, the fact is that for my first hearing in front of the general public I sat under a table, and to this day whenever I hear a song of mine sung in a nightclub or on a CD but not in the context of the show it was written for, my impulse is the same: I want to get under the table. Perhaps it's because I fear that the flaws will be more apparent than the virtues, perhaps it's because I'm anticipating a wrong harmony or the singer taking so much liberty with the melody that it loses its shape. In any event, somehow it's an embarrassment first and a pleasure second.

I still have a recording of that broadcast. Their arrangement was terrific, although they did play a wrong note in the melody.

Rap Of all the forms of contemporary pop music, rap is the closest to traditional musical theater (its roots are in vaudeville), both in its vamp-heavy rhythmic drive and in its verbal playfulness. At first glance it would seem an inappropriate medium for most shows, except for those dealing with the recording industry, or stories which take place in milieus where rap might be the natural expression of the characters, as in the case of Lin-Manuel Miranda's *In the Heights.* But it need not be site specific. Meredith Willson's startling use of rap for the opening number in *The Music Man* (which I'll talk about later) demonstrated this, and I would have expected more songwriters to pick up on it, including myself. But not until rap became omnipresently popular did I try to make it work: I imitated it in a passage for the Witch to sing during the opening number of *Into the Woods.* But I was never able to find another appropriate use for the technique, or perhaps I didn't have the imagination to.

Miranda does. Rap is a natural language for him and he is a master of the form, but enough of a traditionalist to know the way he can utilize its theatrical potential: he is already experimenting with it in a piece about Alexander Hamilton. This strikes me as a classic example of the way art moves forward: the blending of two conventional styles into something wholly original, like the marriage of Impressionism and Japanese prints in the late nineteenth century. It's one pathway to the future.

Sanskrit When I first heard that the libretto of Philip Glass's opera *Satyagraha* was written in Sanskrit (by him and Constance de Jong), I giggled inwardly at what I deemed its pretentiousness and, delightedly reverting to my snotty adolescence, made many a witty remark at its expense. Then I saw it. Not only was I mesmerized for most of it, I was brought up short by the realization that Sanskrit was the best possible language for an opera libretto. It has the two necessary qualities: it utilizes predominantly open vowel sounds (listen to the title), and it doesn't invite you to try to understand the language, which is something you automatically do at the opera if you know a smattering of German or Italian or French. With Sanskrit, you are relieved of every bit of concentration except where it counts: on the music and the singing and, if you're interested in the story, on the surtitles. Even librettos in English need surtitles, since distended vowels, vocal counterpoint and the overtrained diction of many of the performers make it effortful and difficult to understand. Every librettist should have a smattering of Sanskrit; it will save them, and their audiences, a huge amount of work.

Standing Ovations are now de rigueur in the theater. They used to be rare, awarded only to extraordinary performances. In straight (non-musical) plays, especially, the highest compliment audiences could pay would be to sit pinned in their seats by the power

of the experience they'd had. I can remember a number of occasions when not only did I not want to get out of my seat, I didn't want to talk to anyone until I had shaken off the effect of what I had seen. No longer—you don't get the chance. The audience is on its feet even before the first bow, no matter how limp or shallow the piece. They are, of course, giving the ovation to themselves for having been part of a participatory experience rather than a passive one, and for having spent their time and money on it. They're reminding themselves that they're alive. Which is not a bad thing, but which makes the extraordinary ordinary.

Surprise Many years ago, I went with the playwright Peter Shaffer to an off-Broadway play about Mad Queen Juana of Castile. It was a melodramatic affair, Jacobean in scope and intensity: my kind of theater. During the first act alone, there were two rapes, one murder, a torture scene and a fire, and I was bored to distraction. I spent a lot of time calculating the number of seats in the house, which is what I like to do on such occasions. I would gladly have left at intermission, but the playwright responsible was a friend of mine, so Peter and I cooled our heels out on the sidewalk, smoking (those were the days of cigarettes). I asked him how it could be that a play with so much happening could seem so monotonous. His answer was that it had many incidents but no surprise. He didn't mean surprise plot twists—there were plenty of those—but surprises in character and language. Every action, every moment, every sentence foretold the next one. We, the audience, were consciously or unconsciously a step ahead of the play all evening long, and it was a long evening.

As I said in the previous volume, and I haven't changed my mind, surprise is the lifeblood of the theater. It comes in many flavors: a plot twist, a passage of dialogue, a character revelation, a note in a melody, a harmonic progression, startling moments in staging, lighting, orchestration, unexpected song cues (more about them below)—all the elements of theater. There are surprises to be had everywhere if you want to spring them, and it behooves you to do so. What's important is that the play be ahead of the audience, not vice versa. Predictability is the enemy.

The problem with surprise is that you have to lay out a trail for the audience to follow all the while you're keeping slightly ahead. You don't want them to be bored, but neither do you want them to be confused, and unfortunately there are many ways to do both. This applies to songs as well as to plays. You can confuse an audience with language by being overly poetic or verbose, or you can bore them by restating something they know, which inserts a little yawn into the middle of the song. It's a difficult balancing act, but when you do find that balance, the song acquires quickness, even if it's a slow song: A dramatic tension arises that makes the audience eager to know what happens next, which is the whole point of narrative art.

The principle applies even within a given line of lyric. In the song "Finishing the Hat," for example, George sings about "How you're always turning back too late / From the grass or the stick or the dog or the light." If I had used a list of related images, such as "the grass or the tree or the cloud or the leaf" it would have made for a pretty but placid picture, whereas switching from a natural image to a man-made one to an animal to a generalized quality has the effect of giving the ear and the mind's eye a set of tiny surprises which keep the line alive.

As you know by now, the prose of this book is full of expected words and phrases, but they're less noticeable when there's a sea of them. A lyric, however, is brief and bald, and expected phrases and ideas stand out like—wait for it—sore thumbs.

Surprise, Part II: Song Cues Controlling the moment when a character switches from speech to song is crucial to the suspension of disbelief. To be absorbed in a scene and then to hear the orchestra abruptly start underscoring, announcing the advent of a song, yanks you out of the reality of the show (artificial reality, but reality nonetheless). And it ruins any sense of surprise.

Making the transition from speech to song used to require no skill at all. Not only didn't the audience mind having a scene interrupted by a song; they welcomed it. Almost every song in musicals, including the revolutionary Rodgers and Hammerstein shows (and, I should add, *Saturday Night*), had a verse which served as a transition from the dialogue to the song proper—a preamble which announced what the song was going to be about. The verse related faintly to the scene that preceded it, but even that wasn't necessary. I remember a comedian named Bobby Clark in a musical called *Sweethearts* being suddenly assaulted by a group of chorus girls dressed as milkmaids who came out of nowhere, one of them inquiring excitedly, "Have you heard about Jeanette?" To which Clark replied, "No, but I have a feeling I'm going to now—and with music," at which point he gestured to the conductor and the girl began singing a verse to introduce the subject of Jeanette, a character who hadn't yet appeared. The song which followed was called "Jeanette and Her Little Wooden Shoes," and neither she nor the shoes were heard of again.

Despite, or perhaps because of, instances as outrageous if not outrageously funny as this, I recognized the value of verses as lead-ins to songs, even while I recognized that they were an abrupt reminder to the

audience that it was attending a musical. I also recognized that verses were a boon to the composer. They allowed freedom of form and harmony; it was the chorus of the song that had to conform to the popular stencil. In fact, some verses were as beautiful or arresting as the songs themselves. Yet even though Rodgers and Hammerstein used verses, the concentration on story and character in their shows increasingly blurred the line between dialogue and song, so that eventually verses were precluded as such and became, as in the case of the seminal bench scene in *Carousel* and the "Twin Soliloquies" in *South Pacific*, songs themselves.

If a show has a great deal of underscoring, the transition from dialogue to song becomes easier for the audience to accept, and there is one other huge advantage: when the conductor is constantly waving his arms, it is less startling to see him raise them to cue the singers. Nothing announces the coming of a song like seeing the conductor's head pop up out of the pit and his arms rise and hold their position in anticipation of the downbeat. This is one reason that I use as much underscoring as I can and why I also favor sudden entrances of songs whenever possible—that is, when a sudden change of mood is a virtue, not a disruption, as in the case of "Some People" in *Gypsy* or at the first moment of *Into the Woods*, where there are four spoken words and the orchestra bursts in like an explosion.

The Frogs Rereading *Finishing the Hat* for this Reintroduction, I was taken aback and chagrined by how dismissive I had been about Nathan Lane's 2004 revision of *The Frogs*. I wrote only a few sentences about it, the weight of which was that it was too long ("inflated") and therefore not as good as Burt Shevelove's original, and I indicated elsewhere that I had written the additional songs "to suit the requests of the star and director." This book affords me a chance to apologize for my earlier comments and to expound a bit on what Nathan and I and our co-conspirator, Susan Stroman, who directed and choreographed the show, were trying to do.

When Nathan first became acquainted with *The Frogs* at a Library of Congress concert in 2000, it struck him that Aristophanes' fury at the corruption of the state had an echo in this country which it had not had when the show was first presented in 1974, and that we could use up-to-date tools to sharpen his points. In Burt's version, there had been no references to living figures, only to specific artists, not specific politicians. The play, of course, is relevant to every country at any time, and in 1974 at the end of the Vietnam War its relevance seemed particularly acute. But where Aristophanes had poked fun at his countrymen and politicians for being Philistines, Nathan wanted to work in more specific contemporary references, the kind of topical, even slanderous, satire that Aristophanes himself had used, only raunchier (although Aristophanes was no slouch at raunch). He wanted this version of *The Frogs* to err on the side of ambition rather than frivolity—to be an overtly political piece for a divisive time.

It didn't quite work. Although it was richer than the original, both sillier and more stinging, it still felt inflated—by all of us. Nevertheless, it was worth more of my attention than a couple of sentences.

Valuable Excuse Paul Valéry said, "A poem is never finished; only abandoned." All writers should be grateful to him forever.

Writing is a form of mischief.

Now, what was I saying in volume one? Oh, yes, I was in a morass of despair after the joyful public slaughter of *Merrily We Roll Along*. Then I met James Lapine . . .

Look,
I Made a Hat

SUNDAY in the PARK with GEORGE

A Musical

Music and Lyrics by
Stephen Sondheim

Book by
James Lapine

1. Sunday in the Park with George (1984)

Book by James Lapine

The Notion

Act One concerns the French painter Georges Seurat (1859–1891) and his creation of *Un dimanche après-midi à l'Île de la Grande Jatte* (*A Sunday Afternoon on the Island of La Grande Jatte*), which took more than two years to complete.* Act Two deals with the artistic crisis experienced by his great-grandson, an American conceptual artist in his forties, named George.

General Comments

Unexpected significant moments, moments which happen entirely by chance, keep life surprising and sometimes change its direction permanently—not events, mere moments. My parents' divorce, for example, was an event: it led to my meeting Oscar Hammerstein II and finding a channel into the work I was meant to do. Studying Latin at George School with an inspiring teacher named Lucille Pollock opened me up to the fascinating intricacies of the English language; taking an elective music course at Williams College taught by an ascetic, eccentric professor

named Robert Barrow introduced me to the logic of music and focused my interest for the next sixty-some-odd years—those were events. Running into Arthur Laurents at the opening-night party of a play I hadn't even attended, a fortunate happenstance that brought me the opportunity to write the lyrics for *West Side Story*—that was a lucky moment. So was going on a whim to a small theater half an hour outside central London to see what I thought would be Grand Guignol but which turned out to be Christopher Bond's version of *Sweeney Todd*. And another was in 1982 when I went to see *Twelve Dreams* at the New York Shakespeare Festival. It was a play based on a case of the psychoanalyst Carl Jung in which a little girl had twelve dreams presaging her death, and was written and directed by James Lapine, whose work I had seen only once before (a piece called *Table Settings*). I was stunned by the mixture of sophisticated reality and fanciful incident couched in graceful dialogue, as well as by the elegant imaginativeness of the staging—so much so that I determined to meet him and raise the possibility of collaborating with him on a musical.

I did nothing about it. I'm neither aggressive nor enterprising by nature, and for all I knew he had that condescension toward musicals common to young playwrights and old academics, particularly young off-Broadway playwrights and old university academics. And even if he liked musicals, I feared he might have an antipathy toward mine. But the seed had been planted and it blossomed fortuitously a few months later when I got a telephone call from Lewis Allen, a producer of plays and movies, asking me if I would be willing to meet with a young off-Broadway playwright named James Lapine, who had a project in mind that he'd like to write with me. Somewhat taken aback by the coincidence (I like to think it was

---

*It is one of the half-dozen most popular paintings in the world and is part of the permanent collection of The Art Institute of Chicago. It measures about ten feet by seven feet and depicts approximately fifty people in varying perspectives and proportions strolling and relaxing in a public park outside of Paris. It is composed of hundreds of thousands of daubs of color and contains no outlines as such, the figures and landscape being delineated by the juxtaposition of the colored daubs. Although some of the colors have faded, it is a mesmerizing work, unsettling in its play with perspectives and at the same time still and dreamlike.

kismet, not coincidence), I met with him and discovered that the project was a musical adaptation of Nathanael West's novel *A Cool Million*. This made the kismet even more startling, since *A Cool Million* was one of the very few non-mystery novels I had read since graduating from Williams thirty-two years earlier. Burt Shevelove* had turned me on to it, partly because it was sarcastic and satirical, two qualities I enjoy, and partly because it was short, a quality I enjoy even more. (I had liked West's *Miss Lonelyhearts* for the same reasons.) The story was a version of *Candide,* even bleaker than Voltaire's, set in Depression-era America. I thought that musicalizing it would be a fine idea, but I pointed out to James that Lillian Hellman, Leonard Bernstein and a raft of lyricists had written a musical version of *Candide* already. He wasn't familiar with the show, but when he'd read and listened to it, he agreed that once was enough.† Nevertheless, we got along so well together we decided to look for something else to write.

As we talked and came to know each other over the subsequent weeks, we found that our tastes were surprisingly alike. I say "surprisingly" because I'd never collaborated with someone from an off-Broadway nonprofit theater background, and playwrights nurtured in that protective atmosphere think differently than we Great White Way dinosaurs who were raised in commercial theater do. Nonprofits encourage experimentation—they can afford to, since the plays they present have limited runs and need not attract large audiences—whereas Broadway encourages repetition of formula, the occasional maverick works notwithstanding. Thus with Lapine I found myself suggesting movies and plays to adapt, while he suggested ideas. I came up with plots, while he came up with images. One evening he asked me what kind of musical I most wanted to write and I replied, "Theme and variations." To illustrate, I described my original notion for *A Little Night Music* (described in volume one) and then showed him a French arts magazine called *Bizarre,* which had devoted one issue entirely to variations on the *Mona Lisa*: Mona Lisa with a mustache, Mona Lisa cut up and rearranged, Mona Lisa in a Charles Addams cartoon, Mona Lisa scrubbed with Brillo, and so on, along with dozens of Mona Lisa jokes and anecdotes. This led to a discussion of French paintings, and James brought up the Seurat, which he had used in *Photograph*, an adaptation of a Gertrude Stein play he had devised with students of his when he was teaching poster design at

---

* Co-author of *A Funny Thing Happened on the Way to the Forum.*
† West's idiosyncratic and specifically American take on Voltaire persisted in intriguing James over the years, and he subsequently wrote a straight play version of it called *Luck, Pluck and Virtue,* which was produced off-Broadway in 1995.

Yale. We commented on how much Seurat's depiction of the island looked like a stage set. We discussed the curious fact that of all the fifty-some-odd people in the painting, not one of them is looking at another one, and speculated about the reasons for their avoidances. We realized that we were talking about a theater piece, possibly a musical. James said, "What's missing is the principal character." "Who?" I asked. "The painter," he replied, and we knew we had a show.

I bring this up not simply as an anecdotal history but as an illustration of the theatrical gap between us, a gap that enriched the collaboration. The two youngest collaborators I have written with are John Weidman and James Lapine, each almost a full generation younger than me. They are only three years apart in biological age, but in theatrical terms John is my generation. He and I may flirt with mildly experimental forms, as in *Pacific Overtures* and *Assassins,* but we are Broadway babies. We think in terms of the well-made play, in which intention leads to action leads to consequence leads to intention and so on— our thinking is linear. The off-Broadway playwrights of the sixties and their offspring, like Lapine, lean toward lateral thinking, toward intuition rather than structural logic. They are less interested in plot than in atmosphere and subtext, more in intimation than in statement. This often results in vagueness masquerading as suggestiveness and pretension being mistaken for whimsy or innovation, but it also sometimes results in freshness and surprise.

James was also the first (and only) writer I've worked with who thinks like a director. His first impulse is visual, as is Hal Prince's, but Hal is not a writer. I had worked with Arthur Laurents when he had directed *Anyone Can Whistle,* and his first impulse was literary—he was primarily and always a playwright. In line with what Jerry Robbins had lectured me on about staging numbers, James staged things as he wrote them, something which many playwrights attempt, but with the skills to realize his vision. As a rule, it's a great danger for a playwright to direct his own work when it's new; it's useful, maybe even necessary, for him to have someone to argue with. Few producers are articulate enough to do so and few actors have any perspective except about their own roles, so an outside director, even one less than ideal, is a good idea. It's even more difficult for a librettist to direct, if for no other reason than that musicals are so complicated. And it takes an inordinate amount of restraint and flexibility to gently coax, day after day, a performer who keeps veering from the script or the lyric, or who's struggling to reach an understanding of something you think he should have understood on the first day of rehearsals. In the two-hats field, librettists need patience; directors need hu-

With Mandy Patinkin, Bernadette Peters and James Lapine during rehearsals (1983)

mility. James seems to have both, perhaps because he came to maturity in a laid-back era; more likely, it's a matter of temperament rather than talent. Working with him after so many collaborations with Hal was a mild but noticeable shock. In many ways the two of them are alike: smart, worldly, culturally aware, creatively adventurous, and critical of their own work as much as of others'. Most particularly, their generating ideas are, unlike mine, primarily visual. Temperamentally, the contrast could not be greater. It goes beyond James's coming from a different generation and being able to wear two hats creatively. Hal, with whom I have worked on eight shows, is sharp and brilliant, heartily warm but inwardly removed. His work tends to be distancing; he is drawn to Brechtian presentations in which the audience is constantly reminded that they are in a theater. He likes epic scope in the tradition of Meyerhold and Reinhardt, which is one reason he directs operas whenever he gets the chance: they offer him the possibility of spectacle. Hal is mercurial in mood, given to large swings from high to low although, being a gent, he doesn't spread the lows to his colleagues: he is constantly, even aggressively, encouraging. His energy is dynamic and contagious— I have seldom left a meeting with Hal without wanting to rush home and write songs. James, on the other hand, though just as warm as Hal, is reserved

rather than removed. Like his plays, he is elusive where Hal is open, romantic where Hal is sociological, formal where Hal is freewheeling, subtle and suggestive where Hal is forceful and immediate, as unflappable as Hal is volatile. He likes to work on a small scale, intimate and seductive, the playwright always overriding the director. I have seldom left a meeting with James without feeling that it wasn't quite over. Theatrically and temperamentally, I'm more like him than like Hal. Moreover, I tend to plant red flags in my collaborations; I am always on the lookout for what might be wrong with a proposed song or scene or, in extreme cases, the whole show. This grudging resistance could sometimes drive Hal crazy: he would grumpily mutter that I was just being "negative." But it was less a manifestation of negativity than a matter of caution; unfortunately, the caution would occasionally slide into overcautiousness. In other words, I could be a drag on the creative energy in the room. That difference in process, though, was one of the reasons that we made a good team: Hal's function was to keep the truck moving, mine to see that it didn't fall off the cliff.

The generational difference *was* telling, however. Hal and I are virtually the same age: we are, like Weidman, Broadway babies. We produced work under the pressures of unions, reviews and the obligation to pay

investors back. *Sunday in the Park with George* was developed at Playwrights Horizons, one of the higher-profile off-Broadway nonprofit theaters, and one which had presented some of James's earlier work. Since there was no need to worry about investors or reviews (nonprofit theaters don't bother inviting reviewers until near the end of a play's limited run because the sale of tickets has been substantially accounted for by subscribers), the atmosphere was more relaxed. The fact, for example, that the second act of the show wasn't finished in time for most of the run didn't deter us from presenting only the first act to audiences, because they consisted of subscribers who accepted the notion that it was a work in progress. This left us free to tinker with the show—including finishing it—to our own satisfaction without fretting about word of mouth or the deadline of an opening.

If for me the shock at the difference between commercial and nonprofit theater was a pleasant one, it was less so for James. During the show's first preview a few months later at the Booth Theatre, a commercial Broadway house two blocks and a hundred light-years away from Playwrights Horizons, he was busy taking notes on the performance only to notice small droves of unhappy patrons leaving throughout the first act as well as at the intermission. He had never seen people walk out on one of his plays; I, on the other hand, had seen them do it on every single one since *A Funny Thing Happened on the Way to the Forum,* and although I hardly found the rush for the exits welcome, I expected it and was used to it, if not quite inured to it. James's jaw dropped in dismay and disbelief, but after a few more previews he too had become a Broadway veteran.

These differences, both in temperament and in process, affected not only the score for *Sunday in the Park with George* but my subsequent scores as well. I found myself writing with more formal looseness than I had before, allowing songs to become fragmentary, like musicalized snatches of dialogue, but avoiding the static verbosity of *recitative.* I worried less about punctuating the piece with applause and concentrated more on the flow of the story itself. Even more noticeable was the effect of my new partnership on the tone of the work. I have often been accused of writing "cold" scores: intellectually acute but emotionally dispassionate, not user-friendly. Warmth comes in many guises, however, and one man's passion is another man's sentimentality. When I look back as objectively as I can at the shows I wrote before James and contrast them with *Sunday in the Park with George* and the others I wrote with him, it seems clear to me that a quality of detachment suffuses the first set, whereas a current of vulnerability, of longing, informs the second. It's not that I prefer one to the other, but at this late date I can more easily understand the early and persistent reaction to my songs (although, I'm glad to say, the persistence seems to be wearing down with the passage of time). With James, detachment was replaced by a measure of compassion. When I think of songs like "Sunday" or "Move On" or "No One Is Alone" (from *Into the Woods*), I realize that by having to express the straightforward, unembarrassed goodness of James's characters I discovered the Hammerstein in myself—and I was the better for it.

"Look out at the water. Not at me."

ACT ONE

A white stage. George, a nineteenth-century artist, enters and sits at an easel on the side of the stage with a large drawing pad and a box of Conté crayons. He stares at the pad for a moment, then turns to the audience.

GEORGE
(Speaking)
White. A blank page or canvas. The challenge: Bring order to the whole.

(A chord; a tree flies in)

Through design.

(As chords continue and the scenery assembles)

Composition.
Balance.
Light.
And harmony.

I include this piece of dialogue even though it is not a song, because it is a mantra that becomes a recurring theme in the show.

It is 1884. A hot July morning on La Grande Jatte, a recreational park for the middle and working classes, situated on an island in the Seine, a short distance from Paris. George is sketching Dot, his model and mistress. She is reluctant and uncomfortable in a heavy dress with a high bustle and annoyed that George is looking at her only as his model, as something to draw, all the while badgering her to stay absolutely still and concentrate on posing. George has mollified her by promising to take her to the Follies that evening, but she is also suspiciously curious as to why, as gossip has it, he has been drawing monkeys at the zoo.

Sunday in the Park with George

DOT
(To herself, sotto voce)
A trickle of sweat.

(Twitches slightly)

The back of the—

(Twitches again)

Head.
He always does this—

(Hisses)

Now the foot is dead.
Sunday in the park with George,
One more Sun—!

(Twitches)

The collar is damp.
Beginning to pinch.

The bustle's slipping—

(A hiss and a twitch)

I won't budge one inch.

(Undulating with some pleasure)

Who was at the zoo, George?
Who was at the zoo?
The monkeys and who, George?
The monkeys and who?

GEORGE
Don't move.

DOT
(Becoming elaborately still)
Artists are bizarre. Fixed. Cold.
That's you, George, you're bizarre.
    Fixed. Cold.
I like that in a man. Fixed. Cold.
God, it's hot out here.

Well, there are worse things
Than staring at the water on a
    Sunday.
There are worse things

Than staring at the water
As you're posing for a picture
Being painted by your lover
In the middle of the summer
On an island in the river
On a Sunday.

George races over and rearranges her a bit, as if she were an object, then returns to his easel and resumes sketching. Dot twitches again.

DOT
The petticoat's wet,
Which adds to the weight.
The sun is blinding.

(Closing her eyes)

All right, concentrate.

GEORGE
Eyes open, please.

DOT
Sunday in the park with George!

GEORGE
Look out at the water. Not at me.

DOT
Sunday in the park with George . . .
    Concentrate . . . Concentrate . . .

Her dress opens and Dot walks out of it. The dress closes and remains standing; George continues sketching it as if she were still inside. During the following, Dot undulates and poses around the stage, the music punctuating her movements.

Well, if you want bread
And respect and attention,
Not to say connection,
Modeling's no profession.

(Does mock poses)

If you want, instead,
When you're dead,
Some more public and more
    permanent
Expression—
Of affection—
You want a painter,

Bernadette Peters as Dot and Mandy Patinkin as George

Poet,
Sculptor, preferably:
Marble, granite, bronze.
Durable.
Something nice with swans
That's durable
Forever.
All it has to be is good.

(Looking over George's shoulder at his work)

And George, you're good.

(Then at George)

You're really good.

(Still to herself)

George's stroke is tender.
George's touch is pure.

(Watches him intently as he works)

Your eyes, George.
I love your eyes, George.
I love your beard, George.
I love your size, George.
But most, George,
Of all,
But most of all,
I love your painting . . .

(Looking up at the sun)

I think I'm fainting . . .

She steps back into the dress, resumes her pose, gives a twitch and a wince, then sings sotto voce again.

DOT
The tip of a stay,

(Winces)

Right under the tit.
No, don't give in, just—

(Shifts)

Lift the arm a bit . . .

GEORGE
Don't lift the arm, please.

DOT
Sunday in the park with George!

GEORGE
The bustle high, please.

DOT
Not even a nod,
As if I were trees.

The ground could open,
He would still say, "Please."

Never know with you, George,
Who could know with you?
The others I knew, George.
Before we get through,
I'll get to you, too.
God, I am so hot!

Well, there are worse things
Than staring at the water on a
    Sunday.
There are worse things
Than staring at the water
As you're posing for a picture
After sleeping on the ferry
After getting up at seven
To come over to an island
In the middle of a river
Half an hour from the city
On a Sunday,
On a Sunday in the park with—

GEORGE
Don't move the mouth.

Dot holds absolutely still for a very long beat, then pours all her extremely mixed emotions into one word.

DOT
—George!

Prior to *Sunday in the Park with George* I had often taken snippets of dialogue and expanded them into song ("Something's Coming" in *West Side Story,* "Someone in a Tree" from *Pacific Overtures*) or even whole speeches ("The Worst Pies in London" from *Sweeney Todd*), and I had written my own stream-of-consciousness soliloquies ("Rose's Turn" [*Gypsy*], "Epiphany" [*Sweeney Todd*], "Franklin Shepard, Inc." [*Merrily We Roll Along*]), but only once before had I asked a librettist to write me a monologue specifically for the purpose of supplying something to musicalize. (It was James Goldman and the song was "I Remember" from *Evening Primrose*.) Because the world of this show was so foreign to me and because the writing style which James chose for it was

Another CHORD. More trees descend.

                                    DOT
                (twitches slightly, mutters)
        A DRIBBLE OF SWEAT.
                (twitch)
        THE BACK OF THE HEAD.
                (twitch)
        HE ALWAYS DOES THIS --
                (hiss)
        NOW THE FOOT IS DEAD.
        SUNDAY IN THE PARK WITH GEORGE.
        ONE MORE SU --
                (twitch)
        BEGINNING TO CREEP.
                (slightly larger twitch)
        BEGUN TO DESCEND.
                (slow twitch)
        I WILL NOT BUDGE ONE --
                (hiss and twitch)
        NOW IT'S MET A FRIEND.
                (perhaps undulating with some pleasure,
                 perhaps twitching tinily with vexation)
        WHO WAS AT THE ZOO, GEORGE?
        WHO WAS AT THE ZOO?
        THE MONKEYS AND WHO, GEORGE?
        THE MONKEYS AND WHO?

                          GEORGE
        Don't move.

                            DOT
                (still)
        ARTISTS ARE BIZARRE. FIXED. COLD.
        THAT'S YOU, GEORGE, YOU'RE BIZARRE. FIXED. COLD.
        I LIKE THAT IN A MAN. FIXED. COLD.
        GOD, IT'S HOT UP HERE.   BY A RIVER   *looking at (ad lib, standing in your pose)*

        WELL, THERE ARE WORSE THINGS   BY (A) RIVER
        THAN POSING IN THE MORNING ON A SUNDAY.
        THERE ARE WORSE THINGS
        THAN POSING IN THE MORNING FOR A PICTURE
        FOR A PICTURE BEING PAINTED BY YOUR LOVER
  BY THE RIVER ON AN ISLAND IN THE RIVER ON A SUNDAY.   (IN THE MIDDLE OF THE MORNING)

        GEORGE rearranges her a bit, as if she were an object, then
        resumes sketching. DOT hisses, twitching again.

                IT'S GATHERING SPEED.
                        (larger twitch)
                THE SMALL OF THE BACK.
                        (slow undulant twitch)
                A LITTLE FURTHER --
                        (hiss of pleasure and sexy twitch)
                NOW IT'S HIT THE CRACK.

                            GEORGE
        Keep the foot still.

A I	Quibble
	Sunday in the park
A II	Quibble
B	Who-was-at the zoo
C I	Artists are bizarre
	It's hot up here.
D	Worse things
C	
A III	I'll move my tree
	Sunday in the park
C II	If you want bread, fuck a baker
	If you want longevity, fuck an artist.
	If he's good. And George is.
	You never know what it's going to be. With the others, I did.
	George is really good.

A IV	But the knuckle itches and I hate it	A II	
V	Sunday in the park	B	
A VI	His studio + work habit	(C variation)	
B II	Never knew with you, George		
	(How can you can't fuck + paint?)	D Coda	
C III	I wake up, I look around — 70 ft. canvas — he's crazy		
D II	It's hot up here — or other complaint		
	Fucking on the ferry... or a / Sunday in Sunday in the park with [George]		

Coda	On a Sunday
G:	

both odd and delicate, I asked him for a stream-of-consciousness version of Dot's thoughts as she was posing in the opening scene, which would elaborate her introduction to us and incorporate any necessary exposition not covered in the brief dialogue preceding the song. The speech, I assured him, need not be polished, as it would never be spoken but would serve only as a guideline for me. This is what he came up with:

First a dribble of sweat, from the back of the head, slowly down the spine. Tickling. Sunday in church, having to sit still on rock hard pews. The right foot. Tingling. Fitted out in a scratchy dress, sitting on a rock hard pew. Hated clothes then. Hate them now . . . (*Sexily*) Shit. Another dribble of sweat. Under the arm, slowly down the side. Titillating . . . (*Change of tone*) Look calm, Dot. Don't give in. Show George the perfect model. Show George—George, who can sketch moving monkeys but not moving girlfriends. The right foot is gone. Dead weight. The fun is waking it up. God, I am so hot. George, the monkeys and who? Don't make a move, Dot. Don't say a word. Obey and pray on Sunday, you'll get your way and stay.

All solos are in some way monologues, but most of them are in song form, with the emphasis on form: refrain lines and the like. Monologues which reflect the loose, disorganized ways of the mind, which reveal and develop character, used to be few and far between, even after Hammerstein's "Soliloquy" in *Carousel* had pointed the way. I had toyed with stream-of-consciousness in "Rose's Turn," but now James had given me a blueprint to go farther, and an appropriate one at that, since he gave Dot a mind that does not burn with a steady flame, but flickers and sputters; she has a short attention span. That justified my juxtaposing images and emotions without transitions between them, such as the instantaneous switches from complaints about her discomfort to her defiant determination to be a model he admires to suspicious jealousy to general observations about art and artists. The clipped phrases of James's speech also supplied me with the rhythmic building blocks of the song's structure. Even the profusion of near-rhymes in the interlude ("attention," "connection," "profession") not only reflects the skittishness of Dot's thinking but helps keep the song from becoming formless. Dot, philosophizing, would not think in perfect rhymes but in imperfect ones if she were to try rhyming long words at all—which she would in her attempt to intellectualize the situation. Most important, the music of this section underpins their love story throughout the evening.

So much is going on in James's monologue that the salient problem for me as lyric writer was to find an organizing principle that could encompass such an embarrassment of riches without skimping on them. The physical discomfort which keeps recurring to Dot was the solution, and emotionally it made for comedy; poor Dot is constantly being dragged back from her fantasies by her dress, by the heat and by George's impatience. I also needed some sort of verbal thread to hold the song together so that it wouldn't lose dramatic focus through diffusion: I needed a refrain line that would imply both complaint and pleasure. The title, flat and inconclusive, served that purpose not only for the song but, divested from the specific situation, for the show as well.

Other people enter the park: an Old Lady who turns out to be George's mother, accompanied by her Nurse; and two household servants, a married couple, Franz and Frieda. The scene is interrupted by shouting and catcalls from across the river. A platform rolls on, bearing a tableau of Seurat's Bathers at Asnières: *a scene on the banks of the Seine across from the island, with a Boy in the water, a Young Man sitting on the bank and an Older Man lying just behind him.*

Yoo-Hoo! (cut)

BOY
(*Loudly, through cupped hands*)
Yoo-hoo! Dumb old bat!
Who you think you're staring at?
In about a minute flat
We're all coming over to get you!

He splashes water toward the island. The Older Man mutters something obscene to the Boy, who nods delightedly and laughs.

Yoo-hoo! Kinky beard!
Everybody knows you're weird!
How'd you like your picture smeared?

YOUNG MAN
Yeah, how'd you like your picture smeared?

BOY
We're coming right over and get you!

Nursie! Nursie!
Help, I'm drowning!

(*Makes gurgling sounds*)

Mercy! Nursie!
I'm not clowning!
Can't you see I'm drowning?

He makes horrifying drowning sounds and disappears underwater, struggling; as the Nurse moves, he suddenly pops up.

Na-na-na-ni-na-na!

He belches gigantically. The Older Man mutters to him again.

BOY
(*To Dot*)
Yoo-hoo! Lady, dear!
Who you hiding in the rear?
Would you like a volunteer?
Why don't you come over here?

(*As the Older Man mutters again*)

Feeling weary, dear?
Don't you worry, dearie, we're
Coming right over to get you!
Yoo-hoooooooo—!

Halfway through the word George gestures as if framing an image: the Boy, the Young Man and the Older Man freeze into the familiar tableau as a picture frame comes in around them.

In the course of transferring the show from Playwrights Horizons to Broadway, we made a number of cuts in the score, most of them having to do with the minor characters in the show. One of the casualties was "Yoo-Hoo!" The tableau remained, the song did not.

Jules and Yvonne, a well-to-do middle-aged couple, stroll on and pause before the framed painting, amused.

No Life

JULES
Ahh . . .

YVONNE
Ooh . . .

JULES
Mmm . . .

YVONNE
Oh, dear.

JULES
Oh, my.

YVONNE
Oh, my dear.

JULES
It has no presence.

YVONNE
No passion.

JULES
No life.

(They laugh)

It's neither pastoral
Nor lyrical.

YVONNE
(Giggling)
You don't suppose that it's satirical?

(They laugh heartily)

JULES
Just density
Without intensity—

YVONNE
No life.
    Boys with their clothes off . . .

JULES
(Mocking)
I must paint a factory next!

YVONNE
It's so mechanical.

JULES
Methodical.

YVONNE
It might be in some dreary
Socialistic peri-
Odical.

JULES
(Approvingly)
    Good.

YVONNE
So drab, so cold.

JULES
And so controlled.

BOTH
No life.

JULES
His touch is too deliberate,
somehow.

YVONNE
The dog.

(They shriek with laughter)

JULES
These things get hung—

YVONNE
Hmm.

JULES
And then they're gone.

YVONNE
Ahhh.
Of course he's young—

(Hastily, as Jules shoots her a look)

But getting on.

JULES
All mind, no heart.
No life in his art.

YVONNE
No life in his life!

BOTH
No—

(They giggle and chortle)

Life.

George's studio. Dot, in the likeness of Seurat's Young Woman Powdering Herself, *sits at a vanity, powdering her face and arms to an intermittent rhythmic figure in the orchestra. George is on a scaffold, a number of brushes in his hand, painting* La Grande Jatte, *a work in progress, covering the canvas with tiny specks of paint to the same rhythmic figure. Both are absorbed in their own thoughts, unheard by the other.*

Color and Light

George dabs and pauses, checking the canvas.

GEORGE
Order.

STEPHEN SONDHEIM

Depth
Reddish radish
Bluish
Greenish
Blue-green

will tiles
needs
wants

Who will win?

pops
sends

Red-orange / Green, G Blue
Yellow, G yellow / Violet-VH. Blue

Semi White
Violet

Red red red red   4/8 Purify purify
Red red red red   (Just be :)   watch it watch it
Red red red red   too much   Watch watch watch watch
Blue against the   Touch the orange   Watch watch what is she
                                            wants
Blue blue blue blue   Other blue   Doing

Blue against the

No we won't it   No no no no

Touch against the   Mustn't touch the   Not so too close

          Orange
          Yellow yellow
          Right against
          Just beside the   Yellow carrying the

Fill in the spaces   Orange orange orange over to the
Fill in the shapes   Green green green green
                      Green green (Just be)   (×3)
       Touch over touch over   Watch it watch it   let it
              "

Red red red red   Not too much   Watch it let it   Dry dry dry
Red red in she Now sky? At her   Dry dry dry dry   Dry dry
Red red sit her   Mirror   Over to the
Red reading her mirror
Blue beside her table
Blue
Needs the orange   Mirror   One one & one another
                              Dot dot dot dot

Green the green

No brown, no black, no earth

Part IV   What what what shall I do do do about it it it   dot dot dot - I know -
                                                                             red.

(He dabs with another color, pauses and checks, continuing to do so as he mutters to himself)

Design.
Composition.
Tone.
Form.
Symmetry.
Balance.

More red . . .

(Dabs with more intensity)

And a little more red . . .

(Switches brushes)

Blue blue blue blue
Blue blue blue blue
Even . . . even . . .
Good

(Humming)

Bumbum bum bumbumbum
Bumbum bum . . .

(Paints silently for a moment)

More red . . .

(Switches brushes again)

More blue . . .

(Again)

More beer . . .

(Taking a swig from a nearby bottle, always eyeing the canvas)

More light!

He dabs assiduously but delicately, attacking the canvas.

Color and light.
There's only color and light.
Yellow and white.
Just blue and yellow and white.

(Addressing the woman he is painting)

Look at the air, miss—

(Dabs at the space in front of her)

See what I mean?
No, look over there, miss—

(Dabs at her eye, pauses, checks it)

That's done with green . . .

(Swirling a brush in the orange cup)

Conjoined with orange . . .

The lights go down on George and up on Dot, now powdering her breasts and armpits.

DOT
Nothing seems to fit me right.

(Giggles)

The less I wear, the more comfortable I feel.

(Checking herself)

More rouge . . .

(Applying rouge)

George is very special. Maybe I'm just not special enough for him.

She picks up tweezers and starts plucking her eyebrows, one after every line.

If my legs were longer . . .
If my bust was smaller . . .
If my hands were graceful . . .
If my waist was thinner . . .
If my hips were flatter . . .
If my voice was warm . . .
If I could concentrate—

Abruptly, her feet start to dance under the table.

I'd be in the Follies!
I'd be in a cabaret!

Gentlemen in tall silk hats
And linen spats
Would wait with flowers.
I could make them wait for hours.
Giddy young aristocrats

With fancy flats
Who'd drink my health
And I would be as
Hard as nails . . .

(Looking at her nails)

And they'd only want me more—

(Grabbing the buffer and buffing her nails)

If I was a Folly girl . . .
Nah, I wouldn't like it much.
Married men and stupid boys
And too much smoke and all that noise
And all that color and light . . .

The lights come up on George, talking to a woman in the painting, the rhythmic figure continuing.

GEORGE
Aren't you proper today, miss? Your parasol so properly cocked, your bustle so perfectly upright. No doubt your chin rests at just the right angle from your chest.

(Addressing the man next to her)

And you, sir. Your hat so black. So black to you, perhaps. So red to me.

DOT
(Spraying herself rhythmically)
None of the others worked at night . . .

GEORGE
So composed for a Sunday.

DOT
How do you work without the right—

(Spray)

Bright—

(Spray)

White—

(Spray)

Light?

(Spray)

How do you fathom George?

GEORGE
(Muttering feverishly, trancelike, as he paints)
Red red red red
Red red orange
Red red orange
Orange pick up blue
Pick up red
Pick up orange
From the blue-green blue-green
Blue-green circle
On the violet diagonal
Di-ag-ag-ag-ag-ag-o-nal-nal
Yellow comma yellow comma

(Humming, massaging his numb wrist)

Numnum num numnumnum
Numnum num . . .

(Sniffs, smelling Dot's perfume)

Blue blue blue blue
Blue still sitting
Red that perfume
Blue all night
Blue-green the window shut
Dut dut dut
Dot Dot sitting
Dot Dot waiting
Dot Dot getting fat fat fat
More yellow
Dot Dot waiting to go
Out out out but
No no no George
Finish the hat finish the hat
Have to finish the hat first
Hat hat hat hat
Hot hot hot it's hot in here . . .

He whistles a bit, steps back from the painting.

GEORGE
(Joyfully)
Sunday!

(Attacking the canvas ecstatically)

Color and light!

DOT
(Pinning up her hair)
But how George looks. He could look forever.

GEORGE
There's only color and light!

DOT
As if he sees you and he doesn't all at once.

GEORGE
Purple and white . . .

DOT
What is he thinking when he looks like that?

GEORGE
. . . And red and purple and white!

DOT
What does he see? Sometimes, not even blinking.

GEORGE
(To the young girls in the painting)
Look at this glade, girls,
Your cool blue spot.

DOT
His eyes. So dark and shiny.

GEORGE
No, stay in the shade, girls.
It's getting hot . . .

DOT
Some think cold and black.

GEORGE
It's getting orange . . .

DOT
But it's warm inside his eyes . . .

GEORGE
(Dabbing intensely)
Hotter . . .

DOT
And it's soft inside his eyes . . .

George steps around the canvas to clean a brush. He glances at Dot. Their eyes meet for a second, then she turns back to her mirror.

DOT
And he burns you with his eyes . . .

GEORGE
Look at her looking.

DOT
And you're studied like the light.

GEORGE
Forever with that mirror. What does she see? The round face, the tiny pout, the soft mouth, the creamy skin . . .

DOT
And you look inside the eyes.

GEORGE
The pink lips, the red cheeks . . .

DOT
And you catch him here and there.

GEORGE
The wide eyes. Studying the round face, the tiny pout . . .

DOT
But he's never really there.

GEORGE
Seeing all the parts and none of the whole.

DOT
So you want him even more.

GEORGE
But the way she catches light . . .

DOT
And you drown inside his eyes . . .

GEORGE
And the color of her hair . . .

DOT
I could look at him forever . . .

GEORGE
(Simultaneously)
I could look at her forever . . .

There is a long beat as they look at each other.

GEORGE
It's going well.

DOT
Should I wear my red dress or blue?

GEORGE
Red.

DOT
Aren't you going to clean up?

GEORGE
Why?

DOT
(Furious at his forgetting)
The Follies, George!

GEORGE
(After a brief pause)
I have to finish the hat.

He returns to his work. Dot slams down her brush and exits.

GEORGE
(As he paints)
Damn. The Follies. Will she yell or stay silent? Go without me or sulk in the corner? Will she be in the bed when the hat and the grass and the parasol have finally found their way?
Too green . . .
Do I care?
Too blue . . .
Yes . . .
Too soft . . .
What shall I do?

(Thinks for a moment)

Well . . .
Red.

He continues painting, as music swells and he is consumed by light.

If there is any song in the score that exemplifies the change in my writing when I began my collaboration with James Lapine, it would be "Color and Light." The flow between spoken and sung monologue, the elliptical heightened language, the stream-of-consciousness fantasies, the abrupt climactic use of unaccompanied dialogue, these are all musical extensions of hallmarks in Lapine's playwriting, particularly his early plays. They were the qualities in *Twelve Dreams* which turned me on so enthusiastically to his work and which I wanted to experiment with as a composer. In response, I organized this song, and much of the score, more through rhythm and language than rhyme.

When I speak of heightened language, I refer to the latent poetry in a line like "He could look forever" and the formality of "Will she yell or stay silent?" or the combination of both in a sentence like "Will she be in the bed when the hat and the grass and the parasol have finally found their way?" All of Lapine's writing has a touch of the formal (the ghosts of writers like Henry James and Edith Wharton visit him quite often) and it served *Sunday in the Park with George* well, lending the show both a nineteenth-century aura and the sense that it was a translation from the French. Thus, "Folly girl" instead of "Follies girl." Even writing the first sentence of this paragraph illustrates Lapine's lingering influence on me. Ordinarily, I say "talk"; he always says "speak."

Speaking of language, *Sunday in the Park with George* gave rise to two memorable remarks. One occurred during my initial encounter with Bernadette Peters. In the first draft of the show, James had written a scene in Act Two based on another of Seurat's major paintings, *Les Poseuses*, which depicts three naked models in the artist's studio, each of them in actuality the same model. This was the draft that we sent Bernadette in the hope that she would accept the role of Dot. Although I had never met her, she telephoned me from California to say how much she liked the script, except for one problem. "I don't do nude," she said. I assured her she wouldn't have to do nude, although I dreaded the prospect of her playing the scene in a body stocking, a ploy that is never effective unless it's on a darkened stage. The problem was obviated when we cut the scene because of a structural change in the story, but she would have looked great—a lot better, in fact, than the skinny androgyne that Seurat chose. In fact, if Bernadette had "done nude," the show might still be running.

The other memorable verbal moment happened during a rehearsal for James's production of *Merrily We Roll Along* in La Jolla in 1985. I was standing on the stage one afternoon when I peered out into the auditorium and saw Sarah Kernochan, James's wife, making her way down the aisle in a vastly enlarged state. I knew she was pregnant, but not having seen her in a while I didn't know she was *that* pregnant. She saw me staring agape at her belly and explained, "It's getting orange."

The park. The Old Lady and her Nurse are there, as are two flighty shopgirls, both named Celeste. Yvonne and Jules stroll about, gossiping about George. George is sketching a surly Boatman and his dog, Spot.

Gossip

CELESTE #1
They say that George has another woman.

CELESTE #2
I'm not surprised.

CELESTE #1
They say that George only lives with tramps.

CELESTE #2
I'm not surprised.

CELESTE #1
They say he prowls through the streets
In his top hat after midnight—

CELESTE #2
No!

CELESTE #1
—And stands there staring up at the
  lamps.

CELESTE #2
I'm not surprised.

BOTH
Artists are so crazy . . .

OLD LADY
Those girls are noisy.

NURSE
Yes, Madame.

OLD LADY
(Referring to Jules)
That man is famous.

NURSE
Yes, Madame.

OLD LADY
(Referring to the Boatman)
That man is filthy.

NURSE
  Your son seems to find him
    interesting.

OLD LADY
That man's deluded.

CELESTES
Artists are so crazy.

OLD LADY, NURSE
Artists are so peculiar.

YVONNE
Monkeys!

BOATMAN
(Muttering to himself)
Over-privileged women
Complaining,
Silly little simpering
Shopgirls,
Condescending artists
"Observing,"
"Perceiving . . ."
Well, screw them!

CELESTES*
Artists are so crazy!

BOATMAN
Artists are pompous prigs.

ALL
Artists are just people.

BOATMAN
And people are pigs.

CELESTE #1
They say his parents are just as
  crazy.

BOATMAN
Laughing like baboons . . .

CELESTE #1
And that's where George gets that
  crazy look.

CELESTE #2
I'm not surprised.

CELESTE #1
They say the father's a freak—
His arm is made of metal.
He doesn't have a hand, just a—

OLD LADY
These people!

CELESTE #1
Hook.

NURSE
Those giggles!

BOATMAN
God!

OLD LADY
That dog!

CELESTE #2
I'm not the least surprised.*

---

*The passages between asterisks were cut
during the transfer to Broadway for reasons
of length. The information about Seurat's
parents, incidentally, is true—but unnecessary.

ALL
Artists are so—

CELESTE #2
—Crazy.

CELESTE #1
—Secretive.

BOATMAN
—High and mighty.

NURSE
—Interesting.

OLD LADY
—Unfeeling.

CELESTE #1*
I hear he paints on the tops of
  boxes . . .

CELESTE #2
I'm not surprised.

CELESTE #1
That when you're near him, he
  smells of chalk . . .

CELESTE #2
It's no surprise.

CELESTE #1
That every night he goes home
To have dinner with his mother . . .

CELESTE #2
Oh?

CELESTE #1
And also says that colors can talk.

CELESTE #2
I'm not surprised.
Artists are so crazy—!

CELESTE #1
Oh, shut up.†

---

†Later in the scene, there was this further interesting but unnecessary information
which was also cut. I include it because I
like the last line: It tells us what we need to
know about the girls' relationship. And after
all the elaborate singing, the shock of its
spoken flatness is funny.

Dot enters with her new beau, Louis (pronounced "Louie," as in France), a baker who wanders about, selling cream puffs to the strollers in the park. Dot sits on a bench, studying a primer, teaching herself to read. George comes over and they have a strained interchange. Louis takes her away as the other people leave. George is left alone sketching Spot, the Boatman's scruffy dog.

The Day Off
(Dog Song)

GEORGE

If the head was smaller . . .
It the tail were longer . . .
If he faced the water . . .
If the paws were hidden . . .
If the neck was darker . . .
If the back was curved . . .
More like the parasol . . .

(Humming)

Bumbum bum bumbumbum
Bumbum bum . . .

More shade . . .
More tail . . .
More grass! . . .
Would you like some more grass?
Mmmm . . .

SPOT (GEORGE)
(Barks)
Ruff! Ruff!
Thanks, the week has been—

(Barks)

Rough!
When you're stuck for life on a
    garbage scow,

(Sniffs around)

Only forty feet long from stern to
    prow,
And a crackpot in the bow—wow,
    rough!

(Sniffs)

The planks are rough
And the wind is rough
And the master's drunk and
    mean and—

(Sniffs)

Grrrruff! Gruff!
With the fish and scum
And planks and ballast . . .

(Sniffs)

The nose gets numb
And the paws get calloused.
And with splinters in your ass,
You look forward to the grass
On Sunday,
The day off.

(Barks)

Off! Off! Off!
Off!

SPOT
    The grass needs to be thicker. Per-
    haps a few weeds. With some ants,
    if you would. I love fresh ants.

Roaming around on Sunday,
Poking among the roots and rocks.
Nose to the ground on Sunday,
Studying all the shoes and socks.
Everything's worth it Sunday,
The day off.

(Sniffing)

Bits of pastry . . .
Piece of chicken . . .
Here's a handkerchief
That somebody was sick in.
There's a thistle.
That's a shallot.
That's a dripping
From the loony with the palette.

Fifi, a pug dog, appears.

FIFI (GEORGE)
Yap! Yap!

(Pants)

Yap!
Out for the day on Sunday,
Off of my lady's lap at last.
Yapping away on Sunday
Helps you forget the week just
    past—

(Yelps)

Yep! Yep!
Everything's worth it Sunday,
The day off.
Yep!

Stuck all week on a lady's lap,
Nothing to do but yawn and nap,
Can you blame me if I yap?

SPOT
Nope.

FIFI*
As I'm powdered and petted,
I keep thinking of mud.
As I'm ribboned and bowed and
    barretted,
All I want is her blood.

So whenever we're out where it's
    leafy,
I play a game:
I run off just as far as I—

MISTRESS
(offstage)
Fifi!

FIFI
Yich! What a sickening name.*
    There's just so much attention a
    dog can take.
Being alone on Sunday,
Rolling around in mud and dirt—

SPOT
Begging a bone on Sunday,
Settling for a spoiled dessert—

FIFI
Everything's worth it—

---

*The passage between asterisks was cut during the transfer to Broadway.

George and Dot in the studio (Playwrights Horizons, 1983)

SPOT
Sunday—

FIFI
The day off.

SPOT
(*Sniffs*)
Something fuzzy . . .

FIFI
(*Sniffs*)
Something furry . . .

SPOT
(*Sniffs*)
Something pink
That someone tore off in a hurry.

FIFI
What's the muddle
In the middle?

SPOT
That's the puddle
Where the poodle
Did the piddle.

Not long before we began working on *Sunday in the Park with George*, I had gone to a Laurie Anderson concert and watched and listened with fascination as she sang into a large sausage-shaped microphone called a vocoder, which transmogrified her voice as she sang into any timbre and range that she chose: crackling, gurgling, soprano, bass, male, female, infinite kinds and infinite combinations. I thought it would be smart and surprising to conceal one of these instruments in George's sketch pad so that his voice would take on the qualities of a growling mutt and a yapping lap-dog in turn. To this end, I went shopping for such a device with Lapine and our conductor, Paul Gemignani. It was a needless expedition—I hadn't counted on Mandy Patinkin, the pro-tean actor and singer whom we had cast as George. He told us that a vocoder was unnecessary and to prove his point auditioned dogs for us—three different Spots and three different Fifis, each one distinctively character-ized: crackling, gurgling, soprano, bass, male, female, and so on. We chose one from Column A and one from Column B, and the result was spectacular. Some day, though, I'd like to hear the song through a vocoder, just to hear what effect the artificiality would have on it.

Franz, Frieda, the Celestes (carrying fishing poles) and the Nurse stroll on.

The Day Off
(Ensemble Songs)

GEORGE
Taking the day on Sunday,
Now that the dreary week is dead.
Getting away on Sunday
Brightens the dreary week ahead.
Everyone's on display on Sunday—

ALL
The day off!

George flips open a page of his sketch-book and starts to sketch the Nurse as she clucks at the ducks in the river.

GEORGE
Bonnet flapping,
Bustle sliding,
Like a rocking horse that nobody's
    been riding.
There's a daisy . . .
And some clover . . .
And that interesting fellow looking
    over . . .

*The Nurse exchanges glances with
Franz.*

OLD LADY
(Offstage)
Nurse!

GEORGE, NURSE
One day is much like any other
Listening to her snap and drone.

NURSE
Still, Sunday with someone's dotty
    mother
Is better than Sunday with your
    own.

Mothers may drone, mothers may
    whine—
Tending to his, though, is perfectly
    fine.
It pays for the nurse that is tending
    to mine
On Sunday—
My day off.

"The Day Off" is a sequence whose primary purpose is to show George sketching—by which I mean inhabiting, as Seurat did, the interior lives of the major figures in his painting or, more accurately, James's interpretations of them. The problem was how to avoid its being an illustrated list, one where the audience waits in bemused, if not dreaded, anticipation of having to sit through a potted history of every person onstage. The most frightening example of this for me occurred in *A Chorus Line*. When the first of the sixteen dancers vying for jobs sang an interior monologue, I thought, "Fifteen more—don't keep a scorecard." Happily, some monologues

were combined into duets and trios and ensembles, but as with "I Fought Every Step of the Way" and "One Hundred Easy Ways" (p. 237 in the *Follies* chapter in the first volume), I felt uncomfortable at having the entire meal laid out for me before I began to eat it. I spent time anticipating instead of being surprised.

This was the problem with "The Day Off." As soon as the audience got to hear one character sing while being sketched by George, they would think with a collective sigh that they'd have to wade through every other character's sketch similarly. Since James had thoughtfully connected two of them in a marriage (Franz and Frieda) and three of them in a romantic dalliance (the Celestes and a Soldier) I was able to combine them into a duet and a trio, varying the structures as in *A Chorus Line*, but also interspersing them with introspective solos for Dot and George, as below. I tied each one into George by having him sing the introductory lines of the characters' verses along with them so that the audience wouldn't feel that they were irrelevant. It would be clear (I hoped) that these were going to be the leading players on the stage of George's canvas.

*George flips a page and starts to sketch
Franz and Frieda.*

GEORGE, FRIEDA
Second bottle . . .

GEORGE, FRANZ
(As Franz looks off at the Nurse)
Ah, she looks for me . . .

FRIEDA
He is bursting to go . . .

FRANZ
Near the fountain . . .

FRIEDA
I could let him . . .

FRANZ
How to manage it—?

FRIEDA
No.
    You know, Franz—I believe that
    artist is drawing us.

FRANZ
Who?

FRIEDA
Monsieur's friend.

FRANZ
(Sees George; he and Frieda pose)
    Monsieur would never think to
    draw us! We are only people he
    looks down upon.

(Pause)

    I should have been an artist. I was
    never intended for work.

FRIEDA
    Artists work, Franz. I believe they
    work very hard.

FRANZ
    Work! . . . *We* work.
We serve their food,
We carve their meat,
We tend to their house,
We polish their
Silverware.

FRIEDA
The food we serve
We also eat.

FRANZ
For them we rush,
Wash and brush,
Wipe and wax—

FRIEDA
Franz, relax.

FRANZ
While he "creates,"
We scrape their plates
And dust their knickknacks,
Hundreds to the shelf.
Work is what you do for others,
Liebchen,
Art is what you do for yourself.

At Playwrights Horizons, we went a little deeper into the restlessness of their
marriage and the monotony of their
lives, with the following lines:

FRANZ, FRIEDA
Monday through Saturday,
Half a day Sunday,
Six in the morning
Till nine p.m.,
Monday through Saturday,
And then again Monday:
Him. Her. Them.

Taking the day on Sunday,
Out of the house, or so to speak
Nothing to say on Sunday,
Nothing we haven't said all week.
Being alone together Sunday—

FRANZ
And Tuesday
And Thursday
And Christmas . . .

*George flips a page and starts sketch-
ing the Boatman.*

GEORGE, BOATMAN
You and me, pal,
We're the loonies.
Did you know that?
Bet you didn't know that.

BOATMAN
'Cause we tell them the truth!

Who you drawing?
Who the hell you think you're
    drawing?
Me?
You don't know me!
Go on drawing,
Since you're drawing only what you
    want to see,
Anyway!

(Points to his eye patch)

One eye, no illusion—
That you get with two:

(Points to George's eye)

One for what is true.

(Points to the other)

One for what suits you.
Draw your own conclusion,
All you artists do.
I see what is true . . .

You and me, pal,
We're society's fault . . .

*George wanders around the park
among the people he has sketched.*

ALL
Taking the day on Sunday
After another week is dead.

OLD LADY
Nurse!

ALL
Getting away on Sunday
Brightens the dreary week ahead.

OLD LADY
Nurse!

*George begins to exit, crossing paths
with Dot and Louis. He gives Dot a
hasty tip of the hat and makes a speedy
exit.*

ALL
Leaving the city pressure
Behind you,
Off where the air is fresher,
Where green, blue,
Blind you—

*Dot looks at the departing figure of
George.*

Everybody Loves Louis

DOT
Hello, George . . .
Where did you go, George?
I know you're near, George.
I caught your eyes, George.
I want your ear, George.
I've a surprise, George . . .

Everybody loves Louis,
Louis's simple and kind.
Everybody loves Louis,
Louis's lovable.

Seems we never know, do we,
Who we're going to find?
And Louis the baker—
Is not what I had in mind.
But . . .

Louis's really an artist:
Louis's cakes are an art.
Louis isn't the smartest—
Louis's popular.
Everybody loves Louis:
Louis bakes from the heart . . .

The bread, George.
I mean the bread, George.
And then in bed, George . . .
I mean he kneads me—
I mean like dough, George . . .
Hello, George . . .

Louis's always so pleasant,
Louis's always so fair.
Louis makes you feel present,
Louis's generous.
That's the thing about Louis:
Louis always is *there*.
Louis's thoughts are not hard to
    follow,
Louis's art is not hard to swallow.

Not that Louis's perfection—
That's what makes him ideal.
Hardly anything worth objection:
Louis drinks a bit,
Louis blinks a bit,
Louis makes a connection,
That's the thing that you feel . . .

We lose things.
And then we choose things.
And there are Louis's.
And there are Georges—
Well, Louis's
And George.

But George has George,
And I need someone—
Louis . . .

*Louis gives her a pastry and
exits.*

Everybody loves Louis,
Him as well as his cakes.
Everybody loves Louis,
Me included, George.
Not afraid to be gooey,
Louis sells what he makes.
Everybody gets along with him.
That's the trouble,
Nothing's wrong with him . . .

Louis has to bake his way,
George can only bake his.

(Licks the pastry)

Louis it is!

*A Soldier enters, attached to a life-size
cutout of another soldier, his Companion. The Celestes attract their attention.*

The Day Off
(Soldiers' Song)

SOLDIER, GEORGE
Mademoiselles,
I and my friend,
We are but soldiers.

SOLDIER
Passing the time
In between wars
For weeks at an end.

CELESTE #1
(Aside)
Both of them are perfect.

CELESTE #2
You can have the other.

CELESTE #1
I don't want the other.

CELESTE #2
I don't want the other either.

SOLDIER
And after a week
Spent mostly indoors
With nothing but soldiers,

Ladies, I and my friend
Trust we will not offend,
Which we'd never intend,
By suggesting we spend—

BOTH CELESTES
(Excited)
Oh, spend—!

SOLDIER
This magnificent Sunday—

BOTH CELESTES
(A bit deflated)
Oh, Sunday—

SOLDIER
With you and your friend.

*The Soldier offers his arm. Both Ce-
lestes rush to take it; Celeste #1 gets
there first. Celeste #2 tries to get in between the Soldiers but can't, and rather
than join the Companion, takes the
arm of Celeste #1. They all start to
promenade.*

CELESTE #2
(Aside, to Celeste #1)
The one on the right's an awful bore.

CELESTE #1
He's been in a war.

SOLDIER
(Aside, to Companion)
We may get a meal and we might get
    more . . .

*Celeste #1 shakes free of Celeste #2
and grabs the Soldier's arm, freeing
him from his Companion.*

CELESTE #1, SOLDIER
(Exiting)
It's certainly fine for Sunday . . .

CELESTE #2
*(Dejected, exiting with the
Companion)*
It's certainly fine for Sunday . . .

During the run of the show at Playwrights Horizons, we realized that we
were asking the audience to spend too

much time with the characters George
sketched rather than with George
himself and that their songs should
indeed be sketches, short and quick:
thus the above. The original Soldier's
song, however, was not merely a
longer version, it was a completely
different number:

Soldiers and Girls
(cut)

SOLDIER, GEORGE
Mademoiselles,
I and my friend,
We are but soldiers.

SOLDIER
Passing the time
In between wars,
However we may.

CELESTE #2
(Aside, to Celeste #1)
Careful, he's peculiar.

CELESTE #1
How is he peculiar?

CELESTE #2
Soldiers are peculiar.

SOLDIER
And after a week
Spent mostly indoors
With nothing but soldiers,
May we venture to say
It's a glorious day!

CELESTE #2
Wasn't that peculiar?

CELESTE #1
No, it's not peculiar.

CELESTE #2
Something is peculiar.
Shouldn't we be going?

CELESTE #1
No, will you be quiet?

"Soldiers and Girls"

Frieda and Franz

Louis and Dot

Mr. and Mrs.

"THE DAY OFF"

SOLDIER
Sundays were made for soldiers and
    girls,
Don't you agree?
Sundays were made
For medals and ribbons arrayed
With red sashes,
Buckles and braid,
And sabers—
And girls.

Sundays were meant for helmets and
    plumes,
Mademoiselles,
Meant for salutes
And epaulettes,
Glistening boots,
The heady perfumes
Of horses and grooms—
And beautiful girls!

Mademoiselles!
I and my friend
Have a suggestion!

CELESTE #2
(Aside)
Anyone can see that
That man is peculiar.

SOLDIER
I and my friend
Wish to be friends
With you and your friend.

CELESTE #1
See, he's very friendly.

CELESTE #2
Yes, he's very friendly.
That's what is peculiar.

SOLDIER
Only just now
I said to my friend
Of you and your friend,
"I suspect they are friends."

CELESTE #1
Both of them are perfect.

CELESTE #2
You can have the other.

CELESTE #1
I don't want the other.

CELESTE #2
I don't want the other either.

SOLDIER
And, see, you are friends!

CELESTES
What can be the harm in
Strolling in the park with
Soldiers even if they *are* peculiar?

SOLDIER
And we shall be friends.

SOLDIER, CELESTES
Sundays were made for soldiers and
    girls.

SOLDIER
Mademoiselles,
Sundays were made for medals—

*(Looks expectantly at Celeste #1, who
picks up her cue)*

CELESTE #1
And ribbons arrayed with red
    sashes.

(Nudges Celeste #2)

CELESTE #2
Buckets and braid—

CELESTE #1
(Whispers)
Buckles!

SOLDIER
And sabers—

*(Looks at his Companion, who appar-
ently conveys something)*

Right!

Sundays were made for banners and
    bells,
Don't you agree?
Made for whatever sparkles,
Whatever is fresh and sweet,

(The Celestes giggle)

Everything casting colorful spells—
For beaches and shells

And scarlet lapels
And vigorous smells.
And soldiers!

(At a nudge from the Companion)

And mademoiselles!

When the show transferred, that song
was replaced by this one:

The One on the Left
(cut)

SOLDIER, GEORGE
*(The Soldier singing to his
Companion)*
The one on the left is nice and pink.

*The Companion replies silently; the
Soldier nods.*

SOLDIER, GEORGE
I'll tip her a wink.

SOLDIER
The one on the right seems
    charming, too,
Although she does look rather blue.

*(Listens to Companion's reply,
shrugs)*

Well, what shall we do?

The Celestes giggle.

The one on the left is awfully bold—
I wonder how old.
The one on the right is more demure
Or less mature,
You can't be sure.
She isn't much over seventeen.
She looks pretty clean . . .

The Companion replies silently.

I see what you mean.

*The Soldier approaches the girls and
starts a conversation.*

CELESTE #2
(Aside)
I don't think he likes me.

CELESTE #1
Certainly he likes you.
You take the other one.

CELESTE #2
That one is peculiar—

CELESTE #1
How is he peculiar?

CELESTE #2
Why is he so quiet?

CELESTE #1
Both of them are perfect.

CELESTE #2
You can have the other.

CELESTE #1
I don't want the other.

CELESTE #2
I don't want the other either.

They all start to promenade.

CELESTE #2
(Aside)
The one on the right seems quite
attached.

CELESTE #1
(Looking over, then back)
As well as scratched.

SOLDIER
(Aside, to his Companion)
Admit it, old man, we're not badly
matched.

ALL
It's certainly fine for Sunday.

SOLDIER
(Aside)
The one on the left seems quite
subdued.

CELESTE #2
(As Celeste #1 tries to elbow her over
to the other side)
I'm not in the mood.

CELESTE #1
You're ruining things and we're
being rude!

ALL
(To each other)
It's certainly fine for Sunday!

SOLDIER, CELESTE #1
(Aside, to their partners)
My only advice
Is don't think twice.

SOLDIER
(To Celeste #1)
Would you care for an ice?

CELESTES
Oh, an ice would be nice!

CELESTE #2
(To Celeste #1)
Will they buy us a drink?

SOLDIER
(To his Companion)
Are they virgins, you think?

ALL
It's certainly fine for Sunday!

CELESTE #2
(To Celeste #1, referring to the
Companion)
Is that a mustache or just a gash?

CELESTE #1
But just look at the sash!

SOLDIER
(To his Companion)
Did you bring any cash?

CELESTE #1
(To Celeste #2)
The buckles and braid—

CELESTE #2
The gold brocade—

CELESTE #1
The boots—

CELESTE #2
The blade—!

SOLDIER
Shall we head for the glade?

CELESTE #1
(Excited, aside)
Heading for the shadows—!

CELESTE #2
Anything can happen—!

CELESTE #1
Wonder what they're planning.

CELESTE #2
(Alarmed)
What they're planning?

CELESTE #1
What they're planning later on!

SOLDIER
(To his Companion)
The one on the right gave you a
look—
Let's hope she can cook.

CELESTE #1
(Aside)
Taking us to dinner—

CELESTE #2
Maybe to the Follies—!

BOTH CELESTES
Anyhow, it's certainly fine for
Sunday!

CELESTE #1
The one on the right is odd, it's true,
But what can we do?

SOLDIER
(To his Companion)
The one on the left—

CELESTE #1
You're odd as he—

SOLDIER
—has great esprit!

CELESTE #2
I don't agree—

SOLDIER, CELESTE #1
The one on the left is right for me—

They switch positions so that Celeste #2 has the Companion.

SOLDIER, CELESTE #1
So the one on the right is left
    for you!

I was sorry to see this lyric reduced to a shadow of its former self, but following Oscar's rules of ruthlessness, I had to agree that it involved spending too much time with unimportant characters, regardless of the linguistic playfulness involved. (One of the pleasures of writing this book is having the opportunity to show off and share these things that would otherwise never have seen the light of day.)

George is now alone in the park, except for Spot, the Boatman's dog. He sits and leafs back through his sketches of the day.

Finishing the Hat

GEORGE
Mademoiselles . . .
You and me, pal . . .
Second bottle . . .
Ah, she looks for me . . .
Bonnet flapping . . .
Yapping . . .
Ruff! . . .
Chicken . . .
Pastry . . .

(Licks his lips, then looks offstage to where Dot exited)

Yes, she looks for me.
Good.
Let her look for me to tell me why
    she left me—
As I always knew she would.
I had thought she understood.
They have never understood,
And no reason that they should,
But if anybody could . . .

Finishing the hat,
How you have to finish the hat,
How you watch the rest of the world
From a window
While you finish the hat.

Mapping out a sky,
What you feel like, planning a sky,
What you feel when voices that
    come
Through the window
Go
Until they distance and die,
Until there's nothing but sky.

And how you're always turning back
    too late
From the grass or the stick
Or the dog or the light,
How the kind of woman willing to
    wait's
Not the kind that you want to find
    waiting
To return you to the night,
Dizzy from the height,
Coming from the hat,

Studying the hat,
Entering the world of the hat,
Reaching through the world of
    the hat
Like a window,
Back to this one from that.

Studying a face,
Stepping back to look at a face
Leaves a little space in the way like a
    window,
But to see—
It's the only way to see.

And when the woman that you
    wanted goes,
You can say to yourself, "Well, I give
    what I give."
But the woman who won't wait for
    you knows
That however you live,
There's a part of you always
    standing by,
Mapping out the sky,
Finishing a hat,
Starting on a hat,
Finishing a hat . . .

(Showing the sketch to Spot)

Look, I made a hat
Where there never was a hat.

If the songs "Good Thing Going" and "Opening Doors" in *Merrily We Roll Along* are personal to me in that they reflect actual experiences I've had, "Finishing the Hat" reflects an emotional experience shared by everybody to some degree or other, but more keenly and more often by creative artists: trancing out—that phenomenon of losing the world while you're writing (or painting or composing or doing a crossword puzzle or coming to a difficult decision or anything that requires intense and complete concentration). The most vivid example in my life had nothing to do with writing songs, however. It occurred in 1965, shortly after I'd gone to Cincinnati to see my friends Phyllis Newman, Jack Cassidy and John McMartin perform in the tryout of a Frank Loesser musical called *Pleasures and Palaces*. The cast had just been informed that the show would close out of town and Phyllis was, understandably, depressed. She murmured that what she needed to lift her spirits on her return to New York would be a game party, a social service I often provided in those days. I not only said yes, but to bolster my generosity I impulsively offered to invent a game for her, inventing games being something I did to avoid working while still maintaining the feeling that I was exercising my brain.

    Phyllis duly returned, a date was set and I found myself one day with a deadline a week away. Dutifully, I set to work that evening around eight o'clock to come up with an idea. I had often thought of trying to fashion a game of Murder to replace the traditional dull one, which involved the dealing of cards, the queen of spades denoting (secretly) the Murderer, the ace of hearts the Detective, the other players as potential victims. The lights would be turned out, the Murderer would put his hands around someone's throat, the victim give a choked cry, the lights would be turned on, and a round of fruitless questioning

Studying the hat

Entering the (world of the) hat

Entering the world of the world

Through a window — like a window

Through to other worlds
To another world beyond that

From this one to that

Even when you're ready to open

The window

Sunshine
You are finishing that

Looking at the face
look at a face

Stepping back to see

Puts a little space between you

Puts you in a different place

Then when you might like to be

But it's the only way to see.

Pressing up as close as you can

To the window

Reaching to the world through the hat

As a window.

Getting you from this one to that

Travelling from this world to that

Getting through to this one from that

Like a window

Making it
Hiding in the rules of the hat

Finishing the hat

Working on the hat

Studying the hat

Entering the world of the hat

How the only way you can see is to
Step back just a bit

Coming to a face

But how else can you see
You have to step close
Where else can you be free

Stepping back to look at the hat
world
Through a window

If you want to
Only way to see

Studying the hat

Entering the world of the hat

Reaching through the

As a window

To a world

Reaching through from this one to
that

Release I

The kind of
And if
Until the woman
But you want won't wait   And when you
While you're redoing the sky   (cloud)   Turn back from the hat, too late
        attend to   Too late
    you refinish
        you are   The kind of
On the grass or the sand   (cloud)   Girl I want won't wait
                                             Wait for me to come back

                                                         From the sky
While you're lost in the sky (hat on the grass or the tree)   And when you
                                             Turn back from the sky, you may find
                                             That there is nothing at all.
The kind of woman who is
Willing to wait
Is not the kind that you want to be   (have in the night)
Waiting when you're finished w/ the hat   There should be
And what you feel like   Someone that I
Turning back   Want who would want   (to)
(From the hat) Too late
(From your trip) (journey)
From the grass or the stick   R.S.:
On the (street) or the sand   (dock)   Until the woman that you want
                                          Won't wait --
                                          But I was sure that she would.

The kind of woman that you want
Will not wait

The kind of woman that will wait for that   (who would) (the hat)
You don't want when you turn from the hat to the room   (or the grass) (world)

would follow, the Detective leading the "investigation" and the game would rapidly deteriorate into repetitive palaver. I wanted to invent a game that had some suspense and a puzzle solution so that even those players who got killed and who knew the Murderer's identity wouldn't have to sit around idly while the rest of the players tried to figure out who it was, but could participate in trying to prove it. I sat down—or, more precisely, lay down, since I write supine—and started to sketch ideas and plot their variations, in the knowledge that I had days to work out the details. The next thing I knew, I could see by the dawn's early light that it was seven in the morning and that, as far as I was aware, I hadn't moved for eleven hours. I must have, of course, if for nothing else than to go to the bathroom, much less get a drink or a snack. But I had no memory of it. I had left the planet for eleven hours, completely absorbed in a world of instructions, gunshots, diagrams, and clues, calibrating every possibility of the players' movements and observations. I've never had a better time making a hat. No matter how trivial the goal may have been, the intensity of the concentration was the same as that of writing a song, and just as difficult and exhilarating. "Finishing the Hat" is an attempt to convey that treasured feeling.

Relinquishing the world may be easier in the privacy of a study or during a walk in the woods, but it can happen in a public place, too. I wrote a great deal of *A Little Night Music* at Christo's Steak House, a block from where I live, in the late hours of the evening and the early ones of the morning, with customers ordering, waiters arguing and Peggy Lee and Frank Sinatra singing through the sound system. I didn't hear a thing. "Liaisons" took shape while "Fever" was playing, with no problem in concentration. When the cocoon is self-created, the surroundings matter not at all.

As befits the creative act, "Finishing the Hat" is a stream-of-consciousness lyric. There is no complete sentence

until the last stanza; each of the preceding stanzas is a subordinate clause. Stream-of-consciousness doesn't think in sentences. It's a technique common in pop lyrics, largely because it relieves the writer of having to say anything coherent; strings of images are always effective, if often meaningless. But a little incoherence seemed appropriate in the case of an artist struggling to reconcile his personal life with his professional one. Looking at the lyric now, it seems to me neat and graceful, except for the glaring flaw of the word "wait's," which should rhyme with "late" but doesn't quite. When I wrote it, I excused myself on the grounds that the "'s" is short for "is" and therefore belongs to the next line, but even so, it *sounds* like a false rhyme, and that's what counts. The sour fact is that I could never get rid of that "s." I was reduced to letting it go and taking refuge in the romantic cliché that all first-rate works of art are imperfect. This comforting notion has saved many an ego, as exemplified by the rehearsals for Leonard Bernstein's theater oratorio *Mass* in Washington, D.C. After a dress rehearsal which lasted for more than two hours, Gordon Davidson, who was directing, suggested that perhaps the piece might benefit from some tightening. Lenny agreed and left Gordon with carte blanche to fiddle with the piece for a day or so. When Gordon was ready to show Lenny what he'd done, Lenny returned to the rehearsals and Gordon ran it for him. The running time had been shortened by half an hour, and Lenny complimented Gordon extravagantly on it. "It's tighter, it's swifter, it's more coherent and dramatic," he gushed. As Gordon started to beam with pleasure, Lenny added, "And I want you to restore it to the way it was." "Why?" Gordon asked, baffled. "I want it to be flawed," Lenny replied. I know how he felt. But I try to fight it.

One more thing about this song: my fondness for the word "hat," which the British critic Michael Ratcliffe pointed out in his program note at London's Royal National Theatre, when *Sunday*

in the Park with George was produced there in 1990. From "You could say, 'Hey, here's your hat'" in *Gypsy* to "Does anyone still wear a hat?" in *Company*, through "Hats off" in *Follies* and "It's called a bowler hat" in *Pacific Overtures*, I seem to be attached to it as an image. Surely some future graduate student in Musical Theater, looking for an obscure subject to write about, will seize on "The Use of Headgear in Sondheim's Lyrics" and conjure up insightful theories for my persistent attraction to the word, but I can save him the trouble: it's the jaunty tone and the ease in rhyming that attract me—two sound reasons.

Dot, very pregnant, visits George in his studio to tell him that she is leaving for America with Louis. He is gruff and impatient and refuses to acknowledge responsibility for the baby. She accuses him of hiding his real self behind his painting and caring about nothing human.

We Do Not Belong Together

GEORGE
. . . I cannot divide my feelings up as neatly as you, and I am not hiding behind my canvas—I am living in it.

DOT
What you care for is yourself.

GEORGE
I care about this painting. You will be in this painting.

DOT
I am something you can use.

GEORGE
I had thought you understood.

DOT
It's because I understand that I left, That I am leaving.

GEORGE
Then there's nothing I can say,
Is there?

DOT
Yes, George, there is!
You could tell me not to go.
Say it to me,
Tell me not to go.
Tell me that you're hurt,
Tell me you're relieved,
Tell me that you're bored—
Anything, but don't assume I know.
Tell me what you feel!

GEORGE
What I feel?
You know exactly how I feel.
Why do you insist
You must hear the words,
When you know I cannot give you
    words?
Not the ones you need.

There's nothing to say.
I cannot be what you want.

DOT
What do *you* want, George?

GEORGE
I needed you and you left.

DOT
There was no room for me—

GEORGE
You will not accept who I am.
I am what I do—
Which you knew,
Which you always knew,
Which I thought you were a part of!

DOT
No,
You are complete, George,
You are your own.
We do not belong together.

You are complete, George,
You all alone.
I am unfinished,
I am diminished
With or without you.

We do not belong together,
And we should have belonged
    together.

What made it so right together
Is what made it all wrong.

No one is you, George,
There we agree,
But others will do, George.

No one is you and
No one can be,
But no one is me, George,
No one is me!
We do not belong together,
And we'll never belong—!

You have a mission,
A mission to see.
Now I have one too, George,
And we should have belonged
    together.

I have to move on.

*She leaves. On the following Sunday in
the park, George is sketching the Old
Lady, his mother. She is looking across
the river at the Eiffel Tower and, with a
failing memory, lamenting the passing
of time.*

Beautiful

OLD LADY
Changing.
It keeps changing.
I see towers
Where there were trees.

Going,
All the stillness,
The solitude,
Georgie.

Sundays
Disappearing
All the time,
When things were beautiful . . .

GEORGE
All things are beautiful,
Mother,
All trees, all towers,
Beautiful.

That tower—
Beautiful, Mother,
See?

(*Gestures*)

A perfect tree.

Pretty isn't beautiful, Mother,
Pretty is what changes.
What the eye arranges
Is what is beautiful.

OLD LADY
Fading . . .

GEORGE
I'm changing.
You're changing.

OLD LADY
It keeps fading . . .

GEORGE
I'll draw us now before we fade,
Mother.

OLD LADY
It keeps melting before our eyes.

GEORGE
You watch
While I revise the world.

OLD LADY
Changing,
As we sit here—
Quick, draw it all, Georgie!

BOTH
Sundays—

OLD LADY
Disappearing,
As we look.

GEORGE
Look! . . .
Look! . . .

OLD LADY
(*Not listening, fondly*)
You make it beautiful.

Oh, Georgie, how I long for the old
view.

Nothing is quite as embarrassing for a writer trying to be elusive as having to explain what he means to an actor, and that is exactly what happened to me when Mandy Patinkin, who played George, asked me to explain the quatrain beginning with "Pretty isn't beautiful . . ." I knew what I meant, but I hoped I would never have to articulate it. I was able to explain it to him enough, however, without reducing its vague mystery, so that he was able to sing it with passionate conviction. It's still a favorite lyric of mine, and I think I know what it means.

Squabbles erupt all over the park: Dot, finally leaving for America with Louis and her baby, whom she has named Marie after a character in her primer, quarrels with George; the two Celestes quarrel over the Soldier; Jules, out for an assignation with Frieda, is caught by Yvonne and Franz and an angry scene erupts; two American tourists, trying to get off the island, have a confrontation with the Boatman; general chaos ensues. George gestures and everyone freezes. As he utters his artistic mantra, we see his ultimate power over his subjects. He nods to them, and with each word they individually take up positions onstage.

GEORGE
Order.
Design.
Tension.
Balance.
Harmony.

They promenade and sing. As they do, George is moving about, setting trees, cutouts and figures, making a picture.

Sunday

ALL
Sunday,
By the blue
Purple yellow red water
On the green
Purple yellow red grass,
Let us pass
Through our perfect park,

Pausing on a Sunday
By the cool
Blue triangular water
On the soft
Green elliptical grass,
As we pass
Through arrangements of shadows
Toward the verticals of trees
Forever . . .

By the blue
Purple yellow red water
On the green
Orange violet mass
Of the grass
In our perfect park,

GEORGE
Made of flecks of light
And dark,

MEN
And parasols . . .

GEORGE
(Hums as he works)
Bumbum bum bumbumbum
Bumbum bum . . .

ALL
People strolling through the trees
Of a small suburban park
On an island in the river
On an ordinary Sunday . . .

They all reach their positions.

Sunday . . .

Everyone assumes the final pose of the painting. George comes downstage to look at what he's done.

Sunday . . .

At the last moment, he rushes upstage and removes Louise's eyeglasses. He dashes back, inspects his work one last time and gestures. Everyone freezes. The picture is complete. The finished canvas flies in.

BLACKOUT

This is the only lyric I've written that consists of one long incomplete sentence. I wanted it to be like the descriptive caption you might read in a museum next to the painting. I hoped that the tone would echo the permanence of the painting, which is not only a miracle of composition and innovative technique, but also a satirical piece of reportage, something Lapine had pointed out to me. Seurat was as much a cartoonist as a painter.

Once during the writing of each show, I cry at a notion, a word, a chord, a melodic idea, an accompaniment figure. Only once in each case, curiously enough, since I'm an easy crier at works of art, particularly those made by others. For example, with *Anyone Can Whistle* it was the phrase "Hold me" at the end of "With So Little to Be Sure Of" against the chord underneath; in *Follies* it was the word "home" in "The Right Girl"; in *Pacific Overtures* the last line of "Someone in a Tree" ("Only cups of tea/And history/And someone in a tree!"); in *Merrily We Roll Along* the vamp to "Our Time." In this show it was the word "Forever" in "Sunday." I was suddenly moved by the contemplation of what these people would have thought if they'd known they were being immortalized, and in a major way, in a great painting. I still cry when I think about it. But then I cry at Animal Planet. Often.

ACT TWO

The curtain rises on everyone in a tableau of the painting. After a long pause, they sing one by one, in a tone of enervation.

It's Hot Up Here

DOT
It's hot up here.

YVONNE
It's hot and it's monotonous.

LOUISE
I want my glasses.

FRANZ
This is not my good profile.

NURSE
Nobody can even see my profile.

CELESTE #1
I hate this dress.

CELESTE #2
The soldiers have forgotten us.

FRIEDA
The boatman schvitzes.

JULES
I am completely out of proportion.

SOLDIER
These helmets weigh a lot on us.

OLD LADY
This tree is blocking my view.

LOUISE
I can't see anything.

BOATMAN
Why are they complaining?
It could have been raining.

DOT
I hate these people.

ALL
It's hot up here
A lot up here.
It's hot up here
Forever.

A lot of fun
It's not up here.
It's hot up here,
No matter what.

There's not a breath
Of air up here,
And they're up here
Forever.

It's not my fault
I got up here.
I'll rot up here,
I am so hot up here.

YVONNE
(To Louise)
Darling, don't clutch Mother's hand quite so tightly.

Louise doesn't move.

Thank you.

CELESTE #1
It's hot up here.

FRIEDA
At least you have a parasol.

SOLDIER, NURSE, YVONNE, LOUISE
Well, look who's talking,
Sitting in the shade.

JULES
(To Dot)
I trust my cigar is not bothering you—unfortunately, it never goes out.

(As she pays him no attention)

You have excellent concentration.

SOLDIER
(To his Companion)
It's good to be together again.

CELESTE #2
(To Celeste #1)
See, I told you they were odd.

CELESTE #1
Don't slouch.

LOUISE
He took my glasses!

YVONNE
You've been eating something sticky.

NURSE
I put on rouge today, too . . .

FRIEDA
(To the Boatman)
Don't you ever take a bath?

OLD LADY
Nurse! Hand me my fan.

NURSE
I can't.

FRANZ
At least the brat is with her mother.

LOUISE
I heard that!

JULES
(To Dot)
Do you like tall grass?

FRIEDA
Hah!

YVONNE
Jules!

BOATMAN
Bunch of animals . . .

DOT
I hate these people.

ALL
It's hot up here
And strange up here.
No change up here
Forever.

How still it is,
How odd it is,
And God, it is
So hot!

"Sunday" (Playwrights Horizon, 1983)

SOLDIER
I like the one in the light hat.

DOT
Hello, George.
I do not wish to be remembered
Like this, George,
With them, George.
My hem, George:
Three inches off the ground
And then this monkey
And these people, George—!

They'll argue till they fade
And whisper things and grunt.
But thank you for the shade,
And putting me in front.
Yes, thank you, George, for that—
And for the hat . . .

CELESTE #1
It's hot up here.

YVONNE
It's hot and it's monotonous.

LOUISE
I want my glasses!

FRANZ
This is not my good profile.

(Overlapping)

CELESTE #1: I hate this dress.
CELESTE #2: The soldiers have
    forgotten us.
CELESTE #1: Don't slouch!
BOATMAN: Animals . . .
JULES: Are you sure you don't like
    tall grass?
NURSE: I put on rouge today,
    too . . .
FRIEDA: Don't you ever take a
    bath?
SOLDIER: It's good to be together
    again.
OLD LADY: Nurse! Hand me
    my fan.
DOT: It's hot up here.
YVONNE: It's hot and it's
    monotonous.
LOUISE: He took my glasses, I
    want my glasses!
FRANZ: This is not my good
    profile.

ALL
And furthermore,
Finding you're
Fading
Is very degrading.
And God, I am so hot!

Well, there are worse things than
    sweating
By a river on a Sunday,
There are worse things than
    sweating by a river—

BOATMAN
When you're sweating in a picture
That was painted by a genius—

FRANZ
And you know that you're
    immortal—

FRIEDA
And you'll always be remembered—

NURSE
Even if they never see you—

OLD LADY
And you're listening to drivel—

SOLDIER
And you're part of your
    companion—

LOUISE
And your glasses have been stolen—

YVONNE
And you're bored beyond
    endurance—

LOUIS
And the baby has no diapers—

CELESTE #1
(To Celeste #2)
And you're slouching—!

CELESTE #2
I am not—!

JULES
And you are out of all proportion—

DOT
And I hate these people!

ALL
You never get
A breeze up here,
And she's (he's) up here
Forever.

You cannot run
Amuck up here,
You're stuck up here
In this gavotte.

Perspectives don't
Make sense up here.
It's tense up here
Forever.

The outward show
Of bliss up here
Is disappear-
Ing dot by dot.

(Long pause)

And it's hot!

*1984. At the art museum where
the painting hangs, George's great-
grandson, also named George, is being
feted at a cocktail party for art lovers,
museum trustees and art critics on the
occasion of the unveiling of his latest
multimedia installation, which he calls
a Chromolume. The guests discuss the
work.*

Putting It Together

HARRIET (A Trustee)
I mean, I don't understand
    completely—

BILLY (Her Boyfriend)
I'm not surprised.

HARRIET
But he combines all these different
    trends.

BILLY
I'm not surprised.

HARRIET
You can't divide art today into
    categories neatly—

BILLY
Oh.

HARRIET
What matters is the means, not the ends.

BILLY
I'm not surprised.

BOTH
That is the state of the art, my dear,
That is the state of the art.

BOB GREENBERG
(The Museum Director)
It's not enough knowing good from rotten—

CHARLES REDMOND
(A Visiting Curator)
You're telling me.

GREENBERG
When something new pops up every day.

REDMOND
You're telling me.

GREENBERG
It's only new, though, for now—

REDMOND
Nouveau.

GREENBERG
But yesterday's forgotten.

REDMOND
And tomorrow is already passé.

GREENBERG
There's no surprise.

BOTH
That is the state of the art, my friend,
That is the state of the art.

BETTY (A Young Artist)
He's an original.

ALEX (Another Artist)
Was.

NAOMI (A Composer)
I like the images.

ALEX
Some.

BETTY
Come on, you had your moment,
Now it's George's turn.

ALEX
It's George's turn?
I wasn't talking turns,
I'm talking art.

BETTY
(To Naomi)
Don't you think he's original?

NAOMI
Well, yes.

BETTY
(To Alex)
You're talking crap.

ALEX
(Overlapping, to Naomi)
But is it really new?

NAOMI
Well, no . . .

ALEX
(To Betty)
His own collaborator—!

BETTY
(Overlapping, to Naomi)
It's more than novelty.

NAOMI
Well, yes . . .

BETTY
(To Alex)
It's just impersonal, but—

ALEX
It's all promotion, but then—

ALEX, BETTY
(To Naomi)
That is the state of the art,
Isn't it?

NAOMI
Well . . .

BILLY
(To Harriet)
Art isn't easy.

HARRIET
Even when you've amassed it.

BETTY
Fighting for prizes—

GREENBERG
No one can be an oracle.

REDMOND
Art isn't easy.

ALEX
Suddenly, you're past it.

NAOMI
All compromises—

HARRIET
And then when it's allegorical—!

REDMOND, GREENBERG
Art isn't easy—

ALL
Any way you look at it.

George enters the gallery with his grandmother, Marie. He surveys the crowd as they applaud him.

GEORGE
(To himself)
All right, George,
As long as it's your night, George—
You know what's in the room,
    George:
Another Chromolume, George.
It's time to get to work . . .

George makes polite small talk with Harriet and Billy.

GEORGE
(To himself)
Say "cheese," George.
And put them at their ease, George.
You're up on the trapeze, George.

Move at end / each stage
to square, stakes, some of which fall

Chorus I

circulation   imagination
communication   inspiration
concentration   accumulation
consideration   conversation
creation   aspiration
dedication

submit   it
admit   quit
sit   fit
lit   split
hit   wait
out

Make then

Bit by bit   Can't just sit
Putting it together   Till when it's lit
How (Tell) when as ( ) Bits must fit   Building it   Got it made
Every (little) detail (tiny) (single) detail [anything making] every plays a part

clout   First of all you need a good foundation
smart   First you need an adequate foundation
heart
cart   Just another part of making art   Getting a foundation for a   start
part
                Everything depends on preparation
                Starting with an adequate foundation   Otherwise you'll never get it built
facts   The art of making art
proportion It's
distortion (Is) putting it together   Nothing can be built up Nothing's good
                                        How you gonna build up a foundation

situation   all
combination   After that the first consideration
demonstration   Everything depends on preparation   Is to have an adequate foundation
appreciation   Map you out Otherwise you're   Or you going off balance
discrimination How you plan the project from the start off
expiration   Takes a little cocktail conversation   Number one, you get a good foundation
exploitation   But it helps you get a good foundation   Have to have
expectation   First you need reliable foundation
exploration   way you make a work   What's
formation   That's the only way of making art   Takes a little cocktail conversation
indication   There you have the art of making art   If it means Sit with
(orchestration)   But it helps you get a good foundation
orchestration   Two Bro So you can begin with
observation   First you have to lay the right foundation
                All it takes is time & perseverance   Otherwise you're squared from the start
                Now & then a personal appearance   Taking a little cocktail conversation
                                    defensive   (Just another part of making art)
                After all, elections are expensive

Machines don't grow on trees,
    George.
Start putting it together . . .

Art isn't easy
Even when you're hot.
Advancing art is easy,
Financing it is not.

A vision's just a vision
If it's only in your head.
If no one gets to see it,
It's as good as dead.
It has to come to light!

Bit by bit,
Putting it together.
Piece by piece—
Only way to make a work of art.
Every moment makes a
    contribution,
Every little detail plays a part.
Having just the vision's no solution,
Everything depends on execution:
Putting it together,
That's what counts.

Ounce by ounce,
Putting it together.
Small amounts
Adding up to make a work of art.
First of all you need a good
    foundation,
Otherwise it's risky from the start.
Takes a little cocktail conversation,
But without the proper preparation,
Having just the vision's no solution,
Everything depends on execution.
The art of making art
Is putting it together
Bit by bit.

He chats with the museum directors.

GEORGE
(To himself)
Link by link,
Making the connections.
Drink by drink,
Fixing and perfecting the design.
Adding just a dab of politician
(Always knowing where to draw the
    line),
Lining up the funds, but in addition
Lining up a prominent commission,
Otherwise your perfect composition
Isn't going to get much exhibition.

Art isn't easy.
Every minor detail
Is a major decision.
Have to keep things in scale,
Have to hold to your vision.

Every time I start to feel defensive,
I remember lasers are expensive.
What's a little cocktail conversation
If it's going to get you your
    foundation,
Leading to a prominent commission
And an exhibition in addition?

GUESTS
Art isn't easy—

ALEX, BETTY
Trying to make connections.

ALL
Who understands it?

HARRIET, BILLY
Difficult to evaluate.

ALL
Art isn't easy—

GREENBERG, REDMOND
Trying to form collections.

ALL
Always in transit.

NAOMI
And then when you have to
    collaborate—!

ALL
Art isn't easy,
Any way you look at it!

*George chats to the press agent for the
museum and poses for a photographer.*

GEORGE
(To himself)
Dot by dot,
Building up the image.
Shot by shot—
Keeping at a distance doesn't pay.
Still, if you remember your
    objective,
Not give all your privacy away,

A little bit of hype can be effective,
Long as you can keep it in
    perspective.
After all, without some recognition
No one's going to give you a
    commission,
Which will cause a crack in the
    foundation.
You'll have wasted all that
    conversation.

*George's assistant, Dennis, comes over
to him and announces that he's quitting because the pressure of mounting
and promoting the work is too much
for him.*

GEORGE
(To himself)
Art isn't easy,
Even if you're smart.
You think it's all together,
And something falls apart.

*Alex, who is competing with George for
commissions, confronts him hostilely.*

GEORGE
(To himself)
Art isn't easy.
Overnight you're a trend,
You're the right combination.
Then the trend's at an end,
You're suddenly last year's sensation.

So you should support the
    competition,
Try to set aside your own ambition,
Even while you jockey for position.
If you feel a sense of coalition,
Then you never really stand alone.
If you want your work to reach
    fruition,
What you need's a link with your
    tradition,
And of course a prominent
    commission,
Plus a little formal recognition,
So that you can go on exhibit—
So that your *work* can go on
    exhibition.

*Blair Daniels, a prominent art critic
who used to support George's work,
now criticizes him for repeating himself. George tries to control himself.*

CRITICS AND THEIR USES

I was advised (by myself, among others) not to deal with the subject of critics, but it would be disingenuous of me to ignore them altogether, and *Sunday in the Park with George* invites a few observations on their opinions and effect. During a long professional life, I have been both a critics' darling and a critics' target, sometimes simultaneously, and this show was a paradigm of that polar split: it was savaged by some and championed by others (notably and luckily, two critics at *The New York Times*). Over the years the darling aspect has gotten stronger, but the target aspect remains. In my more balanced moments, I read that as a good thing: it means that some of the work has maintained its power to abrade as well as please. Irritation is a more gratifying response than dismissiveness or indifference.

The first business of the day is to distinguish between critics and reviewers. Theater critics are not critics, but reviewers. This is not a matter of fussy nomenclature; for me, the words denote significantly different functions. Reviewers are reporters; their function is to describe and evaluate, on first encounter, a specific event, whether a play, a concert, a gallery showing, a building—any public form of artistic expression. On first encounter. Reviewers work for newspapers and magazines and, occasionally, television, and are victims of deadlines. Newspaper reviewers in particular have limited time to think about what they've witnessed, to *consider* the work at hand.* They are of necessity drive-by shooters.

As for critics, they also describe and evaluate, but from a loftier perspective. Time affords them distance; they can take in the whole range of the art and the artist. They can not only afford to consider, they can choose what's worth consideration. Reviewers, even first-stringers, have to see whatever is shoved in front of them, which may account for the hyperbolic enthusiasm as well as the casual disdain that crops up so often in their notices. (At *The New York Times,* the first- and second-stringers pretty much get to choose the shows they want to cover, but they're the exceptions.) The audience can leave a play at intermission and forget about the whole thing over a meal; reviewers not only have to sit through every play they're assigned to, they have to go home (in the old days, it wasn't even home, it was a newspaper office) and describe and evaluate it. Over time even the better reviewers become desensitized, and atrophy sets in—the reviews lose whatever freshness they may have had when the reviewer first eagerly began; passion gets modified and bitchiness seeps in with increasing frequency, if for no other reason than that the reviewer feels the need to keep himself as well as his readers amused. Most reviewers hang on long past their expiration date; the more talented ones soon recognize what a stultifying profession they're in and, if they have the guts, quit the job. Some of them even become critics.

One thing which unites theater critics and reviewers is that most of them have little knowledge of the craft as it is practiced. They don't know how to distinguish among the contributions of the playwright, the actor, the director, and the stage manager; they can't tell a Leko light from a Fresnel or a first pipe from a second pipe, and almost none of them knows anything whatever about how music is made. And why should they? In the case of reviewers, knowledge is not required for the job. People read reviews to decide whether they should spend a considerable sum of money to see for themselves the subject under the microscope, and if it's a musical, they are not interested in whether the reviewer knows the difference between an arranger and an orchestrator or what he thinks of the Rodgers and Hammerstein revolution. People read critical studies to learn something about the cultural landscape, so there is even less need for such arcana, since critics, when they do write about specific theatrical events, usually include them as points in an overview; they're surveyors; they're allowed to generalize. That loftiness sometimes leads them to promote themselves rather than the object of their affection, but loftiness is what their readers look to them for, and often with rewarding results. What readers look for in a reviewer is immediate guidance. The better informed a reviewer is, the more he can function in both capacities. When Walter Kerr wrote for the *New York Herald Tribune* and *The New York Times,* he was a reviewer; when he wrote "How Not to Write a Play," he was a critic.

Having made the distinction between the two terms, I would now like to refer to them all as *critics,* since *reviewer* is a word with

---

* They used to have even less time. Until the mid-1960s, all the daily newspaper reviewers came on opening night and had to make the early editions, which meant that those who worked for a morning paper had about an hour to write their reviews. Only the very best of them could manage this consistently well. As a result, even in the afternoon papers the reviews were often hasty, inaccurate or, more likely, bland (that is, hedging opinions). Harold Prince changed this self-defeating routine by inviting the reviewers to see the shows he produced on any of the three nights preceding the opening as well as the opening itself. That way, he urged them, they would have more time to think about, as well as write about, the show—in fact, they could see it more than once if they found it stimulating enough. The first musical of his that they reviewed under these circumstances was *Cabaret,* and Hal's scheme has been the standard operating procedure in the theater ever since. And though at the time it may have seemed unlikely that any reviewer would feel the need to see a musical twice in order to write about it, Hal's notion paid off in a very particular way twelve years later. One reviewer of *Company* confessed that he had been so baffled and annoyed by it the first time that he had decided to give it a second chance and revisit it. His review was a rave.

no clout, and clout is what reviewers no longer have. There was a time when newspaper and magazine critics (that is, reviewers) did have clout—the time before the Internet burgeoned and newsprint started to lose its position as a prime conveyor of opinion. I was brought up in the newspaper era, and I read the critics avidly and believed what they told me. But then I grew up and became a writer, and gradually got to know better.

It takes a long time to learn not to pay attention to critics, or at least not to let them distract you. For the young writer, critics have a number of destructive effects. If they praise you highly on your IPO, you suffer afterward by disappointing them—few writers who have a smash hit the first time out survive to be more than one-trick ponies. When the critics pan you, your confidence is shattered, but you gain a certain resilience, if for no other reason than that there's nowhere to go but up. It isn't necessarily the criticism that hurts, of course, because you can choose not to believe it; it's the fact that it's out there in public, that thousands of people are witnessing your humiliation. When you're a young writer, critics have you both ways. The praise makes you overestimate yourself, whereas anything less often leaves you disappointed or angry—and impotent. Writing a letter to the newspaper or magazine which has wounded you and having it published will only and always sound like the whine of a sore loser, again in public. Worse, it encourages critics to think that you take them seriously. In either case, you subsequently find yourself brooding, briefly but often, over the unjustified indignities you've suffered, dwelling on everything negative published about you in the past— especially when you hit a snag while working. That's the most pernicious thing about critics: they cause you to waste your time. And did I mention that they can steer people away from your show, just as they can hurt sales of your novel or put a crimp in further gallery showings of your paintings or concerts of your music? They can discourage both

you and your audience, which is their ultimate unfortunate effect. Of course, if it's praise . . . but let's not think about that, let's dwell on the negative.

After a rotten review, no one remembers his good notices—the only pleasure the reviewee has is to reiterate, both to himself and to anyone who'll listen, the bad ones, which he can quote in exquisite detail. Moreover, he has to come to terms with the truth that no matter how doggedly he tries to deceive himself to the contrary, if he's going to believe his good notices, he's going to have to believe the less good ones as well, unless he's deeply self-delusional. I've worked with a few of the deluded, and there's a part of me which envies their blindness. Richard Rodgers was one. For all his success, he was so sensitive to bad notices (of which he got almost none until *The King and I,* after which he got a few) that during the New Haven tryout of *Do I Hear a Waltz?,* his wife and his assistant would cut out any sentences in the reviews unfavorable to the music and then read him the bowdlerized version. This didn't do Arthur Laurents (book writer), John Dexter (director) or me any good, since Rodgers, as the producer, would then blame us for being the architects of the show's problems—after all, he scolded us, the critics made it clear that we were the villains. His ego remained unscathed.

There are theater people who claim to be immune to public criticism, and perhaps some really are, but I haven't met any who have convinced me. When I first entered the arena and for a long while was not treated kindly by most critics, although I was far from immune, the notices had a perversely salubrious effect on me. Every time I felt unfairly trashed, I retreated to my copy of Nicolas Slonimsky's *Lexicon of Musical Invective,* a startling and hilarious, if discomfiting, compendium of published criticism about everyone from Beethoven to Copland. To read the sneering and uncomprehending reviews which the likes of Brahms and Ravel received made me feel akin to them

and by association as innovative, brilliant and misunderstood as they. Slonimsky's display of these monumental misjudgments should be required reading for every artist, particularly those just starting out. Older artists are less vulnerable because they've survived—they've learned that they can be wounded but not killed, that what once was devastating has become merely annoying. And if they survive long enough, they become venerable, which is decent compensation. The solution, of course, is not to read reviews of your own work, although the temptation is hard to resist— who knows, one of them might refer to you as the greatest writer since *(fill in name of most admired writer here)*—but learn to resist you do.

Reading reviews of other people's work is another matter. For many readers a good critic, in whatever field (remember, I'm talking about reviewers), is someone they agree with or who agrees with them. For me, a good critic is a good writer. A good critic is someone who recognizes and acknowledges the artist's intentions and the work's aspirations, and judges the work by them, not by what his own objectives would have been. A good critic is so impassioned about his subject that he can persuade you to attend something you'd never have imagined you'd want to go to. A good critic is an entertaining read. A good critic is hard to find.

Then again, to a certain degree good critics are no longer necessary to find. The phrase "Everybody's a critic" has taken on a universal cast. The Internet encourages people to share their opinions with the world. In the theater, the "buzz" created by chat room chatters has become increasingly important to a show's reputation before it opens, and has actually affected some of the newspaper and magazine critics, who refer to the chatter in their opening-night reviews. The irony is that the Internet is in the process of killing off the critics' jobs. Not long ago there were four or five major New York newspapers, two national magazines and one local one, plus two or three TV stations, all reviewing whatever opened on Broadway.

Now only *The Times* covers the theater completely and regularly. The other newspapers have been downsizing and, as with schools, the first departments to be downsized are the arts. Nor do national magazines report on theater any longer, except to spot the occasional extreme disaster or gigantic hit, and then only as news stories. Even *Variety,* the weekly paper that used to be described as the backbone of show business, doesn't maintain a full-time New York critic on its staff anymore. Jobs have been replaced by blogs. There are thousands of critics tapping away their opinions to whoever will listen, so who needs a paid pontificator to tell you what your opinion should be?

Show business chat rooms reveal that the need to criticize is insatiable, but they also reveal that there are still people who are enthusiastic about the theater, who want not only to go but to talk about what they've gone to. The diffidence and short attention span that pervade so much of our culture were nowhere evident in the liveliness of the chat rooms I looked at, although I soon learned not to keep logging on for the same reason I learned not to read my reviews: every group of compliments about my work that started me preening soon was peppered with potshots that unpreened me, and for every piece of thoughtful observation about other people's work, there was a piece of mean-spirited snottiness—some of which, I regret to say, made me laugh and wish that I were young enough again to participate in those kinds of exchanges as wholeheartedly as I had before I had my baptism by fire.

Back to the distinction between critics and reviewers. The value of true critics is as surveyors; the value of reviewers is as publicists. That, and that alone, makes them necessary. Reviewers' opinions matter less than the fact that they bring up the subject at all—reporting the event is what counts. The influence of critics on an artist's work and reputation is debatable, whereas the influence of reviewers is temporal. In the end, of course, nothing matters except the work, but ironically it's the lesser breed, the reviewers, who wield more power: they can hinder the work's being seen as widely or heard as frequently as it might have been. And they have immediate influence, too. During previews of *Sunday in the Park with George,* anticipation for the show was far from bubbling; audiences had been walking out, not in droves but in driblets, and mild enthusiasm had been the most positive response at the curtain calls. Then *The New York Times* review came out and that same night the show got a standing ovation—this in the days when standing ovations were not yet de rigueur. In any event, both kinds of critics have their uses. Awards are a different matter.

GEORGE
(To himself)
Be nice, George . . .
You have to pay a price, George.
They like to give advice, George.
Don't think about it twice,
  George . . .

"Be new," George.
They tell you till they're blue,
  George:
"You're new or else you're through,
  George."
And even if it's true, George,
You do what you can do . . .

Bit by bit,
Putting it together.
Piece by piece,
Working out the vision night and
  day.
All it takes is time and perseverance
With a little luck along the way,
Putting in a personal appearance,
Gathering supporters and
  adherents—

HARRIET
But he combines all these different
  trends—

GEORGE
Mapping out the right configuration,
Starting with a suitable
  foundation—

BETTY
He's an original—

ALEX
Was.

GEORGE
Lining up a prominent commission
And an exhibition in addition—
Here a little dab of politician,
There a little touch of publication,
Till you have a balanced
  composition.
Everything depends on preparation,
Even if you do have the suspicion
That it's taking all your
  concentration—

(Simultaneously with George)

BETTY: I like those images.
ALEX: Some.
BETTY: They're just his personal
  response.
ALEX: To what?
BETTY: The painting!
ALEX: Bullshit. Anyway, the
  painting's overrated.
BETTY: Overrated? It's a
  masterpiece!
ALEX: A masterpiece? Historically
  important maybe—
BETTY: Oh, now you're judging
  Seurat, are you?
ALEX: All it is is pleasant, just like
  George's work.
BETTY: It's just your jealousy of
  George's work.
ALEX: No nuance, no resonance,
  no relevance—
BETTY: There's nuance and there's
  resonance, there's relevance—
ALEX: There's not much point in
  arguing.

Besides, it's all promotion, but
    then—
BETTY: There's not much point in
    arguing.
You say it's all promotion, but
    then—
GREENBERG: It's only new,
    though, for now
And yesterday's forgotten.
But then it's all a matter of
    promotion—
REDMOND: Nouveau.
And yesterday's forgotten
And you can't tell good from rotten
And today it's all a matter of
    promotion—
HARRIET: You can't divide art
    today.
Go with it!
What will they think of next?
BILLY: I'm not surprised.
What will they think of next?
OTHERS: Most art today
Is a matter of promotion—

            GUESTS
That is the state of the art,
And art isn't easy.

            GEORGE
        (Overlapping)
The art of making art
Is putting it together
Bit by bit,
Link by link,
Drink by drink,
Mink by mink,
And that
Is the state of the—

            ALL
Art!

One of the most overused gambits in
the rhyming game is the use of words
ending in "-tion": "-ation," "-ition,"
"-otion" and "-ution," not to mention
(there we go) diphthong versions such
as "-action," "-estion" and the like.
The possibilities in our Latinized language are innumerable, and since
most such words have at least three
syllables they are not only easy to
rhyme but give off a sheen of erudi-
tion, as well as articulation, precision,

the perfection of expression—I think
I've made my point. I usually avoid
this huge family of words because the
effect invariably glitters with glibness,
but I had dipped into it briefly in the
interlude of the title song and now saw
another justification for it: George's
intellectual rationale for his own glibness as an artist. Also, I hoped that the
increasing repetition of the rhymes
would mirror the increasing tension
in George. In order to prevent monotony of sound, however, I varied the
rhyming vowels (as I had done in the
title song): just as the ear was about to
get sick of "-ation" rhymes I switched
to "-ition." Moreover, I was careful to
avoid identities (false rhymes in which
the accented consonants are the same):
no "nation" rhyming with "consterna-
tion," no "commission" rhyming with
"intermission." The effect of this
rapid-fire Kudzu-like proliferation of
rhymes intensifies George's mounting
anxiety. Or at least, echoing what Charlotte says to Anne in *A Little Night
Music*, that was the plan.
    George's anxiety is something I can
identify with all too easily. I spent a
good part of my early professional life
auditioning for people to produce my
work, then for people to give money to
those people to produce my work,
then for people who run theater party
groups that get people to buy tickets in
advance that encourage last-minute
co-producers, if necessary, to help
raise the money . . . and so on. The
process involved two kinds of performing: playing the piano and making
conversation. If it was in a record
company's office, the conversation
would be an exchange of politeness; if
it was at a backer's audition, it meant
trying to be interested in even what
the sentient listeners had to say. In
either case, it took nerves, not to say
patience, of steel and a talent for
salesmanship. But munificent patrons,
whether personal or conglomerate,
have been necessary to the arts, high,
low and in between, since time im-
memorial; and once I had come to
terms with that fact, over a period of
time I became hardened to it by practice and actually began to enjoy it.

After about twenty-five years I didn't
have to peddle my wares as much, or
as blatantly, and I can't say that I was
sorry.
    Having to plead for the opportunity
to do what you want to do is a humiliation that occurs in higher echelons
than you might expect. In 1985 Barbra Streisand, as successful as any
singer alive, found herself trying to
persuade her record company to let
her do a collection of show songs, to
be called *The Broadway Album*. They
balked, on the reasonable ground that
show songs were passé and that Barbra should record something more
contemporary. She had to fight a bit,
but not a lot, and she got her way (fortunately for me) but, never one to
waste her resources, she thought that
the disagreement might be the basis
for a song to open the album, a song
about the difficulties of putting a
record together. She asked if I could
change the lyric of "Putting It
Together" to describe the record business rather than the art business. I
suggested that all she needed to do
was to change "I remember lasers are
expensive" to "I remember vinyl is
expensive" and the rest of the lyric,
being a generalized set of statements
about patronage and its effects, would
take care of itself. That made her
happy, which made me happy, until I
started to think about so much other
imagery in the lyric: phrases such as
"A vision's just a vision . . . If no one
gets to see it" and words like "commission" and "exhibition," not to mention
the thematic pun of "Any way you
look at it." These were clearly references to the visual arts, not the musical ones. As a result, although the last
thing I wanted to do was rewrite an
old lyric that I was perfectly satisfied
with, I felt beholden to someone who
wanted to make the song so personal,
and guilty about skimping on the
obligation to make it as pertinent as
possible. I started transmuting some of
the images, only to find out, of course,
that I had to start tearing the rhymes
apart, and that it was a more time-
consuming job than it seemed. Here
are the relevant changes:

AUSTRALIAN PREMIERE

Sunday in the Park with George:

A triumph for the School of Arts

High Art

Only Connect:

Sondheim gets
to the point

Down by th

'Sunday' is still a vibrant day i

Pretty as a picture

Sondheim's Intimate Core

Sonntags im Park mit George

Blue Purple Yellow Red Water

he park

By 'George,' dot's a work of art!

Putting It Together

(Barbra Streisand version)

As the orchestra tunes up, Barbra is overheard arguing with her producers, who are telling her to abandon the album for every artistic and commercial reason. Unlike George, who faced his critics last, she has to face hers first.

BARBRA
(To herself)

Be nice, girl.
You have to pay a price, girl.
They like to give advice, girl.
Don't think about it twice, girl.
It's time to get to work.

Art isn't easy
Even when you're hot.
Advancing art is easy,
Financing it is not.

A vision's just a vision
If it's only in your head.
If no one gets to share it,
It's as good as dead.
It has to come to life!

Bit by bit,
Putting it together . . . etc. . . .

Ounce by ounce,
Putting it together . . . etc. . . .

Link by link,
Making the connections.
Drink by drink,
Taking every comment as it comes.
Learning how to play the politician
Like you play piano, bass and drums.
Otherwise you'll find your
    composition
Isn't gonna get an exhibition.

Art isn't easy.
Every minor detail is a major
    decision . . . etc. . . .
. . . Every time I start to feel
    defensive,
I remember vinyl is expensive . . .
    etc. . . .

Dot by dot
Building up the image . . . etc. . . .

. . . Even when you get some
    recognition,
Everything you do, you still
    audition . . . etc. . . .
. . . All they really want is repetition,
All they really like is what they
    know.
Gotta keep a link with your
    tradition,
Gotta learn to trust your intuition,
While you re-establish your position
So that you can be on exhibit—

So that your *work* can be on
    exhibition!

Be new, girl.
They tell you till they're blue, girl.
You're new or else you're through,
    girl.
And even if it's true, girl.
You do what you can do!

Bit by bit,
Putting it together . . . etc. . . .

The record executives argue about her, as in the original: "She's an original." "Was!" and so forth.

Mapping out the songs, but in
    addition
Harmonizing each negotiation,
Balancing the part that's all musician
With the part that's strictly
    preparation,
Balancing the money with the
    mission
Till you have the perfect
    orchestration,
Even if you do have the suspicion
That it's taking all your
    concentration.
The art of making art
Is putting it together—

Bit by bit,
Beat by beat,
Part by part,
Phrase by phrase,
Chart by chart,

(Her voices overlapping)

Track by track,   Take by take,
Reel by reel,   Break by break,

Snack by snack,   Snit by snit,
Deal by deal,   Fit by fit,
Shout by shout,   Hit by hit,
Doubt by doubt,   Bit by bit,

(In unison)

And that
Is the state of the art!

Needless to say, her performance made the rewrite more than worth the trouble.

In 1975 three British performers (Julia McKenzie, David Kernan and Millicent Martin), spearheaded by the writer Ned Sherrin as compere, assembled a revue of my songs called *Side By Side By Sondheim*, which was presented at a small theater in London by Cameron Mackintosh, a neophyte impresario. The show went on to become a hit in the West End and on Broadway, and Cameron went on to become the most successful producer of his time. Over the years, *Side By Side* became popular in theaters big and small throughout the United States and the United Kingdom, but it contained only songs written before 1975, so in the late 1980s Cameron urged me to devise a sequel that would allow for the songs I'd written since to be included. I enlisted Julia to help; she was a good friend, she knew my canon and she had become an experienced director in the interim. What we came up with was a pleasant but awkward revue titled *Putting It Together*, which made the mistake of trying to shoehorn songs of different styles and tone into a story line. It was an effortful evening, but it had its compensations, chief among them the return to Broadway of Julie Andrews in a cast of five. Here is the version of the title song that introduced her.

Putting It Together
(Julie Andrews version)

FOUR CAST MEMBERS
Bit by bit, . . . etc. . . .

(Variously)

Note by note,
Working on projection.
Lips, teeth, throat,
Looking for a moment to inhale.
Keeping the emotional connection
Even when your fellow actors fail—
Pointing up the subtext by
    inflection—
Helping your director reach
    perfection—
Even though you have a strong
    objection
To the way she's handling the
    direction.

Art isn't easy . . . etc. . . .

Even when you're feeling
    apprehensive
That you're looking bland and
    inoffensive—
And you wish your wardrobe was
    extensive—
Don't forget that spangles are
    expensive.

*Julie enters and addresses the spotlight
man.*

JULIE
The light, luv—
A little to the right, luv.

The spotlight obliges her.

It isn't very bright, luv.
And must it be so tight, luv?

*The light brightens and widens. She
addresses the audience.*

He does that every night . . .

ALL
(Variously)
Beat by beat,
Losing inhibition.

Head, hands, feet.
Trying to relax but not too much,
Trying to lay out the exposition
But without exposing it as such,
Trying to perform but not audition,
Trying to establish recognition,
Trying to persuade the electrician
That he should destroy the
    competition . . .

*The light goes out on the others; Julie
blows a kiss to the electrician.*

Art isn't easy.
Every word, every line,
Every glance, every movement
You improve and refine,
Then refine each improvement . . .

Bit by bit,
Putting it together.
Piece by piece,
Working out the vision night
    and day.
What it takes is time and
    perseverance,
Dealing with details along the way:
Dealing with producers'
    interference,
Waiting for the author's
    disappearance,
Filling up the holes with animation,
Covering the flaws in the
    construction.
Lacking any scenic ostentation
(This is not a Mackintosh
    production),
Finding every tiny syncopation
Hidden in the tiny orchestration,
Working for a tiny compensation,
Hoping for a thunderous ovation—

The art of making art
Is putting it together
Bit by bit,
Part by part,
Fit by fit,
Start by start,
Stride by stride,
Kick by kick,
Glide by glide,
Shtik by shtik,
Side by side
By side
By side
By side

By side
By side—

And that is the state of the art!

In 1994 the Academy of Motion Picture Arts and Sciences asked me to write an adaptation of the song for the opening of their annual awards ceremony, which I did. It was sung by Bernadette Peters, the action suiting the word: recording the song, rehearsing the number for the stage and cameras and culminating with her live appearance on the show, all intercut with clips from movies. Thus:

Putting It Together
(Academy Awards version)

Scene by scene,
Working out the story.
In between,
Getting the production under way.
Finding a director who is willing,
Who can take a script and make it
    play,
Lining up a cast who'll make it
    thrilling
If you can negotiate the billing.

Art isn't easy.
Though you start with a dream,
If you don't have the team work
And the right kind of team,
Then you can't make the dream
    work.

Getting the right writers to rewrite it,
The right cameraman to light it,
Hiring designers to design it,
Editors to tighten and refine it,
Carpenters and stagehands to
    construct it,
Certified accountants to deduct it,
Technical magicians to enhance it,
And of course the money to finance
    it . . .

Shot by shot,
Putting it together,

On the lot
Or on a location far away.
4 a.m. the phone rings, that's your
    wakeup,
5 a.m. begins the working day.
6 a.m. it's actors into makeup,
8 o'clock at night at last you
    break up,
Having shot at most one movie
    minute
Which when it comes out may not
    be in it.

Art isn't easy.
Every minor detail
Is a major decision.
From a carpenter's nail
To a punchline revision.

Every single close-up, every angle,
Every little suit and boot and
    spangle,
Up until you reach the final inning
When at last there's nothing more to
    shoot—
Even the executives are grinning.
Actually it's only the beginning.
Now it takes a month to see if
    whether
You can put the freaking thing
    together.

Now you've got the cutting and the
    fixing,
Dubbing, and the opticals and
    mixing,
Music to extend each moment's
    meaning
Till you think it's ready for a
    screening,
Which with any luck will have you
    preening
Or will have you quickly
    reconvening . . .

Back you go,
Putting it together
From hello
To the vision thoroughly revised,
Trying to take care of each objection
But without it being compromised.
Maybe you can never reach
    perfection,
But you've got to head in that
    direction.
Finally you're sure it's a sensation—

Then you have to build anticipation,
Maybe go for sexy exploitation,
Pitch it to the younger generation,
Gamble on a critical ovation,
Leading to an Oscar nomination—

The art of making art
Is putting it together
Bit by bit,
Shot by shot,
Page by page,
Plot by plot,
Stage by stage,
Set by set,
Mic by mic,
Debt by debt,
Strike by strike—

And that
Is the state of the art!

"Putting It Together" seems to be an
inexhaustibly adaptable lyric, suitable
for any occasion. I'm thinking of rent-
ing it out. But I digress. The first version of this song, the one performed at
Playwrights Horizons, was a solo for
George and didn't incorporate any action. It was a song, not a number (for
the difference, see the chapter on *Into
the Woods*). Thus:

Have to Keep Them Humming (cut)

GEORGE
Be nice, George.
Don't make them pay the price,
    George.
It's something they enjoyed, George.
Don't show them you're annoyed,
    George.
Don't tell them it was shit.

Don't sneer, George.
Remember why you're here, George.
You know now you're a fraud,
    George.
So smile when they applaud,
    George.
Start mapping out the year, George.

Making the art's the easy part of it,
Just the start of it,
Getting it out there,
That's the art of it.
Have to keep them humming—
Mm-hm!
If you want a showing.
Have to keep it coming—
Mm-hm!
Just to keep it going.

Have to buy the canvas and the slide
    projectors,
Have to pay the actors and the
    sound technicians,
Have to rent the lighting and the
    synthesizers
Have to keep 'em glowing.
Have to keep on growing.
Have to keep them humming.

Have to keep them purring—
Hm-hm!
Have to use your cunning.
Have to make it stirring—

Hm-hm!
Have to make it stunning.
Have to make a splash or no
    commissions,
And without commissions no
    exposure,
And without exposure,
No one knows you're
Even in the running . . .
Not unless they're slumming.
Have to keep them humming.

*At the end of the reception, George is
left alone with his ninety-eight-year-
old grandmother, Marie, who drifts in
and out of reality. She sings about him
to the figure of Dot in the painting.*

Children and Art

MARIE
You would have liked him,
Mama, you would.
Mama, he makes things.
Mama, they're good.
Just as you said from the start:

Children and art . . .
Children and art . . .

He should be happy.
Mama, he's blue.
What do I do?
You should have seen it,
It was a sight.
Mama, I mean it—
All color and light!

I don't understand what it was,
But, Mama, the things that he
    does—!
They twinkle and shimmer and
    buzz.
You would have liked them . . .
It . . .
Him . . .

(To George)

Isn't she beautiful? There she is—

(Pointing to different figures)

There she is, there she is, there
    she is.
Mama is everywhere,
He must have loved her so much . . .

This is our family, this is the lot.
After I go, this is all that you've got,
    Honey.
Wasn't she beautiful, though?

You would have liked her.
Mama did things
No one had done.
Mama was funny,
Mama was fun.
Mama spent money
When she had none.

Mama said, "Honey,
Mustn't be blue.
It's not so much do what you like
As it is that you like what you do."
Mama said, "Darling,
Don't make such a drama.
A little less thinking,
A little more feeling—"

(As George looks at her sharply)

I'm just quoting Mama . . .

(Indicating Louise in the painting)

The child is so sweet

(Indicating the Celestes)

And the girls are so rapturous.
Isn't it lovely how artists can
    capture us?

You would have liked her—
Honey, I'm wrong,
You would have loved her.
Mama enjoyed things.
Mama was smart.
See how she shimmers—
I mean from the heart.

I know, honey, you disagree,

(Indicating the entire painting)

But this is our family tree.
Just wait till we're there, and you'll
    see—
Listen to me . . .

(Drifting off)

Mama was smart . . .
Listen to Mama . . .
Children and art . . .
Children and art . . .

She falls asleep.

Later that year, George visits the island of La Grande Jatte, where he has been invited to set up his Chromolume. Marie has died and George has brought with him the language primer that Dot had been studying a hundred years ago, which Marie has passed down to him. He is skeptical about this inheritance, half convinced that his grandmother had fantasized her relationship to Seurat.

GEORGE
(Leafing through the book, reading)
"Charles has a book . . ."

(Turns a page)

"Charles shows them his
    crayons . . ."

(Turns a few pages)

"Marie has the ball of Charles . . ."

(Turns the book to read writing in the margin)

"Good for Marie . . ."

(Smiles at the coincidence of the name, turns a page)

"Charles misses his ball . . ."

(Looks up)

George misses Marie.
George misses a lot.
George is alone.

George looks around.
He sees the park.
It is depressing.
George looks ahead.
George sees the dark.
George feels afraid.
Where are the people
Out strolling on Sunday?

George looks within:
George is adrift.
George goes by guessing.
George looks behind:
He had a gift.
When did it fade?
You wanted people out
Strolling on Sunday—
Sorry, Marie . . .

See George remember how George
    used to be,
Stretching his vision in every
    direction.

AWARDS AND THEIR USELESSNESS

Sunday in the Park with George invites a few remarks about awards as well as about critics. I have received enough awards to collapse a mantelpiece and to form some opinions.

Awards have three things to offer: cash, confidence and bric-a-brac. A few offer all three, but even though some of the bric-a-brac is handsome indeed, the only awards that have significant value are the ones that come with cash. They strengthen the artist by helping him to subsist and continue. (I bought a piano with one). The confidence-boosters have a temporary strengthening effect but, like good reviews, are dangerous: they lead the recipient to overestimate himself, and make him vulnerable to the disappointments which inevitably follow.

Awards come in two flavors: competitive (Tonys, Oscars, Grammys) and honorary (degrees, medals, lifetime achievement). The latter are usually awarded to established artists and are created primarily to publicize or raise money for worthy institutions and causes. This is not to cast aspersions on them—good causes and good institutions *need* money—but merely to caution that they should be seen for what they are: promotional tools. For the awardee, the most depressing among them is the Lifetime Achievement, which signifies one more nail in his coffin. It denotes the slippage from respect into veneration. (A retrospective is almost as dismaying, but if you like your own work a retrospective at least comes with an element of pleasurable pride.) In my blacker moments, I think of it as the Thanks-a-Lot-and-Out-with-the-Garbage Award. However, honoring longevity does no damage; I save my aspersions for competitive awards.

In every dominion of the entertainment industry ("industry" is the key word here) there are as many competitive awards as there are subsets of participants within and without who love to bestow them—critics as well as practitioners. By competitive awards, I mean awards

which, in the theater for example, exalt one play or performance or set design over all the others in that category. There are the Antoinette Perry Awards (the Tonys), the Drama Desk Awards, the Drama Critics' Circle Awards, the Outer Critics Circle Awards, the Off-Broadway Awards (the Obies) and the Pulitzer Prize, to mention only the most prominent. All these competitions, of course, are races among unequals. How would you compare *The Man Who Came to Dinner* to *Death of a Salesman* if they had opened the same season? Both are first-rate of their kind, but guess which one would have won the Tony. (Don't assume it would have been *Death of a Salesman*.) Similarly, which is the better performance, Judy Holliday's in *Born Yesterday* or Jessica Tandy's in *A Streetcar Named Desire?* Which is more satisfying, an orange or a potato?

Then one has to consider who nominates and who votes for these awards. In the theater, nominations for the Tonys are bestowed by a Nominating Committee, thirty-five brave souls from various theater disciplines who volunteer to see every play and musical that lands on the boards. They all participate in the nominations, which immediately dilutes the consensus. Nominations in fields of endeavor for Academy Awards are made by craftsmen in each field who know something about the craft: actors nominate actors, sound editors nominate sound editors. In the theater, actors nominate set designers, general managers nominate orchestrators. Moreover, some members of the committee not unsurprisingly have vested interests in the shows under consideration, since they are a ragtag group of producers, directors, authors, etc., whose babies are to be protected and promoted, and they are not above skewing the rules of nomination to minimize competition.

As for the Tony voters, they comprise approximately 750 theater "professionals." "Professionals" is a tricky word in this context, since

over half of them are members of an organization called The Broadway League, which is made up of theater owners, producers, entrepreneurs, retirees and other ancillaries.* The theater owners care chiefly about filling their real estate; some of the producers haven't actively produced anything in years (many of them do nothing but put money into shows) and are voters simply by virtue of paying dues to the League; the entrepreneurs book shows across the country and understandably vote on the basis of what they think will be popular with the audiences in their territories; they see few of the nominated shows, only the ones that present possibilities for touring. In fact, very few Tony voters see all the nominated works and performances. Even with the best will, they can't: some shows close too quickly for them to attend. Most go only to the shows they want to see anyway, even though all tickets are free. (The cost of those free tickets to each production is severe, particularly to the smaller ones.)

Do not read this as sour grapes about the Tony Awards. My own history with them is mixed; *West Side Story* and *Gypsy* were losers and the score for *A Funny Thing Happened on the Way to the Forum* was not considered worthy of a nomination, but subsequently I've been a winner many times. What sours my grapes is the principle of reducing artists to contestants. Competitive awards boost the egos of the winners (until they lose) and damage the egos of the losers (until they win), while feeding the egos of the voters (all the time). Just as there are people who claim to be immune to public criticism, so there are those who claim to be unaffected by being passed over for an

---

* The rest consist of the boards of the craft unions (actors, directors, writers, designers, etc.), press agents, casting directors and the Theater Wing, which administrates the awards, plus a few supernumeraries.

award from their supposed peers, but as in the case of the critic-immune, I've not met any who have convinced me. It isn't so much that you want to be deemed the best as it is that you don't want to be deemed second-best. No matter who the voters are and whether you accept them as worthy of judging you or not, winning means they like you more than your competitors; for that moment, you are the favorite child of the family. Of course, if you make the mistake of looking back at the people who have won before you, it can be a matter of some dismay.

Sunday in the Park with George was snubbed by the Tonys but won the Pulitzer Prize, an award of much greater distinction. It served me as an antidote not only to the Tonys but to the generally negative reviews the show had received, until I bothered to think about it. My thought was this: Distinction or not, why is the Pulitzer any more to congratulate oneself about than the Tony? Who votes for the Pulitzer? Are any of the judges playwrights or directors? No, the Pulitzer nominating committee is made up of academics and critics, which makes them just as flimsy a group to be grateful to as The Broadway League. Moreover, the Pulitzer board, consisting of Columbia University trustees and others who have nothing to do with the arts, can veto the drama jury's choices, as they famously did in the case of *Who's Afraid of Virginia Woolf?*, where the language, along with the occasional "taboo" subject matter offended them and caused

them concern about public reception. These factors do not mean that the Pulitzer is worthless, but again it must be assessed for what it is: an award bestowed by a few particular people, who do not represent a general consensus on excellence. Even the Pulitzer, prestigious as it is, has to be viewed in perspective or you delude yourself, which, as in the case of critics, some people are happy to do.

After a while of winning and losing awards, I realized the obvious, something often overlooked in the interests of maintaining a workable ego: the only meaningful recognition is recognition by your peers or, more accurately, people you consider your peers, and peer-recognition is a very personal matter. An artist's peers are other artists, not necessarily in the same field—musicians for musicians, painters for painters—but people who understand what you're trying to do simply because they're trying to do a similar thing.

In 1983 I was elected to the American Academy of Arts and Letters, an organization founded in 1898 by Mark Twain, Henry James, Theodore Roosevelt, Edward Mac-Dowell, Childe Hassam, Woodrow Wilson and a dozen or so others. Since its roster is limited to 250 members, and new ones can be elected only on the deaths of older ones, it could be considered elitist—and it is. It comprises 250 of the most distinguished and accomplished writers, painters, sculptors, architects and composers in the country, and I am proud to be in

their company. They give a lot of awards to both established and budding artists, and almost all are the good kind—no crystal slab or bronze sculpture, just a piece of paper and a lot of cash. They do give a few honorary awards, however, one of them being the Gold Medal in Music, which is awarded every three years. Nominees are chosen by the musician members but voted on by the whole academy. In 2006 I was the recipient, and it was much the most meaningful award I've ever received. It came from not only my peers but my superiors—the artists I most admire. No cash was involved, and the gold was plated (up until a few years before, the medal had been made of real gold, worse luck), but that was recognition indeed. It had taken me so long to be acknowledged, much less accepted, as a composer that I would have been happy with one made of zinc. And yet—granted, it wasn't the result of a competition among entirely different works (as with the Tonys, the Oscars, the Grammys, and so on), it still was a competition. Songs versus symphonies. Oranges and potatoes.

Competitive awards have existed since at least the days of ancient Greece, and the need to anoint is apparently so strong that their proliferation is not only guaranteed, it keeps expanding. Nevertheless, they are like reviews—useful only for publicity and, at least in the theater, not as effective. They may be good for the ego, but they don't sell tickets.

See George attempting to see a
   connection
When all he can see
Is maybe a tree,
The family tree—
Sorry, Marie . . .

George is afraid.
George sees the park.
George sees it dying.
George, too, may fade,
Leaving no mark,
Just passing through,

Just like the people
Out strolling on Sunday . . .

George looks around.
George is alone.
No use denying
George is aground,
George has outgrown
What he can do.
George would have liked
   to see
People out strolling on
   Sunday . . .

The original title of this song was "Primer." I liked the pun (a base for both Dot and the painter), but then I thought about Alan Jay Lerner's title pun in the song from *My Fair Lady* called "A Hymn to Him," a title I found so self-consciously clever that I almost turned against the lyric, which proved to be the best one in the show, and I reverted to something pointed and straightforward. A wise decision, I think, especially since I get a chance to point out my cleverness here.

Dot appears, summoned by the book, and addresses George as if he were the George of 1884. She asks him if he is working on anything new. He answers "No" and tells her of his conviction that his creativity has dried up.

Move On

GEORGE
I've nothing to say.

DOT
You have many things . . .

GEORGE
Well, nothing that's not been said.

DOT
Said by you, though, George . . .

GEORGE
I do not know where to go.

DOT
And nor did I.

GEORGE
I want to make things that count,
Things that will be new . . .

DOT
I did what I had to do:

GEORGE
What am I to do?

DOT
Move on.

Stop worrying where you're
    going—
Move on.
If you can know where you're going,
You've gone.
Just keep moving on.

I chose, and my world was shaken—
So what?
The choice may have been mistaken,
The choosing was not.
You have to move on.

Look at what you want,
Not at where you are,
Not at what you'll be.
Look at all the things you've done
    for me:
Opened up my eyes,
Taught me how to see,
Notice every tree—

GEORGE
Notice every tree . . .

DOT
Understand the light—

GEORGE
Understand the light . . .

DOT
Concentrate on now—

GEORGE
I want to move on.
I want to explore the light.
I want to know how to get through,
Through to something new,
Something of my own—

BOTH
Move on. Move on.

DOT
Stop worrying if your vision
Is new.
Let others make that decision—
They usually do,
You keep moving on.

DOT	GEORGE
Look at what you've done,	*(Looking around)*
	Something in
Then at what you want,	the light,
	Something in
Not at where you are,	the sky,
	In the grass,
What you'll be.	Up behind the
Look at all the things	trees . . .
You gave to me.	
	Things I hadn't
	looked at
Let me give to you	Till now:
Something in return.	Flower in your
	hat.
I would be so pleased . . .	And your smile.

GEORGE
And the color of your hair,
And the way you catch the light.
And the care,
And the feeling.
And the life
Moving on!

DOT
We've always belonged together!

BOTH
We will always belong together!

DOT
Just keep moving on.

Anything you do,
Let it come from you.
Then it will be new.

Give us more to see.

"Move On" is both an extension and a development of "We Do Not Belong Together," which in turn is an extension and a development of the lyrical section of "Color and Light," the seeds of which, both musical and verbal, have been planted in the interlude of "Sunday in the Park with George." They are four parts of one long musical arc, something more apparent when they are sung than on the printed page. They could be read as a mini-musical of their own: Boy Loves Girl, Boy Loves Art, Boy Loses Girl, Boy Gets Both Girl and Art a Hundred Years Later. All the musical themes of the love story culminate and intertwine in "Move On." The lyric is meant to connect with the earlier ones, distantly, just the way the young George connects with his roots in the painting; words and phrases like "the way she catches light" and "the color of her hair" are echoed along with the music. If it works, if "Move On" feels like a satisfying and touching resolution as it does to me, it's a tribute to my First Principle: Less Is More.

The most profound statement about polishing a piece of work is the famous dictum attributed to the French poet Paul Valéry, which I men-

[handwritten top margin: the vision will bring you to ... and then, most important, bigger!]

[handwritten: Not to take judgments! ... Whatever you create, other people will see it differently than you]

[handwritten: YOU HAVE A]

DOT

AS LONG AS IT <u>IS</u> YOUR VISION,
EXPLORE.
AND IF IT'S THE WRONG DECISION,
MAKE MORE.
YOU HAVE TO MOVE ON.

[handwritten right: I want to see any vision you have / Believe in your vision accept]

[handwritten left: Be one part of it / Don't hold ... if Follow if they]

(simultaneously)

DOT
LOOK AT WHAT YOU'VE DONE,
LOOK AT WHAT YOU WANT,
NOT AT WHERE YOU ARE,
WHAT YOU'LL BE.
LOOK AT ALL THE THINGS
    YOU GAVE TO ME.

LET ME GIVE TO YOU
SOMETHING IN RETURN.
I WOULD BE SO PLEASED...

[handwritten left: THEN]

GEORGE
(looking around)
...SOMETHING IN THE LIGHT,
SOMETHING IN THE SKY,
IN THE GRASS,
UP BEHIND THE TREES...

THINGS I HADN'T LOOKED AT
TILL NOW:
~~LAYERS IN YOUR DRESS.~~ (Flowers in your hat)
AND YOUR SMILE.

[handwritten: your eyes]

[handwritten right: shadows / shadings / colors]

GEORGE
AND THE COLOR OF YOUR HAIR.
AND THE WAY YOU CATCH THE LIGHT.
AND THE CARE.
AND THE FEELING.
AND THE LIFE
MOVING ON.

DOT
WE'VE ALWAYS BELONGED
TOGETHER!

BOTH
WE'LL ALWAYS BELONG
TOGETHER!

[handwritten left: WE WILL]

DOT
JUST KEEP MOVING ON.
IF IT COMES FROM YOU,
THEN IT WILL BE NEW.
GIVE US MORE TO SEE...

[handwritten left: But]
[handwritten left: Whatever comes from you / LET IT]

[handwritten right: Anything you do / If it comes from you only can be / will be new / is / NOTHING ELSE TO DO / DON'T YOU UNDERSTAND / WHAT YOU HAVE TO DO]

Listen to yourself. You always have. More than
anything, you never cared what anyone thought.
That upset me at the time because I wanted you
to care what <u>I</u> thought.

(to 2-41)

STEPHEN SONDHEIM

tioned in the Reintroduction: a poem is never finished, only abandoned. There are many occasions in a lyric writer's life, or at least there have been in mine, when you know a word or phrase needs improvement and you know what the improvement should consist of, but you can't figure out how to do it and the desire for perfection is simply not worth the time spent on it, so you have only that one recourse: abandonment. Every time you hear the song, of course, you pay for that abandonment with a wince of shame, as in the case of the dangling "s" in "Finishing the Hat." In the case of "Move On," the word "usually," in the phrase "They usually do," was and is my bête noire. The word I mean, the word I want to use, is "eventually," but what do I do about that extra first syllable? The musical pattern has been set by the matching phrase "The choosing was not" in the preceding equivalent stanza. I could have

matched the opening stanza phrase ("You've gone"), but that would have given me only one syllable to make my point. Nor did I want to break the pattern in a small fussy way—there's nothing wrong with breaking a pattern in a big way because in effect it makes a *new* pattern, but to add one stingy eighth-note upbeat is to draw attention to the inconsistency. This can be an appropriate thing to do when you want to draw attention to a thought, as with the extra note at the end of "I thought that you'd want what I want" in "Send in the Clowns," but is otherwise a clumsiness. I'd have settled for "inevitably," but it has two syllables too many. "Always," which doesn't have the kick of "inevitably" but carries with it a nice sense of irony, is a syllable too short. "Generally"? "Invariably"? Same problems. "Constantly"? "Ceaselessly"? They're not what I mean, exactly. At least "usually" doesn't have an extra upbeat, but

it's an example of one of those numerous four-syllable adverbs which often get squashed into three-and-a-half when spoken ("gen'rally," "practic'ly"). It's legitimate, but it's imprecise, both sonically and tonally.

The next-to-last lines ("Let it come from you . . .") express something I firmly believe but find it increasingly hard to act on. I use it as a supportive thought when I hit those low moments of taking on the fraudulence of what I'm writing, moments which occur with increasing frequency the older I get. It's a weak mantra, but one worth repeating as often as possible.

Finally, the last line of "Move On" demonstrates that sometimes it's a good idea not to rhyme, even when the music calls for it. With the possible exception of the last line of "Four Black Dragons," this one is my favorite. And as I look back at it now, it reminds me of how much I wanted to write another show with James Lapine.

"Move On"

Heidi Landesman   Rocco Landesman   Rick Steiner
M. Anthony Fisher   Frederic H. Mayerson   Jujamcyn Theaters

present

Bernadette Peters
Joanna Gleason   Chip Zien
Tom Aldredge   Robert Westenberg

in

INTO THE WOODS
A New Musical

Music and Lyrics by
Stephen Sondheim

Book by
James Lapine

2. Into the Woods (1987)

Book by James Lapine

The Notion

In a folktale time and setting, a childless baker and his wife are told by a witch that they will be able to conceive if they can find and bring to her four objects: a cow as white as milk, a cape as red as blood, hair as yellow as corn and a slipper as pure as gold. In the course of their quest, the Baker and his Wife encounter Cinderella, Little Red Riding Hood and Jack (of "Jack and the Beanstalk") and become part of their stories. At the end of the first act, they achieve their goal. The second act deals with the consequences of what they did to get there.

General Comments

After the exhilaration of *Sunday in the Park with George,* I wanted immediately to write another show with James Lapine. I suggested that we write a quest musical along the lines of *The Wizard of Oz,* the one movie musical I had loved in which the songs not only defined the characters and carried the story forward but were wonderful stand-alone songs as well. James replied that it would be frustratingly difficult to invent a fantasy quest that could sustain itself for two hours or more because there were too many possibilities: a shining irony when you consider that the last line of *Sunday in the Park with George* comes from the young artist looking at a blank canvas and exalting, "So many possibilities." But indeed, how do you go about inventing a picaresque adventure peopled with fantastic creatures? When you have infinite choices and no point to make, every plot is possible and every character arbitrary except for the princi-

pals. In *Candide,* for example, Voltaire had a simple moral observation to propound and tailored a plot to illustrate it, but the episodes are arbitrary (which is one reason the musical *Candide* has had no definitive script and score since its premiere in 1956). We had nothing we wanted to say, merely a desire for a form, which is not a good way to begin writing a play. (Content Dictates Form.)

Then James came up with the notion of inventing a fairy tale in the tradition of classic fairy tales, one that could be musicalized and fleshed out into a full evening, which excited us but died aborning. After a couple of tries, James realized that fairy tales, by nature, are short; the plots turn on a dime, there are few characters and even fewer complications. This problem is best demonstrated by every fairy-tale movie and TV show since *Snow White and the Seven Dwarfs,* all of which pad the lean stories with songs and sidekicks and subplots, some of which are more involving than the interrupted story itself. And those are all less than two hours long. It seemed to be an insoluble, self-defining problem until we remembered something he'd concocted a year before when we were looking for a quick way to make a buck.

It was an idea for a TV special: a story involving TV characters from situation comedies (for example, Ralph and Alice Kramden, Archie and Edith Bunker, Mary Richards and Lou Grant, etc.) in a car accident which brings to the scene characters from the cop shows (T. J. Hooker, Joe Friday, Cagney and Lacey, etc.) who take them to the hospital where they are treated by Dr. Kildare and Marcus Welby and Ben Casey, etc. I loved the idea and proposed to James that we write a brief treatment and sell it to Norman Lear, the most imaginative producer of such fare. Lear loved the idea, too, and declared he couldn't wait to see the script. We explained that we weren't interested in writing the script, just in selling the idea. He in

turn explained that he wasn't interested in buying the idea, just in reading the script. This concluded our conversation. Now, in 1986, James came up with the notion of applying the TV idea to the Brothers Grimm. We would write a story in which the lives of famous fairy-tale characters would collide and intertwine in a mutual meeting ground, and where else but the woods, where so many of the stories take place? To weave them together, James invented his own fable, that of a Baker and his Wife, a pair who would go on a quest that would touch and involve such characters as Cinderella, Little Red Riding Hood, Jack, Rapunzel, the Three Little Pigs, Snow White and, of course, a Wicked Witch. The pigs and Snow White got left behind in San Diego, where the show tried out, but the others remained to populate an olla podrida of (mostly) farcical and (finally) tragic events. We ate our cake and had it, too: it would be a fairy-tale quest.

And ah, the woods. The all-purpose symbol of the unconscious, the womb, the past, the dark place where we face our trials and emerge wiser or destroyed, and a major theme in Bruno Bettelheim's *The Uses of Enchantment,* which is the book that everyone assumes we used as a source, simply because it's the only book on the subject known to a wide public. But Bettelheim's insistent point was that children would find fairy tales useful in part because the protagonists' tribulations always resulted in triumph, the happily ever after. What interested James was the little dishonesties that enabled the characters to reach their happy endings. (Dishonesty was something Bettelheim preferred not to deal with, as the posthumous revelations about his falsifying his academic credentials would seem to indicate.) James was also skeptical about the possibility of "happily ever after" in real life and wary of the danger that fairy tales may give children false expectations. As his play *Twelve Dreams* had demonstrated, he was drawn not to Bettelheim's Freudian approach but to Carl Jung's theory that fairy tales are an indication of the collective unconscious, something with which Bettelheim would be unlikely to agree. James and I talked about fairy tales with a Jungian psychiatrist and discovered that with the exception of "Jack and the Beanstalk," which apparently is native only to the British Isles, the tales we were dealing with exist in virtually every culture in the world, especially the Cinderella story. African, Chinese, Native American—there is even a contemporary Hebrew version in which Cinderella wants to dance at the Tel Aviv Hilton.

In inventing the story of "The Baker and His Wife," James contributed his own cultural fairy tale, an American one. The Baker and his Wife may live in a medieval forest in a fairy-tale medieval time, but they are at heart a contemporary urban American couple who find themselves living among witches and princes and eventually giants. Cinderella gets transformed into a princess, Little Red (which is how we always referred to her) gets eaten by a wolf and comes back to life, Rapunzel gets rescued by a prince, but the Baker and his Wife are merely trying to earn a living and have a baby. Their concerns are quotidian, their attitudes prototypically urban: impatient, sarcastic, bickering, resigned—prototypical, except that they speak in stilted fairy-tale language and are surrounded by witches and princesses and eventually giants. This makes them funny and actable characters, and their contemporaneity makes them people the audience can recognize.

In any event, the gimmick—or, more respectably, the idea—of mashing the tales together gave us a form, much as gimmicks have done in the past (see Schnitzler's *La Ronde*). If we were to focus on the consequences of the little transgressions each character makes in pursuit of his or her heart's desire, it followed naturally that the first act would deal with the traditional telling of the tales up to the Happily and the second with the Ever After. The first would be farce, the second melodrama (still with laughs, of course). As I say, Content Dictates Form—or should.

Having learned so much about the subject of farce from my four-year observation of Burt Shevelove and Larry Gelbart struggling over the intricacies of *A Funny Thing Happened on the Way to the Forum,* I generously offered to give Lapine the benefit of my knowledge to help him construct the plot. To this end I suggested he draw a detailed linear map which would chart the progress of each character's journey through the woods and how it intersected with each of the others. He gave me a tolerant smile, said he'd think about it and plunged headlong into the woods, into the middle of the story, with minimal ideas as to where things would lead (or so he led me to believe) and emerged from them with the best-constructed farce since *Forum*. The elegance with which he crosscuts among the four stories simultaneously throughout the show still astonishes me. It is a lesson in play construction.

I must add that at one point in the collaborative joy of our early discussions I brashly predicted that if the piece worked, it would spawn innumerable productions for many years to come, since it dealt with world myths and fables and would therefore never feel dated. Moreover, it would appeal to schools and amateur theaters as well as professional ones, especially in conservative parts of the country which are hesitant to support shows that deal with contemporary themes in contemporary ways and use four-letter words (there are none in the show). I predicted that *Into the Woods* could be a modest annuity for us, and I'm surprised to say I was right.

ACT ONE

A kingdom long ago. The curtain rises on three structures: On the left, the home of Cinderella; she is in the kitchen, scrubbing the floor. In the center, the home/workplace of the Baker and his Wife; they are preparing tomorrow's bread. On the right, the cottage where Jack lives with his mother; he is inside, milking his pathetic-looking cow, Milky-White. Behind these homes there is a drop depicting a large forest separating these dwellings from the rest of the kingdom.

A Narrator steps forward.

Into the Woods

NARRATOR
Once upon a time—

CINDERELLA
(To us)
I wish . . .

NARRATOR
—in a far-off kingdom—

CINDERELLA
More than anything . . .

NARRATOR
—lived a young maiden—

CINDERELLA
More than life . . .

NARRATOR
—a sad young lad—

CINDERELLA
More than jewels . . .

JACK
I wish . . .

NARRATOR
—and a childless Baker—

JACK
More than life . . .

CINDERELLA, BAKER
I wish . . .

NARRATOR
—with his Wife.

JACK
More than anything . . .

CINDERELLA, BAKER, JACK
More than the moon . . .

WIFE
I wish . . .

CINDERELLA
The King is giving a Festival.

BAKER, WIFE
More than life . . .

JACK
I wish . . .

CINDERELLA
I wish to go to the Festival—

BAKER, WIFE
More than riches . . .

CINDERELLA
And the Ball . . .

JACK
I wish my cow would give us some milk.

CINDERELLA, WIFE
More than anything . . .

BAKER
I wish we had a child.

JACK
(To Milky-White)
Please, pal—

WIFE
I want a child . . .

JACK
Squeeze, pal.

CINDERELLA
I wish to go to the Festival.

JACK
I wish you'd give us some milk
Or even cheese . . .

BAKER, WIFE
I wish we might have a child.

ALL FOUR
I wish . . .

Cinderella's Stepmother and Stepsisters, Florinda and Lucinda, enter.

STEPMOTHER
(To Cinderella)
You wish to go to the Festival?

NARRATOR
The poor girl's mother had died—

STEPMOTHER
You, Cinderella, the Festival?
You wish to go to the Festival?

FLORINDA
(Overlapping)
What, you, Cinderella, the Festival?
The Festival!?

LUCINDA
(Overlapping)
What, you wish to go to the Festival!?

ALL THREE
The Festival?!
The King's Festival!!!???

NARRATOR
—and her father had taken for his new wife—

STEPMOTHER
The *Festival*!!!???

NARRATOR
—a woman with two daughters of her own.

FLORINDA
Look at your nails!

LUCINDA
Look at your dress!

STEPMOTHER
People would laugh at you—

CINDERELLA
Nevertheless—

CINDERELLA	STEPSISTERS	STEPMOTHER
I still wish to go	You still wish to go	She still wants to go
To the Festival.	To the Festival—	To the Festival—

STEPSISTERS, STEPMOTHER
—and dance before the Prince?!

NARRATOR
All three were beautiful of face, but vile and black of heart. Jack, on the other hand, had no father, and his mother—

JACK'S MOTHER
I wish . . .

NARRATOR
Well, she was not quite beautiful—

JACK'S MOTHER
I wish my son were not a fool.
I wish my house was not a mess.
I wish the cow was full of milk.
I wish the walls were full of gold—
I wish a lot of things . . .

(*To Jack*)

You foolish child! What in heaven's name are you doing with the cow inside the house?

JACK
A warm environment might be just what Milky-White needs to produce his milk—

JACK'S MOTHER
It's a she! How many times must I tell you? Only "she"s can give milk.

Two knocks on the Baker's door; the Wife opens the door and there stands Little Red Riding Hood.

WIFE
Why, come in, little girl.

LITTLE RED RIDING HOOD
I wish—
It's not for me,
It's for my Granny in the woods.

Jack (Ben Wright) and Jack's Mother (Barbara Bryne), with Milky-White

A loaf of bread, please,
To bring my poor old hungry
Granny in the woods . . .
Just a loaf of bread, please . . .

The Baker gives her a loaf of bread.

NARRATOR
Cinderella's Stepmother had a surprise for her.

The Stepmother throws a pot of lentils into the fireplace.

STEPMOTHER
I have emptied a pot of lentils into the ashes for you. If you have

picked them out again in two hours' time, you shall go to the ball with us.

The Stepmother and Stepsisters exit.

LITTLE RED RIDING HOOD
And perhaps a sticky bun? . . .
Or four? . . .

CINDERELLA
Birds in the sky,
Birds in the eaves,
In the leaves,
In the fields,
In the castles and ponds . . .

LITTLE RED RIDING HOOD
And a few of those pies,
Please . . .

CINDERELLA
Come, little birds,
Down from the eaves
And the leaves,
Over fields,
Out of castles and ponds . . .

JACK
No, squeeze, pal . . .

CINDERELLA
Ahhhhhh . . .

*Cinderella falls into a trance and birds
descend into the fireplace.*

CINDERELLA
Quick, little birds,
Flick through the ashes.
Pick and peck, but swiftly,
Sift through the ashes.
Into the pot . . .

*The birds start picking at the lentils
and dropping them into the pot.*

JACK'S MOTHER
Listen well, son. Milky-White must
be taken to market.

JACK
But, Mother, no—he's the best
cow—

JACK'S MOTHER
Was. Was! *She's* been dry for a
week. We've no food nor money
and no choice but to sell her while
she can still command a price.

JACK
But Milky-White is my best friend
in the whole world!

JACK'S MOTHER
Look at her!

There are bugs on her dugs.
There are flies in her eyes.
There's a lump on her rump
Big enough to be a hump!

JACK
But—

JACK'S MOTHER
Son,
We've no time to sit and dither
While her withers wither with her—
And no one keeps a cow for a friend!

Sometimes I fear you're touched.

LITTLE RED RIDING HOOD
Into the woods, it's time to go,
I hate to leave, I have to, though.
Into the woods—it's time, and so
I must begin my journey.

Into the woods and through the
    trees
To where I am expected, ma'am,
Into the woods to Grandmother's
    house . . .

*(She grabs a cookie and takes a bite;
    mouth full)*

Into the woods to Grandmother's
    house . . .

WIFE
You're certain of your way?

LITTLE RED RIDING HOOD
The way is clear,
The light is good,
I have no fear,
Nor no one should.
The woods are just trees,
The trees are just wood.
I sort of hate to ask it,
But do you have a basket?

BAKER
Don't stray and be late.

WIFE
And save some of those sweets for
Granny!

LITTLE RED RIDING HOOD
Into the woods and down the dell,
The path is straight, I know it well.
Into the woods, and who can tell
What's waiting on the journey?

Into the woods to bring some bread
To Granny who is sick in bed.

Never can tell what lies ahead,
For all that I know, she's already
    dead.

But into the woods,
Into the woods,
Into the woods
To Grandmother's house
And home before dark!

*She scampers out of their house, grab-
bing another cookie on the way. Meanwhile, the birds have helped Cinderella
with her task and are flying off.*

CINDERELLA
Fly, birds,
Back to the sky,
Back to the eaves
And the leaves
And the fields
And the—

*Florinda and Lucinda enter, dressed for
the ball.*

FLORINDA
Hurry up and do my hair,
Cinderella!

(To Lucinda)

Are you really wearing that?

LUCINDA
(Pointing to her sleeve)
Here, I found a little tear, Cinderella!

(To Florinda, eyeing her hair)

Can't you hide it with a hat?

CINDERELLA
You look beautiful.

FLORINDA
I know.

LUCINDA
She means me.

FLORINDA
(To Cinderella)
Put it in a twist.

CINDERELLA
(To herself, as she obeys)
Mother said be good,
Father said be nice,
That was always their advice.
So be nice, Cinderella,
Good, Cinderella,
Nice good good nice—

FLORINDA
Tighter!

CINDERELLA
What's the good of being good
If everyone is blind
And you're always left behind?
Never mind, Cinderella,
Kind Cinderella—

*(Accenting each word with a twist of a
strand of hair)*

Nice good nice kind good nice—

*Florinda screams and slaps Cinderella
across the face.*

FLORINDA
Not that tight!

CINDERELLA
Sorry.

FLORINDA
Clod.

LUCINDA
Hee hee hee—

Florinda glares at her.

Hee hee—

(She stops)

*A Witch who lives next door to the
Baker enters and explains to him why
the Wife can have no children.*

WITCH
In the past, when you were no
more than a babe, your father
brought his young wife and you to
this cottage. They were a handsome couple, but not handsome
neighbors. You see, your mother
was with child and she had developed an unusual appetite. She took
one look at my beautiful garden
and told your father that what she
wanted more than anything in the
world was

Greens, greens, and nothing but
    greens:
Parsley, peppers, cabbages and
    celery,
Asparagus and watercress and
Fiddleferns and lettuce—!

He said, "All right,"
But it wasn't, quite,
'Cause I caught him
In the autumn
In my garden one night!
He was robbing me,
Raping me,
Rooting through my rutabaga,
Raiding my arugula and
Ripping up the rampion
(My champion!
My favorite!)

I should have laid a spell on him
Right there—
Could have turned him into stone
Or a dog or a chair or a sn—

*She drifts off into a long momentary
trance, then abruptly snaps out of it.*

But I let him have the rampion,
I'd lots to spare.
In return, however,
I said, "Fair is fair:
You can let me have the baby
That your wife will bear,
And we'll call it square."

BAKER
I had a brother?

WITCH
No . . . But you had a sister.

NARRATOR
However, the Witch refused to tell
him any more of his sister, not even
that her name was Rapunzel. She
went on:

WITCH
I thought I had been more than reasonable, and that we all might live
happily ever after. But how was I to
know what your father had also
hidden in his pocket?! You see,
when I had inherited that garden,
my mother had warned me I would
be punished if I ever were to lose
any of the

Beans.

BAKER, WIFE
Beans?

WITCH
The special beans!

(Getting worked up)

I let him go,
I didn't know
He'd stolen my beans!
I was watching him crawl
Back over the wall,
And then bang! Crash!
And the lightning flash!
And—well, that's another story,
Never mind.

Anyway, at last
The big day came
And I made my claim.
"Oh, don't take away the baby,"
They shrieked and screeched,
But I did and I hid her
Where she'll never be reached.

And your father cried
And your mother died,
When for extra measure—
I admit it was a pleasure—
I said, "Sorry,
I'm still not mollified."
And I laid a little spell on them—
You too, son—
That your family tree
Would always be
A barren one . . .

So there's no more fuss
And there's no more scenes
And my garden thrives—
You should see my nectarines!
But I'm telling you the same
I tell Kings and Queens:
Don't ever never ever
Mess around with my greens!

Especially the beans.

Jack is reluctantly preparing to take Milky-White to market.

JACK'S MOTHER
Now listen to me, Jack. Lead Milky-White to market and fetch the best price you can. Take no less than five pounds. Are you listening to me?

JACK
Yes.

JACK'S MOTHER
Now how much are you to ask?

JACK
No more than five pounds.

Jack's mother pinches his ear hard.

JACK'S MOTHER, JACK
Less! Than five.

JACK'S MOTHER
Jack Jack Jack,
Head in a sack,
The house is getting colder.
This is not a time for dreaming.

Chimney stack
Starting to crack,
The mice are getting bolder,
The floor's gone slack.
Your mother's getting older,
Your father's not back,
And you can't just sit here dreaming pretty dreams.

To wish and wait
From day to day
Will never keep
The wolves away.

So into the woods, the time is now.
We have to live, I don't care how.
Into the woods to sell the cow,
You must begin the journey.

Straight through the woods and don't delay,
We have to face
The marketplace.
Into the woods to journey's end—

JACK
Into the woods to sell a friend—

NARRATOR
Meanwhile, the Witch, for purposes of her own, explained how the Baker might lift the spell:

WITCH
You wish to have the curse reversed?
I'll need a certain potion first.
Go to the wood and bring me back
One: the cow as white as milk,
Two: the cape as red as blood,
Three: the hair as yellow as corn,
Four: the slipper as pure as gold.

Bring me these before the chime
Of midnight in three days' time,
And you shall have, I guarantee,
A child as perfect as child can be.

Go to the wood!

She disappears. Fanfare.

STEPMOTHER
(*To the Stepsisters*)
Ladies. Our carriage waits.

CINDERELLA
(*Showing her the plate of lentils*)
Now may I go to the Festival?

STEPMOTHER
The Festival—!
Darling, those nails!
Darling, those clothes!
Lentils are one thing but
Darling, with those,
You'd make us the fools of the Festival
And mortify the Prince!

Cinderella's Father enters.

CINDERELLA'S FATHER
The carriage is waiting.

STEPMOTHER
We must be gone.

She and the Stepsisters exit with a flourish.

CINDERELLA
Good night, Father.

Cinderella's Father grunts and exits with the rest of the family.

CINDERELLA
I wish . . .

She sits dejectedly. The Baker, having gone off, returns in hunting gear.

BAKER
Look what I found in Father's hunting jacket.

WIFE
Six beans.

BAKER
I wonder if they are the—

WIFE
Witch's beans? We'll take them with us.

BAKER
No! You are not coming.

WIFE
I know you are fearful of the woods at night.

BAKER
The spell is on *my* house.
Only I can lift the spell,
The spell is on *my* house.

WIFE
No, no, the spell is on *our* house.
We must lift the spell together,
The spell is on *our* house.

BAKER
No. You are not to come and that is final. Now what am I to return with?

WIFE
You don't remember?

The cow as white as milk,
The cape as red as blood,
The hair as yellow as corn,
The slipper as pure as gold—

BAKER
(*Memorizing*)
The cow as white as milk,
The cape as red as blood,
The hair as yellow as corn,
The slipper as pure as gold . . .

NARRATOR
And so the Baker reluctantly set off
to meet the enchantress's demands.
As for Cinderella:

CINDERELLA
I still wish to go to the Festival,
But how am I ever to get to the
Festival?

BAKER
The cow as white as milk,
The cape as red as blood,
The hair as yellow as corn—

WIFE
(Prompting)
The slipper—

BAKER
The slipper as pure as gold . . .

CINDERELLA
I know!
I'll visit Mother's grave,
The grave at the hazel tree,
And tell her I just want to go
To the King's Festival . . .

BAKER
The cow, the cape,
The slipper as pure as gold—

WIFE
The hair—!

BAKER, CINDERELLA
Into the woods, it's time to go,
It may be all in vain, you (I) know.
Into the woods—but even so,
I have to take the journey.

BAKER, CINDERELLA, WIFE
Into the woods, the path is straight,
You (I) know it well,
But who can tell—?

BAKER, WIFE
Into the woods to lift the spell—

CINDERELLA
Into the woods to visit Mother—

WIFE
Into the woods to fetch the things—

BAKER
To make the potion—

CINDERELLA
To go to the Festival—

BAKER, WIFE, CINDERELLA,
JACK, JACK'S MOTHER
Into the woods without regret,
The choice is made, the task is set.
Into the woods, but not forget-
Ting why I'm (you're) on the
journey.

*Little Red Riding Hood comes skipping
by and joins in.*

Into the woods to get my (our) wish,
I don't care how,
The time is now.

JACK'S MOTHER
Into the woods to sell the cow—

JACK
Into the woods to get the money—

WIFE
Into the woods to lift the spell—

BAKER
To make the potion—

CINDERELLA
To go to the Festival—

LITTLE RED RIDING HOOD
Into the woods to Grandmother's
house . . .
Into the woods to Grandmother's
house . . .

ALL
The way is clear,
The light is good,
I have no fear,
Nor no one should.
The woods are just trees,
The trees are just wood.
No need to be afraid there—

BAKER, CINDERELLA
(Fearfully)
There's something in the glade
there . . .

*The Stepmother, Cinderella's Father
and the Stepsisters are seen riding in
their carriage.*

ALL
Into the woods without delay,
But careful not to lose the way.
Into the woods, who knows
what may
Be lurking on the journey?

Into the woods to get the thing
That makes it worth the journeying.
Into the woods—

STEPMOTHER, STEPSISTERS
To see the King—

JACK, JACK'S MOTHER
To sell the cow—

BAKER, WIFE
To make the potion—

ALL
To see—
To sell—
To get—
To bring—
To make—
To lift—
To go to the Festival—!

Into the woods!
Into the woods!
Into the woods,
Then out of the woods,
And home before dark!

As with "A Weekend in the Country,"
"God, That's Good!" and "Opening
Doors," this is the kind of number I
love to work out: the playlet, or what
Leonard Bernstein liked to call in his
linguistic cups the musical *scena*—a
brief plot tightly and tidily laid out
in a fluid combination of song and
speech. But this one was an *opening*
number and would allow me to set up
all the musical themes for the show
because it encompassed all four stories. I use the word "number" as opposed to "song" carefully. It may seem
to be a trivial matter, but it's an important distinction. A song concentrates

on one idea, one story, one emotion—it is a distillation. A number is an extension of ideas and/or stories and/or points of view; it involves development. I bring it up to point out a painful truism that it's taken me a long time to learn: numbers are easier to write than songs, much easier. Concentrating matter is hard—but then, Less Is More.

Rodgers and Hammerstein wrote a pleasant, tepid musical of the Cinderella story for television and I've sometimes wondered what Oscar would have made of our version. I mean, what is this weird thing she has with birds? And where is the Fairy Godmother? Where are the mice and the pumpkins? Most audiences seeing *Into the Woods* probably were as startled as Oscar would have been because their exposure to the tale via school and Disney had been to the one by Charles Perrault, not that of the Brothers Grimm, whose version more tellingly reflects the homonym of their name. On Broadway, the audiences gasped with delight at the bloody mutilations of the Stepsisters trying to fit themselves into the slipper. The gentrification of this extremely cruel story at the hands of a Frenchman may or may not be a convenient metaphor for the differences between the French and the German, but it certainly makes for a less strange and enchanting story. Lapine's choice of the Grimms' version is that of a dramatist rather than that of an illustrator.

The woods. Late afternoon. Cinderella stops at the hazel tree which has grown from a branch she planted at her mother's grave and which has been watered by her tears.

Cinderella at the Grave

CINDERELLA
I've been good and I've been kind,
   Mother,
Doing only what I learned from you.
Why then am I left behind, Mother,
Is there something more that I
   should do?
What is wrong with me, Mother?
Something must be wrong.

I wish . . .

The ghost of Cinderella's Mother appears within the tree.

CINDERELLA'S MOTHER
Do you know what you wish?
Are you certain what you wish
Is what you want?
If you know what you want,
Then make a wish.
Ask the tree,
And you shall have your wish.

CINDERELLA
Shiver and quiver, little tree,
Silver and gold throw down on me.

A gold and silver dress and fancy slippers drop down from the tree.

I'm off to get my wish . . .

In case you're wondering about glass slippers dropping, they don't break, because they're not glass, they're gold. Perrault's version of the story refers to slippers made of "verre" (glass) and a persistent mistaken belief is that he mistook "vair" (medieval French for fur) for "verre," but that theory has been disproved. The roots of the story date back to ninth-century China, and in that version the heroine loses a gold slipper.

Little Red Riding Hood meets a Wolf and exchanges pleasantries with him. He watches her skip off on her way to her Grandmother's house.

Hello, Little Girl

WOLF
(Grunting lasciviously)
Mmmh . . .
Unhh . . .

(To himself)

Look at that flesh,
Pink and plump.
Hello, little girl . . .
Tender and fresh,
Not one lump.
Hello, little girl . . .
This one's especially lush,
Delicious . . .
Mmmh . . .

He smacks his lips, then runs over and pops up in front of her.

Hello, little girl,
What's your rush?
You're missing all the flowers.
The sun won't set for hours,
Take your time.

LITTLE RED RIDING HOOD
Mother said,
"Straight ahead,"
Not to delay
Or be misled.

WOLF
But slow, little girl,
Hark! And hush—
The birds are singing sweetly.
You'll miss the birds completely,
You're traveling so fleetly.

Little Red Riding Hood stops to listen.

WOLF
(To himself)
Grandmother first,
Then Miss Plump . . .
What a delectable couple.
Utter perfection:
One brittle, one supple—

(Seeing her start to move off again)

One moment, my dear—

LITTLE RED RIDING HOOD

Mother said,
"Come what may,
Follow the path
And never stray."

WOLF

Just so, little girl—
Any path.
So many worth exploring.
Just one would be so boring.
And look what you're ignoring . . .

Gestures to the trees and flowers; Little Red Riding Hood stops to look around.

WOLF
(*To himself*)

Think of those crisp,
Aging bones,
Then something fresh on the palate.
Think of that scrumptious carnality
Twice in one day . . .
There's no possible way
To describe what you feel
When you're talking to your meal!

LITTLE RED RIDING HOOD

Mother said
Not to stray.
Still, I suppose,
A small delay—
Granny might like
A fresh bouquet . . .

(*Starts collecting flowers*)

Goodbye, Mr. Wolf.

WOLF

Goodbye, little girl.

(*Starts off*)

And hello . . .

He howls and exits swiftly.

Jack, on his way to market, meets a Mysterious Man in the woods who advises him to sell his cow as soon as possible. The Baker and his Wife, who to the Baker's annoyance has followed him into the woods, encounter Jack and, seeing one of the objects of their quest, persuade him to sell it to them for five of the Witch's six beans, which they claim have magic powers. Jack bids Milky-White a tearful goodbye.

I Guess This Is Goodbye

JACK

I guess this is goodbye, old pal.
You've been a perfect friend.
I hate to see us part, old pal.
Someday I'll buy you back.
I'll see you soon again.
I hope that when I do,
It won't be on a plate.

This is the only song I've ever written that has no rhyme at all. It's so brief that it hardly qualifies as a song, but it's a continuation of the fragmentary approach that I had developed with Lapine for the "Day Off" sequence in *Sunday in the Park with George*. It seemed fitting that innocent, empty-headed Jack be so dimwitted that he couldn't even rhyme. But it's not so easy to make nonrhymes work when the music rhymes—that is, when the music has square and matching rhythms, as this ditty deliberately does. Just as the vowel sounds must match exactly in a good rhyme, so must they bear no resemblance to each other in a nonrhyming pattern. If "I'll see you soon again" were the fourth line, the approximate rhyme of "friend" and "again" would make for a sloppily imperfect rhyme. The word "back," however, is so shockingly different to the ear from "friend" that it emphasizes Jack's mindlessness. (When the word "again" does appear, it doesn't land on a phrase of matching music, so it feels fresh.) Not only are the vowel sounds from different realms, so are the consonants (soft in the first, hard in the second). The same principle applies to "again," "do" and "plate" and ratchets up the laugh at the image (which, inciden- tally, was Lapine's). Subtle as it may seem, the lack of rhyme makes Jack all the more appealing.

After they have the cow, the Baker reprimands the Wife for pretending the beans have magic powers when she knows no such thing. He tells her to go home and let him carry out the quest by himself.

Maybe They're Magic

WIFE

If you know
What you want,
Then you go
And you find it
And you get it—

BAKER
(*Pointing off*)

Home.

WIFE

Do we want a child or not?
—And you give
And you take
And you bid
And you bargain,
Or you live
To regret it.

BAKER

Will you please go home?

WIFE

There are rights and wrongs
And in-betweens,
No one waits
When fortune intervenes.
And maybe they're really magic,
Who knows?

Why you do
What you do,
That's the point,
All the rest of it
Is chatter.

BAKER
(Referring to Milky-White)
Look at her. She's crying.

WIFE
If the thing you do
Is pure in intent,
If it's meant,
And it's just a little bent,
Does it matter?

BAKER
Yes.

WIFE
No, what matters
Is that everyone tells tiny lies.
What's important, really, is the size.

Pause; the Baker just looks at her.

Only three more tries
And we'll have our prize.
When the end's in sight,
You'll realize:
If the end is right,
It justifies
The beans!

The Baker tells the Wife to go home. They exit, irritated, in different directions.
Meanwhile, the Witch, having isolated her daughter, Rapunzel, from the world in a doorless tower deep in the woods, visits her.

Our Little World

RAPUNZEL
(Singing wordlessly, brushing her hair)
Ah-ah-ah-ah-ah . . .

WITCH
(Looking up lovingly)
Children are a blessing—

RAPUNZEL
Ah-ah-ah-ah-ah . . .

WITCH
If you know where they are.

RAPUNZEL
Ah-ah-ah-ah-ah . . .

WITCH
Nothing's so distressing,
Though,
As when they keep you guessing,
So
Be sure you don't leave any doors
    ajar.
Make a little world . . .

RAPUNZEL
Our little world—

WITCH
Our little world—

RAPUNZEL
Is big enough for me . . .

WITCH
Perfect . . .

BOTH
Our little world—

RAPUNZEL
Is all it needs to be.

WITCH
Perfect!

RAPUNZEL
Brushing my hair, combing my hair,
Only my mother and me and my
    hair—

BOTH
Our little world is perfect—

RAPUNZEL
If she just didn't drool.

WITCH
Rapunzel, Rapunzel, let down your
    hair to me!

Rapunzel lowers her hair for the Witch to climb.

"Our Little World" (Regent's Park, London, 2010)

WITCH
Look at that complexion,
Still untouched by the sun.
Children need protection
Just the way they need affection
Or they wonder, and they wander,
    and they run
From your little world . . .

RAPUNZEL
Our little world—

WITCH
Our little world—

RAPUNZEL
Is all I have to see . . .

WITCH
Perfect . . .

BOTH
Our little world—

RAPUNZEL
Is everything a world ought to be.

WITCH
Perfect! Perfect!

RAPUNZEL
Washing my hair—

WITCH
Tending her hair—

RAPUNZEL
Drying my hair—

WITCH
Stroking her hair—

RAPUNZEL
Unravelling my hair—

WITCH
Looking at her hair—

RAPUNZEL
Winding and binding and minding
    my—

WITCH
Something we can share:

BOTH
Hair.
Our little world is perfect—

RAPUNZEL
Or at least so she says.

WITCH
Nothing to change her . . .

RAPUNZEL
If she only would cut her nails . . .

WITCH
Each day like the other . . .

RAPUNZEL
Didn't have those funny teeth . . .

WITCH
Nothing to divert her,
To disconcert her . . .

RAPUNZEL
Tiny eyes . . .

WITCH
Nothing that can possibly hurt
    her . . .

RAPUNZEL
Otherwise—

BOTH
Our little world is perfect—

RAPUNZEL
And world enough for me.

WITCH
Our little world . . .

RAPUNZEL
Growing my hair—

WITCH
Raising her hair—

RAPUNZEL
What do I care what they're doing
    out there?

WITCH
If what was growing was only her
    hair
And not her,
That I'd prefer.
Nevertheless—

BOTH
Our little world
Is perfect . . .

The Witch starts to climb Rapunzel's hair; Rapunzel grunts with pain.

WITCH
Delicious . . .

    (Rapunzel grunts again)

Fulfilling . . .

    (Another grunt)

Exclusive . . .

    (Two more grunts)

Unchanging . . .

    (Grunt)

Exemplary . . .

The Witch reaches the top of the tower.

This song was added for the London production. Having seen the show in its final form a number of times, I realized that we never observe the Witch having a happy maternal moment with her daughter, which makes the Witch unrelentingly possessive and Rapunzel's mixed feelings about her inexplicable. In order to avoid sentimentality, however, which might seem a bit forced considering the bizarrerie of the Witch's persona, I made the song an accompaniment to what I hoped would be the hilarity of the action: the hair-climbing. Sometimes the moment has been funny and sometimes it just lies there—not a good sign. Hedging my bets, I've labeled it "optional" in the score that is leased for performance.

The Wolf, having eaten Little Red Riding Hood's Grandmother, waits in her bed until Little Red Riding Hood enters, and then eats her, but they are rescued from his stomach by the Baker, who kills him. Little Red pauses to assess the situation.

I Know Things Now

LITTLE RED RIDING HOOD
Mother said,
"Straight ahead,"
Not to delay
Or be misled.
I should have heeded
Her advice . . .
But he seemed so nice.

And he showed me things,
Many beautiful things,
That I hadn't thought to explore.
They were off my path,
So I never had dared.
I had been so careful
I never had cared.
And he made me feel excited—
Well, excited and scared.

When he said, "Come in!"
With that sickening grin,
How could I know what was in
    store?
Once his teeth were bared,
Though, I really got scared—
Well, excited and scared.

But he drew me close
And he swallowed me down,
Down a dark, slimy path
Where lie secrets that I never want
    to know,
And when everything familiar
Seemed to disappear forever,
At the end of the path
Was Granny once again.

So we wait in the dark
Until someone sets us free,
And we're brought into the light,
And we're back at the start.

And I know things now,
Many valuable things,
That I hadn't known before:
Do not put your faith
In a cape and a hood,
They will not protect you
The way that they should.
And take extra care with strangers—
Even flowers have their dangers.
And though scary is exciting,
Nice is different than good.

Now I know:
Don't be scared.
Granny is right,
Just be prepared.
Isn't it nice to know a lot?

And a little bit not . . .

Early on in the game, James proposed that each of the familiar folktale figures (Little Red, Jack and Cinderella) should have a musical soliloquy directed to the audience about their adventures in Act One, setting up a climactic soliloquy of the same sort for our newly invented character, the Baker's Wife, after her adventure with the Prince in Act Two. For some reason, defying my Germanic instinct for writing in chronological order, I tackled Jack's song first, probably because his adventure lent itself to incident and images most fertilely. It didn't turn out well. It was neat, descriptive and somehow unnecessary: Why tell the audience a story they already know unless you dramatize it? Moreover, we never showed Jack (or the others) in the course of their adventures: Jack in the Giant's kingdom, Little Red inside the Wolf's stomach, Cinderella at the ball. James's wife, Sarah, suggested that these songs would be more interesting if they dealt with what the adventures *meant* to the adventurers, rather than simply being narrative descriptions. Not only was she right, her suggestion gave me a thematic idea which tied all four lyrics together, baldly stated in the title of Little Red's song: the experience of learning.

Aren't such songs dangerous in a farce, you may not be asking yourself (but you should)? If even fragments like "I Guess This Is Goodbye" are potential speed bumps when a farce is just beginning to bubble, aren't these internal monologues showstoppers in the worst sense? The difference, a subtle but defining one when it comes to the pace of unfolding a plot, is the difference between songs that slow down the action merely to savor the moment and songs that stop it com-

pletely, that serve as punctuations. The first have to be brief, but the second can take their time and hold their own. "I Know Things Now" is a case in point. It is a signpost on the road of the story. The words of the title recur and resonate in each of the other soliloquies about experience, culminating, in Act Two, in the self-assessment of the Baker's Wife, who, contrary to the others, decides that she likes life as it is—an ironic decision in view of what happens to her immediately afterward.

Cinderella, running away from the Festival, encounters the Wife, who wants to know what the Prince was like.

A Very Nice Prince

CINDERELLA
He's a very nice prince.

WIFE
And—?

CINDERELLA
And—
It's a very nice ball.

WIFE
And—?

CINDERELLA
And—
When I entered, they trumpeted.

WIFE
And—?
The Prince—?

CINDERELLA
Oh, the Prince . . .

WIFE
Yes, the Prince!

CINDERELLA
Well, he's tall.

WIFE
Is that all?
Did you dance?
Is he charming?
They say that he's charming.

CINDERELLA
We did nothing but dance.

WIFE
Yes—?
And—?

CINDERELLA
And it made a nice change.

WIFE
No, the prince!

CINDERELLA
Oh, the Prince . . .

WIFE
Yes, the Prince.

CINDERELLA
He has charm for a Prince, I
    guess . . .

WIFE
Guess?

CINDERELLA
I don't meet a wide range.

WIFE*
Did he bow?
Was he cold and polite?

CINDERELLA
And it's all very strange.

WIFE
Did you speak?
Did he flirt?
Could you tell right away he was
    royalty?
Is he sensitive,
Clever,
Well-mannered,

Considerate,
Passionate,
Charming,
As kind as he's handsome,
As wise as he's rich,
Is he everything you've ever wanted?

CINDERELLA
Would I know?

WIFE
Well, I know!

CINDERELLA
But how can you know what you
    want
Till you get what you want
And you see if you like it?

WIFE
Would I know?

CINDERELLA
All I know is—

WIFE
I never wish—

CINDERELLA
What I want most of all—

WIFE
Just within reason.

CINDERELLA
—Is to know what I want.

WIFE
When you know you can't have
    what you want,
Where's the profit in wishing?

BOTH
He's a very nice prince.*

CINDERELLA
And it's all very strange.

*The first chime of midnight. The
Wife tries unsuccessfully to get hold of
Cinderella's golden slipper. The second
chime. Jack's beanstalk sprouts up. As
the chimes continue, each of the characters (now including Rapunzel) appears moving through the woods,
pursuing their errands, mostly oblivi-*

*ous to one another. The lines are spo-
ken rhythmically as each character appears and disappears.*

First Midnight

BAKER
One midnight gone . . .

MYSTERIOUS MAN
No knot unties itself . . .

WITCH
Sometimes the things you most wish
    for are not to be touched . . .

PRINCES
The harder to get, the better to
    have . . .

CINDERELLA'S PRINCE
Agreed?

RAPUNZEL'S PRINCE
Agreed.

FLORINDA
Never wear mauve at a ball . . .

LUCINDA
Or pink . . .

STEPMOTHER
(Glaring at them)
Or open your mouth . . .

JACK
(Looking up and off at the beanstalk)
The difference between a cow and a
    bean
Is a bean can begin an adventure . . .

(Runs out)

JACK'S MOTHER
(Looking off in Jack's direction)
Slotted spoons don't hold much
    soup . . .

LITTLE RED RIDING HOOD
The prettier the flower, the farther
    from the path . . .

CINDERELLA'S FATHER
The closer to the family, the closer to
the wine . . .

RAPUNZEL
Ah-ah-ah-ah-ah . . .

WITCH
One midnight gone! . . .

GRANNY
The mouth of a wolf's not the end of
the world . . .

STEWARD
A servant is not just a dog to a
prince . . .

CINDERELLA
Opportunity is not a lengthy
visitor . . .

WIFE
You may know what you need,
But to get what you want,
Better see that you keep what you
have.

ALL
One midnight one midnight one
midnight gone . . .

Into the woods,
Into the woods,
Into the woods, then out of the
woods,
And home before—!

Not only are these "lyrics" spoken,
they are for the most part written by
Lapine; I include them to exemplify
the songs I referred to above as punctuations in the action rather than interruptions. In this story they act as
echoes of the opening "Once upon a
time," variations on the traditional
summing up of The Story So Far. More
important, this "First Midnight" sets
up the "Second Midnight," a long and
substantial number which was intended (by me, anyway) to be the
philosophical center of the show—and
which turned out to be both senten-
tious and unnecessary, and conse-
quently was gradually whittled down
to a nub. I liked it a lot.

*Jack returns from his trip to the top of
the beanstalk and recounts his adventure to the Baker, from whom he is trying to buy back Milky-White.*

Giants in the Sky

JACK
There are giants in the sky!
There are big tall terrible giants in
the sky!

When you're way up high and you
look below
At the world you left and the things
you know,
Little more than a glance is enough
to show
You just how small you are.

When you're way up high and you're
on your own
In a world like none that you've ever
known,
Where the sky is lead and the earth
is stone,

You're free to do
Whatever pleases you,

Exploring things you'd never dare
'Cause you don't care,
When suddenly there's

A big tall terrible giant at the door,
A big tall terrible lady giant
sweeping the floor.
And she gives you food
And she gives you rest,
And she draws you close
To her giant breast,
And you know things now that you
never knew before,
Not till the sky.

Only just when you've made a friend
and all,
And you know she's big but you
don't feel small,
Someone bigger than her comes
along the hall
To swallow you for lunch.

And your heart is lead and your
stomach stone
And you're really scared being all
alone,
And it's then that you miss all the
things you've known
And the world you've left and the
little you own.

The fun is done.
You steal what you can and run!

Jack's Mother, Jack and Milky-White (Regent's Park, London, 2010)

And you scramble down
And you look below,
And the world you know
Begins to grow:

The roof, the house, and your
    mother at the door.
The roof, the house, and the world
    you never thought to explore.
And you think of all of the things
    you've seen,
And you wish that you could live in
    between,
And you're back again,
Only different than before,
After the sky.

There are giants in the sky!
There are big tall terrible awesome
    scary
Wonderful giants in the sky!

The first version of this song, the one I
described earlier that looked right and
seemed wrong, the one that spurred
Sarah Kernochan to make her observation, was this:

Giants in the Sky
(original version)

CINDERELLA'S PRINCE

JACK
(To the Baker)
Good fortune, sir!
Hello, I'm back!
Remember me?
My name is Jack,
And when you see
What's in my sack
You'll more than be
Repaid.

How right you were
When you persuad-
Ed me to trade,
Though I'm afraid,
My mother, sir,
When I displayed
The beans to her,
Was quite dismayed—

For with a shout
She threw them out
And said I'd made
Without a doubt
The dumbest trade
She'd heard about,
But no, sir, you were right!

'Cause in the night I woke to find
The beans had sprouted,
Intertwined,
And all combined
To form a stout
And stately kind
Of beanstalk!

Up and up and up it grew
Up past the trees and up and
    through
The clouds and up and up into
The sky and up it climbed,
And so did I,
And up and up and up so high
I thought I'd drop . . .

(Running out of breath)

I'd fall and die
A violent death . . .
I had to stop . . .
And catch my breath . . .

(Pauses to catch his breath)

But then I reached the top!

There are giants in the sky!
There are big tall terrible giants in
    the sky!

At the top of the stalk
I looked around:
The sky was chalk,
Just like the ground.
I began to walk
A road that wound
Through countryside
All stark and bare,
With not a sound
Upon the air.

My throat was parched,
My eyes a-blur,
But on I marched
Until I spied
A mansion, sir,
Three meadows wide!
And standing there,

A big tall terrible giant
At the door,
A big tall terrible lady giant
Sweeping the floor!

And I asked for bread
And I asked for rest,
And she saw me fed
And she made me guest
And she nestled me in her big soft
    giant breast
Up in the sky!

*And there the song stopped, unfin-
ished, rescued by Sarah.*

*The Prince, searching through the
woods for the beautiful girl who danced
with him at the ball and who left her
slipper behind, runs into his younger
brother, who has been vainly trying
to woo Rapunzel. They compare
complaints.*

Agony

CINDERELLA'S PRINCE
Did I abuse her
Or show her disdain?
Why does she run from me?
If I should lose her,
How shall I regain
The heart she has won from me?

Agony—!
Beyond power of speech,
When the one thing you want
Is the only thing out of your reach.

RAPUNZEL'S PRINCE
High in her tower,
She sits by the hour,
Maintaining her hair.
Blithe and becoming,
And frequently humming
A lighthearted air:

(Hums Rapunzel's theme)

Ah-ah-ah-ah-ah-ah-ah—

Agony—!
Far more painful than yours,
When you know she would go
    with you,
If there only were doors.

BOTH
Agony!
Oh, the torture they teach!

RAPUNZEL'S PRINCE
What's as intriguing—

CINDERELLA'S PRINCE
Or half so fatiguing—

BOTH
As what's out of reach?

CINDERELLA'S PRINCE
Am I not sensitive, clever,
Well-mannered, considerate,
Passionate, charming,
As kind as I'm handsome,
And heir to a throne?

RAPUNZEL'S PRINCE
You are everything maidens could
    wish for!

CINDERELLA'S PRINCE
Then why no—?

RAPUNZEL'S PRINCE
Do I know?

CINDERELLA'S PRINCE
The girl must be mad.

RAPUNZEL'S PRINCE
You know nothing of madness
Till you're climbing her hair
And you see her up there
As you're nearing her,
All the while hearing her
"Ah-ah-ah-ah-ah-ah-ah-ah—"

BOTH
Agony!

CINDERELLA'S PRINCE
Misery!

RAPUNZEL'S PRINCE
Woe!

BOTH
Though it's different for each.

CINDERELLA'S PRINCE
Always ten steps behind—

RAPUNZEL'S PRINCE
Always ten feet below—

BOTH
And she's just out of reach.
Agony
That can cut like a knife!

I must have her to wife.

Night falls, the second night of the Festival. Once again Cinderella, running away from the Prince, encounters the Wife and once again the Wife wants to know everything about the Festival.

A Very Nice Prince
(reprise)

CINDERELLA
Oh, it's still a nice ball.

WIFE
Yes—?
And—?

CINDERELLA
And—
They have far too much food.

WIFE
No, the Prince—

CINDERELLA
Oh, the Prince . . .

WIFE
Yes, the Prince!

CINDERELLA
If he knew who I really was—

WIFE
Oh? Who?

CINDERELLA
I'm afraid I was rude.

WIFE
Oh? How?

CINDERELLA
Now I'm being pursued.

WIFE
Yes—?
And—?

CINDERELLA
And I'm not in the mood.

In its original version, this brief reprise was a precursor to "Moments in the Woods," the song sung by the Baker's Wife in Act Two. Just as I connected the dilemmas of Little Red Riding Hood and Jack to that of Cinderella, so did I (musically) connect Cinderella's to that of the Wife. The lyric:

Just Like Last Night
(cut)

CINDERELLA
It was close,
It was hot.
I was wet
As a blotter.
He kept chattering,
He was flattering,
Just the same as last night.

As we danced—
Quite a lot—
He got close,
I got hotter.
He was clutching me,
Not just touching me,
Even more than last night.
And it's bothered me since.

He's a very nice prince.

The Wife tries to snatch one of Cinderella's golden slippers but fails. By now the Baker has the cape and the

Agony Reprise

bad fair   SM is disguised   SW = Goldilocks in Dwarf's home
pricked < fight   tie up   evil stepmother
thickets   corset laces   fasten Spurns Snow White
                   poisoned comb   Boris heat
                   ~ apple   Friend in the last — — cures
                                                              hint
                   disl. 2nd apple   snow
                      from Prince   ebony
                        who inherit   blood (rose)

_____

suffer   What is more   My thing about Thickets
yearning   What else is worth winning
hunger   Basically what's out of reach
desire   And guarded by dwarfs   makes me sick, it's
frustration   Thorns, Roses
itchy   Thickets
nuisance   A dwarf standing guard   The tiniest prick, it's
torment   At his mistress   My thing about blood.
affliction   I did keep my destiny
addiction   guarded'er   Every   rising
titillate   My problem is harder   Is a reminder
tantalize   Of what's out of reach

pang   Why do you fall most
ache   For something always,   And it's
anguish   whatever always they that are Worse, how annoying
torment   In reach?   almost   To know you're enjoying
                I a reach?
maiden   Always in thrall most
                                         What an affliction
beauty   This awful addiction

                What could be stranger
                         older
                                         My love lies sleeping
                                         off in
                                         Alive in a coffin
                                         tiniest
                                         casket

                                         Love's little lunacies

cow and the Wife has found the hair. After having repeatedly urged her to go home to no avail, the Baker, with the second midnight rapidly approaching, agrees to let the Wife stay and assist him on his quest.

It Takes Two

WIFE
You've changed.
You're daring.
You're different in the woods.
More sure,
More sharing.
You're getting us through the woods.

If you could see—
You're not the man who started,
And much more open-hearted
Than I knew
You to be.

BAKER
It takes two.
I thought one was enough,
It's not true:
It takes two of us.
You came through
When the journey was rough.
It took you.
It took two of us.

It takes care,
It takes patience and fear and
    despair
To change.
Though you swear
To change,
Who can tell if you do?
It takes two.

WIFE
You've changed.
You're thriving.
There's something about the woods.
Not just
Surviving,
You're blossoming in the woods.

At home I'd fear
We'd stay the same forever.
And then out here

You're passionate, charming,
    considerate, clever—

BAKER
It takes one
To begin, but then once
You've begun,
It takes two of you.
It's no fun,
But what needs to be done
You can do
When there's two of you.

If I dare,
It's because I'm becoming aware
Of us
As a pair
Of us,
Each accepting a share
Of what's there.

BOTH
We've changed.
We're strangers.
I'm meeting you in the woods.
Who minds
What dangers?
I know we'll get past the woods.

And once we're past,
Let's hope the changes last
Beyond woods,
Beyond witches and slippers and
    hoods,
Just the two of us—
Beyond lies,
Safe at home with our beautiful
    prize,
Just the few of us.

It takes trust.
It takes just
A bit more
And we're done.
We want four,
We had none.
We've got three.
We need one.
It takes two.

The second chime of midnight. Once again all the characters move through the woods on their errands. In the Broadway production they spoke a broken set of gnomic maxims, as in the "First Midnight." In the show's initial incarnation, however, they sang.

Second Midnight
(original version)

CINDERELLA'S MOTHER
Careful with what you say,
Children will listen.
Careful with what you do,
Children will see.
And learn.

JACK'S MOTHER
Children may not obey,
But children will listen.
Children will look to you
For which way to turn,
To learn what to be.

PARENTS
Careful before you say,
"Listen to me."

BAKER, WIFE
How do you say to your child in the
    night,
Nothing's all black, but then
    nothing's all white?

Chip Zien as the Baker and Joanna Gleason as the Baker's Wife (San Diego, 1986)

How do you say it will all be all
  right,
When you know that it mightn't be
  true?
What do you do?

PARENTS

What do you leave to your child
  when you're dead?
Only whatever you put in its head.
Things that your father and mother
  had said,
Which were left to them, too.
Careful what you say.

CHILDREN

How do you show them what they
  want to see,
Still being true to what you want
  to be?
How do you grow if they never agree
To your wandering free
In the wood?

PARENTS

How do you say to a child who's in
  flight,
Don't slip away and I won't hold so
  tight?

What can you say that, no matter
  how slight,
Won't be misunderstood?
What, except:
Be good.
Make me proud.
Have a little patience.
Watch out for the wolves.

CHILDREN

I will.

PARENTS

Don't be foolish.
Don't be frightened.

CHILDREN

I won't.

PARENTS

Be sure of what you want.

CHILDREN

I promise.

PARENTS

Wait.

CHILDREN

Don't worry.

PARENTS

Think.

CHILDREN

I love you.

PARENTS

I love you.

Careful with what you say,
Children will listen.
Careful you do it, too.
Children will see.
And learn.

Guide them but step away,
And children will glisten.
Tamper with what is true,
And children will turn,
If just to be free.

The more you protect them,
The more they reject you.

CHILDREN

The more you reflect them,
The more they respect you.

PARENTS

Don't worry.

"Second Midnight" (Phoenix Theatre, London, 1990)

CHILDREN

I'm fine.

PARENTS

Be polite.

ALL

It will all be all right.

Into the Woods played its tryout for six weeks at the Old Globe Theatre in San Diego. James and I spent our time there not only cutting and rearranging songs and dialogue, as is the custom out of town, but—a far more difficult task—tightening the focus on what the show was about, something we had never felt the need to decide on. Under ordinary circumstances, articulating such a thing isn't necessary. You do have to know what it is that you're saying in order to keep the piece from flying off in all directions and becoming amorphous, but you don't have to spell it out. In fact, if you do, you run the risk of becoming preachy (a practice which didn't prevent Rodgers and Hammerstein from becoming the most successful writers in modern musical theater history). But folktales all have an axiom to grind, whether implicit or explicit, and in this case we decided to interrupt the narrative at each midnight with aphoristic fragments which gently satirize themselves. To avoid such pronouncements would have been easy but lazy: a folktale without a moral is merely a whimsy. And because the show dealt with a number of these tales, we felt an obligation to center the evening on one prevailing idea. Examining things as best we could in the balmy listlessness of California, we saw that our narrative primarily illustrated two: the relationships between parents and children, which pervade the stories we chose; and the notion of community responsibility, which dictates (or is dictated by) the plot. "Second Midnight" was the encapsulation of the first, but we decided to focus emotionally on the idea of community, which led me to write "No One Is Alone" for the climax of the piece. We didn't abandon

"Second Midnight" entirely, however; we kept some of the spoken fragments and retained the "Children Will Listen" motif, expanding it as a coda to the show so that it became a traditional moral, an add-on sung at the end of the evening by the Witch, the outsider who has observed the events.

As is my wont, I fretted less about the point of the show than I did about the word "wood." Up to this moment, two-thirds of the way through Act One, the setting had for the most part been known as "the woods." But "woods" is much more restrictive to rhyme than "wood." A lot of useful "ood" words like "stood" and "could" can't be pluralized except in special circumstances (see "Moments in the Woods," in Act Two) and when they can be, they have less flexibility. For example, "good" has a wide range: it can be used straightforwardly, ironically, as an expletive or anywhere in between—it can have many tones. "Goods" has one meaning and one tone only. What justification was there to use "wood" here (and in the "Finale") and "woods" everywhere else? I finally hit on an explanation: "wood" sounded statelier and therefore suited a lyric sung by someone outside the action. It takes almost as much imagination to justify what you write as it does to write it.

The Witch, having discovered that Rapunzel has been dallying with a Prince, drags her from the tower, brandishing a pair of scissors.

Stay with Me

WITCH

What did I clearly say?
Children must listen.

(Grabs Rapunzel's hair)

RAPUNZEL

No, no, please!

WITCH

What were you not to do?
Children must see—

RAPUNZEL

No!

WITCH

And learn.

(Rapunzel screams in protest)

Why could you not obey?
Children should listen.
What have I been to you?
What would you have me be,
Handsome like a prince?

Ah, but I am old.
I am ugly.
I embarrass you.
You are ashamed of me.

RAPUNZEL

No!

WITCH

You are ashamed.
You don't understand.

(Tender but intense)

Don't you know what's out there in
    the world?
Someone has to shield you from the
    world.
Stay with me.

Princes wait there in the world, it's
    true.
Princes, yes, but wolves and
    humans, too.
Stay at home.
I am home.

excused   misuse   use   C
fewer   news
compress   ooze   relax   Am, Coda
disturb   ones
whose   clues   ensues   views
                                        as   knows   dues   reviews
                                             cues   glues

1

replied
guide
divide
pride
provide
slide
stride
wide
defied
denied
out-died
implied
lied
pried
replied
satisfied
supplied
tried
untied

collide

Then from out of the blue   And you suddenly think
You decide what to do.   And then suddenly born.
And/Or you know what your   And yours made you ... in
When your first big decision is
Whether or not to decide
Just to give him a clue   Then from out of the blue
Meaning leave him a shoe   And suddenly he will do.
Then you suddenly think   Then it comes like a flash
It's your first big decision   And within ...
                                               Without now ... to guide

Which you take in your stride   Then it's suddenly clear

And you suddenly know
It's your first big decision

                                               Why should you have to choose
If he's really pursuing   And then if he pursues
You can give him a clue   You've got nothing to lose
say   You can leave him a shoe   You can always refuse

And you suddenly know/see   Why   Drop a couple of merely
You can face him & hide   You can leave him some clues,
But without any morning guide   Maybe one of your shoes
Without mother as guide
                                               And then, as he pursues,
Go if you need ...   You think
you don't have to collide
And the knot is untied   And you know what to do
2   With a feeling of pride   ... leave him a clue
And you take it in stride   You think, leave him a shoe
                                               If he wants to pursue
                                               You, he'll know what to do.
                                               And it's he & not you
                                               Who is stuck with a shoe
                                               In a stew in the zoo

Who out there could love you more
     than I?
What out there that I cannot
     supply?
Stay with me.

Stay with me,
The world is dark and wild.
Stay a child while you can be a child.

With me.

*Cinderella returns from her third night
at the ball, hobbling, wearing only one
shoe.*

On the Steps
of the Palace

CINDERELLA
He's a very smart prince.
He's a prince who prepares.
Knowing this time I'd run from him,
He spread pitch on the stairs.
I was caught unawares.
And I thought: Well, he cares—
This is more than just malice.
Better stop and take stock
While you're standing here stuck
On the steps of the palace.

You think, what do you want?
You think, make a decision.
Why not stay and be caught?
You think, well, it's a thought,
What would be his response?
But then what if he knew
Who you were when you know
That you're not what he thinks
That he wants?

And then what if you are
What a prince would envision?
Although how can you know
Who you are till you know
What you want, which you don't?
So then which do you pick:
Where you're safe, out of sight,
And yourself, but where everything's
     wrong?
Or where everything's right

And you know that you'll never
     belong?

And whichever you pick,
Do it quick,
'Cause you're starting to stick
To the steps of the palace.

It's your first big decision,
The choice isn't easy to make.
To arrive at a ball
Is exciting and all—
Once you're there, though, it's scary.

And it's fun to deceive
When you know you can leave,
But you have to be wary.

There's a lot that's at stake,
But you've stalled long enough,
'Cause you're still standing stuck
In the stuff on the steps . . .

Better run along home
And avoid the collision.
Even though they don't care,
You'll be better off there
Where there's nothing to choose,
So there's nothing to lose.
So you pry up your shoes.

Then from out of the blue,
And without any guide,
You know what your decision is,
Which is not to decide.
You'll just leave him a clue:
For example, a shoe.
And then see what he'll do.

Now it's he and not you
Who is stuck with a shoe,
In a stew,
In the goo,
And you've learned something, too,
Something you never knew,
On the steps of the palace!

The story of Cinderella has always
struck me as the most incomprehensible of all the moral fables known as
fairy tales. Here is a plain, depressed
slave of a girl, beaten and maltreated
by her family (her stepfamily,
actually—as is usual with these
matriarch-oriented narratives, the

father is absent), whose miserable life
consists of cleaning pots, waiting on
tables and sleeping on straw, who
suddenly finds herself magically
transformed into a radiant, opulently
dressed beauty, sought after by the
Prince of the Kingdom, and who three
times flees the palace where she is the
belle of the ball to return to the hole
in a corner of the house where she is a
virtual prisoner. And she can't decide
which place to choose? (In the anodyne Perrault version, she is forced to
be back by the stroke of midnight or
be exposed as the fraud she is, but in
the Grimm version it is her choice.) It
takes an accidental circumstance to
solve her problem: she loses a slipper,
leading the Prince to find her and take
matters into his own hands. But what
exactly *is* her problem? No one in five
hundred–plus years has given a plausible explanation of her indecisiveness
until Lapine came along with a startling solution: Cinderella doesn't lose
her slipper, she deliberately leaves it
behind. She knows she's an impostor
and doesn't want willingly to mislead
the Prince (and the world). She figures
that if the Prince really cares to see
her again, he'll follow the clue she has
left. She doesn't want an accident of
fate to fix her life, she wants to be
loved for herself. Viewed in this light,
the story makes sense; not only that, it
explains the universality of its appeal
and why, more than any other fable, it
exists in every culture. No one, as far
as I know, has ever made this observation, and if there were no other reason
to write this book, the opportunity for
me to point out James's insight would
be justification enough.

Misc.

Though it's dangerous, a palace can be fun
you might prefer a prince.

Do you wish in either one

What you really wish is both and neither one.

choice

                                              Let   be applied

wile
slide
ride   Neither   nor hide
provide
pride   If what
              since your wish can't be tried
                                                  the shoe   as a
decide   Let your wish be your guide
abide   By deciding you needn't decide
              You decide that you needn't decide
died
denied
tried   And. at last you decide   When the
implied   After one shoe is pried
hide   your decision
guide

pried   Leave And will   You've decided at last
tried   Let Fate to fit the foot   You deny your decision by proceed.
                  permit the foot to fit
applied
supplied   And Fate will find the foot that fits the shoe.
sighed Cried
satisfied

              You decide not to make up your mind.   A decision is tried
                                                    your The decision
              are   You decide your don't
              When you've pried up the   shoes
              You decide that you don't have to choose.

                    run a tried
              You decide on the spot   You decide no decision be made

Back to the Palace

CINDERELLA
When you're off in a palace
Where there's no one who
    knows you,
You're whoever you say.
You can leave, you can stay.
When you're far from the malice
And the envy of those you
See day after day,
Far, far away,

Where it's new and it's grand
And you're scared and excited,
And a prince takes your hand,
And he makes you feel as if you'd
    been invited,

And then just when it seems
Like your dreams,
You look up and he's there
And it's real,
And he's close
And it's like you're being swallowed.

So you run to the woods,
Where you'll never be followed,
You run to the dark
Till you're safe,
Till you're where you belong:
Home.

But is home what you wish?
Though it's dangerous, a palace can
    be fun.
Do you wish neither one?
You must return,
Just to learn
If Mother's right or wrong.

So it's back to the palace;
And although at the start you're
Not intending to leave,
Like the previous eve,
Since he may think you callous
For your hasty departure,
You may well not receive
A reprieve.

But a prince is a prince,
So he's even politer.

He gleams and he glints
And he draws you closer,
Holds you even tighter—
So you run once again,
Through the dark
Till you're where you belong:
Home.

Now you know what you wish.
What you wish is something
    somewhere in between.
You'll decide when you've seen
A little more
And explore.
Is Mother right or wrong?

So it's back to the palace
Which is getting familiar,
But it's once and for all.
Still, it's even more gala,
So it's no time until you're
Again in his thrall,
And you rush from the ball.

But he's played you a trick,
And your shoes seem to stick
To the ground.
You'll be found.
Have to pry them out quick
Or be caught.
And it's then while you're stuck
That you're struck
With a thought:

You decide on the spot.
Your decision is not
To decide.
Just leave something behind
He can find.
Leave a clue.
Let him choose what to do.
Leave fate to find the foot that fits
    the shoe.

As I look at it now, it seems senten-
tious, prosy and humorless, probably
because I was overly eager to echo the
adventures of Jack and Little Red Riding Hood, with the references to swallowing, feelings of being in between
and the like. Also, like the original
version of "Giants in the Sky," it relies
too much on the details of the adventure rather than the effect the adventure has on the character. It's one of

those songs that reads better than it
functions, and my decision to replace
it seems wise.

The Baker and his Wife locate the four objects and break the Witch's spell. The Witch regains her beauty but in return loses her magical powers. Jack comes back from another trip to the Giant's Kingdom and cuts down the Beanstalk, killing the Giant.

Ever After

NARRATOR
As for the Prince, he began his search for the foot to fit the golden slipper.

Cinderella's Prince and his Steward enter.

NARRATOR
When he came to Cinderella's house, Cinderella's Stepmother took the slipper into Florinda's room.

Florinda tries on the shoe; the Step-mother struggles to help her cram her toe into it.

FLORINDA
Careful, my toe—!

STEPMOTHER
Darling, I know—!

FLORINDA
What'll we do?

STEPMOTHER
It'll have to go.

(Florinda reacts)

But when you're his bride
You can sit or ride,
You'll never need to walk!

She looks at her encouragingly and cuts off her toe.
    The Prince puts the shoe on Flo-rinda's foot and lifts her onto the back of his horse. As they travel in the woods, they pass Cinderella's Mother's grave.

CINDERELLA'S MOTHER
Look at the blood within the shoe.
This one is not the bride that's true.
Search for the foot that fits.

*The Prince looks at Florinda's foot and
sees the blood trickling from the shoe.
They return to Cinderella's home.*
  *The Stepmother takes the shoe and
tries forcing it onto Lucinda's foot.*

LUCINDA
Why won't it fit?

STEPMOTHER
Darling, be still.
Cut off a bit
Of the heel and it will.
And when you're his wife
You'll have such a life,
You'll never need to walk!

*She looks at her encouragingly and
cuts off her heel. The Prince puts the
shoe on Lucinda's foot and lifts her onto
the back of his horse. As they travel in
the woods he notices the blood trickling
from the shoe.*
  *He removes the shoe from Lucinda's
foot and, ashen, returns Lucinda to the
Stepmother.*

CINDERELLA'S PRINCE
Have you no other daughters?

NARRATOR
To which the woman replied:

STEPMOTHER
No, only a little stunted kitchen
wench which his late wife left behind, but she is much too dirty; she
cannot present herself.

CINDERELLA'S PRINCE
I insist.

NARRATOR
And when Cinderella presented
herself and tried on the blood-
soaked slipper, it fit like a glove.

CINDERELLA'S PRINCE
This is the true bride!

NARRATOR
And much to the dismay of the
Stepmother and her daughters, he
took Cinderella on his horse and
rode off.

*Cinderella's Prince and Cinderella ride
by the grave.*

CINDERELLA'S MOTHER
No blood at all within the shoe.
This is the proper bride for you,
Fit to attend a prince.

*They ride off. Rapunzel joins her
prince, leaving the Witch alone.
Florinda and Lucinda, attending Cinderella's wedding, are blinded by birds
who peck out their eyes. The Wife enters, very pregnant, followed by the
Baker.*

CINDERELLA
I didn't think I'd wed a prince.

CINDERELLA'S PRINCE
I didn't think I'd ever find you.

**CINDERELLA, CINDERELLA'S
PRINCE, BAKER, WIFE**
I didn't think I could be so
  happy! . . .

The company comes onstage.

NARRATOR
And it came to pass, all that seemed
wrong was now right, the kingdom
was filled with joy, and those who
deserved to were certain to live a
long and happy life ever after . . .

ALL
Ever after!

NARRATOR
Journey over, all is mended,
And it's not just for today,
But tomorrow, and extended
Ever after!

ALL
Ever after!

NARRATOR
All the curses have been ended,
The reverses wiped away.
All is tenderness and laughter
For forever
After!

ALL
Happy now and happy hence
And happy ever after!

NARRATOR
There were dangers—

ALL
We were frightened—

NARRATOR
And confusions—

ALL
But we hid it—

NARRATOR
And the paths would often swerve.

ALL
We did not.

NARRATOR
There were constant—

ALL
It's amazing—

NARRATOR
Disillusions—

ALL
That we did it.

NARRATOR
But they never lost their nerve.

ALL
Not a lot.

NARRATOR, ALL
And they (we) reached the right
  conclusions,
And they (we) got what they (we)
  deserve!

ALL
Not a sigh and not a sorrow,
Tenderness and laughter.

Joy today and bliss tomorrow,
And forever after!

FLORINDA
I was greedy.

LUCINDA
I was vain.

FLORINDA
I was haughty.

LUCINDA
I was smug.

BOTH
We were happy.

LUCINDA
It was fun.

FLORINDA
But we were blind.

BOTH
Then we went into the woods
To get our wish
And now we're really blind.

WITCH
I was perfect.
I had everything but beauty.
I had power,
And a daughter like a flower,
In a tower.
Then I went into the woods
To get my wish
And now I'm ordinary.
Lost my power and my flower.

FLORINDA, LUCINDA
We're unworthy.

FLORINDA, LUCINDA,
WITCH
We're (I'm) unhappy now, unhappy
    hence,
As well as ever after.
Had we used our common sense,
Been worthy of our discontents—

ALL
To be happy, and forever,
You must see your wish come true.
Don't be careful, don't be clever.
When you see your wish, pursue.
It's a dangerous endeavor,

But the only thing to do—

(In groups, in canon)

Though it's fearful,
Though it's deep, though it's dark,
And though you may lose the path,
Though you may encounter wolves,
You mustn't stop,
You mustn't swerve,
You mustn't ponder,
You have to act!
When you know your wish,
If you want your wish,
You can have your wish,
But you can't just wish—
No, to get your wish

(In unison)

You go into the woods,
Where nothing's clear,
Where witches, ghosts
And wolves appear.
Into the woods
And through the fear,
You have to take the journey.

Into the woods
And down the dell,

"So Happy"

In vain perhaps,
But who can tell?
Into the woods to lift the spell.
Into the woods to lose the longing.
Into the woods to have the child,
To wed the Prince,
To get the money,
To save the house,
To kill the Wolf,
To find the father,
To conquer the Kingdom,
To have, to wed,

To get, to save,
To kill, to keep,
To go to the Festival!

Into the woods,
Into the woods,
Into the woods,
Then out of the woods—

A giant beanstalk emerges from the ground and stretches to the heavens; none of the characters see it.

NARRATOR
To be continued . . .

ALL
—And happy ever after!

CURTAIN

KAUFMAN'S QUEST

According to theatrical lore, back in the ancient days of the three-act play, George S. Kaufman, master of the genre, found himself one afternoon reluctantly accompanying his girlfriend, the languorous actress Leueen MacGrath, to Bloomingdale's department store, where she wanted to shop in the home furnishings section for sheets, towels and the like. Trailing around after her and trying to seem interested as she ordered things, he finally asked the salesgirl, "What do you have in the way of second-act curtains?"

Until the end of World War II, most plays on Broadway were in three acts and were built to hoary, and satisfying, structural specifications: Act One, Get the Hero Up a Tree; Act Two, Throw Stones at Him; Act Three, Get Him Down From the Tree. The climax of the play, whether comic or dramatic, came at the end of the second act. Surprise revelations, moments of decision, culminations of previous actions—the Act Two curtain was expected to be the high point of the evening. Kaufman's plays, no matter whom he collaborated with, were models of this blueprint, as were those of Lillian Hellman, Robert E. Sherwood, Maxwell Anderson and all the other distinguished, now dismissed and often forgotten playwrights of the period. It constituted the design of the "well-made" play, currently a term of disparagement. The sequence of events simplistically described above has always been the core

trajectory of theatrical storytelling, but it wasn't until the twentieth century that it got codified into a three-act form. Immediately after World War II, however, television intervened, shortening audiences' attention span, and before long it became apparent that to allow them two intermissions risked testing their impatience level twice. Playwrights quickly adjusted, compacting their plays into the comfortable two-act and one-act forms of today.* (With attention spans getting shorter by the year, it will be interesting to see how long even the two-act form will prevail.)

Musicals, however, had always been the exception. Even in the early twentieth century they were usually presented in a two-act form; only a few of the European operetta imports such as *The Merry Widow* clung to the convention of three. The principal reason is that most of them were concocted as a series of vaudeville turns, production numbers and comedy routines disguised as librettos, and as with an entire evening of vaudeville, there was a danger that tedium would set in very quickly.

With no story to involve the audience beyond farcical romantic

---

* Curiously enough, as plays became more compact, movies became longer and more bloated—also in an effort to compete with the new bite-sized medium of television.

complications, it seemed wise therefore not to release the crowd for more than one intermission—a different reason than the one which subsequently guided the postwar plays, but with the same result. The looseness and leisureliness of these shows, however, soon became a thing of the past, a victim of the Jazz Age, and when Rodgers and Hammerstein came along with their focus on story and character, no longer was it sufficient to end Act One with a breathlessly energetic full-cast showstopper that sent the audience out on a bright rhythmic cloud to smoke their cigarettes and drink their sodas. (Those were the days when cigarettes were the main reason for intermissions; theater liquor licenses were still a dream of the future.) There had to be a good reason for them to come back inside; the second-act curtain had become the first-act curtain.

The average running time of a musical's first act is between an hour and an hour and a half, the second act about an hour. This presents a tricky problem: if a significant climax is reached at the end of Act One, taking an hour to resolve it requires either a good deal of padding or some further plot complications. But if the first act has built convincingly to its cliff-hanging conclusion, further plot complications are likely to seem irrelevant or diversionary. Does anyone remember what happens in the second act of *My Fair Lady* after Higgins has successfully passed Eliza off at the ball? Even

West Side Story, as heavily plotted a musical as there ever was, which brings its first-act curtain down on two dead bodies, pads its second with a dream ballet and a comedy number, since the rest of the plot contains only a few brief incidents, dramatic though they may be. There are not many musicals which *demand* a two-act structure (one example would be, *Into the Woods*), and so arbitrary Act One curtains have to be considered or invented from the first day of conception.

One-act shows, in addition to holding audiences by maintaining atmosphere, pace and story, have the advantage of holding them in their seats as well. It is not easy to leave the theater when the curtain is up, the actors are acting, the singers are singing, and any disturbance in the house such as rising from a seat and trying stealthily to sneak up an aisle, is a noticeable distraction for everybody nearby; the playgoer is trapped for the duration by social responsibility.

The one-act form would seem to be ideal, then. The only problem is that of length; how long will the customers sit without the need to escape, to congregate and socialize and go to the bathroom? (I'm postulating a good show, not a bad one where escape *is* the distraction.) *Follies* was conceived as a two-act musical until James Goldman and I decided over a succession of rewrites to jettison the plot and make it a mood piece, which called for the one-act treatment. However, when it premiered in Boston, the mood went on for two hours and twenty minutes and the audience, even though they seemed to be having a good time, became restive around the hour-and-a-half mark: tushes were numbing and throats were thirsting. Therefore, when we began previewing in New York we experimented with a couple of arbitrary act breaks: one after "Who's That Woman?," which brought the curtain down on a breathlessly energetic full-cast showstopper, the other after "Too Many Mornings," which brought it down on the minimally dramatic note of Buddy seeing his wife sing a lush duet with her ex-lover. Neither worked because they didn't occur at a genuinely climactic moment—the only climax in *Follies* occurs just before the "Follies" sequence, which lasts less than half an hour and would result in a very short second act indeed.* Perforce, and thankfully, we wound up on opening night with our original one-act intention, trimmed to just over two hours.

Assassins and *Passion,* like *Follies,* were also conceived as one-acts: *Assassins* because it's a plotless revue, *Passion* because its intense concentration on just three characters makes it feel more like a short story than the novel from which it was adapted. With *Sunday in the Park with George,* of course, the structure was built in: the creation of the painting had to be one act, its consequences another. This simplicity was both the good news and the bad news. Some people who saw the show thought it should have been a one-act: the first. James and I never even considered such a possibility. The second act is the point of the show, whether we conveyed it or not. To confine the piece to the first act only would be little more than a stunt; in fact, our worry was not that people might think the second act unnecessary but that they would leave after the first simply because they felt satisfied.

That may seem like a complacent joke, but the actuality came to pass during the San Diego tryout of *Into the Woods.* A large group of seats had been sold to a women's theater club which attended local attractions a couple of times a month. On the matinee of their attendance, at the end of the first act when all the plot points but one have apparently been resolved, the assemblage applauded lustily and headed for their cars to beat the traffic, having failed to notice the giant beanstalk sprouting from the stage floor, accompanied by the Narrator saying, "To be continued." Luckily, they were spotted dashing to the parking lot and advised that there were more delights to come. Happily, they returned and enjoyed the second act even more.

It will probably not come as a surprise that theater owners abhor one-act shows. Without intermissions, what happens to the concession stands and bars, of which they have a significant percentage? Once the tickets are sold and the drinks consumed, they couldn't care less about Act Two, but if the first-act curtain doesn't entice the customers back to the diversionary world, said customers may leave for a better bar or a restaurant, and revenue will be lost.

Writers aren't the only ones with structural problems.

---

* Readers who have no idea what I'm talking about should read the *Follies* chapter in *Finishing the Hat.*

ACT TWO

Three structures: The palace, where Cinderella now sits on her throne; Jack's cottage, dramatically improved, Jack and his Mother inside, along with Milky-White and the golden harp he has stolen from the Giant; the cluttered home of the Baker and his Wife, replete with baking supplies and nursery items, the Wife holding their baby, who will not stop crying. The Narrator steps forward.

So Happy

NARRATOR
Once upon a time—later—

CINDERELLA
I wish . . .

NARRATOR
—in the same far-off kingdom—

CINDERELLA
More than anything . . .

NARRATOR
—lived a young princess—

CINDERELLA
More than life . . .

NARRATOR
—the lad Jack—

CINDERELLA
More than footmen . . .

JACK
I wish . . .

NARRATOR
—and the Baker with his family—

BABY
Waaah!

JACK
No, I miss . . .

CINDERELLA, BAKER
I wish . . .

BABY
Waaah!

JACK
More than anything . . .

CINDERELLA, BAKER, JACK
More than the moon . . .

WIFE
(To the baby)
There, there . . .

CINDERELLA
I wish to sponsor a Festival.

BABY
Waaah!

BAKER
More than life . . .

JACK
I miss . . .

CINDERELLA
The time has come for a Festival . . .

BABY
Waaah!

WIFE
Shh . . .

BAKER
More than riches . . .

CINDERELLA
And a ball . . .

JACK
I miss my kingdom up in the sky.

CINDERELLA, BAKER
More than anything . . .

WIFE
I wish we had more room . . .

JACK
Play, harp . . .

BAKER
Another room . . .

Interspersed throughout the first version of "So Happy" were echoes of the characters' Act One Prologue solos, reflecting the changes in their lives, such as:

CINDERELLA
Clean out the moat,
Hang out the flags,
Send for the steward,
We'll gild the stags!
I'm going to sponsor a Festival
And notify the Prince!

And:

JACK'S MOTHER
I wish the cow were in the yard . . .
I wish the hen would lay some
 eggs . . .
I wish he'd leave the harp alone,
I wish it knew another tune,
I wish a lot of things . . .

And:

CINDERELLA
Princesses are good,
Princesses are nice.
Princesses must pay a price,
So just smile, Cinderella.
Style, Cinderella!
Nice good good nice . . .

Don't forget your place,
Don't be thought a fool,
Learn benevolence and grace.
Calm and cool, Cinderella.
Rule, Cinderella.
Nice good smile
Rule good nice . . .

And:

JACK
Play, harp, play.
Do it all day.
You set my mind to dreaming
Of far away

Castle turrets gleaming
And giants to slay . . .

And I just can't sit here
Dreaming pretty dreams.

JACK'S MOTHER
Jack, Jack, Jack,
Head in a sack,
The money's getting lower.
This is not a time for dreaming.

Hen won't lay,
How shall we pay?
Your mother's getting slower.
And you can't just sit here,
Dreaming pretty dreams.

The time has come
For you to go.
But that would make me
Worry so.

Unfortunately, that old devil length led
to their excision. Meanwhile, back at
the number as eventually performed:

*Cinderella's Prince enters the castle,
followed by the blind Stepsisters and
Stepmother.*

CINDERELLA
I never thought I'd wed a prince . . .

CINDERELLA'S PRINCE
I never thought I'd find
    perfection . . .

BOTH
I never thought I could be so happy!

CINDERELLA
Not an unhappy moment since . . .

JACK, JACK'S MOTHER
I didn't think we'd be this rich . . .

CINDERELLA'S PRINCE
Not a conceivable objection . . .

BAKER, WIFE
I never thought we'd have a baby . . .

CINDERELLA, CINDERELLA'S
PRINCE, JACK,
JACK'S MOTHER
I never thought I could be so happy!

BAKER, WIFE
I'm so happy!

STEPMOTHER
Happy now,
Happy hence,
Happy ever after—

STEPMOTHER, FLORINDA,
LUCINDA
(To Cinderella)
We're so happy you're so happy!
Just as long as you stay happy,
We'll stay happy!

CINDERELLA, CINDERELLA'S
PRINCE
Not one row . . .

JACK'S MOTHER
Pots of pence . . .

JACK
With my cow . . .

BAKER, WIFE
Little gurgles . . .

CINDERELLA'S PRINCE
(To Cinderella)
Darling, I must go now . . .

(Exits)

JACK'S MOTHER
(To Jack)
We should really sell it.

BAKER
(To Wife)
Where's the cheesecloth?

ALL OTHERS
Wishes may bring problems,
Such that you regret them.

(The Baker joining in)

Better, that, though,
Than to never get them . . .

CINDERELLA
I'm going to be a perfect wife!

JACK
(Overlapping)
I'm going to be a perfect son!

WIFE, JACK'S MOTHER
(Overlapping)
I'm going to be a perfect mother!

BAKER
(Overlapping)
I'm going to be a perfect father!
I'm so happy!

CINDERELLA, JACK, JACK'S
MOTHER, WIFE
I'm going to see that he (she)
Is so happy!

ALL
I never thought I'd love my life!
I would have settled for another!

CINDERELLA
Then to become a wife . . .

JACK, JACK'S MOTHER
Then to be set for life . . .

BAKER, WIFE
Then to beget a child . . .

ALL
That fortune smiled . . .
I'm so happy.

BAKER, WIFE, JACK,
JACK'S MOTHER
We had to go through thick and
    thin.

STEPMOTHER, LUCINDA,
FLORINDA
We had to lose a lot to win.

CINDERELLA
I ventured out and saw within.

ALL
I never thought I'd be so much I
    hadn't been!
I'm so hap—

Suddenly, a loud rumbling noise followed by an enormous crash. All the structures are damaged. The Witch enters the Baker's house. She informs him that her house has been damaged, too, her garden flattened, a gigantic footprint left behind.

BAKER
Do you think it was a bear?

WITCH
A bear? Bears are sweet.
Besides, you ever see a bear with
    forty-foot feet?

WIFE
Dragon?

WITCH
(Shakes her head)
No scorch marks—
Usually they're linked.

BAKER
Manticore?

WITCH
Imaginary.

WIFE, BAKER
Griffin?

WITCH
Extinct.

BAKER
Giant?

WITCH
Possible.
Very, very possible . . .

It seems that the Giant's Wife has come down the second beanstalk and is laying waste to the Kingdom in her search for the boy who killed her husband. The Baker and his Wife decide to flee the neighborhood; Little Red Riding Hood wants to move in with her Grandmother; the Baker wants to accompany her and the Wife doesn't want to be left behind, so, with her baby, joins them. Cinderella, told by her birds that her mother's grave has been desecrated, determines to investigate;

Jack excitedly wants to search for the Giant's Wife and kill her. They all head for the woods, becoming increasingly unsettled.

Into the Woods (reprise)

BAKER
Into the woods,
It's always when
You think at last
You're through, and then
Into the woods you go again
To take another journey.

WIFE
Into the woods,
The weather's clear,
We've been before,
We've naught to fear . . .
Into the woods, away from here—

JACK
Into the woods, to find a giant!

LITTLE RED RIDING HOOD
Into the woods, to Grandmother's
    house . . .

BAKER
Into the woods,
The path is straight,
No reason then
To hesitate—

WIFE
Into the woods,
It's not so late,
It's just another journey . . .

CINDERELLA
Into the woods,
But not too long:
The skies are strange,
The winds are strong.
Into the woods to see what's
    wrong . . .

JACK
Into the woods,
To slay the Giant!

WIFE
Into the woods,
To shield the child . . .

LITTLE RED RIDING HOOD
To flee the winds . . .

BAKER
To find a future . . .

WIFE
To shield . . .

JACK
To slay . . .

LITTLE RED RIDING HOOD
To flee . . .

BAKER
To find . . .

CINDERELLA
To fix . . .

WIFE
To hide . . .

LITTLE RED RIDING HOOD
To move . . .

JACK
To battle . . .

CINDERELLA
To see what the trouble is . . .

JACK
I miss . . .

CINDERELLA
The time has come for a Festival . . .

In the woods, the trees have fallen, the birds no longer chirp, the natural order has been broken. The Princes enter; each is surprised to see the other. Cinderella's Prince claims that he is investigating news of a giant wandering about; Rapunzel's Prince claims that Rapunzel has run off and that he has been searching for her. Each asks the other why he is really in the woods.

Agony (reprise)

CINDERELLA'S PRINCE
High in a tower
Like yours was, but higher—
A beauty asleep.
All 'round the tower
A thicket of briar
A hundred feet deep.

Agony!
No frustration more keen,
When the one thing you want
Is a thing that you've not even seen.

RAPUNZEL'S PRINCE
I found a casket
Entirely of glass—
No, it's unbreakable.
Inside—don't ask it—
A maiden, alas,
Just as unwakeable.

BOTH
What unmistakable
Agony!
Is the way always barred?

RAPUNZEL'S PRINCE
She has skin white as snow—

CINDERELLA'S PRINCE
Did you learn her name?

RAPUNZEL'S PRINCE
No,
There's a dwarf standing guard.

BOTH
Agony
Such that princes must weep!
Always in thrall most
To anything almost,
Or something asleep.

CINDERELLA'S PRINCE
If it were not for the thicket—

RAPUNZEL'S PRINCE
A thicket's no trick.
Is it thick?

CINDERELLA'S PRINCE
It's the thickest.

RAPUNZEL'S PRINCE
The quickest
Is pick it
Apart with a stick—

CINDERELLA'S PRINCE
Yes, but even one prick—
It's my thing about blood.

RAPUNZEL'S PRINCE
Well, it's sick!

CINDERELLA'S PRINCE
It's no sicker
Than your thing with dwarves!

RAPUNZEL'S PRINCE
Dwarfs.

CINDERELLA'S PRINCE
Dwarfs . . .

RAPUNZEL'S PRINCE
Dwarfs are very upsetting.

BOTH
Not forgetting
The tasks unachievable,
Mountains unscalable—
If it's conceivable
But unavailable,
Ah-ah-ah-ah-ah-ah-ah—

Agony!

CINDERELLA'S PRINCE
Misery!

RAPUNZEL'S PRINCE
Woe!

BOTH
Not to know what you miss.

CINDERELLA'S PRINCE
While they lie there for years—

RAPUNZEL'S PRINCE
And you cry on their biers—

BOTH
What unbearable bliss!

Agony
That can cut like a knife!
Ah, well, back to my wife . . .

This reprise offers two nice examples of the difference between literary jokes and character jokes, between clever and funny. "Dwarves/Dwarfs" is clever. When I wrote it, I was concerned that the laugh it would get would cover the next line. I needn't have worried—at the most it got a chuckle. It was the next line ("Dwarfs are very upsetting") that got the laugh, and a large one, because it came from character. "Cry on their biers," like most puns (and it isn't even a very good one), evokes admiration at best, impatience at worst, but I needed a joke there because that phrase of music in the pattern of the song both here and in Act One featured a joke. Needless to say, it was greeted with silence. "Ah, well, back to my wife," on the other hand, got the kind of response the end of a comedy song is supposed to get: a big laugh and a large hand. The biggest laugh in the lyric, however, was "There's a dwarf standing guard." Not only is it evidence of the gap between the Prince's nobility and his cowardice, it also evokes the audience's collective memory of Disney fairy tales as they realize who the Prince is talking about. The line, like a number of my best jokes in all the shows, was filched from my collaborator's dialogue.

The Princes exit and the travelers reenter, meeting the Stepmother and Stepsisters, accompanied by the Steward, all of whom are fleeing the castle, which has been destroyed. The group is joined by the Witch, who warns them that the Giant's Wife is in the neighborhood. Indeed, the ground begins to shake and they are confronted by her. She demands that they give her the boy who killed her husband. When they protest that the boy is not there, she refuses to believe them and roars that she will not move until they deliver him to her. In an early draft of the script, they argued about what to do.

Have to Give Her Someone (cut)

WITCH
We'll have to give her someone.

LITTLE RED RIDING HOOD
Who?

WITCH
Well, maybe—
How about the baby?

BAKER
The baby?

WIFE
The baby!

WITCH
You can have another.

WIFE
I'm his mother!

BAKER
Never!

WITCH
All right, what do you suggest
   we do?

The earth rumbles menacingly.

GIANT
I'm waiting.

They look up, frozen with fear.

WITCH
(*Referring to Little Red Riding Hood*)
What about the brat here?

BAKER
The brat here—
The girl?

LITTLE RED RIDING HOOD
Me?

WIFE
She doesn't want the girl!

BAKER
No!

LITTLE RED RIDING HOOD
Do you mean me?

WITCH
Fine.

We'll stand around and chat here
And get stamped flat here—

LITTLE RED RIDING HOOD
Me!!??

WITCH
Just give her anyone—

LITTLE RED RIDING HOOD
We ought to give her you!

In order to keep up the swift pace of the storytelling, a particular necessity for fairy tales, this song became dialogue, as did the following commentary by the Narrator.

Interesting Questions (cut)

NARRATOR
A fundamental issue,
One of many that arise.
Does morality reflect what others
   wish you?
And is "moral" always wise?
In tales like these
One often sees
How crisis can be instructive,
Even perhaps a bit seductive,
Part of the process of becoming self-
   reliant.
But who do you feed to the Giant?

These are interesting questions,
Fundamental issues,
Archetypal figures.
You. Me.
Problematic choices.
Difficult decisions.
Life. Death.
Right. Wrong.
Fairy tales:

(*Rumble*)

What we feel,
Not what we do.
Fairy tales:
Not what's real,
Only what's true.

This song was intended to prepare us for what happens next. I wanted something properly pompous that would cause the characters one by one to get an idea, much the way in *Sweeney Todd* that Mrs. Lovett and then Sweeney got the idea of how to dispose of his victims. The idea: feed the Narrator to the Giant. Thus, the Narrator continues:

NARRATOR
These are universal struggles
Basic confrontations,
Natural transitions.
Guilt. Growth.
Patterns of behavior,
Mutual adjustments.
Hopes. Needs.
Fears. Dreams.
Fairy tales.
These are parables
Drawn from the myths of our—

And they push him into the path of the Giant.

James and I discovered soon enough that the vamp to the song alone, an ominous one, was all that was necessary—the characters could come up with the notion simultaneously. Which they did. And do.

The Giant picks up the Narrator, sees that it's not Jack and drops him, killing him. The Narrator having been disposed of, the characters' stories speed toward chaotic resolutions. First, Rapunzel runs in, distraught, followed by her Prince. She sees her mother, runs in the other direction and is squashed by the Giant, who is leaving, having been told she will find Jack hiding in a nearby bell tower. Everyone watches in shock as the Witch, standing alone, stares off in her daughter's direction.

Lament

This is the world I meant.
Couldn't you listen?
Couldn't you stay content,
Safe behind walls,
As I
Could not?

*Now you know what's out there in
   the world.
No one can prepare you for the
   world.
Even I.
How could I, who loved you as you
   were,
How could I have shielded you from
   her?
Or them!*

(Looking out front)

No matter what you say,
Children won't listen.
No matter what you know,
Children refuse
To learn.

Guide them along the way,
Still they won't listen.
Children can only grow
From something you love
To something you lose . . .

*The Baker and his Wife decide to search
for Jack separately, leaving the baby behind with Little Red Riding Hood. The
Wife encounters Cinderella's Prince,
who flirtatiously compliments her on
her courage under the circumstances.*

---

* The passages between asterisks were cut,
although they were recorded on the original
Broadway cast album.

Any Moment

CINDERELLA'S PRINCE
Anything can happen in the woods.
May I kiss you?

(As the Wife blinks)

Any moment we could be crushed.

WIFE
Uh—

CINDERELLA'S PRINCE
Don't feel rushed.

*He kisses her. She is taken aback, steps
away and turns to us.*

WIFE
This is ridiculous,
What am I doing here?
I'm in the wrong story.

CINDERELLA'S PRINCE
Foolishness can happen in the
   woods.
Once again, please—

(Kisses her)

Let your hesitations be hushed.

Any moment, big or small,
Is a moment, after all.
Seize the moment, skies may fall
Any moment.
*Days are made of moments,
All are worth exploring.
Many kinds of moments,
None are worth ignoring.
All we have are moments,
Memories for storing.
One would be so boring.*

(Kisses her again)

WIFE
But this is not right!

CINDERELLA'S PRINCE
Right and wrong don't matter in the
   woods,
Only feelings.
Let us meet the moment unblushed.

Life is often so unpleasant—
You must know that, as a peasant—
Best to take the moment present
As a present for the moment.

*The Prince picks her up and carries her
into a glade. Time passes. Later:*

CINDERELLA'S PRINCE
I must leave you.

WIFE
(Flustered)
Why?

CINDERELLA'S PRINCE
The Giant.

WIFE
The Giant. I had almost forgotten.
Will we find each other in the
woods again?

CINDERELLA'S PRINCE
This was just a moment in the
   woods,
Our moment,
Shimmering and lovely and sad.
Leave the moment, just be glad
For the moment that we had.
Every moment is of moment
When you're in the woods . . .

He exits. The wife sits, stunned.

Moments
in the Woods

WIFE
What was that?

Was that me?
Was that him?
Did a prince really kiss me?
And kiss me?
And kiss me?
And did I kiss him back?

Was it wrong?
Am I mad?
Is that all?

Does he miss me?
Was he suddenly
Getting bored with me?

(Stands)

Wake up! Stop dreaming.
Stop prancing about the woods.
It's not beseeming.
What is it about the woods?

(Firmly)

Back to life, back to sense,
Back to child, back to husband,
No one lives in the woods.
There are vows, there are ties,
There are needs, there are standards,
There are shouldn'ts and shoulds.

Why not both instead?
There's the answer, if you're clever:
Have a child for warmth
And a baker for bread,
And a prince for whatever—
Never!
It's these woods.

Face the facts, find the boy,
Join the group, stop the Giant,
Just get out of these woods.
Was that him? Yes, it was.
Was that me? No, it wasn't,
Just a trick of the woods.

Just a moment,
One peculiar passing moment . . .

Must it all be either less or more,
Either plain or grand?
Is it always "or"?
Is it never "and"?
That's what woods are for:
For those moments in the woods.

Oh, if life were made of moments,
Even now and then a bad one—!
But if life were only moments,
Then you'd never know you
    had one.

First a witch, then a child,
Then a prince, then a moment—
Who can live in the woods?
And to get what you wish,

Only just for a moment—
These are dangerous woods . . .

Let the moment go.
Don't forget it for a moment,
    though.
Just remembering you've had
    an "and"
When you're back to "or"
Makes the "or" mean more
Than it did before.
Now I understand—
And it's time to leave the woods!

One of the many reasons that I would make a bad director is that I have a limited tolerance for actors who can't resist suggesting changes in the script. It is problematic enough that some of them change lines and lyrics unintentionally, their ears for grammar and rhythm being defective, but their overview of the piece more often than not is bounded by the perspective of the characters they play—good for the characterization, bad for the small nuances and large shape. In musicals particularly, since numbers are seen as chances to shine (versus scenes, which so often depend on the circumstances of the situation and the presence of other actors), most of their suggestions are useless. The ones that are tolerable are the trivial ones: a change of word or phrase, which to them is important, since it means that they have contributed to the creative fabric—not a bad thing, since it heightens their performance. Only once in my experience has an actor said something that I immediately latched onto—not only a good notion for a lyric line, but also an insight into a character that hadn't occurred to me. It came from Joanna Gleason, who played the Baker's Wife and who, in a late-night conversation about the character, noted in passing that she felt like she was "in the wrong story."

With a jolt, I suddenly saw the Baker and his Wife in a way I hadn't seen them before, a way James and I had never discussed with this particularity: They were not only in the wrong story, they were in the wrong

play. They were a contemporary urban couple who had awakened one morning to find themselves in a medieval fantasia, surrounded not only by their own anxieties but by all the fairy-tale figures they had grown up with and probably loathed. The line in the song got a huge laugh, partly because it broke the fourth wall (it was the only time in the evening that a character, apart from the Narrator, delivered an aside directly to the audience) but, more trenchantly, encouraged them to identify with someone from their own era. In an instant, the Wife's problem became the contemporary soap-opera dilemma: adventure versus dependability, romance versus fidelity. It connected her with the traditional characters she found herself surrounded by: like Cinderella, Jack and Little Red Riding Hood, she was caught "in between." I wanted to use the words "excited" and "scared" as I had used them in the other soliloquies, but the song had to be about the present rather than the past—her decision of the *moment*. I took care of the past in the first twelve lines and then toyed with the dilemma, not merely with her conflicted emotions, but with the language she used: inadvertent puns and plays on words, semi-tongue twisters to mirror her confusion. Unlike the word-juggling in "Pretty Little Picture" (the song often cut from *A Funny Thing Happened on the Way to the Forum*), playfulness here serves a purpose. Puns are two-sided words—they are, in fact, verbal dilemmas.

The Wife wanders into the path of the Giant and is killed. Meanwhile, the Baker, accompanied by Cinderella, returns to his baby, whom he has left in Little Red Riding Hood's care. The Witch appears, dragging Jack along, eager to sacrifice him to the Giant. Jack has discovered the Wife's body and tells the Baker that she is dead. The Baker rounds on him with a fury, blaming him for planting the beanstalk, stealing the Giant's gold, then killing him, which brought the Giant's Wife down for revenge.

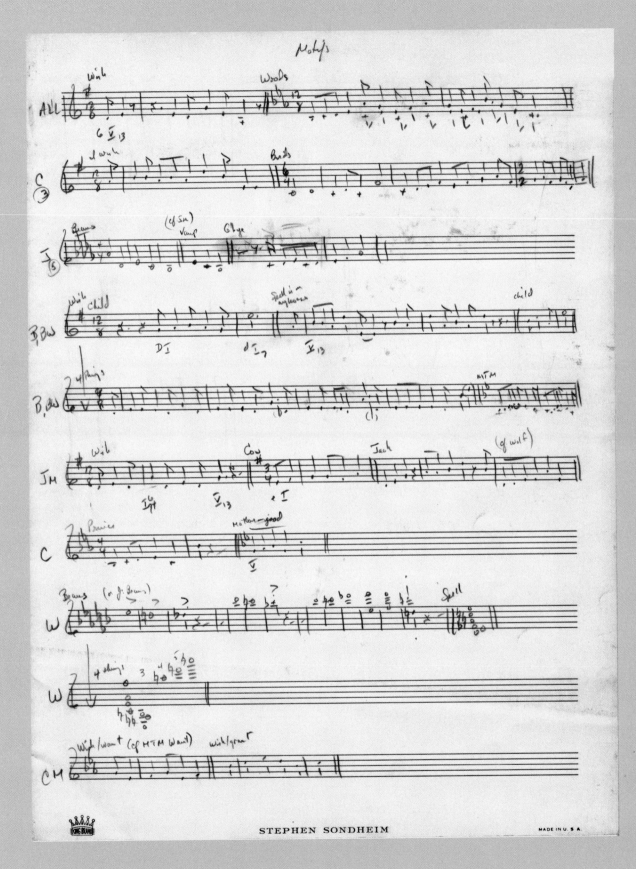

STEPHEN SONDHEIM

"The Dance at the Gym"

The set (Regent's Park, London, 2010)

"Any Moment" (Robert Westenberg as Cinderella's Prince, with Joanna Gleason)

Your Fault

JACK
But it isn't my fault,
I was given those beans!
You persuaded me to trade away
My cow for beans!
And without those beans
There'd have been no stalk
To get up to the Giants
In the first place!

BAKER
Wait a minute—
Magic beans
For a cow so old
That you had to tell
A lie to sell
It, which you told!
Were they worthless beans?
Were they oversold?
Oh, and tell us who
Persuaded you
To steal that gold!

LITTLE RED RIDING HOOD
(To Jack)
See, it's *your* fault.

JACK
No!

BAKER
So it's *your* fault.

JACK
No!

LITTLE RED RIDING HOOD
Yes, it is!

JACK
It's not!

BAKER
It's true.

JACK
Wait a minute, though—
I only stole the gold
To get my cow back
From you!

LITTLE RED RIDING HOOD
(To the Baker)
So it's *your* fault!

JACK
Yes!

BAKER
No, it isn't!
I'd have kept those beans,
But our house was cursed.

(Referring to the Witch)

She made us get a cow
To get the curse reversed!

WITCH
(Referring to the Baker)
It's his father's fault
That the curse got placed
And the place got cursed
In the first place!

LITTLE RED RIDING HOOD
Oh.
Then it's *his* fault!

WITCH
So . . .

CINDERELLA
It was *his* fault.

JACK
No.

BAKER
Yes, it is,
It's his.

CINDERELLA
I guess . . .

JACK
Wait a minute, though—

I chopped down the beanstalk,
Right? That's clear.
But without any beanstalk,
Then what's queer
Is how did the second Giant get
   down here
In the first place?

(Confused)

Second place . . .

CINDERELLA
Yes!

LITTLE RED RIDING HOOD
How?

BAKER
Hmm . . .

JACK
Well,
Who had the other bean?

BAKER
The other bean?

CINDERELLA
The other bean?

JACK
(To the Baker)
You pocketed the other bean.

BAKER
I didn't!
Yes, I did.

LITTLE RED RIDING HOOD
So it's *your*—!

BAKER
No, it isn't,
'Cause I gave it to my wife!

LITTLE RED RIDING HOOD
So it's *her*—!

BAKER
No, it isn't!

CINDERELLA
Then whose is it?

BAKER
Wait a minute!

(To Cinderella)

She exchanged that bean
To obtain your shoe,
So the one who knows what
    happened
To the bean is you!

CINDERELLA
You mean that old bean
That your wife—? Oh, dear—
But I never knew,
And so I threw—
Well, don't look here!

LITTLE RED RIDING HOOD
So it's *your* fault!

CINDERELLA
But—

JACK
See, it's *her* fault—!

CINDERELLA
But—

JACK
And it isn't mine at all!

BAKER
(To Cinderella)
But what?

CINDERELLA
(To Jack)
Well, if you hadn't gone
Back up again—

JACK
We were needy—

CINDERELLA
You were greedy!
Did you need that hen?

JACK
But I got it for my mother—!

LITTLE RED RIDING HOOD
So it's *her* fault then!

CINDERELLA
Yes? And what about the harp
In the third place?

BAKER
The harp—yes!

JACK
(Referring to Little Red Riding Hood)
She went and dared me to!

LITTLE RED RIDING HOOD
I dared you to?

JACK
You dared me to!

(To the others)

She said that I was scared—

LITTLE RED RIDING HOOD
Me?

JACK
—To.
She dared me!

LITTLE RED RIDING HOOD
No, I didn't!

BAKER, CINDERELLA, JACK
So it's *your* fault!

LITTLE RED RIDING HOOD
Wait a minute—!

CINDERELLA
If you hadn't dared him to—

BAKER
(To Jack)
And you had left the harp alone,
We wouldn't be in trouble
In the first place!

LITTLE RED RIDING HOOD
(To Cinderella, overlapping)
Well, if you hadn't thrown away the
    bean
In the first place—!
It was *your* fault!

CINDERELLA
(Referring to the Witch, overlapping)
Well, if she hadn't raised them in the
    first place—!

JACK
(To the Witch, overlapping)
Yes, if you hadn't raised them in the
    first place—!

LITTLE RED RIDING HOOD,
    BAKER
(To the Witch, overlapping)
Right! It's you who raised them in
    the first place—!

CINDERELLA
You raised the beans in the first
    place!

JACK
It's your fault!

CINDERELLA, JACK, LITTLE
    RED RIDING HOOD, BAKER
You're responsible!
You're the one to blame!
It's your fault!

WITCH
Shhhhhhhhhhh!

They stop in their tracks.

Last Midnight

WITCH

It's the last midnight.
It's the last wish.
It's the last midnight,
Soon it will be boom—

(Stamps her foot)

Squish!

(Grinds it into the ground)

Told a little lie,
Stole a little gold,
Broke a little vow,
Did you?

Had to get your prince,
Had to get your cow,
Have to get your wish,
Doesn't matter how—
Anyway, it doesn't matter now.

It's the last midnight,
It's the boom—
Splat!
Nothing but a vast midnight,
Everybody smashed flat!

Nothing we can do—
Not exactly true:
We can always give her the boy.

*They protect Jack as she reaches
for him.*

WITCH

No?
No, of course what really matters is
    the blame,
Somebody to blame.
Fine, if that's the thing you enjoy,
Placing the blame,
If that's the aim,
Give me the blame—
Just give me the boy.

LITTLE RED RIDING HOOD,
    CINDERELLA, BAKER
No!

WITCH

No . . .

(To them all)

You're so nice.
You're not good,
You're not bad,
You're just nice.
I'm not good,
I'm not nice,
I'm just right.
I'm the Witch.
You're the world.

I'm the hitch,
I'm what no one believes,
I'm the Witch.
You're all liars and thieves,
Like his father,
Like his son will be, too—
Oh, why bother?
You'll just do what you do.

It's the last midnight,
So goodbye, all.
Coming at you fast, midnight—
Soon you'll see the sky fall.

Here, you want a bean?

(Starts to scatter beans)

Have another bean.

*They scramble to collect the beans as
she scatters them.*

Beans were made for making you
    rich!
Plant them and they soar—
Here, you want some more?
Listen to the roar:
Giants by the score—!
Oh well, you can blame another
    witch.

It's the last midnight,
It's the last verse.
Now, before it's past midnight,
I'm leaving you my last curse:
I'm leaving you alone.
You can tend the garden, it's yours.
Separate and alone,
Everybody down on all fours.

(Looks up at the sky)

All right, Mother, when?
Lost the beans again!
Punish me the way you did then!
Give me claws and a hunch,
Just away from this bunch
And the gloom
And the doom
And the boom
Cruuunch!

She disappears.

The first version of this song, as presented in the San Diego tryout:

Boom Crunch! (cut)

WITCH
(To the Baker)

Told a little lie,
Did you?
Naughty naughty.
Now boom crunch!
Pretty clever, pretty sly,
Wasn't it?
Pretty soon boom crunch!

Just a tiny fib,
Really,
And you got your wish.
Nothing more than being glib,
Really—
Soon boom crunch
Squish!

Got your heart's desire.
Liar.

(To the others)

Liar! Liar! Liar!
Little lies from little liars—
What harm is that?
Fool a prince,
Break a vow,
Grab a bag of gold,
Get your cow,
Doesn't matter how!
Anyway, it doesn't matter now

'Cause any minute—
Boom splat!
Smashed flat.

(To Little Red Riding Hood)

Strayed a little from the path,
Did you?
Rumble rumble
Wham! Boom crunch!
Bringing down a little wrath
On yourself?

(Menacingly)

Here it comes—

(Smiles; quietly)

Just a cloud.

(To Cinderella)

Fooled them at the ball,
Did you?
And you got your prince.
Selfish little liars all,
All of you! Oh well, soon—

(Stamps her foot suddenly, grinds it
into the ground)

Mincemeat.

Just a small upheaval—

(Pointing to each of them)

Evil.
Evil! Evil! Evil!
Want to know what's evil?
Nice people's lies.

Well, goodbye.
You could use a good witch now,
But why?
You don't want me around?
I'm just crushed.
You're just crushed.
I'm just going.

No one likes a witch,
Which is why I don't have to lie.

I'm unpleasant.
No one likes a witch,

But we all need someone to curse.
Well, goodbye, get another witch
For whatever's left
Of the present
And keep getting better
At making things worse:

Letting lie
Lead to lie
Lead to cheat a little
Lead to steal a little
Lead to kill a little
Lead to—

(Cocking an ear, looking around)

Uh-oh.
Time to call a halt.
Too late.
Everybody's fault!
Boom . . .

(Getting louder)

Boom . . .
Boom . . .
Boom . . .

Can't believe your eyes,
Can you?
Couldn't happen.
Just bad luck.
Only harmless little lies,
And surprise!
Rumble boom crunch—

(She looks down at what she has
stepped on)

Yuck.

Here, you want my greens,
Do you?
Take the whole damn bunch!

(Flings them at the Baker)

And my money!

(Flings money at Jack)

Oh, and as for beans,
Here—you want some more?

She flings a handful of beans into
the air; everyone scrambles to pick
them up.

Get 'em by the score,
But get 'em quick before—!

(She begins growling a low growl at
first, then growing in intensity and
volume until she is screaming)

Boom.
Right—
Take boom everything you boom
    want,
Do boom anything you boom wish,
Tell bumbaboom each other all the
    lies you like,
But hurry up because
Rumble boom pound
Thump
Whoosh crackle roar
Slam bang
Cruuunch—!

She shrieks the last word and waves
her hand. A puff of smoke. When it
clears, all that remains is a black rab-
bit, which hops offstage.

On first reading, this lyric may not
seem significantly different from "Last
Midnight," but it sounded discursive
when performed, and on closer examination I realize the reason for it. It
spends too much time describing each
lie—information we already know—
and too little time on the central idea,
disposed of in a single line ("Want to
know what's evil? / Nice people's
lies"). It was an echo of the same mistake I had made with Cinderella's,
Jack's and Little Red's soliloquies:
concentrating on the event rather
than the notion. And instead of cli-
maxing the song with the menace of
the "Boom" passage (which I must
confess I rather miss), I brought it
back to the curse on the Witch herself
in order to personalize it. A lot of theater buffs and theater journalists gos-
siped that I had changed the song to
try to give Bernadette Peters, who
played the Witch, a showstopper. They
were wrong.

The Baker, disgusted with the group
and even more with himself, leaves

them. Deep within the woods, he comes across the Mysterious Man, who has been present throughout the show and who was revealed earlier as the Baker's long-lost father. He is a man who speaks in gnomic riddles and who now questions the Baker's decision to desert his friends and his baby.

No More

BAKER
No more questions.
Please.
No more tests.
Comes the day you say, "What for?"
Please—no more.

MYSTERIOUS MAN
They disappoint,
They disappear,
They die but they don't . . .

BAKER
What?

MYSTERIOUS MAN
They disappoint
In turn, I fear.
Forgive, though, they won't . . .

BAKER
No more riddles,
No more jests.
No more curses you can't undo
Left by fathers you never knew,
No more quests.
No more feelings.
Time to shut the door.
Just—no more.

MYSTERIOUS MAN
Running away—let's do it,
Free from the ties that bind.
No more despair
Or burdens to bear
Out there in the yonder.

Running away—go to it.
Where did you have in mind?

Have to take care:
Unless there's a "where,"
You'll only be wandering blind.
Just more questions,
Different kind.

Where are we to go?
Where are we ever to go?

Running away—we'll do it.
Why sit around, resigned?
Trouble is, son,
The farther you run,
The more you feel undefined
For what you have left undone
And, more, what you've left behind.

We disappoint,
We leave a mess,
We die but we don't . . .

BAKER
We disappoint
In turn, I guess.
Forget, though, we won't . . .

BOTH
Like father, like son.

The Mysterious Man disappears.

BAKER
No more giants
Waging war.
Can't we just pursue our lives
With our children and our wives?
Till that happier day arrives,
How do you ignore
All the witches,
All the curses,
All the wolves, all the lies,
The false hopes, the goodbyes,
The reverses,
All the wondering what even
    worse is
Still in store?

All the children . . .
All the giants . . .

(After a moment's thought)

No more.

He returns through the woods to the group. They hatch a plan to kill the Giant. Cinderella tells them the birds will help.

The Plan (cut)

CINDERELLA
They have it all planned.
They'll attack
Her when she's back
And peck her eyes out.

(Brief pause)

BAKER
And—?

(Another pause)

CINDERELLA
Then you take a stick
And you hit her quick,
Or whatever you do to kill a giant.

BAKER
Wait a minute!

Once she's blind,
She will either fall
Or go staggering about
Until she's crushed us all.
With a thing that tall,
You can only stall.

LITTLE RED RIDING HOOD
And you don't take the word
Of a bird
In the first place!

BAKER
It's hopeless.

CINDERELLA
No, it's not!

JACK
It's hopeless.

CINDERELLA
No!

LITTLE RED RIDING HOOD
So we might as well just run.

CINDERELLA
Wait a minute!
We can smear the ground—

BAKER
Smear the ground with pitch!

CINDERELLA
She'll get stuck
In the muck
And won't know what is which—!

LITTLE RED RIDING HOOD
And she'll squeal and squirm—!

JACK
And she'll twist and twitch—!

CINDERELLA
And you'll do what you do to kill a
giant!

LITTLE RED RIDING HOOD
This is fun!

JACK
And I'll climb the nearest tree
And wait till she
Gets near to me,
And then I'll strike her mightily!

BAKER
And I'll be there with you!

JACK
You will, too?

BAKER
It may well take more than
One of us to do.

LITTLE RED RIDING HOOD
I'm excited!
This is scary!

This was sung to the tune of "Your
Fault," indicating that what had been
contention had become, under the
pressure of impending group doom,
cooperation. As in so many other
shows in these pages, however, stop-
ping to sing a song, no matter how relevant, impeded the pace of the story.
The situation was better presented in
dialogue which was briefer and more
immediate. The song was cut.

*Jack and the Baker climb a tree and
wait for the Giant to appear. Cinderella*

*sits nearby, comforting Little Red Rid-
ing Hood, who is uncharacteristically
frightened and misses her mother.*

No One Is Alone

CINDERELLA
Mother cannot guide you.
Now you're on your own.
Only me beside you.
Still, you're not alone.
No one is alone, truly.
No one is alone.

Sometimes people leave you
Halfway through the wood.*
Others may deceive you.
You decide what's good.
You decide alone.
But no one is alone.

LITTLE RED RIDING HOOD
I wish . . .

CINDERELLA
I know . . .

*The Baker informs Jack that his
mother has been killed, not by the
Giant but by the Prince's Steward. Jack,
enraged, vows to kill the Steward. The
Baker tries to tell him that killing only
begets killing.*

CINDERELLA
(To Little Red Riding Hood)
Mother isn't here now.

BAKER
(To Jack)
Wrong things, right things . . .

CINDERELLA
Who knows what she'd say?

_____
*The "wood" vs. "woods" problem again.
This time I have no justification except that
I needed the rhyme.
_____

BAKER
Who can say what's true?

CINDERELLA
Nothing's quite so clear now.

BAKER
Do things, fight things . . .

CINDERELLA
Feel you've lost your way?

BAKER
You decide, but you are not alone.

CINDERELLA
You are not alone,
Believe me.
No one is alone.

BAKER
No one is alone,
Believe me.

CINDERELLA
Truly . . .

BAKER, CINDERELLA
You move just a finger,
Say the slightest word,
Something's bound to linger,
Be heard.

BAKER
No one acts alone.
Careful, no one is alone.

BAKER, CINDERELLA
People make mistakes.

BAKER
Fathers,

CINDERELLA
Mothers,

BAKER, CINDERELLA
People make mistakes,
Holding to their own,
Thinking they're alone.

CINDERELLA
Honor their mistakes.

BAKER
Fight for their mistakes—

CINDERELLA
Everybody makes—

BAKER, CINDERELLA
One another's
Terrible mistakes.

Witches can be right,
Giants can be good.
You decide what's right,
You decide what's good.

CINDERELLA
Just remember:

BAKER
Just remember:

BAKER, CINDERELLA
Someone is on your side.

JACK, LITTLE RED RIDING
HOOD
Our side.

BAKER, CINDERELLA
Our side.
Someone else is not.
While we're seeing our side—

JACK, LITTLE RED RIDING
HOOD
Our side—

BAKER, CINDERELLA
Our side—

ALL FOUR
Maybe we forgot:
They are not alone.
No one is alone.

CINDERELLA
Hard to see the light now.

BAKER
Just don't let it go.

BAKER, CINDERELLA
Things will come out right now.
We can make it so.
Someone is on your side—

We hear the Giant approaching in the distance.

Because fairy tales, folktales, fables, myths, whatever you want to call them, are considered parables, many people have asked what the Giant in *Into the Woods* "represents." To this day, I receive a couple of letters each year from theatergoers, directors, academics and even psychoanalysts, as well as others in the think business, inquiring, theorizing and analyzing what James and I "meant," especially since it's a lady giant. (We've been accused of misogyny many times, especially since it's the women who keep getting killed off.) The predominant assumption is that the Giant represents AIDS—after all, the show was written and produced in the 1980s, when AIDS was at its most prominent. Given a moment's thought, it becomes apparent that if the Giant represented anything, it wouldn't be AIDS. The Giant is not a natural phenomenon but a force roused to vengeance by greed, prevarication and irresponsibility. It could just as easily be the atomic bomb, global warming or the economic meltdown that is occurring as I write this. To James and me, it is a giant. Enough said.

The Giant is killed and the group— Cinderella, Jack, Little Red Riding Hood and the Baker and his baby— reunite. The Baker laments the loss of his wife while the baby continually cries.

Finale: Children Will Listen

BAKER
Maybe I just wasn't meant to have
children—

The spirit of his Wife appears behind him.

WIFE
Don't say that!
Of course you were meant to have
children . . .

BAKER
But how will I go about being a
father
With no one to mother my child?

(The baby cries)

WIFE
Just calm the child.

BAKER
Yes, calm the child.

WIFE
Look, tell him the story
Of how it all happened.
Be father and mother,
You'll know what to do.

BAKER
Alone . . .

WIFE
Sometimes people leave you
Halfway through the wood.
Do not let it grieve you,
No one leaves for good.
You are not alone.
No one is alone.

Hold him to the light now,
Let him see the glow.
Things will be all right now.
Tell him what you know . . .

The baby cries.

BAKER
(To the baby)
Shhh. Once upon a time . . . in a
far-off kingdom . . . there lived a
young maiden . . . a sad young
lad . . . and a childless baker . . .
with his wife . . .

The Witch enters.

WITCH
(To the audience)
Careful the things you say,
Children will listen.
Careful the things you do,
Children will see.
And learn.

Guide them along the way,
Children will glisten.

Children will look to you
For which way to turn,
To learn what to be.

Careful before you say,
"Listen to me."
Children will listen.

ALL

Careful the wish you make,
Wishes are children.
Careful the path they take—
Wishes come true,
Not free.

Careful the spell you cast,
Not just on children.
Sometimes the spell may last
Past what you can see
And turn against you . . .

WITCH

Careful the tale you tell.
That is the spell.
Children will listen . . .

ALL
(In groups)

Though it's fearful,
Though it's deep, though it's dark
And though you may lose the path,
Though you may encounter wolves,
You can't just act,
You have to listen.
You can't just act,
You have to think.

There are always wolves,
There are always spells,
There are always beans,
Or a giant dwells
There,
So:

Into the woods you go again,
You have to every now and then.
Into the woods, no telling when,
Be ready for the journey.

Into the woods, but not too fast,
Or what you wish you lose at last.
Into the woods, but mind the past.
Into the woods, but mind the future.
Into the woods, but not to stray
Or tempt the Wolf
Or steal from the Giant.

The way is dark,
The light is dim,
But now there's you,
Me, her and him.
The chances look small,
The choices look grim,
But everything you learn there
Will help when you return there.

Negotiating with the Giant

W/FCH: So To hungry   I-1 Finale - Woods   To C's house & 5th?
                                         III   Out of the woods

Into the woods   To get my wish

Bw   To fetch   My dearest wish

        To pray,   My heart's desire

Jm   To sell,

J   To buy, to make

SS, SM To dance

        To save   To lift, to fetch

        To fix   To ask, to sell

Bw   To lift, To fetch   To make, to dance

C   To ask, To go   To Grandmother's House

B   To mine, To fetch

cJ/Rd To Grandmother's House   ① To lift the spell

                                  B, Bw ② To fetch the thing

                                      To make the potion   To lift the spell

        also   To keep the child

To lift the spell

To keep the child   To sell the cow

To make the money   To ask the spirits   ③ To ask the spirits

To save the house   To help me go

To ask the spirits   (To dance before the)

                 (Prince at the Festival)

                 { To fetch,   ④ To sell the cow

                 To lift,   ⑤ To make the money

                 To sell   To save the house

                 To ask make

                 To make the money

                 To ask   To Grandmother's House

                 To see   before the Prince

                 To dance

                                    ⑥ To dance before the Prince

                    To C's house   At the Festival

BAKER, CINDERELLA, JACK,
LITTLE RED RIDING HOOD
(Softly)
The light is getting dimmer—

BAKER
I think I see a glimmer—

ALL
Into the woods—you have to grope,
But that's the way you learn to cope.
Into the woods to find there's hope
Of getting through the journey.

Into the woods, each time you go,
There's more to learn of what you
    know.
Into the woods, but not too slow—
Into the woods, it's nearing
    midnight—
Into the woods to mind the Wolf,
To heed the Witch,
To honor the Giant,
To mind,
To heed,
To find,
To think,
To teach,
To join,
To go to the Festival!

Into the woods,
Into the woods,
Into the woods,
Then out of the woods—
And happy ever after!

CINDERELLA
I wish . . .

**BLACKOUT
END OF PLAY**

In 1995 Columbia Pictures and Jim
Henson approached James and me
with a plan to make a movie of the
show, using Henson creatures as the
animals. A script was written by Low-
ell Ganz and Babaloo Mandel, and two
readings were held in Los Angeles, followed shortly by one of those periodic
studio shake-ups where a new platoon
of executives replaces the old one,
eager to throw out all projects begun
before their arrival in order to demonstrate the freshness of their rethinking. The readings, therefore,
were as far as the production went. I
wrote two songs for the project before
the axe descended, however. The
opening number would have been
this:

*The camera looks down onto a small,
charming storybook village from centuries ago. It swoops around and finally down behind the royal palace and
into the village streets.*

I Wish

NARRATOR (voice-over)
(Music underneath)
Once upon a time . . .
In the distant past . . .
In a far-off kingdom . . .
In a wide green valley . . .
Lay a little village
At the edge of the woods.

And everybody in it
Was busy
And cheerful
And thriving
And full of contentment
And yet—

*During the following, the camera glides
by various villagers going about
their everyday business. They sing their
thoughts, sometimes in voice-over.*

VILLAGER
I wish . . .

NARRATOR (v.o.)
—beset—

ANOTHER VILLAGER
I wish . . .

NARRATOR (v.o.)
—with unfulfilled longings—

ANOTHER VILLAGER
I wish . . .

MALE VILLAGER
I wish my house was made of
    gold . . .

NARRATOR (v.o.)
—or, as some would say, dreams.

MALE VILLAGER
I wish my well was filled with
    beer . . .

ANOTHER VILLAGER
I wish . . .

OLD VILLAGER
I wish my feet were not so cold . . .

BOY VILLAGER (JACK)
(Trying to milk his cow)
I wish my cow were not so old . . .

MIDDLE-AGED FEMALE
VILLAGER
I wish my son-in-law would
    disappear . . .

BALDING VILLAGER
I wish I had more hair . . .

ANOTHER VILLAGER
I wish . . .

ANOTHER VILLAGER
I wish . . .

SLOVENLY VILLAGER
I wish I'd something nice to wear . . .

ANOTHER VILLAGER
I wish . . .

JACK
I wish my cow could go with me to
    school . . .

JACK'S MOTHER
I wish my son was not a fool . . .

GIRL VILLAGER
(CINDERELLA)
(Hanging wash)
I wish I had a family—

ANOTHER VILLAGER
I wish . . .

GIRL VILLAGER
(CINDERELLA)
—that really liked me . . .

GROUP OF VILLAGERS
I wish . . .

The camera approaches a little house,
which serves as the village bakery.

NARRATOR (v.o.)
Now in this village at the edge of
the woods lived a baker—

BAKER
I wish . . .

NARRATOR (v.o.)
—and his wife . . .

WIFE
I wish . . .

NARRATOR (v.o.)
And what they wished for more
than anything—

BAKER, WIFE
I wish . . .

NARRATOR (v.o.)
—was—

BAKER
I wish we had a baby . . .

WIFE
I want to have a child . . .

BAKER
A pink and shiny baby—

WIFE
A tiny baby—

BAKER
A little whiny baby—

BOTH
The kind that lives
To drive its parents wild.

They go off on their rounds.

BOTH
I wish we had a baby—

BAKER
—who gurgled and who smiled.

WIFE
A pink and twinkly baby . . .

BAKER
A crinkly baby . . .

WIFE
A little wrinkly baby . . .

BOTH
All pink and white—

WIFE
—who cries all night—

BAKER
—whose eyes grow bright
The minute that they see me—

WIFE
A pink and creamy—

BAKER
Screamy—

BOTH
Dreamy baby.

They continue to make their deliveries,
passing various villagers as they do so.

VILLAGER
I wish my wife were not my wife . . .

HOMELY GIRL VILLAGER
(*Looking at a pretty girl*)
I wish I looked like her . . .

VILLAGER
I wish my life were not my life . . .

VILLAGER
I wish . . .

PRETTY GIRL VILLAGER
(*Looking at the homely girl*)
I wish I were as smart as her . . .

VILLAGER
I wish my shoes were not so
tight . . .

YOUNG VILLAGER
I wish my parents wouldn't fight . . .

OLD VILLAGER
I wish I were younger . . .

VILLAGER
I wish I had a dog . . .

BOY VILLAGER
(*Overlapping*)
I wish I were older . . .

BAKER, WIFE
(*Overlapping what follows*)
I wish we had a baby
That burbled and beguiled.
A pink and twinkly baby,
A crinkly baby,
A little wrinkly baby,
A soft and dribbly,
Bubbly, cuddly,
Giggly, teentsy-weentsy, bouncy,
Squishy little baby.
I want a child!

VILLAGERS
(*Variously, singly and in groups,*
overlapping the above)
I wish I had a friend . . .
I wish my husband had a job . . .
I wish I were thin . . .
I wish I could read . . .
I wish I were braver . . .
I wish my clothes were made of
silk . . .

JACK
I wish my cow would give us some
milk . . .

CINDERELLA
I wish I could go to the Festival . . .

VILLAGERS
I wish . . . I wish . . . I wish . . .
I wish I had . . .
I wish I could . . .
I wish I were a . . .
I wish I knew a . . .

I wish I'd find a . . .
I wish—! I wish—!
I wish—! I wish—!

ALL

I wish—!!!

The song ends climactically but like the wishes, unresolved.

The second song occurs a bit later, when the Baker is despairing about his inability to have children and the Wife is trying to conceal her impatience with his pessimism.

Rainbows

BAKER
(In rhythmic speech)
Maybe we just weren't
Meant to have children.

WIFE
Don't say that, of course we were
Meant to have children.
We mustn't give up hope.

BAKER
It's too painful to hope.
I'd rather stop hoping
Than be disappointed.

WIFE
And I'd rather be disappointed
Than give up hope.

BAKER
(Sings)
You're always expecting rainbows.

WIFE
You're always expecting rain.

BAKER
I used to expect a rainbow.
It's no longer worth the pain.
Can't sit around sighing for
The dreams that won't come true.
They're not worth the trying for—
A few less dreams will have to do.

Besides,
Who says that we need a rainbow?
We've lots to be glad about.
We're not guaranteed a rainbow—
Be grateful the sun is out.

As long as we have each other—
Wouldn't you agree?—
That's rainbow enough.
At least for me.

WIFE
(Rhythmic speech)
That's your idea of reality, isn't it?
Life is a mess,

The original Broadway cast

So settle for less.
Maybe you don't really
Want to have children.

BAKER
Don't say that, of course I do!
Yes, I want children!

WIFE
I don't think you want the
Responsibility.

BAKER
I do, I do. But—

WIFE
But—?

BAKER
Can't we just be happy the way
we are?

WIFE
Are we happy?

Stop taking away our rainbow,
Don't tell me it's all in vain.
Why would you expect a rainbow?
I think you enjoy the pain.

You chip away long enough
At every dream we've made,
Things soon will go wrong enough
That more than dreams are going to
        fade.

Don't say they just last a minute,
That rainbows are only air.
Don't tell me there's nothing in it—
We've got to have hopes to share.

The longer we love each other,
More and more it seems
Love isn't enough.
We need some dreams.

The first reading of the movie script
had, among others, Martin Short as
the Baker, Julia Louis-Dreyfus as the
Wife, Neil Patrick Harris as Jack, Mary
Steenburgen as his Mother, Kathy Na-
jimy as Florinda, Janeane Garofalo as
Lucinda, Cynthia Gibb as Cinderella,
Rob Lowe as her Prince, Christine
Lahti as the Witch, Daryl Hannah as
Rapunzel and Michael Jeter as the
Giant.

The second reading was even more
star-studded: Robin Williams (the
Baker), Goldie Hawn (the Wife), Cher
(the Witch), Carrie Fisher (Lucinda),
Bebe Neuwirth (Florinda), Moira Kelly
(Cinderella), Kyle MacLachlan (Cinderella's Prince), Brendan Fraser (Rapunzel's Prince), Elijah Wood (Jack),
Roseanne Barr (Jack's Mother), Danny
DeVito (the Giant) and Steve Martin
(the Wolf). All that and Jim Henson,
too.

I wish. . . .

Pamela Winslow as Rapunzel and Bernadette Peters as the Witch

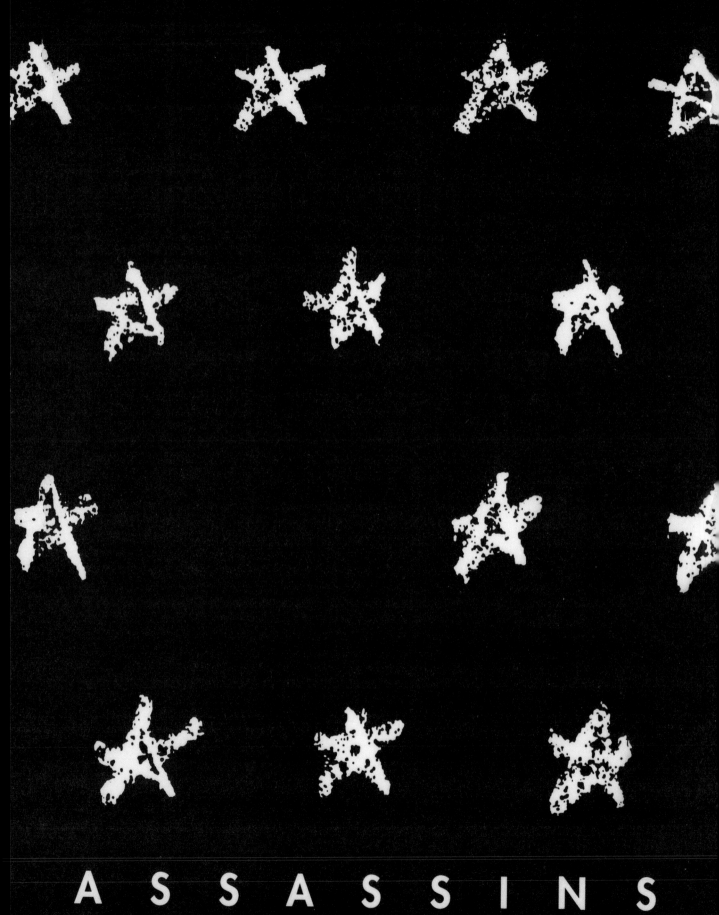

3. Assassins (1990)

Book by John Weidman

Based on an idea by Charles Gilbert, Jr.

The Notion

A book musical masquerading as a revue, featuring nine of the thirteen assassins who have attempted to kill the president of the United States.

General Comments

Writing lyrics is an exasperating job, but there are occasional moments which compensate, such as finding the right word that sits exactly on the right phrase of music or stumbling on the surprising but appropriate rhyme. It is those moments that propel you (me) to continue groping through the morass of banalities and not-quite-good-enough stabs at freshness and grace which constitute the bulk of the writing. And there is no moment more invigorating than reading the initial pages of your collaborator's work, especially if your collaborator is first class, the kind with whom I've been repeatedly blessed (not by chance, I can assure you—I've approached, and agreed to be approached by, only those whose work I like). Suddenly, what have been weeks of theoretical palaver, circling the subject, finding the spine and mapping the trajectory of the story, analyzing the characters, improvising scenes and songs, discussing style—suddenly, all that becomes crystallized in a page or two of dialogue which makes the idea into words, much in the way a first rehearsal makes the word become flesh. Because of the quality of my collaborators, I have experienced that moment often, but the most exhilarating of those

highs was the evening I read the first pages of John Weidman's script for *Assassins*.

We had been talking about the show for months. The idea had first arisen in 1979 when I was serving on the board of the Musical Theater Lab, an organization dedicated to finding and presenting new musicals by unknown writers. The venture lasted little more than a year and produced only one show, but among the projects which came to the table was a piece called *Assassins*, by a composer/lyricist named Charles Gilbert, Jr. The minute I saw the title I thought, "What a great idea for a musical," without having any idea of what I meant. The script turned out to be the story of a disillusioned Vietnam veteran who, urged on by a mysterious and symbolic figure called the Fat Man, becomes a presidential assassin. In between episodes in the protagonist's journey were quotations from some of the assassins who had targeted presidents throughout our history, and the opening scene took place in a shooting gallery over which a lighted sign announces SHOOT THE PREZ AND WIN A PRIZE. The script didn't excite the board members, including me, although I still found the title galvanizing, and there it lay for ten years until the advent of Weidman. John and I had been wanting to collaborate again ever since the good and proud time we'd had with *Pacific Overtures,* and when, in the middle of one of our idea-bouncing sessions about political subjects (John's favorite kind), I told him about *Assassins,* he had the same reaction I'd had ten years earlier: his eyes lit up like the shooting gallery sign. Unknowingly echoing me, he said that he had no idea what the show could be, only that it was a terrific notion. And so it turned out to be, I say without modesty or apology.

Fired with the arrogance of our enthusiasm, I searched out Charlie Gilbert and asked his permission to steal his idea. To John's and my delighted surprise,

The set (Studio 54 production, 2004)

he agreed, with the proviso that he would always be free to present his piece anywhere at any time. To his delighted surprise, we agreed, with the proviso that we would take nothing from his show except the title and the notion of the fairground shooting gallery. What John and I wanted to do had no relation to Charlie's concept other than the subject and the opening image. What we envisioned initially was a kaleidoscopic revue of assassins through the ages, from Brutus through Charlotte Corday via Gavrilo Princip to James Earl Ray. It wasn't long before we realized that we had bitten off more assassins than we could chew. The world's history is filled with them, every one a colorful, passionate story. (Assassins are perfect theatrical fodder: they come with built-in motivations and climactic actions.) We decided to narrow the field by restricting ourselves to American assassins; indeed, the first draft included a scene about Dan White, the man who killed Harvey Milk. But even that proved too broad a selection: Why include Dan White and not Sirhan Sirhan or Mark Chapman or Carl Weiss (the man who shot Huey Long)? It was all too arbitrary, so we narrowed the field further: we would deal only with the people who tried (in four cases successfully) to kill the president. Even that cast proved too populous, so we omitted Richard Lawrence, whose attack on Andrew Jackson was the very first attempt on a president's life, but whose delusional motivation was similar to Charles Guiteau's, the man who killed James Garfield. We also chose not to include Oscar Collazo and Griselio Torresola, the pair who tried to kill Harry Truman, because although like John Wilkes Booth their motives were political, they were less complex psychologically and therefore less interesting dramatically. We did include the character of John Schrank, one of the more bizarre of the lot, who tried to shoot Teddy Roosevelt. (He claimed later that he'd been ordered to do so in a dream by President William McKinley, whom Roosevelt had succeeded when McKinley was assassinated.) However, we dropped Schrank during rehearsals, despite a hilarious performance in the role by occasional actor and full-time playwright Christopher Durang, who, ironically and with self-destructive generosity, murmured to us that he feared the scene was too lightweight for the rest of the show and dangerously close to nothing more than a blackout sketch.

But back to that first draft. Ordinarily, I start reading the librettist's work after he has written one or two scenes—all I really need from him is the flavor of his writing so that I can start mimicking it in the lyrics and (yes) the music. Once I get going, completing the piece is then just a matter of getting in gait with him, filling in the gaps, always a few steps behind. When he is in the middle of Act Two, I'm usually halfway through Act One. In this way, we keep tabs on what each other is doing. With *Assassins*, for some reason that John and I recognized but still can't articulate, I never asked to see the scenes as he was writing and he never offered to show them to me. As I said, we had talked about the show for months; I knew the content of each scene, and we had deter-

mined what most of the songs would be about and where they would occur. The structure of the show was to be a dreamlike vaudeville, skipping backward and forward in time (a hundred years' worth), and would incorporate a number of different theatrical modes, from burlesque comedy to melodrama, with a few straightforward stops in between. I knew that the score would consist mostly of pastiches of different American musical styles and that "Hail to the Chief" would be a useful tune to start with. But apart from the opening, which would take place at the fairground shooting gallery and be almost all sung, I was in the dark.

Luckily, that number took me a long time to write and by the time I had finished it, John had a first draft of the whole script, which he dropped off one afternoon just before I was leaving the city for my house in Connecticut, a place good for concentration (countryside isolation) but bad for concentration (beautiful countryside isolation). Itchy with weeks of pent-up curiosity and anticipation, I started to read it that evening, thinking, "Don't expect too much. Allow for this being a first draft. We're trying something audacious here, and audacious is an inch away from smart-ass, as *Anyone Can Whistle* proved." I assumed that his previous reluctance to show me anything had come from an uncertainty about mixing the different styles of the scenes, orchestrating them and commingling them without their deteriorating into the kind of mishmash that happens when you throw dollops of paint into a bucket and hope that they'll blend. I should have known to expect better from the man who wrote *Pacific Overtures*, which is just such a controlled patchwork. But *Pacific Overtures* was a chronological revue; *Assassins* was something more complicated and dangerous—it was a collage. Within five minutes of reading, I knew the reason for John's hesitation in showing me what he was writing: far from uncertain, he had known exactly what he was doing, and he was on a white-hot roll. All the scenes were assured: where they were supposed to be funny, they were hilarious; where they were supposed to be surprising, they were jolting; where they were supposed to be straightforward, they were touching. And the scenes which combined the characters from different time periods and played them off against one another tied the piece together. All of this was topped off with a nonmusical scene which was a tour de force of rhetoric and political persuasion.

Later on, John told me that when he started writing the show, he quickly realized why he had been so immediately drawn to the material—that is to say, he realized what he was actually writing about. When John was seventeen, President Kennedy was assassinated; that death was his first real experience of loss, a loss he found devastating and bewildering. How could one inconsequential angry little man cause such universal grief and anguish? More important, *why* would he?

That's what *Assassins* is about.

Original cast

ACT ONE

A Shooting Gallery in a Fairground. "Hail to the Chief" plays on a calliope. A Proprietor stands behind the counter, idly picking his teeth. A slow, faintly sinister vamp begins, as a scruffy sullen laborer, Leon Czolgosz, shuffles on disconsolately.

Everybody's Got the Right

PROPRIETOR
(*To Czolgosz*)
*Hey, pal, feelin' blue?
Don't know what to do?
Hey, pal—

(*Czolgosz looks up*)

I mean you—yeah
C'mere and kill a President.

He reaches under the counter and pushes a button; a sign lights up: HIT THE "PREZ" AND WIN A PRIZE.

No job? Cupboard bare?
One room, no one there?
Hey, pal, don't despair—
You wanna shoot a President?

(*Puts a gun in Czolgosz's hand*)

C'mon and shoot a President . . .

Some guys
Think they can't be winners.

(*Smiles, shakes his head*)

First prize
Often goes to rank beginners.

Czolgosz buys the gun. John Hinckley, a soft, plump twenty-one-year-old, ambles aimlessly on.

PROPRIETOR
Hey, kid, failed your test?
Dream girl unimpressed?
Show her you're the best.

(*Proffering a more modern kind of gun*)

If you can shoot a President,
You can get the prize
With the big blue eyes . . .

(*Indicating a sexy doll on the shelf of prizes*)

Skinny little thighs
And those big blue eyes . . .

(*Pressing the gun into Hinckley's hand*)

Everybody's got the right
To be happy.
Don't stay mad,
Life's not as bad
As it seems.
If you keep your goal in sight,
You can climb to any height.
Everybody's got the right
To their dreams . . .

Charles Guiteau enters: quick, furtive, seedy but dapper.

PROPRIETOR
Hey, fella,
Feel like you're a failure?
Bailiff on your tail? Your
Wife run off for good?
Hey, fella,
Feel misunderstood?
C'mere and kill a President . . .

GUITEAU
Okay!

As Guiteau approaches the counter brightly, Giuseppe Zangara, a tiny, angry man, enters, groans and leans against the side of the counter, rubbing his stomach.

PROPRIETOR
(*In stage Italian*)
What's-a wrong, boy?
Boss-a treat you crummy?
Trouble with you tummy?
This-a bring you some relief.

(*Holding out a gun*)

Here, give some
Hail-a to da chief—

Zangara throws money onto the counter, grabs the gun and examines it furiously as the others look at him.

Everybody's got the right
To be different—

Samuel Byck, a fattish greasy man in a sweat-marked Santa Claus suit, enters and parades by, carrying a sign which reads: SANTA SAYS, ALL I WANT FOR CHRISTMAS IS MY CONSTITUTIONAL RIGHT [OVER].

PROPRIETOR
—Even though
At times they go
To extremes.
Aim for what you want a lot,
Everybody gets a shot.

Byck reverses direction, revealing the other side of his sign: TO PEACEABLY PETITION MY GOVERNMENT FOR THE REDRESS OF MY GRIEVANCES.

Everybody's got the right
To their dreams.

Lynette "Squeaky" Fromme, a small intense girl swathed in red religious robes, enters sullenly, eyeing the Shooting Gallery with interest. At the same time, Sara Jane Moore, a bright-eyed, heavy-set middle-aged woman, enters from the other side of the stage and moves toward the booth with cheery curiosity, fishing clumsily in her handbag for money.

PROPRIETOR
(*To Fromme, as she approaches*)
Yo, baby! Looking for a thrill?

(*Points off*)

The Ferris wheel is that way.

(Fromme, impassive, comes closer)

No, baby, this requires skill—

Fromme slams her money down; the Proprietor shrugs, gives her a gun.

Okay, you want to give it a try . . .

As Fromme plays with the gun, aiming it, feeling it, practicing to draw it from under her skirt, Moore is spilling keys, credit cards, lipstick, etc., all over the counter next to Czolgosz.

PROPRIETOR
Jeez, lady—!

(Indicates Czolgosz)

Give the guy some room!

(Points off)

The bumper cars are that way . . .

Moore finds her money and drops it in his hand; reluctantly, he gives her a .38, which she accidentally points at his stomach.

Please, lady—!

(Turning the barrel away)

Don't forget that guns can go
    boom . . .

The music reverts to the sinister vamp that we heard at the beginning. John Wilkes Booth enters, handsome and thoughtful, theatrically but elegantly dressed in black. He contemplates the scene. After a beat, the Proprietor and the Assassins slowly turn and look at him with a certain deference.

PROPRIETOR
Hey, gang,
Look who's here.
There's our
Pioneer.

(To Booth)

Hey, chief,

(Gesturing toward the Assassins)

Loud and clear:

BOOTH
(To the Assassins)
Everybody's got the right
To be happy.
Say, "Enough!"
It's not as tough
As it seems.
Don't be scared you won't prevail,
Everybody's free to fail,
No one can be put in jail
For his dreams.

Free country—!

PROPRIETOR
—Means your dreams can come
    true.

BOOTH
Be a scholar—

PROPRIETOR
Make a dollar—

BOOTH, PROPRIETOR
Free country—!

BOOTH
—Means they listen to you:

PROPRIETOR
Scream and holler—

BOOTH
Grab 'em by the collar!

BOOTH, PROPRIETOR
Free country—!

BOOTH
—Means you don't have to sit—

PROPRIETOR
That's it!

BOOTH
—And put up with the shit.

The Assassins turn front, guns at their sides.

ASSASSINS
Everybody's got the right
To some sunshine.

BOOTH
Everybody!

ASSASSINS
Not the sun,
But maybe one
Of its beams.

ALL
Rich man, poor man, black or white,
Pick your apple, take a bite.
Everybody just hold tight
To your dreams.

Everybody's got the right
To their dreams . . .

As they hold the note, they turn slowly upstage to face the targets, raising their guns. Just as they are about to aim and shoot, we hear "Hail to the Chief" played by a military band, then a voice on the P.A. system:

VOICE
Ladies and Gentlemen, the President of the United States, Abraham Lincoln!

Booth looks up at an imaginary theater box; the Assassins turn front and follow his gaze.

BOOTH
(To the Assassins)
Excuse me.

He exits. A gunshot offstage: BANG!

BOOTH'S VOICE
Sic Semper Tyrannis!

Originally we intended to set the opening scene in the Texas School Book Depository in Dallas. The notion was that Lee Harvey Oswald would arrive at work intending to kill himself, and that the assassins would materialize out of the contents of the room, the depository ironically containing history books giving accounts of the assassination attempts (inaccurate, as the

Assassination is okay if it's Hitler or Huey Long.

The Gun: Czolgosz: Who made this gun? A treatise on American capitalism from the downtrodden 30's Marxist POV. Connect with LHO? And Booth and Guiteau?
    What did they do before guns (Caesar, Marat, etc.)? Ours is a gun culture.

Duelling Diaries: D10/11.

Ballad of LHO: After LHO, Americans no longer need lead lives of quiet desperation (de Lillo).

Love Song: Czolgosz: Free Love (cf. Guiteau). I don't believe in marriage, I don't believe in Presidents.

Opening: Carnival Barker: Hit the Prez and Get a Prize.

You Do What You Can Do (when you're impotent, frustrated) or Why Can't I Do What I Want? All I want to do is shoot the President. (Fromme?)

Byck: Stalking is hard when you've got a suspicious-looking face. Why do they always spot me? (cf. Byck in Santa Claus suit, zoot suit, etc.)

Secret Service: "Security". Protection for (from?) the President.. Bush getting a burger at the airport, keeping everybody else waiting. D109 et seq. (a la Cora and her Boys?)

TR: cf. D144. Make a long speech and wear glasses.

Zangara: Stomach pains. Everyone's got a pain somewhere. Soothe it: kill a king. Long Time Stomach Hurt (Ache). D148/9. Memory of school (151). Everything makes stomach hurt (152/3), including girls. A grumble and a grumbler. Stomach rumble (a rumbler). Bumbler. "I belong to nothin'". A saga? (D155 et seq.)

Corbett: (D212 et seq.) The man who shot the man who shot Lincoln. The man who killed the man who killed the man who killed the country. "God Almighty directed me" (cf. other Assassins)

Sanity: D294/5. Sanity of A's vs. sanity of country. We're sane as long as we can talk about it, write this show, this very song.

Media: cf. TR (D298/9). Provocation.

assassins would indignantly point out). It was James Lapine who persuaded John and me not to begin the story there but to save Oswald and the depository for the show's climax, and not to see them until then. This was as valuable a piece of theatrical advice as I've ever had: when Oswald and the depository did finally appear over an hour later, the audience gasped. They had been so absorbed with the other eight assassins that they'd forgotten he even existed, and the immediacy of his presence in their own lifetime was stunning.

At one point, we toyed with the idea of premiering the show at the book depository itself, which is now a museum and has a large room with vitrines displaying the guns used in the various assassinations. We thought, why not set up some folding chairs, improvise a stage and open the piece there for a limited run, say a week? The show lends itself to minimal scenery, as numerous productions over the last twenty years have proved. Why not, indeed, but then again, apart from the publicity, why? After a little thought, we abandoned the idea not just because of the practical problems involved but because we didn't know what the effect of the show would be or, in fact, if it was any good. Now that it's proved its mettle, of course, I'd like to reconsider. Or maybe not.

In fact, the first production took place at Playwrights Horizons, where *Sunday in the Park with George* had been hatched. It was directed by Jerry Zaks, and during rehearsals he had an idea for a different opening image: an imaginary presidential parade with a crowd of bystanders watching, some of whom turn out to be assassins we get to know later. To accommodate the idea, I wrote the following song during rehearsals.

Flag Song (cut)

BYSTANDERS

You can gripe
All you like,
You can sneer,
"Where are the heroes?"
You can shout about
How everything's a lie.

Then that flag goes by . . .

You can snipe
At the greed,
At the need
To be a winner,
At the hype
You keep hearing
From on high,

And you think, "Why try?"
And you want to cry.
Then that flag goes by,
And you think, "*That's* why:
'Cause of that idea,
That incredible idea."

What you want to do is brag,
"I'm part of that.
Yeah, I know it's just a flag,
Okay, but still . . ."
For a minute you say, "Hey,
We could—we will
Fix everything tomorrow."

For a minute you're aware
Of feeling proud,
And then suddenly you're staring
At the crowd
And you're thinking,
"There's no link I can see,
They're as different from me
As they possibly could be—"

Then you see
The idea . . .

And you know
It's a dream,
And you know
It isn't perfect,
And at times
It may seem
To go awry.

Then that flag goes by,
And no matter how you sigh,
"It's the bright blue sky,
It's just Mom and apple pie,"
There's this thing you can't deny,
This idea:

That it's fixable tomorrow,
We've a chance,
There's a choice.
We can change ourselves tomorrow,
We're in charge,
We've a voice,
An idea about tomorrow
To remember
When the flag has gone by.

Most theater composers have a stock of what in show business parlance are called "trunk" tunes—tunes unused or cut from shows, lying around in desk drawers and file boxes—and they are often tempted to reuse them when the occasion arises. The lineage of such recyclers is wide and distinguished, from Richard Rodgers ("Blue Moon" was reused twice) to Cole Porter ("All of You") to Jule Styne ("Everything's Coming Up Roses," "You'll Never Get Away from Me") to Leonard Bernstein ("Gee, Officer Krupke!," "Somewhere," "America"), so it's an honorable tradition, but it has always struck my puritanical streak as cheating. The composers from the Golden Age were writing generic shows which had neither stylistic conceptions nor demands of character and could therefore accommodate any and every kind of song in the recesses of their trunks. I had relentlessly made it a point of pride not to recycle songs—not a difficult point to make, since each of the shows I'd written had such an individual style and milieu—but in the case of this song (and in only one other) I couldn't let the tune go. I used it again nine years later in *Wise Guys*, reincarnated as *Road Show*, for the song "It's in Your Hands Now." For the tune detectives in the audience who own the *Road Show* CD, I invite you to sing the above lyric to that melody (although, be warned, there are a few changes). My second lapse was also for *Wise Guys*, as you'll see.

reluctant   sulky   touchy
take umbrage   sullen
                        cranky   grumpy   Db
                        moody   grouchy   II
                                    sorehead $ A, B, C, D

violent   to make statements
foolish   outraged
crazy   separate   resentful
mad   choosy   bitter
angry   different   testy
                    feisty

potentate
peers & gowns   Look at all the
        thrones   All the doors are
streams   Nothing near but open doors   Everybody's got the right to be
reams   Spring sunshine   pissed
regions   Everything you want is yours   Day
                    Sometimes things are slow   Every day you've
                                                        Got a chance
                                                        Everyone's allowed
impractical   Be polite or   Everybody's free to make a request
unattainable
                    Raise your voice
                    Everybody's got the choice   a chance   He + she + we are free
                    Of their dreams   For their dream   You and me
                                                            All of us
                                                            Win or lose,

welcomed
accepted   Life is still
                    Everybody's got the right   In your hands control   No one has to be polite
simple modest   Just because you
humble   To say "Me."   Rich man, poor man,
unpretentious   Black or white
                        You just could
                    Everyone can be   you want to be   It don't mean
wielded   Whatever they'll be.   You can't satisfy   The higher
coupled   Yours   just   The higher
noticed   All of us, we're
married   Some have fun   If it's fun   All (Still) unlifted
chosen   By joining us   To be no one

detached   Everybody's got the right   Big, booming   No one has the go to jail
frail hair   To mean something   Unassuming   For his dreams
nail read pale   be someone
rail red scale   Somewhere   grooming   Rich with power
they'll sale   Up there where   Small + scare
                    The spotlight   gleams   In the middle
                    Constantly beams beams   Big or little   High + mighty
mighty   In the shadows   Good counseling
                                                        resurrecting
                    Cover the line   don't be polite   New directions
unassuming   Don't be polite, End a   Simple pleasures
                    Always keep the Quit your job Folks!
                    Goal in sight   And scheme Or
                                    Improbable schemes.   Influential
                                    Unfulfillable   Inconsequential
                                    Unachievable

As Booth's cry of "Sic Semper Tyrannis!" echoes and reverberates, a twentieth-century folk singer, the Balladeer, enters, carrying a guitar.

The Ballad of Booth

BALLADEER
Someone tell the story,
Someone sing the song.
Every now and then the country
Goes a little wrong.
Every now and then a madman's
Bound to come along.
Doesn't stop the story—
Story's pretty strong.
Doesn't change the song . . .

Lights come up on a tobacco barn in rural Virginia. It is the middle of the night. Booth sits huddled on the floor, wet and trembling, a shawl pulled around his shoulders. He is reading newspaper accounts of the assassination and writing his version furiously in a diary.

BALLADEER
Johnny Booth was a handsome devil,
Got up in his rings and fancy silks.
Had him a temper, but kept it level.
Everybody called him Wilkes.

Why did you do it, Johnny?
Nobody agrees.
You who had everything,
What made you bring
A nation to its knees?

Some say it was your voice had
     gone,
Some say it was booze.
They say you killed a country, John,
Because of bad reviews.

Johnny lived with a grace and glitter,
Kinda like the lives he lived onstage.
Died in a barn, in pain and bitter,
Twenty-seven years of age.

Why did you do it, Johnny,
Throw it all away?

Why did you do it, boy,
Not just destroy
The pride and joy
Of Illinois,
But all the U.S.A.?

Your brother made you jealous,
     John,
You couldn't fill his shoes.
Was that the reason, tell us, John—
Along with bad reviews?

Booth hurls one of the newspapers aside and starts dictating a manifesto condemning Lincoln to his assistant, David Herold.

They say your ship was sinkin',
     John . . .

Booth glances at the Balladeer briefly, then turns back to Herold.

You'd started missing cues . . .

Booth glances again, then continues dictating.

BALLADEER
They say it wasn't Lincoln, John.

BOOTH
   Shut up!

BALLADEER
You'd merely had
A slew of bad
Reviews—

BOOTH
   I said shut up!

Herold bolts from the barn, which is now surrounded by Union soldiers. Booth tosses the diary to the Balladeer, who glances at it without opening it, as if he knows the contents.

BALLADEER
   (Front)
He said,
"Damn you, Lincoln,
You had your way—

BOOTH
Tell them, boy!

BALLADEER
—With blood you drew
Out of blue and gray!"

BOOTH
Tell it all!
Tell them till they listen!

BALLADEER
He said,
"Damn you, Lincoln,
And damn the day

"How I Saved Roosevelt"

You threw the "U" out
Of U.S.A.!"
He said:

BOOTH
Hunt me down, smear my name,
Say I did it for the fame,
What I did was kill the man who
    killed my country.
Now the southland will mend.
Now this bloody war can end,
Because someone slew the tyrant,
Just as Brutus slew the tyrant—

BALLADEER
He said:

BALLADEER, BOOTH
Damn you, Lincoln,
You righteous whore!

BOOTH
(To the Balladeer)
Tell 'em!
Tell 'em what he did!

BALLADEER, BOOTH
(Front)
You turned your spite
Into civil war!

BOOTH
(To the Balladeer)
Tell 'em!
Tell 'em the truth!

BALLADEER
And more . . .

BOOTH
Tell 'em, boy!
Tell 'em how it happened,
How the end doesn't mean that it's
    over,
How surrender is not the end!
Tell them:

How the country is not what it was,
Where there's blood on the clover,
How the nation can never again
Be the hope that it was,
How the bruises may never be
    healed,
How the wounds are forever,
How we gave up the field
But we still wouldn't yield,

How the union can never recover
From that vulgar,
High and mighty
Nigger lover,
Never—!
Never. Never. Never.
No, the country is not what it
    was . . .

*The sound of crackling flames. Smoke
begins to seep under the walls of the
barn. Booth bows his head in prayer.*

BOOTH
Damn my soul if you must,
Let my body turn to dust,
Let it mingle with the ashes of the
    country.
Let them curse me to hell,
Leave it to history to tell:
What I did, I did well,
And I did it for my country.

Let them cry, "Dirty traitor!"
They will understand it later.
The country is not what it was . . .

*He draws his gun, puts it to his head.
Blackout. A gunshot—BANG! The
Balladeer strums his guitar.*

BALLADEER
Johnny Booth was a headstrong
    fellow,
Even he believed the things he said.
Some called him noble, some said
    yellow.
What he was was off his head.

How could you do it, Johnny,
Calling it a cause?
You left a legacy
Of butchery
And treason we
Took eagerly,
And thought you'd get applause.

But traitors just get jeers and boos,
Not visits to their graves,
While Lincoln, who got mixed
    reviews,
Because of you, John, now gets only
    raves.

Damn you, Johnny!
You paved the way

For other madmen
To make us pay.
Lots of madmen
Have had their say—
But only for a day.

Listen to the stories.
Hear it in the songs.
Angry men don't write the rules,
And guns don't right the wrongs.
Hurts a while, but soon the country's
Back where it belongs,
And that's the truth.

Still and all,
Damn you, Booth!

I had originally wanted to use gunshots as a rhythmic underpinning for
this song, but soon realized that it
would interfere a bit with Booth's
rhythm, as he'd be startled and duck-
ing, not the best posture for singing a
mellifluous heartfelt prayer. Unwilling
to let such an ostentatiously clever effect go, I tried to incorporate it into
virtually every other song in the show,
but as with a notion I'd had for *Sunday in the Park with George* of equat-
ing the twelve tones of the scale with
the twelve colors on Seurat's palette,
I finally realized what a restrictive
conceit it was. I'd still like to use it,
though, someday.

*Bayfront Park in Miami. 1932. President-
elect Franklin D. Roosevelt, standing
in an open car, has just finished addressing a large rally of supporters
when someone in the crowd shoots
at him but misses and instead kills
Anton Cermak, the mayor of Chicago.
The police have arrested Giuseppe
Zangara. A radio announcer, accompanied by a photographer, interviews a
group of bystanders who were close to
the assassin.*

How I Saved Roosevelt

BYSTANDER #1 (MAN)
(Seizing the microphone)
We're crowded up close,
And I see this guy,
He's squeezing by,
I catch his eye,
I say to him, "Where do you
Think you're trying to go, boy?
Whoa, boy!"
I say, "Listen, you runt,
You're not pulling that stunt—
No gentleman pushes their way to
    the front."
I say, "Move to the back!," which he
    does with a grunt—
Which is how I saved Roosevelt!

BYSTANDER #2 (MAN)
*(Pushing #1 away from the
    microphone)*
Then—!
Well, I'm in my seat,
I get up to clap,
I feel this tap.
I turn—this sap,
He says he can't see,
I say, "Find a lap
And go sit
On it!"
Which is how I saved—!

BYSTANDER #3 (WOMAN)
(Pushing #2 away hysterically)
Then—!
He started to swear
And he climbed on a chair,
He was aiming a gun—
I was standing right there—
So I pushed it as hard as I could in
    the air—!
Which is how I saved Roosevelt!

ALL THREE
Lucky I was there!

BYSTANDER #1
That's why he was standing back
    too far!

BYSTANDERS #2 AND #3
That's why when he aimed, he
    missed the car!

ALL THREE
Just lucky I was there!
Or we'd have been left
Bereft
Of FDR!

*A sudden light on Zangara, strapped
into the electric chair.*

ZANGARA
(Front)
You think that I scare?
No scare.
You think that I care?
No care.
I look at the world—
No good. No fair. Nowhere.

When I am a boy,
No school.
I work in a ditch.
No chance.
The smart and the rich
Ride by,
Don't give no glance.
Ever since then, because of them,
I have the sickness in the stomach,
Which is the way I make my idea
To go out and kill Roosevelt.

First I was figure I kill Hoover,
I get even for the stomach.
Only Hoover up in Washington,
Is winter time in Washington,
Too cold for the stomach in
    Washington—
I go down to Miami, kill Roosevelt.

No laugh!
No funny!
Men with the money,
They control everything.

Roosevelt, Hoover,
No make-a no difference.
You think I care who I kill?
I no care who I kill,
Long as it's king!

BYSTANDER #4 (MAN)
(Into the microphone)
The crowd's breaking up
When I hear these shots,
And I mean lots—

BYSTANDER #5 (HIS WIFE)
I thought I'd plotz!

MAN
I spotted him—

WIFE
(Overlapping)
My stomach was tied in knots!

MAN
So I barreled—

WIFE
Harold—!
No, what happened was this:
He was blowing a kiss—

MAN
She means Roosevelt.

WIFE
(Overlapping)
I was saying to Harold, "This
    weather is bliss!"

MAN
When you think that we might have
    missed
Seeing him miss—!

BOTH
Lucky we were there!

WIFE
It was a historical event—

MAN
—Worth every penny that we spent!

ALL FIVE BYSTANDERS
Just lucky we were there!

BYSTANDER #1
To think, if I'd let him get up
    closer—!

BYSTANDER #3
I saw right away he was insane—

(Dragging Bystander #2 forward)

Oh, this is my husband, we're from
    Maine.

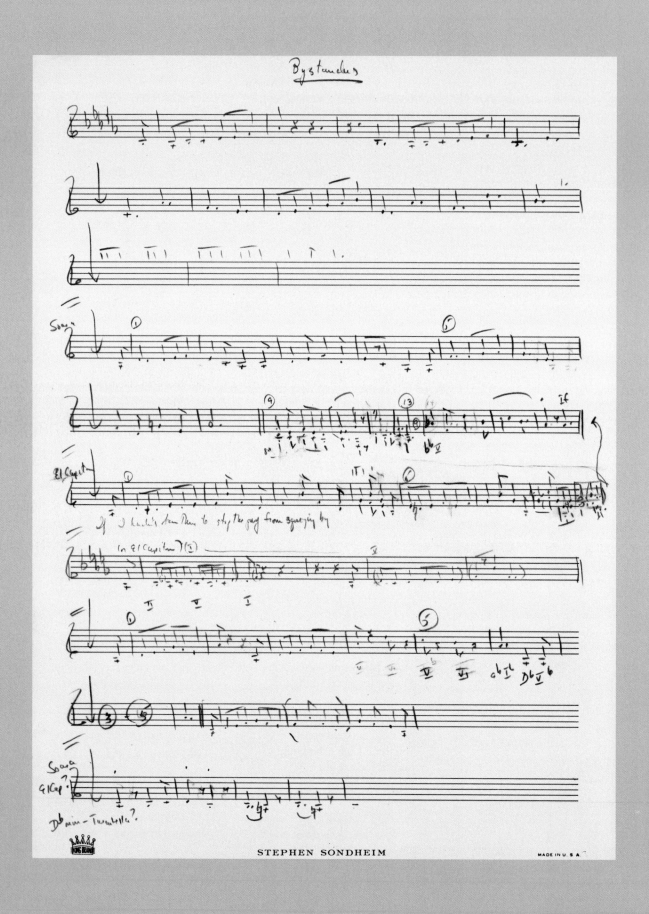

Bystanders

STEPHEN SONDHEIM

I WAS CLOSE TO THE FRONT
WHEN I TURNED TO SPY
THIS TINY GUY
WHO'S SQUEEZING BY

I WAS UP THERE IN FRONT
STANDING DOWN
WHEN I SAW THIS TI-
NY FELLOW TRY   7/14/89
TO SQUEEZE ON BY WHEN I TURN AND SPY

BYSTANDER #1

WE'RE CROWDED UP CLOSE,
WHEN I SEE THIS GUY
WHO'S SQUEEZING BY,
I CATCH HIS EYE,
I SAY TO HIM, "WHERE DO YOU
THINK YOU'RE TRYING TO GO, THERE?"
WHOA, THERE!"
I SAY, "LET ME BE BLUNT,"
I SAY, "BEAT IT, YOU RUNT,
I SAY, "GENTLEMEN DON'T PUSH THEIR WAY TO THE FRONT.
I SAY, "MOVE TO THE BACK!", WHICH HE DOES WITH A GRUNT --
WHICH IS HOW I SAVED ROOSEVELT.

BYSTANDER #2

WAIT, I'M IN MY SEAT,
I STAND UP TO CLAP,
I FEEL THIS TAP,
I TURN THIS SAP,
HE SAYS HE CAN'T SEE, I SAY, "CLIMB ON A LAP --
IT'S A RALLY,
PALLY!"

BYSTANDER #3 (WOMAN)

I WAS STANDING RIGHT THERE AS HE CLIMBED ON THE CHAIR,
IN HIS HAND I SAW SOMETHING REFLECTING THE GLARE,
SO I PUSHED IT AS HARD AS I COULD IN THE AIR
WHICH IS HOW I SAVED ROOSEVELT.

ALL THREE

LUCKY I WAS THERE --

BYSTANDER #1

THAT'S WHY HE WAS STANDING BACK TOO FAR --

BYSTANDERS #2 AND #3

THAT'S WHY WHEN HE AIMED HE MISSED THE CAR --

ALL THREE

JUST LUCKY I WAS THERE --
OR WE'D HAVE BEEN LEFT BEREFT OF FDR!

I SAY
(I SAID SIR I'LL BE BLUNT)
BE A LISTEN YOU RUNT
YOU'RE NOT PULLING THAT STUNT
DON'T PULL

I ASK HIM, JUST

SAID

SAP

SAT

WAIT, NO. WAIT THEN --

THEN

REAR DO

MIGHT
OR HE WOULD HAVE
KILLED

FIND A LAP
LOOK YOU SAP CHAP

(interrupting)

THEN --
#3 THAT'S WHER   (NEXT TO HIM)
HE (CLIMBED) ON (THE) CHAIR -- I WAS STANDING RIGHT THERE --
   GOT UP

Zangara NO
(in chair)

The Great American No to the Great American Yes.

No hit target. No tall enough. No luck. No food

No pool.

No picture? No photographer? (later) No photo! Lousy capitalist!

✓ No scared.

No God, no soul, no mercy, no minister -- only below. No church

✓ No money, no chance.

No cold -- need heat warm. No night air - No good for stomach gut.

✓ No school.

I belong to no thin'. Nowhere. Nobody make no
✓ No matter which is which. Hoover or FDR. No difference. Kill all kings, etc. till same.
(Ideal) No money so everybody is same like. nobody is different

No people, no girls. Just me. And the capitalists. No bother

No work, no luck, no cash. No food

No suffer (then), no trouble (then), no kill President. No hand. Simple No big deal.

No view, no height, no aim.

No repeat speech, no sit still,

No seat to stand on. Till -- no stay still.

(to Warden) No wait. No points. Push the button. No solution. answer

Bali: No one claimed the body.

No.   My stomach hurt long time.
That Roosevelt FDR ... That car ...   I am no one, need nothing. nobody
The speech wasn't long enough   No wait -- push the button

No time. 2nd night   No tall enough   M-
No fair. No care. Too painful. That's all.
(like my life) Too small, No tall enough. No tall. That's all.
It was the chair
I swear

BYSTANDER #2
He told me to sit, but I said, "No, sir!"

BYSTANDER #4
This made our vacation a real success!

BYSTANDER #5
(To the photographer)
Are you with the press?

PHOTOGRAPHER
Yes.

BYSTANDER #5
Oh God, I'm a mess!

BYSTANDER #1
Some left wing foreigner, that's my guess.

ZANGARA
No!

BYSTANDERS
And wasn't the band just fantastic?

ZANGARA
(Overlapping)
No left!
You think I am left?
No left, no right,
No anything!
Only American!

Zangara have nothing,
No luck, no girl,
Zangara no smart, no school,
But Zangara no foreign tool,
Zangara American!
American nothing!

(Furious)
And why there no photographers?
For Zangara no photographers!
Only capitalists get photographers!
No right!

BYSTANDERS
Lucky I was there!
I'm on the front page, is that bizarre?
And all of those pictures, like a star!
Just lucky I was there!
We might have been left bereft
    of F—

ZANGARA
(Simultaneously)
No fair
Nowhere!
So what?
No sorry!
And soon no Zangara!

Who care?
Pull switch!
No care
No more,
No—

A loud electrical hum; the lights dim briefly, then rise.

BYSTANDERS
—D—

Another hum; the lights dim briefly and rise again.

BYSTANDERS
R!

Another hum; the lights dim briefly and go out.

With "Please Hello" in *Pacific Overtures*, I took great care about the accuracy of the information being sung: the order of the countries sending envoys to Japan, the specific demands, the kinds of goods offered, all were historically correct. I can say with gratification that the song has been used in high school and college history classes as a relatively painless outline of the facts. So it is with "How I Saved Roosevelt." There were in fact five bystanders who claimed to take the actions described in the song, although no one deflected Zangara by pushing his arm in the air. He had the misfortune to be only five feet tall and had arrived too late at the arena to get a seat close to the front. Roosevelt's speech was unusually brief, and, as he started to sit down, Zangara was hastening to shoot when the entire audience rose to its feet in applause and blocked his view, forcing him to stand on his seat, which wobbled just enough to ruin his aim. Thus Roosevelt was indeed saved. (I should

add that "El Capitan," the Sousa march to which the Bystanders sing, was the tune playing when Roosevelt entered the park in his car.)

An extraordinary coincidence which we cut from the show concerned an attempt on the life of the other Roosevelt: Teddy. John Schrank fired a shot at him when he was campaigning (unsuccessfully) for re-election in Milwaukee. The bullet would have pierced Roosevelt's heart were it not for the steel eyeglass case and the fifty-page speech lodged in the breast pocket of his jacket. So one Roosevelt was saved by being long-winded and the other by being terse, a ripe opportunity for a song if I ever heard one.

Leon Czolgosz, a laborer who has been radicalized by the leftist politics of Emma Goldman, is alone onstage, examining a gun.

Gun Song

CZOLGOSZ
It takes a lot of men to make a gun,
Hundreds,
Many men to make a gun:

Men in the mines
To dig the iron,
Men in the mills
To forge the steel,
Men at machines
To turn the barrel,
Mold the trigger,
Shape the wheel—
It takes a lot of men to make
    a gun . . .
One gun . . .

Booth appears.

BOOTH
(Softly)
And all you have to do
Is move your little finger,
Move your little finger and—

(Czolgosz clicks the trigger)

GUN
GUITEAU
IA

People tend to pay
/Everybody pays
Attention to you
With a gun.

You can get so much accomplished
There is nothing like a gun

① What a wonder is a gun
② What a wonderful invention

One remarkable invention
Have you noticed with a gun
④ Everybody pays attention
Mostly, when you have a gun
First, for instance, with a gun
Watch how when you have a gun,
With the thunder of a gun (boom!)
Think of all that can be done.

Think of all that you can do
That's the way you get things done
Think of what can be undone

Once you know what it can do
All of that with only one —
Think what you could do with two:

(...Sell twice as many books) And (I'll sell / Twice as many books
And) this gun ...
/ Will make history

And this / gun ...
/ / In the name of the
Lord

Notice Also Note how
Smokers, when you have a gun,
Everybody pays attention

You can great deal accomplished
You get a lot done
With a gun

you stand talking
When your standing w/ a gun

When you want to get things done
When you want to get attention

With a gun you'll be remembered

(boom) Don't you love the way it looks
waves

It will a
Kill the despot
Save Party
Preserve the Union
Help selling
Promote the sales of my books
Be remembered, enter history
What's more inspires useful
more stirring as a gun
What is more an inspiration?
Even more than hearing him

With this old Gun you can
/ Get so much / done:
/ Kill the tyrant
/ Preserve the union

You can change the world.

Why should you be blue
When you've your little finger?
Prove how just a little finger
Can—

(Czolgosz clicks the trigger again)

Change the world.

CZOLGOSZ
I hate this gun.

Guiteau waltzes in cheerfully, holding a gun up admiringly.

GUITEAU
What a wonder is a gun!
What a versatile invention!
First of all, when you've a gun—

He points it out front, slowly panning over the audience, his smile setting grimly; music stops. A long pause.

GUITEAU
(Resuming cheerfully)
Everybody pays attention!
When you think what must be done,
Think of all that it can do:
Remove a scoundrel,
Unite a party,
Preserve the union,
Promote the sales of my book,
Insure my future,
My niche in history,
And then the world will see
That I am not a man to overlook!
Ha-ha!

GUITEAU, BOOTH, CZOLGOSZ
And all you have to do
Is squeeze your little finger.
Ease your little finger back—

(They click the triggers)

You can change the world.

Whatever else is true,
You trust your little finger.
Just a single little finger
Can—

(They click again)

Change the world.

Sara Jane Moore enters, fishing through her large purse.

MOORE
I got this really great gun—

(Fishing)

Shit, where is it?
No, it's really great—
Wait—!

(Pulls out a lipstick, drops it back)

Shit, where is it?
Anyway—

(Continuing to fish)

It's just a .38—

(Pulls out a large hairbrush)

But—

(Drops it back, keeps fishing)

It's a gun,
You can make a state—
Ment—

(Pulls out a shoe)

Wrong—!
With a gun.
Even if you fail.
It tells 'em who you are,
Where you stand.
This one was on sale.
It—
No, not the shoe—!
Well, actually the shoe was, too.

(Drops it back in, fishes around)

No, that's not it—
Shit, I had it here—
Got it!

(Pulls her gun out, waves it around)

Yeah! There it is!
And—

ALL FOUR
(Barbershop style)
All you have to do
Is crook your little finger,
Hook your little finger 'round—

They pull their triggers; the men's guns click; Moore's goes off—BLAM!

MOORE
Shit, I shot it . . .

OTHERS
—You can change the world.

QUARTET
Simply follow through,
And look, your little finger
Can slow them down
To a crawl,
Show them all,
Big and small,
It took a little finger
No time
To change the world.

They all exit, except Czolgosz, who continues to examine his gun.

CZOLGOSZ
A gun kills many men before it's
    done,
Hundreds,
Long before you shoot the gun:

Men in the mines
And in the steel mills,
Men at machines,
Who died for what?
Something to buy,
A watch, a shoe, a gun,
A "thing" to make the bosses richer,
But
A gun claims many men before it's
    done.

Just one . . .
More . . .

If I had to pick one moment among my many favorites in this show, it would be when Guiteau, suddenly and with great purpose points his gun at the audience. In every production I've seen, as his affability froze and he slowly panned over the crowd, not

STEPHEN SONDHEIM

missing a patron, there has been a hush more chilling than at any moment in *Sweeney Todd*. Facing the barrel of a gun, even when it's just in a musical, is the kind of shock that can exist only in live theater—a photograph is always a photograph, and movie shocks are an entirely different animal. The sound of audience relief when Jonathan resumed his cheeriness with a "Just kidding, folks" smile had a Pirandello-like magic: they were reassured then of the distinction between illusion and reality—it was just an actor in a funny costume with a prop—and they were on safe ground again. In a movie, you're always on safe ground.

Czolgosz puts the gun in his pocket as, behind him, lights come up on the Temple of Music pavilion at the Pan-American Exposition in Buffalo, New York. It is September 6, 1901. The Balladeer enters.

The Ballad of Czolgosz

BALLADEER
Czolgosz,
Working man,
Born in the middle of Michigan,
Woke with a thought and away
    he ran
To the Pan-American Exposition
In Buffalo,
In Buffalo.

Saw of a sudden how things
    were run,
Said, "Time's a-wasting, it's
    Nineteen-One.
Some men have everything and
    some have none,
So rise and shine.
In the U.S.A.
You can work your way
To the head of the line!"

Lights come up on half a dozen fairgoers, the epitome of bourgeois prosperity and complacency. They are standing in a line.

ATTENDANT
Single line, ladies and gentlemen. Line forms here to meet the President of the United States. Single line to shake hands with President William McKinley—

BALLADEER
Czolgosz,
Quiet man,
Worked out a quiet and simple plan,
Strolled of a morning, all spick and
    span,
To the Temple of Music
By the Tower of Light
At the Pan-American Exposition
In Buffalo,
In Buffalo.

Czolgosz joins the line.

BALLADEER
Saw Bill McKinley there in the sun.
Heard Bill McKinley say, "Folks,
    have fun!

"Gun Song"

Some men have everything and
    some have none,
But that's just fine:
In the U.S.A.
You can work your way
To the head of the line!"

FAIRGOERS
Big Bill—!

BALLADEER
—Gave 'em a thrill.

FAIRGOERS
Big Bill—!

BALLADEER
—Sold 'em a bill.

FAIRGOERS
Big Bill—!

BALLADEER
Who'd want to kill
A man of good will
Like—?

FAIRGOERS, BALLADEER
Big Bill!

*Czolgosz takes out his gun and wraps
it in a handkerchief.*

BALLADEER
Czolgosz,
Angry man,
Said, "I will do what a poor
    man can.
Yes, and there's nowhere more fitting
    than
In the Temple of Music
By the Tower of Light
Between the Fountain of Abundance
And the Court of Lilies
At the great Pan-American
    Exposition
In Buffalo,
In Buffalo."

Wrapped him a handkerchief 'round
    his gun,
Said, "Nothin' wrong about what I
    done.
Some men have everything and
    some have none—
That's by design.

The idea wasn't mine alone, but
    mine—*
And that's the sign:

In the U.S.A.
You can have your say,
You can set your goals
And seize the day,
You've been given the freedom
To work your way
To the head of the line—

*Czolgosz at last reaches McKinley and
shoots him—BANG!*

To the head of the line!"

*Lights come up on John Hinckley, sit-
ting on the couch in the basement rec
room of his parents' house, picking out
a song on his guitar, staring at a picture
of Jodie Foster.*

Unworthy
of Your Love

HINCKLEY
I am nothing,
You are wind and water and sky,
Jodie.
Tell me, Jodie, how I
Can earn your love.

I would swim oceans.
I would move mountains,
I would do anything for you.
What do you want me to do?

I am unworthy of your love,
Jodie, Jodie.
Let me prove worthy of your love.
Tell me how I can earn your love,
Set me free.
How can I turn your love
To me?

*As he continues strumming, lights
come up on Lynette "Squeaky" Fromme*

---

*This was something Emma Goldman had
said to him, speaking about the idea of civil
rights.

on the other side of the stage, in limbo,
staring at a newspaper clipping of
Charles Manson. She sings to Hinckley's accompaniment, but without ac-
knowledging him.*

FROMME
I am nothing,
You are wind and devil and god,
Charlie,
Take my blood and my body
For your love.

Let me feel fire,
Let me drink poison,
Tell me to tear my heart in two,
If that's what you want me to do.

I am unworthy of your love,
Charlie, darlin'.
I have done nothing for your love.
Let me be worthy of your love,
Set you free—

HINCKLEY
I would come take you from your
    life—

FROMME
I would come take you from your
    cell—

HINCKLEY
You would be queen to me, not
    wife—

FROMME
I would crawl belly-deep through
    hell—

HINCKLEY
Baby, I'd die for you—

FROMME
Baby, I'd die for you—

HINCKLEY
Even though—

FROMME
Even though—

BOTH
I will always know:

I am unworthy of your love,
Jodie (Charlie) darlin',

Let me prove worthy of your love.
I'll find a way to earn your love,
Wait and see.
Then you will turn your love
To me,
Your love to me . . .

*At which point Hinckley goes out and
shoots Ronald Reagan.*

*Guiteau, having assassinated Presi-
dent Garfield, is revealed at the foot of
the gallows, the Hangman waiting at
the top.*

The Ballad of Guiteau

"Unworthy of Your Love"

GUITEAU
(Unaccompanied)
I am going to the Lordy.
I am so glad.
I am going to the Lordy,
I am so glad.
I am going to the Lordy,
Glory hallelujah!
Glory hallelujah!
I am going to the Lordy . . .

*The Balladeer enters. He accompanies
himself on guitar.*

BALLADEER
Come all ye Christians,
And learn from a sinner:
Charlie Guiteau.
Bound and determined
He'd wind up a winner,
Charlie had dreams
That he wouldn't let go.
Said, "Nothing to it,
I want it, I'll do it,
I'm Charles J. Guiteau."

Charlie Guiteau
Never said "never"
Or heard the word "no."
Faced with disaster,
His heart would beat faster,
His smile would just grow,
And he'd say:

GUITEAU
*(Cakewalking cheerfully up and down
the gallows steps)*
Look on the bright side,
Look on the bright side,
Sit on the right side
Of the Lord!
This is the land of
Opportunity.
He is your lightning,
You His sword.

Wait till you see tomorrow,
Tomorrow you'll get your reward!
You can be sad
Or you can be President.
Look on the bright side . . .

*(Finishing a step or two higher than
before)*

I am going to the Lordy . . .

BALLADEER
Charlie Guiteau
Drew a crowd to his trial,
Led them in prayer,
Said, "I killed Garfield,
I'll make no denial.
I was just acting
For Someone up there.
The Lord's my employer,

And now He's my lawyer,
So do what you dare."

Charlie said, "Hell,
If I am guilty,
Then God is as well."
But God was acquitted
And Charlie committed
Until he should hang.
Still, he sang:

GUITEAU
(More shrilly, cakewalking faster)
Look on the bright side,
Not on the black side.
Get off your backside,
Shine those shoes!
This is your golden
Opportunity:
You are the lightning
And you're news!

Wait till you see tomorrow,
Tomorrow you won't be ignored!
You could be pardoned,
You could be President.
Look on the bright side . . .

(Finishing a step or two higher)

I am going to the Lordy . . .

Charlie Guiteau was a man with ambition(s) — Charlie! —
(had a lot / a lot of)

CG was   lad   CG was mad as a hatter
                        So was his mother for that matter

CG was   mad   And his... aunt.
CG was a man with a dream (the / smile) CG was a man who aspired
CG had a bundle of dreams   lived in hope / full of hopes
CG was a natural dreamer   CG wasn't frightened of dreams
CG was a man of good cheer
CG was a (little) bit off (the rails) (inside) CG was an impudent rascal
CG got his orders from God   CG was the dreamer of dreams
CG was a tiny bit odd (guy)

That's why he did what he did.   That's why he had to go "Bang!"
                       That's why he's going to hang

President Garfield went out with a bang.
CG wanted the whole shebang
CG is going to hang.   CG only lived for tomorrow
                     CG said, It's all getting better

CG said, "I am the lightning (& I am the sword)
I bring the message from the Lord."

C would wake up   CG shined his shoes when he...
And look up and say   CG shined his shoes...
And face every new day
                   CG was a man of ambition (with a vision / mission)
CG had a bundle of talents   CG had a parcel of dreams
" was a man out of balance
                   CG had a franchise from God

Who was the man ... with dreams & the greatest ambitions?
Charlie Guiteau. Guiteau, Guiteau. Madness is not what it seems
                   Charlie was crazy with dreams

No one had/was more dreams than CG (way / like)
Never knew a dreamer like CG

GUITEAU BALLAD

STEPHEN SONDHEIM

BALLADEER
Charlie Guiteau
Had a crowd at the scaffold—

GUITEAU
I am so glad . . .

BALLADEER
—Filled up the square,
So many people
That tickets were raffled.
Shine on his shoes,
Charlie mounted the stair,
Said, "Never sorrow,
Just wait till tomorrow,
Today isn't fair.
Don't despair . . ."

GUITEAU
(*Feverishly, cakewalking ever faster*)
Look on the bright side,
Look on the bright side,
Sit on the right side—

(*Reaching the Hangman, he hesitates*)

—Of the—

*He steps backward to the bottom,
hesitates again, then with resolution
cakewalks slowly back up, gathering
momentum.*

I am going to the Lordy,
I am so glad!
I am going to the Lordy,
I am so glad!
I have unified my party,
I have saved my country.
I shall be remembered!
I am going to the Lordy . . .

BALLADEER
(*As the Hangman adjusts the noose*)
Look on the bright side,
Not on the sad side,
Inside the bad side
Something's good!
This is your golden
Opportunity:
You've been a preacher—

GUITEAU
Yes, I have!

BALLADEER
You've been an author—

GUITEAU
Yes, I have!

BALLADEER
You've been a killer—

GUITEAU
Yes, I have!

BALLADEER
You could be an angel—

GUITEAU
Yes, I could!

BALLADEER
(*As the Hangman puts the hood over
Guiteau*)
Just wait until tomorrow,
Tomorrow they'll all climb aboard!
What if you never
Got to be President?
You'll be remembered—

(*Guiteau dances briefly*)

Look on the bright side—

(*Again*)

Trust in tomorrow—

(*Once more*)

GUITEAU, BALLADEER
And the Lord!

*The Hangman pulls the trapdoor lever.
Blackout.*

Only twice in my life have I set someone else's lyric to music. In each case
my collaborator was dead. The lucky
fellows were William Shakespeare
("Fear No More" from *Cymbeline*) and
Charles Guiteau (the opening section
of the song above). "I am going to the
Lordy" et seq. was written the morning of his execution; he recited it from
the scaffold. He had originally re-
quested an orchestra to play as he sang
his poem, but this request was denied.
His last words before the recitation
were:

I am now going to read some
verses which are intended to indicate my feelings at the moment of leaving this world. If set
to music they may be rendered
very effective. The idea is that
of a child babbling to his
mamma and his papa. I wrote it
this morning about ten o'clock.

The following song presages the
climax of the show and involves all
the assassins whom we've met, standing in individual spotlights. It is the
only song in the score which does not
use musical pastiche—not intention-
ally, anyway. It begins with a wordless
lamentation sung offstage. As it continues, the assassins speak in incantation;
then, led by Byck, their speech turns
into song.

Another National Anthem

CZOLGOSZ
I did it because it is wrong for one
man to have so much service when
other men have none . . .

BOOTH
I did it to bring down the government of Abraham Lincoln and to
avenge the ravaged South . . .

HINCKLEY
I did it to prove to her my everlast-
ing love . . .

FROMME
I did it to make them listen to
Charlie . . .

ZANGARA
I did it 'cause my belly was on
fire . . .

GUITEAU
I did it to preserve the Union and
promote the sale of my book . . .

MOORE
I did it so my friends would know
where I was coming from . . .

BYCK
(Sings, muttering)
Where's my prize? . . .

CZOLGOSZ
I did it because no one cared about the poor man's pain . . .

MOORE
I did it so *I'd* know where I was coming from . . .

BYCK
I want my prize . . .

ZANGARA
I did it 'cause the bosses made my belly burn . . .

HINCKLEY
I did it so she'd pay attention . . .

MOORE
So I'd have someplace to come from, and someplace to go . . .

BYCK
Don't I get a prize? . . .

GUITEAU
I did it because they said I'd be Ambassador to France . . .

BOOTH
I did it so they'd suffer in the North the way we'd suffered in the South . . .

BYCK
I deserve a fucking prize! . . .

FROMME
I did it so there'd be a trial, and Charlie would get to be a witness, and he'd be on TV, and he'd save the world! . . .

GUITEAU
Where's my prize? . . .

BYCK
I did it to make people listen.

CZOLGOSZ, FROMME
They promised me a prize . . .

HINCKLEY
Because she wouldn't take my phone calls . . .

ALL
(Except Zangara)
What about my prize? . . .

ZANGARA
Because nothing stopped the fire—!

ALL
(Except Byck)
I want my prize! . . .

BYCK
Nobody would listen!

The Balladeer enters with his guitar and sings to them, in wistful folk-style.

BALLADEER
And it didn't mean a nickel,
You just shed a little blood,
And a lot of people shed a lot of tears.
Yes, you made a little moment
And you stirred a little mud,
But it didn't fix the stomach
And you've drunk your final Bud,
And it didn't help the workers
And it didn't heal the country
And it didn't make them listen
And they never said, "We're sorry"—

BYCK
Yeah, it's never gonna happen,
Is it?
No, sir.

CZOLGOSZ
Never.

BYCK
No, we're never gonna get the prize—

FROMME
No one listens.

BYCK
—Are we?

ZANGARA
Never!

BYCK
No, it doesn't make a bit of difference,
Does it?

OTHERS
(Variously)
Didn't.
Ever.

BYCK
Fuck it!

OTHERS
Spread the word . . .

ALL
Where's my prize? . . .

BALLADEER
I just heard
On the news
Where the mailman won the lottery.
Goes to show:
When you lose,
What you do is try again.

You can be
What you choose,
From a mailman to a President.
There are prizes all around you,
If you're wise enough to see:
The delivery boy's on Wall Street,
And the usherette's a rock star—

BYCK
Right, it's never gonna happen, is it?
Is it?

HINCKLEY, FROMME
No, man!

BYCK, CZOLGOSZ
No, we'll never see the day arrive—

The Assassins divide into two singing groups.

GROUP I
Spread the word—

BYCK, CZOLGOSZ
—Will we?

GROUP II
No, sir!

ASSASSINS · 135

ALL

Never!

BYCK, CZOLGOSZ

No one's ever gonna even care if
   we're alive,
Are they?

GROUP I

Never.

GROUP II

Spread the word.

BYCK, CZOLGOSZ

We're alive.

GROUP I

Someone's gonna listen—!

ALL

Listen!

BYCK

(Quietly, front)

Listen . . .

There's another national anthem
   playing,
Not the one you cheer
At the ball park.

OTHERS

Where's my prize? . . .

BYCK

It's the other national anthem,
   saying,
If you want to hear—
It says, "Bullshit!"

CZOLGOSZ

It says, "Never!"

GUITEAU

It says, "Sorry!"

GROUP II

Loud and clear!

ASSASSINS

It says: Listen
To the tune that keeps sounding
In the distance, on the outside,
Coming through the ground,
To the hearts that go on pounding

To the sound
Getting louder every year . . .
Listen to the sound . . .
Take a look around . . .

We're the other national anthem,
   folks.
The ones that can't get in
To the ball park.
Spread the word . . .

There's another national anthem,
   folks,
For those who never win,
For the suckers, for the pikers,
For the ones who might have
   been . . .

BALLADEER

There are those who love regretting,
There are those who like extremes,
There are those who thrive on chaos
And despair.
There are those who keep forgetting
That the country's built on dreams—

ASSASSINS

People listen . . .

BALLADEER

And the mailman won the lottery—

ASSASSINS

They may not want to hear it,
But they listen,
Once they think it's gonna stop the
   game.

BALLADEER

And the usherette's a rock star—

ASSASSINS

No. They may not understand
All the words,
All the same
They hear the music . . .
They hear the screams . . .

BALLADEER

(To the Assassins)

I've got news—

ASSASSINS

They hear the sobs.
They hear the drums . . .

BALLADEER

You forgot about the country—

ASSASSINS

The muffled drums, the muffled
   dreams . . .

BALLADEER

So it's now forgotten you—

ASSASSINS

And they rise . . .

BYCK

You know why I did it? Because
   there isn't any Santa Claus!

ASSASSINS

Where's my prize?

BALLADEER

And you forgot—

ASSASSINS

What's my prize?

BALLADEER

How quick it heals—

ASSASSINS

Promises and lies . . .

BALLADEER

That it's a place
Where you can make the lies come
   true—

ASSASSINS

Spread the word . . .

BALLADEER

If you try—

ASSASSINS

Gotta spread the word . . .

BALLADEER

That's all you have to do—!

ASSASSINS

Right, all you have to do . . .

*They advance on the Balladeer, forcing
him off the stage, and turn front.*

ASSASSINS
Well, there's another national
  anthem,
And I think it just began
In the ball park.

Listen hard . . .

Like the other national anthem
Says to each and every fan:
If you can't do what you want to,
Then you do the things you can.
You've got to try again!

GROUP I
Like they say—

GROUP II
You've got to keep on trying . . .

GROUP I
Every day—

GROUP II
Until you get a prize . . .

ALL
Until you get a prize . . .

*One by one, they start to disappear into
the darkness.*

GROUP I
Until you're heard . . .

GROUP II
Mustn't get discouraged . . .

GROUP I
Spread the word . . .

GROUP II
Mustn't give up hope . . .

Their voices fade into the distance.

GROUP I
Up to you—

GROUP II
Don't say—

GROUP I
—What you choose . . .

GROUP II
—It's never gonna happen . . .

GROUP I
Spread the word . . .

ALL
You can always get a prize . . .
You can always get your dream . . .

BYCK
Sure, the mailman won the
  lottery . . .

The Texas Book Depository. Lee Harvey Oswald has come there to kill himself, but the assassins, led by Booth, urge him to turn his rifle on President Kennedy instead. They sense that they are about to succeed, and as he is on the brink of making his decision, their urgency grows.

"Another National Anthem"

Family

GUITEAU
I envy you . . .

MOORE
We're your family . . .

HINCKLEY
I admire you . . .

CZOLGOSZ
I respect you . . .

MOORE
Make us proud of you . . .

BOOTH
I envy you . . .

GUITEAU
We're your family . . .

Their voices repeat and overlap, mounting in intensity.

HINCKLEY
I admire you . . .

FROMME, MOORE
We're depending on you . . .

ZANGARA
You are the future . . .

GUITEAU, MOORE
We're your family . . .

CZOLGOSZ
We respect you . . .

BYCK, GUITEAU
Make them listen to us, we've been
    waiting for you . . .

BYCK, ZANGARA
Make them listen, boy . . .

During the above, Oswald has turned and crouched at the window overlooking Dealey Plaza.

ALL
(Variously)
We admire you . . .
We're your family . . .

You are the future . . .
We're depending on you . . .
Make us proud . . .
All you have to do is squeeze your
    little finger.
Squeeze your little finger . . .
You can change the wor—

Oswald fires. Blackout. Music stops for a moment, then resumes, loud and triumphant. A slide is projected, enormous, filling the stage: President Kennedy, slumped over in the backseat of the limousine as Jackie Kennedy scrambles desperately across the trunk. The slide fades and the music returns to the wordless choral lamentation which we heard earlier.

The five Bystanders enter, now dressed in nineteenth-century costumes. They are prototypical Americans: a housewife, an office clerk and a rich gentleman, to begin with. As the number progresses, they change character by simply turning around and adding or subtracting a piece of costume, or even just by characterization: the clerk becomes a factory hand, the gentleman becomes a farmer, etc. Only the housewife remains a housewife throughout.

Something Just Broke

HOUSEWIFE
I was out
In the yard,
Taking down the bed sheets,
When my neighbor yelled across:

VOICE
(An official announcement)
"The President's been shot."

HOUSEWIFE
I remember where I was,
Just exactly where I was,
In the yard out back—

VOICE
"The President's been shot."

OFFICE CLERK
(Gartered sleeves, etc.)
I was getting me a shoeshine—

HOUSEWIFE
—Folding sheets—

CLERK
—When I heard—

GENTLEMAN
We were waiting for a carriage—

CLERK
—Newsboys—

GENTLEMAN
Suddenly there's shouting in the
    street—

HOUSEWIFE
—Lizzie's sheet . . .

VOICE
"The President's been shot."

CLERK
I'll remember it forever—

HOUSEWIFE
And I thought:

CLERK
—Where I was, what I was doing—

HOUSEWIFE
Something just broke.

VOICE
"The President's been shot."

GENTLEMAN
My God—!

FARMER
I was up near the ridge,
Plowing—

FACTORY HAND
We were working at the plant.

SCHOOLTEACHER
I was halfway through
Correcting the exams—

FARMER
—When my wife—

I was plowing out in the field *north 40*
I was writing out tomorrow's lessons *correcting the quiz*
Correcting lessons

And my wife she comes a-running
'Cross the field
Like the devil's at her back *was holin her*
I remember it exactly
Where I /was
And I thought, "The
Country's gone to pieces."

And I thought, "I've
Got to get the/supper" *really*

I remember thinking,
"Something just broke."

I remember just exactly
Where I was
When I heard,
When And I thought

I'll remember *it a long as I live*
to my dying day

And I thought, "So what?
He's the kind that got shot
As a President, he didn't
Really mean an awful lot *matter 'amount to*
Not until he was got shot

no identity / (of a tree) a nonentity

windbag / common / ordinary / traitor / phony faker / muckraker fraud / liar / slippery swindler / vacillator snake / villain shark / saint pirate / mediocrity / apher / small beer / lightweight / climber / trickster / sharpie

When I opened up the paper
(When) Mr. Murphy called the
school to assembly
O was terrible. People sobbing

He was me.
He was us.
He's the idea
And that's all we've got.

Out in the yard,
Hanging the wash up
That's where I was *that*
When I heard
My neighbor yelling.
"The President's been shot."

Standing in the yard,
Taking down the wash

He was harmless
Party-hack.
Politician
Seemed a pleasant sort of fellow.

President who?
Who's President now?
One's no different from the another *the*
well He's a nice fat man

I   Housewife   C: 9:30 AM – neighbor
    Office worker McK: 4:00 PM – newsboy
    Rich lady   A.L: 8:30 PM – torches in the street
                        restaurant supper

#1 ① I was out
   ② In the yard
   ③ Taking down the [washing?] starting out [hanging out?]   Folding up the bedsheets
           across the street
      When I heard my neighbor yell,   ④ When my neighbor yelled across
   ⑤ "The President's been shot."

   ⑥ I remember where I (was) stood   I don't know how long I stood there
   ⑦ Just exactly where I was doing   I can tell you just exactly where I was
   ⑧ In the yard out back folding sheets in the yard   I was reaching up   When I heard my neighbor yelled
                                                           When I heard the news
      I was folding up a sheet holding the blanket   Henry's shirt

   ⑨ "The President's been shot.
  (#2 I was working near the office window)   For a shirt
           near the office
   # 2: I was coming from the office   just + upside   ① I was running in the trolley   getting me a shoeshine
          Henry's shirt (Folding sheets)   riding   going out to
         (And I thought)   sheets   We were coming home from supper
   ② #2   When I heard just + saw outside coming from .   ③ We had just begun our supper were beginning (dinner)
   #3   We were in tiny the restaurant   ④ We were waiting   too big for a carriage   in the trolley
   ③ #2 From Henry The (hawking)   Knots of people
         In the newsboy showing
   ④ #3 (When) we noticed P T.   at the supper from restaurant
   ⑦ (All the) people in the street Torches
   ⑧ #1 And I thought
         Did I really hear ···?

   ⑨ "The President's been shot."
   #1 Mr. Garfield   One was hipped
   #3 Mr./Lincoln   Knots of people.   No one talking
   #6 Bill McKinley   Barns head line   Such confusion a clamor Pandemonium All the tumult uproar
       "The/President been shot."   ⑤ #2 Quiet. Blue.
                                          ⑥ #3   I'll remember it forever.
  All: ① I'll remember it forever.   ⑦ #1 (Folding sheets) things/shirt
       ⑦ #2 Where I was, what I was doing,   ③ #2 Knots of people. in the corners
                                                 (It was raining)
       ⑧ All: When I heard.   ④ #3 Oh the shouting that screaming just that needless

FACTORY HAND
It was Mike—

FARMER
—She comes tearing 'cross the field.

FACTORY HAND
—Mike the foreman—

SCHOOLTEACHER
In runs Billy—

FACTORY HAND
I mean, he was crying—

SCHOOLTEACHER
(Overlapping)
He was crying—

FARMER
She was crying—

ALL THREE
I'll remember it forever . . .

HOUSEWIFE
And I thought:

VOICE
"The President's been shot."

HOUSEWIFE
You know what?
As a President, he isn't worth a lot.

OTHERS
I kept thinking:

HOUSEWIFE
He's the kind that gets elected, then
forgot.

FARMER
Mr. Garfield—

SCHOOLTEACHER
Mr. Lincoln—

FARMER
—He's a hack.

FACTORY HAND
Bill McKinley—

SCHOOLTEACHER
—He's a giant.

FACTORY HAND
—He's a joke.

HOUSEWIFE
Still, something just broke . . .

VOICE
"The President is rallying."
"The President is sinking."
"The President is dead."

HOUSEWIFE
Something just broke.

STOCKBROKER
I was down at the exchange . . .

HOUSEWIFE
Something just made a little dent.

LADY
I'd been shopping . . .

OLD MAN
I'd been sick . . .

HOUSEWIFE
Something just broke—

PAWNBROKER
All I know it was a Friday . . .

HOUSEWIFE
—Only for a moment.

OTHERS
I remember it exactly . . .

HOUSEWIFE
Something got bent.

WAITRESS
I'm taking the order—

HOUSEWIFE
Something just left a little mark.

SCHOOLBOY
I was getting dressed . . .

WAITRESS
—Two potato soups . . .

HOUSEWIFE
Something just went a little dark.

ALL
Ahhhhh . . .

HOUSEWIFE
Something just went.

OTHERS
And I wondered:
I was scared of
What would follow.

HOUSEWIFE
Something to be mended.

STOCKBROKER
Made me wonder who we are . . .

HOUSEWIFE
Something we'll have to weather—

LADY
It was seeing all those torches . . .

HOUSEWIFE
Bringing us all together—

POLICEMAN
He was me . . .

MINISTER
He was us . . .

HOUSEWIFE
—If only for a moment . . .

OTHERS
I'll remember it forever . . .

HOUSEWIFE
Nothing has really ended.

OTHERS
Where I was, what I was doing . . .

HOUSEWIFE
Only just been suspended.

OTHERS
Like a flash . . .

HOUSEWIFE
'Cause something just stirred.

OTHERS
(Variously)
And I thought—
And I thought to myself—

HOUSEWIFE
Something just woke.

OTHERS
And I thought—
I kept thinking:

ALL
Something just spoke,
Something I wish I hadn't heard.
Something bewildering occurred.
Fix it up fast,
Please—
Till it's just smoke,
Till it's only something just passed—

HOUSEWIFE
—Nothing that will last.

OTHERS
Where I was, what I was doing . . .

HOUSEWIFE
Nothing but the moment,
Just an awful moment . . .
But—
Something just—

She breaks down and exits with the others as the lights fade.

This sequence was first performed in the 1992 London production, two years after the musical's premiere run at Playwrights Horizons in New York. *Assassins* inaugurated the new regime at the Donmar Warehouse Theatre under the management of Sam Mendes and it was he who planted the seed. After reading the script prior to directing it, he felt that there was a song missing toward the end of the show, although he wasn't sure exactly what it should be. Around that time Weidman was revisiting the Texas Book Depository and sent me a video being sold there which focused on the reactions of people after Kennedy was shot. It became immediately clear that the missing song should deal with the nation's shock at each of the assassinations—not just the news itself but the way the news was spread, the chain of grief, especially in the days when communication throughout the country was slow and sporadic. The

show up to that point had been claustrophobic, and necessarily so: it took place in an enclosed world of angry and despairing people. What was missing was some musical expression of the outside reality, the emotional impact of these irrational (or rational but misguided) acts on all of us Bystanders.

When *Assassins* was revived (and brilliantly) by the Roundabout Theatre Company in 2004, the song was criticized as being an unnecessary afterthought, calculated to add "warmth" to the piece. I like to think that any additional song would have evoked this reaction, simply because the show was so tight and streamlined in the first place. But for us the song is not only necessary, it is essential.

As the Bystanders exit, one by one the Assassins reappear.

Everybody's Got the Right (reprise)

BOOTH
Everybody's got the right
To be happy.
Don't be mad,
Life's not as bad
As it seems.

CZOLGOSZ
If you keep your goal in sight,
You can climb to any height.

BOOTH, CZOLGOSZ
Everybody's got the right
To their dreams.

MOORE
Everybody's got the right
To be different—

BOOTH, CZOLGOSZ
If you want to be different . . .

GUITEAU
Even though
At times they go
To extremes . . .

BOOTH, CZOLGOSZ, MOORE
Go to extremes . . .

ZANGARA
Anybody can prevail.

BYCK
Everybody's free to fail.

ALL SIX
No one can be put in jail
For their dreams.

ALL
Free country—!

HINCKLEY
Means that you've got the choice:

GUITEAU
Be a scholar!

BYCK
Make a dollar!

ALL
Free country—!

CZOLGOSZ
Means that you get a voice.

ZANGARA
Scream and holler!

FROMME
Grab 'em by the collar!

ALL
Free country—!

OSWALD
Means you get to connect!

MOORE, FROMME
That's it!

ALL
Means the right to expect
That you'll have an effect,
That you're gonna connect.

(Advancing, guns at their sides)

Connect! Connect! Connect!

Everybody's got the right
To some sunshine.

Not the sun,
But maybe one
Of its beams . . .
One of its beams . . .

Rich man, poor man, black or white,
Everybody gets a bite,
Everybody just hold tight
To your dreams.
Everybody's got the right
To their dreams . . .

*They fire their guns into the air—
BLAM!*

I've often been asked to name my favorite show among the ones I've written music and lyrics for and, like most
authors, my reply has been the standard one: I have different favorites,
each for a different reason. But if I
were asked to name the show that
comes the closest to my expectations
for it, the answer would be *Assassins.*
Certainly, John's book does. As to my
own contribution, in every show I've
written there are things in the score I
wish I could have fixed at the time but
didn't know how to, or in hindsight

don't have the patience to return to.
Assassins has only one moment I'd
like to improve (the brief passage I
call "Family," which reeks of the
academic—that is, it resounds with the
voice of the songwriter rather than the
characters). Otherwise, as far as I'm
concerned, the show is perfect. Im-
modest that may sound, but I'm ready
to argue it with anybody.

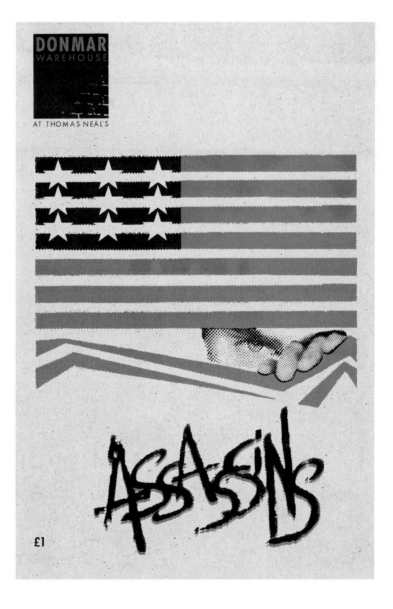

PASSION

A MUSICAL

Music & Lyrics
Stephen Sondheim

Book & Direction
James Lapine

4. Passion (1994)

Book by James Lapine

Based on the novel Fosca *by Iginio Ugo Tarchetti*

and the film Passione d'Amore

The Notion

1863. Milan. Giorgio, a handsome young captain in the Italian army, is having an affair with a beautiful married woman named Clara. He is unexpectedly sent to a remote military outpost, where the commanding officer's cousin Fosca, an unattractive and aggressive young woman given to fits of hysteria, falls in love with and relentlessly pursues him.

General Comments

Iginio Tarchetti, born in a small Italian town in 1839, was an experimental writer, a central figure in a movement of nonconformist artists known as the Scapigliatura, who were the equivalent of the French Bohemians of the time and, like Baudelaire and Rimbaud, among others, were rebellious Romantics, worshipers of Poe, attuned to abnormal psychology and the macabre. Tarchetti's novel *Fosca* was a fictional recounting of an affair he'd had with an epileptic woman when he was a soldier posted to a small provincial town like the one he describes in the story. He fell ill there and was sent home to Milan, where he died of tuberculosis at the age of thirty, before finishing the book. Completed by a friend of his, *Fosca* was published posthumously and, a little more than a hundred years later, made into a movie directed by Ettore Scola called *Passione d'Amore,* which I saw in 1983 and which, suddenly, half an hour into it, struck me as a story worth singing.

In the movie, Fosca is a character much talked about (and derided) by the soldiers on the post but neither we nor Giorgio see her fully until one day she comes down to breakfast in the dining quarters of the commanding officer, her protective cousin Colonel Ricci. We (but not Giorgio) have seen her figure from the back as she sits playing the piano upstairs in her parlor and we (and Giorgio) have seen her dimly descending a staircase behind a glass brick wall one morning when she is about to enter the dining room but decides at the last minute not to. We've heard her screaming in the distance at odd times of the day and we also have heard the military doctor talk about her moribund unhealthiness, but nothing prepares us (or Giorgio) for her entrance a third of the way into the film. As she comes down the stairs and into a close-up, we see a woman neurasthenically thin, with protruding teeth, sharp cheekbones, huge eyes and a face like a skull—and sweating with desire for the young captain. She is an echo of the spiderlike vampire in F. W. Murnau's movie *Nosferatu.* Scola's camera cuts to the look of shock on Giorgio's face and it was then, as Fosca started to speak and the camera cut back to her, that I had my epiphany. I realized that the story was not about how she is going to fall in love with him (she's in love with him already, having watched him from a distance ever since his arrival) but about how he is going to fall in love with her. I was instantaneously upset (that is, moved) and at the same time thinking, "They're never going to convince me of that, they're never going to pull it off," all the while knowing that they would, that Scola wouldn't have taken on such a ripely melodramatic story unless he was convinced that he could make it plausible. And he did. By the end of the movie, the unwritten songs in my head were brimming and I was certain of two things.

First, I wanted to make it into a musical, the prob-

lem being that it couldn't be a musical, not even in my nontraditional style, because the characters were so outsized. This was a lesson I had learned from Billy Wilder, a man whom I met for a little more than three minutes at a Park Avenue cocktail party sprinkled with celebrities, to which I'd been invited by the daughter of the hostess. At the time (around 1960) Burt Shevelove and I were toying with the notion of transforming *Sunset Boulevard* into a musical. We had actually sketched out the first few scenes, so when I found myself introduced to Wilder, the movie's director and co-author, I plunged right in. Blushingly, I allowed as how I was a co-author of *West Side Story* and *Gypsy* and now had an interest in adapting his movie. "But you can't make a musical out of *Sunset Boulevard*," he snapped. Startled and dismayed, I assumed that what he meant was that the rights were not available. I was wrong. He continued, "It has to be an opera. It's a story about a dethroned queen." Instantly, I recognized that he was right and relayed the story to Burt and we abandoned the project; I had no desire to write an opera, which is a form I resist. Years later, shortly after *Sweeney Todd,* the notion came up again: Hal Prince wanted to produce and direct it, with a book by Hugh Wheeler, starring Angela Lansbury. Again, I balked. As the subsequent musical by other hands proved (for me, at least), Wilder was right.

Second, I wanted James Lapine to write it: he was a romantic, he had a feeling for different centuries and different cultures, and he was enthusiastically attracted to weirdness.

Coincidentally, when I approached him, he was already toying with an odd idea of his own that he wanted me to collaborate on: a musical of a memoir called *Muscle,* by Sam Fussell, a young intellectual who became obsessed with bodybuilding. It seemed fortuitous that each of our projects concerned outward physical appearance and furthermore that they were both compact, slightly plotted stories. An even more curious parallel between the two was that on the first page of *Fosca* the narrator refers to the love he felt as a "disease" and on the first page of *Muscle* the narrator refers to his attraction to bodybuilding as a "disease." Both stories deal with obsessions that begin with the flesh and end up breaking the spirit—although both narrators eventually recover. Despite the opera problem, I suggested to James that we treat the pieces as a pair of related one-acts and we started to work, first on *Muscle.*

James wrote a couple of scenes and I began writing the opening, but I wasn't more than five minutes into it when I started to feel acutely uncomfortable with what I was doing. It was more than the usual writer's lack of confidence, it was the conviction that I was the wrong composer for the piece. The characters

were young and the period was contemporary; what was needed was a score that would vibrate with the sensibilities of the day, something rock-tinged. When I wrote *Company,* I was part of the generation I was writing about; *Follies* was about middle-aged show business, something easy for me to relate to; and *Merrily We Roll Along* traveled back to a youth I'd experienced. Everything else I'd written had been a period piece in one way or another (*West Side Story* might seem to be the exception, but in fact it was a fantasy which took place in a romantic never-never land). Rock and contemporary pop are not part of my DNA; worse, I find them unsatisfying when applied to the kind of musicals I like to write because of the limited range of their colors. Perhaps someday (maybe even by the time this book is published) someone will write a rock score that will have suppleness and variety, but the ones I've heard seem to me rhythmically and emotionally restricted, earnest to a fault and, above all, humorless except when they're being "satirical" (that is, sarcastic). This lends them a pretension which rivals the British pop operas that briefly conquered the world during the 1990s. I called James and said that he should get another songwriter, but that if he was willing to plow ahead with *Passione d'Amore* I'd be happy to include it as a companion piece. The result: James decided he wanted to pursue *Muscle,* with William Finn supplying the songs, but floated the idea that instead of a companion piece, the story of *Fosca* might be enough for an evening in itself.

The second of my problems was thus solved—James would write and direct the show. But the first remained: how to write something that had both the colloquial theatricality of a musical and the extravagant flamboyance of an opera. *Sweeney Todd* had been a step in that direction, but its melodramatic arioso moments were balanced by the music-hall flavoring of Mrs. Lovett's character and the occasional comic song and rambunctious chorus number. Most of the score consists of recognizable song forms, distended though some of them may be, as befits an operetta. *Passione d'Amore* is a mesmerizing movie partly because it has not one moment of comedy, and although there's a useful chorus at hand (the soldiers at the post), they have only one relieving color: gossip. And a little gossip goes a long way very quickly (which is one reason that the "Gossip" song in *Sunday in the Park with George* is so brief).

I have successfully avoided enjoying opera all my life. There are many moments in the operatic literature that thrill me, but few complete scores, and even those that do (*Carmen, Peter Grimes, Wozzeck, Porgy and Bess,* most of Puccini, to list the ones that come to mind immediately) I would rather listen to on records because they strike me as way too long. I was

brought up on the swiftness and insubstantiality of musicals, and I'm not as enthralled by the human voice as I would like to be. For me it's the song, not the singer; I don't really care who sings "Vissi d'Arte," I care about what she's singing. I discriminate among singers of popular songs and show tunes, but for some reason I'm both less enthusiastic and less critical when it comes to the higher stratum of the art form. I recognize that this is my loss, and I sometimes envy (but not a lot) the swooning pleasure my opera-buff friends get from it. The thing that puts me off most is that most opera composers seem to have little sense of theater. They spend as much time having their characters sing about trivialities as about matters of emotional importance, and they too often resort to recitative to carry the plot along—for my money a tedious and arid solution to a problem easily solved by dialogue.

Such condescension toward opera, however, wasn't going to help me solve *my* problem: how to treat a story as ripe as *Fosca* and maintain its intensity without the indulgence in vocal opulence and spectacle that is the blood of opera. I chose to think of the show as one long rhapsodic love song: musically relentless, the recitative where necessary morphing into formal patterns, and as much of the dialogue underscored as possible. The danger was that, like my feeling about rock scores, it would be earnest, monotonous and humorless—God knows, the novel is. I would have to find a way of sustaining a mood without losing variety, a problem compounded by the fact that *Fosca* is an epistolary novel. An evening of letter reading, especially *sung* letter reading, would hardly

contribute to the joy of nations and lead to dancing in the aisles. But, of course, such challenges only whet a writer's appetite—or should. I was saved, at least in my opinion, by Fosca herself. Although the music tends to move slowly throughout the evening, Fosca's manic obsessiveness supplies the necessary energy, her volatility the variety, her unpredictable hysteria the surprise and her sophisticated intelligence the biting humor. And, of course, being a self-dramatizing hysteric, she is always theatrical. She drives the piece, and once I'd locked myself into her she was not hard to write. Her behavior is so outrageous that many of the initial audiences had to take refuge in laughing at her. James and I spent the preview weeks flagging and removing the little discomfiting moments which would cause pre-giggle frissons in the house, and by the time we opened there was no unwanted laughter whatsoever. There wasn't much wanted laughter either. I tried to elicit a few chuckles in the soldiers' choruses, but they were murmurs at best. James pushed me to do more, but I argued that the power of the show had to do with its relentlessness, a relentlessness much like Fosca's. Besides which, jokes are hard to write.

The "songs" in *Passion* lie somewhere between aria and recitative, with an occasional recognizable song form thrown in. The lyrics are best read as a versified short story. To this end, I've divided the show into its component scenes rather than individual song titles, and I've included some of the interwoven speech; to include it all, I'd have to reprint the whole play. In any event, there's enough dialogue so that no one could mistake *Passion* for an opera. I hope.

Donna Murphy as Fosca, Jere Shea as Giorgio and Marin Mazzie as Clara

SCENE ONE

1863. A room in Milan. Late afternoon. The sound of military drums rises to a climax as lights come up on Clara and Giorgio making love on a bed. Clara emits a soundless cry of orgasm, the orchestra substituting for her voice. Music continues underneath as Clara shudders a couple of times and falls back into Giorgio's arms. She lies there for a moment.

CLARA
I'm so happy,
I'm afraid I'll die
Here in your arms.

What would you do
If I died
Like this—

(Languishes across him)

Right now,
Here in your arms?

That we ever should have met
Is a miracle—

GIORGIO
No, inevitable—

CLARA
Then inevitable, yes,
But I confess
It was the look—

GIORGIO
The look?

CLARA
The sadness in your eyes
That day
When we glanced
At each other in the park.

GIORGIO
We were both unhappy.

CLARA
Unhappiness can be seductive.

GIORGIO
You pitied me . . .

BOTH
How quickly pity leads to love.

CLARA
All this happiness
Merely from a glance in the park.
So much happiness,
So much love . . .

GIORGIO
I thought I knew what love was.

CLARA
I wish we might have met so much
    sooner.
I could have given you—

GIORGIO
(Overlapping)
I thought I knew what love was.

CLARA
—My youth.

GIORGIO
I thought I knew how much I could
    feel.

CLARA
All the time we lost . . .

GIORGIO
I didn't know what love was.

CLARA
I've never known what love was.

GIORGIO
But now—

CLARA
And now—

BOTH
—I do.
It's what I feel with you,
The happiness I feel with you.

CLARA
So much happiness—

GIORGIO
You are so beautiful . . .

CLARA
—Happening by chance
In a park.

GIORGIO
Not by chance,
By necessity—

CLARA
Surely, this is happiness—

GIORGIO
By the sadness that we saw
In each other.

CLARA
(Overlapping)
—No one else
Has ever felt before!

BOTH
Just another love story,
That's what they would claim.
Another simple love story—
Aren't all of them the same?

CLARA
No, but this is more,
We feel more!

BOTH
This is so much more—!

(A beat; then, smiling at each other)

Like every other love story.

Some say happiness
Comes and goes.
Then this happiness
Is a kind of happiness
No one really knows.

GIORGIO
I thought I knew what love was.

CLARA
(Overlapping)
I'd only heard what love was.

GIORGIO
I thought it was no more than a
    name
For yearning.

CLARA
I thought it was what kindness
    became.

GIORGIO
I'm learning—

CLARA
I thought where there was love there
   was shame.

GIORGIO
—That with you—

CLARA
But with you—

BOTH
—There's just happiness.

CLARA
Endless happiness . . .

*After a silence, Giorgio reveals that he
has been transferred to a frontier outpost and will have to report in five
days. She is devastated. He tells her
they must write each other every day.
Clara says that she has to go. Giorgio
draws her back down to the bed.*

GIORGIO
God,
You are so beautiful.
I love to see you in the light,
Clear and beautiful,

   (Touching her lightly)

Memorize—

CLARA
No . . .

GIORGIO
—Every inch,
Every part of you,
To take with me.

CLARA
(Succumbing)
Giorgio . . .

GIORGIO
Your feet so soft,
As if they'd never touched the
   ground—

CLARA
Don't . . .

GIORGIO
—Your skin so white,
So pure,
So delicate.

CLARA
Don't . . .

GIORGIO
Your smell so sweet,
Your breath so warm.
I will summon you in my mind,
I'm painting you indelibly on my
   mind.

CLARA
Let me go . . .

GIORGIO
We must fill every moment.

CLARA
(Beginning to cry)
All this happiness—

GIORGIO
No, don't.

CLARA
—Ended by a word in the dark.

GIORGIO
Oh, my love, oh, my darling . . .

CLARA
(Overlapping)
So much happiness—

GIORGIO
No, please, you mustn't . . .

CLARA
—Wasn't meant to last.

GIORGIO
I am here,
I am with you,
I am yours.

CLARA
I never knew what love was.

GIORGIO
Your skin,
Your silken hair . . .

CLARA
I always thought I didn't deserve it.

GIORGIO
Your breasts,
Your lips . . .

CLARA
I didn't know what love was.

GIORGIO
(Overlapping)
I want you every minute of my
   life . . .

CLARA
I don't know how I'll live when
   you're gone!

GIORGIO
(Enveloping her)
I will always be here.

CLARA
*(Overlapping, as the lovemaking
   becomes more intense)*
I don't know how I'll live . . .
Giorgio . . .
Don't leave me . . .

*This time, just before the orgasm, the
drums drown the orchestra and the
scene blacks out.*

This scene exemplifies what I mean
by the difference between the semi-
operatic styles of *Sweeney Todd* and
Passion. It is immediately apparent on
reading the lyric, which shorn of the
music lacks any recognizable rhythmic
underpinning. The lyrics of pop songs
and show tunes, with few exceptions,
reflect the rhythmic regularities of
their structures even if the reader has
never heard the melody, just as light
verse does (for example, "The Pied
Piper of Hamelin"). The arioso nature
of the *Passion* score obscures the surface rhythm and makes the lyrics less
compelling to read than others in this
book. I say that not as an apology, but
to illustrate the necessarily underwrit-
ten quality of conversational lyric writing, which is best tilted toward the

"Happiness"

CLARA

I had to hide my eyes
So the others on the train
That carried me away from you
Would think I was asleep.

We hear elegant Chopinesque piano music from above the mess hall. Colonel Ricci informs Giorgio that it is his cousin Fosca playing and that she is in poor health and rarely comes down to meals. He adds that she loves to read, and Giorgio offers to lend her some of his books, an offer which the Colonel gratefully accepts.

Days pass. Giorgio, once again at dinner, reads a letter from Clara.

CLARA

Giorgio . . .
I, too, have cried
Inside.

BOTH

You must not be ashamed of your
    tears.

CLARA

I love you for your tears.

BOTH

Your absence only makes my love
    grow stronger.
And when I cannot bear it any
    longer—

The letter is interrupted by a scream coming from Fosca upstairs. Giorgio rises, concerned; the soldiers continue to eat, unfazed. The Colonel apologizes for the outburst but offers no explanation. A few moments later Fosca screams again. The Colonel nods to the post's Doctor, who wearily gets up to go and attend to her.

In preparing the show for a workshop at Lincoln Center, James became increasingly worried about its lack of comic relief, and since the soldiers were the only characters who seemed capable of it, I wrote a number of raucous

banal even when unrhymed. Rhyme makes a lot of banality seem sparkling, witty and profound which is fine for the characters in *A Little Night Music,* but gratingly unsuitable here. If the characters in *Passion* spoke poetically, the music would inflate the language into bombast, as in opera, where it doesn't matter, since the language is incomprehensible anyway, either because of the singers' diction or because it really *is* written in an incomprehensible language. However, people do not go to opera to listen to the libretto (they used not to go to musicals for that reason either, but times have changed and now sometimes they do).

To keep the above song from morphing into recitative, my bête noire, I sprinkled the lyric with occasional rhymes and even included what the actor Anthony Perkins, a man with an antic sense of language, liked to call a "songette": the section centering on the refrain word "happiness." It not only allows the audience to feel that they're back in (moder-

ately) comfortable territory, it provides a core to the passage and prevents it from shattering into fragments of musical banter, a technique much overused these days in both musicals and operas because it's so easy to write.

SCENE TWO

The outpost. Giorgio, having just met the other officers in his regiment, is at dinner with them in the dining room of Colonel Ricci, the commander. Clara, in Milan, is reading a letter he has sent.

CLARA

Clara . . .

GIORGIO

Clara . . .
I cried.

CLARA

I cried.

verses of a raunchy song they could sing every time they were seen. It was first established at the beginning of Scene Two, around the dinner table. Lieutenants Torasso and Barri and the cook are listening to a boastful story from Major Rizzoli.

RIZZOLLI
. . . Six times—

BARRI
In a single night?

RIZZOLLI
Six times.

TORASSO
That's a pretty fair amount.

COOK
Six times?

BARRI
With the redhead?

RIZZOLLI
Right.

TORASSO
(To the others)
Well, it proves he's got endurance—

BARRI
Or it proves he can't count.

The cook starts serving the meal.

RIZZOLLI
(Staring at the meat on his fork)
What is this?

COOK
It's veal.

BARRI
We had veal on Tuesday.

RIZZOLLI
Is it fresh?

COOK
Of course.

RIZZOLLI
Well, it looks familiar.

COOK
Well, it's *not* familiar.

TORASSO
By the way, Lieutenant Barri,
Did you ever find your horse?

They laugh familiarly. Torasso raises his glass in what is apparently a customary toast.

TORASSO
Nothing's ever new in the army!

BARRI, RIZZOLLI, COOK
Prosit!

They drink.

TORASSO
All you've got to be is fast and fit!

BARRI, RIZZOLLI, COOK
Skol!

They drink again.

TORASSO
All you've got to do in the army—

BARRI, RIZZOLLI, COOK
Salud!

TORASSO
—Is never give a—

BARRI
—Never give a—

RIZZOLLI
—Never give a—

COOK
—Never give a—

TORASSO, BARRI
—Never give a—

RIZZOLLI, COOK
—Never give a—

ALL FOUR
—Never give a—

COLONEL
Enough, gentlemen, enough.

At which point Giorgio entered. The interlude was mildly amusing, but its chief effect was to hold up the story, so out it went.

Weeks pass. Clara is in Milan, reading a letter from Giorgio; Giorgio is overseeing a formation of marching soldiers.

CLARA
Clara, I'm in hell.

GIORGIO
This is hell.

SOLDIERS
Living hell.

CLARA
Living hell.
This godforsaken place—

SOLDIERS
This godforsaken place—

CLARA
This sterile little town,
These pompous little men,

GIORGIO
This military madness . . .

SOLDIERS
This military madness . . .
Uniforms, uniforms . . .

CLARA, GIORGIO
My days are spent in maneuvers—

SOLDIERS
Uniforms, uniforms . . .

CLARA, GIORGIO
My evenings in discussing the day—

SOLDIERS
This is hell . . .

CLARA
My nights are spent in thinking
    of you.

GIORGIO
Don't forget me, Clara . . .

Giorgio has a conversation with the Doctor about Fosca. The Doctor describes her as a woman in her late twenties, a "collection of many ills," including hysterical convulsions, adding that Colonel Ricci is fiercely protective of her. When Giorgio wonders if she might be the Colonel's lover, the Doctor replies that her physical fragility prevents her from being anyone's lover.

Days pass. Giorgio is at the breakfast table in the dining room with some of the other officers. There is an empty place setting, which, they explain, is always there awaiting Fosca, who almost never comes down to eat. They exit and Giorgio begins to read a letter from Clara, who appears at the edge of the stage.

CLARA, GIORGIO
How could I forget you?

A shadowy figure appears at the top of the stairs and begins slowly descending.

CLARA
Yesterday I walked through the park
To the knoll where we met.
Afterwards I sat on the bench
Where we sat
All that sultry afternoon.

I thought about our room,
Our little room,
Where we were happy,
And where we shall be happy again,
Some day.

I see us in our room,
Our little room,
And I don't feel so alone anymore.

I close my eyes,
Imagining that you are there,
Imagining your fingers touching
   mine,
Imagining our room,
The bed,
The secrecy,
The world outside,
Your mouth on mine—

The figure descends the last step. It is Fosca. She carries some books and approaches her empty place setting with an uncertain gait. As she turns from the shadows, revealing herself, we see that she is an ugly, sickly woman, preternaturally thin and sallow, her face all bones and nose, her hair pulled tightly back.

FOSCA
(With a grotesque smile)
Captain . . .

Giorgio sees her and is momentarily shocked, then quickly rises.

I came to thank you for the books.
I would have sooner, but I've been
   so ill.

Music continues underneath.

GIORGIO
Well, now you seem to be feeling
more normal.

FOSCA
(Laughing tensely)
Normal? I hardly think so. Sickness is normal to me, as health is to you. Excuse me. I shouldn't speak of my troubles. I have been going through a period of deep melancholy.

An awkward pause, music continuing underneath.

I so enjoyed the novel by Rousseau.

GIORGIO
It's wonderful. My favorite, really.

FOSCA
The character of Julie is a great mystery.

GIORGIO
You should have kept the book longer to meditate over.

FOSCA
(Impatiently, her moods changing rapidly)
I do not read to think.
I do not read to learn.

I do not read to search for truth,
I know the truth,
The truth is hardly what I need.
I read to dream.

I read to live
In other people's lives.

I read about the joys
The world
Dispenses to the fortunate,
And listen for the echoes.

(Fiercely)

I read to live,
To get away from life!

(Calmer)

No, Captain, I have no illusions.
I recognize the limits of my dreams.
I know how painful dreams can be
Unless you know
They're merely dreams.

(Smiling joylessly)

There is a flower
Which offers nectar at the top,
Delicious nectar at the top,
And bitter poison underneath.
The butterfly that stays too long
And drinks too deep
Is doomed to die.
I read to fly,
To skim!
I do not read to swim.

(Bitterly)

I do not dwell on dreams.
I know how soon a dream becomes
   an expectation.
How can I have expectations?
Look at me.

(As Giorgio starts to protest)

No, Captain, look at me,
Look at me!

(Exalted)

I do not hope for what I cannot
   have!

glance taste.
I read to get a glimpse
Of joy
Of other people's joys
An echo of their joy
I read for echoes of the joys
That others (seem to) have
I read to live
I read to breathe
I read, I read.
And so I read.
I read to have a life

① I do not read for truth
   seek seek to find the in search of
② I know the truth
   The truth is what I   It's something to forget
   I need to forget
   I/read to forget. And so I read.
   I read to live
   I read to breathe.
   I have no need for truth
③ The truth   that's hardly what I need
   I do not read to find the truth
   Who wants to be reminded of the truth
   Indeed.
④ I read to dream
   And that is why I read.
⑤ To live how other people live
⑥ I read for echoes of the joys
⑦ The world
⑧ Dispenses to the lucky ones.
   (Ah, how I do go on.)

regret
set
upset

I do not linger long
The   pollen gets too strong

To get drunk on dreams, (fantasy imaginings)
To flee from life

search for truth search
I do not read to find
The truth,   what's true
I know the truth
The truth is what   Thus I read to ill
I'm ready to forget
The truth is what I need to forget
That is it what I need
That's why
I read
So that I forget
In order to forget
The truth
The truth is not my need.
The truth is best forgotten
The truth is something to forget.
At best
I do not wish to test the truth

The truth
I do not read to be enlightened
I do not read " " " .

fancies fly
I read to let my dreams
                         free

To read is to forget.

I do not cling to things I cannot
keep!

(Tightly)

The more you cling to things,
The more you love them,
The more the pain you suffer
When they're taken from you . . .

(Calming down again)

Ah, but if you have no expectations,
Captain,
You can never have a
disappointment.

(Gives a short laugh)

I must be mad to chatter on about
myself like this to you. Forgive
me . . .

GIORGIO
(At a loss)
I assure you—

FOSCA
No, forgive me, please . . .

GIORGIO
But truly, there is nothing to forg—

FOSCA
(Overlapping, brightly)
Have you explored the town?

(Before he can reply)

It is remote, isn't it?
And provincial, don't you think?

GIORGIO
Yes.

FOSCA
And everything so brown:
The streets, the fields,
The river even,
Though there are some lovely
gardens.

(Anxiously)

You do like gardens, I hope?

GIORGIO
Yes.

FOSCA
Good, I can show you gardens.

Giorgio smiles uncomfortably.

And then of course there is the
castle.

(As Giorgio looks blank)

The ruined castle.

GIORGIO
Ah.

FOSCA
I find it lovely. Probably because it's
ruined, I suppose.

GIORGIO
(Avoiding her intensity)
I didn't know there was a castle.

FOSCA
I like to take excursions there—
When I'm in better health.
Perhaps you'll join me—

(As Giorgio tries to hide his
discomfort)

—And my cousin . . .
One day . . .

Fosca suddenly exits, then just as suddenly reenters and offers Giorgio a
bunch of flowers. A funeral procession
passes outside the window and she has
a hysterical fit, screaming and collaps-
ing on the floor. Two female attendants
enter to assist her. Giorgio turns front,
singing a letter to Clara.

GIORGIO
How can I describe her?
The wretchedness,
God, the wretchedness
And the suffering,
The desperation
Of that poor unhappy creature—
The embarrassment, Clara,
Looking at that loneliness,
Listening to all that self-pity . . .

The soldiers appear in formation.

SOLDIERS
The town—
It is remote, isn't it?
And provincial,
Don't you think?
And everything so brown:
The streets, the fields,
The river even . . .
Of course there is the castle . . .
The ruined castle . . .

If Pamela Myers's audition for *Company* was the most heartwarming in
my experience and Hermione Gin-
gold's for *A Little Night Music* the
most bizarre (see volume one), Donna
Murphy's for *Passion* was the most impressive. Ordinarily, performers simply
audition with songs they like and feel
comfortable singing. If everyone on
the production staff thinks she's good,
she may be asked to learn a song from
the score; and so it was with Donna,
especially because she seemed so
wrong for the part. To begin with, she
is exotically beautiful, a problem we
could never solve even after we'd cast
her—the best we could do was to plaster a mole on her face and pull her
hair back in a knot to make her severe
and spinsterish, like Olivia de Havilland in *The Heiress*. Furthermore,
Donna was known primarily as a
comedienne, having made a hilarious
mark as the leading lady in *Song of
Singapore*, a spoof of 1940s Hollywood musicals. But she could sing,
and auditions had turned up very few
possibilities—the harsh, neurotic intelligence of the character is hard even
for a good actress to capture, much
less a good actress with a good voice.
So we gave Donna "I Read" (my title
for the passage above) to take home
and work on. She came back a couple
of days later and gave a performance
that I would have been glad to have
seen on opening night. The nuances
she found and included, the intensity,
the instinctive rhythm and phrasing
crucial to a rhapsodic song in order to
keep it from falling apart as it's being
sung, were so precise and full and

gripping that I turned to James and said, "Let's open tomorrow." Actors often talk about the moment when they "connect to the part"—Donna connected to Fosca instantaneously. Months later, after the show was up and running, I asked her how she understood so much about the character so immediately, and she replied that there had been an incident in her adolescent life which echoed in Fosca, that the minute she met her she recognized her. It showed—for 280 performances.

SCENE THREE

The castle garden. Giorgio and Fosca are strolling together. On the side of the stage Clara is reading a letter from him. Music continues throughout.

Donna Murphy as Fosca

GIORGIO
All the while as we strolled, Clara—

FOSCA
I hope I didn't frighten you the other day.

GIORGIO
No, not at all.

—I could see you reading my letter.

FOSCA
I'm not afraid of death.

GIORGIO
All the while as we strolled—

FOSCA
I rather think I'd welcome dying. It's everything that follows that I dread. Being shut up in a coffin, smothered in the earth, turning into dust. These images send me into a state of terror.

GIORGIO
—All I saw,
All I knew,
All that I could think of was you.

FOSCA
Even talking of this makes me . . .

Momentarily, Giorgio fears she will suffer another attack.

GIORGIO
Surely if you are sick, there is always the hope that you will get better.

CLARA
—All that I could think of was you.

FOSCA
Hope, in my case, is in short supply.

CLARA
How ridiculous—

GIORGIO
Well then, one must look to life for whatever pleasures it can offer.

FOSCA
And what might they be?

CLARA
—To be looking at her—

GIORGIO
Helping others, for example.

FOSCA
Helping others!

(Laughs)

CLARA
—And be thinking of you.

FOSCA
I have worked in poorhouses, Captain.

CLARA
How could anyone—

FOSCA
I felt no different.

CLARA
So unbeautiful—

FOSCA
Pity is nothing but passive love.

CLARA
—Stir my memory of you?

REVIVALS: ACTORS AND THEIR QUALITIES

Despite its first-rate initial production in New York and subsequent ones in both the United States and Europe, I had never seen *Passion* come properly into focus until its 2010 revival at the Donmar Warehouse in London. The production was imaginatively directed by Jamie Lloyd, gorgeously set and costumed by Christopher Oram, elegantly lit by Neil Austin and superlatively acted by the entire cast, but what made the eye-opening difference was the presence of the leading actor, David Thaxton. *Fosca* may be the novel's title, but the story is clearly about Giorgio, who narrates it. He describes Fosca in detail but himself hardly at all. As written, he is that generic nineteenth-century literary staple, the classic protagonist who observes and reacts rather than acts. Giorgio is a tabula rasa, and it's up to the actor who plays him to body him forth, whereas the actor playing Fosca merely has to personalize a specifically defined character. The one characteristic Giorgio must have is innocence. Even though he is not naive, being in the midst of an affair with a married woman, he has to be in some way unprepared not only for the aridity of frontier life but for the extravagance of Fosca's emotions.

Innocence is hard to act. It has little to do with age and everything to do with the actor's quality; it has to come built in. Thaxton's quality delineated Giorgio; he conveyed an innocent vulnerability not just through acting but by virtue of who he was. Unlike all the other Giorgios I'd seen, he didn't seem to be a fully grown man; he was clearly someone who was on the brink of change, and that was crucial to the story. Giorgio's transformation during the course of *Passion* has always been a source of audience contention: some have accepted it and been moved by it, some have found it impossible to believe. In this case, it was not only unarguable, it was inevitable. Elena Roger's performance as Fosca was intense and powerful, but close up (the Donmar Warehouse is an intimate theater), Giorgio's purity

and fragility made him the magnetic center of attention, a position Fosca had always held in previous productions. For the first time, the story was clearly about him and not Fosca.*

I go into this at length because as I was coming out of the Donmar and wishing that everyone could see this definition of the show, I remembered a conversation I'd had in 1979 at a large cocktail party given for Tony Award nominees, where I found myself haranguing two of the most accomplished directors in the British theater, deploring the fact that plays and musicals in London were not being preserved for posterity the way they were in New York, where Lincoln Center Library for the Performing Arts had been videotaping productions both on and off Broadway since 1970.† The Britishers were surprised, not to say baffled. Preservation had never crossed their minds, they said—why would anyone want to freeze an art that by definition keeps changing shape? The whole point of theater is that every performance is unique; the play may be the same from night to night but not the performance. The tapes are not supposed to be definitive, I replied, they're simply a record of events, and I for one would prefer to see a frozen performance of Laurence Olivier in *Oedipus Rex* than none at all. They shrugged.

I was unsettled; I had never thought about theater quite that way. I was certainly aware that revisiting a show, even without any

changes in the cast, sometimes constitutes an experience noticeably different from the first impression, but until that cocktail conversation I had never paid much attention to the implication: namely, that theater and music, unlike the printed word, the painted canvas, the building, the sculpture, the frame of film, are ephemeral. Each performance disappears as soon as the curtain comes down or the last note fades; each audience has a unique experience and even if it's filmed it can never have its original impact again. Moreover, once a play has closed, the entire production no longer exists; the sets are burned, and the costumes as well if they don't get lent out to other productions or are taken home by the actors. All that's left is the text, which is lifeless until it's performed.

In order to come to life again, a play has to be—yes—revived. The word is exact. Novels, paintings, statues and movies remain the same from generation to generation, only the responses change—one year's shocker is another year's yawn and what seems like a stunning performance a decade later looks like either overacting or underacting (Bette Davis and Montgomery Clift come to mind). But plays and symphonies are open to reinterpretation and to changing with the times. They can be revivified, and even redefined, through something as simple as recasting. Not many performances refocus a work the way David Thaxton's did in *Passion*, because most shows don't allow for it, or need it. Every Rose who's been in *Gypsy* on Broadway (and elsewhere, I would imagine) has brought a different color to the part, simply by being who she is,

---

* A similar shift occurred at the Kennedy Center in 2002, when John Barrowman played Bobby in a revival of *Company*. Many in the audience think of the character as a cipher who, although he's virtually never off stage, is no more than a reflection of his far more interesting friends. Not with Barrowman. His quality, not unlike Thaxton's, was that of a boy in a man's body, and it was clear that Bobby was about to graduate from one to the other, which is what *Company* is about.

† In 1970 the craft unions finally allowed tapings to proceed, after prolonged negotiations aimed (rightly) at guaranteeing that the tapes would never see the commercial light of day and that access to viewing them would be restricted to theater professionals, students and others with specific theater interests.

but to paraphrase Gertrude Stein, Rose is Rose is Rose. The show is never going to be about Herbie or even, despite her epon-ymous role, Louise. New actors may not have the galvanic effect on a show that Thaxton had, but they can bring out different facets of the piece, valleys that were formerly hidden, colors that were swallowed up in the background. With a play worth seeing more than once, each gen-eration of performers allows you to see it afresh. It isn't only actors, of course, who can revivify a piece. Directors can not only revivify it, they can kill it—or at least, wound it. More about them in the next chapter. The point is that what keeps theater alive is the possibility of revival, whether on Broadway, in the West End, Budapest, summer stock or high schools. It leads to a nice paradox: the very thing that makes theater impermanent is what makes it immortal.

Movies are permanent. They can't be revived because they were never alive to begin with; they neither grow nor change, they are born finished; they can only be remade. This is not a sneer at movies, which I've loved since I was a child, it's simply a description of one differ-ence between the two media. Few movies have a chance to be revivi-fied because remakes take a long time and cost a lot of money, and they are almost never as satisfying as the originals (unless they have been truly reconceived, as with *His Girl Friday*, Howard Hawks's remake of *The Front Page*). This is sometimes because so much is riding on them, and they are therefore built to please whatever demographic is prevalent at the time, which leaves them toothless, and sometimes because their writers and directors are so determined to revise the original in order to make it their own that they throw the baby out with the bathwater (and occasionally even keep the bathwa-ter). The same thing can happen with plays, of course: their revivals can be patronizing or effortfully original or any station in between, but there are always more reinterpre-tations waiting down the line.

Reviving a show preserves it; preserving it embalms it. Theater is mercury, and my wish for the world to see that performance at the Donmar was an impossible one. The experience belonged exclusively to me and a roomful of others who had come together at the same time for the same event. It wouldn't have been the same show the next night. In a sense, every night of a show is a revival. Every new audience affects the performance in a different way, as does every aspect of the pro-duction itself—a late lighting cue can change the temperature of a scene as much as an unexpected laugh. The British still don't tape most of their shows, and I admire their reasons. Still, I'd like to see Olivier's Oedipus, even in aspic.

FOSCA
Dead love.

Giorgio is silent as they walk, lost in reverie.

CLARA
To feel a woman's touch,
To touch a woman's hand,
Reminded me how much
I long to be with you,
How long I've been without you
near.
And then to hear a woman's voice,
To hold a woman's arm,
To feel a woman's touch . . .

GIORGIO
These thoughts are bad for you. You must concentrate on every-thing around you that suggests beauty and life. These trees, these flowers, the warm smell of the air—

FOSCA
You make it sound so simple, Cap-tain. As if a flower or a tree could somehow make one happy.

CLARA
Perhaps it was the dress,
The fragrance of her dress,
The light perfume of silk
That's warm from being in the sun,
That mingles with a woman's own
perfume,
The fragrance of a woman . . .

GIORGIO
There is no absolute happiness in anyone's life, Signora. The only happiness we can be certain of is love.

FOSCA
What do you mean?

CLARA
The garden filled with you—

FOSCA
Are you speaking of friendships? Family?

GIORGIO
I'm speaking of a superior kind of love—

CLARA
—And all that I could do—

GIORGIO
—the kind between two people.

CLARA
—Because of you,
Was talk of love . . .

FOSCA
Two people . . .

GIORGIO
Yes.

Giorgio sings to Fosca as Clara contin-ues to sing the letter.

CLARA, GIORGIO
Love that fills
Every waking moment,
Love that grows
Every single day,
Love that thinks
Everything is pure,
Everything is beautiful,
Everything is possible.

Love that fuses two into one,
Where we think the same thoughts,

GIORGIO
Want the same things,

BOTH
Live as one,

GIORGIO
Feel as one,

BOTH
Breathe as one.

CLARA
Love that shuts away the world,

GIORGIO
(Overlapping)
Love that shuts away the world,

CLARA
That envelops my soul,

GIORGIO
That envelops your soul,

CLARA
That ennobles my life,

GIORGIO
(Overlapping)
Your life,

BOTH
Love that floods
Every living moment,
Love like—

CLARA
—Ours.

FOSCA
Love like—?

GIORGIO
Like wine.
An intoxication . . .

Clara retreats and exits.

A great blindness, if you will.

FOSCA
Yes, I've read about that love, but you speak of it as one who lives it.

She stumbles slightly; Giorgio goes to aid her, but she pulls herself away.

FOSCA
I don't feel well. I must go back.

GIORGIO
I'm sorry.

FOSCA
You can be incredibly cruel, Captain.

GIORGIO
Cruel?

FOSCA
To speak to me of love—

GIORGIO
Forgive me. I didn't mean to speak—

FOSCA
To dangle words like "happiness,"
"Beautiful,"
"Superior"—
You can't be that naive.

You with all your books,
Your taste,
Your sensitivity,
I thought you'd understand.

The others—well,
They're all alike.
Stupidity is their excuse
As ugliness is mine,
But what is yours?

I've watched you from my window.
I saw you on the day that you
    arrived.

Perhaps it was the way you walked,
The way you spoke to your men—
I saw that you were different then.
I saw that you were kind and good.
I thought you understood.

(Intensely)

They hear drums,
You hear music,
As do I.
Don't you see?
We're the same.

We are different,
You and I are different.
They hear only drums.

All the time I watched from my
    room,
I would think of coming downstairs,
Thinking we'd meet,
Thinking you'd look at me,
Thinking you'd be repelled by what
    you saw.

Don't reject me.
Don't deny me, Captain.
Understand me, be my friend.
They hear drums,
We hear music.
Be my friend . . .

SCENE FOUR

Giorgio, made acutely uncomfortable by Fosca's insistence, avoids her for the next few days. Desperate to see him, she catches him at the dining table and forces a love note on him. Feeling himself getting trapped, he requests five days' leave in Milan from the Colonel, who reluctantly grants it.

As he leaves at dawn, Fosca intercepts him and blocks his way, begging him to think of her while he's in Milan, finally throwing herself at his feet. Horrified and embarrassed, he promises to write her.

SCENE FIVE

On one side of the stage, Giorgio is passionately embracing Clara on the bed as she strips off his clothes. On the other side, Fosca is reading Giorgio's letter.

FOSCA
I am writing to you,
Signora,
Just as soon as I've arrived,
With a most unhappy heart.

GIORGIO
God, you are so beautiful—

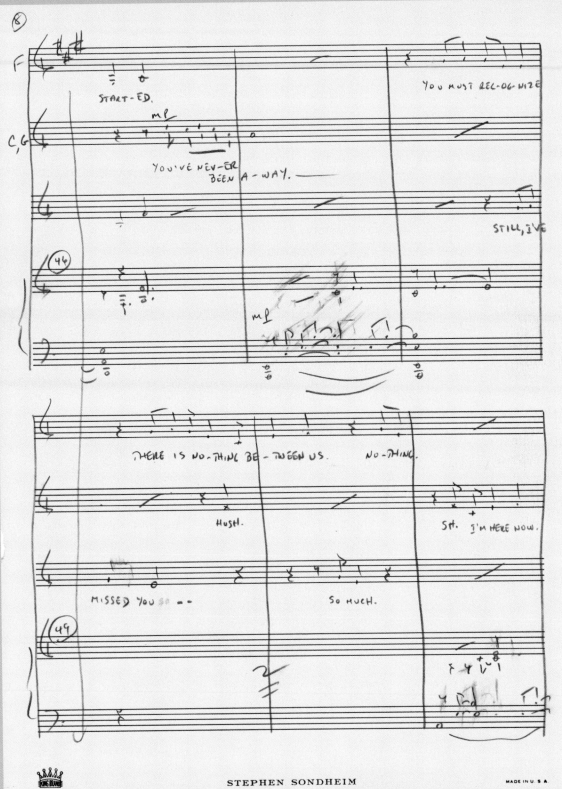

STEPHEN SONDHEIM

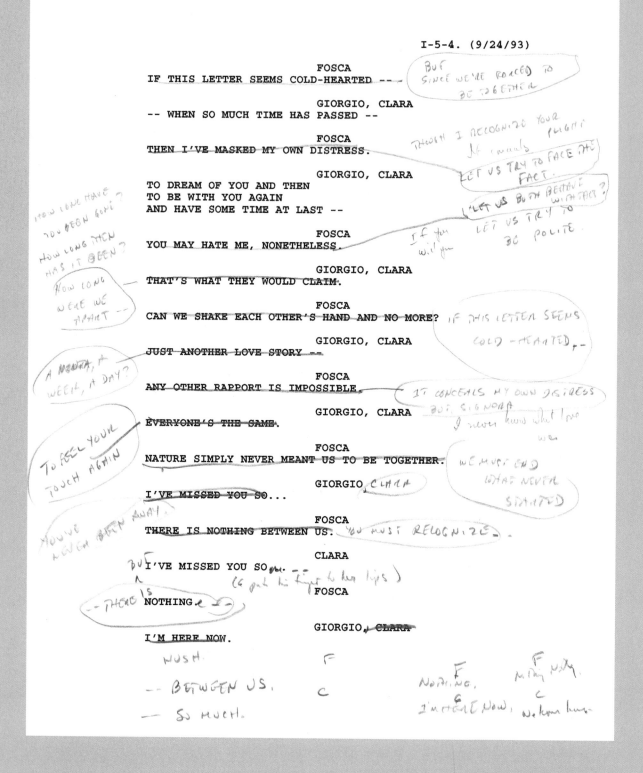

                    FOSCA
IF THIS LETTER SEEMS COLD-HEARTED --   *BUT*
                                         SINCE WE'RE FORCED TO
                                              BE TOGETHER

                    GIORGIO, CLARA
-- WHEN SO MUCH TIME HAS PASSED --

                    FOSCA   *THOUGH I RECOGNIZE YOUR*
THEN I'VE MASKED MY OWN DISTRESS.   *PLIGHT*
                                         let us try to FACE THE
                    GIORGIO, CLARA   *FACT.*
TO DREAM OF YOU AND THEN
TO BE WITH YOU AGAIN   *"LET US BOTH BEHAVE*
AND HAVE SOME TIME AT LAST --   *WITH TACT?*
                                         LET US TRY TO
                    FOSCA   *If you*   *BE POLITE.*
YOU MAY HATE ME, NONETHELESS.   *will you*

                    GIORGIO, CLARA
THAT'S WHAT THEY WOULD CLAIM.

                    FOSCA
CAN WE SHAKE EACH OTHER'S HAND AND NO MORE?   *IF THIS LETTER SEEMS*
                                              COLD-HEARTED, --
                    GIORGIO, CLARA
JUST ANOTHER LOVE STORY --

                    FOSCA
ANY OTHER RAPPORT IS IMPOSSIBLE.   *IT CONCEALS MY OWN DISTRESS*
                                        BUT, SIGNORA
                    GIORGIO, CLARA   *I never knew what love*
EVERYONE'S THE SAME.   *was*

                    FOSCA   *WE MUST END*
NATURE SIMPLY NEVER MEANT US TO BE TOGETHER. *WHAT NEVER*
                                              STARTED
                    GIORGIO, CLARA
I'VE MISSED YOU SO...

                    FOSCA
THERE IS NOTHING BETWEEN US. *YOU MUST RECOGNIZE*

                    CLARA
BUT I'VE MISSED YOU SO... *(he puts his finger to her lips)*

                    FOSCA
-- THERE IS NOTHING.

                    GIORGIO, ~~CLARA~~
I'M HERE NOW.

HUSH.   F

-- BETWEEN US.   C

-- SO MUCH.

NOTHING. *F*

I'M HERE NOW, *C*

How long have you been gone? How long then has it been?

HOW LONG WERE WE APART --

A MONTH, A WEEK, A DAY?

TO FEEL YOUR TOUCH AGAIN

You've never been away.

FOSCA
I do not wish to cause you pain—

GIORGIO
As I remember every night—

FOSCA
So please consider what I say—

GIORGIO
Clear and beautiful—

FOSCA
—With calm.

GIORGIO
—Every night, every day, every part
of you . . .

FOSCA
My heart—

CLARA
You feel so good—

FOSCA
(Hesitating to read on)
My heart belongs—

CLARA
As if you'd never been away—

FOSCA
My heart belongs to someone else.

CLARA
Your breath so warm, your touch so
sure—

GIORGIO
Your skin so delicate . . .

CLARA
Your arms so strong . . .

FOSCA
I am in love,
Hopelessly in love—

(Increasingly upset)

Hopelessly in love,
And am loved hopelessly in turn,
Signora.

GIORGIO, CLARA
All this happiness—

FOSCA
You and I—

GIORGIO, CLARA
—Being here with you in the dark.

FOSCA
—Were not meant for each other.

GIORGIO, CLARA
So much happiness—

FOSCA
If I seemed to imply
Something more—

GIORGIO, CLARA
Even more than what I felt before!

FOSCA
—I apologize.

GIORGIO, CLARA
To feel your touch again—

FOSCA
But since we're forced to be
together—

GIORGIO, CLARA
—When so much time has passed—

FOSCA
—Let us try to face the fact.

GIORGIO, CLARA
To dream of you and then
To be with you again
And have some time at last . . .

FOSCA
Let us both behave with tact.

GIORGIO, CLARA
How long were we apart—

FOSCA
If this letter seems cold-hearted—

GIORGIO, CLARA
—A month, a week, a day?

FOSCA
—It conceals my own distress.
Nonetheless—

GIORGIO, CLARA
To feel your touch again . . .

Scene Five (Jere Shea and Marin Mazzie)

FOSCA
—We must end what never started.

GIORGIO, CLARA
You've never been away.

FOSCA
You must recognize—

CLARA
Still, I've missed you—

FOSCA
—There is nothing—

GIORGIO
(Putting his finger to Clara's lips)
Hush.

FOSCA
—Between us.

CLARA
—So much.

FOSCA
(Repeating to herself)
Nothing . . .

GIORGIO
Shhh.
I'm here now.

FOSCA
Nothing, nothing . . .

CLARA
Welcome home . . .

Clara and Giorgio begin to make love as the lights fade. Fosca, stone-faced, remains alone in her drawing room. She picks up a piece of needlepoint and begins working feverishly at it.

SCENE SIX

Giorgio returns and is summoned by Fosca, who coldly asks about his visit to Milan. On further questioning, she discovers that Clara is married and has a child, and informs him that they need never see each other again.

Three weeks pass, when the Doctor summons Giorgio and tells him that Fosca is mortally ill and is letting herself die because of her passion for him and his rejection of her. He urges him to go visit her at her sickbed, saying that it will save her life, even if just for a little while. Giorgio refuses to accept any guilt, but agrees to go and see her.

SCENE SEVEN

That evening, Giorgio visits Fosca in her bedroom. She talks softly and dreamily with him, then begs him to stay the night, just sitting on the bed with her. He consents, and at dawn starts to leave. She asks one last favor: Would he write a letter that she will dictate to him? He sits at the desk and takes up pen and paper.

FOSCA
(Slowly, dictating)
My dearest . . . Fosca.

He stops writing and looks at her, annoyed.

Please.

After a beat, he resumes writing.

GIORGIO
"My dearest Fosca . . ."

FOSCA
I wish I could forget you,
Erase you from my mind.
But ever since I met you,
I find
I cannot leave the thought of you
  behind.

(Quickly, as Giorgio looks up)

That doesn't mean I love you . . .

GIORGIO
(Writing)
"That doesn't mean I love you . . ."

FOSCA
I wish that I could love you . . .

Giorgio stops writing.

Please . . .

Giorgio shrugs, resumes.

I know that I've upset you.
I know I've been unkind.
I wanted you to vanish from sight,
But now I see you in a different
  light.
And though I cannot love you,
I wish that I could love you.

For now I'm seeing love
Like none I've ever known,
A love as pure as breath,
As permanent as death,
Implacable as stone.

A love that like a knife
Has cut into a life
I wanted left alone.
A love I may regret,
But one I can't forget.

I don't know how I let you
So far inside my mind,
But there you are and there you will
  stay.
How could I ever wish you away?
I see now I was blind.

And should you die tomorrow,
Another thing I see:
Your love will live in me.

There are only three "songs" in the score of *Passion* and this is the first of them. I didn't intend it to have a recognizable form—after all, it's another letter, and the letters throughout are fluid in structure: the line lengths vary and there are few rhymes, in order to make them truly discursive, the way letters tended to be in the nineteenth century. But as I started to write this one, fluidity felt wrong, and I finally figured out why. It's because this letter is a *calculated* one—not just carefully worded, as Giorgio's letter from Milan is, but planned by Fosca in advance as a keepsake. Regular rhythms and neat rhymes bespeak craft—as in crafty. That's why this letter is a song.

After Giorgio gives her the letter, Fosca asks him to kiss her. As he gives her a peck on the forehead, she pulls him to her and embraces him like a lover. Stunned and repelled, he pulls back. She starts to shake, then screams at him to leave, continuing to scream after he has gone.

SCENE EIGHT

The officers are gathered in the billiard room, playing pool.

TORASSO
Did you hear that scream last night?

AUGENTI
Did anybody not?

RIZZOLLI
Four-ball in the side.

COOK
She knows how to scream, all right.

BARRI
Well, she practices a lot.

You were helpful
Now I'm grateful

[I .... love you]

I'm glad I met you. I wish I could forget you. *Such as I have* More than what I've ever felt before.
I've come to feel things *I'm* I keep trying to forget you.
I've never felt before.

Thank you for upsetting me.
Thank you for not letting me

It's true
Yes, you've been a burden.
And yes, at times I've hated you. Something new in my life
But now I know I love you.

tidy I realize I love you. You broke the little circle of my life.
And if you went away *can* I never will forget you Until I met you
To think of you as gone Everything was neat
And should you die tomorrow Everything was ordered *orderly*
You'll still be in my heart. Everything in place
You'll still have changed my life. Everything had grace.
I'll never be the same (again).
And if I hear your name *certain of* I'm not sure of
But should if I never see you again Something's happening
dealt dwelt melt You've made me see things I've never seen Something difficult
There are things There are things Something's happening
I've been cruel I've been cruel Something different
There are things There are things To any thing I've felt before.
shaken I've wanted nothing more
Than for you to go away I'm aware of something *that*
convictions sentiments no peace But mysteriously But now Wonderful & terrible is
What I wanted before Beautiful that happening I realize it now
I don't want any more *All* Now my feelings have changed *are changing*
What I felt I don't feel My convictions have changed
What I thought I don't think
What I thought That I felt *confused & adrift* I'm becoming unmoored
I don't think That I feel (any more) I'm beginning to drift
All these attitudes melt
Are beginning to melt What you have done for me
Can never be undone

AUGENTI
Good shot.

RIZZOLLI
Six-ball in the corner.

COOK
So that wasn't dying, we assume.

BARRI
No, I think she just fell off her
broom.

TORASSO
Or they hung a mirror in the room
Of la Signora!

BARRI
La Signora!

AUGENTI
La Signora!

RIZZOLLI
Please, a little quiet!

*Giorgio enters. The others ask him if he
would care to join them. Politely, he de-
murs and leaves.*

TORASSO
Just a bit aloof, don't you think?

COOK
Not around the Colonel.

RIZZOLLI
Gentlemen, gentlemen . . .

AUGENTI
Never trust a man who doesn't
drink.

TORASSO
And he keeps a journal.

BARRI
Eight-ball off the nine.

RIZZOLLI
Maybe, though, he just prefers his
books.

COOK
Not as much as he prefers his looks.

TORASSO
Which is why he thinks he's got his
hooks
Into la Signora—

BARRI
Gentlemen, I'll make a wager:
Come the summer, he'll be major—

RIZZOLLI
I'll say!

OTHERS
I'll say!

ALL
I'll say!

SCENE NINE
(FLASHBACK)

*Giorgio and the Colonel are discovered
on one side of the stage. As the Colonel
thanks Giorgio for being so kind to his
cousin and aiding her recovery, Fosca
is revealed at her writing table on the
other side. Music continues underneath
throughout the sequence.*

FOSCA
My dear Giorgio. I am writing you
even though the Doctor has forbid-

Scene Eight

den it. What a joy to have someone to whom I can tell my feelings, with whom I can share my past.

COLONEL
I was a young man when my parents died and Fosca's mother and father welcomed me into their house whenever I was on leave.

As a child—

FOSCA
As a child—

COLONEL
She was lonely—

FOSCA
I was happy—

COLONEL
Her parents doted on her—

FOSCA
My parents doted on me—

Fosca's Mother and Father enter.

COLONEL, FOSCA
They said:

MOTHER, FATHER
Beautiful.

MOTHER
So sensitive.

MOTHER, FATHER
So beautiful.

FOSCA
They told me to be:

MOTHER
Careful—

COLONEL
Of course—

MOTHER
—Fosca.

COLONEL
—To them she was.

FATHER
A girl as beautiful as you are
Has to—

FOSCA
And so—

FATHER
—Be careful.

FOSCA
I thought that I was beautiful.

FOSCA, COLONEL
And then I (she) reached the age
Where being beautiful
Becomes the most important thing
A woman can be.

COLONEL
An unattractive man—

FOSCA
As long as you're a man,
You still have opportunities.

COLONEL
(Simultaneously)
—Can still have opportunities.

MOTHER, FATHER
Beautiful.

COLONEL, FOSCA
Whereas, if you're a woman,
You either are a daughter or a wife.

MOTHER, FATHER
A woman is a flower.

COLONEL, FOSCA
You marry—

FATHER
—Now you're seventeen.

COLONEL
—Or you're a daughter all your life.

MOTHER, FATHER
Now is the hour . . .

COLONEL
I'd met this nice young man.

FOSCA
I'd seen this nice young man—

COLONEL
He'd introduced himself—

FOSCA
—Passing by—

COLONEL
—At my club.

FOSCA
—Just below my window.

COLONEL
So—

FOSCA
One day—

COLONEL
—One evening I invited him—

FOSCA
—He tipped his hat to me.

COLONEL
—Home.

He brings a young man over to Fosca's Mother and Father; Giorgio stands to one side and observes.

Count Ludovic—

FOSCA
I must admit that I was flattered—

COLONEL
This is my aunt Theresa and my uncle Bruno.

MOTHER
A count?

FATHER
From where, if I may ask.

LUDOVIC
Austria.

FATHER, MOTHER
(Thrilled)
Austria . . .

MOTHER
What a beautiful place.

COLONEL
(*Calling*)
Fosca, we have a visitor!

FOSCA
Imagine my surprise . . .

COLONEL
I'd like you to meet a new friend.
Count Ludovic.

*Ludovic takes Fosca's hand and
kisses it.*

FOSCA
He was even more handsome up
close.

COLONEL
I was amazed to see the Count take
such an interest in my cousin.

LUDOVIC
(*Floridly, to Fosca*)
If I had known you were here,
signorina—

FOSCA
"If he had known . . ." Of course he
knew.

LUDOVIC
—I would have brought you many
flowers.

COLONEL
If I had known . . .

LUDOVIC
You do like flowers?

FOSCA
Yes.

COLONEL
I should have known.

LUDOVIC
I've seen you at your window.

MOTHER
Won't you stay for dinner, Count?

FATHER
Do. Yes.

LUDOVIC
I've watched you every day since I
arrived.

FOSCA
I had my suspicions.

COLONEL
I had no suspicion.

FOSCA
I chose not to see.

LUDOVIC
The way you move,
The way you gaze at the sky . . .

FOSCA
For love had made me blind—

COLONEL
How could I be so blind?

FOSCA
—Or what I took for love.

COLONEL
Within a month, he had asked for
her hand.

GIORGIO
Signora Fosca has been married?

COLONEL
Yes.

FATHER, MOTHER
Austria . . .
Count Ludovic of Austria . . .

FOSCA
I sensed in him a danger,
Deception,
Even violence.
I must admit to some degree
That it excited me.

FATHER, MOTHER
Austria . . .
Count Ludovic of Austria . . .

COLONEL
Once they were married, once he'd
received my uncle's sizable dowry,
he traveled a great deal, was unavailable to Fosca.

FOSCA
He gambled away the dowry.

COLONEL
It didn't take him long to spend all
their money.

FOSCA
I was forced to go to my parents to
borrow from what little savings
they had left.

COLONEL
Then one day, as she was coming
from market . . .

Ludovic's Mistress suddenly appears.

MISTRESS
Excuse me? You're the wife of a
Count Ludovic?

FOSCA
Yes.

MISTRESS
You fool!
The man's a fraud,
A fake.
The trips he said he had to take
Abroad,
He took them so that he
Could be
With me.

He calls himself a count,
But he's not.
He's never had a title in his life!
He doesn't have a title,
But he does have a wife
And a child
In Dalmatia.

FOSCA
No, you must be mistaken.

MISTRESS
Oh, yes.

He only wants to bleed you—
Until the day he doesn't need you.
I warn you he'll abandon you
As he abandoned her
And me,
And countless others, I've no doubt.

I'm telling you, the man was born without
A heart.

You fool . . .

FOSCA
I confronted him with this information, and he made no attempt to deny it.

LUDOVIC
(Shrugging, pleasantly)
Ah well, at last you know the truth, Signorina.
But you as well must face the truth.
I've no desire to deceive you anymore,
But do admit what you ignore:
We made a bargain, did we not?
And we got
What we bargained for.

You gave me your money, I gave you my looks
And my charm,
And my arm.
I would say that more than balances the books.
Where's the harm?
Now it's through.

If women sell their looks,
Why can't a man,
If he can?
Besides, the money wasn't even yours,
It belonged to those ridiculous old bores,
Your parents.

Fosca starts to strike him, but he catches her arm.

Forgive me, my dear,
But though you are no beauty, I fear
You are not quite the victim you appear.

Well, let us part by mutual consent
And be content.
And so good luck and goodbye.
I must go.

(Starts off, turns back)

Oh, and yes, we haven't paid the rent
Since July.
Just so you know . . .

He exits, as music continues underneath.

FOSCA
I returned home, to find my parents impoverished and in poor health.

COLONEL
Fosca's health failed . . .

FOSCA
(Bitter)
A woman's like a flower . . .

She returns to her writing desk.

COLONEL
She began to suffer her first convulsions. My aunt and uncle nursed her as best they could.

FOSCA
A flower's only purpose is to please . . .

COLONEL
I spent months looking for the man.

FOSCA
Beauty is power . . .

COLONEL
By then, of course, he'd vanished.

FOSCA
Longing a disease . . .

COLONEL
To this day, I dream of finding him and realizing my revenge.

FOSCA
My father died not long thereafter.

COLONEL
How could I be so blind?

FOSCA
I couldn't face the world.

COLONEL
It took her many months to leave her bed.

FOSCA
(Simultaneously)
It took me months to leave my bed.

COLONEL
When her mother died, she had nothing, really. No one.

FOSCA
And so I went to stay with my cousin, who in some way felt responsible for my circumstances.

COLONEL
Why could I not admit the truth?
How could I not have seen through the veneer?
I told myself, "As long as she seems happy,
Why interfere?"
Or was I just relieved to know
That somebody would want her for a wife?
In war you know the enemy,
Not always so in life.

The enemy was love—
Selfishness really, but love.
All of us blinded by love
That makes everything seem possible.

You have to pay a consequence
For things that you've denied.
This is the thorn in my side.

The Mistress, Mother, Father and Ludovic appear in tableau.

MISTRESS
As long as you're a man,
You're what the world will make of you.

MISTRESS, MOTHER
Whereas if you're a woman,
You're only what it sees.

COLONEL, FATHER, LUDOVIC
A woman is a flower
Whose purpose is to please.

p. 7

insatiable all-devouring
hungry ravenous
endless
constant sort of
unremitting
limitless
pursuing
relentless(ness)
maniacal
obsessive(ness)
depending
infect
fill
taint
choke
drown
needliness)
jar
rot
flue new

Scene 9 – Giorgio

Not a snare
I don't care

You blackmail me with talk of death
You are in love with death!
You want me and everyone as dead as you. Ugliness is no excuse
You cannot make me feel anything for you. Not even hatred.
I feel nothing... nothing...
I don't want you to go away. Or to stay. I don't care.
Just leave me alone
I deserve more pity than you do. I have none for you any more
You are entirely selfish, self-involved. You care for nothing but your own feelings
Yes, do die and leave me alone.
They never have dreams, you have nothing but the music of yourself
And your pain
You speak to me of love
You drag me with words like loneliness
Suffering
4 You think that this is love?
Do you think this is love
1 Is this what you call
You really call this love?
I call it hate.
You don't love me, you hate me

Everywhere I turn,
You are there
There you are
You are there! Everywhere
Let me be! Let me alone.
Leave me be! Leave me alone.
2 This (seemingly) insatiable endless and
3 Smothering pursuit of me
You are everything that's joyless,
Everything that's dead!
I am sorry for you.
But I am not the cause
Of your ugliness.

What have I did done to deserve this
You're as selfish self-involved as a beautiful woman

This is the opposite of love

You just want what you can't have

You, you, you!
You think of nothing but yourself,
Your needs, your pain
You smother me blackmail
You wallow in your suffering spray me with
This wallowing blackmail in loneliness
Misery
That's your idea of love
You can't be that naive!
You think that you're magic!
You threaten me with love

Don't you understand?
I want to be alone.

You are death!
You are blackness!
You are walking living despair!

I am not responsible
I will not be responsible

ALL (EXCEPT GIORGIO AND FOSCA)
Beauty is power,
Longing a disease . . .

SCENE TEN

Giorgio is sitting on a rock near a trail on the mountainside, a distance from the outpost, reading a letter from Clara. Clara stands on one side of the stage.

CLARA
Giorgio,
I stand here
Staring at the sunrise,
Thinking how we've never seen a
    sunrise together,

Thinking that the sunrise
Only means another day
Without you,
And thinking:

Can our love survive
So much separation,
Keep itself alive,
Much less thrive?

A faint rumbling of thunder.

If only you were here,
If I could feel your touch,
I wouldn't have such fear.
If only we had more than letters

Holding us together,
If we just could hold each other now,
The sunrise then could be
A thing that I could see
And merely think, "How
    beautiful . . ."

CLARA, GIORGIO
(As Clara exits)
Giorgio,
I now sit
Staring at the mirror—
You may not believe it but I swear,
As I stare,
There it is,
Plain as day:
A gray
Hair,

GIORGIO
Of which I was unaware,
Which is more than I can bear,
Which I'm ripping out right now
And am sending on to you
As a milestone of my age,
As a turning of the page . . .

He removes a hair from the folds of the letter.

Perhaps when next we meet,
I'll be a sorry sight.
You won't know who I am.
My hair completely white,
My face
A mass of wrinkles.

What will you feel then,
My Giorgio?
Time is now our enemy . . .

Fosca enters unsteadily and forces Giorgio to have a conversation, complaining that he has been avoiding her. She admits knowing what she is doing to him but insists he give her a kiss. When he refuses, she grabs his hand and starts kissing it. He pulls away, agitated.

GIORGIO
Is this what you call love?
This endless and insatiable
Smothering
Pursuit of me,
You think that this is love?

(Softly, attempting to control himself)

I'm sorry that you're lonely,
I'm sorry that you want me as
    you do.
I'm sorry that I fail to feel
The way you wish me to feel,

(Growing in anger)

I'm sorry that you're ill,
I'm sorry you're in pain,
I'm sorry that you aren't beautiful.

(Evenly)

But yes, I wish you'd go away
And leave me alone!

(Quietly; intense)

Everywhere I turn,
There you are.
This is not love,
But some kind of obsession.

Will you never learn
When too far is too far,
Have you no concern
For what *I* feel,
What *I* want?

Love is what you earn
And return
When you care for another
So much that the other's

Helen Hobson as Clara (Queen's Theatre, London, 1996)

ABOVE: *Maria Friedman and Michael Ball (Queen's Theatre, London, 1996)*

BELOW: *Elena Roger and David Thaxton (Donmar Warehouse, London, 2010)*

Set free.
Don't you see?
Can't you understand?

Love's not a constant demand,
It's a gift you bestow.
Love isn't sudden surrender,
It's tender and slow.
It must grow.

(Increasingly angry)

Yet everywhere I go,
You appear,
Or I know
You are near.
This is not love,
Just a need for possession.

Call it what you will,
This is not love,
This is the reverse,
Like a curse,
Something out of control.
I've begun to fear
For my soul . . .

A loud clap of thunder. Trembling, Fosca rises and begins to leave, then shudders momentarily and with a muffled cry crumples to the ground. Giorgio turns and sees her lying there; he crosses past her and begins to exit. He stops, pauses for a moment, then reluctantly returns to her, covering her with his coat. He picks her up and carries her offstage.

During the first week of previews, audiences were astonishingly hostile to the show, and this scene was the focus of their disaffection. It drew sniggers, when there weren't snorts, of laughter; the climax came at one performance when after Fosca's collapse, someone from the back of the house shouted to Giorgio, "Why don't you just leave her there?" followed by a hearty round of applause. It became distressingly clear to James and me that although contemporary audiences could enthusiastically accept the notion of an attractive and charming female stalker (Glenn Close in *Fatal Attraction*, for

example) they simply wouldn't accept an unattractive charmless one, especially one given to convenient hysterical fits. They were even more impatient and irritated with her than Giorgio was. I suspect that what bothered them most was how extreme her behavior was, the lengths she went to, her shamelessness—all the things that for James and me ennobled her. It was the moments of opera-sized melodrama that embarrassed them. James and I had experienced something similar during the previews of *Sunday in the Park with George*, but we were still disconcerted and dismayed. We accepted the audience's consistent verdict, however, and as I said earlier, took each of these treacherous moments in turn and cooled it down, reducing the extravagance without, we hoped, eviscerating it. By the end of the first week, there was no more unwanted laughter and, more important, Donna didn't have to go onstage fearing a barrage of flying verbal tomatoes.

I have always attended previews afraid of audience reactions, and often with reason, especially when the previews take place in New York. The desire for failure emanating from people who presumably love musicals is persistently baffling to me. I love to spout my sometimes barbed opinions as much as anybody (and not just on musicals), but I would still rather see a good show than a bad one—unlike many of the show buffs who crowd into early previews, as any theatrical chat room on the Internet demonstrates. I remember a vivid example which I witnessed when *Company* was about to open after its tryout in Boston, where it had received mixed reviews. I was standing on line at the box office to pick up some tickets when I overheard the man in front of me turn to his friend and say, bubbling with excitement, "I hear it's the worst show ever!" "Me too!" the friend cried enthusiastically. They could not have been more thrilled than they were spending their hard-earned money for the pleasure (they hope) of seeing a disaster.

Preview audiences are valuable if you can keep a cool head and not overreact to their overreactions, both good and bad, but it's hard to resist a stroll around the lobby during intermission trolling for overheard compliments (not a temptation with *Passion*, which had no intermission). My advice is, don't: you hear only bad news. Jule Styne was doing just that—eavesdropping—during intermission at a preview of *Funny Girl* and overheard the following exchange between a nicely dressed middle-aged couple, exactly the kind of people he hoped the show would reach:

HE
So what do you think?

SHE
The first act is terrific, but the second is terrible.

HE
We haven't seen the second act yet.

SHE
(Shrugging)
I heard.

SCENE ELEVEN

The Soldiers gossip as they drill on the parade ground.

TORASSO
Both of them were soaked to the skin.

RIZZOLLI
Where had they been?

AUGENTI
On the bluff.

COOK
Were they all alone?

TORASSO
No one knows.

COOK
You don't suppose—?

BARRI
Ugh!

RIZZOLLI
Gentlemen, enough!

TORASSO
Still, it would explain Signora's
attitude—

AUGENTI
Why she comes to every meal.

BARRI
It isn't for the veal.

TORASSO
And it would explain the Colonel's
gratitude.

COOK
I hear he calls him "Giorgio"—

RIZZOLLI
But nobody is *that* brave.

AUGENTI
No, that's cheek.

RIZZOLLI
Nobody is *that* brave.

COOK
Wouldn't you like to peek?

TORASSO
Ugh!

BARRI
Gentlemen, I think I'll change my
wager:
He'll be Major
Next week!

RIZZOLLI
I'll say!

ALL (EXCEPT RIZZOLLI)
I'll say!

ALL
I'll say!

SCENE TWELVE

*Giorgio falls ill from having carried
Fosca back in the rain and the Doctor
gives him forty days' sick leave to go to
Milan. A blanket around his shoulders,
he moves slowly into a train compart-
ment, as Clara appears at the side of
the stage.*

CLARA
Giorgio, darling,
Forty days' leave so soon!
Imagine that,
A whole forty days—
Well, forty matinees.
I'll be there to greet the train
That carried you away from me
Because it brings you home.

I'm filling up the room,
Our little room,
With every flower in bloom.
I'll have the fire lit,
The table set,
I'll wear the blue chemise.

And once we're in our room,
Our secret room,
Where I'll be able to care for you,
Kiss you,
Embrace you,
Be there for you . . .

*She exits. The train whistle blows and
just as the train starts to move, Fosca
enters, carrying a small suitcase. She
announces that she intends to follow
him to Milan, that she will stay out of
his way but always be nearby. He tells
her it will do no good, that it will not
make him love her, that he has no feelings for her, that she has to give him up.*

*GIORGIO
(Quietly, pleading)
Do you know what I feel?
I used to feel respect for you,
Sympathy,
A tenderness.
You know what I feel now?

(Still quiet, almost tender)

I've never felt such anger,
I've never felt such terror and
despair.

The only thing I feel for you is pity.
Soon I won't care.

I couldn't love you then,
I cannot love you now.
Accept it, I will never love you.

And why did you choose me to love?
Please . . .
Leave me alone . . . *

FOSCA
Loving you
Is not a choice,
It's who I am.

Loving you
Is not a choice
And not much reason
To rejoice,
But it gives me purpose,
Gives me voice,
To say to the world:

This is why I live.
You are why I live.

Loving you
Is why I do
The things I do.
Loving you
Is not in my
Control.
But loving you,
I have a goal
For what's left of my life . . .

I will live,
And I would die
For you.

"Loving You" was written during previews to give Giorgio, and the audience, a moment of empathy with
Fosca, a moment to understand her
behavior and find her sympathetic,
but without sentimentalizing her. That
moment clearly belonged in the train
scene, because it's the turning point
for Giorgio. More important, we
wanted the audience to understand

---

*The passage between asterisks was cut
during rehearsals and distilled into two sentences of dialogue.

why he begins to turn, to empathize with his empathy, so to speak. It turned out to be a turning point not only for Giorgio, but for the show, just as "Children and Art" and "Lesson #8" had been for *Sunday in the Park with George.*

Giorgio takes Fosca back to the post rather than continuing on to Milan. The Doctor is appalled at the change in Giorgio and commands him to go to Milan and take his sick leave. Giorgio replies that he must stay, that it is his duty to help Fosca. The Doctor insists that no one can help her and threatens to have Giorgio transferred to another post if he doesn't take his leave.

The Doctor exits and the Soldiers enter drunkenly. They quiet down when they see Giorgio, who acknowledges them and then exits.

TORASSO
Forty days—!

COOK
Where does he get all the luck?

TORASSO
Forty days—!

RIZZOLLI
The man is sick.

TORASSO
But forty days—!

BARRI
Yes, he's sick of being stuck
In the sticks.

AUGENTI
Who isn't?

TORASSO
In Milan—!

COOK
He's gone
Because it's getting pretty thick
With the Signora.

RIZZOLLI
Gentlemen—

AUGENTI
He'd better get out quick
From the Signora.

RIZZOLLI
Gentlemen—

BARRI
That's not an easy trick
With the Signora.

RIZZOLLI
(*Loudly*)
Gentlemen!

They turn to him.

RIZZOLI
You know what I think?

OTHERS
What?

RIZZOLI
We need another drink!

COOK
I'll say.

RIZZOLLI
I'll say!

ALL
I'll say! I'll say!

SCENE THIRTEEN

Clara and Giorgio stroll from the Milan train station to a bench nearby.

CLARA
Giorgio,
I didn't tell you in my letter
Something even better,
A surprise here at home:
In a week my husband goes to
    Rome.
It's the first time he's away,
He'll be gone at least a day,
Maybe two or even three.

I can visit you at night,
We'll be lighted by the moon,
Not a shuttered afternoon.

Just think of having time
That we can call our own,
Together and alone.
Perhaps we'll take a drive
Into the country,
And perhaps at last
We'll share a sunrise.
Wouldn't that be beautiful—?

Giorgio tells Clara that he is forgoing his forty-day leave and returning to the post, assuring her that he loves her, but telling her that Fosca needs him more. If Clara would leave her husband, it would be a different matter, but she can't, so they are at an impasse.

SCENE FOURTEEN

A few days later, during a Christmas Eve party at the post, Giorgio receives a letter from Clara; at the same time the Colonel receives a letter ordering Giorgio back to headquarters in Milan immediately. Giorgio is startled; he realizes that the Doctor has maneuvered the transfer. Fosca, hysterical, rushes to Giorgio, throws herself into his arms and begs him not to go. Everyone in the room stares at her, stunned. Mortified, she runs out, followed by the Colonel, who is infuriated with Giorgio and commands him to stay in the room. Giorgio pauses in confusion, then crosses to a chair and sits, staring off into space. Clara enters.

CLARA
Giorgio . . .

(*He continues staring*)

Giorgio . . .

Suddenly he remembers Clara's letter; he opens it and begins to read.

I am writing to you,
My angel,
Though not long since you've been
    gone,
With a most unhappy heart.

Because, in truth, as time goes on,
I think of nothing else but you—
And us.

Oh, my love, my sweet,
You've changed,
I've watched you change.
You're not the man I thought I knew.

At times, these past few days
        together,
I would wonder whether
You were here,
Really here with me.

I thought, was I naive
To believe
We'd continue year by year?
Is it over forever?

*In her letter, she goes on to ask him to
wait until her son is grown enough to
go off to school, and then she will leave
her husband.*

GIORGIO
(Bitterly, quietly)
Just another love story.

CLARA
No one is to blame.

GIORGIO
A temporary love story.

CLARA
But it needn't end the same.

GIORGIO
I thought that we had more.

CLARA
We had more—

GIORGIO
We had something more—

BOTH
—Than any other love story.

CLARA
All that happiness—

GIORGIO
(Looking at the letter)
Is this what you call love?

CLARA
—We had then—

GIORGIO
This logical and sensible,
Practical arrangement—

CLARA
(Overlapping)
We can have that happiness—

GIORGIO
—This foregone conclusion—

CLARA
—Once again!

GIORGIO
—You think that this is love?

*(His voice rising, as he crumples the
letter)*

Love isn't so convenient.
Love isn't something scheduled in
        advance,
Not something guaranteed
You need
For fear it may pass you by.
You have to take a chance,
You can't just try it out.
What's love unless it's
        unconditional?

Love doesn't give a damn about
        tomorrow,
And neither do I!

CLARA
All that happiness—

GIORGIO
It was fine.

CLARA
—In the past—

GIORGIO
I was yours, you were mine.

CLARA
That was not just happiness,
Love was in that happiness,
That's why it will last.

GIORGIO
Love is more, I want more.

BOTH
I thought I knew what love was—

CLARA
I didn't know that love was a
        complication.

GIORGIO
I do know that it's not a negotiation.

CLARA
We'll take it in our stride.

GIORGIO
What we had—

CLARA
You decide.

GIORGIO
—Wasn't bad.

CLARA
We could have everything.
I want you more than anything.

GIORGIO
How sad—

CLARA
To wait is nothing.
We're young, and time is nothing.

GIORGIO
—That what we have is nothing . . .

CLARA
Nothing . . .

BOTH
Nothing . . .

*The Colonel discovers the letter that
Fosca dictated to Giorgio in her bedroom, accuses him of compromising
her and challenges him to a duel. Giorgio does not reveal that she made him
write it and accepts the challenge. The
Doctor tries to persuade Giorgio to tell
the Colonel the truth, but Giorgio refuses, not only saying that he wants to
protect Fosca but also demanding that
the Doctor arrange for him to see her
immediately. The Doctor protests that
she is too ill, but Giorgio insists.*

GIORGIO
Don't you see what she's endured,
        Doctor,
What this woman has endured?

My rejection, my disgust,
My indifference, my anger, my
    contempt—
And yes, my ugliness.
What that woman has endured,
    Doctor . . .

No one has ever loved me
As that woman has.
No one has truly loved me
Til Fosca,

Love without reason,
Love without mercy,
Love without pride or shame,
Love unconcerned
With being returned,
No wisdom, no judgment,
No caution, no blame.

No one has ever known me
As that woman has.
No one has ever shown me
What love could be like
Until now.
I was wrong, I was wrong . . .

I was wrong.
Love's a demand,
I was wrong.
Love needn't grow.
Love can be sudden surrender,
Not tender,
Not slow,
And I know
Now that

I love Fosca,
Not the way that she loves me,
But I love Fosca—
And nothing can come of it!

And if I should die tomorrow,
Or live and be forced to go,
No one has truly loved her
Like me,
And I want her to know.

*This song is an expansion of the one
below and was written for the London
production. I wanted Giorgio to make a
grand statement of his realization before going to Fosca's room. James felt
that it was grandiloquent, but we tried
it anyway. I liked it, he didn't.*

SCENE FIFTEEN

*Fosca is resting in her bedroom. Qui-
etly, Giorgio enters. He explains that he
had nothing to do with the transfer and
that the affair between him and Clara
is over. Instead of being pleased, Fosca
says she is sorry to hear it. She does not
want him to be unhappy.*

GIORGIO
I feel so much . . . but I'm not
really sad.

FOSCA
I thought you loved Clara?

GIORGIO
I did love Clara. I did, but . . .

(Quietly at first)

No one has ever loved me
As deeply as you.
No one has truly loved me
As you have, Fosca.

(Stronger)

Love without reason,
Love without mercy,
Love without pride or shame.
Love unconcerned
With being returned—
No wisdom, no judgment,
No caution, no blame.

No one has ever known me
As clearly as you.
No one has ever shown me
What love could be like until now:

Not pretty or safe or easy,
But more than I ever knew.
Love within reason—that isn't love.
And I've learned that from you . . .

He sees her trembling.

Are you cold?

FOSCA
No, I'm afraid.

GIORGIO
Of what?

FOSCA
All this happiness,
Coming when there's so little time.
Too much happiness,
More than I can bear.

*Giorgio admits that he has come to love
her, as she predicted. She draws him to
the bed. Giorgio resists, the Doctor
having told him that making love
would be too much of a strain on her
fragile health. But she tells him that "to
die loved is to have lived" and he gently
falls to the bed with her.*

The consummation of Fosca and Giorgio's story is the most extraordinary
scene in Scola's movie. At the moment
of orgasm he photographs Fosca's face
in extreme close-up. Instead of being
transformed into something beautiful,
as one might expect in a fable of this
kind, she is uglier and more grotesque
than ever, her skin more sallow, her
eyes more staring, her ecstatic smile
emphasizing her skull-like look. She
is more herself than she has ever been
and the moment is shocking and joyful
and thrilling all at once. When I first
started to plan the score, I wanted to
open the show with Clara's orgasmic
scream and close it with Fosca's. Unfortunately, there was still a duel to
be dealt with.

SCENE SIXTEEN

*Giorgio and the Colonel fight a duel
with pistols, each firing one shot
simultaneously. Giorgio is in a daze,
disheveled and numb and not concentrating on his aim, but he hits the
Colonel, who falls to the ground. When
he sees this, he lets out a high-pitched
howl, reminiscent of Fosca's screams,
and collapses.*

SCENE SEVENTEEN

*A hospital. Giorgio, almost catatonic,
sits at a desk. A nurse enters and brings
him a box with a letter. It is from the*

Doctor, wishing Giorgio a steady recovery from his breakdown. He reports that Fosca died three days after their night together and that the Colonel has recovered from his wounds. He encloses with the letter a box which contains some of Fosca's personal belongings and a letter she wrote to Giorgio just prior to her death. As Giorgio goes through the box, he summons up the past.

BARRI, RIZZOLLI, TORASSO
The town, it is remote, isn't it?
And provincial—
Don't you think?

CLARA
(Overlapping)
I'm filling up our room,
Our little room,
With every flower in bloom.
I'll have the fire lit,
The table set,
I'll wear the blue chemise.

LUDOVIC
(Overlapping)
The time has come to face the truth,
  Signorina.

ATTENDANTS
(Overlapping)
This sterile little town,
These pompous little men . . .

COOK, AUGENTI, SOLDIERS
(Overlapping)
Military madness . . .

WOMEN
Military madness . . .

COOK, AUGENTI, SOLDIERS,
ATTENDANTS
(Overlapping)
Uniforms, uniforms . . .

CLARA
(Overlapping)
Imagining your fingers touching
  mine.
Imagining our room,
The bed,
The secrecy,
The world outside,
Your mouth on mine . . .

COLONEL
(Overlapping)
An unattractive woman
Is easily deceived . . .

Giorgio picks up Fosca's letter, opens it and starts to read. Music continues underneath.

GIORGIO
My dearest Giorgio. The end is near. The time has come for me to surrender life gracefully. These past two days since you have left, since we were together, have been a revelation.

Now at last
I see what comes
From feeling loved.
Strange, how merely
Feeling loved,
You see things clearly.

Fosca's voice quietly begins to join his from offstage.

GIORGIO, FOSCA
Things I feared,
Like the world itself,
I now love dearly.

Fosca enters and crosses to him.

I want to live.
Now I want to live—

FOSCA
—Just from being loved.

All that pain
I nursed inside
For all those years . . .

GIORGIO
All that vain
And bitter self-concern . . .

BOTH
All those tears
And all that pride
Have vanished into air . . .

FOSCA
I don't want to leave.

GIORGIO
Now that I am loved—

FOSCA
—I don't want to leave.

BOTH
Everywhere I turn,
You are there.

FOSCA
Everywhere I look,
Things are different.

BOTH
Everything seems right,
Everything seems possible,
Every moment bursts with feeling.

Why is love so easy to give
And so hard to receive?

FOSCA
But though I want to live,
I now can leave
With what I never knew:
I'm someone to be loved.

GIORGIO
I'm someone to be loved.

FOSCA
And that I learned from you.

The company becomes visible behind them.

ALL
I don't know how I let you
So far inside my mind,
But there you are, and there you will
  stay.
How could I ever wish you away?
I see now I was blind.

FOSCA
And should you die tomorrow,
Another thing I see:

GIORGIO
Your love will live in me . . .

FOSCA
Your love will live in me . . .

GIORGIO, GROUP 1
Your love will live in me . . .

FOSCA, GROUP 2
Your love will live in me . . .

GIORGIO, GROUP 1
Your love will live in me . . .

FOSCA, GROUP 2
Your love will live in me . . .

GIORGIO, GROUP 1
Your love will live in me . . .

FOSCA, GROUP 2
Your love will live in me . . .

GIORGIO
Your love will live in me . . .

FOSCA
Your love will live in me . . .

GIORGIO
Your love will live in me . . .

The company, Fosca last, leaves Giorgio alone at his desk as the lights fade to black.

As far as I know, *Passion* is the only epistolary musical ever written—that is, a musical whose story is not only developed through letters but one in which the emotional climaxes (Fosca's dictated letter, Clara's farewell letter and Fosca's final letter) are read rather than acted. This was part of the challenge that excited me about writing it: how to make something dramatic out of something inherently static. Fulfilled by James's theatrically inventive staging, the piece worked for me, but certainly not for everyone. As the hostility during previews indicated, the story struck some audiences as ridiculous. They refused to believe that any-one, much less the handsome and saintly Giorgio, could come to love someone so manipulative, relentless and menacing, not to mention physically repellent, as Fosca. As the perennial banality would have it, they couldn't "identify" with either of the main characters. The violence of their reaction, however, strikes me as an example of "The lady doth protest too much." I think they may have identified with Fosca and Giorgio all too readily and uncomfortably. The idea of a love that's pure, that burns with D. H. Lawrence's gemlike flame, emanating from a source so gnarled and selfish, is hard to accept. Perhaps they were reacting to the realization that we are all Fosca, we are all Giorgio, we are all Clara. Which, as far as I'm concerned, is what gives Tarchetti's stodgy novel and Scola's elegant movie such profound power.

The New York Times
Arts & Leisure

Sunday, March 20, 1994

Copyright © 1994 The New York Times

Section 2

Sondheim's
Passionate 'Passion'

Fred R. Conrad/The New York Times

Stephen Sondheim backstage at the Plymouth Theater—At 63, Mr. Sondheim says, "I'm happier now personally than I have ever been." It's not entirely luck, he says. "I think you have to be ready for things."

5. Wise Guys/Bounce/Road Show
A Saga in Four Acts

Act One · **Wise Guys** · The Reading (1998)

Book by John Weidman

The Notion

A chronicle of two brothers, Wilson and Addison Mizner, who were born in the 1880s and died in the 1930s. Wilson was a con man, entrepreneur and wit, among other semi-accomplishments; Addison was chiefly an architect. Their personalities were polar opposites, but their relationship was intense and complicated. The show charts their lives from their beginnings in Benicia, California, through their adventures in the Klondike gold fields of the 1890s to the extremes of New York City society in the early 1900s and into the Florida real estate boom and bust of the 1920s, for which they were largely responsible.

General Comments

I graduated from Williams College in 1950, having received the Hutchinson Prize for Music, a stipend of $3,000 a year for two years, money which I used to study composition with the composer Milton Babbitt in New York City. It was a good, if not great, sum in those days, and I had the blessing of being able to live rent-free at home with my father and stepmother, both of whom I loved. But although my father was proud of my being awarded the prize, he disapproved of my not having a salaried job and made it clear that he wouldn't pay for any of the other basics, such as laundry, dentist and food, with the healthy result that after two years my money had run out and I was forced to find gainful employment, which I did as a co-scripter of the television series *Topper.* I had written a couple of moderately promising unproduced TV scripts, and

they proved good enough to qualify me for the job. My collaborator and boss on *Topper* was George Oppenheimer, a former contract scenarist at MGM and an expert in the craft of writing screenplays. We worked in Los Angeles and I learned a lot about both Los Angeles and screenplays, but after five months, when I'd earned enough to return to New York and rent an apartment for a year (the point of the exercise), I flew back home just as fast as American Airlines could carry me. It was on that flight that I read a pair of articles in *The New Yorker* which struck me as rich material for a musical and which became a sporadic, if mild, obsession—more like an ache than a fever—for much of the rest of my writing life.

The articles were written by Alva Johnston and comprised excerpts from a soon to be published book titled *The Legendary Mizners,* an exaggerated biography (Johnston was a fanciful reporter) of Wilson and Addison Mizner, two flamboyantly eccentric brothers who had a minor cultural and economic impact on this country. What intrigued me was not so much the zeitgeist of the period as the character of Wilson, a brilliant and shifty fellow who, during a colorful life, was at times a gold miner, a saloon keeper, a prize fighter, a cardsharp, a con man, manager of a hotel for criminals as well as the manager of the world's welterweight champion, a celebrated Broadway playwright, the husband of one of the richest women in America, a raconteur known for his wit, an entrepreneur majorly responsible for the Florida real estate boom and bust of the 1920s, a drunk, a cocaine addict, a notorious womanizer and, finally, a Hollywood hack (and a successful one, too). He was a man of numerous gifts, none of them focused, none of them fruitfully equal to their potential. His life was the story of someone with too many talents and too few principles, most of which were skewed anyway but

Guatemala? (W 13, Ad 17)   The theory of the smashed
Shift A's SF adventures (ch. I) to NY later.   hand of "Roebuck device"?
A's Oriental career as a Dancer?   (p. 130,
STRUCTURE OF THE SHOW IN LETTERS? (to allow for "incident
                                        vignettes" + jumps in chronology,
                                            as well as scene-changes?)

1.   Tea — young girl + Ork. Chorus.
                                                        Ballads - p. 206
Belle?   Wilson's letters betraying the truth, with add jobs. P. 142,
(cf. p. 73)   End in Klondike.   Magic Lantern singer
                                                            p. 161
2.   Journey to the Yukon. P. 89 on.   on.
p. 17 on
2a   Addison ~~Kearns~~ enters Klondike (Nome) - W pretends not to
            know him. p. 100 Ad plays along. Edgar + Wm.?
            W takes (Sid) under his wing, teaches him crime.
p. 142-between   Nellie (Belle? Rena?). Rena (p. 88) Willus Britt
p. 100 fight.   Sid-Kearns (prizefighter kid and object of W's immoral
                chiseling lessons in gold-weighing, etc.)
                p. 102-3 con game with Rena

3. ~~Addison (stuff) (Rena)~~

4.   Meeting of Mrs. Yerkes (p. 106) Ballads - cf. p. 206.
        Marriage. Interviews with reporters.   Training of fighter
        Arguments. Valet (boy in Klondike?)   (p. 137 on)
?. 5. Offer to clear debris. No.
6. Run a hotel, with friend's backing. Addison
        designs the bar. Manager is his valet.
        Also p. 159 on.
7. Playwright. First one a flop, but his own with
    Bronson-Howard (fight). also p. 166 on. Opium.
8. Psyke episode (Dance?) (p. 121)
    Man-about-town. Diamond Jim, Bet-a-million, etc.
    He is managing Ketchel, a society Cad. Silk shirt
                                                solvency?
    episode. (Friedlander's confidence in Mizner, distrust of
    Ketchel. The Champ (Mizner as a Con Man).

some of which were admirable. He was that prototypical romantic figure, the iconoclast rogue, a character which appeals to me a lot. But he was more interesting than the traditional loose cannon because of his relationship with his sidekick, his younger brother, Addison, who was himself a rogue, although of another kind.

Addison, after a briefly picaresque life all over the world, became an idiosyncratic architect without portfolio. In this guise he was largely responsible for changing the face and building up the image of southern Florida during the 1920s, in particular the Palm Beach area. He and Wilson developed and promoted Boca Raton, which they left unfinished but which turned into one of the major resorts of the twentieth century. Their closeness was intense, but in most ways they could not have been more different: Wilson the unashamedly public lover of heiresses and celebrities, Addison the closeted homosexual; Wilson the addicted gambler with underworld connections, Addison the obsessed social climber; Wilson the irresponsible cheat and lowlife, Addison the grandiose but moral artist; Wilson the destroyer, Addison the dreamer, Wilson the leader, Addison the follower. I found Wilson charming, but according to those who knew him (George Abbott, for one), he apparently was a slimy, manipulative, irredeemable bastard. This discovery not only didn't diminish my enthusiasm, it stimulated it.

Once I had returned to New York and plunked down the requisite two months' security on a two-bedroom apartment which I was going to share with a classmate from college, I bought a copy of Johnston's book *The Legendary Mizners,* planning to take an option on it. Having written an opening number (called "Benicia"), I discovered to my dismay that a few weeks earlier David Merrick (Broadway's most successful producer) and Irving Berlin had acquired the rights to turn it into a musical with a score by Berlin and a book by S. N. Behrman, one of the savviest playwrights of social comedy at the time. It was to star Bob Hope as Wilson and was to be called *A Sentimental Guy.* "So much for that," I thought with a heavy shrug and sigh, but years later when Merrick was co-producing *Gypsy,* and I asked him what had happened to the project, he replied that Berlin had written half a dozen songs, Behrman had sketched a few scenes and everyone had lost interest, so he, Merrick, had let his option on the book lapse. During the years that followed, I would occasionally think of the Mizner brothers, but each time I did so, another project would come along and steal my energy. Then, in 1993, fresh off the romantic gloom of *Passion* and wanting to write something jazzy and edgy, I mentioned the subject to John Weidman.

John had come to me with an idea for a show about the League of Nations, but interesting as it was, its immediate effect was to make me wonder why I had never brought the story of the Mizners to his attention. From our collaborations on *Pacific Overtures* and *Assassins,* I knew him to be a writer with both an abiding interest in the sociopolitical history of the United States and a sharp, mournful sense of humor about it; the Mizner chronicle touched on many aspects of the first and needed the approach of the second. I gave him Johnston's book and he was duly fascinated, but what sparked his interest was less Wilson than Addison and the symbiosis between the two.

Perhaps it was the Bob Hope connection to the Berlin/Merrick/Behrman musical, but it occurred to us that the tone of the show might be that of a "Road" movie. A "Road" movie back then did not describe an aimless cross-country car trip involving vividly eccentric supporting actors, as it does now—it described an aimless cross-country musical comedy involving Bob Hope and Bing Crosby, although the country crossed was a foreign one. They had made a string of hugely successful pictures in the 1940s, beginning with *Road to Singapore* and following it with titles like *Road to Zanzibar, Road to Morocco* and *Road to Bali,* each of which had a distinct stencil: a freewheeling picaresque in an outlandish locale chronicling the misadventures of two best friends/rivals: a bumbling patsy (Hope) and a suave sly trickster (Crosby), Hope being a popular comedian, Crosby being an even more popular crooner. This adroit concoction was devised to deliver a procession of slapstick incidents and comic duets, punctuated with romantic ballads delivered to and echoed by the leading lady of the series, Dorothy Lamour, Hollywood's reigning exotic but down-to-earth temptress.

It also occurred to us that such a procession was a kind of vaudeville. In fact, Hope and Crosby often began their misadventures as a team of out-of-work vaudevillians or a pair of medicine men using song and dance to sell their wares; we realized that they were a show business version of the Mizners. Once again Content reared its head and Dictated Form: the show would be presented as a vaudeville. We were well aware that metaphoric vaudeville had been used to tell stories before (*Love Life, Chicago, The Will Rogers Follies,* not to mention Brecht's nonmusicals) and was now something of a cliché, but there was apposite justification here: vaudeville had been born in the 1880s and died in the 1930s, as had the Mizners. Our show would be the story of Addison and Wilson, with Hope the pushover and Crosby the deceiver—a sharp, fast, stylish comical musical about two rascals, both gifted, one fatally corrupt. *The Road to Ruin.** In

---

* An entertaining irony in our plan was that Hope, conceived by Behrman and Berlin as Wilson the smoothie, was now to be Addison, the innocent.

the course of time, it evolved into many shows, each one having a distinct personality. As a playwright friend of John's pointed out, *Pacific Overtures, Assassins* and *Wise Guys* (subsequently, in different guises, *Bounce* and *Road Show*) made up in effect an unintended trilogy about this country: its aggressive tendencies, its culture of disenfranchisement and, embodied by the story of the Mizner brothers, its pioneering inventiveness and economic fecklessness.

Wise Guys was intended to be part of the Kennedy Center's twenty-fifth anniversary celebration, which was to take place in 1996, but it took longer to write than we had anticipated and was interrupted by such things as John's creating the book for the musical *Big* and my house burning down. It wasn't until early 1997 that we had a presentable draft and assembled a reading for a small audience of friends and colleagues. The cast included Victor Garber as Wilson and Patrick Quinn as Addison and was supervised by Lori Steinberg, a young director with whom we had worked during the production of *Assassins*. The score was only half finished, but the admittedly biased reception was encouraging enough for us to continue, and six months later we had another reading for another small audience, this time not only with Victor playing Wilson as brilliantly and edgily as he had the

first time, but with Nathan Lane playing Addison. Victor and Nathan looked nothing alike, but they were close friends and their rapport made them believable as brothers.

This second reading turned out to be even more encouraging than the first and led a year later to a third reading, this time with a completed score. Thus began a saga which might well constitute a book in itself, a saga in four acts: Act One an amalgam of the first three readings; Act Two a revision of it, still called *Wise Guys* (although temporarily titled *Gold!*), presented publicly in 1999 for a three-week run at the New York Theatre Workshop; Act Three a modification of it called *Bounce*, presented commercially in 2003 in Chicago and Washington; Act Four a transfiguration of it called *Road Show*, presented by the Public Theater for a limited run in 2008. It is a saga which took fourteen years to play itself out from first draft to last performance. Each incarnation of the show was significantly different from the one preceding, and here they all are. Comparing them will track the tortuous evolution of a musical from promising to derailed to fulfilled. It would be a more effective demonstration if the show had eventually been a hit and the story and songs were therefore familiar.* But you'll get the drift.

---

* Thanks to Nonesuch Records, *Bounce* and *Road Show* can still be heard.

ACT ONE

The stage is framed by a vintage vaudeville proscenium, typical of the 1930s. As the house lights dim, Addison Mizner, a large man in white tie and tails, sporting a top hat and cane, enters a stage-level box. A fanfare announces the beginning of an American Pageant, a series of tableaux vivants featuring important events and personalities of the new (i.e., twentieth) century, decade by decade. As the announcer says, these are the extraordinary American lives that helped shape America's destiny. After 1900–1910 (Theodore Roosevelt, J. P. Morgan, Jack Johnson), Wilson Mizner appears, drink in hand, and settles himself next to his brother. He too is in white tie and tails, also with top hat and cane. He is as tall as Addison, but a good deal less heavy. Addison grouses to him about his lateness as the 1910–1920 decade (Henry Ford, Woodrow Wilson, Alvin York) passes by, accompanied by Wilson's muttered wisecracks. Addison is excitedly awaiting the 1920s, which is the decade when he and Wilson flourished, but the only personalities mentioned are Knute Rockne, Irving Berlin and Charles Lindbergh.

As the next decade begins, Wilson, furious, chases the actors and stage manager off the stage as Addison clambers over the box rail and calls for the act curtain to come in. It is a brightly lit vaudeville olio, filled with generic American scenes: a beach with palm trees, a majestic Western landscape, the Great White Way, the frozen Yukon, and so on. The scenes are organized around a central image: a road disappearing into the distance.

Wilson joins Addison onstage and the two men stroll about, flourishing their hats and canes, vaudeville style.

First Vaudeville

WILSON
On my left—

ADDISON
On my right—

WILSON
Is a prince—

ADDISON
Is a jewel—

WILSON
Never arrogant or cruel—

ADDISON
Never dull or banal.

WILSON
He has heft—

ADDISON
He has height—

WILSON
But he's deft—

ADDISON
And he's witty—

WILSON
Not a morsel
Of self-pity—

ADDISON
Always boosting your morale.

BOTH
He's a gent in a way that
You'll find in no other,
And believe me, I don't say that
Just because he is my brother.

He's a prince, he's a jewel,
And he never needs renewal
As a partner,
As a critic,
As a pal.

BOTH
(Suddenly energetic)
You've heard of
Damon and Pythias—

WILSON
(Aside to Addison, surveying the audience)
I wouldn't count on it . . .

BOTH
—Hell of a pair.

You've heard of
Adam and Eve—

ADDISON
(Aside, also surveying)
Better . . .

BOTH
And, I believe,
Burke and Hare.

WILSON
(Aside)
Lost 'em there . . .

ADDISON
They were each other's very best friend.

WILSON
(Explaining to a woman in the front row)
Nineteenth-century grave robbers . . . British . . .

(Referring to her companion)

Are you with him?

ADDISON
They were each other's, written in stone.

(Yanks Wilson back)

BOTH
They were each other's, right to the end,
Darby and Joan . . .

ADDISON
(Aside)
Leave it alone . . .

BOTH
Forget your Damon and Pythias,
Forget your Darby and Joan.
Think more like table and chair,
Wear and tear,
Flesh and bone.

ADDISON
(Aside)
That's got 'em . . .

BOTH
And yet as
Close as they are,
Closer by far
Than any or all the above
Is brotherly love,
Brotherly love,
Brotherly love!

They resume strolling.

Just a couple of wise guys
On a highway called "life."
Just a couple of wise guys,
Without a kiddie or a wife.

Just a couple of wiseacres,
Heartbreakers,
Or as some would say, "bums."
Just a couple of Joes
Passing time as it goes,
Taking life as it comes.

Just a couple of dreamers
With a gleam in their eyes.
Just a couple of tramp steamers,
Hapless schemers
With no visible ties.

A pair of carefree wits
Who've had their mitts
In more than a couple of pies—
Just a couple of guys,
Cracking wise.

ADDISON
(As music continues underneath)
Speaking of people who called us
bums, did you hear? Henry died.*

WILSON
Henry who?

ADDISON
Big brother Henry.

WILSON
Which one was that, the banker,
the lawyer or the doctor?

---

* I've included more dialogue than usual, in
order to give the flavor of their banter.

ADDISON
The minister. Snapped off to the
Great Beyond.

WILSON
(Thoughtfully)
Henry dead . . .

(Suspiciously)

How can they tell?

ADDISON
He was even stiffer than when he
was alive.

(Pause)

You know, it's a shame.

WILSON
What?

ADDISON
You can choose your friends, but
you can't choose your relatives.

WILSON
I wish I'd said that.

ADDISON
You will.

WILSON
That you cribbed from Oscar
Wilde.

ADDISON
No, actually I cribbed it from
Whistler. Who said it to Wilde.

The music changes to a waltz clog.

WILSON
When your boat's up the creek—

ADDISON
And beginning to leak—

WILSON
That's the time you need—

BOTH
(Close harmony)
—Someone to trust.

ADDISON
When you don't have a crumb—

WILSON
When your life's on the bum—

ADDISON
You need—

BOTH
—Something or someone to trust.

Everyone has to have something to
    trust,
Trust is a must,
And that's fine.
Long as everyone's looking for
    something to trust,
There'll always be fish on the line.

WILSON
Reel 'em in!

ADDISON
Fish were meant to be netted.

WILSON
Reel 'em in! Reel 'em in!

ADDISON
Sheep were meant to be shorn.

WILSON
And that is how suckers get born.

ADDISON
(Searching through the audience,
    aside)
I think I see one.

WILSON
One? It's a veritable ocean out
there.

ADDISON
I mean a big one. Third row.

WILSON
The gink on the aisle?

ADDISON
Next to the old blonde.

WILSON
(Squinting)
Him? He could wear a demitasse
for a hat.

ADDISON
That's the trouble with you, Willie—all fish look alike. You can't discriminate between a minnow and a whale.

BOTH
Just a couple of wise guys—

WILSON
—From a little dumb town.

ADDISON
(With a vaudeville shuffle)
Plenty of fun
If you like sun . . .

BOTH
Just a couple of wise guys—

WILSON
—Who never seem to settle down.

ADDISON
How can you settle down
Till you can settle up?

WILSON
A couple of go-getters—

ADDISON
Trend setters—

BOTH
Or, as some would say, "bums" . . .

Wilson fumbles a tricky dance step.

WILSON
(Recovering)
That used to be easier.

ADDISON
You were younger.

WILSON
How old *are* we?

ADDISON
(Encompassing the house)
Watch it, we're in a field of metaphysics here.

WILSON
(Looking around the auditorium)
And mighty pretty country, too.

They resume strolling.

BOTH
Just a couple of jokers
With a quip and a smile.
Just a couple of rib pokers,
Ego strokers,
With a measure of style.

A pair of busy boys
Who made a noise
But never came home with the prize,
Just a couple of—

WILSON
Ice-skaters—

ADDISON
Spectators—

WILSON
Hook baiters—

ADDISON
Saints and satyrs—

BOTH
Just a couple of guys,
Cracking wise!

As the title implies, *Wise Guys* emphasized both the comic and the con man aspects of the Mizner brothers. It presented them as cynical manipulators, which they were, albeit talented ones. This was not merely Alva Johnston's opinion of them; it was an attitude revealed in their own writings (Wilson's plays and screenplays, Addison's memoir) as well as in books written about them. They saw the world as a community of suckers, and John and I decided that our story would be a history of how Wilson acquired that careless, jaundiced view and how he infected Addison with it, encouraging his architect brother to build a city, and destroyed him in the process. The symbiotic relationship between the two visionaries, one a snake-oil entrepreneur, the other a creative dreamer, struck us as a peculiarly American one. They were performers in the largest sense, people with a need to please the crowd, and that may be es-

sentially what suggested to us Hope and Crosby, with their fast-moving vaudevillian style. Both Mizners had a glib volatility, a characteristic which led me to open the show with four contrasting vaudeville numbers abutting each other in rapid succession. I wanted to establish the sudden changes of pace and tone which were to follow.

Emphasized in this opening and sprinkled throughout the piece were examples of Wilson's public wit. He was widely quoted in his time and continues to be to this day, although some of his *bons mots* have been attributed to people like H. L. Mencken and Dorothy Parker. Example: "Be nice to guys on your way up because those are the same guys you'll meet on the way down."

Taking their bows, Addison and Wilson try to upstage each other, a competition which escalates into a squabble and then a physical fight, each becoming his adolescent self. As they do so, the voice of their mother, Mama Mizner, cuts through, yelling at them to stop fighting, as an olio of an idealized California flies in with a clunk, and we are in the garden of the Mizner home in the early 1890s.

We see the family, with their servant Ying, arranged in an idyllic tableau, posing for a photographer: Lansing, Sr. (Papa), resplendent in a government uniform; Mama behind him, directing traffic; surrounding them their four elder sons Henry, Edgar, Lansing, Jr., and William, high-spirited, handsome Frank Merriwell types, each in his early twenties.

The older boys smirk as Addison and Wilson, on Mama's orders, sheepishly exit to clean up. Mama starts placing her sons for the photograph in rhythm, as music continues underneath.

Benicia

MAMA
Henry there . . .
Edgar there . . .
Lansing, Jr.—

(Shouting into the wings)

And hurry up!

(Back to Lansing, Jr.)

—There . . .
William there . . .

(Into the wings again)

Wilson! Addison!

BOYS, YING
(Close harmony)
Paradise . . .

MAMA
Benicia, California, 1883 . . .

BOYS, YING
Paradise!

MAMA
My boys, my boys,
Just look at them:
Lannie's going into law . . .

LANSING, JR.
Ahhh . . .

(Holds the note)

MAMA
William's going into medicine . . .

WILLIAM
Ahhh . . .

MAMA
Edgar's going into business . . .

EDGAR
Ahhh . . .

MAMA
Henry's going after God . . .

HENRY
Ahhh—men . . .

MAMA
And Papa's in the California
Senate . . .

BOYS
Paradise!

MAMA
(Into the wings)
Addison—!

BOYS, YING
Beautiful Benicia!

MAMA
Wilson—!

Addison re-enters, his clothes neat and clean and teenage; he is rubbing his eye. A moment later, Wilson re-enters, also neatly dressed but with his head tipped back and gingerly feeling his nose. They start blaming each other defensively, for Mama's benefit. She interrupts them.

MAMA
Hush!

Brothers don't snitch,
Not on each other,
Isn't that right?

ADDISON
Yes, Mama.

MAMA
Brothers are rich
Just from having a brother,
'Specially one
Who's as special as yours.
Settle your scores—

(Wipes blood off Wilson's nose)

—But remember: you're brothers.

(Turns to the family)

All right, everyone—

LANSING, JR.
Happy birthday, Papa!

ALL SIX BOYS
Happy birthday!

PAPA
Competition is the cornerstone of
enterprise. The boy who does well
is the boy who does better.

BOYS, YING
Paradise!

ALL
Benicia!

A blinding light from the camera's flash powder, then a momentary blackout. The lights come up on the family, except for Wilson and Addison; all are posing for the photographer as before, but each is a little older (for example, William sports a mustache). Also, there are now a few outbuildings, an orchard and more servants, indicating the Mizners' steady climb to affluence.

MAMA
Henry there . . .
Edgar there . . .
Lansing, Jr.—

(Shouting into the wings)

Wilson!

(Back to Lansing, Jr.)

—There . . .
William there . . .

(Into the wings)

Wilson! Addison!

BOYS, YING
Paradise . . .

MAMA
(To us)
1885, and
William's graduating medicine . . .

WILLIAM
Ahhh—

MAMA
Edgar's got a little business . . .

EDGAR
Ahhh—

MAMA
Henry's still pursuing God.

HENRY
Ahhh—men.

MAMA
And Papa's going to be lieutenant
governor . . .

BOYS, YING, SERVANTS
Paradise!

MAMA
(Looking offstage)
Oh, Lord—

*Addison and Wilson enter, Addison
limping. He has been burned in a
contest of jumping over a pit of hot
ashes, lured by Wilson and his friends.
The brothers start accusing each other,
as before. Once again, Mama hushes
them.*

MAMA
Brothers don't whine,
Brothers don't tattle.
Brothers combine
And fight each other's battle.
Isn't that right?
Tell me, isn't that right?

ADDISON, WILSON
Yes, Mama . . .

OTHER BOYS
Happy birthday, Papa!
Happy birthday!

PAPA
There is no greater loser in the
game of life than the boy who wins
by cheating.

ALL
Benicia!

*Again, a blinding flash and a momen-
tary blackout, and the lights come up
once more on the family posed in front
of the photographer—each, as before,
older and more substantial (for exam-*
*ple, Edgar now sports an expensive
ring and tiepin). There are more buildings as well as a few exotic animals
such as toucans and llamas. Addison
and Wilson are clowning around, ha-
rassing the photographer.*

MAMA
Henry there . . .
Edgar there . . .
Lansing, Jr.—

(The sound of a bicycle bell off)

—There . . .

*A messenger on a bicycle enters with a
telegram and delivers it to her.*

William there . . .

(Sharply)

Wilson!
Addison!

ALL EXCEPT MAMA
Paradise!

MAMA
Benicia, California, 1889,
And it's:

BOYS, YING, SERVANTS
Happy birthday, Papa! Happy—!

*Mama reads the telegram, then inter-
rupts, announcing to everyone that the
president has made Papa ambassador
to Guatemala.*

BOYS, YING, SERVANTS
Happy birthday!

*Papa opens his mouth to deliver an-
other homily, but the music becomes
percussively and seductively South
American, mingled with jungle sounds
slowly growing louder.*

MAMA
And since Lannie's busy at the
firm . . .

LANSING, JR.
Ohhh—

MAMA
William's busy at the hospital . . .

WILLIAM
Ohhh—

MAMA
Edgar's busy with his business . . .

EDGAR
Ahhh—

MAMA
And Henry's closing in on God—

HENRY
Ahhh—men . . .

MAMA
—I'm packing up my little
renegades—

ADDISON, WILSON
Ohhh . . .

MAMA
—And taking them to Guatemala!

*Music explodes into a Latin-American
beat. A generic Spanish republic olio
descends with a clunk: steamy jungle,
Spanish architecture, a presidential
palace, and so on. Mama, Papa, Addison, Wilson and the servants dance
their way into Guatemala, the older
boys freezing into the background. Colorful natives, downtrodden peasants
and uniformed barefooted soldiers
dance by. Mama wheels Papa in and
out of the action.*

MAMA
We're on our way to Guatemala,
The little renegades and me.
We're off to stay in Guatemala,
Where something drips from every
tree.
All steamy and luscious,
Not cozy and dry,
No schedules to rush us,
No neighbors to pry.
All monkeys and mangoes,
No teas or cotillions,
All sunsets and tangos—

ADDISON
Will you look at those vermilions?

An afternoon in Benicia is a lovely afternoon.

Matches
rived
No other town in California
Matches Benicia for the weather

Every day, every day's just like June!
Ho-hum, ho-hum, life in Benicia's so humdrum.
Berenice, please!
It's kind of you, Mrs. Mizner, to invite us here for tea.
One & all agree
That the Mizner house is the place to be
If you're going to have tea.
Sewing, sewing, when will the time for going come?
Berenice, oh!
And how are all your boys? How's Lansing, Junior?
You must be pleased that soon your son will be
The proud possessor of a law degree!
How's Wilson? Berenice, please!
How's Addie — well, I trust? Oh, yes, indeedy!
That boy's a scamp but he deserves respect.
He's going to be a brilliant architect.
How's Wilson? Berenice, please!
How's Edgar? Fine! How's Wilson?
How's Billy? Fine! How's Wilson?
How's Henry? Fine! How's Wilson?
Berenice, really! Berenice, honestly!

"Benicia," 1953

of - TMM - tight checks   BENICIA

Snapshots. Ship cadences like frames. Through the years?

                    nice   sweet
A little dumb town   A nice little town

Paradise; Eden. It's a garden (with no snake/serpent)

M   Everything is so a cappella here. Where's the music?

Boys Happy Birthday, Papa
M: (Fast, articulate, commanding, directing) Henry There, Edgar There...
     Addison correcting, W satirizing   (Lon) Lansing Jr., William There...
                                                Father
                                                Papa ...

little pretty   house
A pretty little home
In a pretty little town   Pranks, escapades
                                           A: I was not the last
              state
Called California Desperation
              mischops
And There's pretty little
Going on there in the pretty little town

Mama loved the brothers, They loved her.   We founded Benicia
And then she died.
M: Boys will Be Boys; unmanageable male giants; ponderous louts
Elegant & eccentric family. Town in awe
Town: The Migners take tea in the afternoon!
      W loved organs (p. 31 TFWM)
      We've been to Guatemala
A: I've been to China & Spain
      Cal's state capital & principal asshole
      Fast talk, repartee (p. 45 TFWM); brevity (46)

A bare-breasted native girl walks by, balancing a bowl of fruit on her head.

WILSON
Will you look at those mangoes?

As the Mizners settle in and the local populace dances around, going through their exotic daily lives, back in Benicia the Messenger delivers letters from Mama to the other brothers, each of whom opens one and sings a line from it.

HENRY
"We're settling in to Guatemala . . ."

EDGAR
" . . . Away from duties and
    routines."

LANSING, JR.
"Until you've been to
    Guatemala . . ."

WILLIAM
" . . . You don't know what 'exotic'
    means."

Mama swans around her adopted country with a parasol. As the song continues, the Guatemalan president greets and chats with Lansing, Sr., who never rises from his chair and hardly changes expression.

MAMA, OLDER BOYS
"Marimbas, machetes, maracas . . ."

ADDISON
I want to go to Spain . . .

MAMA, OLDER BOYS
"Flamingos and orchids and
    guava . . ."

YING
A lot of fucking rain . . .

MAMA, OLDER BOYS
"Volcanoes and earthquakes
And palace revolutions
And instant executions . . ."

ADDISON
The sun could fry your brain . . .

WILSON
(Sniffing some powder that a native
has given him and offering it to
Addison)
They call this stuff cocaine . . .

The music brightens considerably.

MAMA
Paradise!

ADDISON, WILSON
Paradise!

As the celebration continues, shots ring out and there is a revolution. The Mizners flee amid the chaos of gunshots, loud explosions, screeching parrots and pelted vegetables, and return to the tranquillity of Benicia.

MAMA
Well, that didn't work out. But, as Lansing says:

PAPA
If a man can say, "I tried my best," then there is nothing more a man need say.

Mama sighs, starts arranging the positions for another birthday celebration in front of yet another photographer.

MAMA
Henry there . . .
Edgar there . . .
Lansing, Jr.—

(Shouting at Addison, who is peering
under the camera hood)

Addison!

(Back to Lansing, Jr.)

—There . . .
William there . . .

(Shouting at Wilson, who is fiddling
with the flash powder)

Wilson!

(Growling)

Addison . . .

Wilson and Addison scuttle back into position.

ALL EXCEPT MAMA
Paradise!

ALL
Happy birthday, Papa!

PAPA
But if they'd sent me to a place like France, I'd be Governor of California now!

ALL
Happy birthday!

Wilson mimes to Addison with a wicked grin, nods toward the photographer's flash pan.

ALL
(Freezing and smiling)
Benicia!

The photographer takes the picture, which causes a fiery explosion from the camera's flash powder; Papa, startled, puts a hand to his heart and expires; a moment of shock as the family turns toward him.
    A quick blackout, then organ music. Lights come up on the family in black armbands, posing for the photographer around a casket banked with flowers. As before, Mama is placing everybody for the funeral photo—starting with Papa.

MAMA
(Indicating the casket)
Papa there . . .
Henry there . . .
Edgar there . . .
Lansing, Jr. . . . .
Addison . . .

(Pats his hand)

—There . . .
William there . . .
Wilson . . .

(As Addison adjusts her veil)

Addison—!

The photographer takes the picture and leaves. Mama informs everybody that Papa has left them almost flat broke.

OLDER BOYS
Ohhh . . .

LANSING, JR.
Mama, I'm a lawyer,
Come and live with me . . .

WILLIAM
Mama, I'm a doctor,
Come and live with me . . .

EDGAR
Mama, I'm in business,
Come and live with me . . .

HENRY
(Overlapping)
Mama, I'm a minister,
Come and live with me and God . . .

OTHER OLDER BOYS
(Overlapping)
Mama, don't you worry,
Come and live with me . . .

MAMA
My boys, my boys,
Don't fret yourselves.
I've been provided for.
Go forth and prosper.
Lannie, go and be a judge—

LANSING, JR.
Yes . . .

MAMA
William, go and run a hospital—

WILLIAM
Yes . . .

MAMA
Edgar, go and make a fortune—

EDGAR
Yes . . .

MAMA
Henry, go be nice to God.

HENRY
Amen . . .

MAMA
Some day one of you is going to be
   president!

OLDER BOYS
Ohhh . . .

MAMA
Go! Go!

She shoos them offstage, then turns to Addison and Wilson, who are clearly her favorites.

This interminable number, like the clubhouse opening of *West Side Story*, is a play in itself, or, more accurately, an oratorio. It took me a month to write and was completely unnecessary to both the plot and the story. There are two reasons for the mistake. First, I overindulged my delight in organizing plot and exposition within a number. (As such, it's nicely constructed and might have been theatrically effective.) Second, and insidiously, it was emblematic of a subtle trap in the show, and indeed in any show based on fact: the lure of authentic, interesting and irrelevant information. As Oscar Hammerstein had taught me, the opening number must tell the audience everything they need to know— but, as I discovered over many years, only what they *need* to know. They certainly didn't need to know about the other Mizner brothers, none of whom played an important part in our story. (At one point "Benicia" was even more complicated: it included passersby commenting on the Mizners—my attempt to show the class distinctions of the town, all of which was more irrelevant.) This problem— the tendency to utilize incidents simply because they really occurred and characters simply because they really existed—was one which Sam Mendes, our director pro tem, tried to get us to address during the next development of the piece.

As Mama, Wilson and Addison ponder what to do next, Papa sits up in his coffin and gives the boys a rousing pep talk on America and its vast potential, urging them to follow in his pioneer footsteps and make the most of themselves and their country. The boys are eager to find their way in the world, but Mama tells them that Papa has died stone broke. They discuss the situation. Addison wants them to get jobs; Wilson wants to find the opportunity that America is supposedly the land of. They start arguing; Mama stops them.

My Two Young Men

MAMA
Brothers don't fight,
Not with each other,
Isn't that right?

ADDISON, WILSON
Yes, Mama.

MAMA
Brothers are lucky,
Just having a brother.

(To Addison)

'Specially one who's as special as
   yours.

(Addison smiles painfully)

Settle your scores,
But remember, you're brothers.

(Putting an arm around each of them)

My babes, my pets, my scalawags,
It's time to face the world.
We've lived for years
With very few tears.
Now we're all alone,
Strictly on our own.
Darlings, it's the end of paradise.

WILSON
Don't worry, Mama. We can take
   care of ourselves.

MAMA
My two young men—
One to make me smile,

One to make me honest.
My two white knights,
My two adventurers,
My two great rascals—
One who's razor-smart,
One who's warm as wool,
One to lift my heart,
One to make it full.

My two young men—
One to keep me drunk with
    laughter,
One to keep me sober after.
One who's reprehensible,
Indispensable,
One who's sensible—

(Catching Addison's slightly hurt look)

Both of whom I love and adore.
I don't know which one I love more.

As they continue wondering what to
do, a prospector suddenly bounds on,
clutching an enormous nugget of gold.

Gold!

PROSPECTOR
Gold! Yeah!
Bet your little titty, boy!
Gold! Gold!
Nuggets this thick!
Gold! Gold!
Go to Dawson City, boy—
It isn't very pretty,
But it's get rich quick!

Found me a mother lode,
Warn't no trick!
Wanna find another lode?
Dig in any mountain,
Pan in any crick!
All you need's a bucket
And a shovel and a pick
And with a little bit of luck it
Means you get rich quick! . . .

He dances off manically. Wilson, ever
the brash leader, is raring to go. Addison, ever the cautious follower, hangs
back.

WILSON
Haven't you been listening?
Gold!
Sitting there and glistening!
Gold just
Lying around!
Gold dust
Glittering and littering the goddamn
    ground!

ADDISON
I don't know . . .

WILSON
Oh come on, Addie,
The two of us together—!

MAMA
What fun!

WILSON
(An arm around Addison's shoulder)
You and me against the world,
    Addie,
You and me against the world!
You and me together,
Weathering the weather,
Fording the crevasses—

ADDISON
Freezing off our asses—

WILSON
We'll never make our fortune
Just by sitting on the porch 'n'
Looking wistful,
When there are nuggets by the
    fistful . . .

MAMA
Time to leave the nest!

WILSON
Time to venture forth!

WILSON, MAMA
Can't go further west,
Might as well go north,
Where there's all that—

ADDISON
Cold.

MAMA
Gold!
Remember what your papa said:
"Be bold!"

WILSON
"Grab the opportunity!"
That's what Papa said.
"Any opportunity,
Just take the road ahead!"

ADDISON
That's not exactly what he—

WILSON
"Never be content
With what you are,
But think of what you can become!"

WILSON, MAMA
Papa said, "Explore!"
Papa said, "Go far!"
Papa said, "Just grab,
And the world's your plum!"

WILSON
A century's beginning—
Gold will make it tick!
A century of enterprise
For you and me to lick!
That's what Papa meant, you're
Gonna miss the big adventure—
It's the dawning of the century
Of get rich quick!

ADDISON
(Getting caught up in his excitement)
A century's beginning,
Gold will make it tick!
A century of enterprise
For you and me to lick!

ALL THREE
(Overlapping)
That's what Papa meant, you're
    right,
We're off on an adventure!

Just a shovel and a tent, you're right,
We're ending our indenture
As we're entering the century
Of get rich quick!

The original end lyric was:

WILSON
A century's beginning—
Don't you feel the itch?
A century of enterprise
For us to make our pitch!

That's what Papa meant. You're
Gonna miss the big adventure—
It's the dawning of a century,
So let's get rich!

ADDISON
(Getting caught up in his excitement)
A century's beginning,
Gotta find our niche!
We're entering the century
Of let's get rich!

I changed the last phrase because we were having title trouble. "Wise guys" was a phrase that, largely due to the success of books and movies about the Sicilian underworld, had in the public perception suddenly come to connote mafiosi instead of smart alecks and therefore would be, to put it minimally, misleading to an audience's expectations. I thought *Get Rich Quick!* would be a good title for the show, and I still think so, but throughout all four of its incarnations none of my collaborators agreed with me. To them it sounded too much like a TV quiz show. I didn't see anything wrong with sounding like a TV quiz show.

Addison and Wilson go off to Alaska, where they immediately encounter blinding snow, wild animals and frozen tundra, but they start digging. After a few minutes of this, Wilson claims that he has to go back into town to get more equipment. Addison reluctantly lets him go, and Wilson immediately heads for the nearest saloon, leaving Addison alone on the dig.

The saloon has the traditional accoutrements: a barroom piano, shirtsleeved piano player, laconic bartender, a couple of dance hall girls, a passel of drunk and dangerous poker players, and the rest. A prospector stumbles in triumphantly, waving a poke of gold in one hand and a map in the other.

PROSPECTOR
Gold!
Luck of the beginner, boys!
Gold!
Look what I found!
Gold! Gold!

Dug myself a winner, boys!
Let me buy you dinner, boys,
And drinks all 'round!

The denizens of the saloon crowd around him with bonhomie and whoops of congratulations, distracting and confusing him, during which they sing:

ALL
Pluck it from a mountain
Or pan it from a crick,
It's easier to pluck it
Off of someone who has struck it.
There are ways to use a bucket
And a shovel and a pick . . .
If you haven't got a brick . . .

They eventually clobber him with a shovel and toss him behind the bar, during which Wilson enters and stands, observing.

All you need's persistence
If you run into resistance,
And it's get rich quick!

They invite Wilson to play poker. Wilson, protesting that he knows nothing about the game, accedes. The lights fade on the saloon and come up on Addison at the dig.

ADDISON
(Muttering bitterly)
"You and me against the world,
    Addie,
You and me against the world!
You and me together,
Weathering the weather.
Fording the crevasses—"

(Peering ahead)

I wonder where the pass is . . .

Well, anyway,
I'm straining every sinew,
Not to mention I'm continu-
Ally sneezing.
Wolves are howling and I'm
    freezing.
But there's all that—

He swings his pick at the frozen ground. It hits the tundra with a loud clang.

ADDISON
—Ow!

He yowls in agony. In the saloon, Wilson is winning big. The sequence now alternates between the saloon and the dig, as weeks pass.

WILSON
(Sizing up his opponents)
Pluck it from a mountain
Or pluck it from a hick,
All you need is luck or
An accommodating sucker
Who imagines that he's slick,
And you needn't work a lick,
And it's—

(Speaking to the other players)

—my deal, I believe.

At the dig, Addison is standing in a hole up to his waist, hacking at the tundra.

ADDISON
Gold!

(Hack)

How did I get into this—
Gold!

(Hack)

—Knowing the score—
Gold!

(Hack)

Knowing that I've been to this
Dead end before?

(Mimicking Wilson with a sneer)

"Oh, come on, Addie,
The two of us together—
What fun!"

He pauses, huffing and puffing, takes off his hat and waves it over the remains of a fire at his feet.

You can get a fire going,
But just try to keep it glowing
When a gale is always blowing—

Well, at least it isn't snowing,
And it's—

It starts to snow directly on his head in great vaudeville clumps. In the saloon, Wilson continues to rake in the chips.

WILSON
Gold . . .
Found me a mother lode . . .

Addison is now in a hole so deep that he is out of sight.

ADDISON
Gold—Unh!

We hear a mighty grunt, as a large rock is pushed up out of the hole.

Boulders this thick . . .

WILSON
Gold!
I don't need another lode.
Sit around with suckers,
See what makes 'em tick—

ADDISON
Maybe I should chuck it—
I could tell him I got sick.

Another rock appears from the hole. The lights come back up on the saloon.

WILSON
Suckers by the bucket—

ADDISON
On the other hand—Oh, fuck it—

BOTH
With a little bit of luck it
Means you get rich—!

The second rock, which has been resting on the edge of Addison's hole for a moment, rolls back in. A scream.

In the saloon, Wilson has become not only a gambler, conning his opponents with distractions and scams and enlisting one of the dance hall girls as his accomplice, but eventually morphing into a flashily dressed promoter, his latest client being a fighting polar bear who challenges all comers. It is this situation that Addison bursts in on, furious at his brother for having left him at the dig for nearly three months, but triumphantly carrying a pouch of gold dust—he has struck a vein. A large, drunken, bloodthirsty crowd is waiting impatiently for the fight to begin, and Wilson, who habitually peps the bear up with whiskey, has pepped it up too much—the bear is out cold. Wilson is trying to pour coffee down the bear's throat when Addison enters and is overjoyed at his brother's good fortune, but points out that he'll never leave the building alive if he doesn't give the mob a fighting bear. Handily, there happens to be a large bear suit hanging in the closet, and it should come as no surprise (and a good thing too, farce being at its best when the audience thinks it's a step ahead of the playwright) that there follows a classic Hope and Crosby sequence in which Addison fights, disguised as a bear (and wins), only to have the real bear wake up, alerting the crowd to the swindle. The boys narrowly escape with their lives.*

The show olio bangs in, the spotlight picking out a wharf in San Francisco. Top hats and canes are tossed in from the wings. Addison and Wilson catch them and clap them on their heads; from the neck down, they remain prospectors. They quarrel about whose fault the Alaska fiasco was; Wilson cuts Addison off by turning to the audience.

---

* I'm describing book scenes in more detail than usual in order to illustrate the changes of tone and intent in the show as it went through its subsequent transformations.

Second Vaudeville

WILSON
You've heard of
Arthur and Lancelot—

ADDISON
(Following suit)
You've heard of Abel and Cain.

WILSON
You've heard of
Sculptor and clay—

ADDISON
Spider and prey—

WILSON
Ball and chain . . .

Addison is relieved that they at least came away with some gold dust, but of course they haven't—Wilson had bet the entire stash on the other guy. They have only three hundred dollars left. Addison starts to explode, but Wilson again cuts him off.

WILSON
On my left—

ADDISON
On my right—

WILSON
Is a saint and an artist—

ADDISON
Is the smartest of the smartest.

WILSON
If a bit of a twit.

ADDISON
Not to trust—

WILSON
Kind of quaint—

ADDISON
But he's just so seductive—

WILSON
But he's just so self-destructive—

ADDISON

That you find yourself in shit.

WILSON

So he's weak—

ADDISON

So, okay—

BOTH

That is no cause for quibbling.
And believe me, I don't say that
Just because he is my sibling.

*Surreptitiously, between verses, Wilson
has been snorting cocaine. Addison, exasperated, starts to lay into him, but
Wilson again cuts the moment off by
turning to the audience.*

WILSON

When you're caught in a jam
And you've worked out a scam,
You expect things from someone
    you trust.

(Looks askance at Addison)

ADDISON

When you're deep in the snow
And it's forty below,
It'd be nice not to be waiting for
    over three months
For someone you trust.

(Looks askance at Wilson)

WILSON

When you're part of a team
That has dreamed up a scheme—

ADDISON

When you haven't been told
Till you've lost all your gold—

WILSON

When the person you trust,
Like your hand, is a bust—

ADDISON

You've heard of Judas Iscariot—

WILSON

You've heard of Lincoln and Booth—

ADDISON

You've heard of circle and square—

WILSON

Tortoise and hare—

BOTH

Lies and truth—!

*They glare at each other; a beat, then
they turn back to us abruptly and with
bright smiles resume strolling.*

BOTH

Just a couple of wise guys
On the road to "What next?"
Just a couple of wise guys,
Always veering from the text . . .

They do a tricky step together.

Or, as some would say, "bums."

Just a couple of climbers,
Always kidding around.
Just a couple of good-timers,
Wisenheimers,
With their ears to the ground.

A pair of eager lads,
Still undergrads,
Exploring the way the world lies.
Just a couple of guys,
Cracking wise.

ADDISON
(To Wilson)
What are we going to tell Mama?

*Lights up on Mama sitting in her now-
shabby living room. Wilson and Addison burst in and Mama, beaming, asks
them for a report on their Klondike adventure. Wilson charmingly avoids giving her a direct answer.*

Next to You

WILSON

The aurora borealis is a bust,
Next to you.
Every bag of gold was nothing more
Than just a bag of dust,
Next to you.

ADDISON
(Competing for her affection)
Every moment I was digging,
Frozen to the bone—

(Pointedly)

Digging all alone—
All that I could do
Was think of being next—

*Wilson deftly slithers into Mama's
arms and waltzes with her.*

WILSON

Next to you,
Moonlight on the snow was
    unexciting.
Next to you,
The moon is just an accident of
    lighting.

ADDISON
(Cutting in)
Every moment
I was lonely,
What's the only
Thing that saw me through?

WILSON
(Cutting in)
How spiffy could a moon be—?

ADDISON
(Cutting in right back)
Knowing that I'd soon be—

*Wilson cuts in once more so that both
he and Addison are dancing simultaneously with Mama.*

BOTH

—Next to you.

MAMA

Who needs gold,

Who needs moonlight?
Addie is my gold.
Willie, you're my moonlight.
How could any mother,
Any woman,
Ask for more
Than my two young men?

She sings a reprise of "My Two Young Men." The brothers continue their competition, overlapping each other's lines.

WILSON
Next to you—

ADDISON
Next to my best girl—

WILSON
—The aurora borealis is a bust—

ADDISON
—The aurora borealis is a bust—

WILSON
Next to you—

ADDISON
Next to my best girl—

WILSON
—A bag of gold is nothing but a bag
of dust.

ADDISON
—A bag of gold is nothing—

WILSON
 I said that—!

ADDISON
Not the white glow
Of the moon—

WILSON
Not the mellow glow of a spittoon—

Mama squeals with laughter and hits him fondly with her fan.

ADDISON
I will make a home for you—

WILSON
I will take you dancing.

ADDISON
I will come and live with you—

WILSON
I'll leave you alone.

MAMA
My two young men . . .

ADDISON
Anything you want—

WILSON
Anything you want!

ADDISON
Tell me what you want!

MAMA
. . . One to make me melt,
One to make me giggle,
Two to live the life your mama
Wished she could have had before.
Go, lads,
Send me back dispatches from
the war.

(*Pats their cheeks*)

I don't know which one I love more.

Addison, hurt by his mother's favoritism, declares his intention to get out from under Wilson's influence and make a fortune on his own. The scene changes to a steamship office, where he purchases a ticket to Hawaii, which he deems as good a place as any to start.

The following sequence is staged around a gangplank built like a seesaw, which Addison ascends and descends as he arrives at and departs from each destination on his odyssey.

Addison's Trip

ADDISON
(*To us*)
I'm on my way,
Completely on my own.
I'm on my way,
And that's all I'm certain of.
I'm on my way
To worlds I've never known,
Away from those I love . . .

Don't have to stay.
I can either stay or roam.
I'll work, I'll play,
And make up for my half-assed past.
I'm on my way
From the worlds of hearth and
home,
Away from those I love—
At last!

In Hawaii, he is offered the job of assisting a photographer who is taking pictures of the island's topography, and immediately drops a camera down a volcano when it suddenly shoots up flames. He is fired and starts to board a ship, a smaller one, for India. At the foot of the gangplank, three Hawaiian natives hawk their wares: rattan stools, tribal weapons, wood carvings, etc.

HAWAIIAN #1
Souvenir of your visit to Hawaii . . .

HAWAIIAN #2
Souvenir, so the memory will stay in
your mind . . .

HAWAIIAN #3
Souvenir of the day you say
goodbyii . . .

ALL THREE
Souvenir for the girl you left
behind . . .

He sees a vision of Mama at her most loving and benign.

HAWAIIAN #1
Native spear . . .

ADDISON
Just a little setback, Mama . . .

HAWAIIAN #2
Cheaper here . . .

ADDISON
Little setbacks are allowed . . .

HAWAIIAN #3
Souvenir . . .

ADDISON
By the time I get back,
You'll be proud.

He buys a souvenir from the first Hawaiian and turns to Mama, grinning, only to see Wilson appear and waltz her off into the wings. Mama blows Addison a kiss and waves, as the ship's horn sounds. Agitated, Addison hurriedly thrusts money into the hands of the other two Hawaiians, grabs an armful of souvenirs and starts up the gangplank with a determined smile.

ADDISON
I'm on my way,
Discouraged not at all.
I'm on my way
To I don't care where or when.
A brand-new day
And a brand-new port of call—
I'm on my way again!

A small delay
Doesn't shake my confidence.
I'm on my way
To discovering who I am.
I'm on my way
And I've gained experience,
Plus a rattan stool from a
    native hut,
A candle stand made of coconut,
A whatnot made out of God-knows-
    what—
I'm on my way again!
Hot damn!

He arrives in India, where he gets a job restoring paintings. As he is applying a chemical cleaner to the most valuable of the lot, he lights a cigarette and the painting disappears in flames. As before, he heads back to the gangplank, where a group of natives await him with their goods.

INDIAN #1
Sahib like a chair
With inscription of a swami?

INDIAN #2
(Proffering an elaborate jar)
Something very rare—
From a rajah, only one of a kind . . .

INDIAN #3
(Proffering an identical jar)
How about a pair?
One for Daddy, one for Mommy—?

ALL THREE
(As Addison turns away, annoyed)
Don't you care
For the girl you left behind?

Mama appears to Addison, dressed extravagantly and looking at him with an encouraging, but hopeless, smile.

INDIAN #1
Chandelier . . .

ADDISON
I've still got resources, Mama—

Mama holds out her arms to him and moves toward him.

INDIANS #2 AND #3
For your dear . . .

ADDISON
And I'm learning as I go.

ALL THREE INDIANS
Souvenir . . .

ADDISON
Failing merely forces
You to grow.

Mama walks right past him, as Wilson appears from behind, dressed in white tie and tails. She takes Wilson's arm and they stroll off together, as if on a date.
Addison arrives in China, where he is hired to serve writs, one of them on what turns out to be a terrifying warlord. He quickly tears up the writ and leaves for the gangplank, where he boards a Chinese junk. At the foot of the gangplank three natives await him.

CHINAMAN #1
Souvenir—
Can't go empty-handed!

CHINAMAN #2
(Holding up a screen)
Blue veneer—
Very hard to find.

CHINAMAN #3
Gift to cheer
Missy feeling stranded—

ALL THREE
Missy who you left behind!

Wincing guiltily, Addison turns away, only to see Wilson and Mama, laughing exuberantly, sweep by in their waltz.

Souvenir . . . souvenir . . .

ADDISON
(To Mama's departing back)
I've half a dozen letters to mail
    you . . .
Don't worry, Mama, I won't fail
    you . . .

Addison, clearly down to his last few dollars but unable to resist, hands the three Chinamen money, takes another load of stuff and, struggling not to drop everything, heads up the gangplank of a tramp steamer. Exhausted, he stops at the top and rests for a moment.

ADDISON
I'm in my way.
It's a bit disheartening.
I'm in my way,
Still I'm doing as I please,
Facing life's adversities.
I've got lots of memories . . .

(Surveying his possessions)

And a Ming tureen
Made of opaline
And a lacquered tray and a folding
    screen
And an old stone jug
And a fakir's rug
And a chandelier that's a bitch to lug
And a rattan stool and a candle
    stand

And a whatnot I can't get rid of, and I'm on my way again . . .

After a brief stop in Australia where the natives are singing "Waltzing Matilda" and where Addison makes the mistake of winning a boxing match against the local favorite, he picks up more souvenirs.

AUSTRALIAN #1
(Proffering a large canvas)
Picture of a billabong?

AUSTRALIAN #2
(Proffering a bench)
Solid eucalyptus . . .

AUSTRALIAN #3
(Proffering a tribal mask)
Made by Aborigines . . .

AUSTRALIAN #1
Platypus?

AUSTRALIAN #2
Wombat?

ALL THREE
Souvenirs
For you-know-who . . .

Wagner's "Wedding March." Addison has a vision of Wilson and Mama crossing the stage, dressed to get married. Just before they exit, Mama gives Addison a dazzling smile, blows him a kiss and throws the bridal bouquet to him. She and Wilson exit.
  Addison thrusts money into the Australians' hands, grabs an armful of stuff from them, adds them to his other possessions and tries to stagger up the gangplank, dropping things.

ADDISON
(Muttering)
This is ridiculous . . . What am I doing here . . . Where am I?

(Sings)

I give up!

He drops everything, rushes to Australian #3, throws money at him, dumps the man's souvenirs out of his cart, grabs the cart and runs to the ship. He stuffs his collection into the cart and starts up the gangplank again, muttering all the while.

ADDISON
All this time and what have I gotten out of it? Humiliation, embarrassment, malaria—

(Sings)

And a tribal mask and a shepherd's chair
And a painting of a koala bear
And an ego damaged beyond repair
And a sense that worse is to come, but where—?

He lands in Guatemala, where colorful natives, downtrodden peasants and elaborately uniformed barefoot soldiers are parading and dancing to sensual music.

GUATEMALANS
In Guatemala,
Where something drips from every tree!

Two of the crowd turn to reveal themselves as Mama and Wilson, dressed like the natives and dancing together wildly.

MAMA, WILSON
(Disappearing as they dance)
Enjoy your stay in Guatemala,
The land of sensuality!

Addison is offered a job on a coffee plantation but, deploring his own inadequacy angrily, refuses and stalks back to the gangplank, juggling his luggage and souvenirs. Three Guatemalan natives offer him chests, paintings, crucifixes and so on, and before they can even sing, he tosses them his last money and staggers up the gangplank with all his purchases in the cart. He loses his balance and tumbles down the gangplank, landing in New York City in a heap, surrounded by his acquisitions. He kicks at a couple of objects and collapses despondently in the chair he bought.

A beat; he frowns. He picks up the candle stand and sets it on one side of the chair, looks at it critically, then places it elsewhere. Soon he is mentally rearranging all his possessions (carried out in actuality by the natives he has encountered) into first the form of a room and subsequently the form of a house.

ADDISON
(Trying to place the screen)

No, that interrupts the space . . .

(Eyeing something else)

Doesn't really match the rest . . .

NATIVES, ADDISON
Guess you'll (I'll) have to build a place
That holds crucifixes, a Spanish chest,
A hand-carved mirror, a brocade vest
And a tribal mask and a shepherd's chair
And a painting of a koala bear
And a Ming tureen made of opaline
And a lacquered tray and a folding screen—

ADDISON
(Eyeing the screen critically)
No, the folding screen
Should go in between—

(Repositions it)

ADDISON, NATIVES
—And an old stone jug
And a fakir's rug
And a chandelier that's a bitch to lug
And a rattan stool and a candle stand—

ADDISON
And a whatnot I could make look quite grand . . .

He does something ingenious with the whatnot, stands back, appraises it, nods approvingly and, finally, sits back down in the chair, looking around, content at last.

I'm on my way . . .

"Addison's Trip" is the crucial song of the show: it establishes Addison's motive to become an architect and thus leads directly to the events of Act Two, and it's a potential tour de force for the actor playing the part. As it happened, the song (actually, the whole sequence) turned out to be problematic on both counts for reasons which revealed themselves during the workshop, as the next Act of this chapter recounts. It also remains one of only two times I've recycled music from another song (at least consciously): an elaborate number called "Lunch," which I'd written in 1992 for an unproduced movie titled *Singing Out Loud*. Not all the sections are cannibalized, only the refrains ("I'm on my way") and the underlying accompaniments that connect them. I like to think that it wasn't because my inventive powers had run out, but because I kept looking for a motif that mirrored Addie's anxiety, and every time I tried to work one out I couldn't do better than the five-note theme which generated "Lunch." Since by this time the movie was unlikely to be made and since the score of *Wise Guys* was an admixture of styles, it seemed foolish to stick to my lifelong insistence on refusing to recycle music from one show to another, so I threw principles to the wind. I was right to do so, I think. The number may have had problems, but the music was the right music.

A couple of shamefaced observations: "Half-assed" may sound like an anachronism for the 1890s, but in fact it was in use. Nevertheless, it *sounds* anachronistic and is yet another example of theatrical truth trumping the genuine article; reality is always in the ear of the beholder. I used the word because I wanted Addison to sound angry rather than petulant, since his perceived masculinity (or lack of it) was important in preventing him from becoming a cliché, and I thought a small shock of language might do the trick. All it did was draw attention to the writer; by this time in my writing life I should have known better—but I doubt if any author learns to be impeccable from his mistakes, only to be

less peccable. Moreover, "a bitch to lug" is a genuine anachronism and I never even caught it till an eagle-eyed (or its aural equivalent) friend of mine pointed it out. And the penultimate line is unforgivably clumsy-sounding. Even Nathan Lane, who can perform miracles with the diction of lyrics, couldn't make the pile-up of hard consonants in "could make look quite grand" sound graceful. If only that had been the most serious problem with the number—but, as I said above, more about that later.

The lights come up on a box at the Madison Square Garden Dog Show. It is 1903. In it sit two elegantly dressed doyennes of New York society and one vulgar, garishly dressed parvenu in her mid-forties, named Myra Yerkes, widow of Charles Yerkes, the streetcar king. Myra is getting slowly but joyfully potted while the other two ladies do their insufficient best to ignore her. Addison enters, carrying a roll of blueprints. He is in white tie and tails and clearly at home in these surroundings. He surveys the ladies and sings to himself as he approaches them.

Dowagers

ADDISON
Dowagers,
What would we do without
Dowagers,
Flinging-their-weight-about
Dowagers?
Gotta get 'em while they're hot.

Dowagers
Aren't difficult to handle—
Feed them flattery and scandal.
And you know what?
I rather like them a lot.

Dowagers,
What the world needs is more
Dowagers,
Generous-to-the-core
Dowagers,

Bless their cast-iron hearts,
The dear old farts,
The matrons of the patrons of the
    arts.

He explains to us* that he had been working as an architect's apprentice when he had met Mrs. Yerkes, a recently widowed millionairess, and has charmed her into letting him design a house for her in Oyster Bay.

ADDISON
Dowagers
Preening themselves to bits.
Dowagers
Airing their powdered tits,
Dowagers—
Catch 'em while you can.

(Glancing at Mrs. Fisk)

Is that some pan?

When I'm in doubt, despair,
Arrears and gloom,
If I can only look
Around the room
And see my dowagers,
I am a happy man!

His beaming satisfaction is shattered by the unexpected appearance of Wilson, who is gambling on the dogs and whom he has not seen since they parted in San Francisco. Addison is forced to introduce him to Mrs. Yerkes. Wilson, who knows a millionairess when he sees one, flirts with her by being just as vulgar as she is. Addison, seeing his client's attention being diverted, offers to take Mrs. Yerkes home.

ADDISON
(Taking her arm)
I'm getting the carriage and taking
    you home.

---

* One of the reasons for setting the show in a vaudeville framework was that it allowed the characters to address the audience directly whenever we wished.

WILSON
(Taking her other arm)
I'm getting a Stutz and I'm taking
you home.

ADDISON
We're sailing for Europe!

WILSON
We're dining at Rector's!

ADDISON
I'll show you the Prado!

WILSON
I'll show you my etchings!

ADDISON
I'll make you a lady!

WILSON
I'll make you a cocktail!

ADDISON
I'll build you a palace!

WILSON
I'll marry you!

ADDISON
What?!

WILSON
(Seductively to Mrs. Yerkes as he
waltzes her off)
The aurora borealis is a bust,
Next to you.

(As Addison throws up his hands)

Every bag of gold is nothing more
than just
A bag of dust,
Next to you.
And the minute
That we're married
And we're safely snuggled in the
hay—

(Lowering his voice, into her ear)

I'll—

He whispers to her; her face lights up.
The music becomes the "Wedding
March." Wilson marries her, and lights
rise on an enormous canopied bed in
the Yerkes' Fifth Avenue mansion. Mrs.

Yerkes coyly strips down to her under-
wear, settles on the bed and pats the
mattress invitingly as Wilson strips to
his long johns. They are interrupted by
a newsboy entering and shouting headlines about the marriage. Mrs. Yerkes
shrieks and hastily covers up, but Wilson grabs the newspaper and starts
reading, as a flock of reporters and
photographers burst in with questions
about his marrying into millions of
dollars.

The Good Life

WILSON
It's a good life,
I'll admit.
I don't mind the gross extravagance
a bit.
It's a life I can't pretend
That I wouldn't recommend,
If you have just one to spend,
It's a good life.
Want the tour?

The reporters nod. We see projections
of the vast and overdecorated mansion.

WILSON
Gotta be this rich
To keep your taste this poor.

Note the pair of plaster swans
By the real Cellini bronze.
She's got Corots in the kitchen,
She's got Rembrandts in the johns.

It's a good life—
For a while.
Got the shack up in Alaska beat a
mile.
Though it's lacking in restraint,
Call me vulgar, call me quaint,
I like living with "Old Paint"—

He gestures toward Mrs. Yerkes, then at
the paintings. There follows a sequence
of Wilson's encounters with the press
and the eminently quotable witticisms
he spouts about marriage and money.
As he increasingly enjoys himself,

Myra gets increasingly impatient, especially since many of the witticisms
are at her expense, like:

WILSON
(Toasting)
To the good life—

(Looks to Myra)

And the bride.

(Looks upward)

And to Charlie—

(To the reporters, who look baffled)

That's the gent who kindly died.

(Looks upward again)

It's to you I doff my lid.
Thanks for dying when you did.
Though at times I can't help feeling
That you didn't die, you hid.

Whenever Myra dimly senses that she
is being insulted, Wilson swiftly sweeps
her up in a waltz, singing things like:

WILSON
The aurora borealis is a gag,
Next to you.
Every bag of gold is nothing more
Than just another bag,
Next to you.

Time passes with more headlines, more
photographs and more encounters with
the press. Finally, Wilson goes too far
and Myra, fed up and drunk and, in
front of the cameras, throws him out,
pelting him with money, which he
cheerfully picks up. The reporters ask
him how he feels.

The Game

WILSON
Easy come and easy go,
Which one can you trust?

Nothing lasts forever, so
What's to be discussed?
Win one minute, lose the next,
Some things have to fail. You
Can't let that derail you.
Boom's the same as bust,
If you just adjust.

The only thing that matters is the
    game.
It all comes down to staying in the
    game.
The trick is learning how to keep
Both flexible and flexed.
Where now?
What next?

The fact is, boys, when all is said
    and done,
The fun is in the winning, not what's
    won.
When you're hot,
Bet the pot.
When you're not,
Smile a lot,
Change the table,
Raise the stakes,
Adjust your aim.
The only thing that matters is the
    game.

        (After a few more encounters with
                the press)

The point, as I was saying,
Is the game.
It's not the hand you're playing,
It's the game.
The payoff and the blowoff
Both are virtually the same.
The only thing that matters is the
    game.

Sometimes finding the right place for
a song is as difficult as writing the song
itself, and so it proved with this one.
"The Game" constitutes Wilson's philosophy of life and is as important to
his character and to the plot as "Addison's Trip" is to Addison's, since it is
Wilson's recklessness that eventually brings the Mizners' world down
around their ears. It was written to be
sung in the Klondike saloon, where
Wilson's attitude toward life is formed,
but it brought the melodramatic and
comic pace of the scene to a thudding
halt. Placed here, however, it seemed
nothing more than a cynical aside, one
more piece of banter to the reporters. We solved it by restoring it to the
Alaska sequence and *emphasizing*
its static quality: the scene simply
stopped, much the way the nightclub
scene in *Company* simply stops for
"The Ladies Who Lunch." The result
was that Wilson's passion for gambling in the largest sense became as
intense as Addison's passion to build
houses.

*Wilson exchanges a few more quips
with the reporters and they leave. Just
as Addison sang about the usefulness of
dowagers, so Wilson now sings about
journalists.*

Journalists

WILSON
Journalists,
What would we do without
    journalists?
What can we do about journalists?
Gotta greet them with a grin.

Journalists,
Though they fix you with a label,
Help you get a better table.
But watch your skin—
They run a game you can't win.

Journalists—
Maybe you don't adore
Journalists,
Gotta feel something for
Journalists—
The guys who write by rote.
They get my vote.

I never know despair
Or doubt or gloom
If I can only look
Around the room
And see a journalist,
And give him something to
    misquote.

*Addison, upset at losing his only client,
complains to Wilson, who shrugs it off
cheerfully and promises to find him an
even better one, a promise which he
makes again and again during the following sequence.*

What's Next?

WILSON
Some boats sink, what else is new?
Why are you perplexed?
Have to get accustomed to
Changes in the text.
I can't wait to see what happens
    next.

What's done, that's dead.
Full steam ahead.
Too bad. 'Nuf said.
What's next?

Get rich, get burned,
There's lots more stones to be
    turned.
You've lived, you've learned.
What's next?

Anything is possible,
Just as Papa said.
If you can't be this,
Then you go for that
Or go there instead.

Now and then you miss,
Or it all falls flat,
Anything is possible.

I can't wait to see
What I'm gonna be
Next!

*What he becomes next is the manager
of Stanley Ketchel, the middleweight
champion of the world, by charming
him and promising him a world of
wine, women and song. We first see
Ketchel in boxing shorts, having just
won a fight, being dressed in loud
clothes and a Stetson hat by three chorus girls, one of whom hands him a
bottle of beer.*

CHORUS GIRLS
Ooohh, Stanley . . .
Ooohh, Stanley . . .

Ketchel guzzles the beer and grabs at their asses. He looks happily over at Wilson; Wilson shrugs and shakes his head.

WILSON
When I say wine, pal, I don't mean
     beer,
I mean be the best you can be.
When I say women, I don't mean
     hookers—
Although, I grant you, they're not
     bad lookers.
When I say song,
I mean sing along,
I mean string along
With me.
And you'll see . . .

Wilson smiles and beckons offstage. Three soigné society women in resplendent evening gowns glide in and replace the beer with Champagne, the suit with a set of tails and the Stetson with a top hat.

SOCIETY WOMEN
Ooohh, Stanley . . .
Ooohh, Stanley . . .

Ketchel casually pushes the chorus girls offstage and dances more and more elegantly with the women, enjoying everything but the top hat, which he takes off and replaces with the Stetson.

WILSON
A king deserves only royal pleasures,
A champ requires Champagne,
A social circle that's rich and
     varied,
Where all the hookers are rich and
     married.

Wilson nods to one of the women and she offers Ketchel a small open silver box.

And if the stuff you sniff
Isn't up to snuff,
They have better stuff—

KETCHEL
Hey, cocaine!

Ketchel is delighted with the life that Wilson has led him into, but just as Wilson is about to get him to commission a house for Addison to build, a jilted chorus girl enters and shoots Ketchel dead. Reporters rush onstage and interview Wilson for comment.

WILSON
     Start counting ten over him. Maybe
     he'll get up.

The reporters hoot and scribble while a photographer shoots.

REPORTER #1
Gotta hand it to him,
Smart as a whip—

REPORTER #2
—Quick with a quip—

REPORTER #3
Shoots from the lip—

ALL
Good copy!
Gotta hand it to him,
The man has style.

REPORTER #2
(To the others)
     Where you wanna eat?

Addison is crushed by the loss of another possible commission. Wilson calms him down.

The Game
(reprise)

WILSON
Easy come and easy go,
Why get so upset?
Every high spot has a low—
Can't afford regret.

Win one minute, lose the next,
Everything's a sequel.

Think of them as equal:
Place another bet.
Find another table and forget.

The only thing that matters is the
     game.
The trick is getting back into the
     game.
You win, you lose, it's over with.
Don't stick with it, it's gone.
Close shop.
Move on.

Life's full of disappointment,
As you know.
You have to keep inventing
As you go.

Papa said,
"Don't be blind.
Look ahead,
Not behind.
Find a new frontier
And stake another claim."
The only thing that matters is the
     game.

Wilson's new frontier is to collaborate on a play with Paul Armstrong, one of Broadway's most successful playwrights—and another possible client for Addison—who has come to Wilson for advice on how the criminal underworld speaks and acts. We see Wilson ensconced in an opium-filled hotel room with some chorus girls, trying not very hard to finish the play, which turns out to be less than a success, although Wilson's wit with the press, panning his own play, maintains his reputation. Again, Addison complains, and again Wilson reassures him.

WILSON
"Addie Mizner, Architect"—
It's as good as signed.
Failure seen in retrospect
Is just a state of mind.

Look at me, I lose a wife,
Then a protégé, right?
Next day I'm a playwright!
When you're in a bind,
Close the book
And just don't look
Behind.

As is probably becoming apparent, the repetitiousness of the vignettes, here and throughout the first act—Wilson conning Addison, Addison succumbing—begins to get wearisome. Also, too many extended sequences of songs are giving the show a discursive feeling instead of a breezy one.

Wilson's next transformation is to become the manager of a hotel which is nothing but a glorified whorehouse and refuge for criminals, but he promises the despairing Addison that he will get him the job of renovating and redesigning it. Unfortunately, in a fit of exuberance, he throws a couple of guests into the lobby fountain. After charming the judge and jury at his trial for assault and battery, he is acquitted. As photographers descend on him, Armstrong, Mrs. Yerkes and the dead Ketchel step forward.

ARMSTRONG
Gotta hand it to him,
Sonofabitch
Lands in a ditch,
Gives 'em a pitch . . .
Gotta hand it to him,
The guy has style.

MRS. YERKES
Ask how I could be that
Easy to twist,
Quickly dismissed.
Couldn't resist,
Every time I'd see that
Enormous—

(Lasciviously)

Smile.

ARMSTRONG
The man has style.

ARMSTRONG, MRS. YERKES
Gotta hand it to him . . .

KETCHEL
Sure, I was only a kid,
But with my eyes open wide.
I mean, I know what he did,
And it's too bad that I died,
But what a hell of a ride—!

ALL THREE
The man has style.

Wilson, surrounded by admirers, sings to the world.

What's Next?
(reprise)

WILSON
What's done—

REPORTERS
Worth a column—

WILSON
—That's dead.

REPORTERS
—Any day of the week.

WILSON
Full steam—

OTHERS
Never solemn—

WILSON
—Ahead!

OTHERS
—Always tongue in the cheek.

WILSON
Too bad—

OTHERS
Gotta hand it to him—

WILSON
—'Nuf said.

Upstage, a spot picks out an elegant maître d', holding an elegant menu.

MAÎTRE D'
Table at Delmonico's, Mr. Mizner?

Wilson looks at the Maître d' appraisingly.

ALL
—The man has style!

WILSON
Get rich, get burned—

ALL
—He's resilient.

WILSON
—There's lots more stones to be turned.

ALL
—And he's brilliant.

WILSON
You've lived, you've learned—

ALL
Gotta hand it to him . . .

A spot picks out a fight promoter holding a pair of tickets.

FIGHT PROMOTER
Ringside seats at the Garden, Mr. Mizner?

Wilson looks at him, then us, smiles broadly.

WILSON
Anything is possible—

MRS. YERKES, ARMSTRONG, KETCHEL
How can you stay mad—

WILSON
Nothing fails for long.

MRS. YERKES, ARMSTRONG, KETCHEL
—At a guy like that?

WILSON
If it works out, swell.
If it doesn't—well,
Sing another song.

MRS. YERKES, ARMSTRONG, KETCHEL
Have to tip your hat.

WILSON
If it doesn't jell,
Then it doesn't—hell,
Anything is possible.

A spotlight picks out a dealer at an exclusive gambling club.

DEALER
Hand of cards at Canfield's, Mr. Mizner?

WILSON, OTHERS
I can't wait to see
What he's [I'm] gonna be—

WILSON
Next!

Wilson, the center of attention, dances in unison with everybody.

MRS. YERKES
So I had to toss him out on his rump—

WILSON, OTHERS
What's next?

KETCHEL
So he turned me from a champ to a chump—

WILSON, OTHERS
What's next?

ARMSTRONG
So he's pickled and he lives in a dump—

A spotlight picks out a shady character holding a twist of paper.

SHADY CHARACTER
Something to brighten up your evening, Mr. Mizner?

ALL
The man has style!

Addison watches from the sidelines, doing a slow burn, as his brother smiles contentedly, contemplating his choices among the maître d', fight promoter, the dealer and the shady character.

WILSON
Next—!

These incidents were all actual phases of Wilson Mizner's life—although the collaboration with Armstrong was in fact a success—one of two hits they wrote together: *The Deep Purple* and *The Greyhound*. Including these vignettes all might seem to be another example of the add-a-pearl dangers of unnecessary incidents, the kind which killed "Benicia" and threatened to plague "Addison's Trip," but this time there seemed to be a reason for it. We wanted to demonstrate the essence of Wilson's character and a certain aspect of the American spirit: the restlessness inherent in the philosophy of "What's next?," in the idea of reinventing oneself, so often accompanied by irresponsibility because the sheer energy of the optimism has taken over. This is what in large part the show is about, or at least what we intended it to be.

We also wanted to parallel the structure of "Addison's Trip," since both sequences are voyages of self-discovery. As the rest of the chapter chronicles, it took a long circular route for the number to find itself back at its original intention.

Wilson, grinning and shooting his cuffs, is taking a step toward the shady character when suddenly Addison, jaw set, snaps his fingers and the vaudeville olio, filled with column headlines, snippets of gossip and photographs all featuring Wilson, flies in, separating Wilson from the high life upstage. Addison erupts in a rage at Wilson for constantly promising him jobs and botching every opportunity. Wilson cuts him off by turning charmingly to the audience.

Third Vaudeville

WILSON
On my left—

ADDISON
On my right—

WILSON
—Is a man of conviction—

ADDISON
—Is the patron saint of fiction.

WILSON
—Which is why he persists.

ADDISON
He's bereft—

WILSON
Not too bright—

ADDISON
—Of all sense of proportion.

WILSON
—With a weakness for distortion—

The clog waltz breaks in as Addison rounds on him.

ADDISON
When you're eager and broke,
You need more than a joke
From what used to be someone you trust.

WILSON
When you're doing your best
At your brother's request,
And the press is impressed
But your brother's a pest—

ADDISON
So much for Damon and Pythias.

(To the audience)

You've heard of Jekyll and Hyde?

WILSON
You've heard of water and oil—

ADDISON
Brought to a boil?

BOTH
Fratricide?

Suddenly, there is an enormous BOOM! offstage. The theater shakes. It turns out to be the San Francisco earthquake, which Mama survives, but not without some ill side effects. Addison volunteers to take care of her in his small Long Island apartment.

The sequence which follows alternates between Wilson's increasingly dangerous exploits with cocaine and gamblers, and Mama's reading newspaper accounts about him in bed, while Addison tries simultaneously to tend to her and to field the complaining phone calls from the one remaining client he has. As time goes on, Mama, her health fading, keeps waiting for Wilson to visit, but he's always "too busy." Finally, she confesses to Addison that although she loves him, it has always been Wilson who excites her. She starts to fade and announces that she's dying. Addison is distraught.

What's Next?

(reprise)

ADDISON
You aren't! You mustn't! Mama, no!

Next to you,
Nothing is surprising or exciting.
Next to you,
The moon is just an accident of
   lighting.
Every moment
I've been lonely,
You're the only
Thing that saw me through . . .

MAMA
There, there. It's all right, dear. I've had many blessings in this life. And I have no fear of the next one. Only curiosity.

I mean, dead is dead.
Full steam ahead.
That's done. 'Nuf said.
What's next?

Addison is taken aback by her liveliness, by the echo of Wilson.

Can't wait, can you?
The fun is facing what's new.
What's through is through.
What's next?

Anything is possible,
Maybe for the best.

Maybe so my boy,
Loving though he be,
Has to leave the nest.

(Patting Addison's head)

Maybe he'll enjoy
Feeling really free—

(As Addison starts to protest)

Anything is possible.

(Coughs delicately)

I can't wait to see
What you're going . . . to be . . .
Next . . .

She breaks down, coughing genteelly.

ADDISON
What can I do for you? Tell me, what can I do?

I will make a home for you,
I will take you dancing,
I will come and live with you,
I'll leave you alone—

MAMA
My dear dear boy—

ADDISON
Anything you want—
Tell me what you want—
Anything you want—!

MAMA
I want to see Wilson.

And Wilson does come to visit, high and exuberant and carrying a bottle of Champagne—a few minutes after Mama has died. He wheels on Addison for not having warned him of her grave condition. Addison, for once, not only stands his ground but tells his brother that Mama's dying words were a condemnation of Wilson, accusing him of never having thought of anyone but himself and of being a disappointing and unloving son. It is a lie, of course, but Wilson, devastated, storms out. Addison collects himself, and starts to

arrange the bedclothes neatly around Mama's body.

I'm on My Way

(reprise)

ADDISON
I'm sorry, Mama. All these years, I didn't get it, and you never said a word. What a sap I was, huh? Well, I get it now.

I'm on my way,
Completely on my own.
I'm on my way,
And that's all I'm certain of.
I'm on my way
To worlds I've never known,
Away from those I love . . .

Wilson is revealed at the side of the stage, leaning on a lamppost, holding a bottle, drunk. A couple of gamblers step out of the shadows. Addison looks down at Mama. During the following, he folds her hands across her chest, kisses her on the forehead, picks up his blueprints, looks at them and steps away from the bed. The gamblers start systematically beating Wilson, who has welshed on a large gambling debt.

ADDISON
Today's the day.
Mama, I will thrill you yet.
I have to say,
I've been dumb but I catch on fast.
I'm on my way
To a world of no regret.
Away from those I love—

(Glances over at Wilson, then
cheerfully away)

At last!

As the beating continues, Wilson keeps making wisecracks. Addison, growing ever more elated, sings in a higher key.

ADDISON
I'm on my way,
Who's left to tell me "no"?

I'm on my way,
Not the way that was way back then.
I went astray.
Now I know where I want to go.
I'm on my way again!

The beating continues, the wisecracks growing more desperate.

ADDISON
(Ignoring it, a little louder)
Up, down—okay,
Bloody failure, big success,
I'm here to stay.
Papa said, what's past is past.
I'm on my way,
And if I make a mess—

He becomes distracted by Wilson's beating and watches as the gamblers discover that Wilson had the money on him all the time.

ADDISON
(Turning away)
—I'll just close the door, and away
    I'll run.
I'll do the same things that Willie's
    done.
It's time I started to have some fun.
I'm on my way at last!

He takes a long look at Wilson's inert body, then turns to the audience, smiling excitedly.

What's next?

He exits. The show curtain comes in.

END OF ACT ONE

Or at least that was supposed to be the end of Act One. Just before the Reading took place, we cut the reprise of "I'm on My Way" for staleness. It felt like an amalgam of the first-act curtains of *Gypsy* (determination in the face of disaster, sung loudly) and *West Side Story* (body left alone onstage), so we settled for Addison's simply leaving. We kept Wilson's body, however, and added a nice twist: the conductor signaled the pianist to keep playing the first bars of "On My Left" over and over, pausing in between as if urging Wilson to get up and come back to life, and eventually giving up. Then the show curtain came in.

ACT TWO

The lights come up on the show olio. Vaudeville music; a spotlight picks out Addison at one side of the proscenium, dressed as he was at the beginning of the show. A second spotlight picks out Wilson, in a wheelchair, in a hospital gown, slathered with bandages and drugged with painkillers.

Fourth Vaudeville

ADDISON
(To us)
On my left—

Wilson fails to respond.

—Is my wreck of a brother—

Again Wilson fails to answer; Addison pokes him.

    Hello?

    (To us)

You can see he's not well.

Wilson mutters something weakly.

    Speak up, Willie.

    (Explaining, to us)

He feels guilt about his mother—

WILSON
(Croaking it out)
You can fucking go to hell.

ADDISON
(Cheerfully barreling along)

You've heard of arrogant selfishness,
You've heard of truly perverse.
You've heard of coked to the ears,
Crocodile tears—

WILSON
(Weakly)
Get the nurse . . .

ADDISON
They were each other's very best
    friend,
They were each other's, written in
    stone.
They were each other's, right to the
    end—
And this is the end.

WILSON
Leave me alone . . .

Wilson, his hands shaking, takes out a pill bottle and drops it. He looks for it frantically, twisting clumsily over the arm of his wheelchair. Addison picks the bottle up and, smiling, holds it out.

ADDISON
I'm sorry, were you looking for this?

Wilson snarls and snatches it back, emptying the bottle in one gulp.

WILSON
When you're stuck in a chair
In the deepest despair
And there's nobody there
You can trust . . .

ADDISON
When your brother won't come
To the aid of his mum,
And she thought he was some-
One to trust . . .

WILSON
When your own flesh and blood
Sees you drowning in mud—

ADDISON
When you're nipped in the bud
By a self-serving stud—

WILSON
When you're broke and you're sick,
And your brother's a prick—

ADDISON
(Cheerfully)
It's time to move on to what's
    next . . .

*Addison starts recklessly wheeling the
chair around, practically spilling Wilson out of it.*

La-de-da,
La-de-da, la-de-da . . .

WILSON
Jesus, watch it, will you!

*Finally, he launches the wheelchair
downstage toward the pit. The conductor throws his arms up to protect himself, bringing the music to a literally
screeching halt. Wilson slams on the
brakes, and the chair squeals to a stop
at the lip of the stage.*

ADDISON
(Grinning shamefacedly)
Oops.

In the first two readings, Wilson wasn't
the only one beaten up at the end of
Act One. Addison was also, by a group
of young toughs he tried to pick up.
Thus, this song was presented as a
vaudeville routine performed by two
cripples, one with a cane, one on
crutches, each being ostensibly affable
while trying to maim the other even
further. I don't remember why we
changed it, but I'd like to have seen it.

*A beat. As Wilson gasps for breath, a
Real Estate Agent rushes on, clutching
a fistful of greasy deeds. He is a product
of the Florida land boom, a get-rich-
quick artist with a derby hat and a
cheap cigar—the Act Two equivalent
of the Prospector who introduced the
Gold Rush in Act One.*

ADDISON
Pardon me, my good man, what is
    that you have in your hand?

REAL ESTATE AGENT
Land boom!
With a double whammy, boy!

Land boom!
Profits this thick!
Land boom!
Down around Miami, boy—
The weather's kinda clammy,
But it's get rich quick!

Brand-new communities,
Just take your pick.
Lots of opportunities—
All you need is capital,
A little does the trick.
Beg or steal or borrow,
It'll double by tomorrow.
Only get your ass to Florida
And get rich quick!

*He rushes off as quickly as he rushed
on, and Addison hastens to Florida,
leaving Wilson behind, swallowing
pills and trying to score dope.*

1920. Addison at the Royal Poinciana
Hotel in Palm Beach, the only hotel to
winter at for the rich and social, all of
whom complain about the dreariness of
the place. Here he meets Paris Singer,
heir to the Singer sewing machine fortune, who has bought up half the area's
property in the hope of making Palm
Beach an international spa, a truly
American resort. However, none of his
wealthy acquaintances wants to buy or
build anything; they are happy complaining. Addison leaps at the opportunity and, with Paris's connections,
lands a commission from Eva Stotesbury, Palm Beach's dominant social
arbiter.

Palm Beach
Sequence

ADDISON
I'm on my way,
I've got a house to build.
I'm on my way,
Everything that's bad has passed.
Not every day
Do you get your dream fulfilled.
I'm on my way at last!

*Soon his eccentric designs are widely in
demand.*

Another day,
And another house to make.
I'm on my way.
It's the end of all my woes.
I get to play
With an artificial lake
And with Spanish tiles and
    Moroccan chairs,
With indoor fountains and outdoor
    stairs,
With whims and fancies and
    millionaires—
I'm on my way,
Who knows
What's next?

*Addison, with Paris as his partner,
soon becomes the most successful architect in Florida, as more olios bang
in, each depicting bigger and more
elaborate mansions.*

ADDISON
Gold!
Found me a mother lode!
Gold! Gold!
Lucky old me!
Gold! Gold!
Every day another lode:
Gold to build a mansion
Shaped around a tree,
Gold to build a castle
The color of the sea,
Gold for building towers
That are modeled after flowers,*
For commissioning my dreams,
Which are bursting at the seams,
And for—

ADDISON, PARIS
Dowagers—

PARIS
What would we do without—

BOTH
—Dowagers,

---

*One of Addison's many actual whimsical
accomplishments.

ADDISON
Flinging their weight about—

BOTH
Dowagers—
Mustn't let them go to waste.

Dowagers,
Though they may not be the
    smartest,
Are the refuge of the artist,
To be embraced—
If you can live with their taste.

Dowagers—

PARIS
—Toting their millionaires—

BOTH
Dowagers—

ADDISON
Planning their lavish lairs—

BOTH
Dowagers—
Bless their cast-iron hearts,
The dear old farts.

PARIS
The matrons—

ADDISON
—Of the patrons—

BOTH
—Of the arts.

The millionaires and their wives accumulate, as do the bags of money and the houses. They stroll about, examining their commissions, commenting on them competitively and fighting for Addison's attention.

ADDISON
Dowagers,
Where would we be without
    dowagers?
Never beset by doubt,
Dowagers,
Every one of them a peach—
A house for each!

To build a house takes more than
    dreams,
It takes time and thought and plans
    and schemes,
It takes wood and stone and bricks
    and beams
And dowagers.

ALL
Where would we be without—

PARIS
—Dowagers?

ADDISON
—Millionaires?

MATRONS, DOWAGERS
—Architects?

ADDISON, PARIS
All those divine devout
Dowagers—

ADDISON
Every one of them a peach—
A house for each!

ADDISON, PARIS
How does a dream succeed?
Through dowagers.
All that you really need
Is—

ALL
Dowagers and millionaires and
    architects and lunacy
And look what you get:
Palm Beach!

During this, additional olios have been flying in, and Palm Beach is now complete.

Months later, mid-evening, Addison is in his office at home, and a palatial home it is. A hospital bed has been set up in the middle of the room: Addison, partly from guilt and partly from feeling that his success has brought him confidence enough to handle his domineering brother, has had Wilson brought down from the hospital in New York where he was on the brink of dying. A hurricane is brewing as Wil-

son is brought into the room and deposited on the bed, swathed in bandages. The doctor informs Addison that his brother may not last the night, then leaves.

As Addison keeps vigil, distraught, Paris runs in, waving a check for half a million dollars that the DuPonts have given him for a new house. Addison collapses into his arms, weeping that Wilson is going to die. Paris's hand is dangling the check close to Wilson's inert form when slowly, hesitantly, Wilson starts to sit up, reaching out a trembling hand for the check as the hurricane explodes outside and lightning illuminates Wilson's bandaged body. It is a scene out of The Mummy.

Ever faithful to our source, the spirit of Hope and Crosby, of cartoon, of drama by exaggeration, still pervaded the show. Once we reached the Workshop, the next stage of development, this tone had all but disappeared.

Wilson, recuperating, meets Paris and, encouraging Paris's high opinion of Addison as an architect, flatters him into thinking of himself as a grand patron of the arts with Addison as his star—not just as an architect but as a builder of cities. To this end, he informs Paris about an undeveloped tract of land down the coast called Boca Raton (English translation: the Mouth of the Rat) and is just about to foist on him some real estate papers, when Addison enters. The three men freeze, as two straw hats and canes are tossed onto the stage from the wings and caught by Addison and Paris.

Fifth Vaudeville

ADDISON
(*Referring to Paris*)
On my left—

SINGER
(*Referring to Addison*)
On my right—

ADDISON
Is a prince—

SINGER
Is a jewel—

ADDISON
Never arrogant or cruel—

SINGER
Never dull or banal.

ADDISON
He is deft.

SINGER
He is bright.

BOTH
I just love him to pieces.

ADDISON
And believe me, I don't say that
Just because he's rich as Croesus . . .

Addison, generously gesturing for Wilson to join them, snaps his fingers and another straw hat and cane are tossed in from the wings. Addison claps the hat onto Wilson's head, slaps the cane in his hand and yanks him into the dance.

ADDISON
(*His arm around Singer's shoulder*)
You've heard of Arthur and
    Lancelot—

SINGER
(*His arm around Addison's shoulder*)
They were a pair without peer.

ADDISON, SINGER
But come join Paris [Addie] and me.
You can be
Guinevere!

Wilson smiles charmingly to Singer and all three dance. Addison executes a particularly flashy step; Wilson applauds, turns to Singer.

WILSON
Will you look at that grace,
That adorable face?
You can tell that is someone to trust.

Addison does another spectacular turn.

SINGER
In a world full of sham
There's not much worth a damn,
But an artist is someone to trust.

WILSON
That's because now he has someone
    to trust.
Trust is a must, you'll agree.
Plus there's nothing to trust like a
    man with a trust
And you fit the role to a "T."

SINGER
(*Blushing, flattered*)
You mean me?

WILSON
Yes, I do, yes, of course.

SINGER
Do you really mean me?

WILSON
Let me say it with force:
An artist's as good as his source.

Singer does an elegantly intricate step. Wilson applauds him and does his own fancy turn, which Singer applauds. Soon Wilson and Singer are dancing to delight each other. Addison keeps dancing, but is increasingly ignored, until finally he gestures angrily to the conductor and stops the music. Singer, unruffled, tells Addison about his plan with Wilson to build a city in Boca Raton. Wilson grins and sings to Addison.

WILSON
On my left—

SINGER
On my right—

WILSON
—Is a man of decision.

SINGER
—Is a dreamer with a vision.

WILSON
And one hell of a guy . . .

Addison, once again outmaneuvered by his brother, tears off his hat, hurls it and his cane to the ground and stalks out. Singer is baffled; Wilson pats him on the arm and heads off after Addison.

On the beach, Wilson apologizes to the furious Addison for his selfish behavior and for neglecting Mama, adding that he allowed himself to be beaten up because he was feeling suicidally guilty about it. Addison admits to Wilson that he made up Mama's dying words out of spite. The brothers bond for a moment and Wilson quickly takes advantage of it to sell Addison on the idea of Boca Raton. He suggests that it could be both a memorial to Mama and a re-creation of Benicia, a nod to Papa and the good times they had together growing up. Another "You and me against the world, Addie . . ."

Addison caves in, Wilson snaps his fingers and the elements of a boom-time Florida real estate office come together behind them, accompanied by frantic activity: workmen toting furniture; art directors carrying mock-ups of brochures; a bathing beauty posing with a "Boca Raton" sash across her chest and holding a basket of grapefruit; a salesman grilling two eager trainees; and two songwriters at a piano, composing a jingle.

Boca Raton Sequence

SONGWRITER #1
(As Songwriter #2 hammers the keyboard)
So:
Boca Ratone!
You've got a charm all your own!

SONGWRITER #2
(Stops playing)
Not "tone," "ton."

SONGWRITER #1
(A beat)
So:

(Gestures for Songwriter #2
to resume)

Boca Raton!
You've got the charm of a swan!

SONGWRITER #2
(Stops playing)
Great.

*A giant thermometer, calibrated to reflect real estate sales, rolls on, and a sign flies in—*THE MIZNER DEVELOPMENT CORPORATION. *Wilson passes by.*

SONGWRITERS
(Auditioning for Wilson's approval)
The Mouth of the Rat
Is where everyone's at!
It's where everyone goes,
It's where everyone's gone,
Come down and lease a piece of
    Boca Raton!
The spot that's hot
Is Boca Raton!

The scene becomes the swimming pool area of a newly constructed luxury hotel. A choir of young men and women, wearing robes over bathing suits, stands at one microphone. Wilson is at another. It is a national broadcast. Two buglers, dressed as if to ride to the hounds, blast a fanfare and the choir sings joyfully.

CHOIR
Florida! Florida! Florida!

Wilson the entrepreneur makes an eloquent pitch for Boca Raton real estate, backed up by enthusiastic endorsements from sports stars (a Bobby Jones type), movie stars (a Mae West type) and foreign royalty (Princess Ghika of Romania) who supposedly have bought lots.

CELEBRITIES
Boca Raton!
Come down to Boca Raton—

GOLFER
Where every golf course shimmers
    with green . . .

PRINCESS
Where all the famous peoples are
    seen . . .

SEXPOT
It's awful hot—y'know what I
    mean? . . .

ALL THREE
Sea and surf
And sun and sand.
See a perf-
Ect wonderland.

Boca Raton,
Come down to Boca Raton—

GOLFER
For health—

PRINCESS
And relaxation—

SEXPOT
And fun.

ALL THREE
Nice and Venice rolled into one!

CHOIR
Florida . . .

Wilson begins a litany of extravagant statements about the real estate investment opportunities of Boca Raton, culminating in a description of a road about to be built, "A road like no other in the world," that will lead the entire world into the city. It will be, he claims, more than two hundred feet in width and boast twenty lanes for traffic, an illuminated canal running down its middle, plied by gondolas with "genuine Italian gondoliers" singing as they sail ("Call out your favorites as you motor by—they take requests!"), banked by royal palms and lit by spotlights embedded in marble curbstones.*

He is interrupted by an excited man running on, carrying a pirate chest. The man explains that he had just purchased a beachfront lot and discovered a chest of buried treasure on it.

Wilson responds that although that may be exciting, the man has purchased something "far more valuable than gold and jewels," he has purchased a piece of America: the land itself. "Up in the Klondike we shoveled it aside to get at the wealth which it contained. Down here, it is the wealth!"

On cue, testimonials pour in from investors: housewives, farmers, bookkeepers, and the like, all of whom have made a fortune buying and selling Mizner Development Corporation lots.

INVESTORS
Boca Raton,
Come down to Boca Raton,
Where everybody's wearing a smile
'Cause everybody's living in style
While all the while they're making a
    pile.

Don't think twice,
Take our advice:
Get your slice
Of paradise.

Boca Raton,
Come down to Boca Raton,
Where you can swim and mingle
    and play
And invest in the U.S.A.

---

* This road was not just a figment of Wilson's overheated promotional imagination. It was partially built, and a small remnant of it exists today, narrowing into a dirt road that leads into a swamp. That road became a basic metaphor for us, stemming from Papa's deathbed speech, and was emphasized in a song subsequently written for the Workshop and eventually giving us the proper title for the show.

As the giant thermometer climbs, Wilson announces that advertisements for the resort will shortly appear in newspapers throughout the country. Bathing Beauties rush on with beach balls and start to sing and dance.

ALL

Stow your woes,
Stop being frantic.
Dunk your toes
In the Atlantic.
Thumb your nose
At the blizzards and ice.

Getting tanned,
Playing the courses,
Fishing and
Betting the horses,
Life is grand
At an affordable price.

Take a boat or a bus,
Come by road or by river,
Throw your bags in a flivver
Or take the sunshine express
To your new address . . .

The Bathing Beauties form a train, which gradually accelerates among many cries of "Woo-woo!" and "All aboard!"

Buy a lot,
Or maybe two.
Have we got
A lot for you!
Boca Raton—

SEXPOT

You'll love it—

ALL

Boca Raton!
But you'll regret it if you delay!

Come and see
The new frontier!
Come and be
A pioneer!
You'll agree,
Tomorrow's here
Today!
Boca Raton!

Paris starts to become troubled about Wilson's real estate promises, such as "Where the sun is guaranteed to shine three hundred and twenty-seven days per year," but Wilson shrugs them off as nothing more than the everyday practice of advertising. Addison, amused by Wilson's exaggerations, at first disabuses Paris of his worries and assures him that everything is in proportion, but as the sequence progresses, he too begins to become alarmed by Wilson's promotional extravagance and increasing loss of control. Paris demands that Wilson make a public retraction of the promotional lies. Wilson not only refuses, but knocks Paris down. Paris grabs the microphone and announces to the world that the Boca Raton promotion is a dishonest and deceptive one and that investors should withdraw their money. Which they do. The thermometer, and everything around it, crashes to the ground.

This, simplified though it may be, is exactly what happened in Florida in the mid-1920s. Gigantic fortunes were made and lost in short order. Some investors made hundreds of thousands of dollars between a morning buy and an afternoon sell. But, presaging the Wall Street crash of 1929, the boom became a bust virtually overnight, and suicides were not uncommon. The Mizners weren't wholly responsible for it, of course, but they were instrumental in causing it.

Addison's bedroom. Feeling guilty about investors losing their savings, he is packing his suitcase to leave. Wilson enters and tells him not to feel so bothered by it.

Get Out of My Life

WILSON

Easy come and easy go—
So it up and went.

No point in regretting, though,
What you can't prevent.
One two three,
It's time to re-
Invent.

Addison accuses him of not caring about anyone but himself, of using people "Like they were table stakes."

ADDISON

Easy come and easy go,
One and then another
Finally your brother.
Don't you ever stop?

(Sighs)

All because you couldn't stay on top.

He suddenly slams the lid of his suitcase closed.

Get out of my life!
Get the hell out of my life!
No more making me feel
Like I'm the heel,
Like you're the man and I'm the
    wife!

Get out of my way,
Get out of my song.
I'll never be able to sing
With you singing along.

I don't give a damn
Who's weak, who's strong,
Who's right, who's wrong.
So long,
Goodbye,
I have to get on with my life—!

(Losing steam)

So just—
Go . . .

WILSON

Hey, you're upset. It's understandable. One minute you're king of the

world, the next minute you're busted and you're back with me. You'll get used to it—

ADDISON
No!

(Quieter, but with the same intensity)

Get out of my life,
Stay out of my life.
Whatever this race we're in,
Okay, you win.
It's done.
And now that you've won,
Get out of my life.

It used to be fun
To watch you work,
And even be a part of it—
At the start of it.
Such fun to stand and smirk
At the suckers—
But I got that from you.

I used to savor every scheme.
But then
I used to think we were a team.
Amen,
No more,
I've looked at the score:

You owe me a life,
A life of my own!
I wanted to be like you—
Before I do,
Please—
Leave me alone.

Get out of my life,
So I can live it . . .
Please . . .
Go away.

Wilson shrugs, starts to leave, only to turn back; a beat.

Go

WILSON
This will amuse you: I want to stay.

(As Addison stares at him)

More than that—you don't want me to go.

(Softly)

Come on,
You don't want me to go.

You may think, yes, you do,
Right now—
That's now,
But it just isn't so.

ADDISON
Go away, Willie, please . . .

WILSON
(Increasingly in fervor)
You remember the bad.
Not me,
I remember the good.
You remember the things that failed,
But what about the heights we
    scaled?

And this isn't the end of the trip.
No, it's just the reverse.
Face it, brother, we're joined at
    the hip.
And that is our curse,
And that is the miracle!

You don't want me to go.
Admit
You don't want me to go.

ADDISON
Yes I do, Willie, damn it!

WILSON
I know why you're so hurt.
I may be dirt,
But I've never been slow.

ADDISON
I'm just one of a hundred you've
hurt . . .

WILSON
Don't you know that I know,
That I've known all along—?

ADDISON
Everything that you touch, you
ruin . . .

WILSON
(Overlapping)
—What you never could say,
What you don't want to show?
That's the only thing wrong.

ADDISON
All right, Willie, enough—

WILSON
(Furious)
Come on, Addie, you love me!
Come on, say it out loud!
Come on, say it:
You love me, you love me,
You've always been—

ADDISON
(Overlapping)
All right, yes!
I love you, I always have loved you!
Does that make us even?
Does that make you happy?

(Quietly)

And I want you to go.

(Beat)

And no,
I don't want you to go . . .

Wilson embraces Addison. Another beat, then Addison pushes him away.

ADDISON
No!

Wilson smiles, shrugs, and turns to leave, but just as he's about to exit:

Where will you go?

WILSON
I don't know. But somewhere out there there's gotta be a place where they aren't quite so hard on self-centered bastards who don't think twice about wrecking other people's lives.

Lights up on a sign: HOLLYWOOD. Wilson gives Addison a wave and strolls off, as lights come up on the Brown Derby restaurant in Hollywood in 1933. Wilson, drunk and strung out on cocaine, is being interviewed by a reporter about his notorious life. As he looks around the room, he sees that all the patrons are figures from his past. A telegram arrives, announcing

Addison's death. Wilson yells at every-one to get out and promptly crashes to the floor. Addison appears and helps him up. Wilson slaps his hand away disdainfully.

Final Vaudeville

WILSON
(To us)
On my left—

ADDISON
On my right—

WILSON
—Is my boob of a brother.

ADDISON
—Is a man I'd gladly smother,
If he hadn't just died.

WILSON
He's all heft.

ADDISON
He's all height.

WILSON
He's a rat—

ADDISON
He's a cynic—

WILSON
—Went and left me in a clinic—

ADDISON
—Kept on tossing me aside—

Wilson reacts to Addison's line and re-alizes he's dead, too. He takes this in stride.

BOTH
Still, it cannot be denied:

WILSON
As a rat, he's okay.

ADDISON
As a thief, he's D'Artagnan.

BOTH
And believe me, I don't say that
Just because he's my companion.

They wonder whether their lives have added up to anything. Papa Mizner ap-pears and tells them how disappointed in them he is.

ADDISON, WILSON
Just a couple of wise guys,
On the highway of life—

ADDISON
Doing our dance, singing our
song . . .

BOTH
Just a couple of wise guys
Without a kiddie or a wife . . .

WILSON
Making it up as we go along . . .

Mama appears and frets over how their friendship soured.

ADDISON, WILSON
Just a couple of jokers
With a quip and a smile.

ADDISON
Could have been—what?

WILSON
Anything.

BOTH
(With a shrug)
But—

Just a couple of rib pokers,
Ego strokers,
With a measure of style.

Wilson frowns as they saunter around.

WILSON
You don't suppose this is Heaven,
do you?

ADDISON
God keeps better books than that,
Willie.

WILSON
Then where do you think guys like
us go after we die?

ADDISON
I don't think they go anywhere. I
think they just keep going.

The show olio comes in behind them. They look at the central image on the drop—which we now recognize as the road Wilson described in Boca Raton.

BOTH
Just a couple of wise guys,
Looking forward, not back,
Just a couple of wise guys,
Trying not to lose track.

A pair of busy boys
Who made a noise
But never came home with the prize,
Just a couple of—

WILSON
Ice-skaters—

ADDISON
Spectators—

WILSON
Hook baiters—

ADDISON
Saints and satyrs—

BOTH
Just a couple of guys—
Cracking wise!

They look out over the audience's heads and spot something in the distance. It is Papa's road. Ever optimistic, they head off toward it, still pioneering, still rein-venting themselves.

C U R T A I N

The Reading turned out to be some-thing of a triumph, not only because Victor and Nathan were such outsized and engaging personalities, but be-

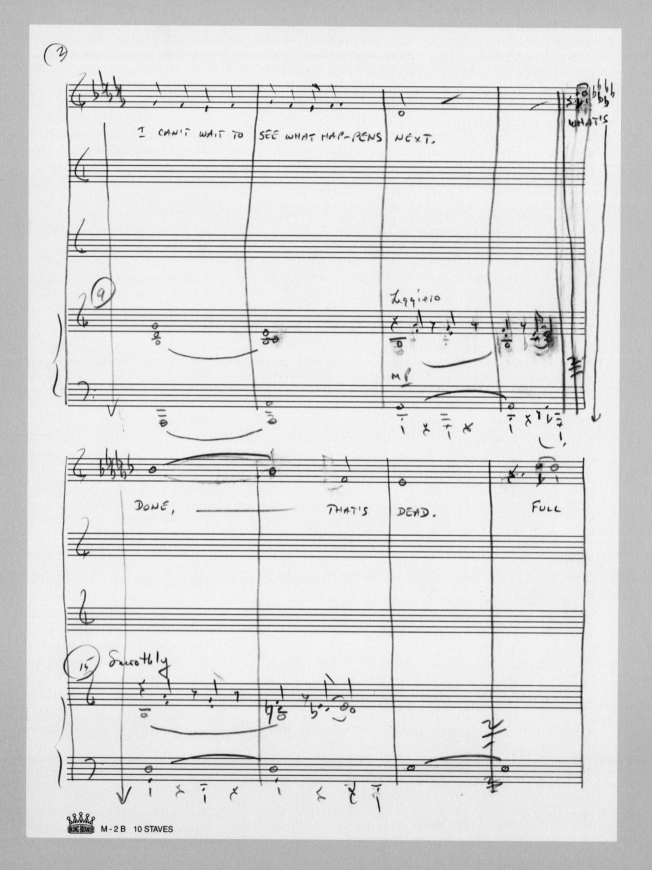

I CAN'T WAIT TO SEE WHAT HAP-PENS NEXT.

WHAT'S

DONE, ——— THAT'S DEAD.

FULL

cause they instinctively knew how to make the vaudeville approach simultaneously stylized and true to character. Everybody connected with the show—producers, director, actors, even John and I—was enormously pleased. We planned to tinker with it a bit, do a full-blown three-week-long workshop at a theater and polish it in front of a paying audience, then transfer it to a Broadway house for a commercial run.

We were overly optimistic. The tinkering took ten years, three directors, two out-of-town tryouts, a rotation of six actors in the leading roles, the writing of more than a dozen new songs, the discarding of more than two dozen, and we never did open on Broadway. Each subsequent incarnation was transformed by and reflected the individual stamp of its director. It was a long journey, but we finally reached our optimal destination, that of the authors.

And now for something completely different.

A Special Workshop Presentation of

WISE GUYS

Book by
John Weidman

Music & Lyrics by
Stephen Sondheim

with

Brooks Ashmanskas Jessica Boevers Candy Buckley
Kevin Chamberlin Christopher Fitzgerald Victor Garber Michael Hall
Nathan Lane Jessica Molaskey Nancy Opel William Parry
Clarke Thorell Lauren Ward Ray Wills

Directed by.. Sam Mendes
Choreographed by ....Jonathan Butterell
Music Director ....Ted Sperling
Scenery Designed by ....Mark Thompson
Costumes Designed by ....Santo Loquasto
Lighting Designed by .... Jules Fisher &
Peggy Eisenhauer
Sound Designed by ....Jonathan Deans
Musical Supervisor ....Paul Gemignani
Orchestrations ....Jonathan Tunick
Casting .... Jim Carnahan
Production Stage Manager.......................................Bonnie Panson
Production Manager...David Bradford
General Press Representation ....Barlow•Hartman public relations

---

Cast of Characters
(in order of appearance)

Wilson Mizner ....Victor Garber
Reporter ....Christopher Fitzgerald
Addison Mizner..Nathan Lane
Papa..William Parry
Mama ....Candy Buckley
A Prospector.. Kevin Chamberlin
Poker Players .... William Parry, Ray Wills, Kevin Chamberlin, Brooks Ashmanskas
Assayer...Clarke Thorell
Ticket Seller ....Ray Wills
Business Man #1 ....Michael Hall
Business Man #2 .... Nancy Opel
Solicitor ....Brooks Ashmanskas
Chinese Warlord ....Kevin Chamberlin
Plantation Owner..William Parry
Doorman .... Kevin Chamberlin
Mrs. Myra Yerkes...Jessica Molaskey
Paul Armstrong...Brooks Ashmanskas
Stanley Ketchel..Ray Wills
Flatbush Phil...Clarke Thorell
Newsboy ....Christopher Fitzgerald
Gladys ....Jessica Boevers
Souvenir Sellers and Club Patrons ....Brooks Ashmanskas, Jessica Boevers,
Kevin Chamberlin, Christopher Fitzgerald, Michael Hall, Jessica Molaskey,
Nancy Opel, William Parry, Clark Thorell, Lauren Ward, Ray Wills

---

Band

Conductor/Keyboards .... Ted Sperling
Keyboards...Robert A. Berman
Drums .... James Baker

Staff

General Management..Dodger Management Group
Sally Campbell Morse, Robert C. Strickstein,
Staci Levine, Matt Olin
Company Manager.. Kimberly Kelley
Stage Manager..Kenneth J. McGee
Assistant Choreographer...Gustavo Zajac
Assistant Lighting Designer ....Jack Jacobs
Assistant Costume Designer..Mitchell Bloom
Production Electrician/Followspot Operator .... John Anselmo
Light Board Operator...Jason Strangfeld
Followspot Operator..Jason Szalla
Production Sound Engineer .... David Gotwald
Production Propertyman ....George Wagner
Wardrobe Supervisor .... Leah Redmond
Casting Associate ....Geoffrey Soffer
Music Preparation Supervisors...........................Emily Grishman Music Preparation
Katharine Edmonds/Emily Grishman
Production Assistants... Joel Derfner, Donald S. Fried,
Courtney E. Golden, Suzanne Menhart
Assistant to Stephen Sondheim ....Steve Clar

Act Two · **Wise Guys** · The Workshop (1999)

Book by John Weidman
Direction by Sam Mendes

The Notion

A chronicle of two brothers, Wilson and Addison Mizner, who were born in the 1880s and died in the 1930s. Wilson was a con man, entrepreneur and wit, among other semi-accomplishments; Addison was chiefly an architect without portfolio. Their personalities were polar opposites, but their relationship was intense and complicated. The show charts their lives from their beginnings in Benicia, California, through their adventures in the Klondike gold fields of the 1890s to the extremes of New York City society in the early 1900s and into the Florida real estate boom and bust of the 1920s, for which they were largely responsible. It begins and ends in Hollywood.

If you think you've read this outline before, you have, except for the last sentence. But there are significant changes within it.

General Comments

In 1992, Sam Mendes, the artistic director of the newly renovated Donmar Warehouse Theatre in London, decided to open it with, of all things, an American musical: namely, *Assassins*. Not only were John (Weidman) and I chuffed, as the British would say, by the choice but, as it turned out, delighted by his direction of the show. This happy experience was repeated for me a few years later when he directed *Company* at the same venue,* so it seemed natural for us to continue the collaboration with *Wise Guys*. To this end John and I invited him to supervise the second and third Readings of the show and subsequently to direct a workshop production at the New York Theatre Workshop, with actors holding scripts and with no scenery, no props and a combo instead of an orchestra, but fully and meticulously staged.

Although Sam had been happy with the results of the Reading, he felt that John and I were hindering the show from finding its proper weight and tone in a number of ways. To begin with, as exemplified by the Benicia and New York sequences, he felt that we were allowing ourselves to be hamstrung by facts, that in an attempt to cover every colorful incident in the Mizners' lives we were shortchanging the emotional content of the material: the convoluted love story between the brothers and with their parents, especially their mother. Moreover, he noted, Addison wasn't a major enough talent in the history of architecture to justify our sticking to the facts of his life. He urged us to take the same liberties with the lives of the Mizners that we had taken with the lives of Kayama and Manjiro in *Pacific Overtures*, who were also real historical figures, or the ones which James Lapine and I had taken with Georges Seurat, who *was* a major artist, but whose life was so secretive and mysterious that we could make up almost anything about him that we chose. Sam also worried that by intermittently

---

* A footnote hard to resist, given my fondness for hyperbole: the Donmar Warehouse is to my taste the best theater space in the English-speaking world. Oscar Hammerstein once told me that with the right opening number for a musical you could read the telephone book for the next forty-five minutes and the audience would be enchanted. At the Donmar, you don't need the opening number.

retreating into the low comedy territory of Hope and Crosby, John and I were avoiding the substance of the piece, as if we were excusing ourselves from taking it too seriously. In the first instance, he went so far as to suggest that we not base the show on the Mizners at all, but on two characters we could invent, who would merely represent what the Mizners meant to us and thus allow us to be looser and freer with the facts of their lives. This seemed such a far-reaching overhaul that after the briefest of thought we dismissed it. Sam's second observation, however, was more difficult to set aside, and it seemed reasonable enough; besides, it was subversively flattering to be told that our work was more substantial than we deemed it to be. John and I started to rewrite accordingly, leaching out the wilder cartoon flavors bit by bit in favor of a more "realistic" approach, although still well within the realm of musical comedy, which is the realm where *Wise Guys* in all of its incarnations belongs.

The process of rewriting, however, was somewhat slowed by the requirements of Sam's inaugural stint as a movie director. In the year since the 1998 Reading, he had directed his first movie, *American Beauty,* and the months directly preceding the Workshop were consumed by post-production and promotional work, as well as previews and film festivals and the like, all of which often made Sam unavailable to us to discuss the rewrites we'd done as well as the ones he was urging us to do. The result was that he began rehearsals distracted by the excitement of this new part of his life, and feeling uncertain about our show, a feeling which over time conveyed itself to the actors. This uncertainty reached its peak exactly where you'd expect it to: at the first public performance. Nathan and Victor entered to wild applause and performed the hell out of the opening number, but what had rocked the house at the readings now drew polite enthusiasm at best.

Perhaps it was partly because of the audience. New York Theatre Workshop patrons would probably have better welcomed a musical with more cutting-edge peculiarity, such as *Pacific Overtures* or *Sunday in the Park with George;* they may not have been ready or willing to greet a traditional Broadway musical comedy with the same generosity, even though we had gone to great lengths in all the pre-production publicity to emphasize exactly what kind of show *Wise Guys* was. Whatever kind, they chose not to go with it, and the effect of subdued laughter and mild response disconcerted the actors as well as the rest of us and set the tone of the evening. To compound matters, I hadn't finished the score—most of Act Two remained to be written, one reason being that the book was still in flux.

Feeling discouraged and panicky, Sam asked John and me and the producers to stay away from rehears- als and to let him tinker a bit with the structure of the piece until he had a reworked first act to show us. We encouraged him to feel free; we didn't expect him to feel quite as free as he did. When he was finally ready, and presented us with a run-through, we discovered to our dismay that for the opening of the show he and the actors had cobbled together a revision of what had been the last scene of the Reading: the scene in The Brown Derby, where the dead Addison appears and the brothers bond together in a vaudeville routine. Sam hoped that this flashback framework would provide the missing (in his view) conceptual connection between style and substance. In his scenario the Mizners, upon being reconciled in death, turned toward the audience and explained that they were about to tell us the story of their lives.

This made for a flaccid and familiar opening. The brothers became merely emcees, guiding us into the story in paint-by-numbers expository style. Flashbacks in shows (and movies) have become such a common narrative crutch over the years that if they are ever to have a chance of being effective they have to pop up unexpectedly, which is why we had written ours to erupt suddenly from the middle of a fight. Announcing it to the audience in advance made it something expected instead of something surprising, and the tone of the number, or rather lack of it, colored everything which followed. Moreover, opening the show on a note of death didn't contribute a lot toward making the first vaudeville funny. But we tried it in performance, anyway.

The flashback framework not only didn't accomplish its goal, its desperate improvised feel unsettled the company, corroding the sense of community that every theater project needs. And since John and I hadn't shown up at rehearsals and the performers hadn't been told why, they felt, as one of them put it later, like children caught in the middle of an imminent parental breakup. The toxic atmosphere worsened as the run continued and was particularly hard on Victor and Nathan: John was their friend, but Sam was their leader. After a week or so, feeling beleaguered by a show that wasn't working but which they had to keep performing, the actors as well as the director lost their faith in John's script.

Of all the performing arts, theater is the most collaborative, and by the middle of the run, the worst had happened: the collaboration—between writers, director and actors—had broken down. The actors became reluctant to take changes in the script, the director supported them, and a kind of chaos set in. The producers, caught in the middle, were forced to declare their sympathies; they did not choose the authors. It was then that I suddenly, and despairingly, realized I was living the show business nightmare I had so naively yearned for and babbled on to Jerome

Robbins about when we were in Washington with *West Side Story:* the legendarily melodramatic dysfunctional out-of-town tryout. This one was exacerbated by taking place in full view of the customary New York mixture of supporters, curiosity-seekers and ill-wishers—no out-of-town shelter for us. I thought I had run up against the genuine article with the tryout of *A Funny Thing Happened on the Way to the Forum,* but in that case, although we all—writers, director, actors—were baffled and too often contentious, there was no choosing up sides; we remained a company working together, triumph or disaster. And we had a producer (Hal Prince) who,

in the face of daunting odds, was convinced that the show was worth working on and determined that it should survive. Whatever hostilities surfaced in that venture, they weren't about the show; they were personal—they concerned feelings of friendships challenged and frayed, but they didn't affect the work.

All things considered, however, the Workshop of *Wise Guys* was not the mess that the chatterati made it out to be (and still do). It was a misfire, but not by a wide margin. It was lurching forward on the first leg of its journey rather than launching smoothly, but it was moving in the right direction.

SONDHEIM STRIKES GOLD!

Judge bars Rudin from interfering with new musical

rk Post, Wednesday, December 5, 2001   nypost.com

By DAREH GREGORIAN

The show can go on for legendary Broadway composer Stephen Sondheim.

A Manhattan judge yesterday barred big-time producer Scott Rudin from interfering with or claiming exclusive rights to the "West Side Story" lyricist's latest musical, "Gold!"

Sondheim and co-writer John Weidman had claimed in a $5 million lawsuit that Rudin was trying to scuttle the musical by claiming he owned the rights to it, a claim that scared off Tony award-winning director Harold Prince from a planned September 2002 production of the new work in Chicago.

In an emergency hearing, state Supreme Court Justice Ira Gammerman sided with Sondheim, ruling that Rudin apparently has "no rights at all" to the musical. He issued a temporary restraining order barring him from interfering with the production.

Rudin's lawyer, Jonathan Zarin, told the judge his decision "violates the federal Constitution" and his client's right to free speech.

Despite the losing battle, Rudin, who produced the steamy Nicole Kidman play "The Blue Room" and a slew of Hollywood hits including "The Truman Show," is continuing the war.

The 43-year-old filed an $8 million countersuit yesterday, charging Sondheim and Weidman with fraud, breach of contract and unjust enrichment.

The counterclaim says he had first dibs on the rights to the completed musical because he invested hundreds of thousands of dollars in it, but that the pair never showed him the finished product before they signed on with Prince.

And, Rudin says, his involvement with "Gold!" is more than monetary; he also contributed "significant creative elements" to the work.

The two were once friends and had worked together. Rudin produced Sondheim's flop, "Passion," and a successful revival of his "A Funny Thing Happened on the Way to the Forum."

Their discord dates to 1997, when Sondheim and Weidman entered into a deal with Kennedy Center to write a musical about

STEPHEN SONDHEIM
On with the show.

the infamous con men, the Mizner brothers, then titled "Wise Guys."

Rudin joined in to fund a workshop of the musical, essentially an early draft, that eventually was performed in New York in 1999.

According to Sondheim's suit, Rudin "saw [Gold!] and hated it." It says Rudin had a six-month window to buy the rights, and let it pass. He also ignored other invitations from the pair involve himself with the project, the suit says — until he found it was supposed to hit the stage in Chicago, and fired off a "cease and desist" letter to Prince, who was producing and directing it.

The letter made the "Evita" director back off, and nearly cost them the theater engagement. Asked if the judge's order might convince Prince to get back on board, Sondheim's lawyer, Gerard Harper, said, "I hope so."

He said this kind of legal ugliness is brand new to his 71-year-old client.

"He's led a charmed life. He's never sued and never been sued. Only Mr. Rudin," he said.

Daily News Dec 5/01

B'way honchos to mine 'Gold!'

A Manhattan judge sided in favor of Broadway bigs Stephen Sondheim and John Weidman yesterday, ruling their show can go on.

The creators of "Gold!" won an injunction against stage and movie producer Scott Rudin that temporarily bars him from claiming he has exclusively rights to the musical.

Although "Gold!" was due to open in Chicago in September, Sondheim and Weidman contended Rudin's claims and threats of legal action have scared off theater operators and their Tony-winning director, Harold Prince.

Rudin claimed he has exclusive rights to produce the musical, but Sondheim and Weidman contend those rights expired when he failed to exercise them by May 20, 2000.

In a hearing shorter than a Broadway intermission, Manhattan Supreme Court Justice Ira Gammerman told the parties "I don't think he [Rudin] has any rights" — and granted the injunction. Another hearing was set for Jan. 30.

Helen Peterson and Leo Standora

Stephen Sondheim

ACT ONE

The Brown Derby restaurant in Hollywood. 1933. Wilson, drunk and strung out on cocaine, is being interviewed by a reporter about his notorious life. A telegram arrives, announcing Addison's death. Wilson screams at the reporter to get out and promptly falls over, dead. Addison appears, and he and Wilson step out of the set.

First Vaudeville***

The opening number comprises the same set of songs as in the Reading (omitting "Someone to Trust"), performed in the same vaudeville style but with a distinct difference in tone: the edgy competitiveness of their banter is now just as lighthearted but more straightforward and expository.

After the applause, the brothers, instead of trying to upstage each other, simply inform the audience that they will now tell the story of their lives. Mama yells for them and we go to Benicia, as before—this time, however, without the unnecessary other brothers, family trappings and history. Instead, Mama has summoned the boys to Papa's deathbed, and Papa now exhorts them, as before, but in song rather than dialogue.

It's in Your Hands Now

PAPA
There's a road straight ahead,
There's a century beginning.
There's a land of opportunity and
    more.
It's in your hands now.

*** The lyrics here and in other songs marked by a triple asterisk can be found in the previous section of this chapter.

We have left you resources beyond
    measure, possibilities undreamt of
    in the history of mankind. Make of
    them what you will, but use them
    well.

There are dreams to be fed,
There's a world that's worth the
    winning,
There's a legacy of riches that's in
    store.
Now it's up to you.
There's a lot to do,
But you'll see it through
If your road stays true.
It's in your hands now.
Time to start the journey now!

Never falter, never rest
Until you know
You've achieved the very best
That you can be,
Never pausing in your quest
For something better just around
    the corner.

Up to you to set the course
Of where we'll go,
With the limitless resources
You can plumb.
Keep your eyes on what's afar,
Not on what we are
But what we can become!

Follow on where we led,
Make the past an underpinning
For the future, for the road you must
    explore . . .

He sits bolt upright and stretches his hand toward the future: the audience.

As the road extends,
You can see it never ends.
No, it just ascends
And it never bends.
Doesn't matter how
Or where it goes, as long as it keeps
    going.

*(Suddenly weakening, his voice
    dropping)*

It's in your hands now,
Go forth and make your papa
    proud—!

He falls back on his bed with a thud and dies.

In the Reading, Papa's pep talk from the coffin was surreal and funny, not least because it was pompous, as Papa is pompous. But we wanted to have it both ways, because what he says is what the show is about: American possibilities, their potential for greatness and their concomitant potential for careless squandering. The Mizner story embodies this for us as a cautionary tale about transforming America's pioneering spirit into the get-rich-quick sensibility that blossomed in the twentieth century. By turning Papa's rant into a stirring Sousa-like march, I hoped to make the point felt rather than funny. I had written just such a patriotic song about the American flag in *Assassins* and I recycled the music here—the only time other than "Addison's Trip" that I've ever done so. The fact that I did such a thing twice in the same show makes me wonder if indeed, like so many composers in what could delicately be called late middle age, I was running out of inventive steam. At the time, I told myself that if a tune was never going to see the light of day in the show for which it was written, why not utilize it in an appropriate elsewhere? I didn't wait around for the answer.

Mama tells the boys that Papa died stone broke. They discuss what to do about it, and the boys begin to argue.

My Two Young Men***

The same as before. In the Reading, this song had struck John and me as holding up the action, but we included it here because Sam felt, and rightly, that it encapsulated the core of the story—the brothers' relationship with each other and with their mother—and provided the springboard for Addison's behavior: his feeling of rejection by her.

As in the Reading, a prospector bounds on, clutching an enormous nugget of gold.

Gold!***

The song as before, including the departure for Alaska, but with a significant change of plot: When the brothers arrive in the Yukon, they start hacking at the tundra together, back to back.

WILSON
(Swinging his pick)
Gold!

ADDISON
(Also)
Gold!

WILSON
Ready for acquiring!

(Pause, as they wiggle their picks out of the frozen ground)

Gold!

(Swings his pick again, to no avail)

ADDISON
Gold!

WILSON
I've got a hunch.
Gold!

(Swings his pick at a new spot)

ADDISON
Gold!

(Sniffing himself)

God, am I perspiring?

WILSON
Jesus, this is tiring,
Let's break for lunch.

He takes a sandwich out of his pocket, Addison a thermos from his knapsack.

Wilson starts to bite the sandwich, eyes it suspiciously and raps it against the end of his pick. It clangs, hard as a rock. As he stares at it in dismay, Addison opens the thermos and tips it to his lips. Nothing comes out. He frowns and turns it over. A solid brown cylinder slides out and hits his foot. He yelps in pain and grabs the foot, dancing around. A moment's recovery, and he starts hacking away again. Wilson just stares.

ADDISON
Gold!

(Hack)

What's a little storm or two?
Gold!

(Hack)

Good for the skin!
Gold!

(Hack, glancing at Wilson)

Wouldn't you be warmer to
Just dig in?
Oh, come on, Willie,
The two of us together—
Let's dig!

You and me against the world,
    Willie,
You and me against the world . . .
You and me together,
Weathering the weather.
Living out the drama—
Wait till we see Mama!

They sing a slight variation of the song on the dig, dividing the lines between them, and are just about to give up when they hit a vein.

Although in this Workshop we included comic vaudeville moments like the sandwich and the thermos bottle, we tried to make the relationship between the brothers more even-handed, to avoid the repetition of Addison's constantly being the subservient patsy and Wilson the domineering trickster. We started the realignment by having

them work the dig together, strike a vein together and return to the Skagway saloon together to register their claim.

In the saloon, it is the Mizners who offer to buy drinks all around—the gold they bring back assays to $24,300. The boat to San Francisco doesn't leave till the next morning, however, so in order to kill time they accept the poker players' invitation to join the game. On the very first deal Wilson, with a full house, wants to bet $20,000. Addison tries to stop him, but Wilson draws Addison aside and excitedly explains that what took them three months of digging to earn he can double in a few minutes at a card table; he has discovered his talent.

The Game

WILSON
Never let a chance go by, Addie,
Isn't that what Papa said?
When you see it, grab it,
Soon it's like a habit.
Now and then you miss one,
But I guarantee you this one
Is a winner.
I'm no longer a beginner . . .

Addie, take the chance
Or it disappears!
Every card you're dealt opens new
    frontiers—
Let's be pioneers!

ADDISON
We could lose everything we've worked for!

WILSON
Exactly!

It's more than just the money, it's the game.
The thing that really matters is the game.
That moment when the card is turned

And nothing is the same—
Then bang!
New game!

The fact remains, when all is said
    and done,
The fun is in the winning, not what's
    won.
What you've made, what you've
    spent,
That is not the main event.
With every hand you stake a whole
    new claim.
The only thing that matters is the
    game.

Better than girls, better than booze,
Beating ace high with a pair of twos.
Better to win, but if you lose,
You've had that moment!

Better than smoke, better than snuff,
Hooking a sucker just enough,
Betting your bundle on a bluff,
Jesus, what a moment!
Still, the point, as I keep saying, is
    the game.
Not just the hand you're playing, but
    the game.
And what's around the corner,
If by chance you lose your pants?
New deal,
New chance!

It's never really money that's at stake.
That's nice, but it's just icing on the
    cake.
It's your life, every pot,
What you are, not what you've got.
Compared to that, the world seems
    pretty tame.
The only thing that matters is the
    game.

We realized that by eliminating the
cross-cutting between the dig and
the saloon and restricting the poker
game to one hand, we undermined
the story. We couldn't have a montage
of deals over time for the simple reason that stage poker is boring—it can
be interesting only if you see the individual hands, as in movies. But we also
couldn't show Wilson's growth into a

full-fledged gambler in just one hand,
and that discovery, the recognition
of his vocation, is the raison d'être
for the whole Alaska sequence. My
solution was to musicalize Wilson's
epiphany by transferring "The Game"
from its casual function in the Reading (the banter with reporters) and
rewriting both lyric and accompaniment to make it intense and personal.
It worked surprisingly well: the audience understood Wilson's passion and
transformation, even though it apparently took only one hand of cards to
effect it.

*Wilson's full house loses to four eights,
and he and Addison run back into their
vaudeville, arguing. Addison is furious
about losing the money, but Wilson
cuts him off by gesturing to the conductor, who starts their music as the olio
thuds in.*

Second Vaudeville***

As before, up to "Just because he is my
sibling," at which point Wilson announces to Addison that he doesn't
want to go home to Mama empty-
handed and is staying in Alaska to
make good.

*The scene shifts to Benicia. Addison
returns to Mama with the leftover
$300, apologizing for his failure. Mama
wants a report anyway.*

Next to You

ADDISON
The aurora borealis is a sight
To behold.
When the moon is out, the world
    becomes
A fairyland of white,
Blue and gold.

*Wilson suddenly appears, back from
Alaska, interrupting Addison's moment
with Mama.*

WILSON
The excitement, the adventure
Was an anticlimax next to you . . .

*He has returned with $4,000 from
gambling successfully and offers it to
Mama, who responds by singing her
section of "Next to You,"*** *as she did
in the Reading, and Addison leaves for
his trip around the world, but this time
with Mama saying to him, "Bring me
back a souvenir."*

The additional line from Mama was
intended to strengthen the motivation
for Addison's becoming not only artis-
tically but emotionally obsessed with
collecting objets d'art on his trip. It
helped, but it did not, sad to say, solve
the larger problem with the number
(elucidation to follow).

Addison's Trip***

*The song as in the Reading. Addison
tries to fulfill himself in all the same
places as before, except for Australia,
which we omitted in order to tighten up
the sequence. I was sorry to see it go, as
it also meant omitting some of my favorite words: "koala bear," "billabong,"
"platypus" and, above all, "wombat."
In line with Sam's desire to make the
show less cartoonlike, however, Addison fails to get jobs in Hawaii and India
for lack of experience rather than in-
competence. His adventures in China
and Guatemala remain the same.*

Nothing discourages a performer in a
musical like being the centerpiece of
a number which is designed as a showstopper and doesn't stop the show.
"Addison's Trip" turned out to be a
shivery example: it *almost* stopped it,
which is in some ways worse—the audience can feel what is expected of it
and becomes conscious of trying to
help the number out. This left a hole
in the middle of the act and, I suspect,
something of a hole in Nathan Lane's
heart as well. He worked ferociously—

to appreciative applause, the most discouraging kind there is. In the Reading the sequence had worked stunningly, so why had it lost its emotional kick?

The presumed value of readings and workshops is that the audience, no matter what size or sophistication, sees the work unembellished, undistracted by the attendant and sometimes deceptively enhancing commercial pleasures of scenery, costume and orchestra in a full production. This leads to the dangerously self-deceptive, although common, practice among most producers and many authors, of excusing a number or scene for not working because it needs props and sets to have its proper effect. If the writing is strong enough, the presumption goes, the audience's imagination will supply perfect decor and lighting. Nevertheless, John and I chose to think that this case was the exception, that without the souvenirs we couldn't possibly convey Addison's obsessional acquisitiveness—the audience had to see the tchotchkes he accumulated and the way they could be assembled into a room at the climax of the song. That is why the number didn't land the way it should, we told ourselves. Unlike the old pros we were, we ignored what was wrong at heart: we hadn't made clear what the sequence was about. Addison stated it, but the number didn't illustrate it clearly. Was Addison an incompetent or merely an innocent abroad? Tellingly, except for the Alaska sequence, "Addison's Trip" was the most difficult section of the show for John to write because, although the lyric articulated Addison's hopes, disappointments and penchant for collecting things, we didn't bring into focus what the vignettes of his journey should be saying about him. Had we gotten trapped, as Sam had warned us, by sticking to actual incidents in Addison's life? (There was a basis in reality for each of his appearances in the countries we had him visit.)

Missing the mark even more crucially was our fudging of his epiphany: it looked as if the whole sequence was designed to lead to his discovering that he had a talent for being an interior decorator, rather than an architect.* Trying to solve this problem, I made a change in the lyric at the end; at the moment when Addison is sitting, discouraged, surveying his possessions.

ADDISON
(*Surveying his possessions*)
All this junk, and no place to put it . . . Guess I'll have to find a place . . .

(*Pondering it all*)

Buy a place . . . Maybe I could *build* a place . . .

(*Starting to get excited*)

A place . . . A place—!

As he continues singing, he is gradually joined by all the souvenir vendors he has met in his travels, who assemble his possessions into a room.

ADDISON, SOUVENIR VENDORS
—That holds crucifixes, a Spanish chest,
An inlaid table, a condor's nest
And a tribal mask and a swami's chair
And a whatnot here and a whatnot there,
And a Ming tureen made of opaline,
And a lacquered tray and a folding screen—

ADDISON
No, the folding screen
Should go in between—

ALL
And a rattan stool
And a candle stand

---

* Although Mizner did indeed travel intercontinentally in his twenties, there's no evidence as to when his interest in architecture began. It may have started in Guatemala, when he was twelve years old and his father was appointed ambassador there. But clearly, from his beginnings he was attracted to the visual, and he was an eccentric—which almost always is an asset in art.

ADDISON
And a whole new future I hadn't planned:
I'll build myself a house!
I'm on my way!

ALL
At last!

A small point: ordinarily, I try to avoid the use of "and" as a connective in a list song, since it tends to be unnecessary filler, but here I think it's effective—it helps keep Addison's breathlessness going. Another small point: The reason I called this sequence "Addison's Trip" rather than the more appropriate "I'm on My Way" is that the latter is the name of the great song at the climax of *Porgy and Bess*, and I don't like to tread on giant toes. The only point that matters: It wasn't until *Road Show* that we solved all the problems of this number, but persistence paid off and solve them we did, and it was worth all the trouble.

Lights come up on an exclusive enclosure at the Madison Square Garden Dog Show. It is two years later. Elegant men and women swirl about, sipping Champagne. Addison enters, carrying a roll of blueprints. He has been invited by his new client, Myra Yerkes, one of the richest and most vulgar women in America, who is about to commission him to design a garage for her. As he looks for her, Wilson suddenly appears; the brothers have not seen each other in a couple of years and embrace effusively. They fill each other in on their recent histories. Wilson has become a man-about-town who knows everybody in high and low society and dabbles in many trades: gambler, playwright, prizefight manager, horse-race aficionado; Addison excitedly reports that he has discovered his purpose in life—as Papa would say, his road: he will be an architect, a builder of houses and cities. He is about to begin his career by designing a garage for Mrs. Yerkes. Wilson, recognizing the name, chides him for setting his sights so

lackey bearer
coolie steward
ayah flunky
[illegible] valet

Moorish [illegible]
Turkish

Time passes—ticking clock

get a new [illegible]

I didn't know the music that my brother knows.
Pleasing both Papa & Mama, [illegible] myself
Ends up w/ preoccupation w/ art.

Any things can go together if you have taste

Chorus in diff. native costumes carrying all his acquisitions—
the servants he acquires (plantation lackey, etc.)
Coffee plantation

Servants carry things from place to place
End w/ [illegible] (vs. I'll build a house). He abandons
making a future [illegible]-like, sees another way of life (non-specific)
Taste replaces fortune. I'm on my way—making something beautiful &

Hawaii — Businessman office or Absconder. I'm [illegible] to the [illegible]
Servant left behind. Starter set for a room of furniture,
just a bit exotic (desk, chair, Colonial, pineapples (in brass). Bamboo ceiling fan, [illegible] desk, palm tree, [illegible]
bamboo screen, campaign desk, wicker screen, peacock chair

[illegible] — Rajah's Palace—cushions, cobras, incense, etc. added to
starter set, screen, elephant footstool, Buddha, carpet, satin
cushions; hookah, temple bells, ivory screen, [illegible] fans

China — English Man kills himself instead of [illegible] room, pagoda, beaded curtain, silk
monkeys, opium table + pipes, gong, someone fanning, ivory screen

Papa's instructions keep echoing

gilded

NYC
(1st trip 2050)

Make everything beautiful
Harmonize, combine
Taste replaces fortune.

shrouds

A million objects I'll never need
What little's left of the native fan
And a ton of other assorted junk

Spanish, [illegible]
Moorish trunk

[illegible]

A dresser made by a Spanish monk

Because everything shines
Finds to find
Has a place to go somewhere
And the only trick
Is to find out where
Has to find its place
In the scheme of things

bunk
[illegible]
hunk
shrunk
sunk

It needs a window, a wall
A door, a ceiling, a floor
Something's missing, I know, of course
They need arches

They need other walls, windows
And They need different doors
Needs a place somewhere
Has to find out where

an stair
chair flair
chiffonier
somewhere
share space

I know

A [illegible] painted a bilious green
An alcove here & an archway there

And a ton of other delicious things
Things that deserve a home, some room

It needs a window to show it off
They need a place of their very own

What I need's a bigger space
What they need is room to breathe

A place for them us to live

dome
home

It needs a dome
It's like the others they all need a home
They need a background

And the chandelier needs a bigger room, dome above
And the tapestry needs a stuccoed wall, parquet floor
And the [illegible] rug needs a painted floor

wall
[illegible]

But it needs a wall, and a window there

To give an object its proper place, space
But first need
You have to build a house
Of course, that's who I am

Of course, of course, of course

peacock chair
campaign desk
piece of fruit
feathered fan
bamboo screen
flowered lei

carpet

2 Hawaii 2000
II

And a flowered lei
That's begun about to rot
Only fools would wear

And a wicker screen desk
And a wicker chair

fronds
[illegible]
[illegible]
[illegible]
strung [illegible]
swans
[illegible]
[illegible]
[illegible]
[illegible]
[illegible]

A wicker peacock chair & campaign desk
A pair of fruit [illegible] beyond your tongue
Who damned [illegible] on my way!

A feather fan & a bamboo wicker chair
And a wicker campaign desk, bothering That's the worse for wear
And a feathered fan from some native [illegible]

A wicker screen sort of vaguely [illegible]

Perhaps I'll stay
I can [illegible]

And a bamboo screen that's beyond repair
jungle lair

And a
no, worse, a pair
And a hanging fan made of native hair

air anywhere
bare bears
care compare
despair
everywhere
fair flair
hair [illegible]
[illegible]
spare square
there wear
ordinaire
God knows where

got cut
shut

Plus a feathered fan from a native hut
And a dozen [illegible] of leis that I'll never wear

Plus a piece of fruit, made of carved in coconut

And a seashell carved [illegible] whatnot from God knows where

China 2000

screen
ivory boxes, statue
scroll
calligraphy
Ming vase
lacquered table

Never say die

And a ton of other assorted junk stuff
from everywhere

Anyone can flop
Next time you'll come out on top

gewgaws

An accumulation of failures
Assorted knickknacks
And a hundred other unneeded things

And an ocean scene
That's painted green

A wicker chair & a bamboo desk
And a (carved wood) whatnot which is beyond your tongue

1014 green
green scene
[illegible] opaline

Lightning struck
Don't you learn — Just bad luck — Worst one yet
You got stuck — Wrong again
Not too so good — Next time, duck — What's the use
You've got pluck
stung — Son, go home
Bite your tongue

buck truck
duck tuck
pluck struck

Comb your hair
Mustn't let it [illegible] get you — You look tired, pale
Don't you fret

[illegible]
crest invest
[illegible]

Someday, you'll come out on top
You'll come up a winner soon.

Don't get stuck
Have to look ahead

Everybody's done it

Happens to the best of all, all the time
Lightning struck—
Won't occur again
Never happens twice

That's the thing that matters, what matters really
Try again, Next time out I bet you

This time you'll succeed
This'll be the one — You can pass the test
You'll be on the dime — You can do it right

Mustn't get depressed

low—a garage, no matter how stylish, is still just a garage. Give me ten minutes alone with this woman, he says, and you'll be building a house for her. Addison reluctantly points her out.

Stay Right Where You Are

WILSON
(Suddenly yelling across the floor)
Don't move!

MRS. YERKES
(Freezing)
What's wrong?!

WILSON
(Staring at her)
Stay right where you are—

ADDISON
(Whispering)
What are you doing?

WILSON
You're perfect like that.

(Aside, to Addison)

Ten minutes.

(To Mrs. Yerkes)

This moment we're at,
Make it forever.

MRS. YERKES
(Thoroughly soused, to Addison)
Who's this asshole?

WILSON
If I've gone too far—

MRS. YERKES
You're full of it.

WILSON
—I'm just too far gone.

MRS. YERKES
Get outta here!

WILSON
This rainbow I'm on
Says to me, now or never.

(As Mrs. Yerkes starts to protest)

Don't break the spell.
We've a rapport
I want to store
In my mind.

MRS. YERKES
You can't kid a kidder.

WILSON
You rang the bell
And I fell,
And I find
That my fate has been sealed—

MRS. YERKES
G'wan!

WILSON
—And I willingly yield!
I'll
Just follow your star—

MRS. YERKES
You're full of it—!

WILSON
—Succumb to your charms.

MRS. YERKES
Just terrible—!

WILSON
Stay right where you are—

(Stepping quickly toward her and grabbing her)

—Here in my arms.

They dance. Every few bars he whispers something salacious in her ear and she squeals in delight with phrases such as "Stop that!" and "Behave yourself!," occasionally swatting him with her fan. The club begins to close up. Finally, no one is left onstage but the two of them.

WILSON
Stay right where you are.

MRS. YERKES
Who's movin'?

WILSON
You're perfect like that.

MRS. YERKES
Ah-ah-ah-ah-ah . . .

WILSON
This moment we're at,
Make it forever.

MRS. YERKES
Anything you say—

WILSON
If I've gone too far—

MRS. YERKES
You haven't at all.

WILSON
—I'm just too far gone.
This roll that I'm on
Says to me, now or never.

Don't look for wings.
Tactfully put,
I've had a toot-
Sie or two.

MRS. YERKES
Who cares?

WILSON
Trivial things,
Little flings.
Now there's you,
And it's not only lust.
It's forever or bust.

He leers at her chest.

What happens, we'll see.

MRS. YERKES
You're terrible!

WILSON
What will be will be.

MRS. YERKES
(Faint with excitement)
I can't stand it . . .

WILSON
There's just you and me
Forever—

Addison applauds slowly from the other side of the stage. The vaudeville olio comes in and the brothers go into their vaudeville mode. In stylized banter they reveal that Wilson married Mrs. Yerkes and was thrown out after seven months, thereby losing Addison his commission. Addison complains that he should never have listened to Wilson; Wilson counters by pointing out that many people have benefited (if temporarily) from knowing him. He brings some of them on.

That Was a Year

Wilson introduces New York's leading playwright, Paul Armstrong.

ARMSTRONG
Willie had style,
Willie had class,
Willie told stories that had color and
    sass.
Couldn't predict
What he would say.
That's why I said, "Willie, let's write
    a play."

But where the hell was Willie
Came the time to rewrite?
Way the hell in Philly,
Off promoting some fight.
Half a play with Willie
Closes opening night,
But oh, what a year!
That was a year . . .

Wilson introduces Stanley Ketchel, middleweight champion of the world.

KETCHEL
Willie had taste
Up the kazoo,

Said to me, "Stan, I'm gonna give
    you your due."
Taught me to dress,
Made me a sport,
Gave me social status and something
    to snort.

Learned a lot from Willie,
Havin' laughs, gettin' tight,
Coked till we were silly
By the dawn's early light.
Learned so much from Willie
I forgot how to fight,
But oh, what a year!
That was a year . . .

Wilson introduces Flatbush Phil, a flashy racketeer.

PHIL
Willie had cash,
Willie had gals,
Willie could deal, and not just cards.
Willie was lightning with a
    comeback or a gag.
When I got nicked,
Willie was pals,
Willie was right there bribing
    guards,
Even though Willie was the one
Who'd left me holding the bag.

ARMSTRONG
Now I write a show,
It doesn't get on—

KETCHEL
Offer me some dough,
I dive like a swan—

PHIL
Once I was a pro,
And now I'm a con,
But oh, what a year—!

ARMSTRONG, KETCHEL
That was a year . . .

MRS. YERKES
(Entering unexpectedly)
That was a year . . .

WILSON
Uh-oh . . .

MRS. YERKES
(The music turning sultry)

Willie was bad,
Bad all along—
Only he had this big enormous—

(Measuring vaguely with her hands)

Gorgeous—
Smile!

He was a hoot,
Even in bed.
All he had his eye on was what was
    ahead.

KETCHEL
(The music becoming lively again)
Sure, I lost the crown, but the things
    that I seen . . .

ARMSTRONG
One thing, though, with Willie it's
    never routine . . .

PHIL
I was voted "biggest wit" in cell
    block eighteen* . . .

ALL FOUR
Thanks to nimble Willie Mizner,
Cock of the walk—

MRS. YERKES
You're telling me?!

ALL FOUR
King of Noo Yawk!

ALL FOUR
Stick around with Willie,
You run out of luck.
Stick around with Willie,

---

* Apart from all the other problems with the show, one of the things that nagged me was why this line rarely got even a murmur of pleasure from the audience. Granted, it's not immortally funny, but it wasn't until after the Workshop's run that I realized I had committed one of the cardinal Sins I have subsequently preached against many times. I had perpetrated an identity (see *Finishing the Hat*, if you don't know what that means) instead of a rhyme, which is death to a comic lyric: namely, "routine" and "eighteen." If the setup in the penultimate line (" . . . routine") had been a proper rhyme, the punch line would have elicited at least a chuckle. I solved it, however, in *Bounce*, the next generation of the show.

You feel like a cluck.
Stick around with Willie,
You're gonna get stuck,
But you'll get a year—!

PHIL
Maybe ten to twenty—

ALL FOUR
Only a year—

MRS. YERKES
A year if you're lucky . . .

ALL FOUR
But oh, what a year!

This condensation of what had been the chronicling of Wilson's adventures in the Reading demonstrates two of my mantras: not only Less Is More, but Content Dictates Form. In the Reading, the number had seemed entertaining but repetitive, as if each episode, no matter the difference in event and tone, was the same. The old and only important question in drama had once again reared its ugly head: What is the point of the sequence? Why detail these adventures, charming, funny or melodramatic though they may be? The point, we realized, is neither the adventures themselves nor the exploration of Wilson's character, it's the effect he has not merely on his brother but on everyone else who enters his orbit: they all succumb to his spell. The song's function is to establish the charm that constitutes his talent for exploitation, because that's what drives the story later on. Also, I like to think the pun on "pro" and "con" is something even E. Y. Harburg might have found worthy.

As the singers exit, Wilson applauds them heartily. Addison resumes his complaint. They argue, leading into their edgy version of "On My Left"*** when a loud BOOM! is heard, heralding the San Francisco earthquake and Mama's sudden arrival. As before, she settles in with Addison while Wilson, now a media darling, goes off to make further headlines, promising to come and visit her every Sunday.

A Little House for Mama

In Addison's small apartment, Mama lies in bed as Addison brings her tea and newspapers. He murmurs shyly that he has a surprise for her, something he's been working on for weeks, and goes back to his drafting table.

ADDISON
(To himself, sketching)
A pink and yellow skylight
To let the sun come streaming in.
A Chinese courtyard
Filled with trees and flowers.
A little house for Mama . . .

(Sketches a bit)

A terra-cotta kitchen,
A paneled den for dreaming in,
An open porch to while away the
    hours.
A little house for Mama—
No, a nice big house for Mama . . .

The phone rings. Addison hears that his latest commission has fallen through. Mama, meanwhile, is reading delightedly about Wilson's raffish exploits. The phone rings again; Wilson apologizes, saying that he can't come to visit. Addison defends him to Mama and tries to ease her disappointment.

ADDISON
(Resuming work)
M is for the mullioned windows,
O is for the oriels,
T is for the terrace made of tile.
H is for the—

The phone rings; Addison tries to ignore it.

H is for the hearthstone—

The phone rings again; annoyed, he picks it up, muttering:

Put them all together, they spell
    "moth."

(Into the phone)

Hello? . . .

Again, Wilson is not coming to visit. Addison is angry, but loyally excuses him to Mama and resumes work. Once again Mama is reading the papers and chuckling over Wilson's latest adventure, which only serves to make Addison work more boldly and confidently.

ADDISON
A fireplace in every room
To keep her warm and cheerful
If she gets a chill.
A bedroom facing south,
So she can look at the ocean
When she awakens.
A place to rest for Mama . . .

(Sketches)

A cozy nook
To read a book,
With wallpaper from France.
Mama likes to dance,
So:
A mirrored ballroom, not too
    large . . .

(Sketches)

A sitting room where we can visit
Tête-à-tête,
A sitting room I'll make my most
    exquisite
Yet.

(Sketches)

A shady trellis breezeway
When summer heat comes
    steaming in,
To keep her cool and shield her from
    the showers.
A little gift from Addie to Mama . . .

He whistles as he finishes sketching and looks at the drawing with satisfaction.

As I've said before, in every score I write I like to include at least one

Harold Arlen imitation, by which I mean something bluesy but hopeful, glowing with those aching, melancholy harmonies that define his music, songs (mine) such as "Sorry-Grateful" in *Company*, "I'm Still Here" in *Follies*, even "There Is No Other Way" in *Pacific Overtures*. In *Wise Guys* I had at least two: this song and the one which follows. Only one of them survived the saga.

The phone rings. Once more Addison is forced to tell Mama that Wilson isn't coming and that he should be ashamed for constantly breaking his promises. She shrugs it off. "It's who he is," she explains.

Isn't He Something!

MAMA
Seldom comes to see me,
Hardly ever calls.
When he sends me letters,
They're just two-line scrawls.

(*Smiles*)

Isn't he something!

Things he says out loud I wouldn't
    dare,
Or I'd have to hide.
Skates along through life without a
    care
Or a shred of pride.
But look at him glide!
Isn't he something?
See how he glides!

He's having the time of his life,
Life filled to the brim.
And I've had the time of my life,
Living through him.

Some men are tender souls
With worthy goals
They keep fulfilling.
Some men ignore the rules,
Are rogues and fools,
And thrilling.

Honey,
If he had the slightest sense of
    shame,
It would be a shame.
And isn't he shameless?
Doesn't he glide?
Isn't he something!

ADDISON
Something that I'm not. That I'll
never be.

MAMA
What you are is my dear, beloved
boy. Who's sustained me, and taken
care of me. Who's been my comfort
and my strength—

ADDISON
Second place. Not bad.

MAMA
(*Tenderly, opening her arms to him*)
Carelessness and being free of care,
Aren't they the same?

Some men live to be good,
Some men live to be bad,
Some men live just to sparkle.
And doesn't he sparkle?
See how he glides!
Isn't he something . . .

She lies back, still.

ADDISON
Mama—?

Addison sees that she has died. He stares at her for a moment, at which point Willie enters drunkenly, as in the earlier version, but this time with a chorus girl on his arm. He discovers Mama is dead and is furious. He shoos the girl away and yells at Addison for not telling him. Addison, as before, responds angrily by lying to Wilson about Mama's dying words. Wilson, shattered and dumbstruck, trying not to believe him, turns to the audience.

Third Vaudeville

WILSON
On my left . . .

(*Trying to recover his composure*)

On my left . . .

(*Again*)

On my left—

ADDISON
On my right—

WILSON
Is my louse of a brother—

ADDISON
Is an error of my mother—

WILSON
And a liar as well.

ADDISON
Prince of theft—

WILSON
King of spite—

ADDISON
With not one single scruple.

WILSON
(*To Addison*)
You're the teacher, I'm the pupil.

ADDISON
(*To Wilson*)
May you choke and go to hell!

(*To the audience*)

You've heard of arrogant selfishness.

WILSON
(*To Addison*)
You've heard of spineless disdain.
You've heard of left on the shelf.

ADDISON
Full of himself,
And cocaine!

BOTH
They were each other's very best
   friend,
They were each other's, written in
   stone.
They were each other's, right to the
   end—

ADDISON
And this is the end!

WILSON
You're on your own!

The orchestra tries to finish the number, but both Addison and Wilson refuse to continue, and leave the stage in opposite directions. The show curtain comes in.

END OF ACT ONE

ACT TWO

Lights come up on the show olio. Vaudeville music begins, the same as at the start of Act One. Addison peeks around the edge of the proscenium, smiling and bright-eyed. He strolls around the stage with his cane, seeming to look expectantly for Wilson.

Fourth Vaudeville

ADDISON
Willie! . . . Willie, we're on!

A beat; he shrugs to us cheerfully, as the orchestra keeps vamping the introduction.

   You'll have to excuse my brother,
   folks. Everybody else does.

On my left . . .

He gestures to Wilson's spotlit area as the orchestra plays the missing Wilson's answering phrase.

Is a space
Where there used to be my brother,
But he hasn't been well.

He's a case . . .

   (Orchestral reply)

Like no other.
All that guilt about his mother—

   (Lightly)

He can fucking go to hell.

Who says that Damon needs
   Pythias?
No more than Abel needs Cain.
Had Lincoln got rid of Booth,
Tell the truth,
Who'd complain?

Just a couple of wise guys,
Through with sharing the bow.

   *(Hopping into Wilson's spotlight,
   imitating him)*

This you'll regret.

   (Hopping back into his own)

You want to bet?

   (Interrupting himself, as Wilson)

Just a couple of wise—

   (As himself)

Just a couple of wise—

   (As both)

Who both are much wiser now.

   (As Wilson)

You're going to carry the act?

   (As himself)

As a matter of fact . . .

He grabs a violin from the wings and plays along with the orchestra for a

while, *then tap dances for a few bars, then does both simultaneously, ending in a clog waltz.*

* When you start to feel dumb
'Cause you cling to the crumb
That there's somebody somewhere to
   trust,
It's a weight off your mind
When you finally find
That there's nobody nowhere to
   trust.

Everyone wants to have someone to
   trust.
God knows, it's well worth the try.
And if you can find somebody
   somewhere to trust,
I know of a bridge you can buy.

La-de-da.
Yes, I once was a sucker.
La-de-da, la-de-da,
That was ages ago . . .
And now let's get on with the show.

The orchestra builds toward a finish. Addison dances, plays, whistles and does tricks in a frantic display of virtuosity.*

A pair of eager gents
Who learned some sense,
Whose troubles are over and done,
Just a couple of guys—
Just a couple of guys—
Minus one!

As in the Reading, a seedy Real Estate Agent rushes on and entices him to Florida.

ADDISON
   You hear that, Papa? A new land of
   opportunity! I'm on my way . . .

On the train to Florida, Addison meets Paris Singer, a handsome, snobbish, nervous young man who is heir to the Singer Sewing Machine fortune. He is

---

* The passage between asterisks was cut— the idea of Addison's doing a duet as a solo had outrun its course to a shattering degree.

on his way to a small town called Palm Beach, where his socialite aunt, Eva Stotesbury, is looking for a place to build a house. His father has disowned him because of his artistic interests and he is hoping to persuade his aunt to sponsor an artists' colony. Why an artists' colony? Addison asks.

Talent

PARIS
(Against the sound of the train wheels)
When I was a tyke,
I said, "What I like
Is art.
I know I'm a boy,
But what I enjoy
Is art."

Looking at paintings, going to plays,
Music and books informing my
      days,
Filling my mind,
Flooding my heart
With art!

I had this dream of becoming an
      artist—
A painter, a poet, who knows?
I had a nice little talent for drawing,
And a natural feeling for prose.
I even began to compose.

So many talents,
Wasn't I blessed!
All of them good,
A few of them better,
None of them best,

Just enough talent to know
That I hadn't the talent.
So I laid my dream
And my self-esteem
To rest.

ADDISON
That must have been difficult to do.

PARIS
At the time, yes. But it didn't matter. I merely had to find what I was meant to be.

I couldn't decide,
Then one day I spied
Palm Beach.
A speck on the map,
No more than a gap:
Palm Beach.

Jungle and seashore, muddled and
      raw,
But in a flash I suddenly saw
What it would take,
What I could make
Palm Beach!

I had this dream of a city of artists,
Versailles by the Florida sea.
A sort of world congregation of
      artists,
All encouraged to set themselves
      free.
I knew what I wanted to be!

I'd be their host and supporter,
The patron saint
Of the things that they write
And compose and paint.
I would wander among them with
      lavish praise
As they carve their statues,
Construct their plays,
Design their buildings,
Recite their rhymes,
Making modern art
Fit for modern times—!

So many talents,
Gathered en masse!
Painters and poets,
Artists and dreamers,
Watered like grass.

And if the talent I have
Is for nurturing talent,
Then succeed or fail,
I will see they sail
First-class.

And my father can go stick it up
      his ass.

In the Reading, there had been no scene on the train; Paris and Addison simply met by chance in Palm Beach. Here we dramatized the meeting to set

up their relationship as something more than casual, and established Paris's character with a song.

At the Royal Poinciana Hotel, Addison does what his brother would do: he woos Mrs. Stotesbury by intruding into her conversation with Paris and showing her architectural drawings for a spectacular house. Mrs. Stotesbury instructs her husband to give Addison money to build it. Paris draws Addison aside and complains that he's not interested in selling his property to build houses on but in starting an artists' colony.

Palm Beach Sequence

ADDISON
Never let a chance go by, Paris—
Treat it as a small detour.
Satisfy the matrons,
Then you'll get the patrons.
All you have to do
Is keep them happy with a few
Extravaganzas,
Which will turn into bonanzas.

Leave it up to me,
And they'll feel fulfilled.
Wait until you see
What I'm going to build,
And you'll have your guild!

He waves his rolled-up blueprint like a wand. Grandiose chords. The hotel vanishes and a house appears—the Stotesburys' Palm Beach mansion.

MRS. STOTESBURY
Look at it!

More chords; the house moves into place.

Look at it!

MR. STOTESBURY
Look at it!

BOTH
Look at it!

Mrs. Stotesbury, in a transport of delight, informs Paris that she will sponsor his colony, as long as Mr. Mizner designs the administration building.

PARIS
(To Addison, rhapsodically)
You . . .
Where have you been all my life?

MR. AND MRS. STOTESBURY
Look at it, look at it, look at it!

PARIS
You . . .
You're the answer to my prayers.

MRS. STOTESBURY
(In rhythm, swooning)
Notice the details . . .

PARIS
You . . .
You're one in a million.

MR. STOTESBURY
(Pointing to an enormous structure)
What's that?

MRS. STOTESBURY
The breakfast nook.

PARIS
You . . .
Where have you been all my life?

MRS. STOTESBURY
(Patting Mr. Stotesbury's hand)
Wait till Lily Cosden sees it.

The Cosdens enter.

MRS. COSDEN
Mr. Mizner, the house you built for Eva is a work of art. You must build me one exactly like it.

ADDISON
No.

MRS. COSDEN
No?

ADDISON
No, it has to be something for *you.*

He frames her with his hands, like a painter.

ADDISON
I see cypress arches, mosaic floors
Reminiscent of the conquistadors,
I see colonnades
In a hundred shades,
With a Roman cloister to house the
    maids,
I see:

Again, Addison waves his plans. Again, stately chords sound; the Cosden mansion appears and starts moving into place.

MRS. COSDEN
(To her husband, who is gaping at the elaborate extravaganza)
Lovely, isn't it?

Mr. Cosden nods sheepishly and starts to write a check.

ADDISON
(To Paris)
You . . .
You're the answer to my prayers.

MRS. COSDEN
Lovely. Absolutely lovely.

ADDISON
You . . .
You're one in a million.

Mrs. Cosden stays her husband's hand as the mansion halts in mid-movement.

MRS. COSDEN
(Pointedly, to Addison)
Lovely. But why is it smaller than Eva's?

Music stops; Mr. Cosden stops writing; Addison's face falls.

PARIS
(Smoothly)
That's merely the west wing . . .

He nods surreptitiously to Addison, who gestures with his plans. Another wing pops out; the mansion is now clearly larger than the Stotesburys' and

promptly moves into place. Mrs. Cosden beams; music resumes.

ADDISON
(To Paris)
You . . .

PARIS
You . . .

BOTH
Where have you been all my life?

PARIS
You . . .

ADDISON
You . . .

PARIS
You have a vision—

ADDISON
They have the money—

PARIS
We—

ADDISON
We—

BOTH
Both have a dream.

PARIS
Me,
I'd say we're a team.

ADDISON
Me, too.

BOTH
Who knew
That you'd come into my life?
Where have you been?

Other dowagers and their husbands, among them the Trumbauers, enter and vie for Addison's attention. Addison and Paris accept all offers.

ADDISON
(Framing Mrs. Trumbauer's face)
I see Gothic arches, Moroccan
    chairs,
With indoor trees and with outdoor
    stairs,

I see gingerbread,
I see Chinese red
And a huge Victorian potting shed—

MRS. TRUMBAUER
(Uninterested)
Fine, just as long as it's finished on
time.

ADDISON
(Under his breath, as Mr. Trumbauer
hands Addison a check)
And a fountain where you can go
soak your head . . .

*Paris hastily grabs the check and
waves Addison's plans. More grandiose
chords, and the Trumbauers' new house
moves in.*

TRUMBAUERS
Look at it!

ADDISON, PARIS
Look at it! Look at it!

*As Addison and Paris become more and
more successful, there are grumbles
along the way.*

MRS. STOTESBURY
(Not happy, to her husband)
Theirs has a view of the ocean . . .

(Smiling politely, to Addison)

Lovely, Addie—

(The smile turning to ice)

And such a view of the ocean—!

PARIS
(Quickly)
Yours has the acreage . . .

She looks at him quizzically.

Yours has the privacy . . .

She turns to go, not mollified.

Yours has the cupola—

MRS. STOTESBURY
(Turning back)
The cupola?

PARIS
—That Addie's just designed for
you—

*He glances at Addison, who gestures; a
tower rises from the Stotesbury house.*

Looking down on the Trumbauers
And out toward the ocean . . .

*Mrs. Stotesbury signals to her hus-
band, who hands Addison another
check. Addison and Paris turn to each
other.*

ADDISON, PARIS
You, where have you been all my
life?

MATRONS
(Overlapping, to Addison)
You, where have you been all our
lives?

ADDISON, PARIS
You, you're the answer to my
prayers.

MATRONS
(Overlapping)
You, you're the answer to our
prayers.

ADDISON, PARIS
We'll make a paradise here!
Where have you been all my life?

MATRONS, MILLIONAIRES
(Overlapping)
You're one in a million . . .
Where have you been all my life?

*Three more matrons enter—Mrs.
Wanamaker, Mrs. Phipps and Mrs. Livermore, followed by their husbands.*

MRS. WANAMAKER
(A large lady)
Yoo-hoo, Mr. Singer,
A house for me, too . . .
Something in blue . . .

ADDISON
Blue is for Norwegians, dearie,
Blue is not you.

MRS. WANAMAKER
No?

ADDISON
No.

(Stepping back to frame her figure)

I see you as a hacienda, a happy
fusion
Of Indonesian and Andalusian—
I see stuccoed walls,
I see paneled halls,
I see carpets woven from native
shawls—
You're a hacienda—

MRS. PHIPPS
(Overlapping)
Yoo-hoo, Mr. Singer, dear,
A house for me, please . . .

ADDISON
—If I ever saw one . . .

*Throughout the following, houses keep
appearing and filling the stage or the
backdrop, or both.*

MRS. LIVERMORE
(Overlapping)
Yoo-hoo, Mr. Singer, dear,
A house for me, too, please . . .

*More couples appear, and the competi-
tion gets keener.*

MRS. STOTESBURY
(To Paris, referring to another couple)
Their house has twenty-one
bedrooms.

PARIS
Yes, but yours has a Renaissance
courtyard . . .

MRS. STOTESBURY
Ah . . .

ADDISON
(Framing another client,
Mrs. Livermore)
You're a medieval villa,
All vermilion and vanilla . . .

MRS. TRUMBAUER
(Overlapping, to Paris, referring to the
Stotesburys)
Theirs has a Renaissance courtyard.

PARIS
Yes, but yours has a view of the
ocean . . .

MRS. TRUMBAUER
Ah . . .

ADDISON
(To Mrs. Livermore)
You're a neo-Gothic ruin—

(Hastily, as Mrs. Livermore reacts)

That's the setting I see you in . . .

MRS. COSDEN
(To Paris, referring to the
Trumbauers)
Theirs has a view of the ocean.

PARIS
(Mollifying)
Yours has a pool for the staff . . .

MRS. WANAMAKER
(To Paris, referring to the Cosdens)
Theirs has a pool for the staff.

PARIS
But yours has a moat
With a boat,
And twenty-one bedrooms . . .

ADDISON
(Admiringly, to Paris)
You—!

PARIS
(Ditto)
You—!

Addison and Paris look at each other
delightedly and embrace, Addison a
trifle too warmly. Paris pulls back
slightly, looks at him. Addison is embarrassed, but Paris, ever the gentleman, covers the moment by embracing
Addison a second time, hugging him
even closer; they are pulled out of the
moment by another prospective client,
Mrs. DuPont.

MRS. DUPONT
Yoo-hoo, Paris darling,
A house for me . . .

MRS. CONKLING
And one for me!

MRS. GEIST
I'll take two . . .

MRS. DUPONT
Make that three . . .

The following lines tumble over one
another as the stage keeps filling up
with ever more elaborate estates.

MRS. CONKLING
(One client to another)
Pardon me, but I was next.

MRS. GEIST
Don't be ridiculous.

MRS. CONKLING
(To her husband)
Willis, tell her I was next.

MRS. DUPONT
It happens to be my turn!

PARIS
(Simultaneously with the above,
to Addison)
A house for Mrs. DuPont . . .
A house for Mrs. Geist . . .

ADDISON
("Framing" Mrs. DuPont)
I see minarets . . .

(Then Mrs. Conkling)

I see parapets . . .

(Then Mrs. Geist)

I see gargoyles . . .

PARIS
(Gesturing to Addison)
A house for Mrs. Conkling!

Another extraordinary house immediately appears.

ADDISON
Grottoes . . .

PARIS
Another house for Mrs. Geist—!

A MATRON
A house for me!

A HUSBAND
A house for us!

GROUP #1
A house for them!

GROUP #2
A house for me!

GROUP #1
Us!

GROUP #2
Them!

ALL
Us!

ADDISON, PARIS
You—

The matrons and husbands babble, ad-
miring, criticizing and ordering.

—Where have you been all my life?

MRS. DUPONT
The ambiance—!

MRS. WANAMAKER
The travertine—!

MRS. LIVERMORE
The finials—!

ADDISON, PARIS
You, you're the answer to my
prayers . . .
You, you're one in a million . . .

ADDISON
And with your permission—

PARIS
And your ambition—

BOTH
And their tradition
Of acquisition,
We'll build a place
Where America can play.

ALL
Where have you been all my life?
Don't go away!

MRS. PHIPPS
(To her husband, in dismay)
Theirs has a floating gazebo . . .

Palm Beach is now complete.

While writing this chronicle of *Wise Guys*, in the interests of reportorial accuracy I spoke to my fellow show-makers, among them John, Nathan, Victor and Sam, as well as Scott Rudin, who was one of the producers and the one among us with the most dependable memory. There were so many versions of each version of what eventually became *Road Show* that discussing any given stage of the saga plunged us into a *Rashomon*-like tangle of recall. What follows is, I think, a reasonably correct account of what went on.

In the course of the conversations, Nathan remembered that in most of the performances, he didn't feel the audience warming to the show until the introduction of Paris and the blossoming of the relationship with Addison during "You," which, if he's right, was a little late in the course of events for the audience to become involved. Ironically, I had written the song for precisely that reason. I had wanted to retain Addison's cynicism from the Reading, but the song I had written for the Palm Beach sequence ("Dowagers") had been terminally static, nothing but commentary from both Paris and Addison, and commentary that had been made before as well (Addison had already sung a version of "Dowagers" in Act One). I wanted to replace it with something that not only had dramatic action in it, but would counterpoint the cynicism with the comic (I hoped) tenderness of the two entrepreneurs falling in love. Although it was the right decision and seemed funny and warm as well as stageworthy, it brought to the front some more problems in the storytelling which we clearly hadn't solved.

After the Reading, John and I decided we had to deal, however tentatively, with Addison's homosexuality. We had debated how important it was to the story, as we wanted to be neither exploitative nor banal (the years we were writing these first two stages of the show were years when the novelty of homosexuality in public enter-

tainment was wearing off and virtually every play, movie and TV show had gay characters disporting emotions of every color and stripe). We had to be tentative because we were dealing with historical figures, and in reality Paris Singer could not have been less homosexual. He was internationally known as a ladies' man and had met Addison in Florida while he was recovering from the breakup of a long affair with Isadora Duncan, the famous and infamous "modern" dancer of the pre–World War II era. We dealt with these problems first in *Bounce*, by changing Paris's name and by digging a bit into Addison's romantic life, and later in *Road Show*, by digging even deeper. We wanted to take liberties with our characters, but not misrepresent them. Or be sued by Singer's descendants.

As before, Paris and Addison are living together. In this version, however, Wilson, rather than being brought in unconscious, shows up suddenly out of the storm, coughing, exhausted from riding the rails, racked with guilt about neglecting Mama and begging Addison for a job. Addison rejects him, and Wilson collapses. Addison doesn't take it seriously at first, putting it down to another of his brother's scams, but soon sees that the collapse is real and calls for a doctor. While he waits, he sings to the unconscious Wilson.

Make It Through the Night

ADDISON
Make it through the night.
Come on,
Make it through the night,
Like you've made it through the
    night
All those times before.
Just this one time more.

Wilson doesn't move.

Make it through the night.

(Brightly)

I mean,
Think of what you'll miss:
All those plans to be made,
All those fish to be played,
All those girls to be laid . . .
Stay in the parade,
Make it through the night . . .

(Suddenly erupting)

Goddammit, don't die!
Don't quit on me.
Not now,
Not yet.
Skies are looking blue,
Dreams are coming true,
Good as they can get.

I'm finally who I meant to be.
I want you to see.
I need you to care.
Dreams are to share.

Make it through the night,
And soon
You'll be back on top.
You'll be painting the town,
You'll be wearing the crown,
You'll be putting me down,
Calling me a clown . . .
You don't have to stop.

Make it through the night.
Jesus,
Make it through the night.
You're just dying out of spite,
Which I won't forgive.
So you better live.

There are good times to come.
You can still be a bum.
Still get drunk till you're numb,
Dying would be dumb.

(Kisses Wilson's hand)

Honey—
Make it through the night.

The scene fades.

The "honey" was intended as a time bomb that would explode in the final scene. As with "The Beggar Woman's Lullaby" in *Sweeney Todd*, some of

the audience got it and some didn't. It's the kind of detail that serves the actor more than anyone else.

The terrace of Addison's house. Wilson has convalesced quickly and proceeds immediately to flatter Paris, trying to persuade him that Addison should build a city. In turn, Paris tells Wilson about his dream of an artists' colony, and Wilson begins to come up with ideas for it when suddenly Addison barrels in, waving the biggest check for the biggest house yet. Wilson turns proudly to the audience.

Fifth Vaudeville

WILSON
Ladies and gentlemen, the King of Palm Beach, Addison Mizner.

ADDISON
Thank you very much. I don't deserve it. Well, perhaps I do.

On my left—

WILSON
On my right—

ADDISON
Is a prince—

WILSON
Is a jewel—

ADDISON
Never arrogant or cruel—

WILSON
Never dull or banal.

ADDISON
He is deft.

WILSON
He is bright.

BOTH
I just love him to pieces.

WILSON
And believe me, I don't say that
Just because he's rich as Croesus . . .

They recall, still in vaudeville style, how Papa promised them they could be anything they wanted. Wilson says that from now on he wants to be Addison. Addison replies that for a while he played around with being Wilson and that, considering his present circumstances, it didn't work out too badly. Wilson shrugs and turns to the audience.

WILSON
He's a prince—

ADDISON
He's a jewel—

BOTH
And he never needs renewal
As a partner,
As a critic,
As a pal.

Paris tells the audience how Addison, and now Wilson, has made him a happy man.

ADDISON
You've heard of Arthur and
    Lancelot—

WILSON
They were a pair without peer.

ADDISON, WILSON
(To Paris)
But come join Willie [Addie]
    and me.
You can be
Guinevere!

PARIS
Right! I'm here!

ALL THREE
Just a trio of partners
On the road to success.

WILSON
(To Paris)
Welcome aboard!

PARIS
Thank you, my lord!

ALL THREE
Just a trio of partners:

ADDISON
Vision—

WILSON
Guidance—

PARIS
And finesse.

ADDISON
Ain't we got fun!

WILSON
Two against one.

ALL THREE
A triad of bell-ringers,
Humdingers,
Three remarkable gents.

WILSON
Rich—

PARIS
Creative—

ADDISON
And smart.

ALL THREE
Wit and money and heart—
The potential's immense.

The real estate market is heating up, and they agree that a new city, designed by Addison, would be a smashing success.

ALL THREE
Just a trio of dreamers,
With a gleam in their eyes.
Three idealist upstreamers,
Crafty schemers,
With their heads in the skies.

ADDISON
(Referring to Wilson)
The one who can't stand still—

PARIS
(Referring to Addison)
The one with skill—

WILSON
(Referring to Paris)
The one not as dumb as he seems.

ALL THREE
Just a trio of path breakers,

PARIS
Tastemakers—

WILSON
Risk takers—

ADDISON
Buy some acres!

ALL THREE
Three exceptional guys,
Building dreams!

Essentially, the song has the same function as in the Reading, but with a difference in the dynamics of the relationships: instead of Wilson's seducing Paris into persuading Addison to build a city, it is now Addison and Wilson who seduce Paris. This not only avoids the repetitiousness of having one more betrayal by Wilson and one more fight between the brothers, it builds up Paris's enthusiasm and excitement, so that the eventual collapse of their plans makes his disillusion and rejection of the Mizners more dramatic as well as believable.

The backstage area behind a platform which has been erected on the seafront. Stagehands, Bathing Beauties, vocalists and assorted salesmen and photographers bustle past, swirling around Wilson, Addison, and Paris. It is five minutes to show time and all three are going to participate in the broadcast. Paris exuberantly informs Addison and Wilson that he has used all the Mizner Development Corporation capital (most of which is his) to buy up land in the area. This makes Wilson and Addison apprehensive, but Paris is determined that with Addison's vision and Wilson's promotional skills the venture will succeed.

Boca Raton Sequence

The platform revolves so that it faces the audience. A robed choir enters. Stately chords resound.

CHOIR
(Religioso)
State of fun and state of leisure—

TENOR SOLO
Florida . . .

CHOIR
Florida!
State of sun and state of pleasure,
Too—ooh.
State of joy, the nation's treasure—

TENOR
Florida . . .

CHOIR
Florida says your
Daily cares are through.

TENOR
Balmy, breezy—

ALL
Life is easy.
Every town is like the fountain of
   youth—

TENOR
In truth—

ALL
In Florida, Florida,
Florida, state of grace.

The Choir hums reverentially underneath as Wilson, Addison, and Paris take their places at three podiums onstage. Wilson gives a pitch for Boca Raton and introduces the Boca Girl.

BOCA GIRL
(Sweet and innocent and cheerful)
Boca Raton,
Come down to Boca Raton,
Where every sky's the bluest you've
   seen,
Where all year long the grass
   remains green,

Where every beach is clean and
   pristine.

Sea and surf
And sun and sand.
See the perf-
Ect wonderland.

Boca Raton,
Come down to Boca Raton,
Where every sidewalk sparkles and
   gleams—
City beautiful of your dreams!

Wilson introduces Addison, who gives a further pitch and makes a gesture to the women in the Choir, who strip off their robes and reveal themselves to be Bathing Beauties.

BATHING BEAUTIES
Stow your woes,
Stop being frantic . . . etc. . . . . ***

They form a train, as in the Reading.

Boca Raton . . .
Boca Raton . . .

They keep repeating the name softly as Wilson introduces "Paris Singer, financier, real estate developer and chief sponsor of Boca Raton, the City Beautiful." Paris, buoyant and eager as a teenager, gives an enthusiastic pitch and nods at the men in the choir, who strip off their robes and reveal themselves in various sports outfits.

CHOIR
Boca Raton,
Come down to Boca Raton,
Where everybody's wearing a smile
Where everybody's living in style,
Where everybody's making a pile.

Don't think twice,
Take our advice:
Get your slice
Of paradise.

Boca Raton,
Come down to Boca Raton,
Where you can swim and mingle
   and play
And invest in the U.S.A.!

Wilson continues his pitch while sales-men pass through the audience, offer-ing brochures.

CHOIR

Buy a lot
Or maybe two.
Have we got
A lot for you!

Boca Raton—

WOMEN

You'll love it—

MEN

Boca Raton!

ALL

But you'll regret it if you delay.

WOMEN

Come and see
The new frontier!
Come and be
A pioneer!
You'll agree,
Tomorrow's here
Today!
Boca Raton!

Addison and Paris are delighted with the response and are ready to end the proceedings, but Wilson has planned something further. A sudden fanfare, and Wilson resumes his pitch with heightened intensity. The Bathing Beauties reappear and sing to a bur-lesque beat.

BATHING BEAUTIES

Boca Raton,
Come down to Boca Raton,
Where you can let your fancies go
    free,
Where every home has views of the
    sea—

Addison looks over sharply, but Wilson pays no attention.

Where life is all you want it to be—

WILSON
(Overlapping)
Yes, Boca Raton. The sweetest piece
    of real estate to hit the market since

the Good Lord foreclosed on the Garden of Eden! What's your plea-sure, friends?

MEN

Tennis courts ?

WILSON

We got 'em.

MEN

Croquet lawns?

WILSON

We got 'em.

BATHING BEAUTIES

Country clubs and plush casinos?

WILSON

Got 'em!

CHOIR

Movie palaces? Yacht marinas?

WILSON
(Starting to become manic)
Got 'em! Got 'em!
Got 'em! Got 'em!
Got 'em all!

WILSON, CHOIR

Boca Raton!
Come down to Boca Raton
And buy a piece of heaven on
    earth—
Then get rid of it at twice its worth!

Wilson continues his pitch, becoming more manic by the moment. He promises that the next twenty buyers of lots will each have a house designed by his brother. Addison makes an effort to demur, but they are on microphones and he has no choice but to go along with the scheme. He tries to draw Wilson aside but, as in the Reading, the man with the pirate chest rushes on, followed by Wil-son rhapsodizing about the country, only this time in song, and to the tune of Papa's "It's In Your Hands Now."

WILSON
(Holding up the dirt from the side of the chest)
Land—yes! Land with
    opportunities!

Dirt—yes! Dirt, as in pay dirt!
Filth—yes! Filth, as in filthy lucre!

It's to buy, it's to sell,
It's all here to bring you riches,
It's a land of opportunity and more.
It's in your hands now—

The testimonials from investors pour in as before. Wilson makes claims that turn more and more extravagant. Addi-son becomes alarmed, as he sees his brother spinning out of control.

ADDISON
(Hastily, into his microphone)
Thank you! Thank you, every-body! We're going to take a break now—!

WILSON
Take a break? And deprive these people of a once in a lifetime op-portunity?! . . . Friends, let me ask you something. What is life? I say:

Call It Home

WILSON

Life is just a journey.

A road down which we travel, ever seeking, never satisfied, an endless quest for

Something different, something better.

Onward we go, following the road unrolling at our feet. Restlessly re-inventing ourselves. Searching for something which remains elusive, just beyond our grasp.

Until now. Till tonight.
'Cause tonight the road will take us
To a paradise so perfect
We can finally stop searching—

ADDISON
(Increasingly alarmed)
Willie—

WILSON
(Overriding him, feverishly)
Where, you ask?
Where, indeed?
Where's the place the road is
    leading?

Call it home.
It's a place for us to rest.
Journey's end,
Coming home
At last.

It's the home that you've sought
Ever since you left the nest,
It's a place to stop your wandering,
Stop the squandering
And the restlessness,
It's a place to stop regretting what is
    past.
The only thing that matters is—
We're home.

Call it home,
Like the place where you began.
Leave the world
And its woes
Behind.

Woes will melt, cares will cease.
The relief and the release—!
There is nothing like the peace
You will find
Once you're home.

When you're weary of the chase,
And you're looking for a place
That you never want to leave,
Here it is!

When you're tired of the race

(Increasingly messianic)

And the betting and the bluffing,
And the winnings and the failures
And the looking round the corners
And the need to keep on moving
As if something needed proving,

When you're spent
And confused
And you realize it's over,
Then it's time
To go home!

ADDISON
(Panicky, into his microphone)
And that isn't all, ladies and gentle-
men—!

WILSON
(Overriding him)
Until now it was gone.
Call it home. This is home.
This is Boca Raton!

"Call It Home" was added late in the Workshop run. It was my attempt to dramatize Wilson's breakdown—his exhaustion and his need for a place where he can stop being himself—by injecting John's prose version of his messianic speech with music, the best intensifier that exists in a musical's arsenal. I wanted to connect Wilson's intemperate project to his feelings about himself and the principles his father had instilled in him. It was a miscalculation: the song seemed as if it had come from another show, something with large anthemic pretensions.

Wilson gestures: the music swells and an enormous painting drops down, a heroic rendering of a mammoth, futuristic city. Across the top is written, "Addison Mizner's Boca Raton." Paris loves it; Addison is appalled: he didn't draw it; it isn't his design; it's Wilson's wild elaboration of it. Wilson barrels on and Addison, desperate, urges him to stop, gently at first. But when Wilson pushes him away, he makes a grab for the microphone and they struggle for control of it. Paris tries to stop Addison and Addison erupts. He accuses Paris of supporting the fraud, of being a fool to believe Wilson and become his stooge. Paris, angry and ashamed, agrees—the Mizners have made a fool of him. He accuses them of taking advantage of him. Wilson retorts that Paris never cared about the artists' colony anyway, that he was merely using it as a way of getting back at his father. Paris, in a cold rage, steps to the microphone and, as in the Reading, denounces the Mizner Development Corporation, which collapses.

Addison is distraught, not least be-cause the investors will sue them. Wilson suggests that Paris ask his father for the money they lost. It seems like nothing more than a nasty remark, but to Addison's surprise, Paris agrees. This is a crisis, and blood is thicker than water. He will phone his father this minute—on the condition that any arrangement must exclude Wilson. Addison has been a help and a support and Paris will be glad to help him in return, but Wilson is a con man and a bastard and deserves nothing—he will have to fend for himself. The choice is Addison's.

After a brief moment, Addison crosses to Wilson.

WILSON
(Smiling, to Paris)
How'd you put it? Blood is thicker
than water.

PARIS
You have each other. You deserve
each other.

He leaves. Wilson moves to embrace his brother. Addison shoves him away.

Get Out of My Life***

Go***

The scene changes to the Brown Derby, as at the beginning of the show, with Wilson drunk and the impatient reporter asking him to sum up his life. "It was a vaudeville," Wilson replies. "A tap dance followed by a juggler, followed by a dog act." The scene proceeds as before, going into the First Vaudeville, but after a chorus of "On My Left,"*** Papa appears, to say how disappointed he is in his sons, followed by a beaming Mama, to say how happy she is that her boys have finally gotten together. As the parents fade from view, the brothers go into their final vaudeville.

Final Vaudeville

ADDISON, WILSON
Just a couple of dreamers
On the road to "what's next?"

ADDISON
Could have been—what?

WILSON
Anything.

BOTH
(*With a shrug*)
But—
Just a couple of schemers,
Always veering from the text.

WILSON
Pick up and pack—

ADDISON
Never look back—

WILSON
Just a couple of wiseacres—

ADDISON
Heartbreakers—

BOTH
Or as some would say, "bums."
Just a couple of Joes
Passing time as it goes,
Taking life as it comes . . .

The olio flies out, revealing an actual version of the road to nowhere, disappearing into the distance upstage. They begin heading up the road, Wilson leading, Addison hanging back.

ADDISON, WILSON
Just a couple of footnotes
Who were once all the rage.

WILSON
Toast of the town,
Soaked in renown . . .

BOTH
Just a couple of footnotes,
When they might have been a page.

ADDISON
Could have been—what?
Anything.

BOTH
(*With a shrug*)
But . . .

A pair of busy boys
Who made a noise
But never came home with the prize.
Just a couple of—

WILSON
Yarn-spinners—

ADDISON
Mule-skinners—

WILSON
Small winners—

ADDISON
Might-have-been-ers—

BOTH
Just a couple of guys,
Cracking wise!

They start up the road.

ADDISON
Where do you think it goes?

WILSON
It's the road to opportunity.

ADDISON
It's the road to eternity.

WILSON
The greatest opportunity of all!
Sooner or later we're bound to get
it right.

ADDISON
You're an optimist, brother.

WILSON
I'm an American.

Arms linked, they head up the road and disappear.

In the Workshop, *Wise Guys* was a completely different show from that of the Reading: the same story, the same characters, but a weightier, less exuberant experience. The piece became more earnest and sober, and perhaps stronger, although some of its giddiness and bounce (yes) was lost in the process. Nevertheless, it was invaluable in the ways that workshops should be.* Among other things, it demonstrated that we had solved one major problem that had been revealed in the Reading: the repetitiousness in the relationship between the brothers. In this go-round, Addison wasn't always the disappointed victim and Wilson wasn't always the successful outsmarter. This time there was some variety to the story.

However, the Workshop also demonstrated that we had a number of other major problems. One was that, as Nathan noted in retrospect, the audience didn't warm to the show until the Palm Beach sequence, specifically the introduction of Addison's relationship with Paris and the burgeoning of it in the Palm Beach sequence. We asked ourselves if we could be suffering from the *Merrily We Roll Along* problem: the leading character was a dislikable opportunist. Was it that we didn't have a leading character; we had two of them? Should the story be primarily about Addison, the sympathetic one?

Then again, could it be that we had distanced the audience too much by the repeated intrusion of vaudevillizing our main characters, that perhaps because Paris was introduced straightforwardly, the audience was able to get involved with him and Addison? Were the picaresque aspects of the story and the many milieus disorienting? Or was our storytelling simply not good enough? Whatever the cause or causes, some of the show worked,

---

* See the chapter on *A Funny Thing Happened on the Way to the Forum* in *Finishing the Hat.*

Interiors created by Addison Mizner for his Palm Beach home

some of it didn't, but one thing was clear: it never accumulated; it didn't gather force.

For all the Workshop's revelations, *Wise Guys* was in one sense damaged by it. The high expectations for the show and the air of uncertainty that hung over it throughout the revisions and the nightly performances, together with the disappointed public reaction, saddled it with a reputation of being unfixable, from which it has never quite recovered—as in the case of *Merrily We Roll Along*. But just as George Furth and I worked on that show till we got it right, with the consequence that its reputation has kept improving through subsequent productions, so the transformation of *Wise Guys* into *Road Show* may have the same restorative effect. I hope so; I even think so.

And now for something *completely* different.

Harold Prince • 10 ROCKEFELLER PLAZA • SUITE 1009
NEW YORK, N. Y. 10020

Telephone
(212) 399-0960
Facsimile
(212) 974-8426

NICK - Don't switch A + W

II-59 p. 12

GOLD!
reading cast breakdown

PLEASE NOTE: ALL ENSEMBLE ASSIGNMENTS ARE SUBJECT TO CHANGE.

1.1

Addison Mizner	TOM McGOWAN
Club Steward	DAVID PITTU
Man in Rumpled Suit	MICHAEL McCORMICK
Young Woman	MICHELE RAGUSA
Wilson Mizner	HOWARD McGILLIN
Mama Mizner	ANITA GILLETTE

1.2

Papa Mizner	BILL PARRY
Man in a Frock Coat	MICHAEL McCORMICK
Laborer	DAVID PITTU
Prospector	HERNDON LACKEY

1.3

Prospector	MICHAEL McCORMICK
Poker Player #1	HERNDON LACKEY
Poker Player #2	DAVID PITTU
Poker Player #3	BILL PARRY
Poker Player #4	MICHAEL McCORMICK
Clerk	DAVID PITTU
Bartender	HERNDON LACKEY
Dance Hall Girl/Nellie	MICHELE PAWK

1.5

Salesman (steamship office)	HERNDON LACKEY
Businessman (Hawaii)	MICHAEL McCORMICK
Servant (Hawaii)	DAVID PITTU

Act Three · Bounce (2003)

Book by John Weidman
Directed by Harold Prince

The Notion

A chronicle of two brothers, Wilson and Addison Mizner, who were born in the 1880s and died in the 1930s. The show charts their lives from their beginnings in Benicia, California, through their adventures in the Klondike gold fields of the 1890s, where they meet Nellie, a woman who will play a significant part in their chronicle, thence to the extremes of New York City society in the early 1900s and into the Florida real estate boom and bust of the 1920s, for which they were largely responsible. It begins and ends in Palm Beach.

In other words, the same story as before, but with the addition of a leading lady.

General Comments

When John and I began the first draft of *Wise Guys* in 1994, the director we hoped to get was our *Pacific Overtures* colleague, Hal Prince. I told him the story one night over dinner; he not only took to the idea, he recognized immediately that the tone of the piece should be like the movie *Tucker,* the chronicle of a real-life entrepreneur and doomed visionary (the man who invented the Tucker car), who fails but is never defeated: an embodiment of American enterprise. This was not exactly our take, but close enough. However, for a reason never entirely clear to me, Hal was wary of our working together again. He had always been honest with me—outspokenly so, in fact—and therefore I knew he was genuinely enthusiastic about the idea, but something was bothering him, and whatever it was, I recognized that even at my most persistent and persuasive I could do nothing about it. I did make a second pitch six years later, and this time, happily, for an equally unknown reason, he said yes.

One of the first things Hal urged us to do was to get rid of the vaudeville armature, on the ground that its banality outweighed its usefulness. He needn't have bothered; John and I had discovered to our chagrin at the New York Theatre Workshop that the audience had taken our metaphor literally and assumed that the Mizners were actual vaudevillians, which made the story confusing, to say the least. And why shouldn't they have made that assumption, since the plot was continually being interrupted by vaudeville interludes? We had every reason to assume such a *modus interruptus* would work: *Sweeney Todd* is constantly interrupted by iterations of a commentary ballad, *Cabaret* by the emcee's numbers, and both those shows work. But on closer examination, *Sweeney Todd*'s interruptions are segments of narration and *Cabaret*'s emcee is not a character in the story—he speaks *only* to the audience. The Mizners were both emcees and characters, and they didn't function as narrators, so what were they?

Worse yet, vaudeville as metaphor, vaudeville as commentary, vaudeville as satire, all were becoming as tired and tiresome to me as they were to musical theater in general. It was a technique that had attracted me sporadically for a long time, ever since *Anyone Can Whistle* more than thirty years earlier, partly because it allowed me to use pastiche, something I love to write, and partly because using vaudeville to treat a serious subject is an easy pathway to irony—and using irony gives you an excuse to say anything, no matter how crass or banal or pretentious, and get away with it. Irony is a made-to-order refuge from emotion or criticism; the author is asserting with a

smile, "You can't criticize what I'm saying, you can't even accuse me of believing it, because I'm fully aware of it and I'm making fun of it while I'm saying it; I'm making fun of it before you can." The irony of irony is that it is often taken to indicate intelligence, and in theatrical circles is aggrandized by the sobriquet "Brechtian," a reference to the playwright Bertolt Brecht, who dealt heavily (very heavily) in irony. He distanced his audiences by direct address in a music-hall tradition, which served to entertain them and make them feel comfortably smart at the same time, as if they were in complicity with the author. Brecht's target audiences were peasants and workers rather than theater sophisticates and he shrewdly painted his plots and theses in primary colors, a defining characteristic of music hall and vaudeville. The apotheosis of the "Brechtian" vaudeville approach in commercial musical theater was probably reached with *Chicago,* the 1975 musical by John Kander, Fred Ebb and Bob Fosse, in which almost every number is a manifestation of vaudeville, no matter what the character, subject or dramatic moment. The technique persists today, especially in rock musicals, because rock is not a vehicle for humor as much as it is for comment, and irony is in itself comment. Irony appeals to almost every young writer, because it immediately confers upon them a badge of sophistication. Metaphoric irony, the kind that sets a show about presidential assassins in a shooting gallery, has become such a useful cliché in musicals that it will probably never be abandoned. Its attraction persisted with me for a long time, but the use of vaudeville—the practice of applying an inappropriate style to an idea, sentiment or situation—had peaked for me with *Assassins.*

Given this sour assessment, it might seem that the first thing John and I should have done in this new incarnation would be to cut the vaudevilles altogether, but we hesitated. We clung to the idea that the inconsistency of vaudeville, its charges and retreats, its constant threat of immediate chaos, was a theatrical reflection of the Mizners' lives, as well as an indication to the audience that they were going to see a set of picaresque adventures. As with Papa's song in the Workshop presentation, we decided to eat our cake and have it, too. We used vaudeville, but only twice: to frame the show, as prologue and conclusion, and to keep the vaudeville flavor alive, Hal and his set designer, Eugene Lee, used painted flats as scenery: painted books, painted beds, painted tables, with no actual props. Unexpectedly, however, the elimination of the vaudeville punctuations, with their sharp contrasts between strolling affability and verbal anger and their rhythmic jolts during the course of the story, made for a less volatile relationship between the brothers and a blander show overall.

The use of vaudeville was of less concern to Hal than his feeling that John and I were cheating our subject by the lack of sex in the show—heterosexual sex, that is. He said that what we were trying to do was to tell a "robust" (his word, and a good one) story about the history of our country, but that having as its kernel an incestuous relationship between two brothers and their mother was another matter altogether and a lessening of the larger picture: the country's reluctance to distinguish between opportunity and opportunism. The reason he thought that the addition of sex would make the story more epic is lost to history (none of us remembers it), but it seemed like a good idea at the time, so John and I, as we had with Sam, set to work accordingly. It occurred to us that we could take a minor figure from the Reading and the Workshop, the dance hall girl in the Alaska sequence who became Wilson's accomplice, and expand her role rather inventively by making her a recurrent figure in their lives.

Next came the problem of what to call the show. After the reception given the Workshop production, the title *Wise Guys* connoted predetermined failure. Above all, Hal wanted the show to present itself as something entirely new, an idealist's hope if ever there was one, but worth a try. He wanted the title to reflect something larger than the story of two con men hooking "fish," yet what? A title should suggest to an audience what a show is about, but *Wise Guys,* like most plays, was about many things: the difference between opportunity and opportunism, the transformation of the pioneer spirit, the ability to reinvent oneself, the effect of parents on children, and more. What was the salient point? As we rewrote, we decided that the central idea had to do with America's resilience, its combination of talent and impatience, its ability to reinvent itself, for good and ill, as exemplified by both Mizners, particularly Wilson. I've always been fond of the word "bounce" for its near-onomatopoeic sound (and it's not too hard to rhyme—for a chorus or two), so *Bounce* it became.

The title is reflected in the score. As with *A Funny Thing Happened on the Way to the Forum* and *Merrily We Roll Along,* most of the songs are rhythmically square and in traditional forms with traditional accompaniments, although somewhat disguised by inserting sections of one song into another. The harmonic language is very tonal (that is, not dissonant), with the kind of moderately simple key relationships that I was writing in the late 1950s and early 1960s while I was warming up in the wings. I wanted the score to be crisp and bright and simple and direct and made up of primary colors. And fast. Not that all the songs would be fast, but they would make their point and get off. At least, that was the intention.

ACT ONE

To the sound of celestial voices the lights come up on a lanai in Boca Raton, Florida, circa 1930. Addison, lying in a beach chair, airily accepts a subpoena for a court appearance to defend against a real estate lawsuit. This scene cross-cuts with another in a hotel bungalow in Los Angeles, where Wilson, a screenwriter, is attempting to bed an aspiring actress. In quick succession, each of the brothers dies of a heart attack, Addison in the middle of a martini, Wilson in the middle of an attempt. They meet in a kind of heavenly limbo, beyond which we can glimpse a road stretching far into the distance. They greet each other, with affection on Wilson's part and suspicion on Addison's. Wilson, with a big smile, presents Addison to the audience.

On My Left*

WILSON
On my left,
Let me state,
Is a prince
Of a fellow.
He pretends he's made of Jell-O,
But that's strictly pretend.

Addison stands, unmoved, observing him.

He has heft,

(Quickly indicating gravity as opposed to fat)

Meaning weight.
He's a great goddamn artist,
He's the wildest and the smartest,
He's the guy who sets the trend.

_____
* This version of "On My Left" was cut before the show's Chicago tryout.

He's himself in a way that
You'll find in no other,
And believe me, I don't say that
Just because he is my brother.

He's a prince,
He's a jewel,
And he never needs renewal
As my partner,
As my conscience,
As my friend.

Addison presents Wilson to the audience.

ADDISON
On my right
Is a child,
But a child with dimension
Who's a master of invention
And has charm without end.

He's as bright
As he's wild,
He gets people's attention,
And it's past my comprehension
How he sees around the bend.

If he's weak—well, okay, that
Is no cause for quibbling,
And believe me, I don't say that
Just because he is my sibling.

WILSON
There's a prince.

ADDISON
That's a jewel.

BOTH
And he never needs renewal—

WILSON
As my conscience—

ADDISON
As my brother—

BOTH
As a friend.

They stroll about for a few moments, reminiscing about their lives together and apart.

Bounce

WILSON
We've come a long way.

ADDISON
We've been through a lot.

WILSON
We've learned how to bounce.

As Papa would say:

BOTH
"You're hot, then you're not,
You better learn to bounce."

If something goes wrong,
That's all right.
Bounce along,
Just travel light.
You go off the track,
Don't look back,
That's the thing that counts.

ADDISON
You hit a few bumps,
You make a few gaffes,
You learn how to bounce.

WILSON
You take a few lumps,
You have a few laughs,
And all the while you bounce.

BOTH
Don't dwell on the times
That you fail,
Remember the times
When you sail.
Find a new road,
Forge a new trail,
Bounce.

WILSON
You don't suppose this really *is* Heaven, do you?

ADDISON
If guys like you get to go to Heaven, Willie, who has to go to Hell?

WILSON
Point taken—

W6

OPENING – PART VIII – WISE GUYS #2

(WILSON, ADDISON)

Stephen Sondheim

(As they resume strolling)

Although if this isn't Heaven, then
where the hell are we?

ADDISON
Yeah. And where do we go next?

WILSON
No cause for concern,
We'll get by,
Live and learn—

(As Addison shoots him a look)

All right then, die.
So what if we're dead,
Gotta look ahead!

ADDISON
How true, how true.

WILSON
The road may get rough—

ADDISON
Who knows in advance?

WILSON
Be ready to bounce.

ADDISON
You needn't have brilliance,
Just resilience.

WILSON
You do it enough—

BOTH
You look for the chance,
You see it and you pounce.

WILSON
When you're spent,
Reinvent.

During the next few lines Wilson turns upstage, slips something surreptitiously out of his pocket and quickly sniffs it.

BOTH
We've bucked a few trends—

WILSON
And with style.

BOTH
We made a few friends—

ADDISON
For a while.

WILSON
From all we've been through—

ADDISON
From dealing with you,
I've learned how to—

(Noticing what Wilson is doing)

Goddammit, Willie! Could you for
once just—!

WILSON
(Turning back, bright-eyed, flinging his arm around Addison's shoulder)
The time up in Nome,
Gold up to our ears—!

ADDISON
We lost every ounce.

WILSON
Come on, it was fun—

ADDISON
At the point of a gun!*

WILSON
Well, then we get home
And who disappears?

ADDISON
(With a shrug)
I had to learn to bounce.

WILSON
But we were a team.

ADDISON
No, *you* were a team.

---

* The original couplet was sharper but a
little too much of a jolt this early in the
proceedings:

WILSON
Come on now, admit
It was fun—

ADDISON
It was shit.

WILSON
The horse that we doped—

ADDISON
That *you* doped . . .

WILSON
Just trying to help further your
career.

ADDISON
When you were finished helping, I
didn't have a career.

WILSON
It's the thought that counts.

Addison stops dead, glares at Wilson.

No, you're right, you're right,
And when you are right, you're
right!*

(Singing front, lightly, with a smile)

On my left—

(Gesturing to Addison, who still glares, refusing to pick up the cue)

On my left—

(As Addison still refuses to respond)

On my left—

(Jumping in front of Addison, gesturing to an imaginary Wilson)

On my "right"—

(Jumping back, gesturing to Addison)

Is a saint and an artist—

ADDISON
(Giving in)
—Is the smartest of the smartest.

WILSON
—Though he can let you down.

ADDISON
Rather sly—

WILSON
Kind of quaint—

ADDISON
—But a guy to rely on—

WILSON
—But a shoulder you can cry on.

ADDISON
—When he isn't skipping town.*

They continue to stroll, but their banter turns into recrimination.

WILSON
(With a bitter smile)
You're stuck in a jam,
Your brother says "Scram!"
You pack up and—!

ADDISON
(An equally bitter smile)
"Scram," yes, indeed. "Scram" as in, "Scram, sucker, I'm getting married. I'll get back to you—"

The brother you prize
Keeps telling you lies,
You better know goddamn well how to goddamn bounce!

WILSON
Lies? Oh, please! You wouldn't recognize the truth if it jumped up and bit you in the ass!

ADDISON
That was *my* line.

WILSON
Sorry. But then the really good lines were all mine, weren't they?

ADDISON
On my left—

WILSON
On my right—

ADDISON
—Is my waste of a brother.

_____
* The passage between asterisks was cut.
_____

WILSON
—Is an error of my mother—

ADDISON
(To Wilson)
A woman you abandoned the moment she became an inconvenience!

WILSON
The hell I did!

ADDISON
(To the audience)
He's bereft—

WILSON
Call it spite—

ADDISON
—Of all sense of proportion—!

WILSON
—And a weakness for distortion—!

After a few more recriminations, they calm down.

WILSON
I mean, here we are,
Team or not.
It's bizarre
How far we've got.
Together again,
Two old men,
Settling our accounts.

ADDISON
You're right, and when you're right,
Which isn't too often—

WILSON
The problem was mine.

ADDISON
All I did was whine.

WILSON
You did sort of flounce—

(Hastily)
With justification.

ADDISON
Just frustration.

WILSON
No, I was a fink.

ADDISON
I drove you to drink.

WILSON
What saved us was our bounce.

ADDISON
That's how you survive.

WILSON
We may just come out of this whole thing alive.

BOTH
With someone to give
You a hand,
You not only live,
You expand.
You learn to adjust.
You do what you must:

Bounce.

As in the Reading, their contentiousness takes over and they soon wind up pummeling each other, interrupted by the voice of Mama, yelling at them to stop fighting. They become their adolescent selves and the scene changes to the Mizner home in Benicia at the turn of the century. Papa lies in bed, railing against the state senators who have bankrupted him by declaring Sacramento the capital of California when he had invested all his money in local real estate, certain that Benicia would be chosen. He is dying, and furious about it.

Opportunity

PAPA
One day lose, the next day win,
Splash and then it's splat!
Giving in's the only sin
And boys, this land is fat!
We can all be rich again—
Like that!

BOYS
Like what, Papa?

PAPA
(Cocks an ear)
That!

(A knocking sound)

Hear that knocking?
Hear that sound?
Opportunity!

*(As knocking sounds continue
throughout)*

What's that knocking
All around?
That's your heritage,
Opportunity!

See what's new!
Something more!
Me, I'm through.
Up to you—
Go explore!

Only one thing never dies—
Opportunity!
Something better always lies
Around the corner!

Once you spot an opportunity,
Don't just make a note.
Take it by the throat,
Pounce, or miss the boat.
There's a land of opportunities—
Grab your hat and coat!

*He starts to become delirious and
struggles to rise.*

You just keep heading west,
Crossing mountains and plains,
Planting roots, building towns
As you go.

Pressing on as you're pressed,
Through the winds and the rains,
Taking risks, tempting fate,
Till you open every gate,
That's what's made this country
    great—!

Westward ho, boys!

ADDISON
But, Papa, we're in California—

Papa falls back, mumbling.

MAMA
Speak up, dear.

*She leans down and listens, conveying
what he says to the boys.*

We've been poor . . .
But we're in Michigan . . .

Papa mumbles impatiently.

Oh—

(Correcting herself)

We'll be rich again . . .
Never say die . . .
New ideas
Are always just around the
    corner . . .

Find the new frontiers . . .
Be the pioneers . . .
Learn to bounce . . .
That's what counts . . .

*Papa summons his last strength and
suddenly rises.*

PAPA
We'll be rich again! . . .
Opportunity! . . .
Never say die—!

*He crashes back on the bed and dies.
Mama hastily leans in, as if to hear his
final words.*

MAMA
(To the boys)
And take care of your mother . . .

This song went through many changes.
It was not only the first song in the
narrative, a position which always carries extra weight, it was also a statement of the philosophy that both
motivates the main characters and un-
derlies the show, so it was centrally
important that its tone be right. The
sententiousness of "It's in Your
Hands," the song Papa sang in the
Workshop, seemed wrong for the return to lightheartedness that we hoped
would invigorate *Bounce*, but if a
deathbed scene was treated comically,
would it make the rest of the evening a
cartoon? And how feeble could Papa
be if he were to espouse a passionate
cause that was supposed to have an effect on his sons? Hal was taken with
the notion of mumbling; in hindsight,
I think transforming the song into the
comic meanderings of an old man instead of presenting him as an avatar of
the pioneering spirit was a mistake.
But it seemed like a good idea at the
time.

In the first version of the song,
Papa was even more delirious, but also
fiercer:

Never Say Die (cut)

PAPA
One day up, the next day down—
That's what life's about.
Time to build another town,
This one's up the spout.
Lansing Mizner's down, but he's not
    out!

We've been rich
And we'll be rich again.
Never say die!
Life is full of empty bank accounts.
That's the challenge, boys—
Have to learn to bounce.
Gloom today,
Tomorrow, Fourth of July!
Never say die!

(Feverishly)

Want to know why?
Simple as pie—!

*Mama and the boys try to calm him,
but he holds up his hand to shush them.*

PAPA
(Cocking his ear)

Hear that sound?

Knocking sounds begin.

That's opportunity knocking!
Opportunities!
Possibilities!
New frontiers
For pioneers!
Let me up
And we'll be rich again—
Let me out of here—!

He struggles to get out of bed. The boys gently prevent him.

Dying is for quitters, boys!
Get my coat and hat!
Rest just gives me jitters, boys.
And boys, this land is fat!
I can make us rich again—

    (Trying weakly to snap his fingers)

Like that.

He sings the "Westward Ho!" section of "Opportunity." When Addison points out that they've gone as far west as they can go, Papa is stopped for only a moment.

          PAPA
That's a hitch,
But we'll be rich again!

          (Coughs)
Never say—

          (Coughs again)
—Die!

Past mistakes—
Sure, they're regrettable,
But, believe me,
They're forgettable.
Don't look back,
And don't let chances go by.

He has a severe comic coughing fit. When it is over, he recovers vigorously but is clearly in a state of mild delirium.

Once you spot a tooneroppity—

Mama and the boys exchange glances.

Don't just make a note.
Grab it by the throat,
Or you'll miss the boat!
All these goddamned tuberosities—

    (Trying to correct himself)

Tooneroppities—
Topperoonities—
Where's my hat and coat?! . . .

Find the new frontiers . . .
Be the pioneers . . .
Don't look back . . .
Learn to bounce . . .
Take the chance . . .
That's what counts . . .

He fades away and is still. Mama and the boys look at each other in alarm for a moment.

    ADDISON, WILSON
Papa?

          PAPA
    (Suddenly bolting upright)
Opportunities!!!

He falls back onto the pillows and starts mumbling. Mama leans in and translates for the boys, as in "Opportunity," but goes on a little longer.

          MAMA
. . . Life goes on,
It's time to switch again . . .

Papa mumbles a bit louder. She corrects herself.

Find an itch again . . .

Papa mumbles angrily.

Niche again . . .

Papa mumbles approvingly and continues, getting weaker.

New ideas . . .
Are always just around the
    corner . . .
Something . . . high . . .

Something . . . west . . .
Listen to your mama . . .
She knows best . . .

          PAPA
    (Erupting for the last time)
We'll be rich again!
Never say d—!

And he dies, bankrupt. Mama and the boys ponder what to do next. Addison suggests opening a florist shop, but Wilson spots a headline in the newspaper Papa had been reading. A Prospector appears and gives his pitch, and the Mizners go off to Alaska as before.

Gold!***

Wilson leaves Addison at the dig as in the Reading, but he is a slightly more naive and honest Wilson than the previous one; he actually intends to return to Addison after staking the claim. "Gold!" continues as before with Wilson entering the saloon, but this Wilson, when he is invited into the poker game, is reluctant to gamble, and the song fades away. He starts to leave, but one of the poker players, spotting him as a sucker, signals to a dance hall girl to slow him down. She sidles over to block the doorway.

*** The lyrics here and in other songs marked by a triple asterisk can be found in previous sections of this chapter.

What's Your Rush?

DANCE HALL GIRL
Hey!

(Softer)

Hi . . .

What's your rush?
Too bad you're in such a rush—
Honey,
Stick around,
Relax and get warm.

WILSON
(Starting out again)
My brother's waiting for me.

DANCE HALL GIRL
What's out there?
A lot of lousy weather.
What's in here?
A chance for you and me to be
    together.

Celebrate.
Believe me, kid, the gold will wait.
I won't.

(Gesturing to the bartender)

Gettin' late,
And listen to that storm . . .

The wind howls; the bartender steps up behind Wilson with a shot glass of whiskey; the girl reaches over Wilson's shoulder, takes the glass and hands it to him, smiling.

What's out there?
Snow and slush.
If you're so determined, though,
Mush, boy, mush.
Otherwise—
Ooh, those eyes—
I mean, what's your rush?

    I'm Nellie.

WILSON
Willie.

They dance together slowly.

NELLIE
When you're through,
There's lots of things I'd like to do—
Bad things.
Maybe you
Could help me to reform.

I could get
Such a crush . . .
What's the matter, baby,
Is that a blush?
Trust me, hon . . .
Just for fun . . .
C'mon, what's your rush?

He stays and joins the poker game. The action cuts back and forth between the poker table and the dig, as in the Wise Guys Reading ("Gold!"***). The lyrics remain as they were, with a few minor changes, the most important being that as Wilson keeps winning, Nellie switches her allegiance from the first poker player to him, fetching him drinks, lighting him cigars and draping herself over him for good luck. As he plays, he thinks.

The Game

WILSON
One day lose, the next day win—
Nothing goes as planned.
When you feel like giving in,
Comes a brand-new hand.

What you've lost, that's where you've
    been.
Long as you keep moving,
Things will keep improving—
Prospects will expand.

(Picking up his last card)

Okay, Papa, now I understand . . .

He goes on to sing an abridged chorus of "The Game"*** with slightly emended lyrics, the song now an intro-spection about the thrill of gambling rather than an inducement to his brother. The climactic bet is about to be made when Addison bursts in, nugget in hand, but Wilson has already bet the claim. He defends himself by singing a brief chorus of "The Game" and Addi-son agrees to go along with the bet.

"The Game" (Howard McGillin as Wilson and Richard Kind as Addison)

This new verse and introspective chorus were designed to emphasize how Wilson had distorted Papa's principles and mistaken opportunism for opportunity, a major theme of the show. Sometimes it's useful to spell things out.

To Addison's horror, Wilson's straight flush loses to the first poker player's four jacks, but Nellie catches Wilson's eye and indicates the poker player's vest pocket. Wilson reaches over and takes two more jacks out of it. Addison, appalled, accuses the poker player of cheating and reaches for the pot. The accused punches him in the face, and he and his cronies draw their guns. They are about to gather the money in the pot when Nellie takes a gun from her garter and shoots the poker player in the leg, shoving the pot money at the boys and urging them to run, which they do. She pockets the claim.

   Addison and Wilson return to San Francisco, where Mama is now living, bringing her their winnings.

Next to You***

Addison leaves to go on his trip around the world.

Addison's Trip***

"Addison's Trip" remains the same as in the Workshop, but with the Indian section omitted and a few minor changes in the lyric. There is a notable difference in the individual episodes, however. In each instance Addison fails because he gets cheated rather than because he is incompetent or inexperi-

enced. In Hawaii the plantation owner takes his investment money without telling him that the pineapple company has already gone into receivership. In China, he invests in a fireworks company whose owner is about to commit suicide because he is bankrupt and bequeaths Addison's money to his wife. In Guatemala, Addison invests in a coffee plantation just before the country undergoes a revolution and he is forced to flee. In each of these disasters, Addison still succumbs to his addiction for collecting, and even with Guatemalan natives rioting and firing guns around him, buys souvenirs.

As in the Workshop, lights come up after the song on an exclusive enclosure, only now it is at the Belmont Park racetrack instead of Madison Square Garden. There are potted palms, a bar, little gilded tables and chairs, the sound of a salon orchestra drifting in from offstage. A cross-section of the New York Social Register is clustered at the windows, staring out at the track. Among them is the grandly dressed Eleanor Yerkes, surrounded by an entourage of middle-aged aristocrats, among them a self-styled ladies' man named Bessemer, accompanied by his handsome son, Hollis.

   Wilson is trying to charm his way into the enclosure without an invitation, but a white-gloved bouncer is too smart for him. Wilson's clothes are sporty and well tailored, but on second glance threadbare and slightly shabby. Addison appears, carrying a card of invitation from his new client Mrs. Yerkes, along with the blueprints for a gazebo she has commissioned. The brothers ebulliently greet each other. Addison discloses that he has discovered his vocation; Wilson discloses that he has been crossing the country with Mama, looking for opportunities, with no luck. He cons Addison into letting go of his invitation, pockets it, shows it to the bouncer and enters the enclosure, leaving Addison unable to gain entrance. Wilson heads straight for Mrs. Yerkes and flirts with her. She accepts it coolly for a moment, then starts to leave. He stops her with a gesture.

What's Your Rush?
(reprise)*

WILSON
What's your rush?
Too bad you're in such a rush . . .

(As Mrs. Yerkes stops and turns)

Lady . . .
Stick around,
Relax and stay warm.

MRS. YERKES
My friends are waiting for me . . .

WILSON
What's out there?
A lot of lousy weather.
What's in here?
A chance for you and me to be
   together . . .

Mrs. Yerkes looks toward the exit, then once more back to him.

Celebrate . . .

He nods to a waiter, who begins pouring two glasses of Champagne. Mrs. Yerkes keeps looking at Wilson fixedly.

I promise you the crowd will wait—

MRS. YERKES
(Overlapping)
I promise you the gold will wait—

WILSON
(Faltering)
I . . . won't . . .

(Realizing)

MRS. YERKES
Getting late,
And listen to that storm . . .

She gestures to the outside: a huge shout of people cheering the horses. Wilson has now recognized the words

---

* This reprise was cut in Washington. Explanation to follow.

and the woman, as have we. She is
Nellie from Alaska, grown rich and
elegant.

NELLIE
What's out there?

(Gesturing toward the sound of the
crowd)

So much slush . . .
Goodness, Mr. Mizner,
Is that a blush?

(As Wilson opens his mouth to
answer)

Big surprise!
Ooh, those eyes,
They're still—

WILSON
Nellie . . .

NELLIE
(Correcting him)
Eleanor.

Wilson asks her about her transforma-
tion. She explains that she took his
claim off the deserted poker table as a
stake, got a ticket to New York, bought
an expensive gown, hung out at places
where the social set convened and
landed an elderly millionaire named
Charles Yerkes; she is now the richest
widow in New York. She asks Wilson
what he has been up to in the interven-
ing years.

The rest of their conversation is mostly
spoken but completely musicalized in
waltz rhythm: every line has an accompanying melody in the offstage
salon orchestra, but only the lines referring to Alaska are sung. This was an
experiment, an attempt to make an
amalgam of dialogue, lyric and music
without resorting to either recitative or
song form. Thus:

WILSON
Where shall I begin?

NELLIE
The top.

WILSON
Whatcha want to know?

NELLIE
A lot. Everything you'd rather Nellie didn't.

WILSON
I think a man's entitled to his
secrets.

NELLIE
That isn't all a man thinks he's entitled to.

WILSON
You sound as if you'd learned the
hard way.

NELLIE
Is there another?

WILSON
Easy, girl.

(Sings)

We aren't in Alaska.

(Speaks)

Would you care to dance?

NELLIE
Right now?

WILSON
I don't see why not.

NELLIE
In here? Everyone will stare.

WILSON
I can only hope they do.

NELLIE
Well, let me have a drink.

(Drains the rest of her glass)

Right.

(Getting up, sings)

Dance me to Alaska . . .

They begin to dance—or, more accu-
rately, sway to the music, as they did in
the Yukon. They continue the musical-
ized conversation, flirting with each
other while Wilson fills her in on his
various failed scams and business
ventures.

I print the above as a sample, but omit
the rest of the extended sequence because on the page and without the
music it reads simply as dialogue and
gives no sense of its quality as a lyric.
Moreover, the experiment didn't work:
the frustration of hearing the words
spoken rather than sung, while all the
time the music underneath clearly
echoed the rhythm and even the in-
flection of the speech, turned cleverness into tedium in the blink of an eye,
or its aural equivalent, and quickly
became interminable. I worked on
the damn thing for a month, which
proves that it takes just as long to
write a wrong song as a right one.
When we got to Washington, we cut
the reprise of "What's Your Rush?"
(Wilson discovered who Mrs. Yerkes
was more quickly without benefit of
song), and I reduced the musical banter to a verse, as in the following,
which is all sung and which is cued by
Wilson asking Nellie how she feels in
her new station.

The Best Thing That Ever Has Happened

NELLIE
Life is pretty smooth.

WILSON
Indeed.

NELLIE
If a little dull.

WILSON
I bet.

NELLIE
Still, it isn't bad.

Howard McGillin as Wilson and Michele Pawk as Nellie

WILSON
Or it isn't bad enough.

NELLIE
Oh, badder than you think.
Though nothing like Alaska . . .

WILSON
(Gets up, extends his hand)
Would you care to dance?

NELLIE
Right now?

WILSON
I don't see why not.

NELLIE
In here? Everyone will stare.

WILSON
I can only hope they do.

(A beat)

NELLIE
Well, let me have a drink.

(Drains the rest of her glass)

Right.
Dance me to Alaska . . .

They dance briefly.

WILSON
You're still the best thing that ever
has happened to me.

NELLIE
(Just as intently)
Bullshit.

WILSON
Okay, the best thing that could ever
happen to me.

NELLIE
Bullshit.

WILSON
How could I realize
What rich was really?
Ideally,
Somewhere I should have been told,
"Kid, you've struck gold."

NELLIE
*(Simultaneously, nodding in
anticipation)*
"—You've struck gold."

You were the best thing that ever
had happened to me—

(As Wilson starts to beam)

Back then.
Of course not much very good ever
happened to me
Back then.

WILSON
(Smiles)
Things change as time goes by.
You never know when
The best thing that happened can
happen again.

*Wilson tells her he deserves a percent-
age of the money from the claim that
she stole. She laughs. He comes on to
her even more.*

WILSON
I'd like to still be the best thing
That's happened to you.

NELLIE
Really?

WILSON
Another moment like this
May not happen to you.

NELLIE
Really?

BOTH
To think I'd meet someone
Who could surprise me
And size me up without cutting me
    down—

NELLIE
Ain't this a town?

BOTH
With all the best and the worst
That have happened to us,
Why not?
We just might be the best thing
That has happened to us.
Why not?

WILSON
When all is said and done—

NELLIE
I have to agree—

BOTH
You're still the best thing that's
    happened to me.

NELLIE
(Appraising)
You're good.

WILSON
You're great.

BOTH
Let's see.

Hollis enters, holding a betting slip.

HOLLIS
Eleanor, your horse came in!

NELLIE
You're telling me . . .

NELLIE, WILSON
All the way from Alaska . . .

This song had been introduced in
Chicago, but not until the next scene.
More about that after the next scene.

Addison pushes his way in, bouncer in
tow, and authenticates his credentials
by showing his blueprint to Mrs.
Yerkes, not recognizing her as Nellie at
first. Wilson snatches the blueprints
away and, as Addison begins to erupt,
assures him that "we" will commission
him for something much grander than a
pavilion. The "we" turns out to be Wilson and Nellie, whom Wilson manages
to marry immediately, with Mama in
attendance and not too happy about it.
    Lights come up on Wilson and Nel-
lie's bedroom, which consists of a number of doors and a monumental bed
which takes up most of the central
playing area. Off to one side is an architect's table, at which Addison
stands, drawing.

I Love This Town

ADDISON
One day modest, next day grand,
Thick with millionaires.
Willie's wish is my command.

(Contemplating the drawing)

. . . Where to put the stairs? . . .

On my way, the way I planned—
Still, though, who could plan it?

(Erasing a word on the drawing)

. . . Travertine, not granite . . .
Willie's got a wife—
Even better, Willie's got a life.

Light dims on Addison and comes up
on Wilson, who is starting to undress
Nellie slowly.

WILSON
You are the best thing that ever has
    happened to me,
You are . . .
You are the best thing that ever
    could happen to me,
You are . . .

Two reporters and a photographer race
on through the upstage doors; Nellie,
startled, hastily buttons up.

*REPORTER #1
(To Wilson)
How's it feel to snag
The second-richest woman in New
    York?

REPORTER #2
(To Nellie)
Does it bother you he hasn't got a
    nickel?

REPORTERS,
PHOTOGRAPHER
Anything you wanna say
You think the public oughta know?

WILSON
We've got it all, boys. Love, happi-
    ness and fifty million bucks!

The reporters chuckle.

NELLIE
(Rolling her eyes and pulling Wilson
    away)
Willie . . .

Wilson dutifully ushers the reporters
out, as music resumes.

REPORTER #1
(As they exit)
No dummy . . .

REPORTER #2
Real phony . . .

ALL THREE
Good copy . . .

WILSON
(Turning back to Nellie)
Where were we? . . .

NELLIE
I was the best thing that ever had
    happened to you,
So far—

---

* The section between asterisks was cut
after the Chicago production, for an interesting reason, to be discussed below.

WILSON
(Starting again to undress her)
Right.
Just you're the best thing that ever
has happened to me, you are.

NELLIE
(Starting to undress him)
Right.*

They keep undressing each other and
have gone moderately far when suddenly a bell rings, Gong!, and two
prizefighters burst into the room, one
of them Stanley Ketchel, the other
Sailor Boy Mackenzie. A crowd roars,
a harsh white light snaps on over the
fighters' heads, and they begin to mix it
up, traveling around the bedroom. Wilson looks on, beaming; Nellie shrieks
and hastily covers up.

The following passage is spoken
rhythmically.

WILSON
(To Ketchel)
Kid!

The fighters trade punches and grunt
rhythmically.

KETCHEL
Hiya, Willie!

WILSON
How you doing?

KETCHEL
Just great!

NELLIE
Who's that?!

WILSON
Stanley Ketchel,
Fighting Sailor Boy Mackenzie
For the title.

NELLIE
For the title?

WILSON
For the middleweight crown.
We bought his contract
For a measly fifty thousand.

NELLIE
We did?

WILSON
(To Ketchel, as he flails away at
Mackenzie)
Looking thick around the middle,
kid. Behaving yourself?

KETCHEL
(Turns to Wilson, still boxing)
Meet the Sailor—

WILSON
Hey.

KETCHEL
(Sings to Mackenzie, after
jabbing him)
Willie gets me fights—

(Mackenzie jabs him back)

Willie gets me dope—

(Jabs Mackenzie)

Willie gets me broads—

(A bimbo pops through one of the
doors)

Say hello to Myrna.

MYRNA
(Waves to Mackenzie)
Hi . . .

Mackenzie turns to say hello, which
gives Ketchel the chance to punch him
three times and knock him out. Loud
cheers. Ketchel holds his arms up in
victory as an announcer speaks.

ANNOUNCER
The winner and new middleweight
champion of the United States—
Stanley Ketchel!

WILSON
(Sings, to Nellie)
God, I love this town!

The other upstage door opens. Two
trainers enter and start carrying
Mackenzie out, followed by a strutting
Ketchel, as the first door opens and the

reporters and photographer rush in,
pencils and camera at the ready. Nellie
rolls her eyes and during the following
pours herself a stiff drink from the
night table.

REPORTER #1
(To Wilson)
How's it feel to own
The biggest little fighter in New
York?

REPORTER #2
Any comment on the rumor
That Mackenzie took a dive?

NELLIE
(Impatiently, as Wilson is about to
answer)
Willie—!

WILSON
Right . . .

As he obediently ushers the assemblage
out the doors, light comes up on Addison, working at his drafting table.

ADDISON
A salon for her, a saloon for him,
And I guess I'd better include a gym,
But with parquet floors and a
    Georgian trim . . .

Light comes up on Wilson, who turns
back to Nellie and begins undressing
her.

WILSON
God, I love this town!
Don't you love this town?
It's got all of these
Opportunities,
Can't afford to turn them down.
Some may not work out.
Some go up the spout,
Plenty more around the corner—

(Seductively)

And what's 'round the corner,
    sweetheart,
That's what life's about.

You are the sexiest thing that has
    happened to me,
You are.

NELLIE
You are the best thing that still hasn't
    happened to me,
You are . . .

*They laugh and resume undressing
each other. Just when Nellie is almost
naked, thunderous applause and shouts
of "Bravo!" usher in Paul Armstrong.
Footlights shine up at him as he acknowledges the imaginary audience's
approval. Nellie squeals and dives
under the bedclothes.*

NELLIE
Who's *that*?

WILSON
Paul Armstrong, Broadway's leading playwright. We're producing
his new play.

NELLIE
We *are*—?

ARMSTRONG
. . . And let me just say that I could
not have achieved this soul-searing
portrait of the New York underworld without my good friend Wilson Mizner, who was more than my
producer, he was my *collaborator*,
my entry card into the underworld
and its lingo—!

*The footlights go out and Armstrong
turns upstage to toast Wilson with a
pocket flask.*

Merde, *my friend! And come join
us for a celebratory libation at
Delmonico's! . . .*

*He gestures, and a trio of giggling
chorines emerges from the other door
into the bedroom, tap-dancing.*

CHORINES, ARMSTRONG
Broadway Willie,
Prince of bons vivants—
Everybody wants
Broadway Willie Mizner!

*Wilson joins them, dancing, drinking,
whatever. During the following, a*

*dealer offers him a whiff of cocaine.
Nellie sits on the bed and drinks.*

CHORINES, ARMSTRONG
Knocks 'em silly,
Lowlifes and DuPonts,
Cops and debutantes—

GONG! *The roar of the crowd, and
Ketchel barrels through a door, fighting
furiously with another opponent, Kid
Callahan.*

*The following passage is spoken
rhythmically.*

KETCHEL
Hiya, Willie.

WILSON
Hiya, champ.

KETCHEL
(To Callahan)
Say hello to Willie.

CALLAHAN
Hey.

KETCHEL
(Sings)
Willie gets me fights—

(Jabs Callahan)

Willie gets me dope—

Callahan jabs back.

Willie gets me broads—

*A door opens and Myrna appears, gun
in hand.*

Say hello to Lulu—

He stops in surprise.

Myrna?

MYRNA
You sonofabitch, you'll never two-
time me again!

*She shoots Ketchel, who bellows and
crashes across the bed. Nellie screams.
Myrna dashes out as the Reporters and*

*Photographer dash in. Callahan raises
his arms over his head in victory to the
roar of the crowd.*

REPORTER #1
Any comment, Mr. Mizner,
On this terrible event?

REPORTER #2
Anything you want to say
About the shooting of the champ?

WILSON
Try counting ten over him, maybe
he'll get up.

*The Reporters chuckle approvingly and
scribble on their pads.*

NELLIE
(Snapping)
Willie—!

WILSON
(Cutting her off)
Stop right there—

REPORTERS,
PHOTOGRAPHER
(To each other)
Good copy!

*Wilson claps his hands and everybody
starts to exit through the doors as
lights dim a bit on the bedroom and
come up on Addison.*

ADDISON
. . . And a little room for Mama,
When she comes to stay . . .

*As he continues, Nellie arranges her-
self in the bed seductively, drink in
hand; Wilson flings himself onto the
covers and takes a twist of cocaine out
of his pocket.*

Willie says that he wants dazzle,
He'll get dazzle
All the way . . .

*Lights dim on him and come back up
on the bed, where Wilson begins to
snort the cocaine, Nellie drinks and
they both resume undressing each other
under the bedclothes. Suddenly, Wilson
notices the time on his watch and snaps*

on the radio. Out of it comes the voice
of an excited announcer.

RADIO ANNOUNCER
And here they come, down the
stretch. It's Whirligig by half a
length, then Tender Trap! Whirligig and Tender Trap! Whirligig
and Tender Trap!

Nellie glares at him and snaps the
radio off.

WILSON
Hey, we own that horse!

NELLIE
We *do*?

WILSON
(Snapping the radio on again)
Whirligig! Plus we bet a hundred
grand on Tender Trap!

RADIO ANNOUNCER
And here they come! They're neck
and neck! Whirligig and Tender
Trap! Whirligig and Tender Trap!
And at the wire, it's . . . Tender
Trap!

Wilson pumps the air in victory, as the
bathroom door bursts open and a
jockey strides in, chuckling, counting a
fistful of cash.

JOCKEY
What a nag! The dope slowed him
down, but I almost had to break his
neck trying to hold him back.

WILSON
Anybody cotton?

JOCKEY
Not so much as a raised eyebrow.

Two gamblers explode out of the doors,
guns drawn.

GAMBLER #1
You cheatin' bastard!

They shoot at the Jockey, who ducks.
Nellie screams. Shouting and shooting,
the Gamblers chase the Jockey around

the bedroom. The closet door bursts
open and a Policeman runs on, gun
drawn.

POLICEMAN
(To the Gamblers)

Stop or I'll shoot!

General chaos, as all the people in the
sequence, including the dead Ketchel,
chase each other, until they abruptly
stop, face front and sing in simultaneous near-cacophony.

WILSON
God, I love this town!
Don't you love this town?
It's got all of these
Opportunities!
Mustn't turn them down!
Papa said, "Explore!"
Papa knew the score—

REPORTERS,
PHOTOGRAPHER, OTHERS
(Simultaneously)
Broadway Willie,
Prince of bons vivants,
Everybody wants
Broadway Willie Mizner!
Knocks 'em silly,
Cops and debutantes—

POLICEMAN
Stop or I'll shoot!

GIRLS
(Overlapping)
Did you read about Willie in the
Trib? . . . I tell you, Willie's a
hoot! . . . I tell you, Willie's a
scream! . . . Willie introduced me
to the mayor! . . . Willie says,
"Meet Ty Cobb!" . . . Willie knows
Fanny Brice! . . . Willie!

WILSON
God, I love it here!

(To Nellie)

Don't you love it here?
Every place you look
Is an open book,
Every street a new frontier!

REPORTERS,
PHOTOGRAPHER
(Simultaneously)
Broadway Willie is the king of the
    street,
Broadway Willie never misses a beat,
Everybody in New York wants to
    meet
Good time Willie Mizner!

OTHERS
(Simultaneously)
Nightclub fillies,
Bluebloods, racketeers,
Everybody cheers
Good time Willie Mizner!

ALL (EXCEPT NELLIE)
Things may not work out,
Things go up the spout,
Plenty more around the corner,
And what's waiting 'round the
    corner,
Isn't that what life is all about?

Addison enters with his plans. He
stops, stands and observes for a
minute, then rolls his eyes and leaves.

WILSON
(To Nellie)
God, I love your face!

OTHERS
Ziegfeld lilies—

WILSON
And I love this place!

OTHERS
Financiers—

CHORINES
Willie gets them hot—

OPPONENT, POLICEMEN,
GAMBLERS
Willie gets them pot—

ARMSTRONG, KETCHEL,
JOCKEY
Willie gets them shot—

NELLIE
Willie gets me not—

ALL
What has Willie got
That makes him king of New York?
Broadway Willie! Broadway Willie!
  Broadway Willie!

WILSON
God, I love this town!

Furiously, Nellie throws everyone out and, after a brief but heated conversation, throws Wilson out, too.

Like "Someone in a Tree" in *Pacific Overtures*, this number exists on more than one time level: the real-time level of Wilson and Nellie's single wedding night occurring simultaneously with months of Wilson's New York career. Initially, I had intended to hold it together with "The Best Thing That Ever Has Happened" as a sort of coitus interruptus, a wedding night love song that would continually be interrupted by the intrusions of Wilson's escapades and not be consummated until the marriage would be, on the morning after, at which point it would go like this:

The Best Thing That Ever Has Happened
(Chicago version)

NELLIE, WILSON
You are the best thing that ever has
  happened to me,
You are.
You are the best thing that ever
  could happen to me,
You are.

To think I'd meet someone
Who could surprise me
And size me up without cutting me
  down—

NELLIE
Ain't this a town?

BOTH
I am the best thing that ever will
  happen to you—

Trust me.
I want to know I'm the best thing
  that has happened to you,
Just me.

If I were sure of that,
That might even be
The best thing of all that could
  happen to me.

What's next?
Who cares?
We'll see.

As it turned out, however, at that moment in the story the action was piling up and getting swifter, and a full-bodied love song held up the proceedings. I didn't want to use it earlier at the racetrack because it was too sentimental for the edginess of their meeting and would make the romantic use of it in the bedroom redundant. Much as I liked it, I was ready to throw the song out, but both John and Hal urged me to find some way to use it, and I got the bright notion of making it comic. The word "bullshit" saved the day. It not only got a large shocked laugh from the audience, it was completely in keeping with the laconic streak in both characters. I realized that I was sacrificing my chance to have a simple straightforward ballad in the score, but Oscar had taught me to be ruthless with my own material and, desire being as much a mother of invention as necessity, I did figure out a way to salvage it in Act Two. Eventually, in *Road Show*, I found an even better use for it.

Getting an audience to grasp the two simultaneous time levels proved to be a problem. They seemed confused during the Chicago run and, as it turned out, for a surprisingly subtle reason, which had to do with the first entrance of the reporters. It would be a natural sequence of events that a notorious wedding of a penniless upstart and a millionairess would be followed by hungry journalists making inquiries, and their intrusion into the couple's bedroom would be a farcical metaphor (for bedrooms as public

celebrity thoroughfares) which would not disturb the time continuum. But that very naturalness was what was wrong; it led the audience to expect a cause-and-effect series of incidents, so that when the fighters appeared a few moments later there was a breach of temporal logic. Reporters in a bedroom? Yes. Prizefighters? No. It took us a while to understand this, but when in Washington we cut the reporters and began the sequence with the surreal intrusion of Ketchel mid-fight, the audience grasped right away that this was not going to be a chronological number. I had wanted the reporters to keep interrupting Wilson periodically because in reality he courted the press a lot and was widely quoted. That was the reason I'd written the song "Journalists" in the first draft of *Wise Guys*. But in that version, Mrs. Yerkes was a throwaway character, a joke who meant as little to Wilson as she did in real life. Now she was a character whom the audience was expected to take seriously and even care about and the New York sequence was about the dissolution of a marriage instead of merely a hustler's climb. Unlike in any of the previous versions, Wilson's relationship with the press no longer had any importance; it was just a color that fleshed out his character. Again, Sam Mendes's caution about adhering to reality had proved itself worth listening to.

The scene changes to Addison's apartment and remains pretty much as it was in the Workshop. Addison is tending to Mama, who is reading about Wilson's exploits and waiting for him to visit. Addison does not sing "A Little House for Mama," however, which we felt had made the scene too slow and too long. Mama sings, though, as she did before:

Isn't He Something!***

and promptly dies. Wilson enters, drunk and snorting coke. Addison spitefully shocks him with the discovery of her death, but does not lie to him about her final words, as he did in the Workshop. Instead, he throws Wilson out in a rage, and, after a long pause, takes a moment to collect himself.

Bounce
(reprise)

ADDISON
Up then down, what else is new?
That was Papa's song.
Mama, what he said was true—
I just heard it wrong.
Willie's been the wise one all along.

I'm fine, it's okay,
The past is the past,
I know how to bounce.
As Papa would say,
You have to learn fast—
Well, Mama, watch me bounce.

The ones you love die
Or move on.
No goodbye,
Just bang! They're gone.
Whatever's been said,
Dead is dead.
Isn't that what counts?

From years on the side
As second in line,
I bounce pretty well.
All right, I can't glide,
But, Mama, I'm fine,
And you can go to hell.

(Turning front)

Whenever there's change
In the text,
You're bound to feel strange
And perplexed.

On to what's new,
On to what's next—
Bounce . . .
Bounce . . .
Bounce . . .

He begins to move downstage.

Bounce . . .
Bounce . . .

(Glaring at the audience)

Bounce!

BLACKOUT

Without the vaudeville, we needed an ending for the act, and this seemed a neat solution: establish Addison's defiance and determination to be as ruthless as his brother, thus counteracting the danger of his pervasive wimpiness, and reprise the title song at the same time. It was so neat it was pat, and we weren't able to solve the moment until *Road Show.* But it seemed like a good idea at the time.

ACT TWO

A triptych: Addison, drinking alone at an outdoor café in a bohemian Greenwich Village; Nellie, a flapper at the Ritz Bar in Paris, in the company of two dandies; Wilson in Storyville, with a flashy madam and a jazz musician or two. All three face front.

The Game
(reprise)

ADDISON
The hell with him.

NELLIE
The hell with him.

WILSON
The hell with them.

ALL THREE
What's next?

WILSON
It all comes down to staying in the
   game.

ADDISON
The thing that really matters is the
   game.

NELLIE
You win, you lose,
There's no one but yourself
That you can blame.

ALL THREE
The only thing that matters is the
   game.

NELLIE
Just a bad bet.

WILSON
Just a slight dent.

ADDISON
Slam the door shut
On what
You spent.

ALL THREE
Every exit is an entrance
Into something else!

The only thing you have to bear in
   mind
Is close the book
And never look
Behind.

WILSON, ADDISON
"Straight ahead," Papa said.

NELLIE
Take a chance or else you're dead.

ALL THREE
You find a new frontier and stake a
   claim.
The thing that really matters is the
   game.

WILSON
Cut a new deck.

NELLIE
Make a new move.

ADDISON
When you've got nothing left to
    prove—

ALL THREE
Doesn't take long to see that you've
Got to go somewhere else . . .

As music continues, Nellie dances
briefly with the gigolos, Wilson drinks
whiskey and snorts coke, and Addison,
trying to study some architectural
plans, becomes distracted by the street
life around him, especially the gay
street life. Suddenly, Wilson and Nellie
turn and face each other.

WILSON, NELLIE
You were the best thing that ever has
    happened to me—
Still are.
The best and worst thing that ever
    has happened to me,
So far.

We missed the boat, my friend.
It sailed, forget it.
We let it
Pass right in front of our eyes.

(Ironically)

What a surprise.

Sometimes I wish that you never
    had happened to me—
Sometimes.
You were the best thing that ever
    had happened to me—
Sometimes.

But if I'm lucky, pal,
You shortly will be
The second-best thing that has
    happened to me.

They turn front again.

NELLIE
The hell with him.

WILSON
The hell with her.

ADDISON
(Discouraged, rolls up his plans)
The hell with it.

ALL THREE
What's next?

Addison starts to read a newspaper. As
in the Workshop, a Real Estate Agent
rushes on and sings about Florida to
him, rushing off as quickly as he
rushed on. Addison looks at the news-
paper, then turns front.

NELLIE, WILSON, ADDISON
The thing that really matters is the
    game.
The trick is getting back into the
    game.
You lose the pot, it's over with.
Don't stick with it, it's gone.

NELLIE
Just stop.

WILSON
Close shop.

ADDISON
Move on.

ALL THREE
To lose the hand you're sure of is a
    shame,
But life without the strife is pretty
    tame.
When you've lost all you've got,
Go and find another pot:
Switch tables,
Raise the stakes,
Adjust your aim.
The only thing that matters is the
    game.

They each start to exit in different di-
rections.

NELLIE
Where's the next bar?

WILSON
Where's the next ounce?

ADDISON
Where's the next chance for me to
    bounce?

ALL THREE
Winning may be what really counts,
But all the same—

WILSON
(Exiting)
The only thing that matters is the
    game . . .

NELLIE
(Exiting, overlapping)
The only thing that matters is the
    game . . .

ADDISON
(Exiting, overlapping)
The only thing that matters is the
    game . . .

Note how I slipped a full, straight chorus of "The Best Thing That Ever Has
Happened" into the action. I was able
to manufacture a love song between
two people who in storytelling reality
would have no possibility of eye contact with each other. That's one of the
advantages of writing musicals rather
than straight plays: you need no justification to be surreal, because the
form itself is. An audience comes to a
play expecting a certain amount of
"reality" (theatrical reality, that is) and
the playwright has to lead them,
whether gradually or suddenly, into
surreality; when they come into a musical, surreality is a given. And once
you have carte blanche permission to
be surreal, you can take any liberties
with logic or plausibility that you
want. Of course, you run the risk of
baffling the audience, but audiences,
exposed to more and more surrealism
all the time, are getting increasingly
sophisticated—not in their taste, perhaps, but in their perception.

As in the Workshop, Addison meets
Paris on the train to Florida, only
Paris's name is now Hollis Bessemer—
he is the handsome young man first
seen at the Belmont racerack in Act

One. *The rest of the scene remains the same, with Hollis singing "Talent."*

Talent***

Addison and Hollis land in Palm Beach. Addison shows Mrs. Stotesbury the house he designed for Wilson and Nellie, and she commissions him to build it. The other dowagers and their millionaire husbands follow suit, and Addison's career is launched.

You***

Among the dowagers is Nellie, dressed in black, who is now the Comtesse de Chevigny by virtue of another marriage and widowhood. She is delighted to see Addison and commissions him to build her a house.

A year later Addison and Hollis, now living together, are ensconced with Nellie in her not-quite-finished mansion. It is a stormy night and Addison is working diligently at his drafting table in the solarium, as Hollis and Nellie go off to a necessary dinner party at a new client's house. Shortly thereafter, Wilson enters, wet and bedraggled and pleading for help. Addison turns him down and, as in the Workshop, Wilson collapses.

With *Bounce* we finally faced the problem of Addie's homosexuality, but circumspectly. Although he and Hollis are clearly lovers in this version of the show, the romantic aspects of their relationship remain unexplored. To be continued.

The next day, on the patio, Addison and Nellie are making plans to get rid of

the recuperating Wilson when Hollis, under Wilson's spell, bounces in with him to report that Wilson has a wonderful idea: Addison should build a city. Addison retorts that he is not interested in any scheme of Wilson's and that the only city he wants to build is the artists' colony Hollis has been dreaming of. Wilson nods to Hollis, who addresses Addison fervently.

Addison's City

HOLLIS
That's what I wanted, a city for
 artists,
Versailles by the Florida sea.
A kind of haven for hundreds of
 artists,
Whose protector and saint would be
 me!
And then I meet Willie—

Nellie and Addison exchange glances.

And he says to me,
"Look what Addie's done,
And he's just begun!
Why be saint to hundreds?
Be saint to one!
Think what he can do—!"

 (Softer, more intense)

Think what *we* can do,
Willie, me and you!

ADDISON
 "Willie?"

He glances at Nellie again.

HOLLIS
 (To Nellie)
And you . . .

WILSON
You'll design a city, Addie,
Like no city ever seen before.
Think of it: a city, Addie,
Every single window, every door—

HOLLIS
You could build a Paris, Addie,
But Paris made anew,
A Paris for today.

WILSON
Paris, U.S.A.—

HOLLIS
A Paris made by you—
Addison's city . . .

WILSON
Venice and jazz combined—

HOLLIS
Addison's city.

WILSON
Every last stick and stone designed
By the same screwy brilliant mind—

BOTH
Addison's city.

HOLLIS
Newport with fizz—

WILSON
Rio with shade.

HOLLIS
Capri as it is,
But not so staid.

WILSON
Not so much a city—a parade!

BOTH
Addison's city!

WILSON
The time is now,
The place is now,
Your chance to do what you were
 born to do
Is now.
A chance like this will never come
 again,
Believe me,
Embrace it now.

 *(Relentlessly, as Addison begins to
 waver)*

The moment's now.
The door is wide.
An opportunity
That mustn't be
Denied.
Don't muff it now.

NELLIE
What's there to muff? He's got everything he wants as it is.

WILSON
Then it's time to want something else.

He should build a city, Countess,
Not just fancy forts for rich old farts.

HOLLIS
Much more than a city, Countess,
More like an amalgam of the arts.
Something international but
    bold—

WILSON
Everything too much.

HOLLIS
European verve—

WILSON
New York City nerve—

HOLLIS
Only with the Mizner touch—

BOTH
Addison's city!

Nellie also begins to waver. Wilson presses in.

WILSON
Your chance is now.

A sound of knocking, as during Papa's deathbed exhortation.

WILSON
You hear that sound?
I mean your chance to bounce,
Not merely bounce around.
You think it's all just men
And money and martinis.
You know what you need?

He unfurls a map, the way Addison unfurled his house plan.

(To Addison)
You make it up—

(To Hollis)
You make it real.

(To Nellie)
You make us a sweetheart of a deal.
Everybody gets to spin the wheel!

NELLIE
And what do you get?

WILSON
A chance for now,
To make amends,
A chance to ditch the blues
And pay my dues
To friends.

(Looks at them all)
And if I chance to make a buck or
    two
Along the way, and so do you,
Why not?

(As Addison still hesitates)
Oh, come on, Addie—
The four of us together, what fun!

HOLLIS
(To Addison)
How about it, honey, what do you say?

WILSON
You and me against the world,
    brother,
You and me against the world!
You and me together,
But in very different weather—
Now it's pretty.

WILSON, HOLLIS, NELLIE
Don't you want to build a city?

HOLLIS, NELLIE*
Something serene but brash—

HOLLIS, NELLIE, WILSON
Addison's city!

HOLLIS, NELLIE
Something where cultures mix and
    clash—

WILSON
But with American panache—

HOLLIS, NELLIE, WILSON,
    ADDISON
Addison's city!

ADDISON
(Catching fire)
Like the golden city
That Papa planned!

WILSON
Only twice as golden
And twice as grand!

ADDISON
Promenades and plazas,
Some small lagoons—

WILSON
And a few saloons—

NELLIE
(As Addison looks askance)
But with gold spittoons—

ADDISON
And an English mall
And a Greek town hall
And a Great Canal running through
    it all!

WILSON, NELLIE, HOLLIS,
    ADDISON
The city of the century!*

---

* The section between asterisks was cut for reasons of length, which was too bad because not only did it accurately describe what in actuality Addison Mizner planned to build, it also related the brothers to the fulfillment of Papa's dream for them—one of the major motifs of the story.

WILSON, NELLIE, HOLLIS
Your chance is now.
Don't settle in.
You're wasting time
When what you are
Is what you've been.
This city's something new,
A door into the future—

The future's now!

WILSON
Gotta make tracks!

NELLIE
Gotta make hay!

HOLLIS
Gotta take the risk and seize the day!

ALL THREE
Gotta travel on—

ADDISON
All right, okay!!!

There is a brief pause as the others let this sink in.

ALL
(Triumphantly)
The time is now!
The place is here!
This is our chance to open up a new
    frontier!
And if there ever was a time to
    pioneer,
The time is now!

Boca Raton Sequence

Light changes. A heavenly Choir in-tones as a wall of doors comes in, a promotional "credo" about Boca Raton printed on them. Addison appears in a spotlight.

ADDISON
(To the audience)
My name is Addison Mizner and
    with all due modesty, I am the man
    who created Palm Beach.

A resounding chord; he brandishes a set of furled plans.

Wait till you see what I'm going to
    build next!

Addison exits, as four Bathing Beauties enter through the doors.

BATHING BEAUTIES
Boca Raton,
Come down to Boca Raton,
Where every sky's the bluest you've
    seen,
Where all year long the grass
    remains green,
Where every beach is clean and
    pristine.
Buy a lot
Or even two.
Have we got
A lot for you!

Boca Raton,
Come down to Boca Raton,
Where every vista sparkles and
    gleams,
City beautiful of your dreams!

The Yacht Club Boys, a male vocal group, enters, dressed in blazers and white ducks.

YACHT CLUB BOYS
The city beautiful,
A work of art in itself.
The city beautiful
Could be displayed on a shelf.

A picture-perfect place,
A place of grace and space,
A world of seaside sports
And leafy malls,
A world of tennis courts
And concert halls,
A world of boating, hot springs,
Golf links, tennis—
Newport, Saratoga, Venice . . .

MEN
Boca Raton!

WOMEN
You'll covet—

MEN
Boca Raton!

WOMEN
You'll love it!

ALL
Best, though, not to delay!

WOMEN
Come and see
The new frontier!

MEN
Come and be
A pioneer!

MEN, WOMEN
You'll agree,
Tomorrow's here
Today
In Boca Raton!

Addison and Hollis appear at the top of the wall, looking down at their creation.

HOLLIS
We're on our way . . .

ADDISON
What?

HOLLIS
We're on our way!
My biggest dream for you
Starts coming true
Today.

ADDISON
Whatever's going to be,
It's you and me
Together—

I love you, Holly.

Wilson and Nellie enter.

WILSON
Still a bit rough.

NELLIE
Pretty good stuff.

WILSON
Think it's too much, or not enough?

NELLIE
All I know is, you've come up to
  snuff.

*Wilson grins and puts an arm around
her shoulder; she stares at him; he
takes it off. A beat, then she puts it
back.*

BOTH
I think we've struck gold . . .

*Addison starts to exit, brandishing his
furled plans.*

ADDISON
You go sell it, I'm behind it,
Just go slow till I've designed it . . .

*Nellie and Wilson exit in the opposite
direction, as the Bathing Beauties,
Yacht Club Boys and various other
Florida denizens fill the stage.*

CHORUS
Take a boat or a bus,
Come by road or by river,
Throw your bags in a flivver
Or take the Sunshine Express
To your new address:

(*Softly*)

Boca Raton . . . Boca Raton . . .
Come down to Boca Raton . . .

*The doors split, revealing a Conestoga
wagon, sporting an advertising banner:
"Boca or Bust!" Wilson stands in the
wagon, addressing both the Chorus
and the audience.*

WILSON
My friends, when our forefathers
first set foot on these shores, they
were given a great gift. A New
World, pristine and unspoiled,
where anything was possible. A
land of limitless frontiers. A home
for enterprising pioneers.

(*As the wagon is pulled downstage*)

And we're still heading west,
Crossing mountains and plains,
Planting roots, building towns as
  we go.

ALL
Pressing on as we're pressed,
Through the winds and the rains,
Taking risks, tempting fate,
Till we open every gate—
That's what makes this country
  great!

WILSON
(*Jumping down from the wagon*)
  America, my friends! A Land of
  Opportunities! And here it is! The
  land itself—

He scoops up a fistful of earth.

Land—yes! Land to build a
  future on!
Dirt—Yes! Dirt, as in pay dirt!
Filth—Yes! Filth, as in filthy lucre!

CHORUS
Yes!

WILSON
Up in the Klondike we shoveled it
aside to get at the wealth it contained. Down here, it *is* the wealth!

Buy it now,
Sell it later
And get rich quick!

Pick a spot,
Buy a plot,
When the spot gets hot,
Sell the lot.
My friends, you know what
You just got?
You got really rich—!

CHORUS
Really quick!

WILSON
Bound to make a bundle!
Sure thing!

CHORUS
Bound to make a bundle—!

*A door bangs open, revealing a dowdy-
looking housewife, wearing an apron,
holding a rolling pin.*

HOUSEWIFE
My name is Mary Monahan.

WILSON AND CHORUS
Bound to make a bundle, just a
  matter of time . . .

HOUSEWIFE
The day the sales office opened in
Boca Raton I bought myself a lot . . .

The chorus hums underneath.

HOUSEWIFE
I paid seven hundred dollars for
that lot. Last week I sold it for
seven *thousand.*

*The man who bought it from her waves
the deed triumphantly.*

CHORUS
Yes!

*A woman yells to the man with the
deed.*

WOMAN
I'll give you ten!

MAN
I'll give you twenty!

WOMAN
Thirty!

MAN
Thirty-five!

*As the song continues, it becomes a
kind of round dance of paper, everyone
exchanging money and deeds, the
money initially ending up in the hands
of Wilson and Hollis, the money gradually being replaced by deeds, until
deeds are all they have left.*

WILSON
Can you hear the knocking?
Hear that sound!

*More knocking and another door
opens, revealing an owl-eyed bookkeeper, wearing an eye shade and
clutching a ledger.*

BOOKKEEPER
My name is Winthrop Tippet.

WILSON
What is that that's knocking
All around?

*More knocking, which continues spo-
radically throughout.*

WILSON, CHORUS
Opportunity!

BOOKKEEPER
A month ago I bought a piece of
property in Boca Raton for two
thousand dollars.

WILSON
Through these gates
Your fortune waits
Around the corner.

BOOKKEEPER
Yesterday I sold it for five times
that.

WILSON AND CHORUS
Boca Raton . . . Come down to Boca
Raton . . .

*A door opens, revealing a Grant Wood
farmer's wife.*

FARMER'S WIFE
My name is Ethel Mudd.

WILSON AND CHORUS
Boca Raton . . .

FARMER'S WIFE
(As the chorus hums underneath)
Last month my Bert and I bought a
lot in Boca Raton with our life's
savings of eight thousand dollars.
This morning we were offered
thirty thousand for that lot and do
you know what we said?

FARMER, WIFE AND CHORUS
No!

FIRST BUYER
(To the Farmer's Wife)
I'll give you forty!

The music starts to become frantic.

HOLLIS
Buy it now,
Build it later
And get rich quick!

SECOND BUYER
Fifty!

THIRD BUYER
Seventy!

*The Farmer's Wife screams with excite-
ment.*

NELLIE
(Dancing with Hollis)
Pick a spot,
Build or not,
When the spot gets hot,
Sell the lot—

NELLIE, HOLLIS
And with what you've got,
Buy another plot
And get even richer even quicker!

*As the sequence progresses and every-
one becomes increasingly frenzied,
one figure remains static: Addison. He
just stares at everything going out of
control.*

NELLIE, HOLLIS, CHORUS
Bound to make a bundle!

*Buyers and sellers start waving deeds
and money.*

FIRST BUYER
Make that eighty! . . .

FIRST SELLER
Footage on the ocean . . .

SECOND SELLER
This one's worth a hundred, at
least . . .

NELLIE, HOLLIS, CHORUS
Bound to make a bundle!

THIRD BUYER
A hundred twenty-five!

CHORUS
Just a matter of time . . .
Just a matter of time . . .

BIDDERS
A hundred fifty! . . . Sixty! . . .
Eighty! Ninety! . . .

*Bidding continues through the follow-
ing, the numbers escalating.*

ALL (EXCEPT ADDISON)
Boca Raton!
Come down to Boca Raton
And buy a piece of heaven on
  earth—
Then go sell it at twice its worth!

*Everyone dances joyfully, still ex-
changing money and deeds. The crowd
parts, revealing Mama and Papa. Addison reacts, as lights change, and Mama
and Papa link arms with the Chorus
and cakewalk downstage.*

MAMA, PAPA, WILSON,
NELLIE, HOLLIS, CHORUS
Buy today, sell tomorrow,
And get rich quick!

BUYERS, SELLERS
Two hundred . . . Two twenty . . .
etc. . . .

*The bidding numbers start tumbling
over each other as the song continues.*

MAMA, PAPA, WILSON,
NELLIE, HOLLIS, CHORUS
Don't delay,
Beg or borrow,
Or come what may,
To your sorrow
You'll rue the day
That you didn't say,
"I want to get rich quick!"

*During the following, Wilson makes
his way to the Conestoga wagon and
leaps on.*

MAMA, PAPA
Can you hear the knocking?
Hear that sound!

HOLLIS, NELLIE
What is that that's knocking
All around?

CHORUS, MAMA, PAPA,
NELLIE, HOLLIS
Bound to make a bundle!
Just a matter of time!
Just a matter of time!

As Wilson sings from the wagon, every-
one dances.

WILSON
Buy it now,
Sell it later
And get rich quick!

CHORUS
Sure thing!

WILSON
Buy for two,
Ask for four—

CHORUS
Yes!

WILSON
If the deal falls through
Prices soar—

CHORUS
Yes!

WILSON
There'll be someone who—

CHORUS
Yes!

WILSON
Offers even more—!

CHORUS
Yes!

WILSON
Then it's toodle-oo
And you're out the door—

CHORUS
Yes!

WILSON
'Cause you're well-to-do,
'Cause you've made your score
And you got rich quick!

Bound to make a bundle!

CHORUS
(Overlapping, to Wilson)
You, where have you been all my
life?

WILSON
Bound to make a bundle!

CHORUS
You're the answer to my prayers!

WILSON
Bound to make a bundle!

HOLLIS
(Opening his arms wide to Wilson)
You, you're one in a million!

The music stops momentarily as Addi-
son reacts, then resumes frenetically.

CHORUS, MAMA, PAPA
Boca Raton, come down to Boca
Raton,
Where once again he's killing your
dreams
Because he keeps on cooking up
schemes
Until they fall apart at the seams.

By now, money and deeds have stopped
changing hands. Nobody is buying,
even though sellers keep waving deeds
and shouting prices. Mama and Papa
climb up on the wagon, along with
most of the sellers.

CHORUS
All alone
And fucked for good,
Fucked as on-
Ly Willie could.

Boca Raton,
Come down to Boca Raton,
Where every sidewalk sparkles and
gleams.
City beautiful, bye bye—!

SELLER #1
(Desperately)
Two hundred and fifty!

CHORUS
(Fast and furious)
Boca Raton, come down to Boca
Raton,

Where Willie's gone and done it
again,
Done it again, done it again, done it
again . . .

The wagon rolls off, stranding Wilson,
Addison, Hollis, Nellie and a small
group of desperate sellers. The music
grinds to a halt; Wilson and Hollis now
hold only deeds, not money.

SELLER #1
(Brandishing a deed)
Two twenty-five . . .

(No response)

Two hundred.

SELLER #2
One fifty—!

(No response)

One hundred!

SELLER #3
Fifty?! . . . Twenty-five?!

SELLER #4
Ten?

(Plaintively)

Five . . . ?

A moment of dead silence. The stage
freezes. Then there bursts from the
orchestra a long, loud, cacophonous
chord, which diminuendos with a wail.
The boom has become a bust.

One of the things we learned about
the Boca Raton sequence in the Workshop was that the focus was wrong: it
was too much about Wilson and not
enough about the crash. We had focused it on Wilson's madness instead
of the madness of the investors, the
madness of crowds. We saw that we
had to explain more clearly to the audience what was happening, which
meant that I needed to write lyrics
which emphasized buying and selling.
Emphasize I did. It would have been
more effective, and a lot less loqua-

cious, if we could have had a visual correlative onstage. I wanted to have the giant thermometer we'd called for in the first draft of *Wise Guys* or else a large metaphoric balloon on the side of the stage that would keep swelling until it actually burst. But Hal didn't take to either of those images, either because he thought they were too obvious or because he thought they would be clumsy to stage. He had a spectacular notion of erecting a city diorama during the song, made of stock certificates, which would all come tumbling down in a mass of paper at the end, but that died aborning. Still, by the end of the Washington tryout the audience understood the crash, while at the same time Wilson retained enough of his madness.

After the crash, everyone exits except Addison, Wilson, Hollis and Nellie.

HOLLIS
(Dazed)
What happened?

They stand looking at each other, as if coming out of a trance.

NELLIE
It's simple, kid. The boom went bust. We got 'em drunk; they sobered up. Hell, I've got a hangover myself . . .

Hollis explodes, accusing Wilson of cheapening and ruining the whole plan. Addison tries to intercede, adding that nothing is as important as their (his and Hollis's) relationship, but Hollis accuses both brothers of seducing him and then using him for his money and connections. Nellie attempts to stop the situation from boiling over, but boil over it does until finally it is Addison who explodes and tells Hollis off for being a spoiled rich kid who wants nothing more than to get back at his father. Hollis slaps Addison and starts to leave; Nellie, just as fed up, offers to go with him. Before she exits, she turns back to Wilson.

NELLIE
(Touching Wilson's cheek)
One day lose, the next day win,
Like the poet said.
Got to give the wheel a spin,
Otherwise you're dead.
I can't wait to see what lies ahead.

(Hooking Hollis's arm and leading him off)

God, I loathe this town . . .

And they leave. The minute they are gone, Addison wheels on Wilson.

Get Out of My Life***

Go***

"Get Out of My Life" is sung exactly as in the Reading, but "Go" has a significantly different finish. Instead of ending like this:

ADDISON
All right, yes!
I love you, I always have loved you!
Does that make us even?
Does that make you happy?

(Quietly)
And I want you to go.

(Beat)
And no,
I don't want you to go . . .

It ends like this:

ADDISON
All right, yes!
I love you, I love you,
And worse, I deserve you . . .

Wilson opens his arms to embrace Addison. Addison, with a roar, slams into him. The two start fighting, as they did at the top of the show. Addison threatens to kill him, but Wilson points out that they're already dead, at which

point the stage is transformed into the limbo in which they found themselves when they died at the beginning of the story—but with the Conestoga wagon still center stage. They look around, assess the situation and reminisce a bit about the disappointment of their lives, then turn to the audience.

Bounce
(reprise)

WILSON*
On my left—

ADDISON
On my right—

WILSON
Is my boob of a brother.

ADDISON
Is the man I'd gladly smother,
If he hadn't just died.

WILSON
He's all heft—

ADDISON
He's all height—

WILSON
He's all wimp—

ADDISON
He's all schemer—

WILSON
He's a patsy and a dreamer—

BOTH
Still, it cannot be denied:
At the end of the day,
He's a guy you don't fuck with,
And believe me I don't say that
Just because he's what I'm stuck
  with . . . *

---

* The half-chorus of "On My Left" between asterisks was cut. It was one beat too many. I include it here because I like it.

A chord, like the one which accompanied the appearance of Addison's first house in Palm Beach. Voices are heard offstage.

VOICES
Look at it!

Addison and Wilson stare at the back of the house, over the heads of the audience.

Look at it! Look at it!

WILSON
Addie, look at it!

He smiles with excitement, Addison with resignation.

You see what's ahead?

ADDISON
I thought we were done.

WILSON
Get ready to bounce.

ADDISON
You'd think, once you're dead—

WILSON
Come on, we'll have fun!
What's happened to your bounce?

ADDISON
A road without end—
I can wait.

WILSON
Round the bend,
There's something great
To grab by the throat—

(As Addison looks at him askance)

That's a quote—

BOTH
"When you see it, pounce."

ADDISON
Right, you're right,
And Papa's right, you're right—

As they continue, Wilson climbs back up on the buckboard of the Conestoga wagon, picks up the whip and extends a hand. Addison takes it and joins him on the wagon.

BOTH
We're still on our way—
That's what we do best—
Improving our bounce.
As Papa would say,
We're still heading west,
And that's the thing that counts.

WILSON
We're still pioneers,
Like before—

A scrim flies in downstage: a map of the United States.

BOTH
A lot of frontiers
To explore.
Ready, set, go,
Bro!

As in the Workshop, they start up the road, but this time in a pioneer wagon, their eyes fixed on the horizon.

CURTAIN

When *Bounce* opened in Chicago, audiences were cool to it—not hostile, cool. By the end of the run two months later, they were enjoying it immensely. This is standard operating procedure for a musical (or play, for that matter), especially during a tryout. Once performers have the chance to play the same piece night after night, with no changes in the scenes or the songs or the staging, and in front of different audiences, they acquire a kind of confidence that informs the evening and conveys itself to the audience, which then feels that it's in good hands and makes allowances for the weaknesses of the piece while enjoying its strengths. In this case, however, they shouldn't have had that chance. The point of a tryout is to fix a show, and by the end of the Chicago run, we should have been making changes in the scenes and the songs and the staging. But we couldn't, because the day after the show opened, Hal had to go to Germany to receive an award and then leave for his summer vacation. Not that he thought the show was in perfect shape when he left; he simply felt that whatever changes we wanted to make could be accomplished on paper and put into practice later when we went back into rehearsal for the Washington engagement. As far as John and I were concerned, interrupting the momentum was upsetting, but since there were six weeks between the end of the Chicago run and the Washington rehearsals, it seemed reasonable.

It was a serious miscalculation. We were all experienced enough to know that the time to fix a show is when it's still raw, before it has started to become slick and rigid, when no one, neither the creators nor the performers, not to mention the audience, is satisfied. Without constant attention while a show is taking shape, it doesn't need many performances before it becomes so efficient that what's bad becomes acceptable. A performer's confident panache can sell a weak song, an actor's practiced passion or timing can infuse a fuzzy scene with enough style that it passes for substance, and in short order some of the cracks in the piece acquire enough varnish to be ignored. But eventually, when the show is frozen and officially opens and the spotlight of New York hits it and it is exposed to journalists and commentators, when everyone knows that no more improvements are going to be made, the cracks can look like chasms, and with justification. Writers, producers and directors can all too easily become blind, or just relaxed, about their creations. This is what distinguishes the professional from the amateur; it's what accounts for Oscar's ruthlessness toward his work. And indeed, the vast majority of shows undergo scrutiny and change from their makers, who watch the performance every night immediately after the show's initial exposure to an audience. Unfortunately, this was not

the case with *Bounce*. The makers left after opening night.

The first problem we should have attended to, as Oscar had imprinted in my DNA, was the beginning of the show. In this instance, not the opening number, which with its introductory scene effectively welcomed the audience and set a style for the evening, but Papa's death scene and song, which muddied it: Was the evening to be a set of cartoon characters or were we supposed to take them seriously and care about them? Papa was written and played in the song as a comic-strip character, but in the scene the mother and the boys were not.

The next problem, or pair of problems, was the presence of two unwieldy lumps in the storytelling: the confusion of the New York sequence in Act One and the endlessness of the Boca Raton sequence in Act Two. John and I thought and talked about these problems over the summer hiatus, but there was no way to try out our solutions until they could be staged and tested with our final collaborator, the audience. And indeed, when Hal returned and we all had a chance to look at them, they got solved, but only to

some extent. We clarified the New York sequence and cut a lot of Boca Raton, and I took some of the jokiness out of Papa's song. (If I'd had more time to look at it in the context of the show, I'd probably have written a new one or gone back to the old one—which I eventually did.)

But neither of these problems was as important as the big one: the introduction of Nellie into the story. It was the wrong blood type for the transfusion. As I said at the start of this chapter, it seemed like a good idea at the time: the notion of a leading lady turning up at unexpected points during the brothers' lives and in different stages of her own transformations—another echo of our theme of reinvention—seemed colorful and appropriate, as well as adding a dollop of traditional sexy musical comedy romance to the love story. But instead of strengthening what the show was about, it dissipated it. Stifling or not, the love story at the heart of our take on the Mizners is between Addison and Wilson. Hal thought it too claustrophobic, but in fact it wasn't claustrophobic enough, as was proved a few years later in its next incarnation.

Then again, everything seemed like a good idea at the time: the invention of Nellie, Papa's mumbling, the flat vaudeville-style sets, the heavy metaphor of the Conestoga wagon, and so on. And they were—at the time. Unfortunately, you can't find out an idea is bad until you've tested it. And by the time we found out that ours were bad, that in practice they served only to blur the focus of both the story and the style, it was too late. As a friend said to me during the Chicago run, "The trouble is, I don't know where the train is going, and it makes too many stops." What had happened was that the show had lost its sense of direction; it had moved sideways rather than forward. We'd learned a lot from it and had been able to attend to a few squeaks in the wheels, but the public and critical reaction was, as in the case of the Workshop and both out-of-town tryouts, mild at best and disappointed at worst. Most destructive of all, it added to the show's reputation as being a perfectly respectable attempt that had outrun its course. But then a couple of white knights came charging to the rescue.

And now for something complete.

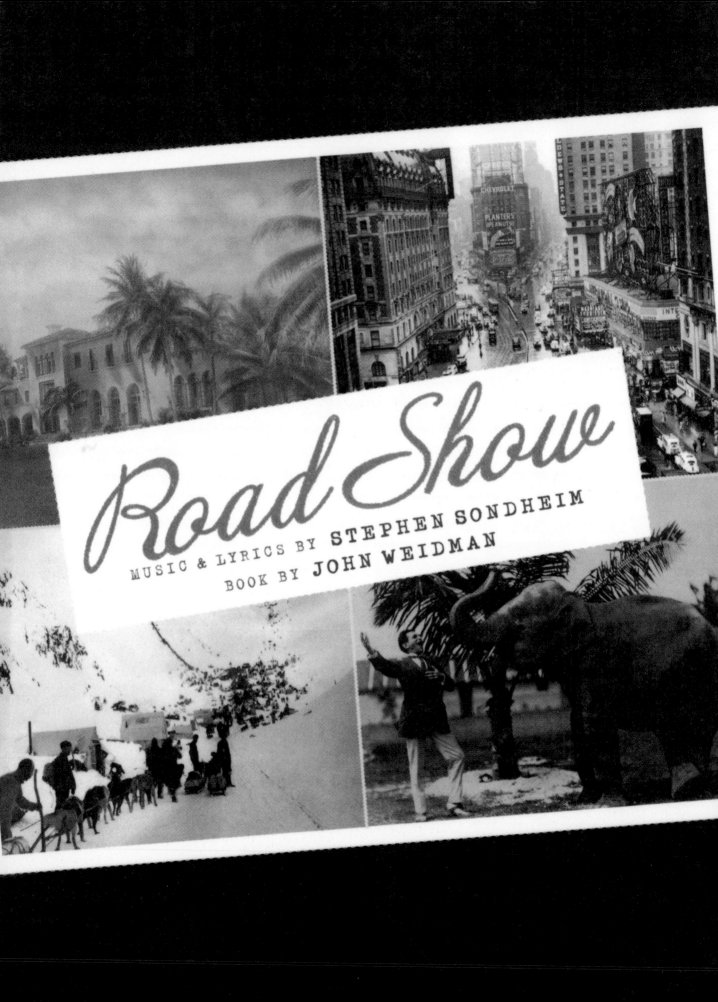

Road Show

MUSIC & LYRICS BY STEPHEN SONDHEIM
BOOK BY JOHN WEIDMAN

Act Four · Road Show (2008)

Book by John Weidman
Directed by John Doyle

The Notion

A chronicle of two brothers, Wilson and Addison Mizner, who were born in the 1880s and died in the 1930s. It begins and ends in bed. There is no leading lady.

General Comments

John and I returned from the Washington tryout of *Bounce* disheartened and baffled as to what to do next with a piece we had nurtured sporadically but persistently for more than nine years, and one which we still loved. Feeling we had lost our perspective (and we had), we decided to step away from it for a while and move on to other things, but we found ourselves thinking and talking about it, even if only occasionally, and always with the same enthusiasm we'd felt when we'd finished our first draft. After a year's hiatus, we couldn't resist the siren call, and we began to rewrite it, with a new director in mind. For a long while, we had both been fans of the work of Eric Schaeffer at his Signature Theatre in Arlington, Virginia, especially his direction of musicals we had written, together and separately. I had worked with him in 2002, when he not only organized a summer's worth of six of my shows at the Kennedy Center, a triumph of executive skill in itself, but also directed two of them, and beautifully. John had worked with him in 1997, when Eric directed the road company of John's musical *Big*, which sported a score by Richard Maltby, Jr., and David Shire. *Big* had been a respect-

able failure on Broadway, but all three authors felt that Eric had reinvigorated it. Trying to reinvigorate failed material was familiar territory to Weidman and me, so we asked Eric to direct our new version of *Wise Guys*.

It didn't work out as well as we expected. Eric liked the show and we liked Eric, but in our discussions creative sparks were rare. Such sparks usually arise from the friction of argument, but whether Eric liked us or the show too much, he was singularly unargumentative. Nevertheless, we made some changes (the first being to eliminate the character of Nellie and restore the original story) and under Eric's supervision held a reading at the Public Theater, home ground of the New York Shakespeare Festival, primarily for ourselves but with an audience of a dozen or so invited friends and professional colleagues. The result was not encouraging: the piece seemed meandering and unfocused. Luckily, one of the spectators there was Oskar Eustis, CEO of the Public, which had lent us the space for the reading. He was an experienced director as well, and had been for many years that hybrid bugaboo of mine: a dramaturge.

I've grumbled before (in *Finishing the Hat*, among other places) that dramaturges tend to know everything about plays and nothing about playwriting; they have a heightened sense of history and little sense of theater. Oskar proved to be a stimulating exception. John, Eric and I met with him the next day more as a measure of politesse, a way of saying thanks for the use of the hall, than with the expectation of hearing anything valuable. But quietly and with an unerring eye, Oskar drew our attention to the places where we were losing the path, where we seemed to be telling the story but were not. He would indicate a passage and say, "See this page? *This* is what the show is about." He rarely suggested cures for the problems,

but that was unimportant; what he did was draw our attention to things we had either not noticed or deliberately overlooked, having been so close to the material for so long: things unresolved under the surface of the dialogue, songs that were blurry or missing or not to the point. In short, he did what a dramaturge is supposed to do. It was an exhilarating meeting and by the end of it, John and I knew two things: that we had to talk more with Oskar and that we wanted a firmer critical hand than Eric's to guide us into port. Indeed, over the next months we met with Oskar a number of times, each meeting as provocative as the first, and a couple of drafts later we were ready to approach a new director.

John Doyle is a Briton (actually, a Scotsman) who had conceived startling and provocative productions of *Sweeney Todd* and *Company* in London and on Broadway, productions in which the actors were their own orchestra, singing and playing instruments simultaneously and providing underscoring for each other, a notion which at first glance might appear to be nothing more than a gimmick but one which, when applied to appropriate material, can be surprisingly effective. Those two experiences with him had led me to know that he was an imaginative inventor with a probing critical attitude which, like Oskar's, was just what we were looking for. We gave him the script, I played him the songs, and to our delight he responded to them with both passion and dispassion. He was enthusiastic about the story and understood the style, and at the same time saw what the show was trying to say about America with the objective, yet sympathetic, eye of a foreigner. He also saw that what the show needed was compression, to give it the kind of pace that defines the American image: speedy, impatient, determined, brash and humorous, all of which was expressed in what we had written—except for the speed, which wasn't speedy enough. His first suggestion was to cut all the stage directions. This seemed to be nothing more than cosmetic surgery, but it gave the script, stripped of its parenthetical asides, a vivid shimmer of what it could, and should, and did, become.

Doyle (best to refer to him by his last name in order to distinguish him from the other John) then made an audacious, not to say presumptuous, request: he said he would like to ponder the script by himself and, with no consultation from us, cut some of the dialogue a bit and reposition sections of the songs in an effort to tighten the action and blend the scenes into each other. Ordinarily, as authors, John and I might have taken this as an outrageous threat to the integrity of our sacred, if mutable, urtext, but in the interest of harmony and given Doyle's clearly genuine enthusiasm for the piece, we agreed. Most good directors of musicals have a fine sense of mise en scène, a fair sense of character and a fuzzy sense of story. As with Oskar's being an exception among dramaturges, Doyle turned out to be an exception among directors; the script he handed us after his tinkering, although it had its fair share of misguided and awkward moments, brought the mix of family dynamics and American penchant for reinvention into one focus, and that was what we had never properly been able to accomplish. *Wise Guys/Bounce/Road Show* was about so many things: American enterprise, American conniving, American promotion, American greed, the class system, sibling love and rivalry, road movies— a soup that Doyle (and Oskar) boiled down for us, which is what a good director, like a good editor, can do. Sam and Hal had also focused the show but on the wrong things. Doyle did nothing drastic to it, he merely—crucially—compressed it; he made the scenes catapult into each other, sometimes by staging one so that its final tableau became part of the tableau at the beginning of the next, which gave the show a flow so swift that it verged on the surreal, leaving the audience a little breathless and having to catch up. Once again, Less proved to be More and John and I, revitalized, rewrote with Doyle's blueprint in mind and, new script in hand, confidently and successfully petitioned Oskar to produce it at the Public.

The first thing we did was to conceive the show as a one-act play, an express train. The next was to retitle it. A title's function is to tell the theatergoer what the show is about, something we thought we knew when we began, and to a certain extent, did. But it took us a long time to return to our beginnings. Perhaps the tortuous process you are witnessing would be more instructive if *Road Show* had been a popular success, in that the plot and characters and relationships and songs which we eventually settled on would be more familiar and the journey to them therefore more involving. Perhaps some day they will be. Anyway, here they are.

ACT ONE

Palm Beach. 1933. Addison lies in a bed, surrounded by a pyramid of trunks, packing crates, old furniture and people. They too are furniture.

Waste

A WOMAN
Mr. Mizner. There's a gentleman to see you.

Addison sits up, looks forward and then falls back on the pillows, dead. The door of one of the packing crates bangs open, revealing Wilson. Lights pick out the people on the boxes, all looking at Addison.

A MAN
Think that he's dead?

ANOTHER MAN
Has been for years.

A WOMAN
God, what a waste.

A MAN
Genius, they said . . .

A WOMAN
Opened frontiers—

ANOTHER WOMAN
Really, such a waste.

ANOTHER WOMAN
All of that style—

A MAN
All that flair—

ANOTHER MAN
All that guile—

ANOTHER MAN
Now, let's be fair.
He had a real spark—

ANOTHER MAN
Made a mark—

A WOMAN
Instantly erased.

A MAN
Could have been rich—

A WOMAN
Could have lost weight—

A MAN
God, what a waist.

ADDISON
(Sitting up)
Excuse me . . .

TWO MEN
Sonofabitch
Could have been great—

A WOMAN AND A MAN
Now he's just disgraced.

ADDISON
Excuse me—?

A WOMAN
Such an ascent—

"Waste"

A MAN
Such a fall—

ANOTHER MAN
Such a nice gent—

ALL
He had it all.
How could he miss,
Finish like this?
Waste.

A MAN
(To Addison)
Remember me?
I'm the one that you bought the
    plantation from.
Boy, what a waste.
That was a waste . . .

A WOMAN
(Overlapping)
Remember me?
I'm the one with the house you
    designed.
What a waste, what a terrible waste,
What a waste . . .

A MAN
(Overlapping)
Remember me?
I'm the one that you baited the
    suckers with—
Waste.
Waste of your money and waste of
    my time.
Remember that? Remember that?
What a waste, what an asinine
    waste . . .

TWO WOMEN
(Overlapping)
Remember me?
I'm the one that you used in the ads.
Honey, that was a waste,
That was a waste and a half.
Remember that? Remember that?
What a waste, what a silly old
    waste . . .

A MAN
(Overlapping)
Remember me?
I'm the one with the fireworks
    business—
A waste if I ever saw waste.
And, believe me, I recognize waste
When I come across waste . . .

ANOTHER MAN
(Overlapping)
You come into my office
And buy all those pineapples
Going to waste.
I mean, talk about waste!
That was a waste, no, a waste and a
    half . . .

A WOMAN
(Overlapping)
Not to mention
The door you forgot to include
And the stairs that went nowhere.
There was a waste,
There was a terrible waste . . .

A MAN
(Overlapping)
Remember me?
I'm the one with the Klondike
    saloon.
What a waste, what a god-awful
    waste.
I mean, that was a waste . . .

A WOMAN
(Overlapping)
Remember me?
I'm the one that you promised a
    mansion to . . .

HANDSOME YOUNG MAN
Remember me?
I'm the one that you fucked.

Addison blinks at him, stunned.

ALL
Such a good start,
Such a bad end—
Still, he had taste.

HANDSOME YOUNG MAN
I'm the one that you fucked.

ALL
Squandered his art—
Cheated his friend—
All of it a waste.

ADDISON
(To the Young Man)
You're the one that I loved.

THREE MEN
Destined to fail—

TWO WOMEN
Poor old guy—

GROUP I
Losing the trail—

GROUP II
And you know why.

WILSON
Everybody shoo!
I said shoo!
I mean you . . . shoo!

*They disappear; Wilson opens his
arms.*

WILSON
A hug for your old brother?

(Climbing into bed beside Addison)

Wasting your time,
Listening to them—
That was the waste.

ADDISON
Willie—

WILSON
What was your crime?
You were a gem,
They were strictly paste.

ADDISON
Willie, listen to me—

WILSON
So it got rough,
Why the guilt?
Look at the stuff
That you built.
So you got burned.
Look what you've learned—!

ADDISON
You know what I learned, Willie? I
learned that the only thing wrong
with my life was you. You conniving son of a bitch!

*And before long they are fighting on the
bed, reverting to their childhoods, until
Mama calls them.*

Of all the openings we had discussed
and tried, this one worked best. An

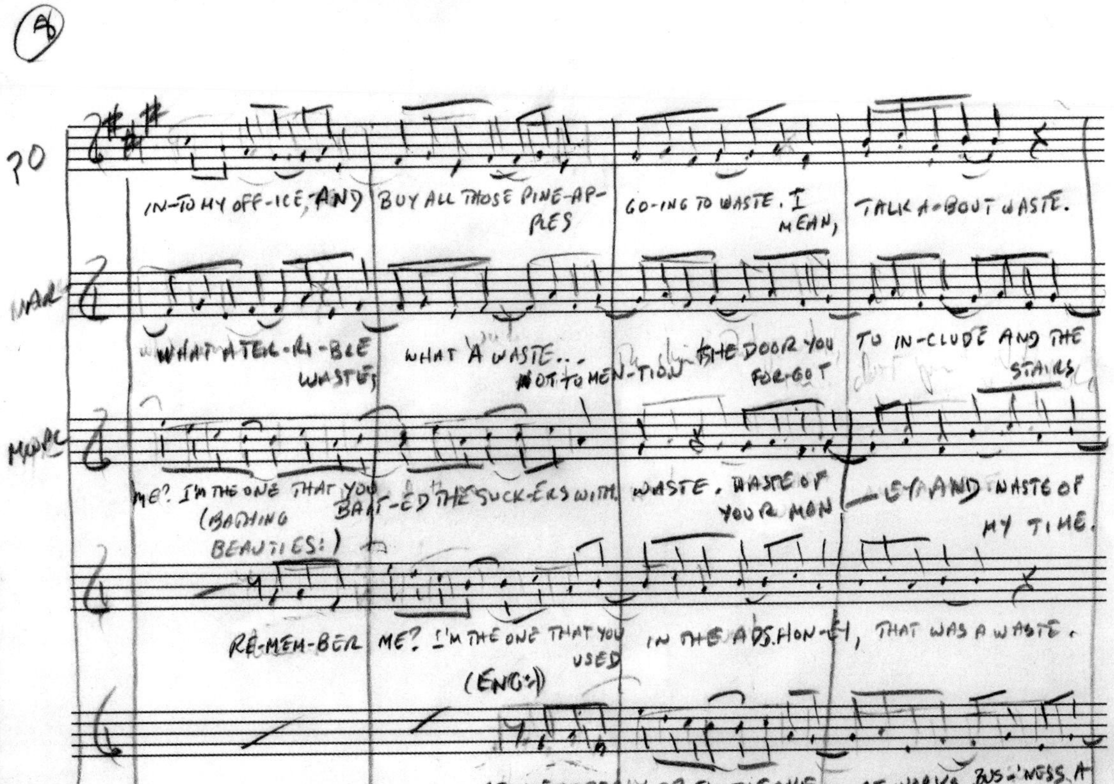

REVIVALS: DIRECTORS AND THEIR NOTIONS

Revivals are what keep theater alive; reinterpretation is renewal. But actors can reinterpret only so far—major revitalization is the province of the director. I'm not talking about the creative suggestions directors make which affect the rewriting of a show, as with John Doyle and *Road Show*. I'm referring to the reconceiving of established texts. Shakespeare, of course, is the Fountain of Youth here; the opportunities for reconceiving his work in cast and setting abound, and directors grab at them with all the imagination they can muster: *Macbeth* set in Haiti, complete with voodoo witches (Orson Welles); *Richard III* in a 1930s Fascist state (Richard Eyre); *A Midsummer Night's Dream* in a bare white wonderland (Peter Brook); admixtures of period and contemporary—the possibilities are virtually infinite. This is partly because Shakespeare's plays are so distant in time and language that one can do almost anything to them without distorting them (except to rewrite them), and partly because they're great plays and worth reviving.

Musical revivals are frequent; rethinking them is not, but then how many musicals invite a director's re-attention? Shows like *Into the Woods* and *Company* are ripe for reinvention because they are fantasies to begin with, but in how many ways can you reinterpret *Cabaret* or *Candide* or *Annie Get Your Gun*? Actually, quite a few: *Cabaret* as a cabaret (Sam Mendes); *Candide* as a carnival (Hal Prince); *Annie Get Your Gun* set in a diner (Richard Jones).

If that last seems startling, it was. It appeared in London in 2009 and was quite wonderful. Richard Jones has a fondness for rooms: for the 1990 London premiere of *Into the Woods*, he set the entire show in a Graustarkian hunting lodge with antlered furniture and wallpaper woods that peeled away in Act Two. When the Giant came looking for Jack, she made her presence felt by peering through a doorway at the back with one gigantic eyeball and inserting a twenty-foot long finger through another at the side. Jones sprinkled the evening with other surreal effects, and the net result was that the show became a grotesque dream, capturing the essence of Grimm's fairy tales. Both Lapine and I loved the production, not least because it had nothing to do with ours. Unlike revivals which are

hybrids of the original source and the director's additions, this one was a complete reinvention. As was John Doyle's revival of *Sweeney Todd*: set in an asylum and performed by a cast who played instruments and thus supplied their own orchestral accompaniment, the show acquired a claustrophobic tension it had never had before. Doyle applied the same cast-cum-orchestra technique to *Company* but for a different purpose. It became a metaphor for the whole piece: Bobby was the only one without a musical instrument, but when he finally came to his climactic realization and sang "Being Alive," he accompanied himself at the piano, playing an instrument for the first time. Again, it intensified the moment as never before.

Not that hybrids are inferior by definition. Declan Donnellan's production of *Sweeney Todd* at the National Theatre in London was nothing startling, but its minimalist approach gave the show a whispered intimacy, which was new to it; Mario Gas directed a Catalan production in Barcelona filled with doorways and balconies slightly smaller in scale than normal, so that the actors loomed over them, which made the evening stark and frightening to a degree I had never seen. Then there was the production of *Into the Woods* performed in Regent's Park among real trees (Tim Sheader); *Sunday in the Park with George*, which animated Seurat's painting (Sam Buntrock); Sam Mendes's *Assassins* with its cheerful fairground atmosphere, as opposed to Joe Mantello's dark one. Both were true to the spirit of the piece. Sometimes the director's approach to casting can alone change the tenor of a show, as Jamie Lloyd's did in *Passion,* and as Lapine's did in his version of *Merrily We Roll Along* in La Jolla, where he cast young adults who could play kids as well as themselves instead of, as in the original, kids who could only play themselves.

Revivals may keep theater alive, but they have two potential drawbacks, one of which I have alluded to before. Directors, as I said, can not only revivify a show, they can kill it—or at least, wound it. I gave some examples of this practice in *Finishing the Hat* in the chapter about *The Frogs; Merrily We Roll Along* played backwards, for instance; or Bobby shooting himself at the end of *Company*. I could cite more from my own roster alone, but I

suspect that every writer who has had the pleasure of seeing his shows revived, whether on Broadway or in a community theater, has also suffered the chagrin of seeing it distorted almost beyond recognition—if it were truly unrecognizable, it would be a relief.

The problem is that a great many directors, not just the academics or the amateurs, reconceive for the sake of reconception, usually in the name of "relevance" or of "fixing" the show's flaws. They want to be considered creators so desperately that they think nothing of rewriting the authors' work. Good directors shine a new light on a piece; the others shine a light on themselves. Setting Chekhov in Connecticut or Strindberg in Miami doesn't really illuminate the script, but it often illuminates the director. Nevertheless, these egregious mistakes are only temporary and actually may help to keep the play alive by encouraging another director to fix the fixes.

The second drawback revivals can have is that reevaluation is a double-edged sword. Sometimes seeing a play afresh is seeing how much staler it is than what was previously thought, the net result being that it gets thrown into the scrap heap of plays that should never have been revived. Bad movies are always available; bad shows don't get revived more than once; they die. Mediocre ones and mediocre revivals of good ones, however, have appeared with alarming frequency over the past few years. The onerous economics of Broadway is virtually the only consideration behind many, if not most, of them. Producers (usually corporations) believe a well-known title coupled with a well-known star is a hedge against the increasingly poor odds of having a financial success. These productions have nothing to do with a director's fresh approach, and rather than reinvigorating the shows, they turn them into zombies. There is a difference between a rehash and a revival.

opening number should tell the audience what the show is about, whom the show is about and how the story is to be presented. It was the whom requirement which none of the other openings had made clear, and this one tilted solidly toward Addison rather than either Wilson or the symbiotic pair of them: the song was clearly about *him*. John and I had been aware of this central problem from the show's beginning—could we ask people to invest their interest equally in both brothers, and if not, which brother should it be, the visionary idealist or the visionary salesman, the inventor or the reinventor, the builder or the destroyer? The answer became clear only as we rewrote through each incarnation, which is where the best answers come from—nothing is potentially as stifling as predetermination.

The scene dissolves to Benicia in the 1890s.

There are no delineations between the scenes: one dissolves into another. This is how Doyle kept the pace going.

It's in Your Hands Now***

As in the Workshop, Papa dies and Mama announces that they are stone broke, at which point the Prospector appears.

Gold! (part I)***

On the first night in Alaska, with both wind and wolves howling, the brothers are miserable and freezing. When Wilson's sleeping bag splits open, Addison offers to share his. Forced into confinement, they huddle together awkwardly.

*** The lyrics here and elsewhere marked by a triple asterisk can be found in previous sections of this chapter.

Brotherly Love

ADDISON
You know what this reminds me of?

WILSON
No. What?

ADDISON
Remember when I was in bed with
    the mumps
And had to stay in New Year's Eve?

WILSON
Frankly, no.

ADDISON
Remember how I was so down in the
    dumps
When everyone started to leave?

WILSON
Jesus, it's cold!

ADDISON
Are you sorry we came, Willie?
You sorry we came?

WILSON
Yes. No. Go to sleep.

ADDISON
At midnight with everyone down at
    the lake
To take in the fireworks show—

WILSON
(Remembering)
Oh, yeah.

ADDISON
I cried till I fell half-asleep by
    mistake—

WILSON
And I snuck upstairs and I shook
    you awake—

ADDISON
You bundled me up in a couple of
    quilts
And you carried me up all the way
    to the roof—

WILSON
(Simultaneously)
Up all the way to the roof—

ADDISON
And that slippery patch—!

WILSON
Yeah, we nearly got killed—!

ADDISON
But we got to see everything!

WILSON
(Simultaneously)
But we got to see every—
Remember the whizbangs—?

Alexander Gemignani as Addison and Michael Cerveris as Wilson

Sleeping Boy

I

the night of that weird
That night in the spot

Remember the fireworks night NY Eve   The time I came down
                                             and When I was in bed w/ the mumps
                 night
      The time that we kept

Remember the NYE I had the mumps   And I was confined to my room

Remember the NYE I was in bed
                 timing that party did   The fireworks set but starting
Remember the party we had NYE   The fireworks slowly & I couldn't hear
                                            The party beginning

I thought I am gonna miss all of the less   Festivities starting

                                    be running   and show
mumps   I thought I'd miss all of the fireworks but
lumps
                         Remember the time & came down w/ the mumps
conceive believe   The day we kept before NY Eve
reprieve deceive   were just
make believe   When   down in the dumps
recieve   While
+leave   And Mama said I couldn't leave

                       when I lost
            Remember are coming down w/ the mumps NY Eve

            When Mama said stay in your room & don't leave
            And I'm stuck in
            Confined to my room but   I got a reprieve
            Confined to my room & forbidden to leave

            Remember when I was in bed w/ the mumps
            And had to stay home New Years eve

The wind howls, drowning them out as they tumble over each other in reminiscences, singing in pantomime.

WILSON
(As the wind dies down)
. . . We had lots of good times . . .

ADDISON
We slept there till dawn,
All wrapped up in those quilts . . .

WILSON
Boy, Mama was madder than hell . . .

(They snicker; pause)

ADDISON
You always looked out for me, no
  matter what . . .

WILSON
Just brotherly love, brother,
  brotherly love—

(Sniffs)

Jesus, I smell.

ADDISON
I'm not sorry I came, Willie,
I'm just glad that you're here . . .

This song was the last written for the show—a crucial one, as it gave the brothers a moment of closeness which they had never had before, a moment which informs everything that subsequently happens between them. Moreover, it's a musical moment, which distills their feeling of camaraderie with more emotional immediacy than a scene would have done.

Addison, acutely uncomfortable with his physical closeness to Wilson, squirms around. Wilson irritably scrambles out of the sack and heads for Skagway to get a new sleeping bag in the general store, which is also the saloon and where the poker players inveigle him into the game.

Gold! (part II)***

The song, with minor emendations and cuts, follows the pattern of Bounce, *the action cutting just once between the saloon and the dig, but with this addition when Addison is in his deepest despair:*

ADDISON
Maybe this is not the road, Papa,
Maybe not the road for me.
Maybe it's for Willie—
Yes, I know I'm being silly,
But this isn't what I want.
I don't think it's what I want.
At the moment all I want
Is Willie . . .

A small addition, but it reiterates the road image and emphasizes Addison's feelings about Wilson.

Back at the saloon, Wilson is becoming a gambler when Addison bursts in at the climax of the game with a huge nugget of gold. Wilson persuades Addison to bet the nugget by telling him that he has found his calling.

The Game***

The song remains as it was in the Workshop and in Bounce, *with a few minor emendations. There is, however, a change in the ending.*

What do you think Papa would say?
"Boys," he'd say, "seize the goddamn
  day!
This is your chance—"

ADDISON
All right, okay!

I made the change from the previous version of the song for two reasons: to keep Papa's influence alive, so that his admonitions become thematic, and

to presage Addison's capitulatory "All right, okay!" in the Boca Raton sequence.

Unlike in previous versions of the show, Wilson wins the hand and ten thousand dollars. Addison is eager to go and work the claim, but Wilson has already swapped it for the saloon, which he plans to expand. Addison, furious, grabs his share of the winnings and storms off around the world.

This remains as it was in Bounce, *but with the visit to India restored (where Addison invests in a gem emporium that is wiped out by a cyclone) and with this change in the opening stanza:*

Addison's Trip***

ADDISON
I'm on my way!
Look, Mama, on my own!
I lost my way—
That was just an episode.
I'm on my way,
Off to worlds I've never known—
I'm looking for my road!

Let Willie stay,
I mean, Willie's found his niche.
I have to say
We were getting just too entwined.
But I'm okay,
And who knows? I might just get
  rich!
I'm on my way to find
My road!

And this change in the closing stanza, where Addison is rearranging all his possessions in his mind:

ADDISON
No, they all seem out of place . . .

(As the company rearranges things)

Now it all looks too compressed . . .

(Pondering)

What I need to have is space
That holds crucifixes,
A Bombay chest,
A temple bell
And a condor's nest
And commodes and mirrors and all
	the rest—
I'll need a hundred rooms!

	(Quietly)

So I'll make a hundred rooms . . .

The company assembles the room.

. . . Give the Chinese scroll an entire
	wall,
The gilded mirror a separate hall,
Build an atrium for the chandelier,
Give the rug a room with some
	atmosphere,
Build a marble niche for the Ming
	tureen
And a mezzanine for the lacquered
	screen,
And an archway here and a skylight
	there
Until everything has a place
	somewhere—

I'll build a goddamned house!

	I'm on my way . . .

The alterations to the lyric are few but
salient: first, they continue keeping
the road image central to the show;
second, they maintain Addison's sense
of his bothersome feelings about Wilson; third, and most important, they
clarify his transformation into an architect, as opposed to an interior
decorator.

*New York. Addison's tiny apartment.
He has his first commission from Myra
Yerkes, the richest widow in America,
to build a pool house. Wilson arrives
with Mama in tow; they have been
making their way across the country
ever since Wilson lost the saloon in a
card game, living hand to mouth,
sneaking out of hotels, hitchhiking and
so forth. Mrs. Yerkes enters; Wilson
courts her with compliments and, in
the blink of an eye, marries her. He*

*promises Addison a commission to de-
sign a new house for himself and his
bride.*

With Doyle at the helm, these scenes
tumbled into each other and the
whole sequence took three minutes
and fifteen seconds. The following section was even swifter, the scenes not
only tumbling but overlapping during
the transitions.

That Was a Year*

*Mrs. Yerkes and Wilson kiss. A bell
rings and Stanley Ketchel, a prizefighter, appears.*

MAMA
(*Who has acquired a newspaper*)
	Addie, look at this! Your brother's
	in the prizefight business!

*The following passage is spoken rhyth-
mically.*

WILSON
Kid!

KETCHEL
Hiya, Willie!

WILSON
How you doing?

KETCHEL
Just great!

MRS. YERKES
Who's that?!

WILSON
Stanley Ketchel,
Fighting Sailor Boy Mackenzie
For the title.

---

* Although large sections of this lyric appear in earlier parts of this chapter, I reprint
them here so that the reader can follow the
reassemblage without having to flip pages
back and forth, thus losing the pace.

MRS. YERKES
For the title?

WILSON
For the middleweight crown.
We bought his contract
For a measly fifty thousand.

MRS. YERKES
We *did*?

	Remind me, when exactly did we
	buy his—?

KETCHEL
	I just wanna say thank you to our
	Lord and Savior Jesus Christ, to my
	sainted mother, may she rest in
	peace, and most of all to the great-
	est manager a fighter ever had,
	Willie Mizner!

The crowd roars.

Willie had style,
Willie had brass,
Willie said, "Stan, I'm gonna give
	you some class."
Taught me to dress,
Made me a sport,
Gave me social status and something
	to snort.

Learned a lot from Willie,
Havin' laughs, gettin' tight,
Coked till we were silly
By the dawn's early light.
Learned so much from Willie
I forgot how to fight,
But oh, what a year,
That was a year!

MRS. YERKES

	Next time you go shopping with
	my dough, let me know, okay?

WILSON
God, I love this town!
Don't you love this town?
It's got all of these
Opportunities,
Can't afford to turn them down!

Some may not work out.
Some go up the spout,
Plenty more around the corner—

I don't need Willie   A's Trip (2008)
I'm thinking of you, Mama   I

I'm on my way,   On a road I know nothing of
Say, mate,
Look, payee, on my own   But now I'm grown
                                          Ibg

N, Trying to be frightened of
code steward   I'm not sure exactly where
episode   But I'll explore   I'm looking for my road
explode   Off to world's I've never known
mother-lode   I'm off to find my road
overload
owed   Look, Mama, are you proud?   I'm on the my road to find
                        all grown up,   My Way.
sword snored   But, Mama, I am on
good   Little Addie is fully grown   My way
                I can find my own mother-lode

hey hey hey   I gotta say   And I'm silly   That was just an episode
  hay
making   I say hurray   It's hard, okay
fair play   And who's to say
may pay   Let Willie play
                I'm scared, okay?   Before Willie gets left behind
                                              Out of sight Willie's out of my mind
blind   Out of sight & out of his mind
                Now that Willie's found his anchor. Gotta leave what you leave behind
                                              Sure this stey I'm sad to say
speak bleak   When you leave you could leave behind
  all   I can leave what I love behind
cheek Greek   Gotta learn not to look behind
creak leak   I have to say   Out of sight will mean out of mind
hide + seek   Brought of my own & let of pique
meek peak   I'm on my way to seek
pique sleek
streak squeak
unique weak

                My Road —
                The Road of Opportunity

And what's waiting 'round the
 corner,
Isn't that what life is all about?

*Addison is in his apartment, tending
Mama and waiting for Wilson to
visit and bring the fee for the promised
commission.*

ADDISON
(On the phone)
I know you're busy, Willie, I read
the papers. But Mama thought she
was going to see you Sunday and
she—this Sunday? You're sure?
Okay, just as long as you're sure.
And don't forget to bring my fee!

(Hangs up)

MAMA
Addie, you won't believe it! Your
brother's written a Broadway play!

*Paul Armstrong, a flamboyant theatri-
cal type, appears.*

ARMSTRONG
Willie had wit,
Willie had brains,
Willie had contacts in the lower
 domains.
Knew how they lived,
Knew what they'd say.
That's why I said, "Willie, let's write
 a play."

But where the hell was Willie
Came the time to rewrite?
Way the hell in Philly,
Off promoting some fight.
Half a play with Willie
Closes opening night,
But oh, what a year!
That was a year!

MRS. YERKES
You're saying I *invested* in this play?

WILSON
God, I love it here!
Don't you love it here?

MRS. YERKES
That I invested *fifteen thousand
bucks* in this play?

WILSON
Every place you look
Is an open book,
Every street a new frontier!
If you sizzle, swell.
If you fizzle—well,
Nothing fails for long.
If it doesn't fly, it doesn't,
And it's time to sing another
 song!

CHORINES, KETCHEL,
ARMSTRONG
Broadway Willie,
Prince of bons vivants—
Everybody wants
Broadway Willie Mizner!
Knocks 'em silly,
Lowlifes and DuPonts,
Cops and debutantes . . .

ADDISON
(On the phone again)
You didn't make it last Sunday or
the Sunday before, Willie, what
makes you think you're going to
make it—fine, I'll tell her. And
Willie, please, I need that fee!

MAMA
Look at this picture, dear! Your
brother kissing a racehorse!

*Addison hangs up. A jockey in hand-
cuffs appears.*

JOCKEY
Willie and me, we had a run,
Doin' some things we shouldn't of
 done,
Till we get rumbled for this race we
 try to fix.
Willie says, "Kid, I'm your support.
Let me explain things to the court."
So he explains and beats the rap
And I get sent up for six.

ARMSTRONG
Now I write a show,
It doesn't get on . . .

KETCHEL
Offer me some dough,
I dive like a swan . . .

JOCKEY
Once I was a pro,
And now I'm a con.
But oh, what a year!

KETCHEL, ARMSTRONG
That was a year!

WILSON
From the mayor to the cop on the
 beat,
Who's the only guy they all want to
 meet?
Who's the man they call the king of
 the street?

THE COMPANY
Good time Willie Mizner!
When you write about New Yorkers
 of note,
Who's the wittiest by popular vote,
Always ready with a quip or a
 quote?

WILSON
Be nice to the people you meet on
the way up, 'cause they're the same
people you're gonna meet on the
way down.

THE COMPANY
Night club fillies,
Writers, racketeers,
Everybody cheers
Good time Willie Mizner!
Ziegfeld lilies,
Pimps and financiers—

ADDISON
(Back on the phone)
What fee? The fee for the pool
house, Willie! *That's* what fee!

MRS. YERKES
Willie had style.
Willie had gall.
Willie had ladies 'round the block
 and down the hall.
Perfect in looks,
Perfect at sex,
Not so goddamn perfect at forging
 my checks.

KETCHEL
Sure, I lost the crown, but I made
 lots of green . . .

ARMSTRONG
Sure, he took his time, but we wrote
a great scene . . .

JOCKEY
I was voted "biggest wit" in cell
block eighteen . . .

ALL THREE
Thanks to Willie Mizner,
Nimble Willie Mizner—

KETCHEL
Sharp as a hawk—

THEATRICAL TYPE
Cock of the walk—

MRS. YERKES
You're telling me . . .

JOCKEY
King of Noo Yawk!

ALL
Stick around with Willie, you run
out of luck.
Stick around with Willie, you feel
like a cluck.
Stick around with Willie, you're
gonna get stuck,
But you'll get a year—!

JOCKEY
Maybe ten to twenty—

ALL
You'll have a year—!

MRS. YERKES
One is more than plenty—

ALL
You'll have the time of your life!

MRS. YERKES
(Overlapping)
I had the time of my life!

WILSON
God, I love this town!

ALL
Broadway Willie,
King of New York!

Mama is tucked up in bed. Addison is at her bedside with his drafting table. The scene proceeds as in Bounce *and once again Mama sings.*

Isn't He Something!***

She dies. The rest of the scene also proceeds as in Bounce *until the moment when Addison throws Wilson out, but there is no reprise of the title song; in fact, there is no song at all because there is no need to end the act with a punctuation because there is no act ending because with Doyle's encouragement we compressed the show into one act the way these sentences have been compressed into one with no punctuation and therefore speeded up. Punctuations in the show are not the ends of scenes but the beginnings of the next ones: for example, the immediate appearance of the Real Estate Agent from* Wise Guys *and* Bounce.

Gold
(Real Estate Promoter reprise)***

As before, Addison meets Hollis on the train.

Talent***

They join forces and build Palm Beach.

You***

As it was in Bounce, *but with a slight change in the verse:*

ADDISON
Never let a chance go by, Hollis—
Don't you see that here's your
chance?
How to stoke the fire
Is the problem in acquiring
A patron.
Every patron has a matron.

Let her feel fulfilled.
Trust me, she'll be thrilled
Once she sees the house
That I'm going to build!
And you'll get your guild . . .

In the Workshop version, this last stanza had a different rhyme scheme:

Leave it up to me,
And they'll feel fulfilled.
Wait until you see
What I'm going to build,
And you'll have your guild!

The reason for the lyric change was a fussy one. I was bothered by the word "guild," which is not really what Hollis wants to establish. He wants to found an artistic community, a "congregation," as he describes it in "Talent," but "community" and "congregation" are not very seductive words, and Addison is seducing Hollis on two levels, whether he knows it or not. I could have changed the music to accommodate a longer word, of course, but the form and music of this verse was a recurrent theme of Wilson's, and I wanted to show that Addison had picked it up from him, since the story in the second half of the show concerns Addison's attempt to become his brother. Wilson's verses culminate in short, sharp final words and "guild" was the only one that came to mind. I tried to strengthen it by making it the ultimate of four rhymes in quick succession, but it meant what it meant and I wasted time trying to justify it: "guild" was simply not the right word. Worse yet, it didn't matter—the audience understood the intention. God is not the only one in the Details; sometimes, as many believe, the Devil is, too.

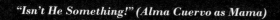
"Isn't He Something!" (Alma Cuervo as Mama)

By the end of the song, as in previous versions, Addison and Hollis are involved with each other; this time the song ends with a kiss.

A tropical night. Hollis and Addison are at home, going over their social schedule.

The Best Thing That Ever Has Happened

HOLLIS
First there's cocktails at the
    Cosdens'—

ADDISON
Oh, Jesus . . .

HOLLIS
Hon, we've got fish to fry.

ADDISON
Why don't you do this one without me?

HOLLIS
Then there's dinner at the Dodges',
The reception at the Roosevelts'—

ADDISON
I think I'm going to die.

HOLLIS
And every party filled
With millionaires who want to build
The biggest villas since the days of
    ancient Rome.
So what do you say
We just stay
Home?

ADDISON
You are the best thing that ever has
    happened to me,
You are.

(As Hollis waves him away, blushing)

Okay then, one of the best things
    that's happened to me,
You are.

They say we all find love—
I never bought it.
I never thought it
Would happen to me.
Who could foresee?

You are the goddamnedest thing that
    has happened to me,
Ever.
When did I have this much
    happiness happen to me?
Never.

I can't believe my luck,
And all I can do
Is be the best thing that's happened
    to you.

HOLLIS
So what do you say
We just stay home?
What do you say we just go
Out on the boat and get smashed
And make love on the beach
And stare up at the moon—?

ADDISON
Holly . . .

HOLLIS
You might just be the best thing that
    has happened to me,
So far.
Of course not much ever really has
    happened to me,
So far.

I didn't much like love,
I always fought it.
I never thought it
Would happen like this.

ADDISON
Give us a kiss.

BOTH
We may just be the best thing that
    has happened to us—

ADDISON
Kiddo . . .

HOLLIS
Partner . . .

BOTH
Another moment like this may not
    happen to us—

ADDISON
Partner . . .

HOLLIS
Lover . . .

BOTH
When all is said and done,
I have to agree:
You are the best thing that's
    happened to me.

HOLLIS
Who knew?

ADDISON
Who dreamed?

BOTH
Beats me.

As I said in the introduction to this chapter, what we'd learned from *Bounce* was that the show had to be more claustrophobic, not less, that it had to concentrate on the small compass of the central love story, which had nothing to do with a woman, and so, in *Road Show*, we broadened the love story. At the end of fourteen years' gestation, we were back at our first perception: what the show was about at its core was these two particular people, the Mizner brothers, not the dangers of entrepreneurship, not the difference between opportunity and opportunism, not the persistence of American resilience or the conflict between artistry and promotion. Those were all ancillary themes which put flesh on the musical's bones and were reflections of the central relationship, but the story was, and is, a tale of two brothers. Thematic "relevance," a favorite word of producers, directors, actors and especially publicists, in describing a show, is an outgrowth of character or it is nothing.

Addison snorts a line of cocaine. The lights go down on Hollis. A crack of thunder, and Wilson appears, pleading for help, as in Bounce, *but this time in song.*

The Game (reprise)

WILSON
One day up, the next day down,
That's the way it goes.
One week you can own the town—
Next week, hey, who knows?
You and me, though, brother mine,
   we're pros.

The whole thing's nothing more
   than just a game.
And what we both are good at is the
   game.
Believe me, I'm not asking for
Forgiveness—all the same,
I'm asking to get back into the game.

Given up booze, given up coke,
Given up girls, don't even smoke.
Got a bad break and wound up
   broke,
Jesus, my life is one sad joke . . .

Pause. Addison just stares at him.

Want me to beg? Want me to crawl?
Want an apology? Your call.
I was a prick, but after all,
Jesus, I'm your brother!

   (With increasing desperation)

It's more than just the money that's
   at stake.
It's even more than begging for a
   break.
Joke or not, it's my life!
If you want to twist the knife,
Then twist the knife . . .

Only please—!

Wilson tilts forward and collapses. The next morning, as in Bounce, *Hollis and Wilson (this time without the participation of Nellie) set about persuading Addison to build a city.*

Addison's City***

The same number as before, with a few emendations to account for Nellie's not being there: for example, Wilson's "He should build a city, Countess" becomes "You should build a city, Addie" and "You make us a sweetheart of a deal" becomes "Leave it to me to make the spiel" (with a dropped syllable—for the better).

Boca Raton Sequence***

This also is the same number as in Bounce, *but in keeping with the warp-speed of Doyle's version, we cut it by a half, omitting a lot of the promotional redundancies and the short reprise of Papa's song, but including the publicity stunts and exaggerations and the patriotic pitch about "land." Punctuated by the recurrent repeat of the sung word "Gold!" underneath, the investors pile in, singing about getting rich quick and concluding with:*

CHORUS
Every property's prime
And the views are sublime
And the values just climb
And climb and climb and climb . . .

Wilson describes to the radio audience in extravagant terms the magnificent twenty-lane highway with a Venetian canal that he described in the Reading. Then, with evangelical fervor, he continues with a version of what he sang in the Workshop, this time spoken:

WILSON
. . . Life is a journey. A road down which we travel, ever seeking, never satisfied. An endless quest for something different, something better. Onward we go, restlessly reinventing ourselves. Searching for something that already lies before us. For in America, the journey *is* the destination! . . .

He goes on to exalt Boca Raton as the Chorus sings, but during the sequence Hollis grows increasingly suspicious of the project's integrity and finally confronts both brothers, accusing them of colluding with each other against his best interests. Wilson impatiently smacks him and when Addison, forced by Hollis to choose between him and his brother, chooses his brother, Hollis explodes in a rage and in a national broadcast divests himself of Boca Raton stock and recommends that everyone else do the same.

In the song "Brotherly Love," we emphasized the closeness between Addison and Wilson in their early years. Here we showed them operating as a team once again, even if just as promoters, after decades of traveling separate roads. That camaraderie had been the heart of the story fourteen years earlier and our reunion with it was not unlike that of the Mizners.

There is a sudden cacophonous noise of things falling and breaking, and the boom has become a bust as before, but it is not only Wilson who has the nervous breakdown, it is Boca Raton, and it is Addison who tells Hollis off, not his brother. He has become Wilson, with Wilson's ruthlessness, but he is prepared to pay the price for it: he gives Hollis up not only because he thinks Hollis ought to be smacked but because he thinks that as a punishment he himself deserves to be left alone with his brother, whom he rounds on the minute Hollis has exited.

Get Out of My Life***
Go***

"Go" ends with Addison, as in the Reading, yearning rather than bitter, alone in bed as at the top of the show, Wilson having gone.

Once again, the door of one of the packing crates bangs open and Wilson strides back in. This time, however, both of them realize that they're dead. Wilson climbs into bed with Addison. Addison bewails the waste of his talent, which Wilson acknowledges.

What a Waste
(reprise)

WILSON
Still, you got rich.
Still, you got laid.
Not such a waste.
Only one hitch:
Me, I'm afraid.
Still, you were embraced.

ADDISON
It wasn't enough, Willie. It was also too much.

WILSON
So you fell short
Of your dream—
Come on, sport,
We're still a team,
We're made the same way—

ADDISON
So you say—

Suddenly, a spotlight on Papa.

PAPA
Boys, boys—

ADDISON
Oh, shit.

PAPA
A doting father's dying words, boys . . .

There's a road straight ahead,
There's a century beginning.
There's a land of opportunity and more . . .

I expected you to make history, boys. Instead, you made a mess.

WILSON
A *mess*? What does he mean, "a mess"?

ADDISON
You know what he means.

"Boca Raton Sequence"

Michail Jibson, left, as Addison and David Bedella as Wilson (Menier Chocolate Factory, London, 2011)

WILSON
Yeah. Well. One man's mess is an-other man's . . . something or other.

ADDISON
God, you had charm,
God, you had guts.
God, what a waste.

WILSON
Hey! We built a city!

ADDISON
Actually, we didn't.

God, we did harm.
What, were we nuts?
And where was our taste?

WILSON
So we went overboard a little bit.
Where's the harm in that?

ADDISON
Where's the *harm*—?

WILSON
So if we fell,
And fell fast,
Why should we dwell
On the past?
Looking ahead—

ADDISON
Willie, we're dead.

Grandiose chords, like those which ac-companied the appearance of Addison's first house in Palm Beach.

THE COMPANY
Look at it!
Look at it! Look at it!

WILSON
(As music continues underneath)
 Addie, look at it! You know what that is? It's the road to opportunity!

ADDISON
It's the road to eternity.

WILSON
The greatest opportunity of all.
Sooner or later we're bound to get it right.

Blackout.

E N D   O F   S H O W

This final dialogue is the same as in the *Wise Guys* Workshop, but with the last two lines snipped to make our point less sententiously. As we did throughout the revisions, whenever we reverted to an earlier version of the show, we returned to *Wise Guys*, ei-ther the Workshop or the Reading, rather than to the hybrid *Bounce*, where we had lost our compass. As often happens with work that under-goes a lot of changes over a long pe-riod of time, original instincts prove to be best.

 And it was a long period of time,

indeed: a saga of fourteen years with four distinct scripts; three distinct directors;* nine leading actors; numerous producers, designers and conductors; and a dramaturge. Also, by last count, more than thirty songs (the exact number is hard to determine, as some are rewrites of others) plus numerous variations on them. Not many songs survived through all four incarnations, but the ones that did are a telling selection: "Gold!," "Addison's Trip," "The Game," the Boca Raton sequence, "Get Out of My Life" and "Go." They comprise a microcosm of the story: the boys setting out on their own, Addison discovering what he wants out of life; Wilson discovering what *he* wants out of life; their partnership, their dissolution, their reunion. All the other songs were either added or subject to change and omission. The narrative sustained; the refinements, whether they dealt with Papa, Mama, Hollis or style, were mal-leable. The story was sturdy; it just took us fourteen years to find out what it was—fourteen years and four scripts, reflected in their titles: *Wise Guys* (opportunity vs. opportunism); *Gold!* (greed vs. morality); *Bounce* (resilience and reinvention); and *Road Show* (finding your destiny). *Road Show* is the right title for what we arrived at, but it's a bit drab; I still prefer *Get Rich Quick!*, which hints at all four. Like Wilson, the show kept reinventing itself. "What's Next?" could have been our theme song, and maybe even our title.

It took four scripts and three directors, each of whom had an idea of how to arrive at what the show should be: Sam's to enlarge its scope by freeing us from the facts of the Mizners' lives; Hal's to aerate it by introducing a heterosexual element to the story; Doyle's to blur its picaresque quality with quick cuts and the telescoping of scenes. All the ideas seemed reasonable enough at the time, and John and I, like the Mizners, felt we should explore each road. It was the last one that hit the mark: Doyle's approach was an exemplary manifestation of Less Is More and Content Dictates Form, and the piece became the one we were trying to write but didn't know it.

Road Show was greeted dismissively: respectfully, but unexcitedly. Part of this response, I think, was that in different guises it had already received two productions, neither of them satisfying, and was per-ceived unconsciously (or maybe consciously) by the critics and theater cognoscenti as having passed its sell-by date.

Perhaps it always will be greeted dismissively, and perhaps my fondness for it and my pride in it exemplify the parent's defensive love of the homelier child, but what matters to me is that John and I finally got the show we wanted. The last line of the show proved to be prophetic.

---

* Sam Mendes, Hal Prince and John Doyle, all of whom presented stage versions. Eric Schaeffer directed a reading only.

6. Other Musicals

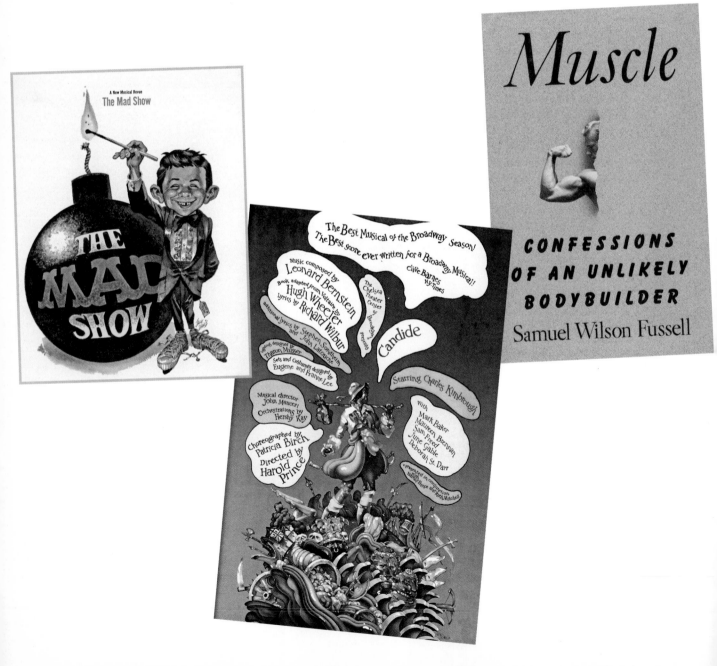

The Last Resorts (Unproduced, 1956)

Book by Walter and Jean Kerr

Based on the title of a social study by
    Cleveland Amory

The Notion

A scruffy Midwestern newspaper reporter is persuaded to cover the weekend visit of the Duke and Duchess of Windsor to a grand mansion in Palm Beach and falls in love with Janet, the daughter of the vulgarly rich host and hostess who own the place. Many romantic and satirical complications ensue.

General Comments

In 1956 Hal Prince, fresh from two triumphs as a fledgling producer (*The Pajama Game* and *Damn Yankees*), bought the rights to *The Last Resorts,* a bestselling book by Cleveland Amory, a social critic, about resort life in America. He then persuaded Jean Kerr to write a libretto based on nothing but the subject, since the book, a compendium of societal observations, was plotless. Jean Kerr, an essayist and playwright, was the wife of Walter Kerr, drama critic for the *New York Herald Tribune* (and much the best writer in the profession until the advent of Frank Rich). She was an old colleague of Hal's: he had been assistant stage manager of a sharp, smart, funny revue the Kerrs had written in 1949 called *Touch and Go,* and he thought she was ripe to write a sharp, smart, funny musical with a plot. The one she concocted concerned a Midwestern hayseed novelist-reporter, very much like Richard Bissell, the Midwestern hay-

seed novelist-reporter who had written *7½ Cents,* the book on which *The Pajama Game* had been based. This arrangement made it a very homey Hal Prince affair, and he shored it up by asking me, his ambitious pal, to audition for the Kerrs, which I was happy to do. Although I was at work on *West Side Story,* nothing I had written had yet breached the walls of Broadway, and I had liked *Touch and Go* a lot. So, *Saturday Night* score in hand, I nervously but eagerly set out to audition for them.

They lived in a mildly forbidding castlelike structure in Westchester, and they turned out to be just as forbidding as their surroundings.* I auditioned for them in a room that had the coziness, and size, of an armory. Jean sat in a tall armchair and rarely moved except to cross and uncross her legs. She was a tall woman and, even seated, seemed to tower over her husband, who was probably about five-feet-three. Apart from that, I remember nothing except that every few minutes Jean, a chain smoker, would bark in a murmur, "Butt me, Walter!" and Walter would dutifully give her a cigarette and light it for her.

The show never got beyond a first draft, but here are the three songs that I wrote for it, with brief synopses of the situations that lead to them.

---

* I later got to know Jean when I joined the Council of the Dramatists Guild, and we became fond of each other. Walter was another matter entirely: as a critic, he disliked almost everything I wrote, sometimes cordially, usually not, and always dismissively.

*Janet is in RB's** hometown, trying to persuade him to come to Florida and write an article about the royal visit to her parents' home. It is a lazy Sunday, and RB's neighbors are hanging around. It should also be noted that RB is a fancier of old automobiles.*

High Life

WOMAN
(To her baby)
Sun is high and warmin' up the
    river,
Orange peels are floatin' on the
    grease.
Go to sleep, my baby, by the river.
So your ma can drink her beer in
    peace.

JANET
Go and see how the vanishing
Other half lives:
Forty rooms and a special wing
Where the staff lives.
Private trains on the hour there
And a private zoo with a tower
    where
The giraffe lives.

That's the high life!

RB
I like my life . . .

My life is a slow life on the river,
Sleepy as a weepy willow tree . . .
Easy, 'cause I know life on the
    river—
What's the high life to a lowlife
    like me?

Don't like to shave
Or wear a tie,
Just sit and wave
As the boats go by.
When things go on,

---

* The script was in such a preliminary stage that the hero is known only as RB, Richard Bissell's initials—Jean hadn't bothered to name him yet, and rightly so, since that was a good deal less important than inventing a plot.

I write 'em down—
Lucky nothin' ever goes on in this
    here town!

Love my easy-go life on the river,
Countin' beer cans floatin' out
    to sea.
Leave me be—I got a job,
Listenin' to those engines throb,
Learnin' how to be a slob
For free,
And the high life isn't no life
For me!

JANET
Anything that you'd like to do
Can be done there:
Golf, or Scrabble or Peekaboo
In the sun there,
Bridge, Canasta and lawn croquet—

RB
Ginger-peachy, but what do they
Do for fun there?

JANET
You can sleep at night
On a downy white
French Provincial bed
And get up at two
Or whenever you
Leave a call.

RB
Here I take a nap
Any place I hap-
Pen to rest my head;
And what's better yet,
I don't have to get
Up at all!

JANET
They've got two swimming pools,
    one's a kid-
Ney shape, one's a liver.

RB
Swell, but I can outbid
Them—I got a river.

JANET
Cars they've got—you can have your
    choice
Of a Thunderbird or an old Rolls-
    Royce—

RB
What did you say?

JANET
I said:
A Thunderbird or an old Rolls-
    Royce—

RB
(Perking up)
Is it old? Really old?

JANET
So I'm told—
And the fittings are gold!

RB
Should've said so before!
Where's my bag? Hold the door!

Gonna see how the millionaire
Other half lives,
Take a room in the tower where
The giraffe lives!

LITTLE BOY
Why they got a giraffe?

RB
Always good for a laugh.

Goodbye,
All my friends!
Don't cry—
Don't take on
'Cause I'm gone—
I'll be back!

ALL
Goodbye!
Goodbye, old pal, and go ahead,
So we can all go back to bed!

RB
Goodbye to a houseboat on the
    river,
Hello to a boathouse in Palm Beach!
Gonna leave my houseboat on the
    river,
Gonna live a life as high as I can
    reach!

I'll smoke cigars
And put on shoes
And count the cars
That they never use.
She'll tell her life—
I'll write it out—
Just hope her life is too damn dull to
    write about!

So long to my neighbors on the
    river,
So long to their warm and friendly
    smile.
Gonna take a brand-new job
Learnin' how to be a snob,
Gonna be the same old slob
In style!
Tradin' my life
For the high life
For a while!

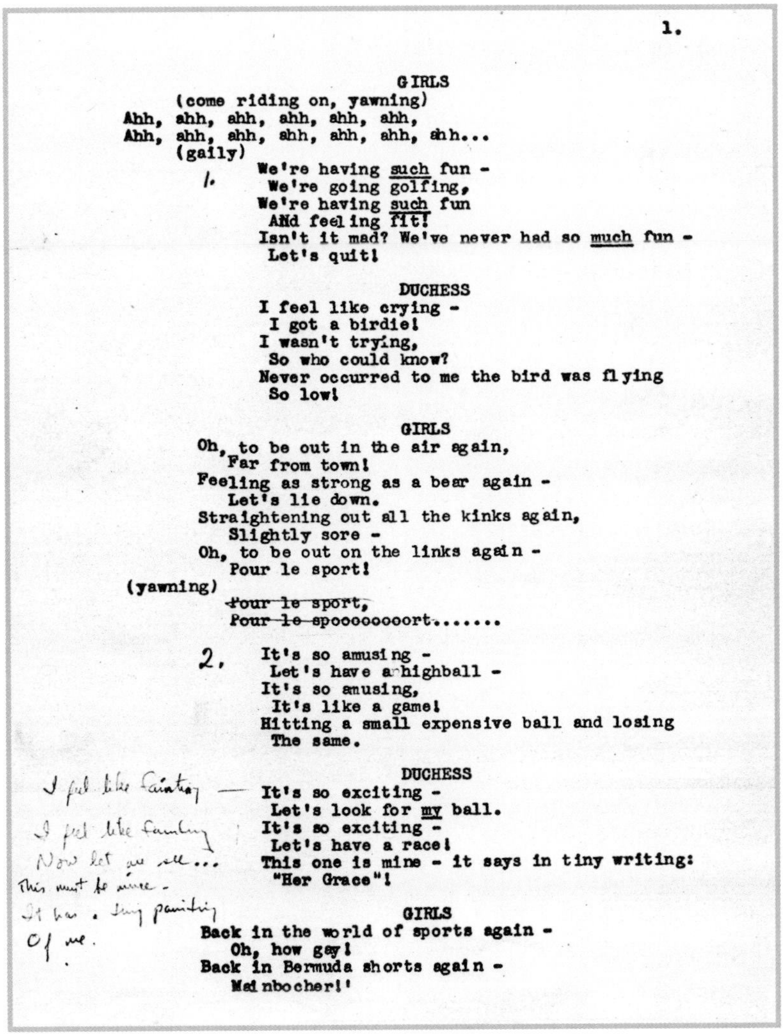

*The Duchess and three Palm Beach so-
ciety women are playing golf.*

Pour Le Sport

ALL

We're having *such* fun—
We're going golfing,
We're having *such* fun,
And feeling fit!
Isn't it mad? We've never had so
    much fun—
Let's quit!

DUCHESS

I feel like crying—
I got a birdie!
I wasn't trying,
So who could know?
Never occurred
To me the bird
Was flying
So low!

ALL

Oh, to be out in the air again,
Far from town!
Feeling as strong as a bear again—
Let's lie down.
Straightening out all the kinks again,
Slightly sore—
Ah, to be out on the links again,
Pour le sport!

It's so amusing—
Let's have a highball—
It's so amusing,
It's like a game!
Hitting a small
Expensive ball
And losing
The same.

DUCHESS

It's so exciting—
Let's look for *my* ball.
It's so exciting—
Let's have a race!
This one is mine—
It says in tiny
Writing:
"Her Grace"!

GIRLS

Back in the world of sports again—
Trés trés gay.
Back in Bermuda shorts again—
Mainbocher!
Nudging the ball with your toe
    again—
Who keeps score?

Ah, to be out with the pro again,
Pour le sport.

WOMAN #1

I want the niblick,
Whatever that is.
It's just a niblick,
But it's divine.
Even if it's
A simple little
Niblick,
It's mine.

WOMAN #2

I need the three-wood—
It's silver-plated.
I need the three-wood,
But which is which?

WOMAN #3

Harriet told
Me hers is gold . . .

```
                                                                1.
                        GIRLS
              (come riding on, yawning)
           Ahh, ahh, ahh, ahh, ahh, ahh,
           Ahh, ahh, ahh, ahh, ahh, ahh, ahh...
              (gaily)
            1.        We're having such fun -
                      We're going golfing,
                      We're having such fun
                      ANd feeling fit!
                Isn't it mad? We've never had so much fun -
                Let's quit!

                        DUCHESS
                I feel like crying -
                I got a birdie!
                I wasn't trying,
                So who could know?
                Never occurred to me the bird was flying
                So low!

                        GIRLS
           Oh, to be out in the air again,
                Far from town!
           Feeling as strong as a bear again -
                Let's lie down.
           Straightening out all the kinks again,
                Slightly sore -
           Oh, to be out on the links again -
                Pour le sport!
           (yawning)
                Pour le sport,
                Pour le spoooooooort.......

            2.        It's so amusing -
                      Let's have a highball -
                      It's so amusing,
                      It's like a game!
                      Hitting a small expensive ball and losing
                      The same.

                        DUCHESS
                      It's so exciting -
                      Let's look for my ball.
                      It's so exciting -
                      Let's have a race!
                      This one is mine - it says in tiny writing:
                      "Her Grace"!

                        GIRLS
                Back in the world of sports again -
                      Oh, how gay!
                Back in Bermuda shorts again -
                Mainbocher!'
```

Handwritten annotations in left margin:
I feel like fainting —
I feel like fainting
Now let me see...
This must be mine -
It has a long painting
Of me.

WOMAN #2
Well, she would—
The bitch.

ALL
Oh, to be out on the green again,
In the pink.
Getting deliciously lean again—
Where's my drink?
Fresh as a girl of eighteen again
And what's more,
We could keep at it yet for hours,
    getting thinner;
Nevertheless, we've *got* to dress for
    dinner.

DUCHESS
Look at the time!
Let's say that I'm
The winner—
Fore!

ALL
What'll we do tomorrow
Pour le sport?

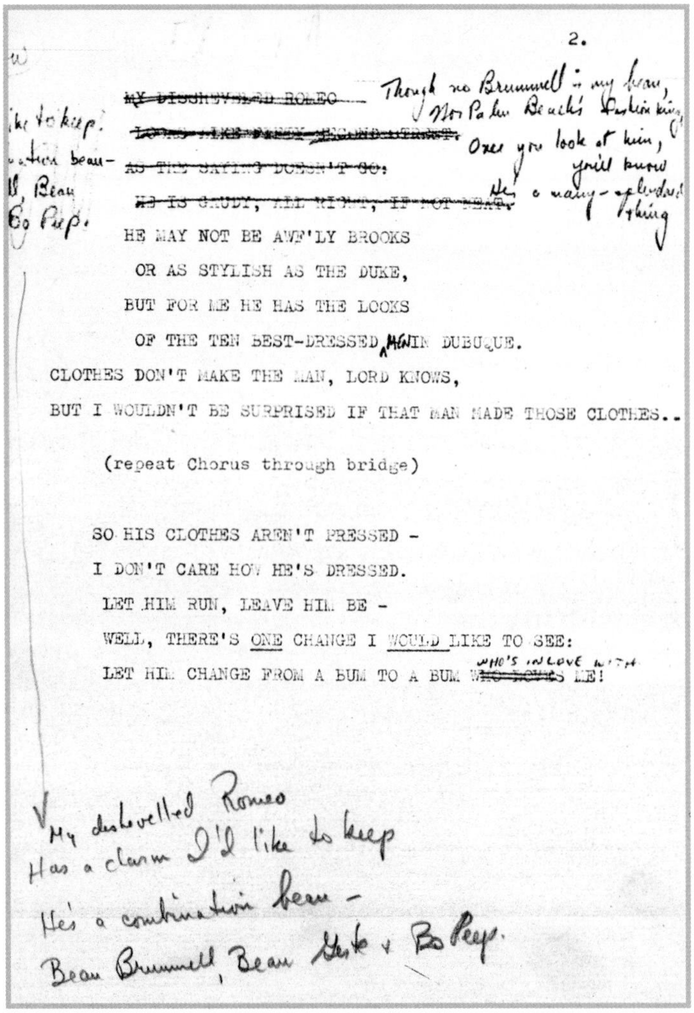

*Janet, falling in love with RB, assesses
the object of her affection.*

I Wouldn't Change a Thing

2.

~~MY DISHEVELLED ROMEO~~

~~AS THE SATIN DOESN'T GO:~~

~~HE IS GAUDY, ALL RIGHT, IF NOT NEAT:~~

HE MAY NOT BE AWF'LY BROOKS

OR AS STYLISH AS THE DUKE,

BUT FOR ME HE HAS THE LOOKS

OF THE TEN BEST-DRESSED MEN IN DUBUQUE.

CLOTHES DON'T MAKE THE MAN, LORD KNOWS,

BUT I WOULDN'T BE SURPRISED IF THAT MAN MADE THOSE CLOTHES..

(repeat Chorus through bridge)

SO HIS CLOTHES AREN'T PRESSED -

I DON'T CARE HOW HE'S DRESSED.

LET HIM RUN, LEAVE HIM BE -

WELL, THERE'S ONE CHANGE I WOULD LIKE TO SEE:

LET HIM CHANGE FROM A BUM TO A BUM WHO'S IN LOVE WITH ME!

[handwritten annotations:]
Though no Brummell is my beau,
Nor Palm Beach's fashion king,
Once you look at him, you'll know
He's a many-splendored thing

My dishevelled Romeo
Has a charm I'd like to keep
He's a combination beau—
Beau Brummell, Beau Geste & Bo Peep.

JANET
One man says he'll be my slave;
This man doesn't even shave.
One man dresses like a prince.
And this one appears in a hat that's
    squashed,
President-elect of the great
    unwashed.
I say to myself, *Chacun à son goût,*
But this one—
This one—
Oooooohhh!

*Her expression changes mid-sound
from irritation to delight.*

He's a bum, he's a clown,
With his socks hanging down,
With his hair taking wing—
And I wouldn't change a thing.

Yellow shirt, red cravat,
Orange coat, purple hat,
Slightly green college ring—
And I wouldn't change a thing.

He's a walking neon sign
In a state of disrepair.
But his suit suits me just fine,
'Cause I know he's inside it
    somewhere.

Does he look rather gay?
Let him stay just that way.
Does he look rather bright?
Well, I wouldn't change the sight,
'Cause I love the way he looked at
    me tonight!

Though no Brummell is my beau,
Nor Palm Beach's fashion king,
Once you look at him you'll know
He's a many-splendored thing.

He may not be awf'ly Brooks
Or as stylish as the Duke,
But for me he has the looks
Of the ten best-dressed men in
    Dubuque.

Clothes don't make the man, Lord
    knows,
But I wouldn't be surprised if that
    man made those clothes . . .

So his clothes aren't pressed—
I don't care how he's dressed.
Let him run, leave him be—
Well, there's *one* change I *would* like
    to see:
Let him change from a bum
To a bum who's in love with me!

The World of Jules Feiffer (1962)

Book by Jules Feiffer

The Notion

Ella, a chimney sweep, dreams of being a movie star. She is magically transformed into one, is romanced by Flip the Prince Charming, Hollywood's hunkiest leading man. But, like Cinderella, at the supreme moment she is transformed back into a chimney sweep, only to find true love with Flip, who is also a magically transformed impostor.

General Comments

In 1962 my friend Mike Nichols, famous as half of the comedy team Nichols and May, called me to say that he had been asked to direct an evening of work by Jules Feiffer at the Hunterdon Hills Playhouse in New Jersey. It was to consist of an unproduced one-act play called *Crawling Arnold*, a monologue called "George's Moon," an animated film called *Munro* and a one-act musical version of "Passionella," one of Jules's cartoon stories. Mike asked me if I would like to write the score for the whole melange. It was to be his first directorial stint apart from the twenty-minute pieces he'd done with Elaine May, and he was excited. I not only loved Nichols and May, I was a Feiffer fan and I accepted with enthusiasm, which Mike exuberantly dampened by telling me that the opening night was exactly two weeks away. The resultant experience was a movie cliché from the 1940s: adolescent hopefuls putting on a show in the barn (which the Hunterdon Hills Playhouse had once been, I believe), a perennial story line from as far back as Rodgers and Hart's *Babes in Arms* (1937) at least. Mike and Jules and I were hardly adolescents and we'd already real-ized some of our hopes, but it was still a barn, if a moderately elegant one. Nevertheless, with the unifying Feiffer tone of gentle satire (this was in 1962—it got less gentle later), in only two weeks Mike was able to shape the disparate genres into a satisfying evening, despite having to include a musical with a score of only one song. Ordinarily, I can write a song a week when I'm at top speed, and in those days I was at top speed, but for some reason all I could churn out was the following song and some under-scoring for "George's Moon." Still, it's a good example of that rare species, the humorous song, a song that's funny without asking for laughs, a genre of which Sheldon Harnick is the master.

Truly Content

ELLA
Though there's soot on my shoes,
There's a beautiful dream in my heart,
And a life in the flues
Is a life to lament.
If I only could be
A guhlamorous movie star,
Just a glamorous movie star,
I'd be truly content.

I am proud of my craft—
Every girl should be proud of her craft.
I'm at home in a shaft,
It's my natural bent.
But I'd give it all up
If I could be a movie star,
Just a glamorous movie star—

I'd be truly content.
They could double my rent
And I'd still be content.

Other people are movie stars,
Why can't I be a movie star
Like Fay Wray and George Brent?
I'd be truly content.

I needn't be a rich glamorous
Nor a really great glamorous,
Just a simple straight glamorous
Movie star!
It's the principle that counts.

If the world only knew
This is not the real Ella they see.
I may stand in the flue
But I yearn for the vent.
To the world I'm a sweep,
But inside I'm a movie star.
If I just were a movie star
I'd be truly content.

Automation comes to chimney sweeping. Ella can find no work.

Had my head in the flue,
Had a beautiful dream in my heart.
No more head in the flue,
Only flu in the head.
But I wouldn't complain
If I just were a movie star.
If I can't be a movie star,
I'd be better off dead.

That was all. The rest was underscoring. But we figured that if any producer wanted to further the evening professionally, I would have time to write more songs and flesh out the piece into a full-blown one-act musical. Eventually one producer did, but I was not involved.

In 1966, Stuart Ostrow decided to present three one-act musicals, to be directed by Mike, under the umbrella title *The Apple Tree,* with a score by Sheldon Harnick and Jerry Bock. The first, the title piece, was a version of Mark Twain's *The Diaries of Adam and Eve;* the second was an adaptation of Frank Stockton's story "The Lady or the Tiger?" (which, coincidentally enough, Mary Rodgers and I had tried to musicalize in the early 1950s for a proposed television show); the third was to be based on a Bruce Jay Friedman story. As rehearsals approached, Mike became less and less sanguine about the Friedman piece and suddenly thought of his fondness for "Passionella." He called me and asked for permission to go ahead with it; I replied, of course, that the piece belonged to Jules, not to me. Mike was relieved and set Sheldon and Jerry to writing it.

As rehearsals grew nearer, he called me again, this time to say that everything Sheldon and Jerry had written was brilliant except for the opening number, which simply didn't have the heft of "Truly Content." He had sent them back to the drawing board a number of times, but nothing they wrote satisfied him. Did I have any suggestions? Yes, I said. I told him that, as with so many things, the first time is the best and nothing can ever match the expectation of reaching it again. If Sheldon and Jerry had handed him *Porgy and Bess,* it wouldn't have been good enough (or appropriate, either). He finally settled for what they offered, and it was wonderful.

Hot Spot (1963)

Book by Jack Weinstock and Willie Gilbert

Music by Mary Rodgers

Lyrics by Martin Charnin

The Notion

Sally Hopwinder, a feckless American girl, decides to join the Peace Corps in order to give her life a sense of purpose. She is sent to the Far Eastern kingdom of D'hum. The show chronicles her adventures there.

General Comments

Hot Spot starred Judy Holliday, in what turned out to be her last show (she died two years later). It opened in Philadelphia and was immediately in a lot of trouble. Numerous play doctors were invited to attend, I among them. Not surprisingly, the trouble started with the opening number, so Mary Rodgers, Martin Charnin and I wrote a new one, intended to establish character, situation and star.

Sally, ever self-deprecating, is enumerating her faults to the Peace Corps recruiter, a starchy young man with a clipboard, all the while begging for a chance to join anyway.

Don't Laugh

SALLY
(Apologetically)
Maybe it's my name,
Maybe it's my face,
Maybe it's my—both.
All I know is:

(Cheerfully)

Show me a glass of water,
I'll show you a soggy dress.
Show me a tube of toothpaste,
I'll show you a mess.
Show me a fresh-laid sidewalk,
And guess where my footprints are?
Show me a fire hydrant,
I'll show you my car.

Show me the latest dance step,
I'll show you the latest fall.
Show me the train to Boston,
I'll show you St. Paul.
Show me a hundred lighters,
I'll show you the one that won't.
Show me a priceless vase—
No, don't!

Maybe it's my name,
Maybe it's my face,
Maybe it's my—both.
All I know is:

Show me a canceled party,
I'll show you the only guest.
Show me an open manhole,
And I'll do the rest.
Show me a broken window,
I'll show you a bat and ball.
Show me the boat to Europe,
I'll show you St. Paul.

Ask me to give directions,
I'll give you a vacant lot.
Show me a knot that's tangled,
I'll show you a tangled knot.

Maybe it's my name,
Maybe it's my face,
Maybe it's my
Self.

The music becomes wistful.

Maybe I can do—
Don't laugh—
Good.
Maybe I can do—
Don't laugh—
Well.

Maybe you could be—
Who knows?—
Proud.

All right, so laugh—
But not too loud.

If I can convince
(Don't laugh) me,
Why can't I convince
(Don't leave) you?

Give me half a chance,
Just half,
And then—
Don't laugh—
Maybe I could be
Proud of me,
Too.

The recruiter accepts her. Sally's spirits rise and the music becomes martial and triumphant.

Show me a barren hillside,
I'll show you a field of grass!
Show me an empty schoolroom,
I'll show you a class!

Show me an epidemic,
I'll show you a board of health!
Show me a starving people!
Show me an insurrection!
Show me a restless native!
Show me the way to get there!
Show me what's on your clipboard!

Sally is gonna do—
Don't laugh—
Good!

Sally is gonna do—
Don't laugh—
Well!
Everything's gonna be—
You watch—
Fine!
You hear a laugh?
That laugh is mine!

Everything will be done—
I hope—
Right!
Everything will be right—
Don't ask
How.

Look at it all fall into place—
Maybe it's my name,
Maybe it's my face!
Show me a job to do
And I'll show you
Now!

The starchy young man with the clip-board was an actor named George Furth, and it was here, during the Philadelphia tryout of *Hot Spot*, that we met and began a friendship which flowered and endured and along the way led to *Company* and *Merrily We Roll Along*, among other ventures. *Hot Spot*, unfortunately, neither flowered nor endured.

The Mad Show (1966)

Book by Larry Siegel and Stan Hart
Music by Mary Rodgers
Lyrics by Marshall Barer, Larry Siegel
   and Steven Vinaver

The Notion

Although officially credited with a "book," the show
was a revue, a collection of songs and sketches inspired by *Mad* magazine.

General Comment

Most of the lyrics were written by Marshall Barer,
Mary's collaborator on the score of *Once Upon a Mattress*, but early in rehearsals he had a sort of nervous
breakdown and disappeared into the wilds of Florida
while the show was still short a song or two. Steven
Vinaver, the other major lyricist of the piece, was too
busy directing the show to write anything, so Mary
called on me to help out, which I was happy to do.
Since much of the show dealt with topical satire and
spoofs, I thought of writing a parody of "The Girl
from Ipanema," the big hit of the day and the song
which made bossa nova popular in this country. It
was sung by Linda Lavin, hilariously.*

The Boy From

GIRL

Tall and slender,
Like an Apollo,
He goes walking by
And I have to follow
Him, the boy from Tacarembo la Tumbe del Fuego
   Santa Malipas Zacatecas la Junta del Sol y Cruz.[†]

When we meet,
I feel I'm on fire
And I'm breathless
Every time I inquire,
"How are things in Tacarembo la Tumbe del Fuego
   Santa Malipas Zacatecas la Junta del Sol y Cruz?"

Why, when I speak, does he vanish?
Why is he acting so clannish?
I wish I understood Spanish.
When I tell him I think he's the end,
He giggles a lot with his friend . . .

Tall and slender,
Moves like a dancer,
But I never seem to
Get any answer
From the boy from Tacarembo la Tumbe del Fuego
   Santa Malipas Zacatecas la Junta del Sol y Cruz.
I've got the blueth.

Why are his trousers vermilion?
(His trousers are vermilion.)
Why does he claim he's Castilian?
(He thays that he'th Cathtilian.)

---

* I wrote the lyric under the coy pseudonym of Esteban Ria Nido,
a part-translation and part-transliteration of my name.

[†] Pronounced with a Castilian lisp.

Why do his friends call him
    "Lillian"?
And I hear, at the end of the week
He's leaving to start a boutique.

Though I smile I'm
Only pretending.
'Cause I know today's the
Last I'll be spending
With the boy from Tacarembo la
    Tumbe del Fuego Santa Malipas
    Zacatecas la Junta del Sol y Cruz.

Tomorrow he sails.
He's moving to Wales
To live in
Llanfairpwllgwyngyllgogerychwrynd-
    robwllllandysiliogogogoch.

Och!

OTHER LYRICISTS: PART I

In *Finishing the Hat*, I offered some brief assessments of the more celebrated theater lyricists who are no longer alive, the ones generally perceived to be the giants in the field. Here are even briefer assessments of those whom, for various reasons, I didn't include.

First, the one-show wonders:

DuBose Heyward   Heyward's lyrics for *Porgy and Bess*, as exemplified by songs like "Summertime" and "My Man's Gone Now," remain for me the most genuinely poetic and deeply felt in the history of musical theater. They accomplish the rare feat of supplying their own music while demanding a composer to make them complete. Unfortunately, Heyward never wrote another musical, or even tried to. Smart man.

Richard Wilbur   Wilbur's lyrics for *Candide* are unequaled for their combination of wit and skill. Although he did collaborate in 1967 on a musical version of *The Madwoman of Chaillot* with Michel Legrand as composer and Maurice Valency as book writer, the project never traveled beyond the casting stage.

Then there are the visitors who wrote a number of musicals but had other jobs, which interfered with their output:

Howard Dietz   Dietz was chiefly a writer of revues, most of them in collaboration with Arthur Schwartz, whose musical suavity and grace Dietz's lyrics matched perfectly. For polish and skill, listen to the scores of *Inside U.S.A.* and *The Band Wagon*. My feeling about him, however, lies somewhere between admiration and enthusiasm, and the reason is that he lacks a distinctive personality; he's just a very, very good lyric writer—which is why, paradoxically, I didn't comment on him in the first book. He wrote a number of standards such as "Dancing in the Dark" and "By Myself" (a Schwartz tune I wish I'd written), as well as some enviably inventive patter songs, my favorite being "Rhode Island Is Famous for You."

Dietz divided his time between the theater and running the publicity department of MGM. His major contribution to popular culture may well have been his invention of Leo the Lion, the MGM logo, but he also wrote his most brilliant lyric—"That's Entertainment," which contains one of the best couplets ever—for that studio. In it the singer describes *Hamlet* as a play "Where a ghost and a prince meet / And everyone ends as mincemeat." Shakespeare should have been so succinct.

P. G. Wodehouse   Wodehouse's other jobs may have interfered with his theater output, but they certainly didn't interfere with his output—in fact, they *were* his output. He was a discouragingly prolific novelist, playwright, librettist and lyricist. He is also many people's favorite comic writer, though not mine—I get impatient with the archness of his style, the tweeness of his characters and the flimsiness of his plots. It's no coincidence that one commentator has saluted his lyrics as "the wittiest since the best of W. S. Gilbert." Given my lack of enthusiasm for Gilbert, I can't disagree.

However, Wodehouse and Jerome Kern and their librettist Guy Bolton were responsible for the "Princess" shows of 1915–18, which were important in the development of musical theater. The shows were named after the 299-seat Princess Theatre, where they were performed. They depended on intimacy and character, in opposition to the lavish revue-spectacles and operettas which dominated Broadway at the time. They were early attempts to utilize songs in the service of people and story, something more "serious" forms like opera and operetta had been doing for centuries, but as titles like *Very Good Eddie* and *Oh, Lady! Lady!* indicate, the range of their attempts was limited. Still, these musicals were the harbingers of things to come. Kern's scores were what elevated them, but because they were written so quickly (six in three years), even his work is variable, most of it little more than efficient. It was these Princess shows, however, that spurred Kern's interest in character and plot and led, with the not inconsiderable aid of Oscar Hammerstein II, to works like *Show Boat*.* As for Wodehouse, the rest of his life in lyrics was unremarkable.

---

* Coincidentally enough, although Hammerstein wrote all the other lyrics in *Show Boat*, the lyric to "Bill" had been written by Wodehouse earlier as a separate song, and Hammerstein wanted to use it, with revisions, in the show. He retained the best, and most famous phrase in it: "I love him because he's—I don't know / Because he's just my Bill." It's certainly the best lyric fragment Wodehouse ever wrote.

Illya Darling (1968)

Book by Jules Dassin (based on the film
　　Never on Sunday)
Music by Manos Hadjidakis
Lyrics by Joe Darion

The Notion

The story concerns the daily life of Illya, a prostitute in the Greek port of Piraeus, and her relationship with Homer Thrace, an American scholar who tries to improve her education and social status.

General Comments

The subtlety and sophistication of *Illya Darling* can best be gauged by the name of its hero: Homer Thrace. The show was an attempt to cash in on the enormous success of *Never on Sunday* and its star, Melina Mercouri, who became something of a sensation after its release. The musical theme of the film, by Manos Hadjidakis, was also hugely popular, and so once she was hired as the star and he was hired to write the score, the project seemed like a shoo-in, especially as it was to be written and directed by Jules Dassin, the man who had written and directed the movie, co-starred in it as the scholar and conveniently enough was Ms. Mercouri's husband. As with almost all shoo-ins, the piece was in terrible trouble from its first preview in Philadelphia. From there it traveled to Toronto and then to Detroit, still in trouble. It was at this point that I got a call from the producer, a man with the flavorful name of Kermit Bloomgarden, who'd given the world successes like *The Music Man* and disasters like *Anyone Can Whistle,* but who liked

my songs anyway and asked me to come out of town and help with the score. I eagerly agreed, as I was still young enough to think that being called in to doctor a show was about as glamorous and flattering a job as the theater could provide: first-class airfare, luxury hotel room, late-night conferences with famous people—who could ask for anything more? A rhetorical question, whose answer is obvious. I did some touch-ups on a couple of Darion's lyrics, and supplied these in addition:

Opening Number

A shipyard. Men are working in the hot sun. Illya shows up for her daily swim in the sea, and the men want to join her as they usually do, but their supervisor, the Captain, tells them they'll be fired if they so much as make a move. Illya protests to him that she doesn't want to swim alone.

ILLYA
Is very hot,
For me is hot,
And I think hot is not so good to be.
The sea is cool,
Is nice and cool,
For being cool, there's nothing like the sea.

And when I'm swimming in the sea,
Can it be wrong to wish
To meet a lot of friends and not a lot of fish?
It would be nice to have some pretty men for company,
But if it cannot be, it cannot be.

(Looking them over)

Well, some are men . . .

MAN

Well, we are men.

ILLYA

And some are mice . . .

MAN

That is not nice.

ILLYA

And mice, of course, are frightened
of the waves . . .

CAPTAIN

Stay where you are.

ILLYA

But now I see—

CAPTAIN

Nobody move!

ILLYA

Is clear to me—

CAPTAIN

Nobody move!!

ILLYA

Some men are free, and other men
are slaves!

*The men surge forward. The Captain
appeals to Illya.*

CAPTAIN

Illya, Greece is a poor country. We
have very few industries; ship-
building is one of them. You're
going to destroy it single-handed.
Go swim somewhere else!

ILLYA

Capitagno, you are right. I am very
selfish. Three things I do not like to
do alone: to eat alone, to sleep
alone and to swim alone. But you
are right; I will never disturb your
work again.

*She makes elaborate preparations to go
in the water.*

Yorgo   Is very hot
Illya: You think is hot?

Yorgo +
 Illya   Is stinking hot
             For me is not.
             Perhaps we swim a little bit w/you.   for you we swim come for just
                                                    Perhaps we swim w/ you a little while.
             The sea is cool   Captain:... Now just a minute ...
             It might be rough
             You think is cool?
             Is look so cool
             Is cool enough

             A little swim — What harm could it to do?

             Is it a crime to take a minute ... in the ocean waves
             You may to think we're slaves— That's what she called us,—
             And if she never comes again. Captains dear (Then build the boat
                       doesn't come tomorrow   yourself...
             You heard her call us slaves — we are not slaves.   We won't
                                                                  be here!

             Then you can take your boat   What you can do with it.

             The boat will still be here tomorrow but if Illya's not
             If Illya says she won't be here tomorrow
             She said she'll never come again, Captains dear
             If Illya doesn't come tomorrow you can take your boat
                                  we won't be here

             But Illya called us slaves and she was right!

This is the last time I come here to
swim—the very last time.

*The men look at her unhappily, espe-
cially their leader, Yorgo. To placate the
Captain, she urges them to work.*

YORGO

Is very hot . . .

ILLYA

Is not too hot.

YORGO, TWO MEN

Is stinking hot!

ILLYA

For me is not.

YORGO, FOUR MEN

Perhaps we swim a little bit with
you.

ILLYA

When work is through.

MAN

The sea is cool . . .

ILLYA

You think is cool?

MAN

It look so cool . . .

ILLYA

Could be is cool.

MAN

A little swim, what damage could
it do?

MEN

Hey, Capitagno, you are rotten,
stinky man today,
You tell our darling girl that she
must stay away.
But if she doesn't come tomorrow,
Capitagno, dear,
You'll build the boats yourself, we
won't be here!

(Roaring)

For we are Greeks!

ILLYA

Ach, they are Greeks!

MEN

And we are men!

ILLYA

Ach, they are men!

MEN

We are not slaves!
We're men and we are free!

ILLYA

What can I do?

MEN

When Illya swims—

ILLYA

I love them all!

MEN

Piraeus swims!

ILLYA

I love you all!

MEN

So now we go with Illya in the sea!
The sea! The sea!
The sea! The sea!

They all go, undressing, pushing, whooping and triumphantly carrying Illya with them.

I hasten to add that the circumstances of this song, as well as the language, were wished on me. But it worked surprisingly well, and the night it went into the show, I trundled backstage to Ms. Mercouri's dressing room after the performance and she embraced me fervently, proclaiming with the excited seductive verve that had made her famous that she loved the song. I was so pleased that I forgot she was a Star, which was a mistake that taught me a lot. More below.

306 · OTHER MUSICALS

Illya is torn between the possibility of a rise in social stature and the pull of her roots.

Piraeus, My Love

ILLYA

Yes, I hear you there, Piraeus.
Please—it is not fair, Piraeus.
You may sing, but me—I lie awake.
Every sound it makes my heart to
    break.

Do not sing and play, Piraeus!
Do not laugh so gay, Piraeus!
Cry for me, is manly thing to do,
I am man enough to cry for you.

It is cruel when you know how
    much I miss you.
You are coward not to go and let
    me be.
But you come to me with stars
And with little soft guitars
And you tiptoe near my door to
    drive me mad.
Come and take me like a man,
Like a lover if you can,
Or you bloody go to hell and I am
    glad.

Yes, I know you cry, Piraeus.
Not as much as I, Piraeus.
Let me be or tell me what to do.
You're my love and all my loves
    are you.

Yes, I hear your tune, Piraeus.
You forget too soon, Piraeus.
You forget, but I am always true.
You're my love and all my loves
    are you.

This song was a thorough rewrite of one Darion had written, and the night it went into the show, I again went backstage to Ms. Mercouri's dressing room after the performance and she again embraced me fervently, with the same proclamation she had made about the opening number. I then returned to New York, with dim hopes about the show's success, but glowing from Dassin's approval and Melina's sexy enthusiasm. When the show started previewing in New York, I went backstage a couple of times again to tell her, as my job demanded, how smashing her performance was. On opening night, then, you may imagine my subdued astonishment on finding that the opening number no longer existed and that she had reverted to the original "Piraeus, My Love." When I asked Dassin why he had dropped my contributions, he told me to ask Melina, and when I did, she replied that since I didn't care enough to come backstage after every performance, there seemed no reason to sing the songs. This is a true story.

I was shocked (in the "startled" sense of the word) but more relieved than disappointed. Ethnic writing is simply not what I'm good at, even when it's supposed to be authentic. As I said in *Finishing the Hat*, I could never have written *Oklahoma!* with its excursions into supposedly authentic Western dialect, and these cute attempts at pidgin Greek were embarrassing. I include them here for completist purposes only.

Illya Darling is an apt illustration of a common event on Broadway: people who are proficient in one profession (in this case the movies, but equally true of those in pop music) and have enough hidden condescension toward stage musicals that they think they can easily swoop in, make a pile of money and fly back to what they do best. This was codified for me during a moment in one of the show's New York previews. A young lover of Illya's was supposed to climb ebulliently through the window of her apartment for a night of love, but at this particular performance his foot caught on the windowsill and not only did he fall with a crash to the floor, so did the bookcase next to the window, spilling books all over the stage. The audience enjoyed it heartily, as audiences always do when there is a comic gaffe in an otherwise dull evening. Mr. Dassin therefore decided to keep it in the show, and from then on at every performance the young man would catch his foot on the sill, the bookcase would fall down and the audience would have a wonderful time for thirty seconds. As Sweeney Todd says, "These are desperate times, Mrs. Lovett, and desperate measures are called for."

These are the underwriters, by which I mean lyricists who, if I had my way, would have written as much for the stage as they did for movies and nightclubs and pop:

Leo Robin Robin's underappreciated lyrics to Jule Styne's music for *Gentlemen Prefer Blondes* include a gorgeously rhymed comedy song ("Diamonds Are a Girl's Best Friend") as well as a chorus number called "Sunshine," which employs a rhyme scheme where each line ends in a three-syllable rhyme that consists of two identities followed by a masculine rhyme (". . . hum a song / . . . hum along") instead of the universal opposite, a masculine rhyme followed by two identities (come along/hum along). It's an anodyne lyric but it flows, and I don't remember ever seeing a song utilizing that technique anywhere else.

Robin had only one other notable Broadway show, *Hit the Deck,* with music by Vincent Youmans. Most of his songs were written for the movies with the composer Ralph Rainger and some of those lyrics, like "Thanks for the Memory," have the casual, wry poignancy of the best of Dorothy Fields, than which there is no better.

Johnny Mercer Many of Johnny Mercer's lyric phrases are now lodged in the American consciousness: "Blues in the Night," "Ac-cent-tchu-ate the Positive," "That Old Black Magic," to pick three out of dozens—but they were written for movies. His few forays into the theater didn't leave us any of those memorable phrases, apart from "Jeepers Creepers," a song he contributed to a two-week show called *Swingin' the Dream.* St. Louis Woman, on the other hand—a musical he wrote with Harold Arlen, his most frequent, and best, collaborator—contains a trove of first-rate lyrics in his distinctive poetic Southern bad-boy style. Mercer came from Savannah and, happily, never lost touch with the

linguistic roots which gave him his individuality. Songs like "I Wonder What Became of Me" and "Any Place I Hang My Hat Is Home" have the flavor of no no other Broadway lyricist. The songs for *Top Banana,* however, a show for which he wrote both music and lyrics, could have been composed by any of the decently skilled hacks of the time. It was a fast, empty Broadway vehicle for a star comic (Phil Silvers) and would have been better served by a songwriter without personality, something Mercer simply couldn't be.

John La Touche La Touche contributed a number of lyrics to *Candide,* but died before the show was produced (1956). I had the pleasure of making additions to some of them in the "Auto-da-fé" sequence for Hal Prince's revival in 1974. I was also the beneficiary of the unfinished first section of a long-since discarded lyric La Touche had written for Cunegonde and Candide to sing, which consisted of eight words set to a Bernstein tune you may recognize from the general outline "One / Hand, / One / Heart, / Your / Hand / My / Heart . . ." Lenny kidnapped both the lyric idea and the tune for *West Side Story* but granted me a couple of extra notes to play around with.

La Touche, like Mercer, had a poetic sensibility often identified with the South, as was apparent in *Cabin in the Sky,* his most successful show. He had neither the earthiness nor the idiosyncratic inventiveness of Mercer, but he had a large vision of what musical theater could be. He wrote acceptably experimental shows like *Beggar's Holiday,* an updated treatment of *The Beggar's Opera,* with a score by Duke Ellington; *Ballet Ballads,* a combination ballet-musical; and *The Golden Apple,* a through-sung, high-minded version of stories from Homer which, like *Ballet Ballads,* featured music by the classical composer Jerome Moross.

He also wrote the lyrics for *Banjo Eyes,* a free-wheeling adaptation of

Three Men on a Horse, one of the most popular farces of the 1930s. The title referred both to a race horse that figured in the plot and to the nickname of the show's star, Eddie Cantor, a popular comic best known for rolling his eyes and singing in a piercing nasal tenor while bouncing up and down and clapping his hands. He was an acquaintance of my family, and when my father took me at the age of eleven to see the show, Cantor surprised both of us by urging his stage wife, June Clyde, to get dressed quickly because "We're going to the Sondheims' for dinner." It remains one of the most thrilling moments in my theater-going experience, right up there with Jessica Tandy yelling "Fire!" in *A Streetcar Named Desire* and Patty Duke spluttering "Wa–! Wa!"under the pump at the climax of *The Miracle Worker.*

Hugh Martin Hugh Martin wrote both music and lyrics, mainly in partnership with Ralph Blane, who also wrote both. The team composed songs mostly for the movies, notably the score for *Meet Me in St. Louis* (most of whose songs were written by Martin alone), but their one Broadway venture, *Best Foot Forward,* was enormously successful. Martin's first solo score was for *Look, Ma, I'm Dancin'!,* a show about a ballet troupe, which contained some neat lyrical ideas, a particular example being a lament by a dancer in the corps de ballet that "I'm the first girl / In the second row / In the third scene /Of the fourth number/In fifth position / At ten o'clock on the nose." He performed a similar stunt in his second solo show, *Make a Wish,* in a song called "Suits Me Fine." In that one, each line of the verse features a pair of opposing adjectives: for example, "Got my bringin' up down in Arizona / Moved when I was old to New Mexico . . ." Another song from that score, "I Wanna Be Good 'n' Bad," culminates in a spectacular extended climax, consisting of a pileup of six lines, each ending with

a rhyme for "ball," the last word of the lyric, and all in a sequence of ascending musical phrases. Waiting for the song to end is a kind of joyful coitus interruptus.

Hugh Martin's music, lyrics and vocal arrangements (the profession which kept him in demand both in movies and the theater), are the quintessence of 1940s musical comedy: they define what is meant by "show tunes" or "pizzazz." With and without Blane, he is responsible for, among others, "Buckle Down, Winsocki," "The Trolley Song," "The Boy Next Door," "Gotta Dance" . . . Enough said.

Meredith Willson   Of the three musicals he wrote, *The Music Man* is the only one that interests me, but the interest is intense. "Rock Island," the unique opening number, is surely one of the most startling and galvanic openings ever devised. It is performed in a railway car by a group of 1930s salesmen, whose rhythmic chatter mimics the sound of the train they're on while at the same time setting up the circumstances of the play. For the first half of the number, there is no orchestral accompaniment whatever, only the chug, whoosh and whistle of the train along with the conversation. The combination becomes verbal music—it is in fact the forerunner of rap. The orchestra doesn't enter until the mention of Harold Hill, the absent central character, which in effect tells the audience to pay attention to the information of the words rather than just their sound.

The number echoed Oscar's lesson, distilled and intensified, about the first song in a musical. Once you heard "Rock Island," you could have sat through the telephone book and had a good time. Luckily, you didn't have to.

There are secondary explosions of Willson's originality in "Piano Lesson" and "Pick-a-Little, Talk-a-Little," and of course the broad spread of it in "Trouble," but the splendor is in Rock Island, not River City. *The Music Man* was an enormous success, some of which has been attributed to its American family values, some to the charm of its star Robert Preston, some to the presence of children and Americana, but I attribute it to its opening number.

Carolyn Leigh   Carolyn Leigh was the most brilliant technician of them all with the possible exception of Cole Porter, whose tone she adopted, but with more irony and less camp—a little touch of Dorothy Fields in the night. (Contrast Leigh's "You Fascinate Me So" with Porter's "All of You," both of which deal with physical attraction.) This is not coincidental; the lyrics of both Leigh and Fields were proto-feminist, reflections, perhaps, of the fact that they were virtually the only two prominent female practitioners in what was a man's profession at the time (by which I mean writing theater lyrics—a significant number of pop lyrics were written by women). Most of Leigh's best, and best-known, songs were written with Cy Coleman, but for cabaret

rather than for the theater, and with reason—she was not a stage writer. That was something else she shared with Dorothy Fields: her sharpest songs were self-contained commentaries, stories of and for the moment (her own). Character interested her, but only as aspects of herself. Except for gender pronouns, many of her theater songs could be switched among the show's characters with little disruption.

Of the three musicals she wrote (one of which, *Peter Pan,* was only partially written by her and her composer Moose Charlap), only *Little Me* gives us some of the pleasures of her prowess. Her signature sexiness in "I've Got Your Number," the rhyming and non-rhyming surprises of "To Be a Performer" and the language of "The Other Side of the Tracks" ("Gonna sit and fan / On my fat divan / While the butler buttles the tea") are her stamp and hers alone. Unique among her stage pieces, *Little Me* somehow suited her, so much in fact that she actually wrote for it something I would never have expected from her: a (seemingly) simple sentimental song called "Real Live Girl" that Irving Berlin might have envied. Nevertheless, even the lyrics of *Little Me* can't compare with the likes of "When in Rome," "The Rules of the Road," "The Best Is Yet to Come," and at least a dozen others that she and Coleman have given us. But then who else combines the styles and technique of Cole Porter and Dorothy Fields and, on occasion, Irving Berlin?

A Pray by Blecht (1968)

Book by John Guare (based on The Exception
and the Rule *by Bertolt Brecht)*
Music by Leonard Bernstein

The Notion

A wealthy Merchant, accompanied by a Guide and a
Coolie (an Oriental porter), tries to cross a (mythical)
desert to beat his competitors in obtaining an oil concession in the (mythical) city of Urga. In his feverish
desire to get there first, he refuses to let them rest,
browbeating the Guide and beating the Coolie. As he
grows increasingly afraid of the desert on the journey,
he becomes convinced that they are out to cheat him
or, worse, kill him. Eventually, he fires the Guide, the
result being that he and the Coolie become lost.
When the water supplies run low, the Merchant mistakenly shoots the Coolie, thinking he is being at-
tacked when in fact he is being offered some water
which the Coolie still has left in his bottle. He is
brought to trial and ultimately acquitted. The Judge
concludes that the Merchant had every right to fear
a potential threat from the Coolie, and therefore was
justified in shooting him in self-defense regardless of
whether there was an actual threat or the Merchant
merely felt threatened.

General Comments

In 1967, Jerome Robbins asked me to write book,
music and lyrics for an adaptation of Brecht's
play, *The Measures Taken,* one of the playwright's
Lehrstücke, or "Learning," plays, short pieces he wrote

around 1929–30. The objective of *Lehrstücke* was that
they be taken on tour and performed in schools or in
factories by students and workers as a means of edu-
cating the masses about socialist politics. The plot in
The Measures Taken, such as it is, concerns the trial
of three Communists on a secret mission to organize
workers in China, who are inadvertently betrayed by
a young comrade and are forced to shoot him, with
his permission, in order to save the cause. I told Jerry
that there wasn't enough action in the piece to justify
a variety of songs, but that wasn't why I didn't want
to adapt it; the real reason was my Brechtophobia.

I had disliked the plays of Brecht ever since,
shortly after *West Side Story,* I had been asked by Carmen Capalbo, the producer of the Brecht-Weill *The
Threepenny Opera,* off-Broadway's first giant hit, to
adapt the lyrics for a subsequent Brecht-Weill musical, *Mahagonny.* The only work of Brecht's I had ever
seen had been that very production, translated by
Marc Blitzstein. I had enjoyed it, mostly because of
Kurt Weill's spiky and wholly original music, but *Mahagonny* struck me as ham-handed satirical comment,
and the more I read Brecht's plays in the interest of
research, the less I liked them. I found the stagecraft
intriguing, and sometimes the stories as well, but the
cartoonish characters and polemic dialogue were, for
me, insufferably simplistic. They had to be that way,
of course, for Brecht's purposes, but I was simply not
one of his targeted audience and there was just too
much *Lehr* in each *stück* to hold my attention.* I
knew Weill's work better, from his American musicals,

---

* I came close to changing my mind about Brecht only once, when
I was witness to Simon McBurney's astounding production of *The
Caucasian Chalk Circle* in London in 1997, but subsequently I saw
another production and changed my mind right back.

but had never been very fond of it, so *Mahagonny* died aborning.

When Jerry first told me he had a project he wanted us to work on together, I was thrilled and flattered. I admired nobody in the theater as much as Jerry, and I would have given anything to work with him again. Difficult as he was, he was the only genius I had ever associated with, and I knew that anything I would write for him would sharpen my skills and expand my knowledge and eventuate in something startlingly theatrical. I hoped that turning him down on *The Measures Taken* might lead him to come up with another project for us to collaborate on, and indeed it did. Without a moment's hesitation, he said, "Look at the next play in the book." He had given me a paperback of four Brecht *Lehrstücke* and the next one in the book was, as you probably have guessed, *The Exception and the Rule*. My spirits sank, but I read the play and could at least smell how it might be musicalized. I told him I would try. I made a stab at two possible songs, but my heart wasn't in them, so I regretfully said no again and suggested that he get Lenny, who was a Brecht admirer, to write not only the music but the lyrics. I had liked his lyrics for his short opera *Trouble in Tahiti,* and to me they had the right flavor for what Jerry wanted, as evidenced in the recurrent "Little White House" trio. For whatever reason, however, Jerry chose to recruit Lenny for the music only, and Jerry Leiber (of the pop-rock team of Leiber and Stoller) for the lyrics.

A number of months went by and I heard nothing further about the project until Jerry and Lenny drew me aside at a Christmas party and said they had doubts about the way the score was turning out, and would I listen to it and give an opinion? Ordinarily, I would never agree to do such a thing, something that might lead to a writer losing a job, but I felt I owed them a lot and agreed. I was prepared to be uncomfortable, criticizing another lyricist's work to his collaborators, but to my happy surprise the songs were terrific—Brechtian without the humorless sarcasm, unobtrusive, impeccably written and always interesting. Robbins and Bernstein had figured they would get me back into the fold the minute I told them (as they'd anticipated) that I thought they needed a new lyricist, so when I burbled to them about how good I thought the score was, they refused to believe me. Nevertheless, because of their reluctance the project came to a halt, until the intended producer of the piece, Stuart Ostrow, took me to lunch a month later and told me that Jerry had asked John Guare to write the book for the show and John had agreed. John was one of the leading playwrights of the 1960s generation as well as a friend of mine, and to my dismay he had come up with what I thought was a wonderful idea for *The Exception and the Rule*. The theater would be a television studio and the play presented as a television play, complete with cameras, floor managers, control booth and all the other noisy trappings. The star of the TV play (intended to be Zero Mostel) would be white and the Guide and the Coolie black, and the growing paranoia of the star that the blacks were getting all the attention and undermining him would parallel the Merchant's paranoia. This notion appealed to me not just because of the setting but because the Brecht play would be chopped up into scenes that would be interrupted by the conflicts among the cast in the studio and thus not be so relentlessly Brechtian. Blinded by the possibilities, I agreed to work on the show. Lenny and I wrote eight songs and then stopped. Why? All will be revealed—well, almost all.

These are the songs for the play within the play, without the interruptory scenes in the TV studio.

SCENE 1—THE DESERT

The Race Through the Desert

MERCHANT
(To the Guide and the Coolie)

There goes our head start!
You're ruining me!
Pick it up! Pick it up!

Move! Quick! Move! Quick! Mush!
Quick! Rest! Quick! Eat!
Quick! Stop! Quick! Drink!
Pee! Faster!

(To the audience)

My name is—wait, excuse me—
My name is Charlie Harmon.*
I haven't time to chat,

(Pointing to a map)

'Cause here is where I've come from,
And here is where I'm at,
And I have to get to there in seven
days flat!

(To the Guide and the Coolie)

Pigs!
Don't you know time is money, you
dogs!
Do you know what it's costing me?
You!
You're a guide and I hired you cheap,
I admit,
But your job is to drive this
ridiculous coolie,
Not go for a stroll on my money,
But you wouldn't care if I'm ruined
or not.
Serves me right, saving money
on you!

Now let me see, where was I?
Oh yes, the road to Urga,
The road to getting rich.

---

* This name was Lenny's suggestion: Charlie Harmon was his music librarian.

I'm way ahead of schedule,
But there's one little hitch:
So is every other greedy son-of-a
bitch!

I'm dreaming
Oil, oil, mountains of oil!
Slimy-slick,
Gusher-thick,
Grab-it-quick
Oil!
It's streaming
Oil, oil, fountains of oil!
No, but wait, there's something
funny
Going on on the side:
There's a stranger handing money
To my coolie and guide!
Yes, he's bribing them,
He's after them to slow up our
speed!
What's that mortifying laughter?
Who's that group in the lead?
They'll reach Urga in a minute
And the race will be done!
Oh, my God, they're gonna win it!
It's over!
They're—
Run! Run! Run! Run!

*(He urges the Guide and the
Coolie onward)*

What do I see? Look!
Over that sand dune? Hoo-hoo!
Isn't that girls?

Yeah, girls! Girls!
See them in the distance on that hill
just ahead!
Run!
Every one is stripped
And each equipped
With a bed!
Run!

What's that hissing sound to the
rear?
Snakes!
Dozens of them, slithering near!
Snakes!
Don't look 'round, they're practically
here!
Run!!

(Sees another merchant, also racing)

Oops!

SECOND MERCHANT
(To the audience)

My name is Leonard Bernstein.
I haven't time to chat,

(Unrolling an identical map)

'Cause here is where I've come from,
And here is where I'm at,
And I have to get to there in seven
days flat!

MERCHANT

So much for that!

Oh, Lord above me,
Don't be a swine.
Rightfully,
Victory
Ought to be
Mine!
And if you love me,
Give me a sign!

(To the Guide)

Look, let's face it, we're in trouble,
So I'm sorry I cursed.
Look, suppose I pay you double
If you get me there first.
Look, what is this guy, your cousin,
You can't give him a smack?
Look, they come a dime a dozen
And they never hit back!
Look, it's you I'm gonna fire
If he doesn't improve!
I know lots of guides for hire,
Now get him to move!
Beat him! Hit him!

*(To the audience, referring to the other
merchants)*

I'm cleverer than they are,
In case you've any doubt.
Tonight, while they are sleeping,
Ha ha, we're moving out,
And I haven't got a thing to worry
about!

SCENE 2—HAN

*He gets the Guide to beat the Coolie be-
cause he's too tired to do it himself. He
begins to suspect that the Guide is de-*

liberately slowing him down and refuses to let either the Guide or the Coolie rest.

They stop at a way station called Han, where the Merchant hopes to get police protection for his trip across the desert. He sees two policemen and greets them warmly.

Han

POLICEMAN 1
Good morning.

MERCHANT
Ah, Officer!

He reaches in his pocket.

POLICEMAN 2
Good evening.

MERCHANT
You too, Sergeant!

He hands money to the first policeman, who takes it, then offers it to the second policeman, but the first one takes that, too.

POLICEMAN 1
Thank you.
Anything that we can do?

POLICEMAN 2
(Referring to the Guide and Coolie)
Are these characters with you?

POLICEMAN 1
Did you have a pleasant trip?

POLICEMAN 2
Did they give you any lip?

MERCHANT
Yes. No. That is—
Now that we're safely in Urga . . .

POLICEMAN 2
Urga? Man!

POLICEMAN 1
This is Han,
You're in Han!
Here's a tinted photograph of—

POLICEMAN 2
(Overlapping)
Greetings on behalf of—

BOTH
Han.
You're in Han,
You're in sandy little dirty—

POLICEMAN 1
Population thirty—

BOTH
Han!

POLICEMAN 2
Never any trouble—

POLICEMAN 1
Uninhabitable—

BOTH
Han,
Patrolled Han,
In old Han—

POLICEMAN 2
Where things are quiet—

POLICEMAN 1
Ever since the riot—

BOTH
Han,
Serene Han,
Clean Han,
I mean Han.

POLICEMAN 1
Thirty natives and all so quiet—

POLICEMAN 2
Thirty-seven before the riot.

BOTH
Han!

POLICEMAN 1
Goodbye now.

MERCHANT
What's that?

POLICEMAN 2
Good luck, sir.

POLICEMAN 1
May we hope you had a pleasant
stay?

POLICEMAN 2
May we be the last to say—

MERCHANT
You mean you're not coming with
me?

POLICEMAN 1
—That we wish you fortune
On your way.

POLICEMAN 2
Come again another day.

MERCHANT
But I thought you were to be my
escort across—!

POLICEMAN 2
Escort?
Shit—

POLICEMAN 1
This is it:
The last link,

The last drink
Of orange soda—

POLICEMAN 2
And the last pagoda—

BOTH
Han,
The last shave,
The last haven
In the desert—

POLICEMAN 1
Everybody says it . . .

BOTH
Han!

POLICEMAN 2
Out there in the sand, it's—

POLICEMAN 1
Bubbling with bandits—

BOTH
Han,

POLICEMAN 1
The last gasp,
The last asp—

POLICEMAN 2
(Overlapping)
Aspirin supplier.

POLICEMAN 1
Final chance to buy a—

BOTH
Fan.
The last shop,
The last stop,
The last cop.
Goom-bye!

POLICEMAN 2
So sorry—

BOTH
Must fly.

The trick and false rhymes (trou-ble/uninhabitable; desert/says it; sup-plier/buy a) may be a bit cute, but they constituted my desperate attempt to insert some playfulness into Brecht's earnest sarcasm.

SCENE 3—A REST STOP

The Coolie falls asleep, exhausted. The Merchant tries to turn the Guide against him, saying that the Coolie is looking for revenge for the Guide's beatings of him. He goes into the rest-room. The Guide wakes the Coolie and offers him a cigarette; they stretch out and smoke. The Guide takes the oppor-tunity to educate the Coolie on the ways of the ruling class.

Little Secret

GUIDE
They got a little secret,
The one that makes the wheels go.
They keep it in a castle
And wait for it to stir.
And when it starts to murmur,
They come around to hear it.
And we could live forever,
But we ain't gettin' near it,
No, sir!

It tells 'em how to set up the rules,
It tells 'em what we're gonna do now,
It tells 'em what decisions to make,
And how
And why
And when.

And every other Tuesday
They take it out and sweep it.
They guard it with an army,
And brother, they can keep it.
Amen,
Amen,
Amen!

The Merchant emerges from the rest-room and sees them.

The Suspicion Song

MERCHANT

Him he chats with,
Him he smokes with,
Him he trades his dirty jokes with;
Him he sits with,
Him he squats with,
Him he hatches sneaky plots with;
Him he kids with,
Him he sings with,
Probably does dirty things with;
Him he's chewing betel nuts with,
Wonder what's with
Him . . .
And him . . .
Hm . . .

The Guide sees the Merchant observing them.

GUIDE
(To the Coolie)
What's he got to be so smiley about?
Something's up with all those giggles
    and winks.
When they're smiling is the time to
    watch out
With these finks!

MERCHANT
Who's he fooling with that song and
    that dance?
Planning something very crafty, he
    thinks—
When they smile is when you don't
    take a chance
With these Chinks!

COOLIE
O!

MERCHANT
How are you?

GUIDE
Just fine, sir.

MERCHANT
Would you care to have a small
liqueur?

GUIDE
Thank you, no, I never drink.

COOLIE
O!

MERCHANT
Now I get it: insurrection,
Out where I've got no protection!
In the desert they'll attack me,
Two to one and none to back me!
Then they'll rob me, strip my
    rings off,
Hack my toes and other things off.
Two to one is one too many:
Why take any
Risk?
Hm . . .
Hm . . .
Something tells me someone's on his
    way out.

COOLIE
(Aching)
O! Back, O!

GUIDE
(Overlapping)
Something tells me someone's on his
    way out.

COOLIE
Head, O!

MERCHANT
(Overlapping)
Sad to say, but someone's had it, me-
    thinks.

COOLIE
Feet, O!

GUIDE
(Overlapping)
Sad to say, but someone's had it,
    methinks.

COOLIE
O!

MERCHANT, GUIDE
Double-dealing, that's what life is
    about—

COOLIE
O!

MERCHANT
—With these Chinks.

GUIDE
—With these finks!

MERCHANT, GUIDE
With these chinks/finks.

SCENE 4—THE DESERT

The Merchant, overcome with paranoid suspicion, fires the Guide. The Guide gives the Coolie an extra canteen of water for the journey, warning him that the Merchant will steal it if he gets the chance. The Guide leaves, and the Merchant and Coolie resume their march through the desert.

Urga Marches

The Merchant is now backed by a chorus.

MERCHANT, CHORUS
Number one! First in line!
Pick and choose, eenie, meenie,
    mine!
Number one! Letter A!
Mister Delicious, when's the day!
Numero uno!
Gentlemen, you know,
Number one!
Eenie, meenie, mine!

COOLIE
Dune number one to Urga,
Dune number two to Urga,
Dune number three and four to
    Urga,
Only a few to Urga—
'Leventy-seven more to Urga.

Family in Urga,
Not so far away in Urga,
Coolie get his pay,
Sleep for a day in Urga,
Bed will squeak in Urga,
Sleep at least a week in Urga,

Dune number nine to Urga,
Dune number eight to Urga,
Dune number fifty ten to Urga,

Coolie go straight to Urga—
Coolie get home again to Urga.

MERCHANT, CHORUS
First, Front, Number One, Letter A,
    January!
Kingpin, To the fore, To the fray,
    Visionary!
Upper hand, Upper most, Number
    one,
Second to none,
The plural of One is Win, Winning,
    Winner, Won!
One win! In!
First around the track,
Everybody back!
Front!
Number One, Letter A, Winner all
    the way . . .

COOLIE
Urga. Family in Urga.
Not so far away in Urga.
Coolie get his pay,
Sleep for a day in Urga.
Bed will squeak in Urga . . .

SCENE 5—THE RIVER

They come to a rushing river. The Merchant is terrified of trying to cross it, but the Coolie is more terrified: he can't swim. The Merchant will have none of it, and sings a rousing anthem to encourage him.

In There

MERCHANT
There's a dream to be won,
There's a dawn that is breaking.
There are deeds to be done,
There's a world in the making.
There's a place in the sun
And it's yours for the taking!

Get your ass in there.

Where there's now only sand.
There will soon rise a tower!
Then a hamburger stand,
And a city will flower!

And we'll own all the land
And we'll charge by the hour!

Get your ass in there.

Little man, the world looks to you;
Your children's children will be
    proud that they knew you.
Man ought to reach for the sky;
How can you fail till you try?
Never say die till you die!

Little man, this is fate—
You've a call, you've a duty.
You've a chance to be great,
Bringing hope, bringing beauty!
Little man, if you wait,
Little gun makee shootee!

Get your ass in there.

SCENE 6—THE TENT

The Coolie breaks his arm crossing the river, but at their next bivouac the Merchant orders him to put up a tent. The Merchant goes inside, but immediately becomes suspicious that the Coolie has set some kind of trap for him and insists that the Coolie sleep inside the tent. While the Merchant sits guardedly outside in his rocking chair, the Coolie spreads a mat and kneels to pray.

Coolie's Prayer

COOLIE
Coolie thanking Buddha no more
    heat, no more day,
At night.
Coolie thanking Buddha no more
    have to find way
At night.
Coolie thankful master relent,
Giving coolie corner in tent.
Coolie no more fear he will die,
Not while Buddha smile and master
    sleeping nearby,
At night.

Coolie tired, brain not able think
    very deep,

At night.
Coolie tired, body only think about
    sleep
At night.
Cannot pray with usual skill,
Buddha please forgive, if he will,
Coolie not at usual best.
Coolie sleep now, wishing Buddha
    have a good rest
At night.

As night falls, the Merchant tries to rest, but starts at the sound of the cast on the Coolie's arm hitting the floor of the tent.

Paranoia Song

MERCHANT
(Into the darkness)
Eh? What? Who's there? Back, back, come out. Halt. Aha. Don't move!

(Suddenly nonchalant)

Give me the open air,
A rocking chair—
Terrific!
With every breath you take
You come awake—

What's that?
Something went bump just then,
Someone or something odd.
What is that lump in there?
Maybe he'll jump—Oh, God!

(Regaining his confidence)

Me for the great outdoors,
It cleans the pores—
Terrific!
No frills or folderol
Where men are always—

(Hearing a noise)

Help!

(Tiptoeing to the tent and spying on the Coolie)

```
No funny
No foolie
Poor coolie off-base
Not knowing
Where going
Most surely lose place
Master lose race
Coolie lose face
Coolie disgrace

No funny
No money
If coolie forget
Hand shaky
Brain achy
Yours truly in sweat
Makee all wet
Plenty regret
Coolie upset

Hot and pretty          Feelie pretty
No permittee            Coolie pretty
Stop and settee         Missee-fittee      Missee-fittee
Want to splittee        Missee-fittee      Want to sittee
Coolie want to quittee
But no quittee!
Hell, no!
No permittee selfee-pity —
Me, coolie, go on
```

Very clever, very crafty,
He stays warm while I get drafty.
While I'm sneezing he'll come
  creeping.
I don't think he's even sleeping.
There I'm sneezing, all defenseless,
He creeps up and knocks me
  senseless.
Wait, I think I saw him blinking—
Dirty stinking
Creep.

He strides into the tent and wakes the Coolie.

  Up up, get up, up up!

The Coolie stumbles sleepily out of the tent. The Merchant drags his rocker into the tent, lights some candles and sits guard.

Give me the open air,
A rocking chair—
Terrific!

  (Yawning)

With every breath you take
You're wide awake . . .

He falls asleep and snores loudly, waking himself.

Something went (Snore) in there.
What was that (Snore) just then?
You, who went (Snore), hands up!
Dare you to (Snore) again!

  COOLIE
  (Mumbling his prayer in his sleep)
Coolie thanking no more day
At night . . .

  MERCHANT
  What's he mumbling there?

  COOLIE
. . . Cannot pray with usual skill . . .

  MERCHANT
  What's that about kill? He said
  "kill," I heard him!

  COOLIE
. . . Giving Coolie corner in tent . . .

  MERCHANT
  Tent? Cornered? Corner me in
  tent?

  COOLIE
. . . Coolie no fear he will die . . .

  MERCHANT
  Die—?!!

In a panic, he tears out of the tent, rocker and all, and storms over to the Coolie.

  Up! Up! Get up! Up! Up!

He shoves the Coolie into the tent and tries to sit guard outside again, but falls asleep. The song ends with contrapuntal snores.

There follows a montage of scenes as the Merchant and the Coolie continue their journey, the days becoming unbearably hot. They lose their way. The water in their canteens is almost gone. The Coolie worries that if the Merchant dies of thirst and the authorities discover him, the Coolie, still alive, they will blame him for causing the death and hang him on the spot, so he quietly approaches the Merchant to offer him a drink from what's left in his hidden

canteen. The Merchant, by now hysterical, is convinced that the Coolie is creeping up to murder him and shoots him. The Coolie dies, as the water drips out of his canteen and disappears into the sand.

SCENE 7—
THE COURTROOM

The Merchant is on trial for murder. At first he claims that he treated the Coolie with kindness and beneficence and that the Coolie loved him, but when the Judge hints that if the Merchant is going to plead self-defense, he'd better have had cause for wanting to defend himself, the Merchant quickly changes his story. He admits to the Judge that he mistreated the Coolie badly, overworking him, beating him, refusing him sleep and so on, so that the Coolie had every reason for vengefulness, and therefore when he offered the Merchant a canteen, the Merchant thought he was threatening him with a rock. The Coolie may have had good intentions, but it was only logical that the Merchant should think they were bad. The Judge accepts the argument and the Merchant is acquitted.

When I finally succumbed to Lenny's and Jerry's blandishments, I expected the collaboration to be as much fun as writing *West Side Story* had been, with none of the artistic compromises I'd had to make as a neophyte writer. It was not to be. Lenny, although affable and stimulating as ever, treated me as if I were still an apprentice. I had to defend every word I wrote and argue him out of all his suggestions for lyric changes. It became tedious and time-consuming and no fun at all, and after we had written the above eight songs, I asked for a meeting with him and Jerry and John. Over dinner at the Harvard Club (Lenny's choice), I told them that I couldn't go any further with the project, that they were welcome to use any of the lyrics I had written, but that they should get another lyricist to finish the job. I urged them to go back to Jerry Leiber, but shortly thereafter, to my surprise and Lenny's and John's disappointment, Robbins also quit the project.* And there it lay for twenty years, until Jerry renewed his interest in it and approached John once again. John supplied new lyrics to add to a few of the ones Jerry Leiber and I had written and retitled the piece *The Race to Urga.* It was performed in a workshop at Lincoln Center, after which it vanished once again and, most likely, forever.

Incidentally, the title *A Pray by Blecht* was Lenny's. None of us could talk him out of it, but I assure you we had no intention of keeping it.

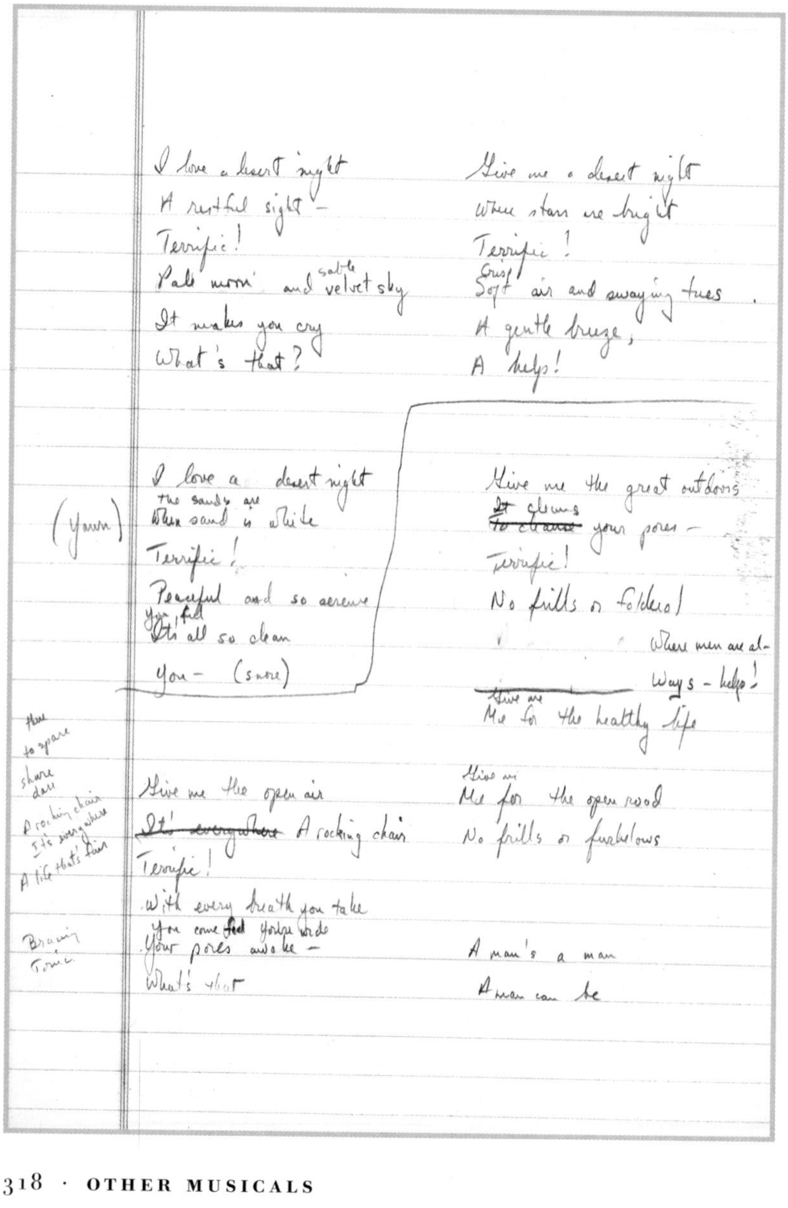

[handwritten manuscript of lyrics]

> I love a desert night
> A restful sight—
> Terrific!
> Pale moon and sable velvet sky
> It makes you cry
> What's that?

> Give me a desert night
> Where stars are bright
> Terrific!
> Crisp/Soft air and swaying trees
> A gentle breeze,
> A help!

> (Yawn)
> I love a desert night
> the sands are
> When sand is white
> Terrific!
> Peaceful and so serene
> You feel
> It's all so clean
> You— (snore)

> Give me the great outdoors
> It cleans your pores—
> Terrific!
> No frills or folderol
> Where men are al-
> ways - help!
> Give me for the healthy life

> Give me the open air
> A rocking chair
> Terrific!
> With every breath you take
> You come ... your pores awake—
> What's that

> Give me for the open road
> No frills or furbelows

> A man's a man
> A man can be

---

* He quit in a bizarre, but not atypical, Robbins fashion. In the midst of holding auditions with Lenny and John one day, he excused himself. When, after fifteen minutes, he hadn't returned, John went looking for him, fearing that he might be ill. Unable to find him, he asked the stage doorman if he had seen him. Yes, was the reply. He had just seen Mr. Robbins get in a cab and tell the driver to go to Kennedy airport. John didn't hear from him again for twenty years.

Candide (Revival, 1974)

Book by Hugh Wheeler (based on Candide,
  by Voltaire)
Music by Leonard Bernstein
*Lyrics mostly by Richard Wilbur, with
  additional ones by John La Touche
  and Leonard Bernstein*

The Notion

The plot deals with the travels and travails of Candide, a hapless young bastard nephew of the Baron Thunder-Ten-Tronckh in eighteenth-century Westphalia. After being expelled from home, he is drafted into the Bulgarian army, brought before the Spanish Inquisition, swindled out of a fortune, shipwrecked on a desert isle, and separated time and again from his true love, Cunegonde, the Baron's daughter, who bears with remarkable dignity a variety of carnal besmirchments by almost everybody she encounters. Also involved in Candide's adventures are Maximilian, Cunegonde's self-infatuated brother, and Paquette, the Baroness's accommodating maid. Through it all, Candide remembers the lesson of his beloved master Dr. Pangloss, that "everything is for the best in this best of all possible worlds."

General Comments

In the early 1950s, Leonard Bernstein had collaborated on a musical of Voltaire's satire *Candide,* with a libretto by Lillian Hellman and lyrics mostly by John La Touche, plus one each by Hellman, Dorothy Parker and Lenny himself. The score was unfinished when La Touche died, and the producers had been unable to raise the capitalization, so the show was put on hold while Lenny (and I) began work on *West Side Story,* in the autumn of 1955. Not long after, the producers found fresh sources of money and told Lenny that they wanted to go into rehearsal the following season. Since both our collaborators, Arthur Laurents and Jerome Robbins, were about to take a few months off (Arthur to attend to the production of his play *A Clearing in the Woods* and Jerry to direct the musical *Bells Are Ringing*), Lenny asked me to take a vacation from *West Side Story* and write the rest of the lyrics for *Candide.* Hal Prince had already asked me to write some songs for his proposed musical of *The Last Resorts,* and since I considered lyric-writing a chore and music-writing a pleasure (and still do), I said no and suggested to Lenny that he ask Michael Flanders, a Britisher who wrote genuinely witty *and* funny (they rarely go together) songs with the composer Donald Swann. Flanders, however, was crippled and confined to a wheelchair, which made traveling difficult, and transoceanic collaboration seemed unsatisfactory at best. Lenny, or someone, had the notion of approaching Richard Wilbur, a poet who had translated Molière and other writers, but had never written a musical. Lenny, or someone, couldn't have made a better choice; for me, Wilbur's lyrics for *Candide* are the most elegantly witty (and funny) ever written for the stage.

When the show was in its Boston tryout, in 1956, Lenny asked me to come to a performance and tell him what I thought. What I thought was that it was a high-class mess and a unique one, in that each of the elements—the score, the book and Tyrone Guthrie's direction—was first-rate; the problem was that they didn't belong together. Lillian's book was sharp but dark, Lenny's music and Wilbur's lyrics were sparkling and Guthrie's direction compounded the

felony by formalizing the show into something between a court masque and a wedding cake. When I told him my dank thoughts, Lenny leapt for joy and demanded that I tell his three collaborators, only one of whom I knew at all (Lillian). This was not what I had expected—I had expected to see the show, chat and get drunk with Lenny and go home. But he insisted, and dragged me to the time-honored out-of-town late-night hotel conference. I was twenty-six years old and had no professional theatrical experience and found myself facing Lillian Hellman, one of the most distinguished playwrights of her day and a fierce lady; Tyrone Guthrie, a six-and-a-half-foot patrician who had directed many a classic if nary a musical; and Richard Wilbur, whose work I admired so much that it made me feel unqualified to make any criticism whatsoever. Lenny introduced me to Guthrie and Wilbur, sat me down and told me to repeat what I'd said to him because he thought it was something valuable they should hear. The three of them looked balefully at me, with understandable disdain—who was this kid, this latest protégé of Lenny's? It was obvious that they were indulging him and couldn't wait to resume their lives. I murmured my comments as shyly and quickly as possible, but without pussyfooting, I'm proud to say, and then raced back to New York on the first available train.

The show was a critical and financial disaster, but the score (my favorite of Lenny's) has outlived every revival, none of which has been very successful—for reasons, I think, having to do with the unfulfilling arbitrary revue-like structure of the show. I became involved in the best of the resuscitations, Hal Prince's production in 1974. He broached to Lenny the no-

tion of presenting the piece as a kind of ragtag circus, performed not like a grand operetta with grand operetta singers, as in the original, but by a troupe of young people imbued with a carnival spirit, all in one swift act and with a small orchestra. Lenny was not happy about the small orchestra, but he knew Hal to be a shrewd producer and an imaginative director and he wisely decided that whatever the compromise, a reduced *Candide* was better than no *Candide* at all.

The minute Lenny said yes, Hal asked me, as a personal favor, to lay aside my composer's hat for a moment and write an opening lyric to Lenny's music. The first song in the original production had been "The Best of All Possible Worlds," a perfect opening song as far as I was concerned, but Hal wanted a number which would introduce the four main characters: Candide, Cunegonde, Maximilian and Paquette. Opening numbers that introduce the main characters being my specialty, and Hal trading on our friendship, I was ready to consent, but on one condition: I would not actively collaborate with Lenny. I had learned my lesson with *A Pray by Blecht*—I couldn't stomach putting myself in the position of being a journeyman apprentice again. I told Hal that if Lenny would give me carte blanche to utilize any of the score's unused music, including music for songs dropped from the original production (he had written many, both finished and unfinished), I would plunge in, but strictly on my own. Lenny, busy with a million other projects anyway, gave his permission, and I dutifully plunged. I wrote not only an opening but, at Hal's behest, two other songs as well, and an additional section to a lyric of John La Touche's.

Candide *revival, 1974*

Life Is Happiness Indeed

CANDIDE

Life is happiness indeed:
Mares to ride and books to read.
Though of noble birth I'm not,
I'm delighted with my lot.
Though I've no distinctive features
And I've no official mother,
I love all my fellow creatures
And the creatures love each other!

CUNEGONDE

Life is happiness indeed:
I have everything I need.
I am rich and unattached
And my beauty is unmatched.
With the rose my only rival,
I admit to one frustration:
What a pity its survival
Is of limited duration!

She rips the petals off the rose.

MAXIMILIAN
(Looking at himself in a mirror)
Life is absolute perfection,
As is true of my complexion.
Every time I look and see me,
I'm reminded life is dreamy.
Although I do get tired
Being endlessly admired,
People will go on about me—
How could they go on without me?
(If the talk at times is vicious,
That's the price you pay when you're
    delicious.)

Life is pleasant, life is simple,
Oh my God, is that a pimple?
No, it's just the odd reflection—
Life and I are still perfection!
I am everything I need,
Life is happiness indeed!

Candide and Cunegonde, joined by Paquette, sing the verses above in counterpoint to Maximilian's singing his. They include two additional lyrics:

CANDIDE, CUNEGONDE,
PAQUETTE
We're innocent and unambitious,
That's why life is so delicious!

MAXIMILIAN
Though it is a heavy duty
To protect my awesome beauty,
I have almost no objection—
Life and I are still perfection!

For the 1997 Broadway revival, I wrote a couple of variations on this song as false entrances for the Old Lady, one following the opening, another shortly thereafter. Thus:

OLD LADY
Life is happiness, or not—
Let's get goink vith the plot.
Vile I'm vaitink in the vings,
Everybody sits and sings.

My importance you're ignoring,
I'm no singer, but I esk you:
Ven the story's getting boring,
Who'll be coming to the rescue?

Life is happiness at last—
You should only know my past.
Hoo, I'll bet you all forgot
I vas comink in the plot.

I am here as her duenna
To invigorate the story.
And I live in such a menna
Life's completely hunky-dory!

Candide's travels take him to Lisbon, where he witnesses an auto-da-fé—the celebratory public burning of heretics. The spectators are having a delightful time, as La Touche's lyric (not included here) illustrates. I made the following addition:

What a Day, What a Day (For an Auto-Da-Fé!)

FIRST COUPLE
What a day! What a treat!

WOMAN
Did you save us a seat?

MAN
In the back,
Near the rack
But away from the heat.
Though we won't see the bones,
We'll hear most of the groans
And we'll still
Get a thrill
Throwing stones.

Two women, one excited, the other bored and dismissive, look into the distance.

FIRST WOMAN
Did you see—?

SECOND WOMAN
Yes, I saw.

FIRST WOMAN
Ugh! They've broken his jaw.

SECOND WOMAN
Don't we know—?

FIRST WOMAN
We should go.

SECOND WOMAN
It's your father-in-law!

FIRST WOMAN
Will he burn?
What's your guess?

SECOND WOMAN
I suppose he'll confess.

FIRST WOMAN
What a bore!
I adore
Your new dress.

BOTH COUPLES
What a nice little bunch
To cremate and to crunch:

There's a dean
And a queen
And a nun with a hunch.
See you soon. We must dash.
When they've swept up the ash,
We can meet
Down the street
And have lunch.

After witnessing so much cruelty and being abused so many times, Candide loses all faith in humanity.

This World

CANDIDE

Is this all then,
This, the world?
Death and envy,
Greed and blindness?
What is kindness
But a lie?
What to live for
But to die?

I would never
Miss the world,
Never this one,
Which is hateful.

Let me die then,
Only grateful
Cunegonde,
Dying sooner,
Was spared this world.

What is kindness
But a lie?
And what to live for
But to die?

Candide lands in Eldorado, a kingdom where everything is perfect and where animals sing. Paquette is with him.

Sheep's Song

FIRST SHEEP

Every sky is blue and sunny,
Every face you see is gla-aad,*
There's no greed or need for money
Or a synonym for ba-aad.

SECOND SHEEP

Here each man is each man's brother,
Here we sleep untroubled sleep.
Every day is like the other,
Even children never weep.

Sheep's Song

After many weeks of treacherous journeying, Paquette and Candide stumble into the country of Eldorado, where everything *does* happen for the best, where the mud is gold and the streets are paved with diamonds. Even the animals are articulate, wise and gentle, including two friendly sheep and a lion. Even in Paradise, though, Candide is not happy and longs to find his Cunegonde once again. He and Paquette decide to load their two friendly sheep with gold and escape from Eldorado.

LION

Roses grow with ruby petals,
Humans grow with perfect grace.
All is joy and precious metals.
Surely there's no better place.

PAQUETTE

Here each man is each man's brother,
Here they sleep untroubled sleep.
Every day is like the other.
Very nice if you're a sheep.

LION

Emerald leaves drip diamond
    flowers,
Silver cows give golden cream.
People laugh and dance for hours,

PAQUETTE

If we don't leave soon, I'll scream.

TWO SHEEP

Farewell, land of peace and order,
Where all pain and woe is pa-aast.
Life awaits across the border,
Au revoir, farewell, goodbye—
At la-aast.

All in all, *Candide* was a happy experience. Even though I was once again supplying just lyrics, Lenny's music was such a shower of delight that I actually had a good, and easy, time writing them. The deeper reason, of course, was that I had no emotional investment in it—it wasn't my blood on the line; it was a lark.

* The sheep bleat each short "a" sound as they sing.

Muscle (Unproduced, 1994)

*Book by James Lapine (based on the memoir
Muscle, by Sam Fussell)*

The Notion

Max, a young intellectual in the publishing business,
becomes at first attracted to, and then obsessed with,
bodybuilding. He shuts himself away from every other
aspect of his life, including his friends, to devote himself to it. He enters a competition, loses and crashes
back into the life he had before.

General Comments

Muscle was not only unproduced, it was unfinished—
at least by me. As I said in the introduction to the
chapter on *Passion*, when I brought that idea as a project to James Lapine and he agreed to do it, we both
felt that it should be a one-act musical, no more than
an hour and a half in length, and that perhaps it
should have a companion piece. James had become
interested in *Muscle*, and since it too concerned the
effects of outward physical appearance on both the
owner and the viewer, it seemed an ideal choice, since
it too demanded a short form. The net result was
shorter than we anticipated: it consisted of one sequence before it was aborted.

Opening Sequence (Poses)

*We see in a montage a succession of people taking poses, il-
lustrating who they are: Max, about to graduate from an
Ivy League college; Mary Ann, a beauty queen; Max's
mother, divorced from his father (both of them are also professors); a bodybuilder in posing briefs; Alice, a ballet
dancer in a tutu; Jack and Dwight, two of Max's friends,
who enter to the sound of jukebox pop-rock.*

*A professor is presenting a literary prize to Max and
keeps speaking through the following.**

PROFESSOR
. . . not that we need wish you success, Max. I've been
teaching here for sixteen years and I don't remember a
single student who has demonstrated such extraordinary analytical skills. Your ability to see through—

*He keeps speaking, occasionally in mime, as music contin-
ues underneath.*

MAX
Two more days
And I'm out of here.

PROFESSOR
. . . Of course, I wasn't around in your father's time—

MAX
Let me out of here.
Two more days . . .

---

* In the interest of brevity, I have omitted some passages of dialogue and described them instead.

occur:

a] he gets panhandled for money
b] he steps in dog shit
c] he almost gets hit by a messenger bicyclist
d] he gets threatened by CRAZY AL, a recurring nightmare of a street-person
e] someone shoves a "Jews for Jesus" leaflet in his hands
f] he passes a vicious fight where someone is getting the shit beat out of them
g] he gets panhandled for money

Eventually Max breathlessly enters the publishing office. He takes a moment to study himself in the mirror before venturing into a beehive of cubicles and bookish looking people. Among them are: ELAINE, mid-thirties, married, ambitious; STUART, mid-twenties, more ambitious than smart; MARIA, early twenties, from the Bronx but with an Ivy veneer; and ALBERT, a total nerd of the "my IQ is bigger than yours" variety. He always carries a copy of the New York Review of Books.)

     ELAINE
You must be Max. Welcome. I'm Elaine Gore. I head this division. This is Stuart, Maria and Albert. We'll all be working together this summer.

  (customary hellos are exchanged)

     STUART
We read your resume and we're all very impressed.

     MARIA
Some of us are already happy that you're only an intern on his way to graduate school.
    (laughter)

     STUART
Do you play squash? I'm dying to find someone to play hooky with me.

     MAX
Sorry, I don't.

         10

PROFESSOR
(Overlapping)
—but by all accounts he was equally amazing.

The Professor continues to mime his speech as Max's father enters and crosses downstage. He is one of those handsome older men who maintain an aura of eternal youth, the type of college professor with whom students fall in love; Max watches him.

MAX
Oh, amazing,
Just amazing—

PROFESSOR
. . . an iconoclast but a classicist . . .

MAX
(Overlapping)
What an entrance,
Isn't he amazing?

The father hits his mark and assumes a pose right out of Gentleman's Quarterly.

The amazing father . . .

PROFESSOR
(Taking in Max and his father)
. . . I'm certain that you two are the only father and son act to win this prize . . .

FATHER
(To himself)
Sycophant.

PROFESSOR
I don't know whether your father would agree with me, Max—

FATHER
(To himself)
Then ask him.

A series of chords. Everyone but Max assumes a different pose.

PROFESSOR
—but I certainly wish you were going straight to graduate school rather than—

MAX
(To himself)
—coming to life.

PROFESSOR
—taking a year off in New York City.

Chords. Everyone changes his pose.

Of course Harvard can wait, but please—

Chords. Everyone changes his pose again.

Academia needs you.

Chords. They change once more.

Your parents can teach only so many courses themselves!

The sound of polite, bored laughter.

In any event . . .

Mary Ann walks downstage to Max's father, who puts his arms around her. They share a long sexy kiss. Everyone but the Professor looks their way.

Laughter.

MAX

Two more days
Of everybody trying to be nice,
Of everybody lying through their
    teeth,
Of everybody offering advice.
Two more days
Of everybody dying underneath,
And it's over . . .

MOTHER
(Eyeing Max's father)

Two more days
Of wandering around here in limbo,
Bumping into him and that bimbo,
Learning how to smile instead
    of run.

MAX

Two more days . . .

FATHER
(Looking at Max)

Two more days,
We'll be just father and son,
Bachelors in more ways than one.

MOTHER, FATHER

Two more days,
And we'll see what we've done.

MAX

Get me out of here . . .

FATHER, MOTHER
(Looking at Max)

See what we've done:

FATHER

Not so bad—

MOTHER

Quite a package—

BOTH

—If I say so myself.

FATHER

Smart.

MOTHER

Charming.

FATHER

Nice-looking.

MOTHER
(To herself)

Give me a fucking break.

MAX
(Internal, snapping his fingers)

Two more days,
And I'm out of here—

PROFESSOR

. . . and so it is with pleasure that I
present—

MAX

Get me out of here . . .

PROFESSOR

—Maxwell Thomas Riddle with
the 1989 Williamson Medal—

MAX

Quick . . .

PROFESSOR

—for excellence in American Literature.

Everyone applauds politely.

FATHER

Where's his check?

MOTHER
Top shelf.

FATHER
What we made . . .

MOTHER
What we had . . .

They glance at each other.

BOTH
What we had.

MOTHER
He'll mature.

FATHER
He'll go forth.

MOTHER
He'll survive.

BOTH
He's been educated.

MAX
Sixteen years
Of learning how to ask the right
    questions,
Coming up with all the right
    answers,
Hoping to leave everyone impressed.

FATHER
Two more days . . .

MOTHER
Two more days . . .

MAX
Sixteen years
Of trying to be better than the
    rest . . .

As he continues, the Bodybuilder struts over and stands directly in front of him; anxiously, Max sidles around him to finish his thoughts.

—Of knowing where I've been,
Where I'll be,
Marking time,
Just excelling,
Watching my reactions and my
    spelling,

Not conforming,
Not rebelling—

MOTHER
What is this New York?
Two more days,
And I won't know where to find
    him—

FATHER
What is this New York?
Three, four months,
He'll start missing what's behind
    him—

FATHER, MOTHER
—I know my son.

FATHER
Smart—

MOTHER
Charming, but—

FATHER
But—

MOTHER
Needs a place to hide.

FATHER
There's still that little boy inside
There.

BOTH
Oh, well . . .

MAX
Two more days—

(Looks at his watch)

—Less forty-seven minutes—
And I'm out of here!

Everyone exits but Max, Jack and Dwight. The music changes to jukebox pop-rock, as at Jack and Dwight's first entrance, but this time ear-shattering. Alice, dressed in street clothes, comes in and hangs on to Jack. A waiter hands them all drinks. The sound of loud convivial boozy chatter transports us to a college tavern; everybody shouts to be heard.

ALL (EXCEPT MAX)
(To the jukebox vamp)
New York is so—
Great!

JACK
(Shouting)
You guys are lucky to be going
there! Me! I'll be stuck in New
Haven!

MAX
Poor Jack!

ALL (EXCEPT MAX)
This town is so—
Great!

DWIGHT
(Screaming, to Max)
Did you find an apartment yet?!

MAX
A sublet on the Upper East Side!

DWIGHT
Enough room for guests?!

MAX
No, not on my salary! It's a studio!

JUKEBOX
New York is real—
Fine!

DWIGHT
(Overlapping)
I'm not picky!

MAX
Forget it!

DWIGHT
Where's your apartment, Alice?!

ALICE
West Side!

JACK
I tried to get her to live in the
Village!

JUKEBOX
This town is hot—
Shit!

ALICE
It's too far from Lincoln Center!

DWIGHT
How big is your place?!

ALICE
Dwight, you're shameless! I have two roommates! My parents won't even—

They continue to mime a conversation; the music becomes light and animated, interrupted periodically by the jukebox.

MAX
(Internal, looking at Alice)
So we'll meet at my apartment . . .

JUKEBOX
So—

MAX
I'll rush home from work at noon.

JUKEBOX
—Great!

MAX
You'll come up from class
With your dancer's ass,
And we'll ride the moon—

JUKEBOX
New York is muy—

MAX
Rip our clothes off—

JUKEBOX
—Bien!
New York is real—

MAX
—Have a nice hot—

JUKEBOX
—Fine—

MAX
Lunch—

JUKEBOX
—Hot—

MAX
Fuck—

JUKEBOX
—Shit!

MAX
God, I love your looks!

The jukebox music continues underneath, softer.

ALICE
(To the group)
I'm only in the corps. You know, seventh swan from the left. I don't know whether I'll ever be a principal dancer. I'm already too old. No one does college *and* ABT.

JUKEBOX
New York is so—
Grock!

JACK
I'm dry. Next round's on you, Riddle.

DWIGHT
Yes, use your prize money.

JACK
(Like an announcer)
These drinks brought to you courtesy of the Williamson Foundation.

(Imitating the Professor)
I don't know whether your father would approve, Max . . .

He continues to mime conversation, as Alice and Max look at each other intensely.

ALICE
(Internal)
So we'll meet at your apartment,
Not the usual motel.
I'll just sweat through class
Till the hours pass
And I ring your bell,
Your private bell . . .

JUKEBOX
New York is so—

DWIGHT
Hey, let's talk about your father's girlfriend, Max.

JUKEBOX
(Overlapping)
Great!

DWIGHT
God, what a bod!

JACK
God, what a bod!

JUKEBOX
This town is real—

ALICE
(Overlapping)
You guys—!

JUKEBOX
(Overlapping)
—Spaz!

JACK
Is it true she was a beauty queen?

DWIGHT
And she's a doctoral candidate in Classics?

JACK
Not possible!

MAX
(Internal)
One more day
Of listening to you and your drivel,
Trying just to sit and be civil,
When I want to smash your fucking
    face . . .
One more day . . .

The music changes to cocktail piano. The scene segues to a restaurant where Max's mother sits at a booth, smoking a cigarette; Max joins her.

PIANIST
One more day
To know each other,
One more meal,
Avoiding
One more way

To show each other
Anything we feel . . .

Max and his mother discuss her ex-husband and his new girlfriend, with references to Schopenhauer, Max's mother's specialty.

PIANIST
One more try
To sing each other
One more song.
One more lie
To string each other
A little farther along.

One more glance
At Schopenhauer,
One more moan.
One more chance
To open our
Hearts, blown.

The piano is replaced by an a cappella student choir. A highly stylized commencement exercise begins. Students file in, dressed in caps and gowns, following their professors, who are in academic robes. The commencement speaker stands at a lectern.

CHOIR
One more long
Supportive speech.
Then we're on the beach.
Commencement speaker . . .
Success . . .

Organ music. The commencement begins. Max, observed by his parents and Mary Ann, finds himself, surprisingly, crying on his way to receive his diploma. We hear five chords, underscoring five poses: Max's mother, father, Mary Ann, Alice and the Bodybuilder.

STUDENTS
One more pose
With the family—

(They pose)

For the photograph—

(Another pose)

And we're out of here . . .

Max graduates and the scene dissolves into a choreographed sequence of his arrival in New York: a hostile place, filled with small, unpleasant incidents and lots of noise, but a recurrent refrain:

ALL
New York is so—
Great!

Eventually, he breathlessly enters the publishing office where he is to begin working. The office consists of four adjacent cubicles. He goes to the first—the largest—in which sits Elaine Gore, an ambitious woman in her mid-thirties. She is taking calls as Max watches, unnoticed, in the doorway. The jukebox music resumes underneath.

No Problem

ELAINE
(Ladylike and tough)
. . . I know, Bob, but you can't dump that kind of load on us with such short notice and expect us to get it back to you by Friday. You want it done well or do you want it Friday? You decide.

She takes a pose as her other phone begins to ring.

MAX
The cheery smile,
The steely voice . . .
Style . . .

ELAINE
(Into the phone, but in rhythm)
No problem.

MAX
Style . . .

ELAINE
And give my love to Joyce. 'Bye.

Max raises his fist to knock, but Elaine picks up the other phone and speaks into it, still in rhythm.

Gore here—hi! Betty, you're back!

(Out of rhythm)

How was Paris? . . . All right, how was London then? Was it fabulous? Did you see Rushdie?

She mimes conversation, twiddling a pencil as she does so.

MAX
The change of tone
From dry to warm,
Before the storm . . .

ELAINE
(Into the phone, in rhythm)
Well, we have to talk . . .

MAX
Style . . .

The first phone rings.

ELAINE
Sorry, darling, there's my other—

MAX
Form . . .

ELAINE
No problem. Ciao.

She runs her hands through her hair.

MAX
The hands through the hair . . .

ELAINE
(Swiveling)
No, the point I was trying to make was that—

As she continues the conversation, sometimes in mime, she takes numerous poses.

MAX
The foot on the desk,
The arabesque
With the chair—
Right. Got it.

Elaine cradles the phone in the crook of her neck, leaving her hands free to grab a yellow pad and take notes.

Holding the phone
In the crook of your neck . . .

          ELAINE
        (Into the phone)
    Who told you that?

          MAX
No problem.
Laying your cards out,
But not the whole deck . . .

          ELAINE
    Let me be frank with you—

          MAX
Check.
Raising your voice just enough—

          ELAINE
    Look—

          MAX
Showing you're easy but tough—

          ELAINE
    No.

          MAX
Filling the pause
While you're grabbing at straws . . .

          ELAINE
    Alex, I promise you there's—

She turns toward the door and finally sees Max; she gives a little wave and he waves back.

      MAX, ELAINE
   (Only Elaine just mouths it)
No problem.

She introduces herself and quickly passes him off to the rest of the office. As he passes each cubicle, he enters, observes, sings and introduces himself.

          MAX
Here a little twiddle,
There a little twaddle,
Knowing when to wheedle
And whom to coddle,

Here and there a doddle,
Now and then a memo—
No problemo . . .

He arrives at the next cubicle and meets Albert.

Staring at the pages,
Not moving for ages,
Lost in what you do . . .

No problem.

Knowing the way
To say, "I deserve credit"
Without ever seeming
You've actually said it.
Treating each day
Like it's something to edit—

He arrives at the next cubicle and meets Stuart and Carmen, who invite him to play games and have drinks with them "to let off steam" when he's done with the "sweat work."

          MAX
  (Heading toward the last cubicle,
      which is his)
Blowing off some steam,
Playing on the team,
Going out for drinks
With a supreme
Asshole . . .

    (Entering his cubicle)

Little monthly dinners
Welcoming beginners—
Perfection . . .

He switches on the light, revealing a neutral white space: an empty desk and blank walls.

Right.

Four chords as he takes four poses: he sits, puts his legs up on the desk, picks up the receiver and puts it in the crook of his neck, then grabs a memo pad and pencil.

So I'll talk on the phone,
And I'll spin in my chair,
While I make a notation . . .

Light up on Elaine, as both she and Max make marks on pads and he speaks what she mouths on the phone.

Darling, not to worry . . .

He hangs up while Elaine continues to mime conversation. Light up on Albert, staring into space, pencil poised.

And I'll sit like a stone
And I'll stare at the air,
And I'll work like a drone
With immaculate care
And intense concentration . . .

Albert continues working as light comes up on Stuart, playing with an executive toy.

And I'll wink
And I'll grin
And I'll sink
Into sweat work,
And I'll try
Not to win,
And I'll drink
And I'll network,
And I'll learn all my lines—

Alice in her tutu glides through the office with the Bodybuilder in a pas de deux.

And I'll play all my roles—

Mary Ann in her beauty pageant guise dances through with Max's father.

I'll follow the signs
And establish my goals—

Max's mother stalks through.

The exemplary employee—

The Professor and Max's fellow students waltz through.

Merely one among many—

Elaine, Albert and Stuart pose in their cubicles as Carmen dances through.

Doing only what's advisable,
Completely recognizable,
So no one will have anything to fear,
Which will let me disappear
With my nice white desk
And my little paper stacks

And my fax
And my phone
And my pads
And my plant
And my books
And my suit
And my work
And my life
And no problem.

New York is sooooooo
Great!

But there *was* a problem. I couldn't write the show the way I felt it ought to be written, as I've explained in the *Passion* chapter. I was the wrong generation for the job. I bowed out, and James and I developed *Passion* into a full-length evening (though still in one act) and he took *Muscle* to William Finn. They finished it and work-shopped it in Chicago, but so far it hasn't developed beyond that stage.

Sondheim on Sondheim (2010)

Devised by James Lapine

The Notion

Sondheim on Sondheim is a revue of songs of mine, performed by eight singers against a set of video and audio collages of me delivering commentaries on the songs and on aspects of my life.

General Comments

The show was conceived as a two-act piece, comprised only of songs I had already written. But James felt that the second act needed an opening to bring the audience back from the intermission into the concept of the evening, and nothing in my work was quite right for the job, so he asked me to write something new. Embarrassed (although flattered) at having an evening not just of my work but with me as photographed host, I immediately fell into a familiar self-deprecating mode and wrote the following number, which was suggested by a *New York* magazine headline that had asked the unanswerable camp question: "Is Sondheim God?"

Mock New York *cover, used in "God" from* Sondheim on Sondheim, *2010*

God

SS is revealed on screen, roaming around his studio, chattering aimlessly. As he does so, the performers enter and take their places. For most of the song, they do not acknowledge the audience and relate only to each other.

SS

So. This is where I work. This is my piano. These are my pencils: they're Blackwings, which are a special kind of pencil . . . etc. . . .

As he continues speaking, a spiky vamp begins. After a few bars his image freezes, his mouth open.

ALL
(Reverently)
God.
I mean, the man's a god.

(Variously)

Wrote the score to *Sweeney Todd,*
With a nod
To de Sade—
Well, he's odd.
Well, he's God!

The music stops. SS's image resumes moving and he continues to pad around the studio.

SS

I write on yellow pads. I prefer the kind that have exactly thirty-two lines on them, which gives enough room to write alternate words in the spaces in between, but that particular kind of pad is hard to find . . . etc. . . . etc. . . .

The music resumes as the performers sing and SS's image freezes again, in a pretentious pose.

ALL
Smart!
The lyrics are so smart!
And the music has such heart—

(Variously)

It has *heart*?
Well, in part.
Let's not start—
Call it art.
No, call it—

The music stops.

ALL
God!

As their voices fade, SS resumes talking.

SS
Of course I do use a computer to transcribe things from longhand and to edit . . . etc. . . .

The music resumes underneath.

I prefer a laptop because I like to write lying down . . . etc. . . .

His voice fades, but this time his image keeps talking silently and moving.

ALL
Well, you have to have
Something to believe in,
Something you can celebrate,
Elevate,
Venerate—
Something like

(Variously)

Italian pottery . . .
Old movies . . .
Butterflies . . .
Politics . . .
Wine . . .
Picasso . . .
Skiing . . .
Stamps . . .
Musicals!
It might as well be musicals.
And when it comes to musicals—

SOLO
(Speaking in rhythm)
I like the score of *Rent.*

ALL
(Variously sotto voce)
Sh . . .
Later . . .
Me, too . . .
Not now . . .
Really, *Rent*?

SS's voice fades in and the performers redirect their attention to him.

SS
. . . Now this piano belonged to Leonard Bernstein. What's interesting about it is that he'd used it only seven times for children's concerts, but . . . etc. . . .

His voice fades but his image continues moving around the room.

ALL
(Variously)
Nice smile.
Sweet face.
Real style.
Such grace.
That wit—
That's it!

SS spills a bowl of pencils off the piano.

SS
Oh, shit.

ALL
(Variously)
And does he know how to rhyme!
Sublime . . .
He'll surprise you every time.

You're never sure just where the
Tune is going next,
Just like the lyrics—
No, the "text."

Just when you think it's going up,
It's going down,
Just when you think it's going on,
It stops.

The music suddenly stops.

It doesn't finish, it just stops.

Cults   Hi everywhere — many images **IV**   SS: Gibberish (Someone on the Sphere)
Obsessions
Allegiances   ( )   Text moving — caught
                                                     on the screens

p. 23 ~~I should make ... you have to keep the ... out~~

Such Con   I think his days
Such grace   He never sleeps
Such style   I love his songs
Such joke   I love every note that he wrote
Such wit   That's an awful lot of fans
              And they're always so cheerful

<u>Such wit</u>

(drops Oh, shit   We're awfully glad that you came
something) Oh, God.   in fact

                                      For coming here to see the sun come out

Well you got it here   have to have you profess is
Something that you can about   that possesses — obsesses you to believe in
(Well you got it here
Something that you can fight for)   And he finds so many objects
                                       At times
Something that you
die for Make yourself a fall for
Something that you can dislocate your life
And tonight you   Something that you tear to pieces
       are you God.   That you be disappointing with
    (SS prattles on)   That can disappoint you
                              That maybe
You never know   So has been anointed with
(unstylized Just where the tune
turn) Is going next   GOD!
And the lyrics
No, the tune   Something that can let you down
He changed the shape of the musical theater   Where's any Wilson?
                                  He's an icon,
Tried where nobody had tried   He's an artifact
                           To me ... fast becoming
                           And be joy to be
                         A fabulous fossil

SOLO
You know what I like best? His flops.

(Freely)

Anyone can whistle,
That's what they say—

SOLO
(Sotto voce)
Later . . .

ALL
But you have to have
Something to believe in,
Something to appropriate,
Emulate,
Overrate—

(Pause)

Might as well be Stephen.

The music reaches a sustained chord.

SS
This box contains my fingernail clippings. They're going to the Smithsonian . . .

SOLO
Or to call him by his nickname:

The vamp resumes.

ALL
God!

(To the tune of "I'm Still Here")

We've got God!
Look who's God!
He's still—

SOLO
Why don't we just sing the songs.

One of the performers clicks SS's image off with a remote.

ALL
(Loud, in elaborate harmony)
Amen!

No further comment necessary.

7. Movies

The Thing of It Is (Unproduced, 1969)

Screenplay by William Goldman,
based on his novel

The Notion

Amos McCracken, a Broadway composer, has written a hit show with a hit song called "No, Mary Ann," but his marriage has fallen apart. In an effort to renew it, he takes his wife on a second honeymoon to Europe, but everywhere he goes, he is pursued by the song, which has become internationally ubiquitous and thus persistently denies him refuge from the world he's trying to leave behind. Every country he visits has its own version playing—on the radio, in restaurants, in outdoor band concerts. In London it is a march, in Italy a tarantella, in Paris a soupy waltz. Nevertheless, by the end of the trip both his marriage and his sanity are saved.

General Comments

The Thing of It Is is a book written in 1967 by William Goldman—novelist, screenwriter and essayist brother of James, with whom I wrote *Follies* and *Evening Primrose*. I met him before I met James and we had always wanted to write something together. We didn't actually do so until 1992, but along the way, in 1969, Bill wrote a screenplay of his novel and it needed the song that, like the posse in his *Butch Cassidy and the Sundance Kid,* relentlessly pursues Amos in his travels, a song that would lend itself to every different national styling.

No, Mary Ann

VOCALIST
You thought it all would be pie—
No, Mary Ann.
Pink little birds in the sky—
No, Mary Ann.
Symphony orchestras reeling
In glorious song,
Nothing but beautiful feeling—
Boy, were you wrong.

Now you say life is a bore—
No, Mary Ann.
Dreary and gray and no more—
No, Mary Ann.
Say it's all pink,
Say it's all gray,
That's too easy to think
And too easy to say,
And I'm just a man,
Mary Ann.

Suddenly now it's all flat—
No, Mary Ann.
Dreary and gray, and that's that—
No, Mary Ann.
Say it's all pink,
Say it's all gray,
That's too easy to think
And too easy to say.

It's what you feel,
And that's the least of it.
Make a meal,
No, make a feast of it!

The thing of it is,
I love you, Mary Ann.

Mary Ann was not the name of Amos's wife, nor of any of the women he meets during the course of the film. It was the name of one of my closest and most necessary friends, a remarkable woman named Mary Ann Madden, best known publicly for many years as the compiler and creator of *New York* magazine's literary competition, the magazine's most popular feature. As I pointed out in the first of these volumes, nothing is as hard to write (at least for me) as a song without a specific situation. When possibilities are infinite, paralysis sets in—there have to be some restrictions, some reasons to make choices, some particular vision. Bill's script called just for a song: any song, any subject, any form, any mood. The only stricture was that it had to sound like a Broadway hit of the period (the sixties), which narrowed the possibilities of the music but not the lyric. Faced with the infinite, all choices are arbitrary, and one night I was laughing over the phone with Mary Ann about her seemingly jaded but deeply romantic view of life and thought, Why not? Amos is a romantic, and he would probably write just such a song. The problem was that I had to decide how good a songwriter he was supposed to be. If the song were such a big hit, it would have to center around a very simple sentiment, neatly but cornily expressed, and that's what I wrote. When I played it for Mary Ann, I had trouble getting through it, we were both laughing so hard—and then we weren't. The eternal alchemy of show music had transformed corniness into feeling, as it so often does.

The Seven Percent Solution (1976)

Screenplay by Nicholas Meyer,
  based on his novel
Directed by Herbert Ross

The Notion

Concerned about Holmes's cocaine use, Dr. Watson tricks him into traveling to Vienna, where Holmes enters the care of Sigmund Freud. Freud attempts to solve the mysteries of Holmes's subconscious, while Holmes devotes himself to solving a mystery involving a kidnapping.

General Comments

Herb Ross was someone I'd known since my *West Side Story* days. He and his wife, Nora Kaye, one of the country's premier ballerinas, were close friends of Jerry Robbins's and we would often see each other at Jerry's parties, but it wasn't until the production of *Anyone Can Whistle* that I got to know him. Herb had been a Broadway chorus boy, a choreographer for American Ballet Theatre, a stager of nightclub acts, and was Jerry's first choice to choreograph for *West Side Story* (although when the producers insisted that Jerry choreograph the show, he hired Peter Gennaro as co-choreographer). He was also a director of musicals, though not successful ones. Arthur Laurents, an old friend of his, asked him to design the dances for *Whistle,* and our resultant collaboration on the "Cookie Chase," an extended ballet based on a dozen waltzes I wrote for it, flowered. In fact, a few years after the show, Herb asked me if I would consider expanding the "Cookie Chase" into a full-length ballet

for American Ballet Theatre. In self-deprecatory mode, I didn't take him seriously and never followed up on it.* He went on to become one of the most successful directors in Hollywood and in 1973 asked me to write a murder mystery for the screen, which, with the collaboration of Anthony Perkins, I did. It was called *The Last of Sheila* and it was not well received, but that didn't matter—writing a murder mystery was something I had always wanted to do.† So when he asked me to write a song for this movie, which took place in Edwardian times and therefore allowed me to exercise my pastiche muscles, I leapt at the chance. There is no need to go into the details of the plot to explain the song's function, suffice it to say that Sherlock Holmes has to go into an upscale brothel to pursue his prey, and when he does, the madam is singing to entertain her customers.

I Never Do Anything Twice

MADAM
When I was young and simple
(I don't recall the date),
I met a handsome Captain of the Guard.
He visited my chambers
One evening very late,
In tandem with a husky St. Bernard.

---

* Twelve years later he directed a memorable concert version of *Follies* with an extraordinary cast, accompanied by the New York Philharmonic Orchestra.
† And did again, with George Furth: a play called *Getting Away with Murder,* which was produced on Broadway in 1996. We didn't get away with it for long.

At first I was astonished,
And tears came to my eyes,
But later when I asked him to
    resume,
He said, to my surprise,
"My dear, it isn't wise.
Where love is concerned,
One must freshen the bloom.

Once, yes, once for a lark.
Twice, though, loses the spark.
One must never deny it,
But after you try it
You vary the diet."
Said my handsome young Guard,
"Yes, I know that it's hard.
Still, no matter how nice,
I never do anything twice."

I think about the Baron
Who came at my command,
And proffered me a riding crop and
    chains.
The evening that we shared
Was meticulously planned:
He took the most extraordinary
    pains.

He trembled with excitement,
His cheeks were quite aglow,
And afterward he cried to me,
    "Encore!"
He pleaded with me so
To have another go,
I murmured caressingly,
"Whatever for?"

Once, yes, once is a lark.
Twice, though, loses the spark.
Once, yes, once is delicious,
But twice would be vicious,
Or just repetitious.

Someone's bound to be scarred—
Yes, I know that it's hard.
Still, no matter the price,
I never do anything twice.

And then there was the Abbot
Who worshipped at my feet
And dressed me in a wimple and in
    veils.
He made a proposition
(Which I found rather sweet)
And handed me a hammer and some
    nails.

In time we lay contented,
And he began again
By fingering the beads around our
    waists.
I whispered to him then,
"We'll have to say Amen,"
For I had developed more catholic
    tastes.

Once, yes, once for a lark.
Twice, though, loses the spark.
As I said to the Abbot,
"I'll get in the habit,
But not in the habit."
You've my highest regard,
And I know that it's hard—
Still, no matter the vice,
I never do anything twice.

Once, yes, once can be nice:
Love requires some spice.
If you've something in view,

Something to do
Totally new,
I'll be there in a trice!
But I never do anything twice—
Except—
No, I never do anything twice.

Herb's request for "a song" might
seem to have presented the same problem as Bill Goldman's request for *The
Thing of It Is*, but even though there
was no specific dramatic situation or
subject, the simple fact that it was to be
sung in a brothel by an elegant madam
gave me something to build on. I knew
immediately that what I wanted to
do was write something filled with
double entendres, something even
Cole Porter, the dirtiest writer on
Broadway, might envy. I'm sorry he
didn't live long enough to hear it.

Dick Tracy (1990)

Screenplay by Jim Cash and Jack Epps, Jr.

The Notion

The famous detective is trying to get the goods on Big Boy Caprice, the leader of the mobsters in the city. His efforts are complicated by his romance with Tess Trueheart and the seductive wiles of Breathless Mahoney, a nightclub singer who is Big Boy's protégée/mistress.

General Comments

In 1981, Warren Beatty asked me to write music for his epic movie about the Russian Revolution, *Reds*. I told him I couldn't write the whole score because not only am I a slow writer (movie composers are forced to write their scores in astonishingly short periods of time) but because there was a good deal of battle music called for, and that kind of noise is largely a matter of orchestration, about which I know relatively little. I told him I'd be happy to supply the music accompanying the love story, which was as important to the film as the political events, and to my surprise he consented, hiring Dave Grusin for the rest. It was a gratifying experience; I was, and am, proud to be a part of that movie. Therefore, when he decided to make one with songs and asked me to supply them, I happily accepted the job. Not only was it for a movie based on a cartoon I had grown up with, it was set in the 1930s and thus invited pastiche, something I loved writing. Better yet, the songs were to decorate the plot rather than enhance it, which made them easy to write, and when Warren hired Madonna, no less, to play Breathless, I thought it might even be my chance to have a hit record. In the fullness of time, I didn't get a hit, but I got an Academy Award and, more important, had another good time working with Warren.

One of Breathless Mahoney's nightclub numbers, which she performs with a chorus of girls.

More

BREATHLESS
(In a fur coat, wearing a large diamond ring)

Once upon a time I had plenty of
    nothing—
Which was fine with me,
Because I had rhythm, music, love,
The sun, the stars, and the moon
    above,
Had the clear blue sky and the deep
    blue sea.
That was when the best things in life
    were free.

Then time went by and now I got
    plenty of plenty—
Which is fine with me,
'Cause I still got love, I still got
    rhythm,
But look at what I got to go
    with 'em!

"Who could ask for anything more?"
I hear you query.
Who could ask for anything more?
Well, let me tell you,
Dearie:

She takes the diamond out of the ring, holds it up and examines it, as chorus girls appear, also dressed in furs.

Got my diamonds, got my yacht,
Got a guy I adore.
I'm so happy with what I've got,
I want more!

Magically, she produces two more diamonds between her fingers.

Count your blessings: one, two,
    three—
I just hate keeping score.

She gathers the diamonds into her fist.

Any number is fine with me,
As long as it's more!

She opens her fist to reveal another three.

As long as it's more . . .

She opens her other hand to reveal six more.

I'm no mathematician.
All I know is addition.
I find counting a bore.
Keep the number mounting,
Your accountant does the
    counting . . .

She mixes the diamonds together, magically transforming them into a necklace.

CHORUS GIRLS
More! More!

BREATHLESS
I got rhythm, music too,
Just as much as before.
Got my guy and my sky of blue,
Now, however, I own the view.
More is better than nothing, true,
But nothing's better than

(Producing other necklaces, brooches, etc.)

More, more, more,
Nothing's better than more!

One is fun,
Why not two?
And if you like two,
Might as well have four.
And if you like four,
Why not a few,
Why not a slew

BREATHLESS, CHORUS GIRLS
More?
More!

Under the following, the chorus girls strip out of their furs, revealing bejeweled dresses.

BREATHLESS
If you've got a little,
Why not a lot?
Add a bit and it'll
Get to be an oodle.
Every jot and tittle
Adds to the pot—
Soon you've got the kit
As well as the caboodle—

CHORUS GIRLS
More! More! More! More!

BREATHLESS
Never say when,
Never stop at plenty—
If it's gonna rain, let it pour.
Happy with ten,
Happier with twenty—
If you like a penny,
Wouldn't you like many
Much more?

Or does that sound too greedy?
That's not greed—no, indeedy,
That's just stocking the store.
Gotta fill your cupboard—
Remember Mother Hubbard!

CHORUS GIRLS
More! More!

BREATHLESS
Each possession you possess
Helps your spirits to soar.
That's what's soothing about
    excess—
Never settle for something less.
Something's better than nothing,
    yes—

CHORUS GIRLS
But nothing's better than
More, more, more—

BREATHLESS
Except all, all, all . . .

CHORUS GIRLS
Except all, all, all . . .

BREATHLESS
(Sentimentally)
Except once you have it all—

capital(ism)
(ist)
(istic)

ample, sample
a few, somewhat
several, slew
sufficient, comp—
past
half, 3/4
whole
little, much
lot(s), swile
pots, couple
minimum, maximum
most
faith in early
extra little god
majority hoard
galore, bundle
good deal, stacks
show, loads
heaps, piles
batch, peck
shooting, bushel
matching, barrel
something
every thing
kit, caboodle
oodles, gobs
scads
bevy
tions, lots
enough, to spare
tons, barrels
the whole shebang
assortment
sweeten
accumulate
amplify, stash
acquire, stack
multiply, change
enlarge, ...
amass
collect
gather
assemble
layaway
stockpile
nest egg(s)
in reserve, dug
for a rainy ...
nuts for winter

dozens
millions
hundreds
thousands

---

increase   double your investment   never stint
plus   triple   any, many, penny
total   bigger   abundant copious
augment   redundant opulent   (mint of) nether lining, mining
accruing   building   luxury   Not to be summoned, determined,
pileups   accumulate   Distinct, minted   ermine!
                                                                   firm and

If you like some,   Gotta start somewhere   Why stop at plenty
Why not plenty   with something
                                                 Stand there firmer chem:
If you like two,   One Thing   Merely murmurs "More ____"
what's wrong with
Why not four   No Thing

Happy with ten,   Why settle for few   All of that "enough's enough" stuff
Happier with twenty   When you can have plenty   54/6
Nice to have something in store. Why settle for two accrued

                    When you can have 20? My first word when just a tot
One is lovely two is swell   was "yacht" (More ____
   Rockefeller
Even sweller is four

                                                 If you're fond of rubies,
When you've got two   I like plethoras,   Not to mention pearls
Then All you have to
know what you do?   I like surfeits   Billionaires are boobies,
Start to accrue   I like gluts   Not to mention earls,
                                                 Remember that
                       Give me surplus   when it comes to girls

Enough is not sufficient,
Sufficient's not enough
                                                 Settle when you're cold,
                                                 (Europe) Sail in Jocque
                                                 London on a liner

         all right   Some   Nothing could be finer than to sail
One is okay   One is just swell   on an ocean liner
Two is even better   Two is even sweller When it comes to gold
Same is swell,   That's how Rockefeller I'm a '49-er
Lots (even) sweller   Started his store fortune Somewhere I was told
I hear tell
                                                 silver lining
From Mr. Rockefeller   Let him dim The mining
                        some crumbs plums thumbs dandelions
Add enough crumbs comes mums becomes drums
                                                 Settle for half?
More is better, period
                                                 Don't make me laugh
         myriad   better Rockefeller   Never be a money thing
                       Surely was nicer..   You can take a taxi
                       It's more.
                                                 min

                                                 max.

ground to Tracy's planting a bug in the club that monitors all of Big Boy's meetings, and subsequently as he raids every crooked establishment that Big Boy owns.

Sooner or Later

BREATHLESS
Sooner or later
You're gonna be mine.
Sooner or later
You're gonna be fine.
Baby, it's time that you faced it—
I always get my man.

Sooner or later
You're gonna decide:
Sooner or later
There's nowhere to hide.
Baby, it's time, so why waste it
In chatter?
Let's settle
The matter.
Baby, you're mine on a platter—
I always get my man.

But if you insist, babe,
The challenge delights me.
The more you resist, babe,
The more it excites me,
And no one I've kissed, babe,
Ever fights me
Again.

If you're on my list,
It's just a question of when.
When I get a yen,
Then baby, amen.
I'm counting to ten . . .
And then . . .

I'm gonna love you
Like nothing you've known.
I'm gonna love you,
And you all alone.
Sooner is better than later,
But, lover,
I'll hover,
I'll plan:
This time I'm not only getting,
I'm holding
My man.

*What I like is gliding
Where the wind takes me to,
Flying high and hiding
Up in a tree.
Live alone and like it,
That's the answer for me.*

On your own with only
You to concern yourself

Doesn't mean you're lonely,
Just that you're free.
Live alone and like it,
Don't come down from that tree.
That's the answer for me.
That's the answer for me.

The following is another of Breathless's nightclub numbers. We first hear a section of it early in the picture, sung by her in the club while the city sleeps. Later, we hear it sung in full as back-

---

* The stanza between asterisks was cut.

CHORUS GIRLS
Have it all—

BREATHLESS
You may find, all else above—

CHORUS GIRLS
Else above—

BREATHLESS
That though "things" are bliss,
There's one thing you miss,
And that's—

ALL
(Brightly)
More! More!
More more more more more!!

In the years between the world wars, a great many popular songs dealt with the idea that material wealth is not a guarantee of personal happiness, a sentiment of particular power during the Depression. (It's a sentiment that persists in popular music to th[is] although it's usually co[...] cosmic, quasi-religious [...] character like Breathles[s...] that the opposite tack wo[...] one to take: as Gordon Ge[c...] greed is good. Thus the man[...] ences, which I trust the know[...] reader will note, to the more fa[...] songs of the period, such as "I G[...] Plenty o' Nuttin'," "I Got the Sun [...] the Morning," "The Best Things in [...] Life Are Free" and "I Got Rhythm."

Also, it should be noted, the stage directions were my intention, but not the result, as is often the case in movies in which the writer and director are not one and the same.

Tracy and Tess adopt an orphaned kid, named Kid, a tough little boy who, during a sequence underscored by the following song, is won over by Tracy and Tess, which makes Tracy happy but emphasizes his isolation as someone obsessively dedicated to his work.

Fr[...]
Onl[...]
As an[...]
Live a[...]
Why is [...]

Free to cal[...]
Free to say i[...]
    or play.
You can have t[...]
But you don't ha[...]
    and day.
Anyway,

---

* In this case, Mel Tormé

"What Can You Lose?" (Mandy Patinkin as 88 Keys, Madonna as Breathless)

ground to Tracy's planting a bug in the club that monitors all of Big Boy's meetings, and subsequently as he raids every crooked establishment that Big Boy owns.

Sooner or Later

BREATHLESS

Sooner or later
You're gonna be mine.
Sooner or later
You're gonna be fine.
Baby, it's time that you faced it—
I always get my man.

Sooner or later
You're gonna decide:
Sooner or later
There's nowhere to hide.
Baby, it's time, so why waste it
In chatter?
Let's settle
The matter.
Baby, you're mine on a platter—
I always get my man.

But if you insist, babe,
The challenge delights me.
The more you resist, babe,
The more it excites me,
And no one I've kissed, babe,
Ever fights me
Again.

If you're on my list,
It's just a question of when.
When I get a yen,
Then baby, amen.
I'm counting to ten . . .
And then . . .

I'm gonna love you
Like nothing you've known.
I'm gonna love you,
And you all alone.
Sooner is better than later,
But, lover,
I'll hover,
I'll plan:
This time I'm not only getting,
I'm holding
My man.

*What I like is gliding
Where the wind takes me to,
Flying high and hiding
Up in a tree.
Live alone and like it,
That's the answer for me.*

On your own with only
You to concern yourself

Doesn't mean you're lonely,
Just that you're free.
Live alone and like it,
Don't come down from that tree.
That's the answer for me.
That's the answer for me.

The following is another of Breathless's nightclub numbers. We first hear a section of it early in the picture, sung by her in the club while the city sleeps. Later, we hear it sung in full as back-

---

* The stanza between asterisks was cut.

CHORUS GIRLS
Have it all—

BREATHLESS
You may find, all else above—

CHORUS GIRLS
Else above—

BREATHLESS
That though "things" are bliss,
There's one thing you miss,
And that's—

ALL
(Brightly)
More! More!
More more more more more!!

In the years between the world wars, a great many popular songs dealt with the idea that material wealth is not a guarantee of personal happiness, a sentiment of particular power during the Depression. (It's a sentiment that persists in popular music to this day, although it's usually couched in more cosmic, quasi-religious terms.) For a character like Breathless, I thought that the opposite tack would be the one to take: as Gordon Gecko says, greed is good. Thus the many references, which I trust the knowledgeable reader will note, to the more famous songs of the period, such as "I Got Plenty o' Nuttin'," "I Got the Sun in the Morning," "The Best Things in Life Are Free" and "I Got Rhythm."

Also, it should be noted, the stage directions were my intention, but not the result, as is often the case in movies in which the writer and director are not one and the same.

Tracy and Tess adopt an orphaned kid, named Kid, a tough little boy who, during a sequence underscored by the following song, is won over by Tracy and Tess, which makes Tracy happy but emphasizes his isolation as someone obsessively dedicated to his work.

Live Alone and Like It

MALE VOCALIST*
Live alone and like it,
Free as the birds in the trees,
High above the briars.
Live alone and like it.
Doing whatever you please
When your heart desires,
Free to hang around or fly at any
    old time.

No equivocation,
Most of all no guarantees,
That can be your motto.
Free of obligation,
Only the murmuring breeze
As an obbligato.
Live alone and like it—
Why is that such a crime?

Free to call the tune,
Free to say if you're gonna work
    or play.
You can have the moon,
But you don't have to have it night
    and day.
Anyway,

---

* In this case, Mel Tormé

"What Can You Lose?" (Mandy Patinkin as 88 Keys, Madonna as Breathless)

BA-BY, YOU'RE MINE ON A PLAT-TER, I AL - WAYS GET MY

MAN. BUT

IF YOU IN-SIST, BABE, THE CHAL-LENGE DE - LIGHTS ME, THE MORE YOU RE-SIST, BABE, THE

STEPHEN SONDHEIM

This was one of my two signature Harold Arlen tunes in the score (the other being "What Can You Lose?"), the one that won me the Academy Award. I'd wanted to win an Academy Award ever since I'd become a movie buff in my early teens, and over the years had imagined half a dozen acceptance speeches, but when the nominations were announced I was recuperating from a broken ankle and was told by my doctor that I would still be on crutches when Oscar night arrived. Warren pressed me to come to the Awards ceremony anyway, but I figured that even if I won, it would take me half an hour to reach the stage and, more important, it would be difficult for me to get out to the bar in the lobby rather than wait in suspense in my auditorium seat (the common practice, I'm told, during the ceremonies), so I reluctantly told him no. A week later, the producers sent me a full-size chocolate Oscar. Perhaps it was in compensation or perhaps it was something they sent to all their nominees, but in any event it arrived with its leg broken. Unlikely as it seems, either the producers or the United States Postal Service had a sense of humor.

This song is sung first by 88 Keys, Breathless's accompanist, who is in unrequited love with her. It begins as ironic background scoring for a sequence of Tracy working futilely and having no time for the increasingly discouraged Tess; halfway through, it becomes a duet for 88 Keys and Breathless, sitting together at the piano in the nightclub after it has closed.

What Can You Lose?

88 KEYS
What can you lose?
Only the blues.
Why keep concealing
Everything you're feeling?
Say it to her—
What can you lose?

Maybe it shows—
She's had clues,
Which she chose to ignore.
Maybe, though, she knows,
And just wants to go on as before—
As a friend, nothing more.
So she closes the door.

BREATHLESS
Well, if she does,
Those are the dues.

BOTH
Once the words are spoken,
Something may be broken—
Still, you love her,
What can you lose?

88 KEYS
But what if she goes?
At least, now you have part of her—

BOTH
What if she had to choose?

BREATHLESS
Leave it alone.

88 KEYS
Hold it all in.

BOTH
Better a bone.
Don't even begin.
With so much to win,
There's too much to lose.

The only reason for this song was Warren's desire to have Mandy Patinkin, who played 88 Keys, sing something in the movie. When I grumbled that since the character was undeveloped, anything he sang would feel arbitrary, Warren urged me to look at his dialogue and see if anything might suggest itself, even just a title. Sure enough, in the scene directly preceding the sequence above, 88 Keys offers Big Boy a proposition to trap Tracy with the enticement, "What can you lose?" Done.

Tracy is framed for murder and put in jail, which leaves Big Boy and his gangsters free to commit heinous crimes all over the city. This song underscores the sequence.

Back in Business

Music: a vamp punctuated with a cash register.

SINGERS
Yesterday it seemed the world was
    about to end,
Didn't it?
Looked as though it wouldn't last
    out the year.
Yesterday disaster waited around the
    bend—
Well, my friend,
Spring is here.

(Cash register)

Back in business,
And ain't it grand?
Let the good times roll!

(Cash register)

Yesterday things were out of hand,
Now they're under control.

(Cash register)

Bye bye, blues,
So long, adversity,
Happiness, hello!
Keep the status quo
Permanently so.

(Cash register)

Back again like a boomerang,
Same old stand,
Same old gang,
Back in business and with a bang!

(Gunshot)

Let the good times roll!

Yesterday it seemed we never would
    smile again,
Didn't it?
Didn't matter what we ventured,
    or how.
Looked as though the fun was over
    till who knew when.
That was then.
This is now.

(Cash register)

Back in business,
And ain't it grand?
Let the good times roll!

(Cash register)

Yesterday things were out of hand,
Now they're under control.

(Cash register)

Back to normal,
Back to usual,
Let the fun resume.

No more doom and gloom.
No more bust, just boom!

(Explosion)

Back in business, and overnight,
In demand—
Well, all right!
Business is just dynamite!

(Explosions)

Let the good times roll!

*Same old play with the same old
    cast,
Like the past,
But at last,
Back in business and with a blast!
Let the good times roll!*

Warren had told me that he wanted to edit according to the song, and so I fashioned a lyric that punned on words like "bang" and "boom," which were designed to coincide with gunshots and bombs—designed to, but not filmed that way. Perhaps it hamstrung him too much, as the scenario for "The Glamorous Life" in the film of *A Little Night Music* had hamstrung Hal Prince. It was a disappointment, but, like the rest of the score, it was a blast to write.

---

* The stanza between asterisks was written for the revue *Putting It Together.*

Singing Out Loud (Unproduced, 1992)

A Musical Movie about a Movie Musical
   That's in Trouble
Screenplay by William Goldman

The Notion

The year is 1992. Charlie Lake, the superstar/actress/ conglomerate, is in the throes of producing her first movie musical, starring herself. A short while into the shooting, the results of which satisfy nobody, the head of production at the studio insists she replace the writer and director. Somewhat reluctantly, she hires Griffith Bean, a prestigious Hollywood filmmaker as well as her ex-lover and a man who needs a hit. Since he is to rewrite it as well as direct it, he in turn hires Jed Lazenby to write the score, Lazenby being the hottest young singer/songwriter/conglomerate in the pop music world. As might be expected, Jed falls for Charlie at the same time her love affair with Griffith is reheating itself. The story chronicles the making of the movie as it is being formed and reshaped by its emotionally tangled creators.

General Comments

In 1990 Bill Goldman was approached by his good friend Rob Reiner, the director of Bill's screenplays *The Princess Bride* and *Misery,* to write a musical movie. Bill in turn approached his good friend me to collaborate on it. Despite my disheartening experience in adapting *A Little Night Music* for the screen, once again I couldn't resist "so many possibilities," as George says in *Sunday in the Park with George,* to write songs for the camera. It was something I'd been

aching to do ever since I'd seen the opening number of Stanley Donen and Gene Kelly's *On the Town* in 1949. Using the editing rhythms of film to parallel and counterpoint musical forms presents infinite chances for invention, as proven by the imaginative movies of Ernst Lubitsch (*The Love Parade*), René Clair (*Sous le toits de Paris*) and Rouben Mamoulian (*Love Me Tonight*) in the 1930s up to those of Richard Lester (*A Hard Day's Night*), Herbert Ross (*Pennies from Heaven*), Baz Luhrmann (*Moulin Rouge!*) and others in the years that followed. Having whetted my appetite with an adaptation, I couldn't wait to try my hand at a piece conceived as a film from the beginning. Moreover, I had an idea for one, which I'd been nurturing for years.

The idea derived from a French film which I'd seen in 1952 when I was a severe movie elitist: *Holiday for Henrietta,* directed by a particular favorite of mine, Julien Duvivier.* Its plot concerned a team of two middle-aged male screenwriters assigned by a film producer about to go into production with a hopeless script, to concoct over a weekend a new one, using the actors and sets at hand.

We see the writers go through their quotidian lives at a country inn where the producer has housed them: waking up, shaving, eating, attending to their companions (one has a wife, one a mistress). All of this is accomplished in short scenes which are sporadically interspersed with the writers' increasingly pressured brainstorming sessions about the scenario

---

* Duvivier's romantic melodramas are a treasure trove of ideas for musicals—or, rather, were in the 1950s. I had wanted to adapt two others: *La belle équipe* and *Un carnet de bal,* the first a linear tale about friendship, the second an episodic one about memory— two subjects that appeal to me.

they're inventing, the constantly shifting plots of which are enacted in a movie within the movie that keeps changing directions as they keep changing their story. It's a delightful film, the kind that used to be known as a Gallic comedy—glancing and indirect, concentrating on the telling details of human behavior, full of small surprises and rhythmic switches.*

Obviously, one of the things that interested me about adapting *Holiday for Henrietta* was the same as one that had interested me in writing *Sunday in the Park with George:* it was about the creative act. In this case it was a narrative act rather than a visual one, which had an advantage: a movie would allow the visualization of the creative process itself as it's taking place. On the stage, you can't dramatize the choices of color, shape and form that a painter makes as he paints, you can show only the result. But you *can* show what goes on in a writer's mind while he imagines a scene or a musical number, and more effec-

tively on the screen than on the stage because of the camera's ability to change course in an instant. For example, a songwriter might begin by imagining a soloist and suddenly in mid-phrase decide it should be a choral number—and in the blink of an eye (literally) the screen fills with fifty people as the musical phrase continues uninterrupted. More important, there was something else which interested me about this project, implicit in the very fact that we would be writing a musical about the making of a musical—it's summed up in the title. (Explanation to follow.)

Singing Out Loud takes place in the remote world of 1992 Hollywood and involves the following cast of characters:

Charlie Lake: 32. For five years, one of the few female movie stars with genuine clout, due to an increasingly popular series of movies about a comic character named Bitsy, which she loathes making. Having started as a musical comedy understudy who never got the chance to go on, she now wants to show the world that she can sing and dance, to which end she is producing her first movie, a musical.

Sid Bergman: Mid-30s. Head of production at the studio where Charlie is producing her movie. A businessman.

Barney Slotkin: Charlie's business partner, formerly her agent. Nervous.

Griffith Bean: Early 40s. Autocratic director, recently divorced and long-ago Charlie's lover.

Jed Lazenby: Late 20s. Singer-songwriter, star in his own right. Also, a worshiper of Griff's movies.

---

* In 1964 it was transformed (to use the word accurately) into a vapid "romantic comedy" by Paramount Pictures called *Paris When It Sizzles,* in which the writers are a youngish man and woman who in the best (that is, worst) Hollywood tradition fall in love and imagine themselves in the different scenarios of the script they're creating. The Duvivier version had two separate casts: one for the "real" movie, grubby and garrulous, the other for the scenarios, outrageously handsome and beautiful. Suffice it to say that in the Paramount version the writers themselves were outrageously handsome and beautiful, being played respectively by William Holden and Audrey Hepburn, and the action, rather than taking place in a country inn, took place on the Riviera.

SINGING OUT LOUD

A Musical Movie

About

A Movie Musical

That's in Trouble

Screenplay by: William Goldman

Songs by: Stephen Sondheim

Fourth Draft

February '92

1

FADE IN ON

A PIN SPOT HITTING A FABULOUS FACE.

The face, we'll find out soon enough, belongs to CHARLIE LAKE. Thirty-two, she has been for five years, one of the few female movie stars with genuine clout.

THE SPOTLIGHT WIDENS.

CHARLIE stands there, motionless, elegant in a glorious long white chiffon evening dress. We realize we're in a 30's nightclub and it's very art deco. Customers fill all the tables, the women in evening gowns, the men in tails.

Now, at a downbeat from the nightclub orchestra, CHARLIE begins to sing "Sand."

                    CHARLIE
          LOVE IS JUST SAND,
          SLIPPERY BUT CLINGING.
          LOVE IS JUST SAND,
          STIR IT AND IT FLIES.
          LOVE IS JUST GRAND
          TILL YOU FEEL IT STINGING
          YOUR EYES.

As she starts the second verse, her body moves gracefully around the beautifully polished dance floor. It's a nice moment, full of memory -- that could be Ginger Rogers or Eleanor Powell up there -- and the song has a certain Gershwin lilt to it.

                    CHARLIE
          LOVE IS JUST SAND,
          SLIPPING THROUGH YOUR FINGERS.
          NOW IT'S IN HAND
          NOW IT ISN'T THERE.
          JUST LIKE SAND,
          EVEN WHEN IT LINGERS,
          ALL IT'S ABOUT
          IS YOU CAN'T GET IT OUT
          OF YOUR HAIR.

The second verse ends and as she spins closer and closer to CAMERA --

-- freeze --

-- and the instant that happens, the music changes, not the tune, but the beat, the orchestration -- it's all rock now, synthesizers blasting away as we

Sand

FADE IN on Charlie, in a long white chiffon evening dress, in a 1930s night-club. The song is a foxtrot in the style of the Gershwins.

CHARLIE
Love is just sand,
Slippery but clinging.
Love is just sand,
Stir it and it flies.
Love is just grand
Till you feel it stinging
Your eyes.

Love is just sand,
Slipping through your fingers.
Now it's in hand,
Now it isn't there.
Just like sand,
Even when it lingers,
All it's about
Is you can't get it out
Of your hair.

The set dissolves into sand dunes and the song instantaneously becomes an MTV rock number, complete with male dancers dressed as Arab brigands, riding camels.

DANCERS
Stir it and it flies,
Flies into your eyes,
Now it ain't there,
Hey, it's in your hair!

The camera keeps cutting back and forth between the nightclub and the desert.

CHARLIE
It can seem smooth,
When really it's bumpy,
It can look soft and be dry,
Warm and be soothing,
Hot and make you jumpy,
Although you'll never know until
    you try:
Is it the Sahara
Or a beach beneath a Caribbean
    sky?

Love is just sand,
You can feel it shifting:
Soon as you stand,
You begin to sink.
Everything's planned,
Then it gets to drifting,
Never to where you think.
Love ain't solid land,
It's just sand.

The number continues in this schizo-phrenic fashion, until:

SID'S VOICE
Okay, enough—I've got a weak
stomach.

The CAMERA pulls back to reveal that we've been watching the rough cut of a musical sequence in a Hollywood screening room. The music and lyrics are by a now-dead legendary song-writer of the 1930s named George Hoffman, and Charlie wanted to do a musical which evoked those innocent times, "but with a contemporary sensi-bility." The number is clearly a disaster and Sid insists that Charlie fire the director-writer and hire someone else. She decides to ask Griffith Bean to take over. Accompanied by Barney, her overly eager agent, she invites Griff to lunch at the Ivy, a Hollywood power-broker restaurant. They haven't seen each other in a long time.

Lunch*

Griff approaches the table where Char-lie and Barney are sitting and holds out his hand.

GRIFF
It's been a while.

---

* Since the songs were conceived for the camera, this and the following lyrics will oc-casionally include detailed scenarios as well as compressed passages of dialogue and camera directions.
† Except where noted, all the dialogue is in rhythm.

A nervous musical phrase. Charlie gives him a polite smile and offers him her hand in return.

CHARLIE (voice-over)
(Speaking in rhythm)†
"It's been a while . . ."

Griff covers her hand with his other hand.

BARNEY
(A bundle of nervous energy, beckoning)
Waiter!

Another brief musical phrase.

CHARLIE (v.o.)
Now we get the wink and the
    smile . . .

Griff winks at her and smiles a warm, intimate smile.

BARNEY
Waiter!

Griff drops into his chair.

CHARLIE (v.o.)
Does the bastard really think that
    I've forgotten? . . .

BARNEY
(To Griff)

Want a drink?

GRIFF
(Gesturing "no")
Thanks.

CHARLIE (v.o.)
Dirty rotten—

BARNEY
(To her)
You?

CHARLIE
(Aloud)
What?

BARNEY
Drink.

CHARLIE
Fine.

(V.O.)
. . . Fink . . .

BARNEY
Waiter—!

CHARLIE (v.o.)
(Smiling ever more brightly)
Creep . . .

BARNEY
(To Griff)
Wine?

CHARLIE (v.o.)
Prick.

GRIFF
(To Barney)
Later.

BARNEY
(Screaming)
Waiter!

He looks up to find the waiter, a bright-eyed young man, standing next to him on the other side.

WAITER
(Cheerfully, in rhythm)
Hi, I'm Nick.

The music stops.

WAITER
(Out of rhythm)
I'm your waiter for today, and our octopus mousse is just outstanding.*

GRIFF
(Amused)
Was that supposed to be funny?

WAITER
I was kind of hoping so.

_____
* The dialogue is Bill's, but the items on the menu are mine.
_____

BARNEY
Two spritzers, and I'm hungry, so tell me, what's with the sprouts?

Percussion underneath.

WAITER
Well, there's always our sprout-and-watercress salad, or if you prefer . . .

Music resumes; his voice recedes into the distance. Griff fiddles with his menu and looks everywhere but at Charlie.

GRIFF (v.o.)
(Speaking in rhythm)
Well, she doesn't seem upset.
That smile a mile long . . .

WAITER
. . . Or we have them foo yong . . .

His voice recedes again, Barney listening intently.

GRIFF (v.o.)
So why isn't she upset?

BARNEY
(To the waiter, ordering)
Vinaigrette.

GRIFF (v.o.)
(Annoyed)
Has she forgotten?

BARNEY
(Turns to Griff)
Which I recommend . . .

His voice recedes also.

GRIFF (v.o.)
(Studying the menu)
I get it,
She's pretending to forget—

Barney turns inquiringly to Charlie, who shakes her head "no." Griff glances up, assessing them.

What's the deal?

Charlie catches his eye with her ever-more-dazzling smile.

BARNEY
(To the waiter)
One vinaigrette.

(To Griff)
Two vinaigrette?

GRIFF (v.o.)
(Returning to the menu)
Is that real?
Is she nervous?
What's the scoop? . . .

(Snapping out of it, to the waiter)

What's the soup?

WAITER
The broccoli gumbo.

GRIFF
(Disbelief)
Broccoli gumbo?

BARNEY
(Simultaneously, encouraging Griff)
Broccoli gumbo . . .

WAITER
(Grimacing)
That's the special.

(His voice receding)

Then of course there's the usual guava madrilène . . .

As he continues, music resumes, growing into a vamp, the background noise (conversation, cutlery, plates, scraping chairs, the occasional phone ring, etc.) becoming a rising and falling hum, playing against it. From here until the end of the sequence, even though we mix dialogue, rhythmic speech and inner thoughts both sung and spoken, the cuts and close-ups are not necessarily on the character we see or the voice-over we hear: rather, they punctuate the moments where singing switches to dialogue, or establish the singer whenever the viewer might be confused. Otherwise, the number is treated as a casual spoken scene, with the camera often observing the whole table

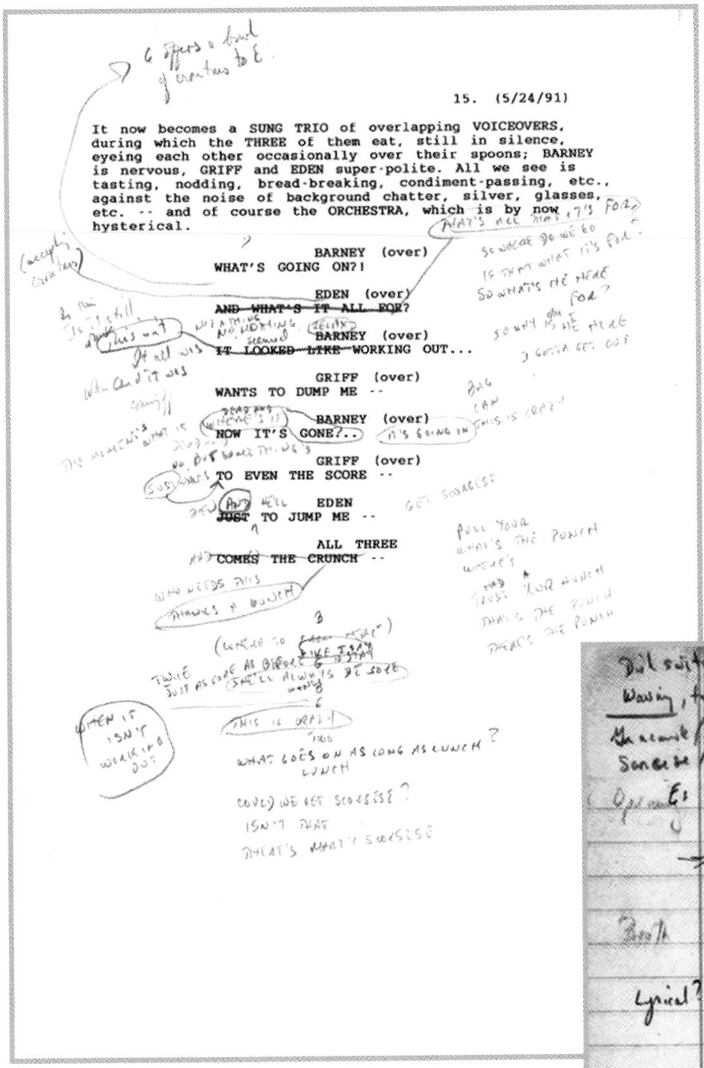

It now becomes a SUNG TRIO of overlapping VOICEOVERS,
during which the THREE of them eat, still in silence,
eyeing each other occasionally over their spoons; BARNEY
is nervous, GRIFF and EDEN super-polite. All we see is
tasting, nodding, bread-breaking, condiment-passing, etc.,
against the noise of background chatter, silver, glasses,
etc. -- and of course the ORCHESTRA, which is by now
hysterical.

                    BARNEY (over)
          WHAT'S GOING ON?!

                    EDEN (over)
          AND WHAT'S IT ALL FOR?

                    BARNEY (over)
          IT LOOKED LIKE WORKING OUT...

                    GRIFF (over)
          WANTS TO DUMP ME --

                    BARNEY (over)
          NOW IT'S GONE?..

                    GRIFF (over)
          WANTS TO EVEN THE SCORE --

                    EDEN
          JUST TO JUMP ME --

                    ALL THREE
          AND COMES THE CRUNCH --

(handwritten annotations throughout, including:)
6 offers a bowl of croutons to E.
WHAT'S HER NAME
SOMEONE DO WE GO
IS THAT WHAT IT'S FOR?
SO WHAT'S HE HERE FOR?
SO WHY IS HE HERE
I GOTTA GET OUT
CAN THIS IS CRAZY
IT'S GOING IN
GET SCARLESS
PULL YOUR
WHAT'S THE PUNCH
WHERE'S
JUST "FOR LUNCH
THAT'S THE PUNCH
THERE'S THE PUNCH
WHO NEEDS THIS
THANKS A BUNCH
WHEN IT ISN'T WORKING OUT
TWICE
JUST AS SORE AS BEFORE
LIKE THAT
SO I'LL ALWAYS BE SORE
THIS IS CRAZY
WHAT GOES ON AS LONG AS LUNCH?
LUNCH
COULD WE GET SCORSESE?
ISN'T THAT
THAT'S MARTY SCORSESE

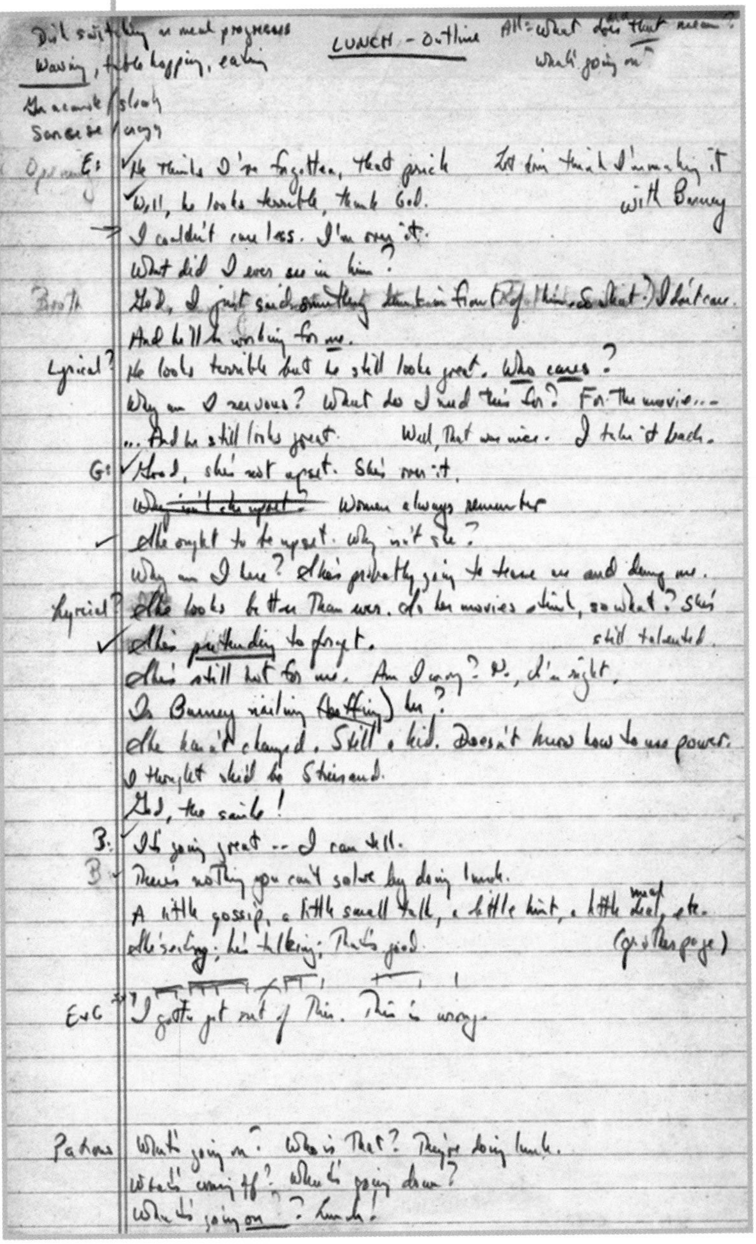

(and room) as well as the details of food, expression, pantomimed speech, etc.

CHARLIE (v.o.)
(Still at the menu)
Well, his hair is thinning,
At least there's that.
And the rest of him's beginning
To turn to fat.
He looks old and sad,
Which he fucking should.
He looks really bad—

BARNEY
(To the waiter)
How's the gumbo?

CHARLIE
(Murmuring)
—Good.

WAITER
(Wryly, to Barney)
Good.

BARNEY
(Gesturing toward Charlie)
Good, one broccoli gumbo.

GRIFF
(To the waiter)
Two broccoli gumbo.

CHARLIE (v.o.)
I could care less . . .

Griff flashes a "We've always liked the same thing" smile at Charlie. She gives him a blindingly phony smile back.

GRIFF (v.o.)
Who'd guess?
She still can't resist
After all this while,
That's the "I'm still pissed
But I've missed you" smile . . .

WAITER
Something else?

BARNEY
(Searching the menu)
Where's the pasta?

WAITER
(Points to insert)
It's polenta with pears.

Barney considers it.

GRIFF (v.o.)
She still cares . . .

CHARLIE (v.o.)
That look . . .

GRIFF (v.o.)
You can read her like a book . . .

CHARLIE (v.o.)
That "We've got a secret no one shares"
Look . . .

BARNEY
(Referring to the polenta)
Griff—?

GRIFF (v.o.)
Am I wrong?

CHARLIE (v.o.)
God, the gall . . .

GRIFF (v.o.)
Am I ever?

BARNEY
(Getting no response from Griff, to the waiter)
No thanks, not for me.

GRIFF (v.o.)
She's still hot for me . . .

GRIFF, CHARLIE (v.o.)
(Smiling up from their menus)
Hasn't changed a bit.

GRIFF (v.o.)
Still a kid . . .

CHARLIE (v.o.)
Still a shit . . .

Barney glances quickly at them.

BARNEY (v.o.)
(Singing for the first time)
So far, so good.

(Speaking, to the waiter)

Any other specials?

(V.O., singing)

I think it's working out . . .

WAITER
Well, there's poi—

BARNEY
Ah.

(V.O.)

I knew it would . . .

WAITER
—With the mango au poivre.

BARNEY (v.o.)
Goes to show you:
Trust your hunch.

WAITER
Diced.

BARNEY (v.o.)
I always say—

WAITER
—And of course today—

BARNEY (v.o.)
—if you want to work things out—

WAITER
Salmon cassoulet.

BARNEY (v.o.)
There's no better way
Than—

WAITER
Brandied.

BARNEY
—Lunch.

GRIFF
(To the waiter)
Okay, broccoli gumbo.

BARNEY (v.o.)
Never saw a meal—

GRIFF
(To Charlie)
Now about this movie . . .

BARNEY (v.o.)
—That a little food could hurt.

CHARLIE
(To the waiter, ignoring Griff)
Is the poi fresh?

BARNEY (v.o.)
I can feel—

WAITER
(Gently, to Charlie)
It's a sort of paste.

CHARLIE
Oh.

She looks with embarrassment at Griff
for an instant.

BARNEY (v.o.)
—They got a real rapport.

CHARLIE (v.o.)
Dumb . . .

BARNEY (v.o.)
We'll have a deal—

Griff smiles at her and shrugs as if to
say, "Who would know about poi?"

CHARLIE (v.o.)
(Back to her menu)
And he's eating it up . . .

BARNEY (v.o.)
By the time we hit dessert.

CHARLIE
(To the waiter, handing back
the menu)
No, that's all.

The waiter turns to Griff for confir-
mation.

GRIFF
(To the waiter, handing back his menu
but smiling at Charlie)
Yeah, that's all . . .

BARNEY (v.o.)
And that's all
That doing lunch
Is for.

(To the waiter, handing back
the menu)

Three broccoli gumbo, and skip
the sprouts.

As music continues underneath, skit-
tish and sporadic, Charlie and Griff
exchange barbed dialogue, first about
their shared past, then the pathway of
their careers; there is an edge of affection, but the tone is mostly hostile.

WAITER
(In rhythm, approaching with plates)
'kay, lemme see, who gets the broccoli gumbo?

(Out of rhythm, putting the plates
down)

Oh, c'mon now, smile, that was
funny—you all do.

Music continues under. Barney goes on
with his mending-fences pitch. As he
does so, he pats Charlie's hand once or
twice in encouragement. Griff glances
back and forth between them.

BARNEY
(Out of rhythm)
It's so exciting, just sitting here—
the sparks are just gonna fly the
minute you two start working
together . . .

CHARLIE (v.o.)
(Simultaneously)
This is all baloney.
He makes us wait,
Says he thinks I'm phony—
Why keep the date?

I'm this big success,
Which he's gotta hate.
Needs the job, I guess.
Boy, is he a mess—

WAITER
Enjoy the gumbo . . .

(Leaves)

CHARLIE (v.o.)
And he still looks great—

BARNEY
(To Griff)
. . . You're here to say "yes"—

CHARLIE (v.o.)
What's going on?

Seeing Griff's look, Charlie squeezes
Barney's hand and holds it, for Griff's
benefit.

BARNEY
I can feel it, you're here—

GRIFF
I'm here to tell you this . . .

He continues to speak aloud, as he
sings.

GRIFF (v.o.)
What is that about?
Is he boffing her,
Or just making out
As if they really were?
What's going on?

GRIFF
(Continuing aloud to Barney, out of
rhythm, simultaneously with
the above)
I've got a big meeting set up—
after agents and lawyers and
accountants—we'll run it through
the computer—

CHARLIE (v.o.)
(Overlapping)
What is that about?
To show he's got clout?

GRIFF (v.o.)
Is this a con?

(Aloud, continuing simultaneously)

—and see what comes out.

The music stops for a moment.

GRIFF
(Out of rhythm)
Did I really say "run it through the computer"?

He laughs and shakes his head. The laugh dies. Barney doesn't know what to say. All three begin to eat their soup in silence—except for the increasingly agitated voice-overs as music resumes.

CHARLIE (v.o.)
I get it:
First he'll work us up
For a week or so—

GRIFF (v.o.)
(Overlapping)
I get it:
First she'll set me up,
Then she'll let me go—

CHARLIE (v.o.)
Then he'll quit—

GRIFF (v.o.)
Just to let me know—

CHARLIE (v.o.)
Just to show me—

BOTH (v.o.)
Who's boss.

CHARLIE (v.o.)
His loss—

GRIFF (v.o.)
Her loss—

BARNEY
Now this I call gumbo!

CHARLIE (v.o.)
And I could care less . . .

A beat. Barney offers Griff a dish of greens from the center of the table.

BARNEY
Watercress?

The song now becomes a trio of overlapping voice-overs, during which the three of them eat, still in silence, glancing at each other occasionally over their spoons; all we see is tasting, nodding, bread-breaking, condiment-passing, etc., against the noise of background restaurant chatter, silver, glasses, etc. The music becomes increasingly frenetic.

BARNEY (v.o.)
What's going on?!

CHARLIE (v.o.)
That's all that it's for . . .

BARNEY (v.o.)
I had it working out . . .

GRIFF (v.o.)
She just wants to dump me—

BARNEY (v.o.)
Now it's gone . . .

GRIFF (v.o.)
Just to even the score.

CHARLIE (v.o.)
And to jump me—

BARNEY (v.o.)
Well—

ALL THREE (v.o.)
Thanks a bunch!

BARNEY (v.o.)
I always say—

GRIFF (v.o.)
She'll always be sore—

BARNEY (v.o.)
If it isn't working out—

CHARLIE (v.o.)
This is crazy—

GRIFF, BARNEY (v.o.)
Jesus—

ALL THREE (v.o.)
What goes on as long as lunch?

CHARLIE
(Speaking sotto voce to Barney)
Could we get Scorsese—?

She waves across the room to Martin Scorsese, who has just entered the restaurant. He waves back, comes over and greets Charlie, who rises and kisses him. The diners register this and the restaurant noise level rises, along with the underscoring. When Scorsese leaves to go to his table:

CHARLIE (v.o.)
(Eyes on Griff, sings)
Into power, is he?
He won't come cheap—

She and Griff reach for the crouton bowl simultaneously. A moment—neither lets go, during which:

CHARLIE (v.o.)
But Scorsese's busy,
And we're in deep . . .

She cedes the bowl graciously. Griff just as graciously offers it back to her. She smiles nicely and grabs a handful, during which:

BARNEY (v.o.)
What's going on?

GRIFF (v.o.)
If instead of dizzy,
She'd play it straight—

BARNEY (v.o.)
What's going on?

Just as Griff is about to take the bowl back, Charlie grabs the rest of the croutons and dumps them in her soup. They acknowledge each other: Griff laughs, she stifles a chuckle, then gives in and laughs, too, during which:

CHARLIE (v.o.)
And he's still a creep . . .

GRIFF (v.o.)
She could be first-rate . . .

BOTH (v.o.)
And does he (she) look great—!

Music continues under, increasingly energetic. As Charlie and Griff laugh louder, a few more patrons turn around

to see what's happening. Barney is baffled but delighted. From here to the
end of the number, everything is in
voice-over and sung. The camera keeps
roaming among patrons and restaurant
activity. To the eye, all is natural: some
patrons just eat or look, others talk
(but never in conjunction with their
thoughts). Most of them (exceptions
noted) are glancing at Charlie's table.

PATRONS (v.o.)
What's going on?

WOMAN (v.o.)
Has she had a lift?

PRODUCER-TYPE (v.o.)
They're working something out . . .

THREE MEN (v.o.)
Griffith Bean?

PATRONS (v.o.)
What's going on?

MAN (v.o.)
She don't have the gift . . .

ANOTHER MAN (v.o.)
(Looking at Griff)
Will he nail her? . . .

MANY PATRONS (v.o.)
What's the deal?
What's going on?

WAITER (v.o.)
(Waiting for an agent-type to figure
the tip)
I'm gonna get stiffed . . .

AGENT-TYPE (v.o.)
(Glancing over at Charlie's table)
That flick's not working out . . .

AGENT-TYPE'S DATE (v.o.)
(Catching the waiter's eye)
Hiya, sailor . . .

VARIOUS PATRONS (v.o.)
(Looking at Charlie's table)
It's a loser,
No matter who they get . . .

BARNEY (v.o.)
They're getting on! . . .

VARIOUS PATRONS (v.o.)
He's a boozer . . .
She's not Madonna yet . . .

BARNEY (v.o.)
They're getting on! . . .

VARIOUS PATRONS (v.o.)
C'mon, she's a flake . . .
Her career's a fake . . .
They got fifty million-plus at
    stake . . .

BARNEY (v.o.)
(Simultaneously, in growing
excitement)
They're getting on!
They're getting on!

ALL PATRONS (v.o.)
What's going on?
What's coming off?
She's getting loud.
He's getting bored.
They're getting up.
I got a hunch
This is the crunch—
WHAT'S GOING ON?

WAITER
(To a large table of patrons)
Sorry, no more broccoli gumbo . . .

A few beats of restaurant pandemonium.

ALL (v.o.)
LUNCH!

In print, this number may appear to
be as long as *Parsifal*, but appearances
deceive; the music barrels along. I invited a group of friends to sing it
through for me and it clocked in at
just under five minutes. I liked the
music enough not to let it go to waste
when the project was dropped and utilized it as the basis of "Addison's Trip"
in *Road Show*. Both numbers were
sung by tense, nervous people, so re-
using the music seemed appropriate, if
not morally justifiable.

*Griff agrees to take the job, providing
that filming stop for a month and that*
Charlie follow his instructions. He tells
her that the movie has to be contemporary in a real way, not a pastiche of the
1930s mashed together with MTV. He
hires Jed, and the three of them have a
brainstorming session in Griff's office.

Griff describes his rewrite to Jed
and Charlie. He will change the plot a
number of times during the course of
the movie (our movie), and we will see
each variation, but in this first version
it is a story about Daisy Plunkett, a
small-town girl who wants to become
a Broadway star. Heedless of her
mother's warnings about the dangers of
big cities, she heads for New York with
her scant savings. Overwhelmed by the
misadventures she has there, including
being mugged, she is befriended by
Billy, a nightclub performer, who gets
her a job at the club as a waitress. As
Griff recounts the details of the story
and Charlie and Jed make criticisms
and suggestions, we see the differences
in their approaches instantaneously,
the camera cutting between the office
and their imaginations. For example,
beginning in the office:

GRIFF
So Billy lands her a job as a waitress
in the club—

CUT TO Daisy (Charlie) in a waitress's uniform, struggling to serve
large plates of food to a big table of
drunken men.

CUT TO Griff's office.

CHARLIE
I was a waitress for years and I
hated it. Isn't there something else?

CUT TO the nightclub and Daisy, now
dressed as a cigarette girl.

GRIFF (v.o.)
I don't know why people find me
difficult.

They decide that at this spot they need
an opening number for Daisy. Jed suggests she should start singing when
she's walking home from work.

GRIFF
Sing? You mean, like out loud?

JED
That's how you know somebody's singing—when you hear them out loud.

Griff grunts.

It's dawn, okay? Listen.

Jed sits at the piano.

I wrote this for my "Urban" album, but we had to cut it 'cause it was too much like some of the others, but I could tweak it and it might fit great.

Dawn

JED
(Playing and singing, slow and romantic)
Gettin' light,
I'll say goodnight,
'Cause it's splittin' time.
Dawn.

Don't
Get uptight.
It was dynamite,
But it's splittin' time.
Dawn.

We're
Caught halfway
Between yesterday
And tomorrow . . .

CHARLIE
Oh, that's pretty.

GRIFF
And wrong.

JED
Well, of course it would need some changing—

GRIFF
Some? Start with the title. Who said "splitting" back in the thirties?

JED
Fine, I'll find another word. It's the right subject and the right atmosphere. Look, she comes out of the club during the vamp . . .

He plays and we see Daisy leaving the club. An empty early-morning city.

DAISY
(Singing, to Jed's piano)
Gettin' light,
I'll say goodnight,
'Cause it's
Whatever-the-new-title-is . . .

CHARLIE (v.o.)
How about "Leaving Time"?

DAISY
(Obligingly)
'Cause it's leaving time.
Dawn . . .

She freezes in mid-frame as Griff interrupts.

GRIFF (v.o.)
C'mon, folks, that's not our situation, that's a song about a one-night stand—

CHARLIE (v.o.)
All right, "Leaving Work."

Daisy continues walking.

DAISY
'Cause I'm leaving work.
D—!

She freezes in mid-syllable.

GRIFF (v.o.)
(Grimly)
That really sings.

The office.

JED
I'll make it about night people. The ones who are going home when all

the normal types are still sleeping. When the whole city is still sleeping—

Daisy reemerges from the club.

DAISY
(Sings, still with piano)
Gettin' light,
Something-about-the-end-of-the-night,
And I'm going home.
Dawn—

Again she freezes as Griff objects.

GRIFF (v.o.)
Why is she telling us she's going home?

The office.

GRIFF
We've got a camera, we can see where she's going.

JED
(Exasperated)
I'm just ad-libbing. You don't have to know the specific lyric to imagine it!

Daisy, frozen as before.

JED (v.o.)
Pretend it's exactly what she'd say—the point is, does the song feel right or not?

Daisy resumes moving, now with an orchestra underneath.

DAISY
Walking home
From working late,
What's around the bend?
Dawn . . .

Again she freezes as Charlie speaks.

CHARLIE (v.o.)
I don't feel any energy.

JED (v.o.)
She's been working all night, she's tired.

Daisy reacts to this; whipped.

CHARLIE (v.o.)
But she's just hit the fresh air—

Daisy perks up considerably.

She should feel bouncy.

The office.

JED
Orchestration. We'll up the tempo
a bit—

(Which the orchestra does)

Daisy, very bouncy as she walks along.

DAISY
(To a pop beat, snapping her fingers)
Walking home
From working late,
And around the bend—

She flings her arms to the sky.

Dawn . . .

*She holds the pose as well as the note
and we see a quick succession of
panoramic shots of an empty New York
City just before the sun comes up: the
Hollywood thirties version of New
York, as Daisy would see it. Each time
she sings the word "Dawn," she holds it
for a few extra beats, during which
we see shots of different city locations
just before daybreak, some with Daisy,
some without. As the song progresses,
the sun comes up and the city is bathed
in golden light.*

CHARLIE (v.o.)
It shouldn't be too contemporary . . .

*The rhythm gets lighter. Daisy resumes
walking, still lighthearted, but a little
less bouncy, and without finger snaps.*

DAISY
You may look grim
But you feel just great,
'Cause you've got this friend:
Dawn . . .

She crosses the deserted avenue.

We're both halfway
Between yesterday
And tomorrow . . .

CHARLIE (v.o.)
I like it. It feels right to me.

GRIFF (v.o.)
Well, it'll have to be real short—she
lives just across the street.

*Daisy arrives at her front door and
stops, as does the music. Abruptly.*

CUT TO the office.

CHARLIE
Why? Billy could ask her to move
in, but she wants to be independent, and the only place she can
find is far away.

GRIFF
How far away?

JED
Three choruses.

CHARLIE
Exactly! And we'd see the whole
city. Fresh. The start of a new day.
Like her new life.

*Music resumes. CUT TO Daisy walk-
ing uptown instead of crossing the
street. During the following she joyfully, and without any geographical
logic, traverses the entire island of
Manhattan in approximately thirty-
two bars. First we see her, apparently
the only person in New York, bopping
up from the Village.*

DAISY
Not a street that doesn't have a
shine,
Not a sound except the milkman's
rattle,
Not a stream of seven million cattle,
And the city's mine,
Yours and mine,
Dawn! . . .

The office.

CHARLIE
Yeah, that feels right.

Daisy in Chinatown.

DAISY
It's when the moon's gone down
But the sun's not up,
Just before this great big town
Becomes a great big buttercup—

*Daisy at the Battery. The sun is just be-
ginning to peep over the horizon.*

DAISY
Your feet are sore,
You're feeling weird,
And then there it comes—

*Getting ready to sing the next note, she
obligingly waits for Jed to speak.*

JED (v.o.)
Feels right to me, too.

DAISY
Dawn! . . .

*She twirls around lampposts in Central
Park.*

The city's roar
May have disappeared,
But the city hums . . .
Dawn!

GRIFF (v.o.)
You know how it feels to me?

DAISY
(Twirling on)
Not a street that isn't clean and
still—

GRIFF (v.o.)
Dead-ass . . .

*The music stops and Daisy does, too—
in mid-twirl. We go back to the office.*

GRIFF
It's not going anywhere. There's no
build.

JED

What do you mean? We haven't begun using the night people yet—all the night people—!

Music resumes. Central Park. Daisy continues to twirl as a milkman and his cart pass by.

DAISY

Not a street that isn't clean and still—

MILKMAN
(Tipping his cap)

Dawn!

DAISY

Not a wall that doesn't gleam and glisten—

She waves to a street cleaner.

STREET CLEANER
(Raising his broom)

Dawn!

DAISY

Not a roof that isn't gold, and listen—

She salutes a passing cop.

COP
(Raising his billy club in greeting)

D—!

DAISY
(Cocking an ear)

Not a single drill—

COP
(Cocks his ear, too)

What a thrill—

GRIFF (v.o.)

Oh, I get it—

DAISY, COP

Dawn! . . .

GRIFF (v.o.)

They all sing with her—the street cleaner, the cop—everybody—

JED (v.o.)

—Sure, absolutely—

DAISY, COP, MILKMAN, STREET CLEANER

Dawn!

GRIFF (v.o.)

You don't think that's a little unreal?

JED (v.o.)

It can be real—the cop can be arresting somebody—

GRIFF (v.o.)

Ah.

The sequence begins again, Daisy twirling, the milkman and his cart passing by.

DAISY

Not a street that isn't clean and still—

MILKMAN
(Tipping his cap)

Dawn!

DAISY

Not a wall that doesn't gleam and glisten—

(Waving to the street cleaner)

STREET CLEANER
(Raising his broom)

Dawn!

DAISY

Not a roof that isn't gold, and listen—!

She looks into an alley, where the cop, his billy club raised, has a clean-shaven, clean-clothed, 1930s young thug spread-eagled against an immaculate brick wall.

DAISY

Not a single drill!

The cop and the thug turn to her.

COP, THUG

What a thrill!

DAISY, COP, THUG

Dawn!

Daisy passes, as the cop and thug turn back and the cop starts to beat the thug unconscious.

MILKMAN
(To Daisy)

And so you're on your own, And you do feel frightened, Only—

STREET CLEANER
(Also to Daisy)

Though you're all alone, Somehow you simply don't feel lonely—

DAISY, MILKMAN, STREET CLEANER

—When it's
Dawn . . .

We see a succession of people: a night watchman, a garbage man, a bum in an alley, top-hatted revellers, customers in a diner, and so on, all singing along with Daisy as the number begins an MGM build, everybody spotting her and waving and smiling. She waves and smiles back.

OTHERS
(Overlapping)

When it's half-past four, You're half-awake, And the town is dead— Yawn!

Shots of Daisy and exhausted passersby, yawning in harmony.

You think, what more
Can a person take?
And then overhead—
Dawn!

DAISY, OTHERS

It's just halfway
Between yesterday
And tomorrow.

Calm and quiet though the city
    seems,
Dead asleep it's still alive and
    teeming,
What with seven million people
    dreaming
Seven million dreams—
Of course it gleams!

You watch the stars go
One by one,
You see the first sign
Of the sun.
It makes you feel that
Done is done
And better things
Have just begun—
It's called
Dawn!

The number continues in this way, half the population of New York exchanging waves and smiles with Daisy—nuns on their way to early-morning Mass, groups of immaculately dressed construction workers, even the birds in the park, all singing "Dawn," the themes building in jazzy counterpoint, getting increasingly exciting—and it looks awful. Phony and awful.

GRIFF (v.o.)
Be quiet and listen to me.

Daisy and all the others freeze, their mouths slightly open.

CUT TO the office.

GRIFF
This may be the single most important thing I ever say to you: *real people, in real life, do not sing out loud.*

All these tricky editing techniques had been used for decades before, of course, but not until *Holiday for Henrietta* (as far as I know) had they been marshaled to demonstrate the creative process of storytelling, particularly cinematic storytelling. Still, utilizing those techniques to show people trying to finish the hat was not the only thing that made me want to write the piece. Inherent was the fact that we were writing a musical about justifying the writing of a musical and it gave me a chance to examine and dramatize the most enduring cliché of the genre, the notion that when an emotion becomes too big and intense for words (a foolish notion, to begin with, as every first-rate playwright has proved), the character experiencing it should sing. As Griff says, people in real life do not sing out loud. (Characteristically, he airily dismisses the problem, saying he'll think about it later.)

In the theater, a completely artificial medium, it is easy to suspend the necessary disbelief when characters burst into song: after all, from the minute the curtain rises (or doesn't, as is more and more frequently the case) they're either addressing you directly or pretending to be overheard through an invisible fourth wall. Theater audiences accept this as part of the compact they make when they buy a ticket. Film is a different matter: it's a reportorial medium, two-dimensional and fixed, however poetically shot and gracefully edited it may be. Characters singing on-screen, unless they're performing numbers in nightclubs, theaters, rock concerts and so on, tend to lose credibility immediately, and usually seem faintly ridiculous. This can be charming and was, for decades; the stories in movie musicals until near the end of the century were deliberately unlikely and more than faintly ridiculous—that was the fun. The Astaire-Rogers movies, the elaborate MGM musicals, the Elvis Presley vehicles—none of those stories was meant to be taken seriously. To involve an audience emotionally requires their accepting a convention that goes against the very medium itself. The most effective modern musical movies use songs either as performance numbers or as interior monologues in voice-over. In the movie *Sweeney Todd*, Tim Burton, its director, tried to prepare the viewer to accept characters singing to each other by having the very first line in the movie sung. For many audiences the convention worked, but not for all.

Instead of sidestepping this problem, *Singing Out Loud* deals with it head-on. In the first part of the film the characters sing in performance mode and in voice-over, but the edges begin to blur as the score progresses, as in the following song, during which Griff and Charlie are moving their lips while they sing their thoughts internally. The climax of the movie comes when they break the bonds of reality and actually sing at each other out loud. The story is thus about two people trying to justify the characters in their movie bursting into song, all the while they are bursting (or not) into song to tell the story. In other words, they are people on their way to singing out loud; they have to learn to overcome the unreality of it and break into song in the conventional manner of all musicals. The emotion that does it, the one that becomes too intense for speech, turns out to be joy. I wanted to write about the joyful noise of singing, about the expressive freedom that comes with song. Perhaps enough freedom to sing your feelings out loud in real life can never be reached, perhaps we can sing such things in artificial circumstances only—that is to say, in art. More's the pity, but we still have musicals.

The fitting room. Griff and Charlie have been arguing briefly about which of two dresses she should wear. Charlie wants to wear the one that conceals her body more, which is also the more glamorous one, but Griff has prevailed and she is being fitted for the dress of his choice. She is standing in front of a three-paneled mirror and getting more and more uncomfortable as the costume designer fusses with details. Finally, Griff gestures matter-of-factly for her to turn. As she does so, she sees him reflected behind her in the left-hand panel. He does not look happy. Music suddenly begins and she sings to him—out loud.

Looks

CHARLIE
(To Griff, in the mirror)
God, I really hate this—
You know how I hate this,
You son of a bitch!

Only it's not really out loud, because Griff doesn't respond—he doesn't hear her. It's all Charlie's fantasy: everything she sings is in her head. Griff merely gestures for her to continue turning, which she does. And indeed, the following sequence is a series of fantasies: Charlie's and Griff's. It is not like "Lunch," where all their thoughts were voice-overs. Here they're singing with their mouths open, because they're feeling more, even though they don't hear each other: they're on their way to singing out loud. What we hear is not only their suppressed thoughts: along with what we see, it's their emotional reactions to each other. It's a romantic sequence, a sequence about eye contact.

CHARLIE
(Into the center panel)
Let me off the hook—
You know I've
Never liked the way I look—

Griff twirls his finger again impatiently to indicate to her that she should keep turning.

CHARLIE
You *know* that!

(Into the right-hand panel)

I'm skinny!
I *know* that!
You *told* me
Maybe fifty thousand times . . .

She completes the turn and faces him. His expression clearly indicates that he feels hopeless about what he sees but that he's taking great pains to conceal it. Infuriated, into her fantasy, Charlie steps away from the mirrors, leaving her three mirror reflections standing behind—and strides aggressively

across the room, invisible to Griff, of course, who is now conferring with the designer.

CHARLIE
(Circling around him)
Well, Buster,
I don't like the way that *I* look,
But I don't like the way that *you* look—
At me—
Disappointed,
Disapproving . . .

If just once you could
Look at me nice—

She yanks him out of his chair and away from the designer.

—You could have me—

The music instantaneously becomes a lilting romantic waltz and we are in an Astaire-Rogers ballroom, black and sleek and twinkling. Griff is in tails and Charlie in the dress he wouldn't let her wear, and they are waltzing together dreamily.

CHARLIE
—Feeling like a million dollars,
When you look at me
Like you like what I look like.

Feeling like a million dollars,
Just to look at you
Looking at me
Like you thought I was beautiful.

Look at me
Like I'm someone who matters—
I'll be beautiful.
Look at me
Like I make you feel good.
Make me feel good.

They continue waltzing for a bit. Griff stops.

GRIFF
(Tenderly)
Take off your bra . . .

CHARLIE
What?

The music suddenly stops; we are back in the fitting room, back to the moment when Charlie completed her turn in front of the mirrors. She is jolted out of her fantasy.

GRIFF
I said take off the bra.

They argue about whether she should wear a bra in the picture or not, about the shape of her body, about whether she can take direction from him. Music suddenly resumes.

GRIFF
God, I really hate this,
You know how I hate this—
You're turning me on!

She doesn't hear him, of course, because now it's his fantasy. She just stands there, looking brightly at him.

Baby, it's bizarre
That you don't know
How beautiful you are—
It's crazy!

And that's what turns me on . . .
It's crazy . . .

Music stops, as Charlie interrupts his fantasy.

CHARLIE
Of course, as an actress, I thought we were going for "real." But as the producer—

A beat, while she lets it hang there. She shrugs.

—it'll save a little something in the budget.

She turns and heads for a nearby screen. Music starts again and Griff, back in fantasy, sings to her with controlled fury.

GRIFF
Look, it's just to help your body,
You're the one who hates your body—

(Exploding)

Not me!

She disappears behind the screen, again leaving her three mirror reflections behind. Griff strides over toward the mirror.

Wear the red dress,
Wear the blue dress,
You don't have to remind me
Who's boss!

(Catching sight of Charlie's left-profile reflection, still furious)

Will you just stop—!

The music instantly becomes a romantic waltz. Griff whirls into the left panel and we are in a smoky but glamorous ballroom, the kind with a spinning mirrored ball. Griff is waltzing with the reflection of the left-profile Charlie. The other two reflections remain frozen in the background.

GRIFF
Looking like a million dollars,
Make that two million—
Like you looked when I met you . . .

As he waltzes, he slowly begins to undress her; as each bit of clothing is removed, it simultaneously disappears from the other two Charlies as well.

Looking like a million dollars—
And I'm feeling that
Same kind of rush,
And I want us to start again . . .

Griff proceeds to dance with each of the three Charlies in turn, slowly undressing each as he does, until all three are completely naked (photographed from a discreet distance, of course)—except for the bra, which is the last to go.

GRIFF
Look at me
Like we never were lovers.
We'll be lovers, then.
Look at me

Like we still haven't met.
Let's just forget . . .

As he is about to remove her bra—with care and delicacy—the Charlie he is dancing with looks up at him lovingly and opens her mouth to speak.

CHARLIE
Allee-allee-allee in fre-eeeee!

The fitting room. Charlie is moving into view from behind the screen. Griff, jolted out of his fantasy, stares at her. She is wearing the same dress, but with no bra. He goes over to examine her a little closer. He straightens a bit of the dress, stands back a step. He clearly approves. She clearly approves of his approval.

GRIFF
(Softly)
You know, as far as "real" goes, they went without bras much more in those days—

DESIGNER
It's true, little one . . .

A long, long beat. Griff smiles at Charlie with something more than approval. She smiles back happily. Music begins again, this time even more sweepingly romantic, and we are back in the Astaire-Rogers ballroom, only now there's some smoke, so that it's both elegant and sexy—and Charlie, of course, is in the simple dress that Griff prefers, because they're in a mutual fantasy now . . .

GRIFF, CHARLIE
(Waltzing)
Feeling like a million dollars,
When you look at me
Like you looked when I met you,
Looking like a million dollars
On that sweltering day in New York
A million years ago—

God, it's happening again!
God, I really hate this,
It's happening again,
And I'm hooked—
Happening, and then

I'll be cooked,
'Cause I'll soon want to kill you—
No, thank you, so will you
Just

Look at me
Like I'm all that you'd hoped for.
I'll be everything.
Look at me
Like you did way back when,
And you'll soon have me
Feeling like a million dollars,
Make that five million—
Do I hear ten?

Mustn't let it happen again . . .

At the far end of the ballroom a tiny light appears: a door slowly opening in the distance. Charlie and Griff waltz toward it, whirling faster and faster, the music becoming more and more lush, and as the door appears larger and larger, we gradually see that it is slowly opening into a bedroom. The figures of Griff and Charlie become tinier and tinier as they disappear into the distant room, and the CAMERA CUTS TO the costume designer, looking at the two of them standing in front of the mirrors. She turns to her silent assistant, the music continuing very faintly underneath.

DESIGNER
Why do I think this isn't a costume fitting anymore . . . ?

The lyric, as you may note, is very conversational, with few rhymes. That's because Griff and Charlie are not ready to sing out loud to each other just yet; their feelings are confused and not ready to be shaped. And if the beginning of this song seems a bit too reminiscent of the sequence in *Sunday in the Park with George*, where Dot steps out of her dress, that's because it is.

The next song takes place in the recording studio, where Charlie is at the microphone, about to record the major ballad of her movie. Jed is in the control room with Army, the recording en-

gineer. After a few false starts due to Charlie's nervousness, the sequence which follows is treated as one continuous "take," but it happens over a period of hours, as is revealed by various shots of clocks and tape recorders and control boards and coffee and tuna fish salad and health food and bottles of water and cups of tea and honey and empty containers of ice cream, all the while Charlie is recording the song. We also hear not only her inner thoughts, some spoken, some sung, but Jed's inner thoughts, too—and, occasionally, dialogue. During this the CAMERA CUTS back and forth between the studio where Charlie is singing and the control room where Jed is listening to her over the monitors. In the interest of brevity, I will not delineate the many shots.

Water Under the Bridge

CHARLIE
(*Over the speakers*)
Here it comes: Love—
What I've been dreading.

Jed rolls his eyes at Army.

ARMY
Let her go through it once.

CHARLIE
Here comes love,
Much too fast.

(*V.O.*)

What am I doing here? . . .

(*Over the speakers*)

If it's not love—

JED (**v.o.**)
And she's got a lisp . . .

CHARLIE
—Where is it heading?

JED
(*Mutters*)
Hit the note, hit the note!

Smiling with false encouragement, he gives her an okay sign through the glass with his thumb and forefinger.

CHARLIE
(*Over the speakers*)
If it *is* love—

JED (**v.o.**)
(*Spoken, in rhythm*)
Oh, Christ . . .

CHARLIE
—Will it last?

JED
(*Into the intercom*)
Look, let's try another take . . .

Later.

ARMY
(*Into a microphone*)
Take two, "Water" . . .

CHARLIE
Sunny on Sunday,
Wake up Monday,
Overcast—

(*V.O.*)

God, I'm killing it . . .

(*Aloud*)

Guess what's past—

JED (**v.o.**)

God, she's killing it . . .

Later.

ARMY
(*into microphone*)
Take four—

CHARLIE
And it's—

ARMY
—"Water" . . .

CHARLIE
(*Simultaneously*)
Water under the bridge, that's all,
Just water under the bridge.

JED
(*To Army*)
This is hopeless.

Army, moving the controls, holds his hand up for silence; Jed blinks.

CHARLIE
(*Overlapping*)
Faded handwriting on the wall,
Just water under the bridge.

JED (**v.o.**)
What am I doing here?

CHARLIE
And I don't even know if it's love
      or not,
It's just what we've got,
It's just hot—

(*V.O., spoken in rhythm*)

That one was worse . . .

Later.

ARMY
Take twelve, "Water" . . .

CHARLIE
And I like it a lot.

JED
(*Smartass, to Army*)
Not me.

JED (**v.o.**)
Jesus, maybe it's the song . . .

CHARLIE
(*Overlapping*)
And I see it tomorrow—

ARMY
She's getting there, Jed.

CHARLIE
—Disappear like a shot.

JED
(Into the intercom, to Charlie, with
more false enthusiasm)
That's great. Look, I want to do a
pickup starting at "You say it's
love—"

Later.

ARMY
Take 20, insert . . .

CHARLIE
You say it's love—

(V.O.)

Wrong rhythm . . .

JED (v.o.)
Wrong rhythm . . .

(Gestures to her to continue)

CHARLIE
—Only you're guessing.

Later.

JED
(To Charlie)
Come in and hear the playback.

Later. Charlie, Jed and Army are listening to the playback of the last take.

CHARLIE
(On playback)
Say it's "love"—

Charlie looks over at Jed for approval,
which he tries to give.

What a pretty sound.

(V.O.)

Not a pretty sound . . .

She heads wearily back into the studio.

Later.

CHARLIE
Well, if it's love—

Later.

ARMY
Take 27, "Water" . . .

CHARLIE
(Over speakers)
Boy, it's depressing.

JED (v.o.)
(Spoken, in rhythm)
Better . . .

CHARLIE (v.o.)
(Spoken, in rhythm)
Even worse . . .

(Aloud)

If it's not love,
Where's it bound?

(Winces)

JED, CHARLIE (v.o.)
Maybe we can fix it in the mix . . .

Later.

ARMY
(Overlapping)
Take 30, "Water" . . .

CHARLIE
Sailing on Sunday,
Sunk on Monday,
Run aground—

JED (v.o.)
Watch the intonation . . .

CHARLIE
All hands drowned—

CHARLIE (v.o.)
Hold it . . .

She means the note; then, aloud:

—In the—

(V.O., spoken in rhythm)

Breathe . . .

(Aloud)

—Water under the bridge—oh, well,
That's water under the bridge.
Yeah, yeah, yeah . . .

JED
(Mutters)
Good . . .

CHARLIE
(Simultaneously)
Good experience—what the hell,
Just more water under the bridge.
Yeah.

JED (v.o.)
(Closing his eyes, shaking his head in
despair)
It's all too pop . . .

CHARLIE
And I don't even know if it's love—

JED
(To Army)
You think it's too pop?

Army glances at him impatiently.

CHARLIE
It looks like love,
It feels like love—

JED
The song, not her.

Army turns back to the board.

CHARLIE
How would I know it's love?

(V.O., spoken)

. . . Two, three . . .

(Aloud)

Love's a place I've never been to.

(V.O., spoken)

. . . Two, three . . .

(Aloud)

Once we're out of what we're into—

(V.O., sung)

Hold it . . .

(Meaning the note again)

Later. Charlie's voice is stronger now, more confident.

ARMY
Take 38, "Water" . . .

CHARLIE
When it's done,
Will we still have fun?

JED (v.o.)
Wait a minute—

CHARLIE
When it ends,
Can we still be friends?

JED (v.o.)
(Hitting his forehead)
—What's that sound like?

CHARLIE
When we're through,
Will you still be you
When it's you and me together?

JED (v.o.)
(Singing the last phrase)
Da-da-da-da-da-da-da-da . . .

CHARLIE
Will we talk about the weather?

JED (v.o.)
(Almost hysterical)
Da-da-da-da—
It's the Beatles—

(Spoken)

Shit!

(Aloud)

Shit!

Army gives him a startled look.

CHARLIE
All I know is it makes me sad,
And I'm feeling scared—

JED (v.o.)
No, it's Hoffman . . .

CHARLIE
And I wanted you to say it.

JED (v.o.)
Only bad Hoffman . . .

CHARLIE
And I thought I was prepared.

JED (v.o.)
Imitation Hoffman . . .

CHARLIE
And I wish you hadn't said it.

JED (v.o.)
Overcomplicated Hoffman . . .

Later: 1:30. Army is gone. Jed and Charlie are listening to the playback, exhausted, their eyes closed.

CHARLIE (on playback)
Here it comes: love.
There it goes: laughter.
In comes love,
Out goes the rest of your life!

JED (v.o.)
(Opening his eyes)
Hey, it's good!

CHARLIE
In comes the doubt,
Two minutes after
Comes the confusion,
Comes the pain.
One day a drought,
Then too much rain,
Then just plain
Disillusion.

JED (v.o.)
(Looking over at Charlie)
God, she's beautiful . . .

CHARLIE
And I don't want to let it go,
But I can't let it just keep going,
Simply follow the flow, not knowing
When it's showing
Signs of slowing,
Till it's

Water under the bridge again,
Just water under the bridge.

(V.O.)

Doesn't sound half bad . . .

Jed sings softly along with the playback.

JED (with Charlie on playback)
Just a journey I took back then,
Just more water under the bridge.

CHARLIE
(Aloud, spontaneously, delighted)
Yeah.

(On playback)

And the truth is that I don't care
If it's love or what.

(V.O.)

I can sing!

(Opens her eyes; aloud, but quietly,
to Jed)

I can sing . . .

(On playback)

This is all that we've got,
So let's give it a shot.

JED, CHARLIE (both v.o.)
(Looking at each other)
Now I know what I'm doing here . . .

CHARLIE (on playback)
Then at least
If we've failed,
Love or not—

JED
(Softly, to himself)
Love or not—

JED, CHARLIE
(Along with Charlie's playback)
We'll have sailed!

They look at each other. Jed wheels his chair over to the control board.

CHARLIE (on playback)
We'll have sailed . . .

JED
(*Starting a fade*)
Now a board fade . . .

CHARLIE
Why?

JED
As they kiss, and the camera pulls back from the window and away from the apartment . . .

CHARLIE
Oh.

CHARLIE (on playback)
(*Fading*)
We'll have sailed . . .
We'll have sailed . . .
We'll have sailed . . .

The music dies away.

Singing Out Loud

The first day of shooting. A huge soundstage, with just a few lights on. Charlie wanders nervously among the sets. Griff moves quietly up behind her. They look at each other with love and remembrance and a jumble of other feelings. An orchestral vamp begins underneath, slow and tender.

CHARLIE
What?

No reply.

Say it.

The vamp repeats it and Griff tries to speak, but can't. For the first time in his life, he is tongue-tied. Music continues under the silence, waiting for him. Finally:

GRIFF
(*In rhythm, but spoken*)
Look, sometimes—

(*A beat*)

CHARLIE
What?

GRIFF
—There is just too much to say.

(*Graduating from speech into song*)

Say.

Charlie smiles, encouraging him.

CHARLIE
And—?

GRIFF
(*Louder, singing*)
And just no other way
To say it,
But sing!

In the distance, a stagehand looks over at him. Charlie sees this.

CHARLIE
(*Lowering her voice, embarrassed*)
Griff, it's okay . . .

GRIFF
(*Getting carried away, louder*)
Well, this is one of those times—!

Suddenly, the orchestra drops out in the middle of the last word. From the stagehand's point of view, we see Griff singing at the top of his lungs with no accompaniment. It looks weird.

GRIFF
—Times!
Everything rhymes!

From across the soundstage, Charlie waves weakly with her fingers to the stagehand, as if everything were normal. But the orchestra immediately resumes underneath.

CHARLIE
(*Sotto voce*)
Griff—this is real life. People don't sing in real life.

GRIFF
(*Also sotto voce*)
Well, they should.

Charlie looks around nervously and is relieved to see the stagehand starting to move off, but just then Griff opens his mouth to sing some more.

CHARLIE
(*Hastily, patting his hand*)
Griff, I get it—

Too late. Griff starts to sing again and, in the distance, the stagehand stops dead in his tracks, transfixed.

GRIFF
(*Starting softly*)
There are times
The feeling gets too strong

(*Getting louder as Charlie gets more self-conscious with every decibel*)

For anything but song, so—

(*Softly, whimsical*)

Fuck it—

Again, the orchestra drops out. From the stagehand's point of view, we see Griff in the distance.

GRIFF
(*At the top of his lungs*)
—You sing—!

An electrician blinks, staring across at Griff. The music resumes mid-word.

—Sing!
I mean, sing it out loud!

Charlie, mortified, covers her eyes and looks down.

You ought to be proud—

The electrician and the stagehand exchange well-what-can-you-expect? looks. The music resumes mid-word.

Proud
You've got something to sing!
Doesn't have to be love,
You know,
Could be one of those bright starry
    skies
Or a problem you solve with
    surprise
And you want to go—

    (At the top of his lungs again)

"Yeahhhhhhh!"

The stagehand and the electrician are now a bit alarmed.

Doesn't have to be love that does it,
Doesn't have to be spring,
Some big thing—
Something silly and small,
Or no reason at all.

        (Tenderly)

Doesn't have to be love,
Only this one is

    (At the top of his lungs once more)

Love!!!

       ELECTRICIAN
       (To the stagehand)
    What are they gonna do now—dance?

Which is exactly what they do. Griff extends a hand to Charlie and leads her gently through the soundstage, past all the sets for their movie. Almost imperceptibly, their walk gradually becomes slow dancing, and as they dance, we see workers: grips, prop people, dressers, stage managers, etc., just as in "Dawn," coming in to work and pausing to observe this peculiar couple half-walking, half-dancing, and singing out loud.

       GRIFF
There are times
There's just too much to say—

CHARLIE

And just no other way to say it,
But sing.
Well, this is one of those times
Everything rhymes!

The movie credits start to roll.

There are times
The feeling gets too strong
For anything but song,
So what the hell—sing!

BOTH

Might as well sing!
Feel like a fool,
Don't be cool.
Who made that rule?

Sing what you feel,
Something that's real,
Draw a crowd.
That's the thing!
Gotta be proud
You got something to sing,
Singing out loud . . .

Bill and I had a couple of our own brainstorming sessions with Rob Reiner, but each one sputtered out and it gradually became clear to us that he and his producers were losing interest. Ever the realists, we faded away. Perhaps it's just as well. If *Singing Out Loud* had ever reached the screen, this title song might well have been the most embarrassing moment in many a musical movie year. After all, it celebrates the conventional wisdom that characters sing only when their emotions are too great for them to speak, when in fact, as I said before, there are many other reasons for them to sing. I only hoped that setting the cliché to music would elevate it beyond sentimentality.

Incidentally, you may have noticed that we did exactly what I deplored in *Paris When It Sizzles*. We used the star in the "real" sequences as the star in the movie within a movie. But this one is the director's fantasy, not the star's, and that makes all the difference. And now that I look at it all again, I must confess that I'm sorry it was never made.

The Birdcage (1996)

*Screenplay by Elaine May (Based on the play
La Cage Aux Folles, by Jean Poiret and
the screenplay by Francis Veber, Edouard
Molinaro, Marcello Danon and Jean Poiret)*

The Notion

The notion of *The Birdcage* must by now be familiar
to almost everybody (if not, see the movie) and, since
the songs have nothing to do with plot or character,
there seems little point in summarizing it here.

General Comments

Mike Nichols asked me to contribute two songs to his
nonmusical remake of the French film *La Cage Aux
Folles*. It seemed like an easy and lucrative job, and I
would be working with someone who was not only a
long-ago colleague and a good friend, but a director I
admired inordinately (well, ordinately).

He wanted two songs: first, a number which could
be performed in the titular drag nightclub and might
also serve as an accompaniment to the opening
credits—a song which would set up the main theme
of the picture.

"Little Dream" (Nathan Lane as Albin)

It Takes All Kinds

FOUR GIRLS
(Men in drag)
It takes all kinds
To make up a world.
It takes all kinds—

TWO OTHER GIRLS
(Men in drag)
All kinds!

#1
(A thin girl)
It takes thin kinds—

#2
(A fat girl)
It takes fat kinds—

#3
(A buxom girl)
It takes round kinds—

#4
(A girl wearing a suit)
It takes flat kinds—

#5
(A "petite" girl)
It takes small kinds—

#6
(A huge girl)
It takes tall kinds—

ALL
—To make up a world!

#2
It takes strong types—

#5
It takes weak types—

#1
It takes French types—

#3
It takes Greek types—

#4
It takes chic types—

#6
It takes freak types—

ALL
—To make up a world!

THREE GIRLS
Everybody's a freak.

THE OTHER THREE GIRLS
Yeah! Yeah!

THREE GIRLS
Everybody is like no other.

THE OTHER THREE GIRLS
No!

THREE GIRLS
Everybody's unique.

THE OTHER THREE GIRLS
Yeah! Yeah!

THREE GIRLS
But we're each of us still like one
   another—

ALL
Members of the club—

TWO GIRLS
From the day we're born.

ALL
Members of the club—

ANOTHER TWO GIRLS
In a long, long line.

FOUR GIRLS
Members of the club—

THE OTHER TWO GIRLS
Baby, you can leave,
But you can't resign!

ALL
No! No!

It takes all sorts
To make up a world.
It takes all kinds—

TWO GIRLS
All kinds!

ALL, VARIOUSLY
It takes bimbos,
It takes dumbos,
It takes Rambos
And Columbos.
It takes slimbos,
It takes jumbos—
To make up a world!

It takes all types
And species.
It takes hims, hers
And He/She's.
It takes peasants
And Maharishis—
To make up this world!

*Second, Mike wanted a number for
Starina (the drag name of Albin, the
central character in the story) which
would lend itself to fanciful staging in a
tiny, tacky nightclub.*

Little Dream

*Ethereal music as Starina conjures
up a young man, frozen in a languid
pose.*

STARINA
What is this dream
I see?
Why does it seem
So real to me?
What if this dream
Turns out to be
More than a dream?

*She gestures; the young man starts to
move.*

Come, little dream,
And play.
Don't be afraid,
Don't fade away.
Quick, little dream,
Before you're gone,
Let's get it on.

You are the dream
And I the dreamer,

Each night anew.
Tell me, my dream,
Are you a dreamer, too?
And of who?

And if you are my dream
Come true,
Why do I feel
Unreal
With you?

Are you my dream,
Or am I yours instead?

Either way,
Little dream
Supreme,
I say,
"Full steam
Ahead!"

I thought the first song was appropriate and clever, the second funny,
but Mike decided not to use the first
and only half the lyric of the second.
His rejection did not affect our friendship, however—it was just a movie.
The theater leaves scars.

8. Television

Kukla, Fran and Ollie (1952)

Television series written by Burr Tillstrom

The Notion

Kukla, Fran and Ollie was an enormously popular fifteen-minute early evening television show in the 1950s, a creation of the puppeteer Burr Tillstrom. It featured Kukla, a sweet, unflappable puppet, and Ollie, a feisty dragon puppet with one tooth; their nonpuppet companion and interlocutor was a singer named Fran Allison. Kukla and Ollie occasionally competed for her affections and in this instance she sings to reassure them.

The Two of You

FRAN

I have made this oath:
I won't play any favorites.
I won't love either of you, save it's
Each or both.

Every day I think anew of you,
How I love
The two of you.
And I fondly hope it's true of you
Two, too.

Dope
That I am,
I can't think what to say,
Just hope

Cake and jam
And happiness
Come your way.

I want no one else in lieu of you,
I prefer
The two of you,
And I'd like to take the two of you
To tea.

Come spend the day;
Oh, what lovely sights we'll see!
But nothing's sweeter than the view of you,
So stay, the two of you,
With me.

I blush to see the rhyme "favorites / save it's" with that extra "r" in there but, as the Old Man in "Someone in a Tree" says repeatedly, "I was younger then"–young enough to want desperately to place a song on a TV show I adored as much as this one. It was rejected by the show's producer, but twenty-five years later Burr became the compere of the Chicago company of *Side by Side by Sondheim*, the revue of my songs that began in London in 1976, transferred to Broadway in 1977, and by 1979 had spawned a tiny cottage industry. There was no Fran, but there were Kukla and Ollie, and Burr sang this song to them. Not only was it touching in itself, but he revealed the puppets on his arms as he animated them, something puppeteers rarely do and which he had never done on the television show.

I Believe in You (1956)

Half-hour television play (unproduced)
by Elaine Carrington

The Notion

I have no idea what the notion was. I've lost the
script and forgotten the plot. All I remember is that
there was a young couple named Sandy and Jo Ann,
and detailed descriptions of food. Many a television
show has been built on less.

General Comments

Elaine Carrington was the inventor of the soap opera.
She was the first practitioner of the five-day-a-week
continuing story on radio; it was a show called *Pepper
Young's Family*. I went to college with her son, Bob,
and by the time I got to meet her she had given up
soap operas for more ambitious fields, such as television plays. Having heard some of my songs at Bob's
insistence, she asked me if I would like to supply a
song for her latest venture. I would and did.

They Ask Me Why I Believe in You

SANDY

Haven't you heard that
Of late
I've been an awful flop?
So it's absurd that
You state
That I can reach the top.

JO ANN

Haven't I heard that
Old moan
Hundreds of times before?
So it's absurd that
You groan.
Don't hear a word that
You groan.
Though you make it tough on you,
I've got faith enough for two.

Take heart, my friend—
I believe in you.
I've bucked the trend—
I believe in you.
Some say I'm blind
Or I'm out of my mind.
They'd be startled to find
Every word is true.

They ask me why
I believe in you.
I only reply:
I believe in you.

So, darling, if you
Don't think half enough of yourself,
It's because you don't love yourself
As I do.

I had titled the song simply "I Believe in You," but because of the popularity of Frank Loesser's song of the same name in *How to Succeed in Business Without Really Trying*, I was persuaded by my publisher to change it into the clumsiness above. Even though you can't copyright a title—there are hundreds of songs called "I Love You" registered with the Library of Congress—the minute a title is a less generic one than that, the situation becomes trickier. For example, registering "Yellow Submarine" as a title, although legal, might open the door to a lot of unpleasantness.

I Believe in You was never produced, but it gave me my first professional opportunity to imitate Harold Arlen's music, so it was a joy. And it's a decent imitation, too.

The Fabulous Fifties (1960)

Television revue

Lyric co-written with Burt Shevelove

The Notion

A children's playground. Kids on a seesaw, bouncing balls, skipping rope, climbing on jungle gyms, the youngest zipping through the activities on a tricycle. All the kids are ten years old or younger.

General Comments

In 1960, Leland Hayward, co-producer of *Gypsy*, co-produced a television special for NBC with what was then known as a galaxy of stars, the excuse for which was to celebrate the end of a decade. Having liked my work in *Gypsy*, he asked me to write a song for it. Although he had a director to oversee the entire operation, each number was to be an autonomous venture, so I turned to Burt, with whom I was writing *A Funny Thing Happened on the Way to the Forum* at the time, to co-write it and direct it. He'd had an extensive career directing television specials and industrial revues (in-house musicals which promoted products such as clothing and cars) and was an excellent lyricist. We came up with a notion for the finale of the show, involving children who were born during the decade. Leland loved the idea and commissioned us to go ahead. The number utilized counting games and nursery rhymes with traditional children's songs, centered around a recurrent chorus, "Ten Years Old," set to the tune of "This Old Man."

Ten Years Old

The CAMERA zooms in on the playground from above.

GIRL ON A SEESAW
Seesaw, Marjorie Daw,
I'll be nine in November.

BOY ON A SEESAW
I was born in 'fifty-two,
But I was too young to remember.

GIRL SKIPPING ROPE
(Always speaks)
Monkey, monkey, in the zoo:
Tell us if you can, how old are you?

(Counting her skips)

One, two, three, four, five, six, seven . . .

GIRL BOUNCING A BALL
A, my name is Amy,
My husband's name is Asa,
I come from Aiken
And I am eight!

BOY #1 ON THE JUNGLE GYM
Ten years old, ten years old,
I am almost ten years old,
with a nick-nack paddy-whack,
Pickle with a beer,
I'll be ten in one more year!

BOY #2 ON THE JUNGLE GYM
When?

JUNGLE GYM #1
I'll be ten in two more years!

JUNGLE GYM #2
When?

JUNGLE GYM #1
I'll be ten in two and a half more
    years!

JUNGLE GYM #2
AND SEESAWS
Ten years old, ten years old,
You're not nearly ten years old,
With a nick-nack paddy-whack,
Meeny-miny-mo,
Who knew you ten years ago?

JUNGLE GYM #1
Ten years old, ten years old,
So I'm under ten years old,
With a nick-nack UNIVAC,
Marilyn Monroe,
Who knew them ten years ago?

GIRL #1 ON A SWING
(To the tune of "London Bridge Is
    Falling Down")
Who had heard of Salk vaccine?

GIRL #2 ON A SWING
Dexedrine?

GIRL #3 ON A SWING
Mister Kleen?

SWINGS #1 AND #2
Who had heard of Fulton Sheen
Or *My Fair Lady*?

SWINGS AND
JUNGLE GYM #1
Under ten, under ten,
Lots of things are under ten!

BOUNCE BALL GIRL
B, my name is Bilko,
My husband's name is Ben-Hur,
We drink Bloody Marys
And we're both beatniks!

JUNGLE GYM #2
(Speaks)
Ah, your mother cheats at Scrabble.

SWINGS AND
JUNGLE GYM #1
Lots of people, lots of things.
Lots of funny happenings,
Under ten, under ten,
Under ten, under ten . . .

SKIP ROPE GIRL
(Overlapping)
Rubirosa lost his head,
How many women did he wed?
One, two, three, four,
Five, six, seven, eight,
Nine, ten . . .

BOUNCE BALL GIRL
F, my name is Fabian.
My husband's name is Faubus.
We come from the Ford Foundation
And we eat frozen foods!

SEESAW GIRL
Oh, dear, who can this Nasser be?

SEESAW BOY
Oh, dear, who can this Nasser be?

SEESAW GIRL
Oh, dear, who can this Nasser be?

BOTH
Him and his Suez Canal!

JUNGLE GYM #2
(Speaks)
Ah, your father drives a Kaiser-
    Frazer!

SWING #1
(To the tune of "London Bridge")
Rock 'n' roll and wash 'n' wear,
Brussels Fair,
You Are There . . .

SKIP ROPE GIRL
Uptown, downtown, I declare,
How much is the subway fare?
Five, ten, fifteen, twenty, twenty-
    five, thirty . . .

TRICYCLE BOY
A-tiska, a-taska,
Is Kiska in Alaska?

SEESAW #1
(To the tune of "Frère Jacques")
Suzy Parker, Suzy Parker,
Desilu, Desilu,
Hi-ya, Judge Medina,
Gimme a subpoena!
Rudolf Bing, Rudolf Bing . . .

ALL
Ten years old, ten years old,
Look what's under ten years old,
With a Bozak double-track stereo
    machine,
Dead Sea Scrolls and wide wide-
    screen.

Ten years old, ten years old,
Look what's under ten years old!
With a Jick Jack Kerouac, General
    de Gaulle,
Castro and cholesterol!

SKIP ROPE GIRL
Charlie on a woodpile, Charlie on a
    quiz,
Tell him in advance what the
    answer is:
One thousand, two thousand,
Four thousand, eight thousand,
Sixteen thousand, thirty-two
    thousand,
Sixty-four thousand, one hundred
    twenty-eight thousand . . .

BOUNCE BALL GIRL
K, my name is Kukla,
My husband's name's Kefauver,
We come from Korea
And we use kredit kards!

SEESAW GIRL
(Speaks)
Elvis pelvis, puddin 'n' pie,
Wiggled at the girls and made
    them cry!

SEESAW BOY
(Speaks)
Deedle deedle dumpling, Juan
    Perón,
All alone by the telephone.

SWINGS
Stop recession, stop inflation,
Automation, segregation,
Stop the overpopulation—
Stop Jayne Mansfield!

BOUNCE BALL GIRL
S, my name is Sagan,
My husband's Willie Sutton,
We come from *The Sea Around Us*
And we are sick, sick, sick!

JUNGLE GYM #2
(Speaks)
Ah, your sister wears a sack dress!

SEESAW BOY
(Speaks)
There was an old fellow named
    Premier Nehru,
He had so many Hindus he didn't
    know what to do.

SEESAW GIRL
Conrad Hilton, have you any rooms?
"Yes, sir, yes, sir,

(Speaks)

We have a lovely suite at the
    Istanbul Hilton, overlooking the
    Black Sea . . ."

JUNGLE GYM #2
(Speaks)
Ah, your brother's still readin' *The
Caine Mutiny!*

SWINGS
Three Gabors, three Gabors,
See how they run, see how they run,

SWING #1
Hungarian accents and marital
    strife—

SWING #2
With every new year they're another
    one's wife—

SWING #3
Did you ever see such a mess in your
    life

ALL THREE
As three Gabors?

SKIP ROPE GIRL
Rocket be good or rocket be bad,
But rocket get off the launching pad:
Ten, nine, eight, seven,
Six, five, four, three,
Two, one—blast off!

TRICYCLE
Twinkle, twinkle, little stars:
Which is *Vanguard*, which is Mars?

JUNGLE GYM #1
AND SOME OTHERS
Ten years old, ten years old,
Look what's under ten years old!
With a finback Cadillac, filter
    cigarette,
Right straight through the alphabet!

ALL
(Speaking, one by one, as in a count-
out game)
A! Angry young men!
B! Brigitte Bardot!
C! CinemaScope!
D! Diners Club card!
E! Eloise!
F! Fallout!
G! Garroway!
H! Hula hoops!
I! Ingemar!
J! Jets!
K! Khrushchev!
L! *Lolita!*
M! Men!

(Hastily, as the others look at him)

Angry young men!

(They speed up the game)

N! *Nautilus!*
O! *Omnibus!*
P! *Pogo!*
Q! Quiz shows!
R! Rumbles!
S! Sputnik!
T! Thruways!
U! Us!
V! Vinyl!
W! Wide-screen!
X! *X-o-dus!*
Y! Young!

(Hastily, again)

Young angry men!
Z! . . .
Z? Z? Z? Z? Z?
Zzzzzzzzzzzzzzzzzzzzzen!

Under ten, under ten,
All the way from angry young men
To Zen!

Ten years old, ten years old,
What a decade, ten years old!
With a nick-nack paddy-whack here
    we go again
—Starting on another ten!

Ten years old, ten years old,
Bigger, better ten years old
With a nick-nack paddy-whack, who
    can go to bed
When the future lies ahead?

Ten years old, ten years old,
Comin' at you ten years old!
With a nick-nack paddy-whack,
    comin' on the run!
We have only just begun—
Wait till nineteen sixty-one!

SKIP ROPE GIRL
Sixty-two!
Sixty-three!
Sixty-four!
Sixty five! . . .

As she continues counting, all the others sing simultaneously, gradually fading out, until only the little boy on the
tricycle can be heard.

SEESAW BOY AND GIRL
Who got married? Don't you know?
The A. F. of L. and the C. I. O.!

Davy Crockett, Little Rock,
Vespas, drive-ins, Dr. Spock!

L.P. records, Budapest,
Gorgeous George and "Mystery
    Guest."

Astronauts and Pay TV,
Juvenile delinquency!

Bridges long and bridges high!
Tappan Zee and River Kwai!

Power steering, Polaroid . . .

SWINGS
Who had heard of Princess Grace,
Nelson Case,

AFL-CIO, Alistair Cooke, Adlai Stevenson, Sherman Adams, Steve Allen, Agonizing Reappraisal

Brubeck		
Ben Hur		
Bruce Swanberg		
Brando - the	**A**	Alaska, automation, Atlas, astronauts, Around the World, Angry Young Men, As seen,
Bridge oe ...		Brigitte Bardot, Brussels Fair, Belafonte, Bergman, Bernstein, Bannister, Sgt. Bilko, Batman
Costello Caspso	**B**	Bloody Marys, Beatniks, Brinks Robbery, Bert & Harry, Black Leather jackets, Bikini(s)
... Camarata		Credit Cards, cholesterol, Caine Mutiny, Candy, Callas, Cliburn, Cooke, Davy Crockett, Cartoon, Commercials
Ray Coli	**C**	Captain Video, Corvette, Charlie Brown, Cinemascope, Cinerama, Castro, Christine Jorgenson
chlorophyl		Jean Shepherd, Drive-ins, Divers Club, Davenport, Sukor, Dragnet, Dealers, Do It Yourself
Chubby	**D**	DC-8, Dagmar, dexedrine, Defense Dep't, de Gaulle, Dead Sea Scrolls, Dr. Zhivago,
Chlorophyll		
	E	Eisenhower, Elvis, Eloise, Electric Everything, Exodus, Eartha Kitt, Earp
		Fulton Sheen, Farouk, Faubus, Four minute mile, Fontainebleau, Flair
	F	Frozen foods, filter tips, Ford foundation, Fabian, Fallout, Funny greeting cards
		Good old Charlie Brown, Gunn, Garroway, Althea Gibson
	G	Gunsmoke, Gorgeous George, Geo. Gobel, Guggenheim Museum, Gigi, Gleason, Ghana
		Hip & Space, Fat Hunter, Rock Hudson, Hal Scardi, Hi-Fi
	H	Hawaii, Hopalong Cassidy, Hula Hoops, Hound Dog, Hilton Hotels (everything)
		Istanbul Hilton, Isolation booth
		Israel, Ike, Ingemar Johansson, Ingmar Bergman, Integration, I Can Hear It Now,
	I	Julie Andrews, Jimmy Dean, Jorgenson, Johansson
	J	Jack Paar, Jonas Salk, Jaguar, Jupiter, Juvenile Delinquency, Jets, Johnny Mathis,
		Kingsize cigarettes
	K	Kubla, Kerouac, Khrushchev, Kathryn Murray, Korea, King Farouk, Kitt, Kefauver
		Levar House, Little Rock, launching pads, Laughlin, Lollobrigida, Loren
	L	Los Angeles Dodgers, Lunik, Little cars, Laika, Lolita, Leonard Bernstein, LPs,
Mambo		Many stars of funny names, Maria Callas, Mambo, Monaco, Nudie, Maverick, McCarthy, Mathis
	M	Miltown, Mad Magazine, Mack the Knife, My Fair Lady, Marilyn Monroe, MG, Mr. Klein, March, Murray
	N	Newtons, Nautilus, Nike, Nasser, Nixon, Nato, Nelson Riddle, Nelson (Ricky)
		Oak Ridge
	O	Only in America, Onassis, Old Man & the Sea, Omnibus, Outer Space, Orbit
		Paperbacks, Playhouse 90, Person to Person, Peyton Place, Pay TV, Power steering, Payola, Paramount
	P	Pogo, Prince Charles, Photons, Polaroid, Peanuts, Presley, Power mowers, Princess Grace, Bert & Harry Piel
	Q	Queen Elizabeth, Quiz shows | Paar, Peter Gunn, P-31, Power of Positive Thinking by Peale
Saccharine		Riddle, Rainier, Rickover,
David Schine	**R**	Roger Bannister, Rock n Roll, Rock Hudson, Ramblers, Ricky Nelson, Rumbles, Rocket ships
stereo,		stereophonic sound, Sick jokes, Sputnik, Sports Illustrated by See it Now, The Sands, Scrabble,
Senate Crime Committee	**S**	Suck, San Francisco Giants, Salk Vaccine, Squeeze bottles, Silly putty, Sammy Davis, Smog,
Suez		Tranquillizers, Three-D, Thailand
	T	Transistors, Tappan Zee Bridge, Thruways, Todd A-O, 21, Tab Hunter, Thor, TV Dinners
		[Sheen, Sutton, Adlai Stevenson, Most Sctd
	U	Uncle Miltie, Univac [Shantrim 90, Cinemascope, 16 Tons
	V	Van Cliburn, Vistavision, Vanguard, Vespa, Vinyl Floors, Vodka Martini, Vampira
	W	Westerns, Wide-screen, Willie Sutton, Wash and wear, World's Fair
	X	Xistentialism, Xodus.
	Y	Young Angry Men
	Z	Zen, Zacherley, Zhivago

GUIDE TO "TEN YEARS OLD"

Some of the references in "Ten Years Old" remain well known, others do not. All of them refer to people, products, places and phrases which came into prominence during the 1950s. The following guide, in order of appearance, is provided for what might be the less familiar ones.

Aiken: South Carolina city whose quiet atmosphere changed dramatically when a nuclear power plant was constructed nearby.

UNIVAC: First American commercial computer, weighing 16,000 pounds, which was delivered to the Census Bureau in 1951.

Dexedrine: Drug approved by the FDA in 1958 to treat attention deficit hyperactivity disorder in children.

Fulton Sheen: Archbishop whose weekly television series made him one of the most influential American Catholics of the twentieth century.

Bilko: Television character portrayed by Phil Silvers on his weekly television program, *The Phil Silvers Show.*

Scrabble: Board game that became a national craze in the 1950s.

Rubirosa: Porfirio Rubirosa Ariza, Dominican diplomat; a tabloid favorite known as an international playboy.

Faubus: Orval Eugene Faubus, the governor of Arkansas who in 1957 ordered the National Guard to prevent black students from attending a high school in Little Rock.

Frozen foods: "TV dinners" were introduced by Swanson in 1954.

Nasser: Gamal Abdel Nasser, Egyptian president who nationalized the Suez Canal and all its assets.

Kaiser-Frazer: Car made by the Kaiser-Frazer Corporation, whose production stopped in 1955.

Brussels Fair: First major World's Fair after World War II (1958).

You Are There: Popular TV series in which the viewer became eyewitness to great events in history.

Suzy Parker: Reportedly the highest-paid model in the world.

Desilu: Production company founded by Lucille Ball and Desi Arnaz.

Judge Medina: Judge Harold Medina, who presided over the most significant political heresy trial in U.S. history.

Rudolf Bing: General manager of the Metropolitan Opera.

Charlie: Charles Van Doren who, after a fix arranged by the producer, defeated his opponent on the television quiz show *Twenty-One.*

Kefauver: Senator Carey Estes Kefauver, whose hearings on organized crime attracted a huge television audience.

Jayne Mansfield: Blond sex symbol of the 1950s.

Sagan: Françoise Sagan, author of the best-selling novel *Bonjour Tristesse.*

Willie Sutton: Celebrated bank robber who, when asked why he robbed banks, famously replied, "Because that's where the money is."

The Sea Around Us: A best seller by Rachel Carson, and one of the most successful books about the natural world ever written.

Sack dress: Designed by Givenchy, it revolutionized women's fashion.

Conrad Hilton: Founder of the international chain of hotels that bears his name.

Three Gabors: Trio of beautiful Hungarian sisters (Zsa Zsa, Eva and Magda) who by 1960 had collectively been married eleven times.

Vanguard: United States rocket, intended to be the first launch vehicle to place a satellite into orbit.

Angry young men: Group of British writers who became known in the 1950s for expressing scorn for the upper classes.

Brigitte Bardot: French actress who became an international sex symbol.

CinemaScope: The process of wide-screen film projection.

Diners Club: The first independent credit card company.

Eloise: Little girl who lived at the Plaza Hotel—titular character of a popular book by Kay Thompson.

Fallout: Residual radiation which falls from the atmosphere after a nuclear explosion; fear of nuclear war became widespread in the 1950s.

Garroway: Dave Garroway, founding host of NBC's *Today* show.

Hula hoops: Plastic hoops twirled around parts of the body, a 1950s fad.

Ingemar: Ingemar Johansson, the Swedish boxer who became the World Heavyweight Champion in 1959.

Jets: Jet airplanes, which began commercial flights in the 1950s.

Khrushchev: Nikita Khrushchev, leader of the Soviet Union, beginning in 1956.

Lolita: Infamous best-selling novel by Vladimir Nabokov.

Nautilus: World's first nuclear-powered submarine.

Omnibus: Live TV program devoted to science and the arts.

Pogo: Newspaper comic by Walt Kelly, noted for its political and social satire.

Quiz shows: Television game shows, whose popularity soared in the 1950s.

Rumbles: Street gang fights—the term came into popularity in the 1950s.

Sputnik: Group of robotic spacecraft missions launched by the Soviet Union.

Thruways: Tolled highway system connecting New York's major cities.

Vinyl: Plastic used to make hundreds of items, notably record albums.

Wide-screen: CinemaScope and subsequent silimar processes were introduced in the 1950s.

X-o-dus: Exodus, blockbuster novel by Leon Uris, about the founding of the State of Israel.

Little Rock: Locale of one of the seminal events of the civil rights movement.

Dr. Spock: Dr. Benjamin Spock, pediatrician whose book about child care influenced generations of parents after World War II.

Gorgeous George: Professional wrestler, famous for his theatrical behavior and flamboyant appearance.

"Mystery Guest": Weekly feature on the television show *What's My Line?*

Nelson Case: Deep-voiced radio announcer, known as "Mr. Radio."

Peyton Place: Best-selling novel and film.

Christine Jorgensen: First person to become famous for changing sexes, from male to female.

Captain Video: Hero of *Captain Video and His Video Rangers*, the first science-fiction program on television.

Dagmar: One of the first female television stars, known for her busty figure and bubbly personality.

Bert and Harry: Fictitious cartoon duo who advertised Piels beer on television and radio.

Toni Twin: Twin sisters featured in Toni Home Permanent commercials, one of whom had her hair done at a beauty parlor and the other who used Toni.

Bobby Thompson: New York Giants baseball player whose game-ending home run became known as "the shot heard 'round the world."

Vampira: Television's first popular horror show hostess.

Zacherley: John Zacherley, host of a cult horror/comedy TV show.

Pasternak: Boris Pasternak, Russian poet and novelist, author of *Doctor Zhivago*.

Hexachlorophene: Disinfectant, one of the first heavily advertised "scientific" ingredients of toothpaste and soap.

Chlorophyll: Green pigment found in plants, touted in toothpaste commercials as beneficial for teeth, another early use of pseudoscientific terms in advertising.

Peyton Place?
Who believed in outer space
Or Christine Jorgensen?

Who had heard of Monaco,
The Fontainebleau,
The Late Late Show?
Where was Captain Video?
Where was Dagmar?

Bert and Harry,
Square and hip,
Gaza Strip,
Sonar blip,
Agonizing brinksmanship . . .

BOUNCE BALL GIRL
T, I am a Toni Twin,
My husband's Bobby Thompson,
We come from Thailand
And we use transistors! . . .

V my name's Vampira,
My husband is Van Cliburn,
Ve both drink vodka
And ve vatch vesterns! . . .

Z my name's Zhivago,
My husband's name is Zacherley . . .

JUNGLE GYM BOYS
Ten years old, ten years old,
Look what's under ten years old!
With a pick-pack Pasternak, *Mad* magazine,
Cha-cha, hexachlorophene!

Ten years old, ten years old,
Look what's under ten years old!
With a swept-back Pontiac,
    tranquilizer pill,
Eartha Kitt and chlorophyll . . .

TRICYCLE
Good night,
Sleep tight,
Don't let the U.N. fight . . .

The CAMERA pulls up to its position at the start of the song, then keeps pulling up and up into the sky as the playground becomes just a blip on the globe.

I loved this song, and still do, but those were the days of live television programs which had to be tailored to finite durations in order to accommodate the commercials, and the day before the broadcast, Leland informed us that the show was seventeen minutes overlong and that some numbers had to be cut. Ours was the only one without a star personality, so we had the honor of being the first off the gangplank. After a brief period of complaint, resignation and mourning, Burt and I decided that as the afternoon's dress rehearsal was not only scheduled but paid for, we would hold a farewell performance for the families of the cast and crew and whatever friends we could round up quickly. We didn't tell the kids what had befallen them until afterward, and they joyfully performed it with all their hearts. That afternoon is a favorite memory of mine.

Do You Hear a Waltz? (1960)

Television musical (unproduced)
Book (unwritten) by Arthur Laurents

The Notion

A young woman in a small upstate New York town, tired of her restrictive life, withdraws all her money from the bank (a few hundred dollars), goes to the railroad station and asks for a ticket to wherever the money will take her, which turns out to be Florida. She admits to the station agent that what she really wants to do is fall in love, an impossibility in this small town, but something she feels sure that travel will open up to her. And how will she know when she falls in love? She'll hear a waltz.

She boards the train and when the conductor asks her for a ticket, she looks up at him and hears a waltz. During the trip south, they begin a romantic relationship, but when she arrives in Florida, gets off the train and hails a cab, she takes one look at the cab driver and starts to hear a waltz. They have a flirtatious conversation on the way to her hotel and make a date to meet that evening. When she gets out of the cab, however, she sees a Boy Scout parade coming down the street, led by a handsome young Scoutmaster, and hears their march turn into a waltz. After a number of romantic misadventures, she finally understands that she's in love with love.

General Comments

If hearing a waltz as an indicator of falling in love sounds like a familiar trope, it's probably because you've been exposed to *Do I Hear a Waltz?*, a musical which Arthur, Richard Rodgers and I wrote a few years later, adapted from Arthur's play, *The Time of the Cuckoo*. The trope originated in a line from that play, and Arthur thought it might be the basis of a television musical we could write for Judy Holliday. It never got beyond the talking stage, but I did write a song for it.

Do I Hear a Waltz?

YOUNG WOMAN
Do I hear a waltz?
I don't understand.
It sounds like a waltz,
But where is the band?

A rose is a rose,
And this isn't Vienna.
It's me, I suppose—
Hold your hat! There it goes
Again, a

Remarkable waltz
That seems to be real.
But is it a waltz,
Or just how I feel?

Peculiar, if true,
But the Danube was never so blue.
Every time I look up and see you,
I hear a waltz!

Evening Primrose (1966)

Television musical

*Book by James Goldman (based on the short
story "Evening Primrose" by John Collier)*

The Notion

Charles, an idealistic young poet, wants to escape
from the pressures and vulgarities of the world. He
hits on the idea of living in a department store, where
all the necessities of daily life are available and where,
if he hides during the daytime and emerges only at
night, he can be left alone. When he carries out his
plan, he discovers that he's not the first person to do
so; there is in fact a whole community of people who
have opted out of society and who live hidden in department stores all over the city. Of necessity they are
secretive, and anyone who tries to escape back into
the real world, anyone who might reveal their secret,
is caught and turned into a mannequin by people
who live in mortuaries.

General Comments

While James Goldman and I were writing *Follies,* his
wife, Marie, became pregnant with their second child
and they needed a larger apartment, which would
stretch their budget to an uncomfortable amount. I
had read about a series that ABC-TV was about to
present, called *Stage 67,* a season of commissioned
plays and musicals. I had also read that the executive
producer was to be Hubbell Robinson, a man who
had been responsible for some of the classier shows
on television and who was married to a canasta crony
of my mother's, Vivienne Segal, a retired star of

Broadway and Hollywood musicals. Knowing Hubbell
slightly, I figured James and I would have an inside
shot, so we set ourselves to thinking of something
easy to adapt. Since we shared a taste for the sinister,
we started looking at John Collier's stories. Collier
was a master of the elegant macabre in the tradition
of Saki, and we homed in on "Evening Primrose,"
a bizarre and romantic piece. Bizarrerie, we hoped,
would enable us to stand out from our competitors,
and romance was something our hearts were drawn
to, so "Evening Primrose" seemed ideal. I met with
Hubbell, subtly drawing on our familial connections
(an irrelevant gambit, I suspect), and James and I
found ourselves on the menu.

If You Can Find Me, I'm Here

Charles is hiding in a gift shop kiosk, just after the store has closed. We hear his excited heartbeat, which serves as the vamp for the song.

> CHARLES
> *(To himself)*

Is it done?
Are they gone?
Am I alone?

(Looks around)

I am alone.
It's done.
They're gone.
I am a genius.

Charles, you are an unadulterated
   genius,
You are an indisputably
   extraordinary—

(Hears a noise)

What was that?

(Shrugs it off)

Not a thing—you're a fool.
You are alone.
And it begins . . .

Careful, careful,
Mustn't get excited,
Mustn't overdo it.
Softly, tiptoe—
You'll get used to it in no time.

He steps out of the kiosk and starts wandering through the deserted store, past the wine coolers, French telephones, dog collars, ceramic bookends and into the yawning cavern of the store.

Look at it:
Beautiful!
What a place to live,
What a place to write!
I shall be inspired.
I shall turn out elegies and sonnets,

Verses by the ton.
At last I have a home,
And nobody will know,
No one in the world,
Nobody will know I am here.
I am free,
I am free!

He roams through the other floors of the store, exploring it, addressing the viewer.

Goodbye, my friends, and good
   riddance,
Pardon, while I disappear.

Come see me soon in my
   hideaway—
If you can find me, I'm here.

Farewell, you bloodsucking
   landlords,
Pouring your threats in my ear.
Good luck forever to you and yours,
If you can find me, I'm here.

And I'll stay,
Cozily hiding by day.
During the day I'll resign,
Waiting till you go away.
But at nine,

Master of all I survey,
Everything gets to be mine
To own,
Mine to use,
Mine to write all the poems I choose.
All alone, only me and my Muse,
And forty pianos and ten thousand
    shoes!

Farewell, Neanderthal neighbors,
Swilling your pretzels and beer.
Fair-weather friends, will you miss
    me now?
If you can find me, I'm here.

Goodbye, despoilers of beauty,
Ruin another career.
When you wake up with one genius
    less—
If you can find me, I'm here.

And I'm free,
Free as a bird in a tree,
Free as the slippers I wear
(Free with a year's warranty).
Free as air,
All of these products and me.
All that I ask is a chair
That tilts,
Books to read,
Light refreshment before I proceed,
And a blazer or maybe a tweed,
The barest essentials a poet would
    need.

Live in your barbarous jungle,
Screaming for ways to get clear.
When all the screaming has died
    away,
Come and visit my hideaway.
I will be glad to provide a way,
If you can find me—
I'm here,
I am here.
I am here! . . .

He hears the night watchman approaching and ducks out of sight, bringing him into contact with the others who live in the store. Among them is Ella Harkins, a girl in her late teens, who has lived in the store since she was eight, when her mother lost her in the Hat department and she was adopted by the night people and raised as their servant. She has grown up entirely within the confines of the store and wants to leave, but is afraid to try. She counteracts her unhappiness with memories.

I Remember

ELLA

I remember sky,
It was blue as ink.
Or at least I think
I remember sky.

I remember snow,
Soft as feathers,
Sharp as thumbtacks,
Coming down like lint,
And it made you squint
When the wind would blow.

And ice, like vinyl, on the streets,
Cold as silver, white as sheets.
Rain, like strings,
And changing things,
Like leaves.

I remember leaves,
Green as spearmint,

Crisp as paper.
I remember trees,
Bare as coat racks,
Spread like broken umbrellas . . .

And parks and bridges,
Ponds and zoos,
Ruddy faces,
Muddy shoes,
Light and noise
And bees and boys
And days.

I remember days,
Or at least I try.
But as years go by,
They're a sort of haze.
And the bluest ink
Isn't really sky,
And at times I think
I would gladly die
For a day of sky.

Barbra Streisand wanted to include this song on her Christmas album, so I wrote the following verse to justify it for her:

I awake on a chilly Christmas
    morning,
Watch the choir singing carols
    on TV.
I gaze out through my window
At a dozen other windows,
Then I plug in my artificial tree.
And like a dream, I begin to
    remember
Every Christmas I used to know,
A thousand miles away,
A million years ago.

The lyric to "I Remember" is as much Jim Goldman's as it is mine. We discussed it at great length, and he wrote this speech for Ella:

I remember snow. It's white as bed sheets and as cold as frozen food. It comes down from the sky. I remember sky. It's blue as ink and very far away, as far away as Mommy. I remember her a little. She was big, as tall as trees. Oh, trees with leaves green as spearmint. Leaves rustle when the wind blows. I can hear them. Nothing in the store sounds like leaves in the wind. I remember rain. It comes down from the sky like shower water and makes the grass grow tall and soft like carpet. But grass is lovelier than carpet and a shower isn't rain and thirteen years of ink aren't like one minute of sky. Oh, I'd do anything for snow. I'd even die I'm so unhappy here.

He didn't write the speech to be spoken in exactly that way, of course; he wrote it to consolidate our ideas about the song. As you can see, everything—and more—is there. All it required was making it into a song. I was taken with the phrase "I remember snow," and I kept trying to work with it. I also knew that I wanted to use the word "die" at the end, but I couldn't see how to connect them. After an unnecessarily long while, I realized that the solution was staring me in the face: the song should start with "I remember sky" instead of "I remember snow," so that then I could repeat it at the end and rhyme it with "die." After that, it was easy.

Charles is commandeered by Mrs. Monday, the autocratic doyenne of the night people, into playing a game of bridge in the Home Furnishings department. Ella serves the players sandwiches as they play. Since Mrs. Monday disapproves of Ella's making any contact with this young stranger, Charles and Ella sing only their thoughts as the game goes on. All the singing is in voice-over.

When

CHARLES
Ella, look at me—
This way, Ella.
Ella, concentrate hard.
Ella, hear me
And turn before I deal another card.

ELLA
No, don't look at me,
Don't look up, Charles.
If you look at me, then
I will look at you happily
And they will see how much I
    like you.

CHARLES
When will I ever see you, Ella?
When will we meet?
When will we speak?
When will I once again touch your
    cheek?
When?

ELLA
When will we meet?
I long to know, Charles.

Charmian Carr as Ella and Anthony Perkins as Charles

How do you dance?
How do you smoke?
What is a party?
What is a joke?
But when? . . .

CHARLES
(Bidding)
I pass.

I pass, I pass the hours planning
  things to teach you.

ELLA
(Overlapping)
I pass the hours planning ways to
  reach you.

BOTH
When? When? When?

CHARLES
(As the bid comes round to him again)
One heart.

One heart, one heart is beating
  wildly,
Can she hear it?

ELLA
One heart is beating wildly,
Charles is near it.
When?

BOTH
(Gazing at each other wistfully)
When will we be alone together?
When can we meet?
When can we speak?
When can I once again touch your
  cheek?
When can I once again touch your
  cheek?
When? . . .

The Office Supplies department. Charles
is trying to write a poem.

CHARLES
"Ella, gay as a tarantella . . ."
"Pure as larks singing a cappella . . ."
"Let my poem be your umbrella . . ."

(Throws his pencil down impatiently)

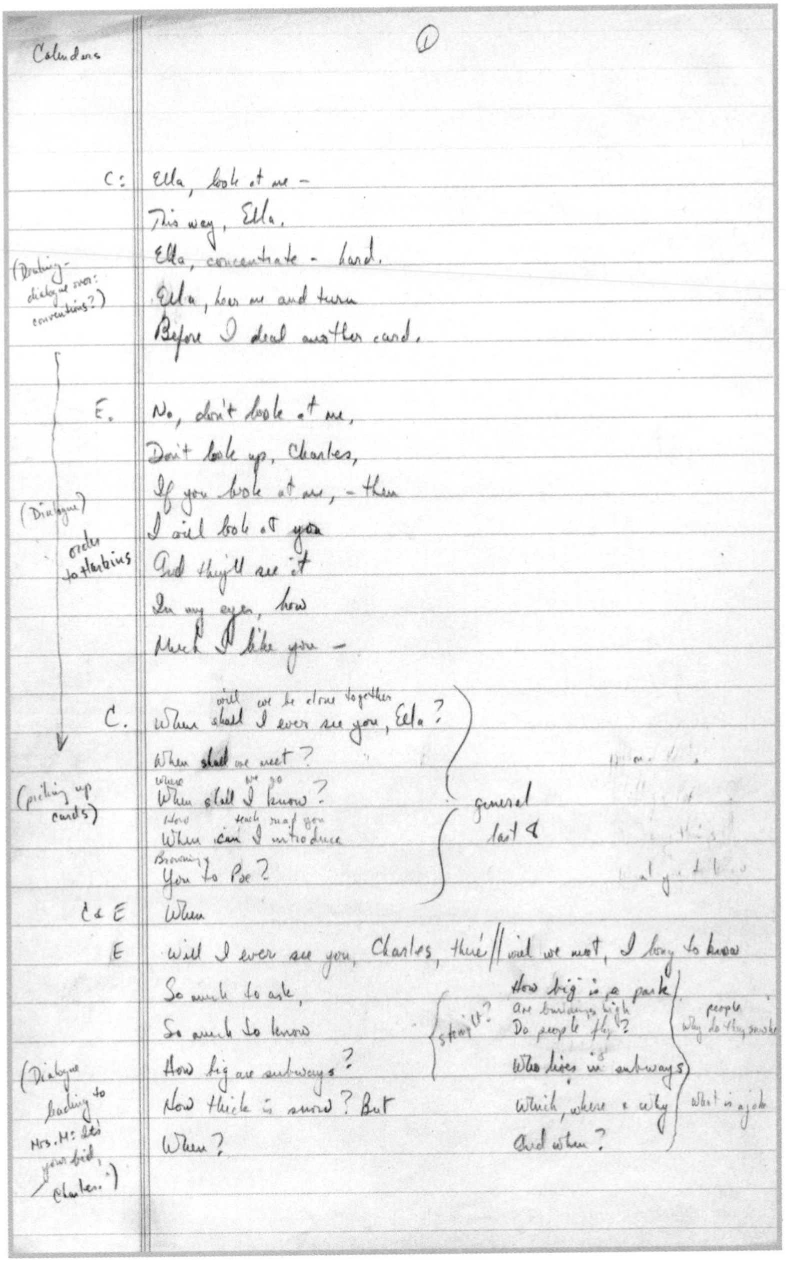

Ella, poets who suffer pain
Should fall in love with girls named
  Jane,
Not Ella.

The basement. Ella is mending one of
her aprons.

ELLA
When will we meet?
I long to know.
What songs do you like?
Where are you from?
Have you been married?

Why did you come?
When?

The Home Furnishings department.
Charles paces.

CHARLES
When, Ella, when?
I long to teach
Your eyes how to read,
Hands how to write,
Lips how to spell,
But night after night—
When?

[Handwritten manuscript draft:]

Calendars ①

C: Ella, look at me —
This way, Ella.
Ella, concentrate - hard.
Ella, hear me and turn
Before I deal another card.

E. No, don't look at me,
Don't look up, Charles,
If you look at me, - then
I will look at you
And they'll see it
In my eyes, how
Much I like you —

C. When shall I ever see you, Ella?
When shall we meet?
When shall I know?
When can I introduce
You to Poe?

C & E When

E Will I ever see you, Charles, ... will we meet, I long to know
So much to ask,
So much to know
How big are subways?
How thick is snow? But
When?

How big is a park?
Are buildings high?
Do people fly?
Who lives in subways?
Which, where & why
And when?

The Music department. Charles is turning pages for a piano recital that Mrs. Monday is giving. Ella is serving. She and Charles exchange furtive glances.

CHARLES
I see you scouring and mending,
Pale and dreamy,
Bending and pretending
Not to see me.
When? When? When?

ELLA
I see you smile at me in Notions,
While I'm cooking.
Cover your emotions—
Charles, they're looking!
When?

Split screen.

BOTH
When will we ever be together?
When is the time?
Where is the place?
When can I once again touch your
    face?
When can I once again touch your
    face?
When? When? When? When?
    When? When?

Mrs. Monday enlists Charles to write a poem for the anniversary of her arrival in the store. As she speaks, Ella, brushing her hair, looks at Charles longingly.

ELLA
When will we meet?
I long to know.
What songs do you like?
Where are you from?
Charles, am I ugly?
Charles, am I dumb?
Charles, do you like me?
Charles, could you love me?
Charles . . .

The Office Supplies department. Charles is still trying to write his poem.

CHARLES
"Harkins absent,
The daylight darkens . . ."

    (*Impatiently*)

Ella, what kind of coward am I?
This I will not allow!

    (*Crumpling up the poem*)

Ella, what if they do their worst?
I'll see you first.
We'll be together!

He makes a plan to meet her in the Lamps department.

Now, Ella, now, girl,
I shall show
Your hands how to touch,
Eyes how to glow,
Lips how to kiss.
I've so much to show!
Then you will blossom,
Then you will grow,
And then—!
Then—!

The Lamps department is too public, so they go to the place least frequented by the night people: the Outdoor Sports department. They lie together in a hammock. Charles turns on a fan for breezes and plays bird calls. All it does, however, is make Ella want to see the real world.

Take Me to the World

ELLA
Let me see the world
With clouds,
Take me to the world.
Out where I can push
Through crowds—
Take me to the world.

A world that smiles,
With streets instead of aisles,
Where I can walk for miles
With you.

Take me to the world
That's real,
Show me how it's done.
Teach me how to laugh,
To feel,
Move me to the sun.

Just hold my hand
Whenever we arrive,
Take me to the world
Where I can be alive.

CHARLES
The world is better here. I know.
I've seen them both . . .

He continues to protest as Ella sings.

ELLA
Let me see the world
That smiles,
Take me to the world.
Somewhere I can walk
For miles,
Take me to the world.

With all around,
Things growing in the ground,
Where birds that make a sound
Are birds.

Let me see the world
That's real,

CHARLES
(*Overlapping*)
I have seen the world—

ELLA
Show me how it's done.

CHARLES
(*Overlapping*)
—And it's mean and ugly.

ELLA
Teach me how to laugh,
To feel,

CHARLES
(*Overlapping*)
We could laugh together here.

ELLA
Move me to the sun.

CHARLES
(*Overlapping*)
Stay here with me.

ELLA
Just hold—

(MUSIC continues under)

* * * * * * *

A world of skies
That's bursting with surprise
To open up your eyes
With joy.

A world that's loud
Where you can watch a cloud (or sit &
Or elbow through a crowd   watch a
To me.   cloud)

CHARLES

(Sings)
Do you want the world?
Why then,
You shall have the world.
Ask me for the world
Again,
You shall have the world.
To walk for miles
On streeets instead of aisles
And smile a hundred smiles
For me.

A world that smiles (with)
With
Where you can walk for miles (run)
With me.
To

▷ ? (on)

BOTH

w/ noise

We shall see a leaf, *(have run)*
A crowd,
We shall have the world.
One where we can laugh
Aloud –
We shall have the world!
Real days, real noise,
A kind you've never known!
You shall have the world
To keep,
Such a lovely world
You'll weep,
We shall have the world
Forever
For our own!

joy,
days

you'll hold any hand, hold chorus
and know you're not close.

We shall see the world
Come true
We shall have the world.
I won't be afraid or
with you
We shall have the world.

CHARLES
Stay here.

ELLA
—My hand—

CHARLES
I love you, Ella.

ELLA
—Whenever we arrive.

CHARLES
But we're happy here!

ELLA
Let it be a world—

CHARLES
Stay with me.

ELLA
—With you.
Any other world—

CHARLES
Stay with me.

ELLA
—Will do.
Take me to a world
Where I can be alive.

She persuades him to escape with her.

CHARLES
Do you want the world?
Well, then,
You shall have the world.
Ask me for the world
Again,
You shall have the world!

A world of skies
That's bursting with surprise,
To open up your eyes
For joy.

BOTH
We shall see the world
Come true,
We shall have the world.
I won't be afraid
With you—
We shall have the world!

You'll hold my hand
And know you're not alone.

CHARLES
You shall have the world
To keep,
Such a lovely world
You'll weep.
We shall have the world
Forever
For our own!

Needless to say, the story does not end happily.

9. Commissions, Occasions, Beginnings

Commissions

The Girls of Summer (1956)

West Side Story was originally to be presented by Cheryl Crawford, one of Broadway's most respected producers. She reneged shortly before rehearsals were to begin, but before she did so, she asked me to compose a trumpet solo to be performed by a character in a play she was producing called *Girls of Summer,* written by N. Richard Nash, author of the recent success *The Rainmaker.* She wanted a theme which I could then set lyrics to, so that she could use it for promotional purposes. Naturally, the lyric had to involve the title, but since the title seemed lyrical enough, I plunged ahead.

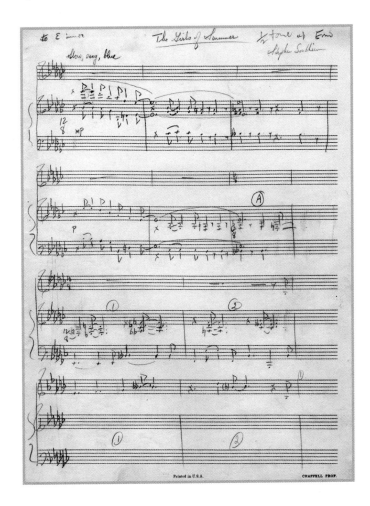

The girls of summer
Get burned.
They start the summer
Unconcerned.
They get undone
By a touch of sun
In June,
Plus a touch of the moon.

The girls of summer
Get fooled,
'Cause soon the summer
Heat has cooled,
And come September
They can't remember
Why
Things were hot in July.

Not me!
It's too easy to fall—
The moonlit sand,
A faraway band,
And that's all.
Not me!
I don't easily thrill,
Never did, never will.

The end of summer's
At hand;
I thought the summer
Was grand,
And here I am
With the same undamaged
Heart
That I had at the start.

The girls of summer
Forgot to run.
The girls of summer
Were bound to lose.
The girls of summer
Have all the fun.
I have nothing but blues.

After "They Ask Me Why I Believe in You" (see chapter eight), this was my second attempt at imitating Harold Arlen, and even closer to the target than the first.

The Night Is the Best Time of the Day (1958)

Kay Thompson was a novelist (the *Eloise* books), actress (the movie *Funny Face*), songwriter and nightclub performer. Her most famous act involved her singing her own highly stylized, elaborately choreographed vocal arrangements with the four Williams Brothers. I was so taken with her work that I used her as the musical model for Cora and the Boys in *Anyone Can Whistle*. I had the nervous pleasure of meeting her at a party and playing some of my songs for her, and the result was that she hired me to write an opening number for a nightclub act she was devising for the movie star Ginger Rogers. To my surprise, she used it. I never got to hear Ms. Rogers sing it, since all her club engagements were far out of town, and I assumed she'd be bringing the act into New York. No such luck.

GINGER ROGERS
There was a time
I got up at five,
Only half alive,
Getting up to
Drive to Metro,
Drive to RKO,
Drive to Warners,
Drive to Twentieth . . .
There was a time
It was quite all right,
Working all the day,
Sleeping all the night.

But being here now
And seeing you all before me,
I know that early to bed
And early to rise would bore me,
'Cause this is the time
People have a ball.
Never more will I sleep
Through this nicest time of all.

The night
Is the best time of the day.
It's the best time for a riot
Or quiet
Café.

I rest
For the best part of the day,
But the first
Burst
Of that neon
Sends me on
My way.

Getting up before noon is out.
I stay in while the sun is high.
But, my friends, when the moon
　is out,
So am I!

The night
Makes the world brilliant and gay.
In the morning it seems run-down.
By sundown,
It's really spinning away,
And for me
The night is the best time of the day.

Smoke and music, I like 'em straight.
Peace and quiet, I don't need *them*.
My day started at half past eight—
P.M.!

And you
Make me feel 'specially glad.
With a low ceiling above us,
I love us,
And by the way, may I add
That I think tonight is the best time
　I've ever had!

All I Need Is the Boy (1959)

While we were writing *Gypsy*, Jule Styne was desperately hopeful that some of the songs would become popular hits, despite the fact that the death knell of the traditional hit song emerging from a musical or a movie was getting louder and clearer with each passing year. Frank Sinatra and Tony Bennett were his choices to sing "Small World" and he was a friend of both of them, so to widen his chances, he persuaded me to adjust the lyric in such a way that it could be sung by a man—which, with a few changes of pronoun and a couple of

Ginger Rogers' nightclub act 1957
opening number and "Mr. A."

In all of my years at the RKO Studio
I certainly met a lot of people there,
I never met Mr. R. or Mr. K, or Mr. O
But I did meet Mr. A — for Astaire.
Now, Mr. A & I
We met
Initially a certain Mr. Y
And then a Mr. B
And also Mr. P
Miss F and Mr. K, the Brothers G

He made a brief reply
And later on that day
We met a Mr. Y
Did I and Mr. A,

(officially introduced) initially

Initially we met a Mr. Y.
we said Hi
to Mr. A

I first met Mr. A
One day at RKO
~~I didn't walk away —~~
~~I surely said~~
~~He greeted me Hello.~~
~~I didn't slap his face~~
~~I didn't walk away.~~

When I was at the RKO Studio
I met a lot 17 people there —
I never met Mr. R or Mr. K, or (Mr.) O
But I did meet Mr. A — for Astaire.

we walked around the place
Did I & Mr. A.

Now you take
We met a Mr. Y
Or Youmans, I should say
We cheerfully met him and said "Hi,"
Did I and Mr A

We said to Mr. Y
Your songs are lovely,
And this was his reply
To Mr. A & me.

It was recorded very nicely by Carol Burnett. A hit it was not.

After Gypsy, Jule wanted to continue our collaboration, but I was determined to write my own music. He couldn't have been nicer about the rejection, which instantly produced in me a gnawing guilt, so when he asked me to write a couple of lyrics for Tony Bennett's new album, I obliged him.

Come Over Here (1960)

TONY BENNETT

Turn off the radio,
I heard the news already.
Take off the shoes already,
Come over here.

Hey! Put out the cigarette—
You smoked a storm already.
If you want to feel warm already,
Come over here.

Hey! Ain't gonna eat you,
Ain't gonna beat you,
I'm gonna treat you
Okay.
I'm gonna meet you
Halfway.

Hey! Stop with the apple pie,
You're gaining weight already,
It's getting late already.
Don't pour that beer,
Dear.
Relax and sit down,
Come over here.

---

other minor adjustments, was easy enough. Jule was also friendly with Doris Day and Peggy Lee, but making "All I Need Is the Girl" suitable for a woman wasn't quite so easy. Here is my attempt:

FEMALE VOCALIST

Got my new gown,
Got my hair down,
All I need now is the boy.

Got my silk net,
Got my heart set,

Got my five yards of beaded crêpe de chine on.
Now, all I need's a strong arm to lean on.

If he'll
Just appear, we'll
Use this big town for a toy.
And if he'll say,
"My darling, I'm yours," I'll throw away
My silk net, yes, and every bead—
All I really need
Is the boy.

Home Is the Place (1960)

TONY BENNETT

Good luck to the boys
With rainbows to chase—
In my time I've chased a few.
Good luck to the runners,

COMMISSIONS · 397

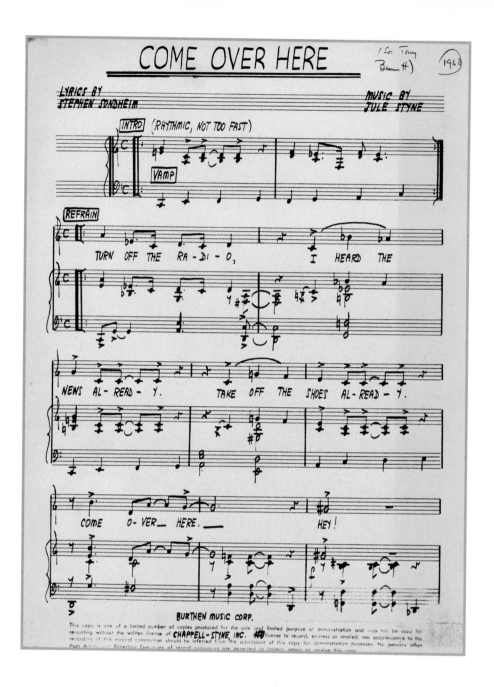

May they all win the race—
Home is the place
With you.

Goodbye to the girls
I'll never embrace,
The dreams that I won't pursue.
But here's to the dreamers
Who can keep up the pace:
I give them my space,
I'm through—
And home is the place
With you.

With Lindsay It's Coming Up Roses

This is the only campaign song I ever wrote; it was for John V. Lindsay when he ran for mayor of New York City. He was a friend and I believed in his politics. The tune should be familiar; not too surprisingly, it was Ethel Merman who sang it:

Poor old New York,
It used to be great, voters—

In nineteen oh eight, voters—
It's still not too late,
But, voters:

We've been down, we've been done,
It's a drought, and in more ways than
  one.
City Hall needs some rain.
Well, with Lindsay it's coming up
  roses!

We were clipped while we slept
With those promises nobody kept.
Where'd they go? Down the drain.
But with Lindsay it's coming up roses!

The prize can be won by somebody else
In my time I've run a few
Good luck to the runners, may they all win the race
('Cause / But) home is the place
with you.

Good luck to the guy who wants to take up my space
I leave it to them to do.
With dreams that they must pursue.
Goodbye to the prizes
Goodbye to the dreamers who can keep up the pace

Good luck to the boys with rainbows to chase
In my time I've chased a few
Good luck to the runners, may they all win the race
But Home is the place with you
I leave them my space
I'm through

I can't keep up with the pace
I'm quitting the race
For me, though, the race
I'm through
So through

What a pity
That we waited so long
While our city
Went to the dogs in committee!

Dirty streets, dirty air,
Dirty deals they pretend aren't there.
In the past
We've been stuck.
Now at last
We're in luck:
What John V. Lindsay says he'll do,
   he'll do!
And with Lindsay it's coming up
   roses for me and for you!

He can do it,
Make us proud once again.
Someone blew it,
Lindsay is gonna see to it!

Crimes are up, jobs are down,
We need someone who cares for
   the town.
We need truth,
Not perfume.
We need youth
With a broom:
John Lindsay is the man to pull us
   through,

'Cause with Lindsay it's less crime
   and more integration;
With Lindsay it's few words and
   much legislation;
With Lindsay it's no deals and all
   dedication;
With Lindsay it's coming up roses
   for me and for you!

As it turned out, he was one of the best
mayors the city ever had.

Hollywood and Vine
(1975)
(Lyric co-written with George Furth)

After *Company,* George Furth decided to write a play, but in a form with which he was comfortable and had had success: a collection of vignettes. The result was *Twigs,* a compendium of four plays about four women, who are revealed at the end to be three sisters and their mother. All four women were played by the same actress, Sada Thompson, and in turn were named Emily, Celia, Dorothy and Ma. Celia is a drudge who had once had a chance to act and sing in the movies but who is now married to an insensitive boor. George asked me to write a song for Celia, who mid-scene is reminiscing about a number she had sung in her movie days.

CELIA

Hollywood and Vine—
That haven,
Hollywood and Vine—
We're savin'
Every cent we earn,
Just so we can journ-
Ey to Hollywood and Vine.

Hollywood and Vine—
The mob's there,
Standing in a line
By Schwab's there.*
Right across the street,
Fingerprints and feet,
All at Hollywood and Vine.

The place where Metro Goldwyn
    Mayer
And Fox and Universal stand,
The place where everybody's always
    tanned.
Take us there!

The place where we can mingle with
    the czars,
Ride in big black chauffeured cars,
Where we'll get more than halfway
    to the stars—
Like Garbo, Gable and Astaire.

Hollywood and Vine—
Things click there.

Hollywood and Vine . . .
There's Pickfair!
Let us off the train
Before we go insane,
And get us to the sign
That's known as
Holly-woo! Woo! Woo!
Holly-woo! Woo! Woo!
Holly-woo! Woo! Wood!
And Vine!

I should add that the false rhyme of "click there" and "Pickfair" was deliberate. I was trying to imply that she was in B pictures. I think.

*Schwab's Pharmacy was apocryphally famous for unknowns who became movie stars after being discovered at its soda fountain.

El Eco (1972)

For some unfathomable reason (unfathomable to me, at least), Art Garfunkel called me one day to see if I would be interested in writing a lyric for a Peruvian folk song that he had found and wanted to adapt. I was flattered that anyone from his songwriting generation and anyone as accomplished as he would want me to collaborate, and I did my best to write something that I hoped would be in his style. I fear it wasn't; he never recorded it.

Whose turn to curtsey and whose
    turn to bow?
Who'll poke the fire and who'll pour
    the wine?

Who cuts the string, is it your turn
    or mine,
As the rain it comes down, as the
    rain it comes down?

Who'll say we tried, but we never
    knew how?
Which of us shows the expected
    despair?
Who murmurs gently, "It never was
    there"
As the rain it comes down, as the
    rain it comes down?

Baby, if ever, the moment is now.
Who'll make the gesture to cushion
    the fall?
Who smiles the smile that means
    nothing at all?
And the rain it comes down, and the
    rain it comes down.

Who'll say we tried, but we never
    knew how?
Who says it's passing and who says
    it's real?
Who takes the chance that it's not
    what we feel
As the rain it comes down, as the
    rain it comes down?

Baby, if ever, the moment is now.
Which of us shows the expected
    despair?
Who murmurs gently, "It never was
    there"
As the rain it comes down, as the
    rain it comes down?

No, I don't know what it means, either,
but it sounds vague enough to be a
contemporary adaptation from the
authentic Peruvian, which it isn't.

Goodbye for Now
(Theme from *Reds*, 1981)

This song is not in the chapter on movies because, although the lyric is set to a motif I wrote for the background music of *Reds*, Warren Beatty's film about the Russian Revolution, it was never heard on-screen. Like "The Girls of Summer," the lyric was written at the request of the producer (in this case, Warren), who hoped to release it as a single, sung by Diane Keaton, his co-star in the movie. She did indeed record it, but it never traveled beyond the studio, for an unavoidable reason: I had written the tune as an instrumental, not a vocal, and its tessitura (the preeminent areas of its range) was very wide; Diane couldn't handle it comfortably—nor could many singers, without noticeably awkward shifts from head voice to chest voice. It looks like a song, it sounds like a song, but it's not a song, although it has been decently recorded a few times. As with "Somewhere" from *West Side Story,* it remains an instrumental with words.

FEMALE VOCALIST
Yes, I know:
Goodbye for now.
How long, a year, a day?
Yes, I love you.
Yes, you're with me
Here, now, next to me,
And worlds away.

See, I free you—
And I'll see you when I see you.
Fine, okay.

Goodbye for now, again.
Goodbye until whenever, then.
We're free,
That's what we said we'd be,
At leave to come and go,
You as well as I.
Somehow, each hello
Makes it worth goodbye . . .

For now.

GOODBYE FOR NOW
(THEME FROM THE MOTION PICTURE 'REDS')

Words and Music by STEPHEN SONDHEIM

GOODBYE FOR NOW
A Hollywood Story

As I said a couple of chapters ago, when Warren Beatty asked me to write the background music for *Reds,* his chronicle of the Russian Revolution, he persuaded me by showing me the interviews he'd filmed over the years with living people who had witnessed the events. He had to persuade me because, as I told him, I could write only songs or background atmosphere, as I had done for Alain Resnais's film *Stavisky* (1974). I told him I was confident I could accommodate the love story between the two leading characters, John ("Jack") Reed and Louise Bryant,* but equally confident that I could not handle the music for the "events," such as rallies and battles, which depend on orchestration, about which I don't know enough. The only possible exception, I said, might be the triumphal march that climaxed the first half of the picture; I like writing marches almost as much as I like writing waltzes. But no, he wanted to use the Communist anthem known as "The Internationale," and gently urged me to find other places in the score for it. I replied equally gently that "The Internationale" was one of the very few tunes I thoroughly dislike—like "The Star-Spangled Banner," it keeps leaping all over the place, making it as graceless to hear as it is difficult to sing—and that I would stick with the love story. He assured me not to worry about it, and I said yes to the project.

Warren, who edits his films close to the chest, parsimoniously doled out scraps of scenes to me as he cut them together (small reels of tape for me to view on the six-inch videocassette screen atop my piano), and I set about underscoring them. Although *Stavisky* was the only film I'd ever scored, it was something I'd loved doing. Timing music to a scene appeals to my

penchant for puzzles; it was probably one of the reasons I wrote *Sweeney Todd,* a show filled with underscoring matched precisely to stage action.

Each time I would score a mini-sequence, Warren would come over to my house at the end of his day (usually midnight—he was an indefatigable worker), and I would play what I'd written. Every gesture, movement and pause that I'd studied on the screen I had carefully, ingeniously and unobtrusively punctuated or emotionally decorated. And each time Warren's reaction was polite, thoughtful, articulate and just enough short of enthusiasm to be noticed. After three or four of these disappointing sessions (disappointing to both of us), I asked him what the problem was. He replied, ever so reticently, that he didn't approve of music that told the audience what was going on in the actors' minds. I, of course, had been brought up on the film scores of the 1930s and 1940s, where the reverse was true, where every on-screen emotion was relentlessly underscored (pun intended) within an inch of its life.

Even as I knew Warren was right, with every word he spoke my spirits fell—telling the audience what was going on in the actors' minds was exactly what I loved about underscoring. Oh, I said, in what was probably an aggrieved tone, all you want is a Love Theme. Yes, he replied, as if surprised I should ask. Okay, I grumped, that's what I'll give you. And that's what I gave him.

Two midnights later, Warren came to the house, and I played him the Love Theme, which he praised without committing himself, as is his wont. He asked me to record it for him, but the only working equipment I had that night was a pocket cassette recorder. Fine, he said; he wanted only to familiarize himself with the piece. I dutifully slogged my way through it; simple as it was to play, I was tired, and my fingers would occasionally blunder and hit two notes simultaneously

instead of the one required. "Never mind, it's great," he said as he snatched the tape. "Promise me you won't play it for anyone else," I pleaded, "Wait till I refine it a bit and perform it properly." "Of course," he replied. Knowing Warren even as little as I did, I should not have been taken aback when I received an excited phone call from him two days later, informing me that Barry Diller, the CEO of Paramount Pictures and producer of the film, loved what I'd written. Naturally, my reaction was mixed: I was annoyed that Warren had broken his promise and played my poorly recorded, sloppily performed demo for anyone, especially his boss, but thrilled that said boss had approved.

The pleasure was short-lived. Two days later, Warren called me again, this time to say that he'd been playing the tape for his film editor and that someone on the editor's staff had pointed out a similarity between my tune and the melody of a well-known popular song of the 1940s, "I'll Be Home for Christmas." "Well known, perhaps, but not to me," I protested. Hearing what sounded like a skeptical pause at the other end of the line, I took a deep breath and confessed to him that I had indeed plagiarized the tune—from his beloved "Internationale." I had merely slowed it down and re-harmonized it, something I hoped he would never discover. The revelation seemed not to rattle him at all—but then I never saw anything that did. Still, the coincidence of the tunes was never mentioned again, and I assured him that "The Internationale" was in the public domain.

Warren is a musician as well as someone who likes to explore every possibility, and the first band session, which was supposed to be devoted to recording the Love Theme and its iterations during the course of the movie, was something of a nightmare: we never got past the initial statement. In the picture it is first heard after Jack and Louise have a violent argument, culminat-

---

*Warren Beatty and Diane Keaton, respectively.

ing in a brief silence, a moment of reconciliation and then a shared, embarrassed laugh; it is the first time we see how deeply in love they are. Warren had a certain emotional color in mind for the underscoring, but he couldn't articulate it and therefore encouraged Jonathan Tunick, the orchestrator, to arrange the thing for every possible size and combination of instruments: piano and orchestra, violin and orchestra, piano and violin, flute and string quartet, trumpet and guitar, ocarina and Jew's harp, you name it. Paramount Pictures was sparing no expense on the project (it cost more than $30 million, which in those days was as expensive as it got), so every combination was orchestrated and recorded. Warren loved them all. But not one of them, he felt, was right.

Finally, when the orchestra had left for their lunch break after the first three-hour session, he drew me aside and confessed that what he missed was the way I had played it for him the night he'd first heard it. He solicitously beseeched me to record it myself to one of the orchestral playbacks while the orchestra itself was out of the room. I replied that I had never performed to a playback and that I was not a member of Local 802, the musicians' union. I would thus be breaking union rules, which might put the whole recording in jeopardy, and therefore I couldn't do it. Unruffled as always, he flung his arm around my shoulders, murmured some more Warren-speak to me—warm, smart and emboldening, but with just enough left unspoken to be seductive instead of merely flattering—and told me not to worry, and five minutes later I found myself ensconced at the keyboard with heavy earphones clamped to my head. I did a number of takes, and Warren liked them all, but softly confessed with a rueful grin that they still weren't quite what he had in mind. I was both chagrined and relieved.

Eventually, with great reluctance, Warren gave up the relentless pursuit of his vision, and the sessions continued after lunch and throughout the week, recording the subsequent entrances of the theme as well as other sections of the score. A few weeks later, he called me to the editing room to help him time the ultimate entrance at the climax of the picture, and that was the last time I had anything to do with *Reds* until I was invited to see the final cut.

The screening took place atop the Paramount offices and was small enough to be glamorous, but Warren wasn't there, so I couldn't ask him which orchestration he had finally settled on for that critical initial moment. My anticipation was such that I found it difficult to concentrate on the first thirty-five minutes; but then Jack and Louise began scowling at each other and by the thirty-eighth minute they were yelling at each other, and in the thirty-ninth they stopped, looked at each other, had a brief, tender exchange of dialogue, laughed with love, and the theme at last reared its romantic head. Warren had chosen a faraway solo piano, a pure, crystalline sound, effective and affecting, but not played very well—every now and then a note would sound a bit blurry, as if two notes had been hit at the same time, only one more strongly than the other. I need not go on. As with Mike Nichols and *The Apple Tree* (see chapter six), Warren couldn't get the virgin impression out of his head, and there it was, and is: The movie cost $30 million, the cassette player cost $36.50, the tape cost $2.50. I came free. And now Local 802 can sue us all.

Occasions

These are "occasional songs," by which I do not mean casual songs or songs written every now and then. I mean songs for special occasions—herewith, seven birthdays and a gala celebration. I hesitated to include them, as they are rife with references to friends, movies, private jokes and the general zeitgeist of my youth. Putting them in this book is the equivalent of showing a family photo album, a collection of strange faces and places, which is of intense interest to the family but a dicey proposition to the guest on whom it is foisted. It can be charming or tedious, depending on the sprightliness of the narrator and the tolerance of the viewer. I will try to keep the narrative sprightly.

A Star Is Born (1954)
(Birthday song for Kitty Lou Hollerith)

"A Star Is Born" is a piece of exuberant camp I wouldn't have exposed in this book were it not for the fact that I had recorded it for the birthday girl's parents (when I was twenty-four) and half a century later allowed it to be reproduced in a 2005 record album called *Sondheim Sings—Volume II*. It has nothing to do with the movie of the same name which was released that year; I merely appropriated the title. The song came into being because at Williams College one of my best friends was a fellow named Charles Hollerith, Jr., who was as obsessed with movies (that is, Hollywood movies) as I was. Later on, I graduated from movies to films (that is, foreign movies), but our interest in studios and stars never waned, so when Chuck's first child, Kitty Lou, née Catherine Louise, was born, it seemed appropriate that I should write a song of celebration.

Unless you're a fanatic about the movies of that era, most of the references to specific pictures, songs and gossip, along with many of the actors, as well as their married names, will baffle you. For this reason, there's a reference guide on a neighboring page.

CELEBRANT
What's the cause of the wild
    commotion in Starland?
Is it merely another tantrum by
    Garland?
Is it Beverly Tyler's return to the
    screen,
Or a beguine
Begun by Nan McFarland?

There's a rumor that the exciting
    event is
Warner Brothers reissuing *Nora
    Prentiss*.
Maybe Crawford and Stanwyck have
    launched a new drive
To try and revive

The loves of Martha Ivers,
Thelma Jordon,
Mildred Pierce
And Harriet Craig.
All these rumors are vague
And untrue.
Then what's the hullabaloo?

It's not the revelations of Garbo
    laying her soul bare,
Telling of her extreme affection for
    Colbert,
Nor is it the discovery that Lizabeth
    Scott
Really is not
A girl!
Then why is Movieland in a whirl?
What is all the to-do?
It's the recent arrival of a rival to
    Merle—
I mean the earth-
Shaking birth
Of Kitty Lou!

Hollywood is all askew,
Topsy-turvy,
From Benay Venuta to
Irene Hervey.
Everyone in Hollywood's gay,*
For a star is born today!

Look at Hepburn weeping on
Shearer's sables,
Vera-Ellen leaping on
Glass-topped tables,
Betty Grable kissing Al Faye,
For a star is born today!

Annie Miller has the gang
    responding to the urge of
Her taps . . .

(Sound of tap dancing)

Piper Laurie's on the verge of
A total collapse!

Praise the miracle of a
New star nearing!
Even Maggie Sullavan
Feels like cheering!
Joan Tone is telling Fay Wray

---
*In those days, to most people the word meant "happy." Period.

That a star is born,
Yes, a star is born
Today!!

While her daddy is handing out the
    cigars,
Kitty Lou's getting presents from all
    the stars.
Everybody who's anybody has sent a
    gift
By starlift:

Ethel Merman
Sent an ermine
Bib in mauve and blue.
Joanie Wanger
Sent a manger
Lined with marabou.

Ann Doran
Sent a can
Of Flit;
Irene Dunne
Sent a nun
To baby-sit.

Swanson sent a
Pale magenta
Mink-upholstered car,
Rita Gam
A silent Sam-
Ovar.
Oliv' de Havilland
Sent some gravel and
Half a ton of tile, cement and tar
To pave the driveway round the
    home of our star.

Ona Munson
Sent a Bunsen
Burner just for kicks,
Osa Massen
Sent a bassin-
Et and swizzlesticks.
Alan Ladd
Sent some mad
Perfume,
Myrna Loy
Sent a toy
Projection room.

Rossellini
Sent martini
Mix for formula,
Anthony Quinn
Sent a sequin

Bra.
A maid of Kit Cornell's
Sent a doll that yells
"Really, Dahling," instead of "Ma!"
A perfect present for the budding
 young "stah."

Dottie Howard
Sent a flowered
Handkerchief of Mag's,
Rita Johnson
Sent a Ronson
And a pack of fags.
Lucille Ball
Sent a call-
Ing card
And the gun
Used in *Sun-
Set Boulevard.*

Brenda Holden
Sent a gold-en-
Ameled telephone,
Sylvia Sidney
Sent her kidney
Stone.
Laraine Durocher
Was strictly kosher,
She sent a case of Manischewitz
 wine.
The other stars are building Kitty a
 shrine.
But let's get back to Hollywood and
 Vine . . .

Ann McNulty, on her knees,
Lights a candle,
Whispers to her rosaries
Some new scandal.
Annie's only trying to pray
For the star that's born today.

Ellie Powell's taking all her tap shoes
 out of mothballs
Tonight,

(*Sound of tap dancing*)

While Veronica de Toth bawls
In utter delight!

Says Ricardo Montalban,
"Dinky's narrow,*

---

*"Dinky" was the nickname of Chuck's
wife, Catherine.

But she'll have more children than
Maureen Farrow,
All as talented as Ida Kay,
Like the star that's born,
Like the star that's born
Today!"

Though time is mean
And though fame is void,
And though film turns green
And a myth's destroyed,
Still, the day we've seen
Kitty Lou employed
On the silver screen,
We'll be overjoyed,
For, like Gloria Jean
And like William Boyd,
She will be the queen
Of the celluloid!

Burgess Meredith,
Even Hed' Lamarr,
The B'nai B'rith
And the D.A.R.,
All their kin and kith,
Whether near or far,
Think Miss Hollerith
Is spectacular!
Like Alexis Smith
And like Deborah Kerr,
She's a junior myth
And a friendly star!
So bring on the rhythm
And the caviar,
And let's go,
While the bids pour in from every
 major studio!

Metro, after flying to
Scout the Midwest,
Says that they are dying to
Bring the kid west;
Dore Schary wants to be called Doré,
'Cause a star is born today.

Fox was given Catherine
Lou's description;
She's replacing Brando in
The Egyptian.
Paramount has bought the Passion
 Play
For the star that's born today.

Junie Preisser has done twenty-
 seven of her dazzling
Routines;

(*Sound of tap dancing*)

Junie's tired, but the jazz ling-
Ers on in her jeans!

Busby Berkeley, sound your horn,
Sound your Claxon,
For today a star is born
Out in Jackson,
Mich!
Make a wish,
And wish that tiny star well;
Be glad she's born beneath the sign
 of Jane Darwell!

Shout hooray!
A star star star star star is born
 today!
Kitty Lou!
Here's to you
From Lena Horne
And Philip Dorn
And Marion Lorne!
It's Californ-
Ia's lucky morn—
A star is born!!!

Like one of the things I deplore about
Noël Coward's lyrics, this one has a
preponderance of jokes about sexual
deviance. Whether or not this was an
attempt to be sophisticated or something I should have consulted a psychiatrist about, I grew out of it.

While some of the names dropped in "A Star Is Born" remain as familiar today as they were fifty years ago (for example, Lucille Ball, Busby Berkeley, Greta Garbo, Katharine Hepburn, Barbara Stanwyck), others have grown more obscure with time. This guide will help.

William Boyd (1895–1972): Early silent film matinee idol who achieved lasting fame as Hopalong Cassidy in the successful B Western series of the same name (1935–1948).

Katharine "Kit" Cornell (1898–1974): Regarded as one of the finest American stage actors of her time, her most noted roles were as Elizabeth Moulton-Barrett in *The Barretts of Wimpole Street* (1931) and as Joan in *Saint Joan* (1936).

Harriet Craig: Title character in *Harriet Craig,* 1950 Columbia drama starring Joan Crawford; it was the third film version of George Kelly's Pulitzer Prize–winning play *Craig's Wife.*

Jane Darwell (1879–1967): Oscar winner for her performance as Ma Joad in *The Grapes of Wrath,* her career spanned fifty years.

Ann Doran (1911–2000): Veteran character actress of five hundred film and one thousand television appearances.

Philip Dorn (1901–1975): Former matinee idol in Holland and Germany who fled to Hollywood before World War II; he portrayed anti-Nazi patriots and continental romancers.

Laraine Durocher (1920–2007): Married name of Laraine Day, MGM contract player of the late thirties and forties; she was known as the "First Lady of Baseball" during her thirteen-year marriage to Brooklyn Dodgers manager Leo Durocher.

Maureen Farrow (1911–1998): Married name of Maureen O'Sullivan, one of MGM's most popular ingenues throughout the 1930s, best remembered as Jane in the six Tarzan movies. Married to Australian writer John Farrow and mother of actress Mia Farrow.

Alice Faye (1915–1998): 20th Century-Fox's reigning singing star of the late thirties and early forties.

Rita Gam (1928–): Stage, film and television actress, primarily from the late forties to the early seventies.

Irene Hervey (1909–1998): Hollywood leading lady of the thirties and forties; wife of musical film star Allan Jones and mother of singer Jack Jones.

Brenda Holden (1915–1992): Married name of Brenda Marshall, Warner Bros. contract player of the early 1940s; she was married to actor William Holden from 1941 to 1971.

Dorothy "Dottie" Howard (1914–1996): Married name of Dorothy Lamour, Paramount star best remembered for her trademark floral-print wrap-around sarong in the Bob Hope–Bing Crosby *Road* pictures.

Martha Ivers: Title character in *The Strange Love of Martha Ivers,* a Paramount melodrama from 1946, starring Barbara Stanwyck, Van Heflin and Kirk Douglas.

Gloria Jean (1926–): Coloratura soprano and Universal contract player of the 1940s.

Rita Johnson (1913–1965): Versatile Hollywood actress of the late thirties and forties, whose career came to a halt in 1948 when she suffered a tragic accident.

Thelma Jordon: Title character in *The File on Thelma Jordon,* a 1950 Paramount drama starring Barbara Stanwyck.

Ida Kay (1917–1985): A graduate student at Williams College in the 1940s, where she choreographed many of the musical shows, including *Phinney's Rainbow.*

Marion Lorne (1883–1968): Made her film debut in Hitchcock's *Strangers on a Train* (1951), but remains best-remembered as the dithering Aunt Clara in the classic TV show *Bewitched.*

Osa Massen (1914–2006): Danish actress hired by 20th Century-Fox in 1936; she played femme fatales in World War II–era Hollywood.

Nan McFarland (1916–1974): TV and stage actress who originated the role of Frau Schmidt on Broadway in *The Sound of Music* (1959).

Ann McNulty (1928–): Married name of Ann Blyth, MGM contract player of the forties and fifties, best-remembered as the daughter in *Mildred Pierce.*

Ona Munson (1903–1955): Stage and film actress, best-known for playing the notorious Belle Watling in *Gone With the Wind* (1939).

Merle Oberon (1911–1979): Indian-born actress best-known for her role of Cathy in *Wuthering Heights.*

Mildred Pierce: Title character in 1945 Warner Bros. melodrama, for which Joan Crawford won the Academy Award as Best Actress.

June Preisser (1920–1984): Acrobatic dancer, contortionist, and blond starlet in MGM musicals.

Nora Prentiss: Title character of a 1947 Warner Bros. melodrama starring Ann Sheridan.

Dore Schary (1905–1980): Head of MGM from 1951 to 1956.

Lizabeth Scott (1922–): Husky-voiced actress, promoted by Paramount in the late 1940s and early 1950s as their leading femme fatale.

Sylvia Sidney (1910–1999): Hollywood star of the 1930s, described as having "the saddest eyes in Hollywood."

Starlift: Title of a 1951 Warner Bros. all-star movie.

Margaret "Maggie" Sullavan (1909–1960): Winsome stage and film star from 1930 to 1960.

Joan Tone (1905–1977): Married name (1935–1939) of film star Joan Crawford when she was married to Franchot Tone, MGM contract player.

Veronica de Toth (1922–1973): Married name of Paramount film star Veronica Lake, of "peekaboo bang" fame; she was married to

director André de Toth from 1944 to 1952.
Beverly Tyler (1927–2005): Radio singer, then MGM contract player of the forties and fifties.
Benay Venuta (1911–1995): Broad-way and Hollywood actress for almost seventy years; she played Dolly Tate in the MGM film and 1966 revival of *Annie Get Your Gun.*
Joan Wanger (1910–1990): Married name of Joan Bennett, Hollywood ingenue turned femme fatale of the thirties and forties; married to producer Walter Wanger.

You're Only as Old as You Look (1955)

(Birthday song for
Julian Beaty, Jr.)

Julian Beaty, Jr. (pronounced "Batey" and known as Jerry), was Mary Rodgers's first husband. He was fourteen years older than she, and to those of us her age, that was ancient. In the case of "A Star Is Born," I had recorded it and sent it to the Holleriths, but in this case I sang the song to Jerry himself at a party Mary threw for him, in front of a large gathering of friends—an aggressive triple act of conveying affection, making someone acutely uncomfortable and showing off, all at the same time. It's something I continued to do sporadically over the years. I should add that the occasion was Jerry's thirty-ninth birthday.

S S

You look flashy, you look sporty,
You look almost as dashing as
    Morty.*
Well, you're only as old as you
    look—
And you look forty.

You look blasé, you look nifty,
When they ask you your age you
    look shifty.

*Morton Gottlieb, an affable, moderately successful and notably frugal producer (*Same Time Next Year, Sleuth*), not known for his sartorial elegance.

Well, you're only as old as you look.
Let me look again—
Fifty.

On your ravaged face
Are more lines than they say on the
    stage.
It's not a sign of sorrow or
    disgrace—
It's age.

Happy Birthday, Jerry Beaty.
May your problems be less and less
    weighty.
Well, you're only as old as you look
And you look eighty-
Five.
You're practically alive.

Of your in-laws,
You've a craw full.
The demands that they make are in-
    lawful.
Well, you're only as old as you
    look—
And you look awful.

You should feel just
Like a baby.
You've got decades ahead of you—
    maybe.
Well, you're only as old as you feel.
What's your ulcer like, J.B.?

You've a rich full store
Of memories in that brain.
Won't you tell us your adventures in
    the War—
With Spain?

You look punchy.
You look drowsy.
The Greeks had a word for it: lousy.

Well, you're only as old as you
    look—
But you can't be as old as all that!

Happy Birthday,
Don't regret it,
'Cause we'll all go right home and
    forget it,
Old friend,
Old pal,
Old Faithful,
Old paint,
Old Greenwich,
Old Crow,
Old shoe,
Old hat!

I should add that I adapted this song for Leonard Bernstein on his actual fortieth. It was the same lyric as the one above, up through "It's age." Then it took off in a more appropriate direction:

You've got more time to write more
    scores,
Whether somebody else's or your
    scores,
'Cause you're only as old as you look
And you look four scores
Five.
Why, you're practically alive.

You look fertile, full of fire,
With your eyes on a goal even
    higher,
If you're only as old as you look,
You should retire.

Count your candles, take a Benny,
You got years yet to go—maybe
    twenny—

OCCASIONS · 409

'Cause you're only as old as you feel.
How's your back today, Lenny?

What great days have gone!
All the debuts, the bravos, the
    bombs!
And the time that you took over the
    baton—
From Brahms.

The last section remained the same.

Mommy on the Telephone (1961)
(Birthday song for
Mary Rodgers Beaty)

By the time she was thirty, Mary
was an exceptionally busy woman:
she was raising three children
(Todd, Nina and Kim) as well as
writing children's books and songs
and composing the score for a musical. She was never too busy, however, to talk to her best phone
crony, Anne Adler. It is not necessary to know who the other people
in the song are, although some of
the names may be recognizable.
What is also not necessary to know
is that I used the dial tone melody
of LEhigh 5-5539 every time it's
mentioned, a detail I'm fond of.
(In those days, Manhattan phone
numbers had an "exchange" prefix
which required dialing the first two
letters before the digits.) What is
necessary to know is that "Grandpa"
is Mary's father, Richard Rodgers.
And although there are three voices
called for, when I performed the
song at Mary's birthday party, I
sang it solo.

SS

Yesterday was Mary Beaty's birthday,
So, I thought I'd get her on the line.
I picked up the telephone
And listened for the dial tone,
Then dialed L-E-5-5-5-3-9.

L-E-5-5-5-3-9.
    Busy.
Well, I thought I ought to buy a
    present,
So I hurried to the five and ten.
Spent about a nickel there,
Then ambled to a pay phone, where
I dialed Mary's number once again:

L-E-5-5-5-3-9.
    Busy.
Now, I'm a very patient sort of
    fellow,
So I started reading *War and Peace*.
Hated it. When I was through,
I went and saw the movie, too.
Came back and got my coin from
    coin release:

L-E-5-5-5-3-9.
    What's going on in the Beaty
    house?

MARY
Toddy's playing softball off the wall,
Using Kimmy as the ball.
Nina's eating lipstick, case and all—

CHILD
Mommy!

MARY
(To the child)
Later—Mommy's on the
    telephone . . .

Todd has hidden Mommy's
    Frigidaire.
Nina hid her extra hair.
Kimmy hid herself and forgot just
    where.

CHILD
Mommy!

MARY
Later—Mommy's on the telephone,
    please!
Children, I'll be with you in a
    minute . . .

But first I must call the Lewines,
Nancy, and Anne Adler,
The Melnicks and the Gelbarts, the
    Dunnes—
And Anne Adler.

Mary Rodgers Beaty

Then I must telephone Hal,
Linda, and Anne Adler,
Minnie, Burt and Susan and Steve—
And Anne Adler.

Then I should call CBS,
Sardi's and Anne Adler.
Bergdorf, Golden Records . . .
Who did I forget now—?
Yes, Jerry, of course—
And Anne Adler!

Nina tore the TV limb from limb.
Todd repaired it—good for him!
Turn on Channel 5—oh, look,
    there's Kim!

CHILD
Mommy!

MARY
Later—Mommy's on the
    telephone . . .

Toddy's hitting Nina with a sledge.
Kimmy's on the window ledge.
Where could she have gone? She
    was on the edge!

CHILD
Mommy!

MARY

Later—Mommy's on the telephone,
    please!
Children, I'll be with you in a
    minute . . .

But first I must call Jule Styne,
Then I'll dial Weather,
Call up Information,
The Time—
And Anne Adler.

Then I must telephone Ruth,
The Zinssers and the Zinssers,
Johnny, D. D., Dinky and Chuck—
And Anne Adler.

Then I should call NBC,
Chappell's, Dr. Sirmay,
Altman's, Leslie Stevens—
Who else do I know now?
Oh, yes! Jerry, of course . . .
And Anne Adler!

SS

Well, anyway, we wish her Happy
    Birthday:
All her friends and neighbors wish
    her well.
And if you want to buy her a
Present, don't buy sable fur.*
Just buy her twenty shares of Tel &
    Tel.†

And for anybody here who may like
    music,
The Beatys have a trio all their own:
Grandpa on the Steinway grand,
Daddy on the spinet, and
Mommy on the telephone!

For those who like to trace music
sources, the "First I must call . . ." sections of the song are set to a sweeping
waltz, which resurfaced in the wordless waltz sections of "Simple," the Act
One finale of *Anyone Can Whistle.*

---

*Pronounced, as in Brooklynese,"fuh"—
a private joke.
†The former shorthand for AT&T.

I Am Content (1978)

(Birthday song for Hal Prince's
fiftieth birthday)

Writing a birthday song for someone is verbal and musical portrait-
painting: instead of trying to
capture the personality of the sitter
through the pose chosen, the clothing worn, the details of the face and
eyes, the compositional tensions
and so on, the songwriter includes
specific details of the subject's life
as well as the nuances of diction
and language and attitude, and his
emotional essence. Hal Prince is a
pleasure to write about—his energy,
his humor, his instantaneous volatility, all make for vivid portrai-
ture. Here I am, as Hal sitting in the
inner sanctum of his office (I sang
this to a crowd of about 150 birthday guests):

HAL
(Quietly, contemplative)

As I sit here, gazing
At my handsome office
With the many pictures
Of my thirty-some-odd shows
And my two large houses
And my two small children
And my shiny shaggy shih tzu
And my multilingual wife,
As I sit here gazing at my
Full rich life,
I am content . . .

(Screams into the outer office)

Ruthie!*

(Contemplative again)

For, as I learn every year,
And after fifty, it's plain,
You need a dream worth pursuing—

(Screams)

Howard!† Ruthie! . . .

(Contemplative)

'Cause in this crazy career,
You won't remain very sane
Unless you love what you're doing—
Howard! Donna!‡

(Mutters)

Jesus . . .

(Quietly)

And when I walk on the stage
And begin to rehearse,
A sort of—
George! GEORGE MARTIN!§

(Quietly)

—Calm comes over me,
I look at the page and I—

---

*Ruth Mitchell, his co-producer.
†Howard Haines, his company manager.
‡Donna Hoffman, his general assistant.
§His stage manager.

ARTIE!*—
—Meet reverses,
Like the Shuberts calling:
Theater not available;
Parties stalling:
Story isn't saleable;
The score isn't done—
Well, you couldn't hum it, anyway—
FLOSSIE!† I said PINK!
Do you really call that PINK?
Jesus Christ!
GEORGE! BORIS!‡
No, wait now, let me think . . .
Let me think—
ARLENE!§
This is consommé, not bean!
I distinctly ordered bean!
Can we please have the scene?
Gang, the scene, not the screen! . . .

(Controlling himself)

Okay, hold it, hold it, let's just sim-
mer down . . .

(After a pause, quietly)

As I sit here, gazing
At my East Side town house
With my Giacometti
And my Hockney and my Grosz,
And my full-length mirror
And my spotless bathroom
And my automatic valet
And my charismatic wife,
As I sit here gazing at my
Rich full life,
I am content . . .
JUDE!‖

For life is not just the play.
If you want real peace of mind,
You need a family beside you—
JUDE! CHARLEY!#
And at the end of the day
You leave your troubles behind,
If you've a home that can hide you.

---

*Artie Masella, his directorial assistant.
†Florence Klotz, his costume designer.
‡Boris Aronson, his set designer.
§Arlene Caruso, his secretary.
‖His wife, Judy.
#His son.

CHARLEY! DAISY!* SOMEBODY!
(Calmly)

I step inside from the street
And I stand in the hall
And all my—
ALMA!†
—Nervous tension vanishes.
My dog runs to meet me,

(Baby talk)

My Choppy Chibby Choobby
Chobby—
DEE!‡ Goddammit,
Can't you hear the phone out there?
It's me, Goddammit!
Doesn't anybody care?

But then, who can hear,
What with Stevie Wonder blaring—
Does it have to be so loud?
JUDY! Why is it so LOUD?
Someone's used my towel!
Please, Charley, get the phone!
Who's been at my desk?
Doody,§ leave my desk alone!
Choppy, I don't want your bone!
Take your bone!
It's all icky,
And will someone get the
phone?!!! . . .

(Controlling himself once more)

Okay, calm down, just everybody
calm down a minute . . .

After a pause, he looks serenely around
the room at the birthday guests.

As I sit here, gazing
At this giant studio,
A thousand chicken legs
And several hundred friends,
All my casts and colleagues
And my wife and children
And my mother and my in-laws,
It's a truly wondrous sight.
When I think why all of you

---

*His daughter.
†Household help.
‡The Princes' cook.
§Daisy's nickname.

Are here tonight,
I am content.

*With the vamp continuing underneath,
one by one his wife, his children, his in-
laws and finally the entire assemblage
sing "Happy Birthday" to him.*

Doug Levine (1993)
(Birthday song for Hal Prince's sixty-fifth birthday)

As the twilight years approach, many of us in sedentary professions suddenly determine to get as fit as possible in an effort to delay the inevitable. We embark grumpily on exercise programs in and out of gyms, guided and prodded by physical trainers, yoga masters and the like. Hal was no exception. Encouraged by his family, he gamely hired a trainer named Doug Levine (pronounced to rhyme with "between").

With this song, all that is necessary to know is that "Hesh" is Judy's nickname for Hal, that "Poppy" was what Charley called his father, and that the entire number is composed of songs from shows which Hal and I did together. For those who know the shows, I will keep a running scorecard of the tunes used; for those who don't, you can make up your own.

It starts with the opening of "Company." Because I sang the whole song solo, some of the overlapping voices are elided into lines of different lengths.

DAISY
Daddy . . .

JUDY
Heshy . . .

DAISY
Dadadada—

JUDY
Heshesheshesh—

CHARLEY
Poppy . . .

DAISY
Daddy . . .

JUDY
Heshy . . .

DAISY
Daddy . . .

ALL THREE
Don't you think you're getting
    sort of—?

JUDY
Heshy . . .

ALL THREE
Fleshy—?
Shouldn't you do something with
    your body?

DAISY
Daddy . . .

JUDY
Heshy . . .

BOTH
Time to think thin.

HAL
Can't wait—
Gang, that's the truth!

DAISY
Daddy . . .

JUDY
Heshy . . .

CHARLEY
Poppy . . .

ALL THREE
Time to begin.

HAL
One sec,
Let me call Ruth . . .

ALL THREE
Dad, we got you a trainer!
He'll be so glad to see you!
Dad, you're gonna start with a
    trainer!

Just be the two of you,
Only the two of you,
You'll love him!

HAL
Phone rings,
Door chimes,
In comes Doug Levine!
Lift things,
Pulse climbs,
Blood hums—Doug Levine!

Biceps,
Triceps,
Quadrupeds,
Stretch, flex,
Delts, pecs,
What do they mean?

Name brand
Headband,
Dirty Keds,
Sweat socks,
Old jocks,
Harold the Lean
Machine . . .
With Doug
Showing the way,
With Doug
Saving the day,
A body by Doug—
Okay,
Let's pump!

        (Starts to lift a weight)

1, 2, 3, 4 . . .

        (To the tune of "Wait" from Sweeney
            Todd*)*

Easy now, mustn't push . . .
Think nice thoughts, like we're rid
    of Bush . . .
Exhale slow, squeeze the tush—
Wait.

9, 10, 11 . . .

Sternum flat on the ground . . .
Come, endorphins, come gather
    round
Me and my twenty-pound
Weight.

18, 19, 20 . . .

(To "In Buddy's Eyes" from Follies*)*

In Judy's eyes,
I'm young, I'm beautiful,
In Judy's eyes
I can't get older . . .
Oh God, my shoulder . . .

28 . . .

(*To "There Is No Other Way" from*
Pacific Overtures)

The arms ache,
The back creaks,
The head throbs—
It's seven weeks.
Is there no other way?

34 . . . 35 . . . 36 . . .

(*To his son, to "Like It Was" from*
Merrily We Roll Along)

Charley,
Why can't we be like we were?
I want us the way that we were.
Charley, you and me,
We were thinner then.

41 . . .

I was thin.
You were thinner, but I was thin.
She was thin.
I don't know how you turned into
    muscle
And we turned into—
No, don't look at me—
Charley,
Can't you just see how we were,
Those days when we read Walter
    Kerr?
God knows, things were easier then.

(*To "Losing My Mind" from* Follies)

Or am I losing my wind?

54 . . . 55 . . .

(*To "One More Kiss" from* Follies)

One more set
Before we part, Doug.
One more set
And farewell.
Never shall we meet again.

Just another ten
And then—
Oh, hell . . .

He rests the weight on his chest.

(*To "Company"*)

DAISY
Daddy . . .

JUDY
Heshy . . .

BOTH
Don't give up now!
Hold on—lookin' good!

DAISY
Daddy . . .

JUDY
Heshy . . .

CHARLEY
Poppy . . .

ALL THREE
Look at you—wow!
That's it! Knew you could!
See, you're getting into condition!
Fittest director in town!
Pop, you're getting real definition!
Aren't you feeling great?
What was that—fifty-eight?
We looooooooooooove
You!

More zest,
Less flab,
Less stress—Doug Levine!

HAL
(*Not quite making it*)
59 . . .

ALL THREE
Big chest,
Flat ab,
God bless Doug Levine!

HAL
(*Making it*)
59 . . .

ALL THREE
Treadmill
Uphill

Strengthens lungs.
Deep squats,
Hard knots,
Who minds the pain?

HAL
60 . . .

ALL THREE
More steps,
More reps
Up the rungs.
Large belts,
Large delts,
If there's no strain—

HAL
61 . . .

ALL THREE
—No gain!

HAL
62 . . .

ALL THREE
It's Doug,
That's who it's for!

HAL
63 . . .

ALL THREE
For Doug, only two more—

HAL
I'll do it for Doug!
64—!
65!
65!
I'm alive!
I'll survive
Sixty—

The haiku chord from Pacific Overtures *sounds.*

The exercise bird,
Whose youth remains within him,
Stays fit forever . . .

Doug Levine didn't last long, but
shortly afterward, Hal bought a house
in the French Alps and took up skiing
and, to everyone's surprise, was good
at it.

The Saga of Lenny

(1988)

(Birthday song for Leonard
Bernstein's seventieth birthday)

Lenny's seventieth was cause for
many celebrations, one of the most
celebratory being a concert at Tan-
glewood, where he had been principal conductor for years, and his
home away from home. It involved
numerous major figures from the
musical and theatrical worlds,
among them his good friend Lauren
Bacall, whom I cajoled into singing
my contribution to the festivities: a
parody of "The Saga of Jenny," by
Kurt Weill and Ira Gershwin from
Lady in the Dark. It will be more
entertaining if you listen to the
original first.

LAUREN BACALL
There once was a boy named Lenny,
Whose talents were varied and
    many,
So many that he was inclined
Never to make up his mind.
In fact, he was so gifted
He seldom felt uplifted,
Just undefined.

Poor Lenny,
Ten gifts too many,
The curse of being versatile.
To show how bad the curse is
Will need a lot of verses
And take a little Weill:

*A sudden intrusion of Lenny's vamp to
"Conversation Piece" from* Wonderful
Town, *then back to Kurt Weill.*

Lenny made his mind up
When he was three,
He'd write a show, a ballet
And a symphony.
But once the winds were tootled
And the first strings plucked,
He decided it was terrible—
He'd have to conduct.

Poor Lenny,
Time and again, he
Complained "I'm in this dreadful
    bind.

I feel for Leonardo—
God, genius is so hard—oh,
You can *not* make up your mind."

A brief passage of ballet music from On
the Town, *followed by the "Conversation Piece" vamp, then back to Weill
again.*

Lenny made his mind up when he
    was nine,
He'd be not only Bernstein,
He'd be Rubinstein.
"But just Rubinstein," he grumbled,
"That's like calling it quits,
When there's Hammerstein
And Wittgenstein
And Gertrude and Blitz."

Poor Lenny
Knew there and then he

Might easily get over-Steined.
From Ein to Ep to Jule
To Liechtenstein*—
No, truly,
He could not make up his mind.

*A snatch of "Gee, Officer Krupke," fol-
lowed by a variation on the "Conversation Piece" vamp, which continues
underneath.*

Lenny made his mind up
At twenty-two,
To do whatever Pinza
Or Astaire could do.

*Pronounced "Lichtensteen"—a reference
to his constant irritation at people mispro-
nouncing his name.

Though his voice was truly base,
He had the charm of a kid,
And if the dance floor didn't
    suit him,
The podium did.

Poor Lenny,
Wondering when he
Could show off all his gifts
    combined,
Began a TV feature.
It's best to be a teacher
When you can't make up your mind.

The vamp of "Carried Away" from On
the Town, *continuing underneath.*

Lenny made his mind up
At twenty-eight,
That marriage and a family
Would be just great.
But he had no time for weddings
Till a moment came
He was free between a tennis
And an anagrams game.

Poor Lenny.
Worse though, poor Jennie,*
Who muttered all those years,
    resigned,
"I don't care if he picks a
Schlemozzle or a shiksa,
He should please make up his
    mind."

A couple of passages from West Side
Story *and* Trouble in Tahiti, *then back
to Weill straight up.*

Lenny made his mind up
At forty-six
That maybe atonality
And rock would mix.
Though it certainly was serial,
With rhythm on top,
It had lots of snap and crackle,
But not enough pop.

Poor Lenny,
Pacing his den, he
Was worried he'd be left behind.
He mumbled, "How ironic,

Atonal is a tonic
When you can't make up your
    mind."

    "So is minimalism . . ."

Another vamp from West Side Story,
then Weill.

Lenny made his mind up
At seven-oh,
To be a modern Renaissance
Like, man, you know.
And there is virtually nothing
That he hasn't done—
So get ready for his club act
At seventy-one.

Poet, pundit, seer,
Politician, skier,
Still at sea at three score ten.
Decked with every laurel,
Lenny, here's the moral:
Do whatever pleases you and when.

Follow all your talents,
Don't attempt a balance,
Shower us with every kind.
Share your every vision.
Stick with indecision.
Don't make up,
You shouldn't make up,
You mustn't make up,
Don't ever make up—

Live another score and
Write another score and
Don't make up your mind!

---

*Lenny's mother.

The Arthur Laurents Eightieth Birthday Song (1998)

Knowing how prickly Arthur was, but wanting to write him a birthday song that had some edge to it, and also knowing that my partner at the time, Peter Jones, was a superb Ethel Merman imitator, I hit on the idea of having the entire song sung in her brassy take-no-prisoners voice. Also, if some of the jokes fell flat, Peter's imitation, I hoped, would carry the day, and it did.

The premise: Ethel returns from the Great Beyond to wish Arthur a rousing Happy Birthday. All the tunes are from Gypsy. *A familiarity with the book as well as the score will help.*

                ETHEL
I had a show,
A wonderful show, Arthur,
A long time ago, Arthur.
And now, so I'm told,
You're eighty years old—
To me you're pure gold!
So, Arthur—

You look swell, you look great.
Shit, you hardly look seventy-eight!
Starting here, from today,
Arthur, everything's coming up roses!

Clear the deck, clear the track,
You're the reason I had to come
    back.
Oh, and hey, by the way,
Loads of love from Benay*—
I'm here to see your wishes all come
    true!
Arthur,
Everything's coming up bigger and
    bigger hits,
Everything's coming up cheering
    and heavy mitts,
Everything's coming up ski trips to
    St. Moritz† . . .

---

*The singer Benay Venuta, one of Ethel's closest friends.
†Arthur was an expert skier who made a yearly visit to St. Moritz.

We have so much in common,
It's a phenomenon.
I think of us as equal,
Let's do a sequel . . .

> But that wouldn't be your style,
> would it, Arthur? Because you
> never repeat yourself! Like some
> others I could mention. And will.

> *(To the pianist—in this case, me)*

> Hit it!

Some playwrights get lots of praise,
Just rewriting their early plays—
That's okay for some playwrights
Who don't know that they're hacks.

Some playwrights get panned a lot,
Grow too bitter and go to pot,
That's perfect for some playwrights
Who stop dead in their tracks.

But you,
You always come through
With something that's
Both tradition and innovation:
*Cuckoo, Clearing, Home of the Brave,
Enclave, Bird Cage, Invitation**—
Each one gets my personal rave!

> And I woulda seen 'em, too, if I
> hadn't been workin' at the time!

Some playwrights can be content,
Making pageants or faking *Rent.*
That's peachy for some playwrights,
For some
Numb
Dumb
Playwrights and their shows.
Well, they can stay and rot—
Or write prose!

> Okay, so I didn't see the plays, but I
> saw the movies. And Arthur, I gotta
> tell ya, they were great! But as my
> old friend Cole Porter said, "Let's
> Face It"—why didn't you think of
> me for some of those roles? With

> what I got inside of me—if I ever
> let it out—*Anastasia—there* was a
> part I coulda sunk my teeth into!
> And what about *Snake Pit? Bonjour
> Tristesse? Rope?* You coulda *written*
> them for me. For me! For me! For
> me! Still . . .

We did a show!
You wrote it for me, Arthur!
It fit to a "t," Arthur!
But you gotta agree:
If it wasn't for me,
Where the hell would you be?

> I made Porter, I made Gershwin, I
> made Berlin—and I made you!
> And I can do it again! I will,
> Arthur, I swear I will! I'm gonna
> make *you* a star! You're gonna write
> a whole new show—all about me!
> It's gonna be better than anything
> you ever did before! Better than
> anything you even dreamed! Fin-
> ished? Why, you're just beginning,
> and there's no stopping you this
> time!

Happy Birthday, Mr. Laurents!
Have a vodka, have a sand dune,*
    have a smash!
Have a memoir, Mr. Laurents—
It'll be a catharsis as well as a source
    of cash.

Have a drink, have a snort,
Read a book, watch the court,
Deal the cards out, overbid.†
Take a bath, take a nap,
Just don't take any crap—
But of course you never did!

Happy Birthday, Arthur Laurents!
Feel the love, the admiration—can
    you feel?
Though the fondness all around you
May astound you,
It's real!
How have you survived the biz,
Full of fight and full of fizz?
Kid, you must be made of steel.

The producers, the actors,
The myriad factors
That make the the-ay-ter insane,
All the Clurmans, the Hermans—
No, there ain't no more Mermans—
Have we heard you complain?

Happy Birthday, Arthur Laurents,
May our wishes for your happiness
    come true.
Our affection comes in torrents
And it warrants
This do.
Sartre, but with sex appeal,
The funniest playwright since
    O'Neill—
Arthur Laurents, we love you!

Happy Birthday!

Hey, Mr. Producer!
(1998)

Hey, Mr. Producer! was a gala tribute to Cameron Mackintosh, Great
Britain's most successful theater
producer. It was an all-star affair in
the presence of the Royal Family,
featuring songs from his shows, and
he had asked me to write something for the evening. Since he is a
good friend as well as someone to
whom I owe a great deal professionally, I said I'd give it some
thought. I didn't have to give it
much, because I came up with an
idea startling and theatrical enough
to obscure any weaknesses in the
song itself: a parody of two of the
most famous songs by two of the
most famous composers whose
work Cameron had produced, performed by them at two pianos. The
composers were Andrew Lloyd
Webber and myself, the songs "The
Music of the Night" and "Send in
the Clowns." I had to give up the
notion of two pianos, as they
proved to be too cumbersome to
move on and off the stage for the
few brief minutes their presence
was required. I settled for four

**The Time of the Cuckoo; A Clearing in the
Woods; Home of the Brave; The Enclave; The
Bird Cage; Invitation to a March.*

*Arthur's second home was a beach house
in Quogue, Long Island.
†He was an avid tennis and bridge player.

hands at one piano, which in any event made for an accompaniment easier to write and simpler to play. Andrew balked at having to perform the piece live and, since I am no more fond of performing in public than he is, we videotaped it. The effect on the audience was as gratifying as I had hoped: the initial sight of the two of us together, publicly perceived as we are to be warring opposites—the aesthete and the populist—was enough to carry the moment. Still, the song is not without a few good jokes.

First, the arpeggiated accompaniment to "Send in the Clowns."

SS
Isn't he rich?

ALW
Isn't he square?

BOTH
Isn't he working the room
Somewhere—

(Indicating a vague placement out front)

—out there?

(Looking at each other)

Send in the crowds.

ALW
Acts on his whims—

SS
Took a big chance—

ALW
Noticed his anagram said:
Cameron: romance.

SS
He went to France.*

BOTH
Send in the crowds.

"The Music of the Night" takes over.

ALW
Night time falling,
Cameron starts calling—

SS
Posing questions—

BOTH
Questions and suggestions.

ALW
Suddenly appearing—

SS
And always interfering—

BOTH
But here we are and cheering,
As we might,
The man who flogs the music of
tonight.

"Send in the Clowns" returns.

SS
Isn't it kitsch?

ALW
Sometimes it's crass.

BOTH
That's when he says to himself:
Bring in the class.

(Looking up to the royal box)

Send in the crowns.

(Calling offstage)

Tee,* get me the crowns.

The accompaniments combine.

SS
Always in charge.

ALW
(Overlapping)
Sees the sketches, signs them—

SS
(Overlapping)
Making things large.

ALW
(Overlapping)
Then he redesigns them.

BOTH
How generous he was to underwrite
The overwritten music of tonight.

Bombastic interlude, consisting of grandiose chords and elaborate arpeggios.

SS
God, but he's rich!

ALW
Richer than me!

BOTH
Lucky he never grew up
Or where would we be?

(Looking front)

Thank you, Sir C.

SS
(To ALW, as the music fades)
Let's do this again . . .

ALW
You're out of your mind . . .

BOTH
Well, maybe next year . . .

---

*Cameron had just bought a chateau in Provence.

---

*Cameron's secretary.

Beginnings

This section is included for the sole purpose of encouraging anyone who wants to write lyrics. I don't consider that the phrase "Collected Lyrics" on the covers of these books obliges me to display all my juvenilia—in particular, school and college songs, and the ones I wrote under the tutelage of Oscar Hammerstein, who advised me to write four apprentice works: an adaptation of a good play, an adaptation of a flawed play, an adaptation of something not written for the stage and, finally, an original. Juvenilia can be fascinating to fans and researchers, but pointless to those less interested in the ex-juvenile who puts it out in public. I have had both those reactions to the catalogs of artists I admire, and I didn't want to take that risk here: I made it clear to the publisher when I agreed to this venture that I had no intention of including anything before *Saturday Night,* which I think of as my first professional work. As I was writing this second volume, however, it occurred to me that a small sampling of my first fumblings might be helpful to other fumblers, that if they could examine my fits and starts and my attempts to become technically proficient and to find my own voice, they might feel more sanguine about the possibility of overcoming their own self-perceived failings.

Here then is a small feast of clichés, redundancies, inappropriate and infelicitous words, cutenesses and confusions (I leave the pleasure of discovering which are which to the reader), all excusable for beginners. Here also, if you look carefully, is every now and then a graceful image, a fresh rhyme, a surprising joke, all recognizable buds of someone who was meant to be a lyric writer, and a lyric writer for the theater. The theatricality is in the phrasing and timing of the ideas and the rhymes, not only the true ones but the false ones, and even worse than the false ones, the ones you can see coming a mile away. Borrowing a page from *Merrily We Roll Along,* I'll present the songs in reverse chronological order so that the would-be lyricist who reads them will grow more encouraged as he proceeds. I've chosen them as exemplary of my attempts to make comment, wax poetic and show sophistication by being variously clever in rhyme, worldly in tone and satirical in approach. To spare myself as well as the reader, I'll include only one from each score. The curtain will fall at my sophomore year at Williams. My prep school years will have to remain shrouded in total obscurity.

New York (1953)
(from *The Clock*)

In 1952, I was living in Hollywood, working on the *Topper* television series. In order to vary the monotony of writing the same thing with minor variations every week, I started to look for something to make a musical of, and thought of *The Clock,* a charming, funny and sentimental MGM movie from 1945 starring Judy Garland (in a nonsinging role) and directed by Vincente Minnelli. The script had never been published, but I happened to be friendly with an executive secretary at the studio and asked her to sneak a copy out of the vault on a Friday after work and lend it to me so that I could retype it in its entirety over the weekend and return it to her Monday morning. Which she did and which I did, with no one the wiser. In between *Topper* episodes, I started adapting it, but once I'd quit my job and moved back to New York, my interest dissipated. Here is a remnant of what I wrought.

The situation is that of a young sailor making his first visit to New York and getting a rundown on the city from a denizen.

NEW YORKER

I love New York.
I've lived here thirty-six years
And buddy, I'm sold.
It's great in New York.
There's so much to see and do—
At least, so I'm told.

There's the Bowery,
And the Battery,
And there's Broadway
And Times Square.
But I'm seldom ever there
Myself.

There's the Statue of Liberty.
It's a lot of fun to climb,
But I've never had the time
Myself.

All week at the office
I think of the city
And how I could do it up brown.
By Friday it's gotten me down,
So I get out of town.

But the Cloisters,
And there's Chinatown—
There's so much to see and do.
How I wish that I were you,
And had time to see
The sights in New York, too!
Ah, New, New York!

I've written a number of better New York songs since then, but you should see the movie, anyway.

(The typescript screenplay page reads:)

Teddy
(Quietly)
Neither did Norman.

David
(His anger mounting)
I'm not interested in Norman. He doesn't pound pavements all day, or wait for hours in offices to beg a crumb from a casting director. For Christ sakes, what else do you want me to do?

Teddy
(Gently, her hand on his arm)
Come up to the apartment.

David
I don't feel like it. Not tonight.

Teddy
Dave, we've spent too much time together to squabble over this. You know that if a part came along that I felt you were right for, I'd see that you got a crack at it.

David
Yeah. Well, I'm going home.
(Sulkily)
I can't afford to stay out late if I have to get up early and start begging.

Teddy
Will I see you tomorrow night? We're *supposed to have dinner* with Norm and Judy.

David
That's right.
(Shrugs)
I suppose so.
(Pause)

Teddy
Well, goodnight.

David
(Shortly)
Goodnight.
(HE exits. TEDDY is left alone)

Teddy
(Sings)

Get tough, Teddy!
You should know.
Be rock-steady,
Let him go!
Get rough, get ready;
He's just a pup!
Get tough, Teddy!
(Sighs) What the hell - give up!
Might as well give up.

I'm in Love with a Boy (1952)
(from *Climb High*)

In the four-musical course that Oscar assigned me to write, the final project was to be an original, and *Climb High* is it. I wrote both book and score for a tale based on the postgraduate life of a college friend* who was a class ahead of me, but who had been in the navy during the war and, like many of the men at Williams, was in the first wave of returning GIs and thus older and far more experienced in the ways of the world than those of us fresh out of high school (although the level of sophistication of men in their early twenties back then was a good deal lower than that of even teenagers today). He wanted to be an actor and immediately after graduation started making the rounds. By the time I had graduated and was living in New York, he had met with some limited success. He was good-looking and good company and something of a ladies' man, and I watched him ply his charms accordingly, especially with one particular older woman, an influential talent agent. In my script her name was Teddy, and I conceived of her as being the kind of smart, world-weary woman

*The title derives from a motto carved at the entrance to a stone staircase on the Williams campus which reads, "Climb high, climb far / Your aim the sky, your goal the star."

This one had music by Mary Rodgers. Neither of us can remember exactly why we wrote it, but at the time we were both hustling to get our work heard, and the song was probably aimed at a television program or a record company. It has a calypso beat.

ISLAND NATIVE

There's an island in the Pacific
Where the weather is perverse.
All year long the heat is terrific,
But at Christmas time it's worse.

Soak me up with a blotter,
Remove me off to a cooler clime.
It's hot and gonna get hotter
On Christmas Island at Christmas
    time.

Last year I write Santa a letter,
Ask him down for Christmas Eve.
Santa come in furry red sweater,
Lose a hundred pound and leave.

Soak me up with a blotter,
Remove me off to a cooler clime.
It's hot and gonna get hotter
On Christmas Island at Christmas
    time.

Everybody north get a present;
If unwanted, can return.
Christmas here not nearly so
    pleasant—
Everybody get bad burn.

Soak me up with a blotter,
Remove me off to a cooler clime.
It's hot and gonna get hotter
On Christmas Island at Christmas
    time.

Mistletoe don't grow in the Tropic;
We kiss under banyan tree.
All year squinting make one myopic.
You kiss you and I kiss me!

Soak me up with a blotter,
Remove me off to a cooler clime.
It's getting hotter and hotter!

played in movies by Joan Crawford and Rosalind Russell—the sort who was always talking crisply on the phone behind an immaculate desk and wearing a suit until late in the movie, when the hero brought out her feminine side. In my story, however, the hero, having duly brought her out, leaves her in the lurch. Here she is, talking to herself:

TEDDY

Get tough, Teddy!
You should know.
Be rock-steady,
Let him go!
Get rough, get ready;
He's just a pup!
Get tough, Teddy!

(Sighs)

What the hell—give up!
Might as well give up.

I'm in love with a boy,
And the boy's just a baby.
He's no bundle of joy—
Well, he may be.
But something's amiss, girl,
Someone's throwing curves.
That bundle of joy leaves this
    girl
A bundle of nerves.

I'm in love with a child,
And the child is a lover.
If the boy hadn't smiled,
I'd recover.
But children destroy,
Recklessly!
And I'm in love with a boy
Too young to love me.

There's not a reason or rhyme
Why anybody should got to be
On Christmas Island at Christmas
time!

The Sun Is Blue
(1950)
(from *Mary Poppins*)

The third musical in the Hammerstein series was to be derived from
a nontheatrical work. I had loved
the Mary Poppins books since I was
a child and thought it would be a
useful challenge to try to make a
coherent whole out of a group of
short, interrelated stories. It was,
but I couldn't meet the challenge
and gave up about a third of the
way through. It did yield the following, however, for a situation in
which the Banks children, Mary's
wards, are complaining that she
doesn't love them enough.

MARY
The universe is small,
The sun is blue;
And summer follows fall
While spring is freezing.

And the ocean's filled with sugar,
And I'm sure that the grass is pink.
And the night is another thing I am
    certain of—
It's a curtain of
Ink.

The moon is made of cheese,
The earth is flat.
And money grows on trees,
And that is that.

And love is just a frivolous game
That soon begins to pall.
Yes, the sun is blue
And I don't love you
At all.

When I was in London late in 1995, to
my astonishment and delight P. L. Tra-

vers, the author of the Mary Poppins
books, tracked me down and called to
invite me to tea. She had a request,
she said: she wanted me to write a musical based on her stories. She assured
me that she and not the Disney corporation controlled the rights. It was no
longer a project that interested me,
but I was certainly interested to meet
the eccentric lady behind the books (I
assumed she was eccentric not just because she was English but because of
the antic imagination that went into
her work). Unfortunately, she called
on the day before I was to leave and I
had no free time left. I assured her
that I visited England often and would
happily accept her invitation when I
next returned. More unfortunately, by
the time I did, she had died. But to

this day I remain flattered that she
asked me, and grateful that I never
had to turn down her request.

The Wonder of You
(1949)
(from *High Tor*)

Maxwell Anderson's 1936 play *High
Tor* was the second in my series of
Hammerstein assignments: to fashion a musical out of a piece I liked
but thought I could improve. This
judgment was something of a presumption on my part, considering
that the play had been a critical and

popular success; in fact, it had won the Drama Critics Circle Award. At the age of nineteen, however, chutzpah is the coin of the realm and my burgeoning confidence in my powers was already tinged with arrogance—something I shed as soon as I started working with professionals.

The story centers on a young idealist named Van van Dorn, who owns a mountain in the Hudson Valley which his father has left him. He works occasionally, but for the most part lives off the land, enjoying the natural life. His girlfriend, Judith, deplores what she sees as his fecklessness; she works at a local hotel and urges him to take a steady job there. At the beginning of the play, they are arguing about it.

JUDITH
. . . I just want you to come down to
    earth.

VAN
Down to earth?
Porter in a hotel,
Lugging up a satchel or
Opening the windows
For the widows in their prime.
Answering the whisper
Of a fat-and-fifty bachelor:
"Where's the nearest cathouse, boy?"
Maybe you get a dime.

JUDITH
I'd see you every day.

VAN
    Yeah—
I could see you on the mezzanine,
Talking to the drummer boys,
Taking their dictation,
How they're always on the go.
Getting little pinches
From the older and the dumber
    boys;
Maybe you can stand that stuff—
I'd choke to death, I know.
And that's my answer—no.

Judith argues that everybody has to make a living.

VAN
Suppose a man makes money
And he works for forty years,
And he slaves and saves and labors
Till the sweat pours off his brow.
Then one day at last the time is up,
He gives three rousing cheers.
What's he do?

JUDITH
Takes a vacation.

VAN
I'm on vacation now.

She berates him for not accepting an offer from a trap-rock mining company to sell High Tor.

VAN
They want to chew the back right
    off the mountain,
Divide it up into a million parts.
They want to blast and sell its soul
    for profit.
These men have rocks instead of
    hearts.
Pop liked this mountain, too,
He would have understood.
Maybe he should have sold,
But he knew he never would.
Neither will I.
I never could.

They talk about getting married, but she says that it's impossible if he doesn't have a job. She thinks that if he's going to be so intransigent, maybe they should stop seeing each other.

JUDITH
. . . Better now than later.

VAN
You don't know what it means to
me if you can say that.

JUDITH
It means as much to me. But I look
ahead a little.

VAN
What do you see?

JUDITH
Two lonely people growing old with
    memories,
Sitting, blinking idly at the
    mountain sun,
Their children running wild and
    having nothing,
Running on the mountain—

VAN
There's no better place to run.

JUDITH
Van, can't you be serious just for
once?

VAN
Things are serious enough without
setting out to do it. But I *had* been
counting on you.

A pause. He looks around, then up at the night sky.

    I can't explain it, but there's some-
    thing about this night . . .

The air is strange,
Its stillness misty-warm.
The clouds foretell
The coming of a storm.
I know the air will change;
I know the storm will go.
I put these facts in words
And yet I also know

There are no words to describe
The sweep of a sunset sky.
I have no words to describe
The mountain, when spring is new.
And you are to me
The mountain view,
The sunset sky—
Then tell me, how can I speak
The wonder of you?

There are no words to express
The peace of a windsoft night.
I have no words to express
The magic of morning dew.
And you are to me
The magic morning, windsoft
    night—
Then tell me, how can I speak
The wonder of you?
Then tell me, how can I speak
The wonder of you?

The sudden intrusion of nocturnal mystery is not just a whim; shortly after the song, the story takes a supernatural turn. The overripe language is partly a consequence of my mimicking Oscar, of course, right down to the repetition of the last line (a signature technique of his) and waxing poetic with words like "windsoft," but behind it all is the heavy touch of Maxwell Anderson, a high-minded, respected and successful playwright who often wrote ornate dialogue, sometimes even in blank verse; I have the excuse of trying to be faithful to his style. The truth is that what probably drew me to the play in the first place was its poetic pretension. Looking back at the lyric now, I realize that I was imitating not only Oscar's weaknesses but some of his strengths as well: his clarity, his attention to character, his use of conversational forms, his fidelity to the material. Therein lies the most important lesson that Oscar, unknowingly, passed on to me: since you start out inevitably by imitating the artists you admire (and sometimes continue to do so throughout your life), be sure to imitate good ones. In that sense, taste is as important as talent. If you allow yourself to grow, the more you write the more you will distance yourself from your influences; imitation may be a form of flattery, but it is also a form of criticism. Standing on the shoulders of giants involves recognizing their weaknesses and improving on them; that's what enables you to see farther than they.

I wrote Anderson for permission to perform the show at college; he politely refused it, replying that he hoped to adapt it for a musical himself, with a score by Kurt Weill. Weill died the following year, but in 1956 Anderson got his wish, writing his own lyrics to Arthur Schwartz's music for a television adaptation. Surprisingly, it was less pretentious than my version but, although it was considerably shorter, it was no better. The era of earnest, idealistic anticapitalism had passed, even if the subject still rears its tired head from time to time, especially in movies.

The Bordelaise
(1949)
(from *All That Glitters*)

My choice for the first exercise in Oscar's list of assignments was a musical adaptation of *Beggar on Horseback*, a 1924 play by George S. Kaufman and Marc Connelly, loosely based on a 1911 German play by Paul Apel whose translated title is *Johnny Sunstormer's Trip to Hell*. I found it imaginative, hilarious and virtually flawless. A parody of the expressionist parables that were popular at the time, it rails against the perils of trading one's artistic talents for commercial gain, an idea which appealed to the adolescent in me, and still does, as *Merrily We Roll Along* and *Sunday in the Park with George* would seem to indicate. Moreover, its structure was startling: a prologue in which the troubled hero falls asleep, a two-act dream sequence (the main body of the play), and an epilogue in which he awakens and resolves his troubles as a result of what he has learned from his dream. The hero is Neil McRae, a poor young composer of classical music, who for financial reasons has gotten himself engaged to Gladys Cady, the airhead daughter of a wealthy industrialist, and is trying to decide whether or not to go through with the marriage. Mr. Cady will approve the union only if Neil promises to give up his "foolish" desire to write symphonies and either write popular songs or go to work in Cady's factory. The extended dream sequence consists of Neil's vision of what life would be like if he married into the Cady family and, as you might guess, is more of a nightmare than a dream. It makes easy but clever fun of the usual targets in the American capitalist system: the acquisitive living style of the nouveaux riches—the ostentatious home, the army of servants, the dinner parties, the golf games and nightclubbing, the sense of entitlement, the mindless waste and neglect and the endless pursuit of leisure. What better subject for an eighteen-year-old?

The following song takes place during a surreal nightclub sequence in the dream. Gladys is out for a good time, as always. She asks Neil to dance with her. Neil, by now regretting his decision to marry her, balks and refuses to dance.

GLADYS
But that music! I can't sit still another minute! It's that new South American number, the Bordelaise—it's marvelous!

*She grabs the headwaiter and dances with him, singing.**

GLADYS
The Bordelaise
Sets my heart ablaze.
I feel the fierce, lonely yearning
For you that is burning
My heart.
And the music brings fire
Of lost love when I hear
It start,
And I perspire
With desire.

The Bordelaise
Puts me in a daze,
Until I all of a sudden
Can feel racing blood in
My veins.
Crazy rhythms which muddle
My heart and befuddle
My brains
Let me drink deep of love's wine,
While violins make you mine.

So then let them begin
That passionate Bordelaise,
For the flames of my love must be
    kindled
Without more delays.

---

*If you know Cole Porter's "Begin the Beguine," you should have no trouble imagining the rhythm of the accompaniment.

Oh, my poor tattered heart and I
Simply abhor delays.
And we surrender
To its joyous, yet tragic,
Enchanting and magical
Splendor.

The Bordelaise!
A kind of morbid craze!
It's the maddest fad
That can be had
Anywhere.
It gets under your skin
And it sticks in your hair,
And where it has been,
Love lights flare.
The violins plink
And orchids stink
In the air,
And you are there,

Faithful and fair,
For me to share.

Music made you for me,
And that music must be
The Bordelaise!
South of the Bordelaise!
The Bordelaise!

Williams College occupies most of Williamstown, Massachusetts, but there are imposing private residences just outside of town and one of the sometime residents was Cole Porter, who maintained a second home there. By sheer and lucky coincidence, Dr. Albert Sirmay, a music editor at Oscar's publishing house, Chappell & Co. (he was a doctor of music and he not only used the title, he wore a white medical coat in his office), had taken an interest in me as a promising young songwriter and proposed that since I was spending my school year in the vicinity of Mr. Porter (walking distance, actually), I might like to play some of my score for him. Yes, I gulped, and in due course an appointment was made.

The sky was gray and the ground was slushy the bleak January morning I was to appear, but score in hand and feeling every inch the promising composer, I tramped the mile or so to Mr. Porter's palatial house, only to be greeted by an elegantly lettered sign adjacent to the front door which read: PLEASE WIPE FEET WHITE RUGS INSIDE. The terseness and lack of punctuation made the request into a demand, and I spent a good two minutes scraping my ski boots against every step and sharp edge I could find, convinced that whatever I did, I would drip gobs of slush into the pristine interior. I considered entering in stockinged feet, boots in hand. After an agonizing two minutes of thought—movies had persuaded me that many a career had foundered on just such a trivial choice—I rang the bell and was admitted to the foyer by the kind of butler you'd expect Cole Porter to have, where I took off my boots. Naked and vulnerable in my athletic socks, I was ushered into Mr. Porter's living room, which looked out onto the countryside through a gigantic picture window and which was dominated by a nine-foot Steinway piano, a magnificent object the like of which I had never seen before. Instead of feeling like a promising composer, I now felt like a clumsy student, which is exactly what I was.

The butler asked me to wait for my host and I listened with eager apprehension for approaching footsteps (at this point in his life, Porter, crippled by a riding accident, was still able to navigate with crutches) and, hearing none, padded my way to the piano, on top of which lay, tantalizingly, an open musical notebook in which were sketched some ideas. As I was about to

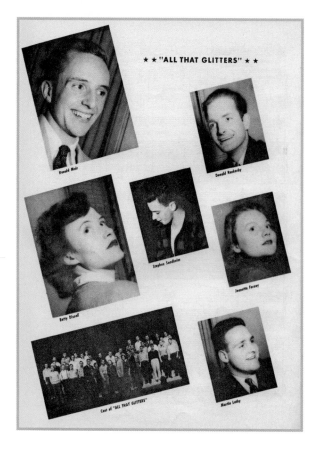

★ ★ "ALL THAT GLITTERS" ★ ★

Ronald Mair

Donald Reckerby

Betty Dissell

Stephen Sondheim

Jeanette Forkey

Cast of "ALL THAT GLITTERS"

Martin Luthy

How Do I Know? (1948)
(from *Phinney's Rainbow*)

During my freshman and sophomore years, the president of Williams had the formidable name of James Phinney Baxter. Also during my freshman and sophomore years, one of the biggest hits on Broadway was *Finian's Rainbow*. This fortuitous concatenation prompted me to write a musical about the college: its customs, its faculty, its fraternity system. Unlike at Harvard and some other bastions of education, there was no tradition of musicals at Williams, no Hasty Pudding Club or Princeton Triangle Club, but there was the Adams Memorial Theater, a state-of-the-art structure run, unfortunately, by the English Department. Williams at the time was a small (1,200 students) all-male college, and the head of the department, a professor with the impressive eighteenth-century name of Clay Hunt, saw to it that only straight plays, and rarely contemporary ones, were presented there. However, with so much money having been spent on the building, there was no reserve left in the bank for productions, and I calculated that I could persuade Professor Hunt that were he to allow a musical on the boards, especially one with local interest, the theater could make some money. Unlike productions of *Faust* and *The Beaux' Stratagem* and such, which at their best just broke even, both students and townspeople would flock to see it I told him. The calculation worked, and they did. We had to schedule two extra performances (out of five), almost doubling the standard run, and ended up with a profit of more than $1,500. (Professor Hunt was so overjoyed that he allowed me to do another musical the next year, which turned out to be *All That Glitters*.)

Once I'd secured the permission, I commandeered a classmate of

memorize what I was seeing (for bragging purposes only), the man himself arrived, greeted me warmly, and without undue small talk asked me to play something from the show. I was only too happy to oblige, having practiced assiduously for hours.

Ordinarily, I would have started with the opening number but, fearful there might be a limit to Porter's time and/or attention span, I had resolved to throw caution to the wind and begin with my blatant parody of his famous song. The minute I sat down at the piano, which stretched out in front of me like a football field, I knew I'd made a mistake. As I played and sang and trembled, all I could think of was how he would take it. Would he be flattered or offended, would he consider it smart or smart-ass, would he sue me for plagiarism? In the event, when I'd finished, he nodded and gave a faint smile, but whether it was cold or amused, I couldn't tell. There followed a pause, which seemed to last

an hour, and then he spoke. "May I make a suggestion?" "Of course," I sputtered. "The ending needs an extension—I almost always extend my endings on songs like that." I was relieved and deflated: relieved that he not only hadn't been offended but was actually helping me to make it more Cole Porter-ish; deflated that he hadn't told me how brilliant it was. Looking at the song now, I find it unlikely that he was impressed by it, but he was generous and gracious enough to encourage a cocky kid who was making fun of his work. In short, he was a gentleman. I extended the ending, and it stopped the show.

mine with the equally impressive name of Josiah T. S. Horton to supply a book, and titled the show we came up with *Phinney's Rainbow*. In the accepted tradition of college musicals at the time, it was a collection of skits masquerading as a plot, satirizing campus life and featuring caricature, puns and men in drag as its main comic ingredients. I wanted to vary the score with a ballad or two, but amid such silliness I could hardly expect an audience to stomach an earnest one, so I wrote a parody, much as I did a year later with my homage to Cole Porter in *All That Glitters*. This time my satirical source was the school of what might be called Uncertain Love Songs, songs which asked questions like "What'll I Do?," "Why Do I Love You?," "How Deep Is the Ocean?" My particular target, melodically and lyrically, was Irving Berlin; it was a slow, simple waltz sung by a character called Miss R, a senior in a dress.

MISS R

My problems are giving me
    indigestion,
They can't be answered in only one
    word.
Why should I love you? That's a
    good question.
That's the best question that I ever
    heard.
With questions of love
I simply drip,
But if you really want a good one,
Here's a pip!

How do I know
That I know I know,
When I really don't know you?
How can I have the heart to do
What my heart tells me to do?

Why do I feel
Just the way I always feel,
When my feelings will never show?

You said goodbye
When I said hello,
And I asked you when,

And you said I would know,
But how will I know
When I know that you said no?
I just don't know.

I expected giggles from the audience. To my amazement, what I got was rapt attention. The song was received as a dreamy romantic ballad, so dreamy and romantic in fact that it became a recurrent theme at the Senior Prom, played tenderly and frequently by the college band with a lead singer crooning the lyric of the chorus while couples (the girls were mostly from Bennington and Smith) danced languorously under the dappled reflections of mirrored balls. This was my first practical lesson in writing lyrics for the theater: if the music is pretty and the words are simple and mellifluous, the audience doesn't listen to or care about what you say. That numbness has changed somewhat over the years with the advent of more sophisticated audiences and more trenchant pop songs and musicals—but not much. Which makes me think that contrary to what I said at the beginning of volume one, assembling all these lyrics on paper wasn't such a bad idea after all.

"How Do I Know?" is my earliest extant song. The score for *By George*, the show I wrote at George School when I was fifteen and showed to Oscar the fateful afternoon I began to take myself seriously, exists only in fragments. We'll leave it at that.

Epilogue

Writing these books has been, unsurprisingly, a mixed experience for me. As my first attempt at extended prose, it has been (also unsurprisingly) both gratifying and dismaying. It has reminded me of how much luck I've had in my life. It has forced me to reread my lyrics—for the most part a (surprisingly) pleasurable surprise. Mostly, it has made me feel my age.

It's not the only thing that has made me feel my age, of course. There's the conventional gradual diminution of creative energy, the dissipation of memory and—a worry particularly prevalent in my field—the fear of superannuation. In popular arts like musical theater, becoming superannuated is as natural a part of the process as dying, just as inevitable and just as unacceptable.

Most theater songwriters sound old-fashioned after the age of fifty, and with good reason: popular music changes with each new generation, and the theater reflects it. I've lived through three generations: the "musical comedy" period of Porter and Gershwin and Rodgers and Hart; the "musical play" era of Rodgers and Hammerstein and me and my contemporaries; and the current stretch, which is dominated by pop and rock. Generations overlap, of course, but these three, together with the Jurassic age of Victor Herbert and operetta, constitute a generalized history of the American musical. No composer I know of has spanned two of them successfully, although some have tried, with embarrassing results. (Burt Shevelove had a wickedly accurate name for a composer who tries to keep up with the younger generation: Rip van With-It.) Gershwin might have been the exception, if he hadn't died at thirty-eight: just as he found a way to incorporate aspects of jazz into his style, he would have incorporated today's pop and rock and made them his own. The best composers and lyricists never go completely out of fashion, but their work eventually and forever carries a whiff of nostalgia and evokes sighs for the past, as in "They don't write songs like that anymore."

The diminution of energy and the fear of superannuation are unpleasant enough, but you learn to put up with the first and ignore the second; the loss of memory is worse, and dangerous. The thing that bothers me the most is not forgetting faces or names, but forgetting trivia. Having to search my dwindling gray cells for who directed *The Sound of Music* upsets me a lot more than not recognizing the stranger who wanders up to me at a party and turns out to be someone I've known for thirty years and worked with half a dozen times. What's dangerous is that not remembering makes you think about remembering, which inevitably draws you into the past. As time goes on, I watch old movies and listen to old songs more and more; when asked my place of residence on a customs form, I always want to write "The Past." I have tried to make a virtue out of it by wallowing in pastiche every now and then, the most acute example being *Merrily We Roll Along*, which actually deals with the subject—the hero keeps rewriting the same song throughout the years. And the past, of course, includes the lyrics in this book and in its predecessor. Compiling them has allowed me to take up residence there for the last few years.

Most jobs get easier over time, or at least less stressful. They may get increasingly tedious and predictable, or even more challenging, but they don't get harder unless they involve physical skills, like bricklaying or surgery. Writing, or at least writing songs for the theater, is different. You would think that the more you write, the easier it would get, but no such luck. Technical facility gets easier; invention does not. It gets harder chiefly because you become—or should

become—more aware of the pitfalls, especially the danger of repeating yourself. I find myself using the same chords and the same tropes over and over, and I fight against it; but when I lose the battle, I rationalize it as being a matter of style, my style, a style I've developed over the years, an identity as unchanging as my signature. And to a certain extent it is—but not as much as I tell myself it is.

Even more daunting, the older you get, the more you see young people making new and different things, each year with increasing speed and proliferation—things you never thought of, just the way your forebears could never have dreamed of what *you* were doing. But making new things out of nothing is less difficult when you're young because almost everything you make is for the first time. After a little experience, especially the kind that's accompanied by success, you tend to get comfortable in your groove, and superficially your work does indeed become easier. It also tends to become more superficial.

I have touched on these subjects before. Still, if repeating yourself in your work is one of the dangers of old age, repeating yourself in your commentaries is one of its perks.

A few random thoughts:

Despite all of the above, I still like lying down, scribbling on a pad, tapping on a computer, thumbing through a rhyming dictionary, riffling through a thesaurus and jumping up sporadically to bang at a piano.

I'll fix the second act of *Allegro* yet.

Having gifts for both words and music, I used to worry that if I was honest with myself, I would admit that one was weaker than the other, that only Berlin and Porter were bestowed with equal portions (not perfect, but equal) and that I should choose only one, probably sticking to lyrics because there were so many more composers than lyricists for me to wish I was as good as. It took me longer than it should have to realize that language *is* music, and that I'm all of one piece.

When Wilson Mizner came out of a coma and saw a priest standing over him, he reportedly said, "Why should I talk to you? I've just been talking to your boss," and promptly died. It's hard to believe he didn't work on it in advance, just as it's hard to believe that Oscar Wilde didn't work on "Either that wallpaper goes or I do" (apocryphal or not) or Goethe rehearse "More light!"—after all, they were writers. If I have the breath to gasp it out dramatically, mine will be a quote from "Our Time," a song in *Merrily We Roll Along*: "There's so much stuff to sing!"

And speaking of "sing," isn't the word "song" a perfect example of onomatopoeia?

Finally, I have a gift to offer to every hatmaker who has waded through these books: read Phyllis McGinley's poem "Love Note to a Playwright." Not only is it a technical marvel, it's as important a piece of advice as you'll ever get, and if I'd listened to it the way I think every artist should, I wouldn't have written these books. I'd have written a couple of musicals instead.

On the last page of *Ulysses*, James Joyce wrote:

Paris-Zurich
1911–1918

I've always envied that pretension and I see no reason not to take this opportunity to do the same. (If only books were as good as the length of their gestation . . .)

New York-Roxbury
1994–2011

Time to start another hat.

Acknowledgments

Once again to my editors Peter Gethers and Christina Malach, for their patient persistence;

Once again to Iris Weinstein, who designed this book as elegantly as the first one, and with far less visual material at her command;

Once again to Frank Rich and Mike Nichols for pumping me full of compliments and courage;

Once again to Jack Feldman for his meticulous corrections of fact and thought;

and special thanks

To Andrew Dorko, the production editor; Roméo Enriquez, the production manager; Kathy Hourigan, the managing editor; and Lydia Buechler, the copy chief—with guilt and gratitude for unnecessarily long hours prompted by my tardiness in delivering the goods;

and

To Scott Rudin, Sam Mendes, Nathan Lane and Victor Garber for dredging up uncomfortable memories and being articulate about them;

To Tommy Krasker and Philip Chaffin for research on "A Star Is Born" and "Ten Years Old";

To James Lapine and John Weidman for permission to quote their work and for correcting my memories of it to the best of their fuzzy recall;

To Bill Goldman for permission to present an outline of his script and to quote dialogue from it;

and above all

To Steve Clar for keeping me syntactically respectable and helping me to avoid as much as possible being condescending, cranky, whiny, mean-spirited and all the other things I like to think I'm not;

To Peter Jones, for archival and editorial assistance enough to make him a co-author;

Finally, to Addie, Willie and Jeff, not necessarily in that order, for being there.

Appendix A: Oversights

As I said in the Reintroduction, the advantage of having this book published a year after the first volume is that the larger mistakes in the first can be rectified here. (The smaller ones were taken care of in subsequent printings.) Among the largest in the first book was the omission of a few lyrics, as follows:

Delighted, I'm Sure
(from *Saturday Night*)

I inadvertently left this song out of the chapter on *Saturday Night* because I was using the first professional production of the show (at the Bridewell Theatre in London in 1997) as a reference rather than the subsequent American productions, where I restored it. The reader who is interested in the details of the song's placement in the plot should refer to that chapter. The song occurs immediately after Gene sings "Class" and should be self-explanatory if you know the situation and characters. Suffice it to say that the gang is short of girls for Saturday night's activities and Celeste has invited a not particularly attractive friend of hers named Mildred to fill in the gap.

CELESTE
I'll do the honors.

(*Sings*)

This is Mildred.

MILDRED
Delighted, I'm sure.*

---

*Mildred pronounces "Sure" as if it had two syllables.

ARTIE
(*Aside, to Ted*)
She's delighted,
I am very unexcited.

Celeste shoots him a look, then abruptly smiles to Mildred.

CELESTE
This is Artie.

MILDRED
Delighted.

CELESTE
And this is Ted.

DINO
(*Aside, to Ray*)
Something tells me we shoulda stood in bed.

Celeste glares at him and turns to Bobby.

CELESTE
This is Bobby.

MILDRED
Delighted, I'm sure.

BOBBY
Now, girls, steady—
I got a date already.

CELESTE
This is Dino.

MILDRED
Hello, there.

CELESTE

And this is Gene.

Gene is in evening clothes.

MILDRED

Ooh, my goodness—

(Aside, to Celeste)

Like from a magazine.

(To the boys)

What's the movie?

TED

I got no idea.

DINO

Hope it's dirty.

RAY
(Looks at his watch)
Hurry up, it's seven-thirty—
Price goes up before eight and
    there'll be a line.

TED
(Aside, to Dino)
Let's get started—Mildred's goes up
    at nine.

CELESTE

Who'll take Mildred?
Ted, you can take Mildred.

ARTIE
(Aside, to Ray)
No world beater . . .

RAY
(Aside, to Ted)
Probably a heavy eater.

DINO

She's no bargain—

ARTIE, RAY, DINO
(Aside, to each other)
But still and all she's a girl.
They're a boy's best friend.

TED
(To Mildred)
Delighted—

MILDRED

Delighted—

ARTIE, RAY, DINO
(To Mildred)
Delighted—

CELESTE

I'm delighted—

ALL

—No end . . .

They all begin to exit, except for Bobby. Celeste starts to hail a cab, but Ray stops her.

RAY

No cabs! . . .

ALL

No end . . .

RAY

No dolls . . .

ALL

No end . . .

RAY

No loge seats . . .

ALL

No end . . .

RAY

No crummy pictures . . .

ALL

No end . . .

By this time, they are only voices in the street offstage. Bobby waves goodbye to them and starts to fluff up the cushions as if in anticipation of his date, as the lights dim.

The Natives Are Restless

(1964)

(cut from *Anyone Can Whistle*)

"The Natives Are Restless" was the working title for *Anyone Can Whistle* and the first song in the show. I replaced it with "Me and My Town" for reasons I can neither remember nor fathom—the lyric is funny and it establishes Cora's venality and ambitions as clearly as its successor. Anyway, here she is: Mayoress Cora Hoover Hooper, surveying her bankrupt town and its bedraggled, picketing inhabitants.

CORA

They're shouting for blood again,
My name will be mud again,
The town is a dud again—
The natives are restless.

They're muttering threats again,
There's nothing but debts again,
I'm on cigarettes again—
The natives are restless.

I give them parks that are sunny—
    oh, ho—
I give them statues and plants.
They say they'd rather have
    money—oh, ho—
Fat chance.

Their patches have holes again
(I bought a new Rolls again).
They'll go to the polls again
And I'll be gone.
I'll never be governess if this
    goes on.

They're running amok again,
I'm learning to duck again.
I'm passing the buck again—
The natives are restless.

The cupboard is bare again,
They've nothing to wear again,
They're selling their hair again—
The natives are restless.

I see my people in trouble—poor
    things—

Oh, it's a shame and a crime.
I see the rabble in rubble—poor
    things—

(She looks at her watch)

Lunch time.

I'm getting depressed again,
I think I'll get dressed again;
I'll make an arrest again—
That helps a lot.
I'll either be governess
Or I'll be shot.

Why don't they rest? . . .
I do my best . . .
I'm so depressed . . .

After a dance break with her Boys, she sings a fast chorus, the Boys joining her on the title line.

The peasants are mad again,
It makes me feel bad again.
They know they've been had again—
The natives are restless!

They're milling about again,
We're having a drought again,
The pickets are out again—
The natives are restless!

If there's a strike I will spike it—
    oh, ho—
They'll have to tighten their belts.
They're gonna love me and like it—
    oh, ho—
Or else.

I need to relax again,
I'd pass a new tax again,
But we have our backs against
The wall.

I've got to do something
Before it's too late.
I talked to the state house
And they're in a state.
I'll never be president
At this rate—!
So rest, little natives,
Wretched little natives,
I'll find a way to save us all.

The Right Girl
(ending, from *Follies*)

Another inadvertency. The ending printed in *Finishing the Hat* is the one I wrote originally. I replaced it years later and for the better, with this:

BUDDY
. . . The right girl—yeah,
The right girl!
She sees you're nothing and thinks
    you're king,
She knows you got other songs to
    sing.
You still could be—hell, well,
    anything
When you got—yeah!
The right girl—
And I got—!

Hey, Margie, I'm back, babe.
Come help me unpack, babe.
Hey, Margie, hey, bright girl,
I'm home.

You miss me? I knew it.
Hey, Margie, I blew it.
I don't love the right girl—

Ah, hell.

Now
(first version, 1973)
(cut from *A Little Night Music*)

Although there are a few similarities to "Now" in its final version, this lyric makes Fredrik a bit more libidinous and desperate. As with "The Natives Are Restless," I have no idea why I replaced it. It's a moderately slow waltz—perhaps that was the reason. The score turned out to be so full of waltz rhythms, even when they're not waltzes, that I may have thought better than to start with one. In the theater you have to conserve variety and surprise any way you can—in any art, as a matter of fact.

FREDRIK
Now,
As you sit at your vanity,
Beaming with vanity,
Now,
As you fuss with your lap—
Now,
I see two possibilities:
A, I could ravish you,
B, I could nap.

How,
If I touch those eyes,
Lips, and/or
Brow,
Could I keep control,
Vow
Not to lose my self-command or
Bow
To the passion whole?
No conclusion.

Now,
If I opt for the former,
I.e., if I ravish you,
Now
In the midst of your dream,
Now,
I see two possibilities:
One, you would welcome it,
Two, you would scream.

How
Can an old man sing
In the blaze of spring
And conceal his despair?
How
Should the winter cling
To an April thing?
What grotesqueries there!

Now,
As you stare at me, wide-eyed,
Now,
As you flirt with your fan,
Now,
If you weren't my bride, I'd
Take you, Anne.
I want you, Anne.
As always.
Now.
Anne.

Appendix B: Original Productions

Sunday in the Park with George

OPENING   May 2, 1984
CLOSING   October 13, 1985
TOTAL PERFORMANCES   604

Produced by the Shubert Organization and Emanuel Azenberg by arrangement with Playwrights Horizons
Music by Stephen Sondheim
Lyrics by Stephen Sondheim
Book by James Lapine
Suggested by the painting *A Sunday Afternoon on the Island of La Grande Jatte* and the life of Georges Seurat
Music orchestrated by Michael Starobin
Musical Director: Paul Gemignani
Directed by James Lapine

OPENING NIGHT CAST

	Act One
Mandy Patinkin	GEORGE
Bernadette Peters	DOT
Barbara Bryne	AN OLD LADY
Judith Moore	HER NURSE
Brent Spiner	FRANZ
Danielle Ferland	A BOY
Nancy Opel	A YOUNG MAN SITTING ON THE BANK
Cris Groenendaal	A MAN LYING ON THE BANK
Charles Kimbrough	JULES
Dana Ivey	YVONNE
William Parry	A BOATMAN
Melanie Vaughan	CELESTE #1
Mary D'Arcy	CELESTE #2
Danielle Ferland	LOUISE
Nancy Opel	FRIEDA
Cris Groenendaal	LOUIS
Robert Westenberg	A SOLDIER
John Jellison	A MAN WITH A BICYCLE
Michele Rigan	A LITTLE GIRL
Sue Anne Gershenson	A WOMAN WITH A BABY CARRIAGE
Kurt Knudson	MR.
Judith Moore	MRS.

	Act Two
Mandy Patinkin	GEORGE
Bernadette Peters	MARIE
Brent Spiner	DENNIS
Charles Kimbrough	BOB GREENBERG
Dana Ivey	NAOMI EISEN
Judith Moore	HARRIET PAWLING
Cris Groenendaal	BILLY WEBSTER

Sue Anne Gershenson	A PHOTOGRAPHER
John Jellison	A MUSEUM ASSISTANT
William Parry	CHARLES REDMOND
Robert Westenberg	ALEX
Nancy Opel	BETTY
Kurt Knudson	LEE RANDOLPH
Barbara Bryne	BLAIR DANIELS
Melanie Vaughan	A WAITRESS
Mary D'Arcy	ELAINE

Into the Woods

OPENING   November 5, 1987
CLOSING   September 3, 1989
TOTAL PERFORMANCES   764

Produced by Heidi Landesman, Rocco Landesman, Rick Steiner, M. Anthony Fisher, Frederic H. Mayerson, and Jujamcyn Theaters
Associate Producers: Greg C. Mosher, Paula Fisher, David B. Brode, The Mutual Benefit Companies, and Fifth Avenue Productions
Music by Stephen Sondheim
Lyrics by Stephen Sondheim
Book by James Lapine
Music orchestrated by Jonathan Tunick
Musical Director: Paul Gemignani
Directed by James Lapine

OPENING NIGHT CAST

Tom Aldredge	NARRATOR, MYSTERIOUS MAN
Kim Crosby	CINDERELLA
Ben Wright	JACK
Chip Zien	BAKER
Joanna Gleason	BAKER'S WIFE
Joy Franz	CINDERELLA'S STEPMOTHER
Kay McClelland	FLORINDA
Lauren Mitchell	LUCINDA
Barbara Bryne	JACK'S MOTHER
Danielle Ferland	LITTLE RED RIDING HOOD
Bernadette Peters	WITCH
Edmund Lyndeck	CINDERELLA'S FATHER
Merle Louise	CINDERELLA'S MOTHER, GRANDMOTHER, GIANT
Robert Westenberg	WOLF, CINDERELLA'S PRINCE
Pamela Winslow	RAPUNZEL
Chuck Wagner	RAPUNZEL'S PRINCE
Philip Hoffman	STEWARD
Jean Kelly	SNOW WHITE
Maureen Davis	SLEEPING BEAUTY

Assassins (Playwrights Horizons)

OPENING   December 18, 1990
CLOSING   February 16, 1991
TOTAL PERFORMANCES   73

Produced by Playwrights Horizons
Music by Stephen Sondheim
Lyrics by Stephen Sondheim
Book by John Weidman
Based on an idea by Charles Gilbert, Jr.
Music orchestrated by Michael Starobin
Musical Director: Paul Gemignani
Directed by Jerry Zaks
Choreographed by D. J. Giagni

OPENING NIGHT CAST

William Parry	PROPRIETOR
Terrence Mann	LEON CZOLGOSZ
Greg Germann	JOHN HINCKLEY
Jonathan Hadary	CHARLES GUITEAU
Eddie Korbich	GIUSEPPE ZANGARA
Lee Wilkof	SAMUEL BYCK
Annie Golden	LYNETTE "SQUEAKY" FROMME
Debra Monk	SARA JANE MOORE
Victor Garber	JOHN WILKES BOOTH
Patrick Cassidy	BALLADEER
Marcus Olson	DAVID HEROLD
John Jellison	BARTENDER
Lyn Greene	EMMA GOLDMAN
William Parry	JAMES GARFIELD
John Jellison	JAMES BLAINE
Marcus Olson	HANGMAN
John Jellison	WARDEN
Michael Shulman	BILLY
William Parry	GERALD FORD
Jace Alexander	LEE HARVEY OSWALD
Joy Franz	ENSEMBLE
Lyn Greene	
John Jellison	
Marcus Olson	
William Parry	
Michael Shulman	

Assassins (Broadway)

OPENING   April 22, 2004
CLOSING   July 18, 2004
TOTAL PERFORMANCES   101

Produced by the Roundabout Theatre Company
Music by Stephen Sondheim
Lyrics by Stephen Sondheim
Book by John Weidman
Based on an idea by Charles Gilbert, Jr.
Music orchestrated by Michael Starobin
Musical Director: Paul Gemignani
Directed by Joe Mantello

OPENING NIGHT CAST

Marc Kudisch	PROPRIETOR
James Barbour	LEON CZOLGOSZ
Alexander Gemignani	JOHN HINCKLEY
Denis O'Hare	CHARLES GUITEAU
Jeffrey Kuhn	GIUSEPPE ZANGARA
Mario Cantone	SAMUEL BYCK
Mary Catherine Garrison	LYNETTE "SQUEAKY" FROMME
Becky Ann Baker	SARA JANE MOORE
Michael Cerveris	JOHN WILKES BOOTH
Neil Patrick Harris	BALLADEER
Brandon Wardell	DAVID HEROLD
Anne L. Nathan	EMMA GOLDMAN
James Clow	JAMES BLAINE
Merwin Foard	JAMES GARFIELD
Eamon Foley	BILLY
James Clow	GERALD FORD
Neil Patrick Harris	LEE HARVEY OSWALD
James Clow	ENSEMBLE
Merwin Foard	
Eamon Foley	
Kendra Kassebaum	
Anne L. Nathan	
Brandon Wardell	
Ken Krugman	SWING
Sally Wilfert	
Chris Peluso	

Passion

OPENING   May 9, 1994
CLOSING   January 7, 1995
TOTAL PERFORMANCES   280

Produced by the Shubert Organization, Capital Cities/ABC, Roger Berlind, and Scott Rudin by arrangement with Lincoln Center Theater
Music by Stephen Sondheim
Lyrics by Stephen Sondheim
Book by James Lapine
Music orchestrated by Jonathan Tunick
Musical Director: Paul Gemignani
Directed by James Lapine

OPENING NIGHT CAST

Marin Mazzie	CLARA
Jere Shea	GIORGIO
Gregg Edelman	COLONEL RICCI
Tom Aldredge	DOCTOR TAMBOURRI
Francis Ruivivar	LIEUTENANT TORASSO
Marcus Olson	SERGEANT LOMBARDI
William Parry	LIEUTENANT BARRI
Cris Groenendaal	MAJOR RIZZOLLI
George Dvorsky	PRIVATE AUGENTI
Donna Murphy	FOSCA
Linda Balgord	FOSCA'S MOTHER
John Leslie Wolfe	FOSCA'S FATHER
Matthew Porretta	LUDOVIC
Juliet Lambert	MISTRESS

Wise Guys (New York Theatre Workshop)

OPENING   October 29, 1999
CLOSING   November 20, 1999

Produced by Scott Rudin, Roger Berlind, Dodger Theatricals, and the Kennedy Center for the Performing Arts
Music by Stephen Sondheim
Lyrics by Stephen Sondheim
Book by John Weidman
Music orchestrated by Jonathan Tunick
Musical Director: Ted Sperling
Directed by Sam Mendes
Choreographed by Jonathan Butterell

OPENING NIGHT CAST

Victor Garber	WILSON MIZNER
Christopher Fitzgerald	REPORTER
Nathan Lane	ADDISON MIZNER
William Parry	PAPA
Candy Buckley	MAMA
Kevin Chamberlin	A PROSPECTOR
William Parry	POKER PLAYER

Ray Wills
Kevin Chamberlin
Brooks Ashmanskas
Clarke Thorell ASSAYER
Ray Wills TICKET SELLER
Michael Hall BUSINESS MAN #1
Nancy Opel BUSINESS MAN #2
Brooks Ashmanskas SOLICITOR
Kevin Chamberlin CHINESE WARLORD
William Parry PLANTATION OWNER
Kevin Chamberlin DOORMAN
Jessica Molaskey MYRA YERKES
Michael Hall PARIS SINGER
Brooks Ashmanskas PLAYWRIGHT
Ray Wills BOXER
Clarke Thorell GANGSTER
Ray Wills STANLEY KETCHEL
Clarke Thorell FLATBUSH PHIL
Brooks Ashmanskas PAUL ARMSTRONG
Christopher Fitzgerald NEWSBOY
Jessica Boevers GLADYS
Kevin Chamberlin REAL ESTATE AGENT
Nancy Opel MRS. EVA STOTESBURY
William Parry MR. STOTESBURY
Lauren Ward MRS. LILLY COSDEN
Ray Wills MR. COSDEN
Jessica Boevers MRS. TRUMBAUER
Brooks Ashmanskas MR. TRUMBAUER
Jessica Molaskey MRS. WANAMAKER
Candy Buckley MRS. DUPONT
Brooks Ashmanskas SOUVENIR SELLERS, CLUB PATRONS AND
MILLIONAIRES, BOCA RATON CHOIR,
BUYERS, SELLERS AND OTHER PARTICIPANTS

Jessica Boevers
Kevin Chamberlin
Christopher Fitzgerald
Michael Hall
Jessica Molaskey
Nancy Opel
William Parry
Clark Thorell
Lauren Ward
Ray Wills

Jeff Dumas
Deanna Dunagan
Nicole Grothues
Rick Hilsabeck
Jeff Parker
Harriet Nzinga Plumpp
Jenny Powers
Craig Ramsey
Jacquelyn Ritz
Fred Zimmerman

Road Show

OPENING November 18, 2008
CLOSING December 28, 2008

Produced by The Public Theater
Music orchestrated by Jonathan Tunick
Musical Director: Mary-Mitchell Campbell
Directed by John Doyle

OPENING NIGHT CAST

Alexander Gemignani ADDISON MIZNER
Michael Cerveris WILSON MIZNER
Claybourne Elder HOLLIS BESSEMER
Alma Cuervo MAMA MIZNER
William Parry PAPA MIZNER
Aisha de Haas ENSEMBLE
Colleen Fitzpatrick
David Garry
Mylinda Hull
Mel Johnson, Jr.
Orville Mendoza
Anne L. Nathan
Tom Nelis
Matthew Stocke
Katrina Yaukey
William Youmans
Kristine Zbornik

Bounce (Goodman Theatre / Kennedy Center)

GOODMAN THEATRE, CHICAGO
OPENING June 30, 2003
CLOSING August 10, 2003
TOTAL PERFORMANCES 47

EISENHOWER THEATER, KENNEDY CENTER, WASHINGTON, D.C.
OPENING October 30, 2003
CLOSING November 16, 2003
TOTAL PERFORMANCES 32

Produced by The Goodman Theatre
Music orchestrated by Jonathan Tunick
Musical Director: David Caddick
Directed by Harold Prince
Choreographed by Michael Arnold

OPENING NIGHT CAST

Richard Kind ADDISON MIZNER
Howard McGillin WILSON MIZNER
Michele Pawk NELLIE
Gavin Creel HOLLIS BESSEMER
Jane Powell MAMA MIZNER
Herndon Lackey PAPA MIZNER
Sean Blake ENSEMBLE
Marilyn Bogetich
Tom Daugherty

Appendix C: Selected Discography

These are the recordings most frequently referred to in the Song List.

Anyone Can Whistle. 1964. Original Broadway cast recording, Columbia Records LP: KOL-6080(M)/KOS-2480(S); CD: 2003 Sony Classical/Columbia/Legacy reissue SK 86860.

Assassins. 1990. Original New York cast, BMG/RCA Records CD: 60737-2-RC.

Bounce. 2003. Kennedy Center cast, Nonesuch (2004) CD: 79830-2.

Candide. 1974. Revival cast recording, Columbia Records, LP: S2X 32923 (2 record set); Sony/BMG CD: 82876-88391-2.

Candide. 1997. New Broadway cast RCA Victor CD: 09026-68835-2.

A Collector's Sondheim. 1985. RCA Records, LP: CRL4-5359 (4 record set); CD: RCD3-5480 (3 disc set).

Company. 1970. Original Broadway cast recording, Columbia Records LP: OS-3530; CD: 1998 Sony Classical/Columbia/Legacy reissue SK 65283.

Do I Hear a Waltz? 1964. Original Broadway cast recording, (1965) Columbia Records LP: KOL-6370(M)/KOS-2770(S); CD: 1992 Sony Broadway reissue SK-48206.

*Follies. 1971. Original Broadway cast recording, Capitol Records LP: SO-761; CD: Broadway Angel reissue ZDM-64666.

Follies in Concert. 1985. RCA Records LP: HBC2-7128; CD: RCD2-7128.

Follies: The Complete Recording. 1998. TVT Records CD: TVT 1030-2.

Follies. 1987. Original London cast recording, First Night Records CD: Encore CD 2.

The Frogs. 1974/2004. Original Broadway cast recording, PS Classics (2005) PS-525.

The Frogs/Evening Primrose. 2001. Nonesuch CD: 79638.

A Funny Thing Happened on the Way to the Forum. 1962. Original Broadway cast recording, Capitol Records LP: WAO (M)/SWAO (S)-1717; CD: Broadway Angel reissue ZDM-64770.

Gypsy. 1959. Original Broadway cast recording, Columbia Records LP: OL-5420(M)/OS-2017(S); CD: 1999 Sony Classical/Columbia/Legacy reissue SK 60848.

Gypsy: 2008 Revival. 2008. Time-Life Records CD: M19659.

Into the Woods. 1987. Original Broadway cast recording, Masterworks Broadway Reissue (2005) CD: 82876-68636-2.

Julie Wilson Sings the Stephen Sondheim Songbook. 1988. DRG Records LP: SL 5206; CD: CDSL 5206.

A Little Night Music. 1973. Original Broadway cast recording, Columbia Records LP: KS-32265; CD: 1998 Sony Classical/Columbia/Legacy reissue SK 65284.

Marry Me A Little. 1981. RCA Records LP: ABL1-4159; CD: 7142-2-RG.

†*Merrily We Roll Along*. 1982. Original Broadway cast recording, Masterworks Broadway reissue (2007) CD: 82876-68637-2.

Merrily We Roll Along. 1994. London cast recording, TER CD: CDTER 1225; 1997, JAY Records CD: CDJAY2 1245, 2 disc set.

Merrily We Roll Along. 1994. Revival cast recording, Varese Sarabande CD: VSD-5548.

Pacific Overtures. 1976. Original Broadway cast recording, RCA Records LP: ARL1-1367; CD: RCD1-4407.

Passion. 1994. Original Broadway cast recording, Angel Records CD: CDQ 7243 5 55251 23.

Patinkin, Mandy. *Dress Casual*. 1990. CBS Records CD: MK45998.

Putting It Together. 1993. Original cast recording, RCA CD: 09026-61729-2.

Road Show. 2009. Original New York cast, Nonesuch/PS Classics CD: 518940-2.

Saturday Night. 1954. Original New York cast, 2000, Nonesuch Records CD: 79609-2.

Side by Side by Sondheim. 1976. RCA Records, LP: CBL2-1851 (2 record set); CD: 1851-2-RG (2 disc set).

Sondheim: A Musical Tribute (also known as the "Scrabble Album"). 1973. Warner Bros. Records LP: 2WS 2705 (2 record set); RCA Records (1990, reissue), CD: 60515-2-RC.

Sondheim at the Movies. 1997. Varese Sarabande CD: VSD-5895.

Sondheim Sings: Volume I (1962–72). 2005. PS Classics CD: PS-9529.

Sondheim Sings: Volume II (1946–60). 2005. PS Classics CD: PS-9533.

Sondheim on Sondheim. 2010. PS Classics CD: PS-1093.

Stephen Sondheim: The Story So Far. 2008. Masterworks Broadway/Legacy 82796-94255-2.

---

*The *Follies* OBC recording was highly abridged. Refer to the listed recordings for the complete original score, as well as auxiliary material.

†Revised extensively in 1985. Refer to the listed recordings for the revised version.

A Stephen Sondheim Evening. 1983. RCA Records LP: CBL2-4745 (2 record set); CD: 09026-61174-2.
Sunday in the Park with George. 1984. Original Broadway cast recording, Masterworks Broadway reissue (2007) CD: 82876-68638-2.
Sweeney Todd. 1979. Original Broadway cast recording, Masterworks Broadway reissue (2007) CD: 82876-68639-2.
Unsung Sondheim. 1993. Varese Sarabande CD: VSD-5433.
West Side Story. 1957. Original Broadway cast recording (1957), Columbia Records LP: OL-5230(M)/OS-2001(S); CD: 1998 Sony Classical/Columbia/Legacy reissue SK 60724.

SONG LIST

"Ah, But Underneath" (*Follies*, U.K., 1987)
  Follies: The Complete Recording, 1998; *Follies*, Original London cast recording, 1987.
"All I Need Is the Boy (Girl)" (*Gypsy*, 1959)
  Burnett, Carol. *Carol Burnett Sings*. Decca (S)7-4437, 1963; CD: *Let Me Entertain You*, Decca 012 159 402-2; Myles, Meg. *Meg Myles at the Living Room*. Mercury MG-20686, (S)SR-60686, 1963; Ross, Annie. *Gypsy*. 1959, 1960. World Pacific Records. LP: (S)ST-1276, WP-1028; Pacific Jazz, (1995 reissue) CD: CDP 7243 8 33574 2 0.
"All Things Bright And Beautiful" (cut from *Follies*, 1971)
  Follies: The Complete Recording, 1998; *Marry Me a Little*, 1981.
"America" (*West Side Story*, 1961)
  Original film soundtrack, Columbia Records LP: OS 2070; Sony Broadway CD: SK-48211.
"Auto Da Fé" (*Candide*, 1974 revival)
  Candide, Revival cast recording, 1974; *Candide*, New Broadway cast (1997).
"Back In Business" (*Dick Tracy*, 1990)
  Stephen Sondheim: The Story So Far; *Sondheim at the Movies*.
"Back to the Palace" (cut from *Into the Woods*, 1987)
  Into the Woods, Original Broadway cast recording, 2005 reissue.
"Bang!" (cut from *A Little Night Music*, 1973)
  Marry Me a Little, 1981; *Putting It Together* 1993.
"Beggar Woman's Lullaby" (*Sweeney Todd*, U.K., 1980)
  Sweeney Todd Live at the New York Philharmonic. 2000. New York Philharmonic Special Editions, CD: NYP 2001/2002 (19054-1855-2); 2 disc set.
"Boom Crunch!" (cut from *Into the Woods*, 1987)
  Into the Woods, Original Broadway cast recording, 2005 reissue.
"The Boy From . . ."(*The Mad Show*, 1966)
  The Mad Show, OBC Columbia Records, LP: OL-6530, OS-2930, 1966; CD: DRG 19072; *Stephen Sondheim: The Story So Far*; *Side by Side by Sondheim*.
"Bring on the Girls" (cut from *Follies*, 1971)
  Follies: The Complete Recording, 1998.
"Can That Boy Foxtrot!" (cut from *Follies*, 1971)
  Follies: The Complete Recording. 1998; *Side by Side by Sondheim*, 1976; *Julie Wilson Sings the Stephen Sondheim Songbook*, 1988.
"Christmas Island at Christmas Time"(1951)
  Anderson, D. C. *All is Calm, All is Bright*. 2001. LML CD-136.
"Country House" (*Follies*, U.K. 1987)
  Follies. 1987. Original London cast recording; *Putting It Together*. 1993.
"Dawn" (*Singing Out Loud*, 1992)
  Sondheim at the Movies.
"Do I Hear a Waltz?"(*Do You Hear a Waltz?*, 1960)
  Sondheim Sings: Volume II.

"Don't Laugh" (*Hot Spot*, 1963)
  Murney, Julia. *The Broadway Musical of 1963*, Bayview RNBW036, 2006; *Phyllis Newman: The Mad Woman of Central Park*, DRG CDSL 5212, 1990; *Hey, Love: the Songs of Mary Rodgers* (titled "Show Me"). 1997. Varese Sarabande CD: VSD-5772; *Stephen Sondheim: The Story So Far*.
"Dueling Pianos" ("Send in the Clowns"/"The Music of the Night"), 1998
  Hey, Mr Producer! (The Musical World of Cameron Mackintosh) 1998. First Night Records/Phillips CD: 314 538 030-2; 2-disc set—video available on DVD.
"Echo Song" (cut from *A Funny Thing Happened on the Way to the Forum*, 1962)
  A Stephen Sondheim Evening.
"Every Day a Little Death" (1976 film version of *A Little Night Music*)
  A Little Night Music Original Soundtrack, 1978 LP: Columbia JS 35333.
"Everybody Loves Leona" (cut from *Do I Hear a Waltz?*, 1964)
  Stephen Sondheim: The Story So Far.
"Farewell" (*A Funny Thing Happened on the Way to the Forum*, 1971 revival)
  Simply Sondheim: A 75th Birthday Salute. 2006. Kritzerland CD: KR 20020-8; 2 disc set.
"Giants in the Sky" (original version cut from *Into the Woods*, 1987)
  Into the Woods. Original Broadway cast recording. 2005 reissue.
"The Girls of Summer" (*Girls of Summer*, 1956)
  Upshaw, Dawn. *I Wish It So*. 1994. Nonesuch CD: 79345-2; *Sondheim Sings: Volume II*.
"The Glamorous Life" (1976 film version of *A Little Night Music*)
  A Collector's Sondheim; *A Little Night Music Original Soundtrack*. 1978. LP: Columbia JS 35333; *Sondheim at the Movies*.
"God" (*Sondheim on Sondheim*, 2010)
  Sondheim on Sondheim.
"Goodbye for Now" (*Reds*, 1981)
  Reds. 1981. Original soundtrack, Columbia LP: BJS 37690 CD: Razor & Tie Entertainment 7940182203-2; *Stephen Sondheim: The Story So Far*; *Unsung Sondheim*.
"Gussie's Opening Number" (*Merrily We Roll Along*, 1985 revised production)
  Merrily We Roll Along. 1994. Revival cast recording; *Merrily We Roll Along*. 1994. London cast recording.
"Growing Up" (*Merrily We Roll Along*, 1985 revised production)
  Merrily We Roll Along. 1994. Revival cast recording; *Merrily We Roll Along*. 1994. London cast recording.
"Happily Ever After" (cut from *Company*, 1970)
  Sondheim: A Musical Tribute; *Stephen Sondheim: The Story So Far*.
"Have to Give Her Someone" (cut from *Into the Woods*, 1987)
  Stephen Sondheim: The Story So Far.
"A Hero Is Coming" (cut from *Anyone Can Whistle*, 1964)
  Sondheim Sings: Volume I; *Stephen Sondheim: The Story So Far*.
"High Life" (*The Last Resorts*, 1956)
  Sondheim Sings: Volume II.
"The Hills of Tomorrow" (*Merrily We Roll Along*, 1981)
  Original Broadway cast recording.
"Home Is the Place" (1960)
  Bennett, Tony. *Yesterday I Heard the Rain*. 1968. Columbia LE-10056.
"Honey" (cut from *Merrily We Roll Along*, 1981)
  Lost in Boston III (Liz Callaway and Jason Graae). 1995. Varese Sarabande VSD-5563; *The Musicality of Sondheim*, 2002. JAY Records CD: CDJAZ 9006.

"The House of Marcus Lycus" (cut from *A Funny Thing Happened
    on the Way to the Forum*, 1962)
    A Stephen Sondheim Evening; A Collector's Sondheim; Broadway
    revival cast, 1996, Broadway Angel: 7243 8 52223 2 0.
"How Do I Know?" (*Phinney's Rainbow*, 1948)
    Sondheim Sings: Volume II (instrumental only).
"I Do Like You" (cut from *A Funny Thing Happened on the Way to
    the Forum*, 1962)
    Julie Wilson Sings the Stephen Sondheim Songbook; Jackie &
    Roy, *A Stephen Sondheim Collection*. 1982. Finesse Records LP:
    FW 38324 (S) DRG Records; CD: DSCD 25102; Bennett,
    Richard Rodney. *A Different Side of Sondheim*. 1979. DRG
    Records LP: SL 5182; CD: 5182.
"I Never Do Anything Twice" (*The Seven Percent Solution*, 1976)
    Side by Side by Sondheim (Millicent Martin); *Stephen
    Sondheim: The Story So Far* (Régine); *Julie Wilson Sings the
    Stephen Sondheim Songbook; Sondheim at the Movies*.
"I Remember" (*Evening Primrose*, 1966)
    *Stephen Sondheim: The Story So Far; The Frogs/Evening
    Primrose; Sondheim at the Movies*; Patinkin, Mandy. *Dress
    Casual*.
"I Wouldn't Change A Thing" (*The Last Resorts*, 1956)
    Sondheim Sings: Volume II.
"If You Can Find Me, I'm Here" (*Evening Primrose*, 1966)
    *Stephen Sondheim: The Story So Far; The Frogs/Evening
    Primrose; Sondheim at the Movies*; Patinkin, Mandy. *Dress
    Casual*.
"I'm Still Here" (rewrites)
    Streisand, Barbra. *The Concert*. 1994. Columbia C2K 66109;
    Shirley MacLaine, Postcards from the Edge. 1990. Columbia
    Pictures.
"Interesting Questions" (cut from *Into the Woods*, 1987)
    Stephen Sondheim: The Story So Far.
"Invocation" (aka "Forget War," cut from *A Funny Thing
    Happened on the Way to the Forum*, 1962)
    Sondheim Sings: Volume I.
"It Takes All Kinds" (*The Birdcage*, 1996)
    Sondheim at the Movies.
"It Wasn't Meant to Happen" (cut from *Follies*, 1971)
    Marry Me a Little. 1981; *The Stephen Sondheim Album*. 2000.
    Fynsworth Alley CD: FA-2101-SE.
"I've Got You to Lean On" (from *Anyone Can Whistle*, 1964—
    truncated on OBC recording)
    Anyone Can Whistle Live at Carnegie Hall. 1995. Columbia
    CD: CK 67224.
"Johanna (Judge's Song)" (*Sweeney Todd*, 1979)
    Original Broadway cast recording.
"The Lame, the Halt and the Blind" (cut from *Anyone Can
    Whistle*, 1964)
    Sondheim Sings: Volume I.
"Life Is Happiness Indeed" (*Candide*, 1974 revival)
    Candide. 1974. Revival cast recording; *Candide*. 1997. New
    broadway cast.
"Like Everybody Else" (cut from *West Side Story*, 1957)
    Lost In Boston (Judy Malloy, Richard Roland, Sal Viviano).
    1994. Varese Sarabande VSD-5475.
"Little Dream" (*The Birdcage*, 1996)
    Music From The Birdcage. 1996. HSE Records, HTCD 33/34-2;
    Sondheim at the Movies.
"Live Alone and Like It" (*Dick Tracy*, 1990)
    *Stephen Sondheim: The Story So Far; Sondheim at the Movies;
    Putting It Together*.
"Love Is in the Air" (cut from *A Funny Thing Happened on the Way
    to the Forum* 1962)
    Sondheim Sings: Volume I; Side by Side by Sondheim.
"Love Takes Time" (1976 film version of *A Little Night Music*)
    A Little Night Music Original Soundtrack. 1978. LP: Columbia

JS 35333; *Stephen Sondheim: The Story So Far; Putting It
    Together*.
"Loveland" (*Follies*, U.K., 1987)
    Follies. 1987. Original London cast recording.
"Make the Most of Your Music" (*Follies*, U.K., 1987)
    Follies. 1987. Original London cast recording.
"Mama's Talkin' Soft" (cut from *Gypsy*,1959)
    Gypsy. 1999 Masterworks Broadway reissue. Original
    Broadway cast, Legacy SK 60848; *Gypsy: 2008 Revival; Lost in
    Boston III*. 1995. Varese Sarabande VSD-5563.
"Marry Me a Little" (cut from *Company*, 1970; restored in 1995)
    Sondheim Sings: Volume I; Marry Me a Little. 1981; *Company*.
    1996. London Revival Cast recording, RCA Victor/BMG
    Classics CD: 09026-68589-2; *Company*. 2007. Broadway
    revival cast recording, Nonesuch/P.S. Classics, 106876-2;
    Callaway, Liz. *The Story Goes On: On and Off Broadway*. 1995.
    Varese Sarabande VSD-5585; *Putting It Together*.
"More" (*Dick Tracy*, 1990)
    Stephen Sondheim: The Story So Far; Sondheim at the Movies.
"Mother's Day" (cut from *Gypsy*, 1959)
    Gypsy: 2008 Revival.
"Multitudes of Amys" (cut from *Company*, 1970)
    Sondheim Sings: Volume I; Unsung Sondheim.
"My Husband the Pig" (cut from *A Little Night Music*, 1973)
    A Little Night Music. 1996. RNT Cast Recording, Tring CD:
    TRING001.
"New York" (*The Clock*, 1953)
    Sondheim Sings: Volume II.
"Nice She Ain't" (cut from *Gypsy*,1959)
    Gypsy: Original Broadway Cast. 1999 Masterworks Broadway
    Reissue. Legacy SK 60848; *Gypsy: 2008 Revival*.
"Night Waltz III" ("Not Quite Night," cut from *A Little Night
    Music*, 1973)
    Stephen Sondheim: The Story So Far.
"No, Mary Ann" (*The Thing of It Is*, 1969)
    *Sondheim Sings: Volume I; Stephen Sondheim: The Story So Far;
    Unsung Sondheim* (Jason Graae).
"No One Has Ever Loved Me" (*Passion*, U.K., 1996)
    Passion London Concert. 1997. First Night Records CD: CAST
    CD61.
"Now You Know" (*Merrily We Roll Along*, 1985 revised
    production)
    Merrily We Roll Along. 1994. Revival Cast Recording. *Merrily
    We Roll Along*. 1994. London Cast Recording.
"Our Little World" (*Into the Woods*, U.K., 1990)
    Into the Woods. 1991. Original London Cast Recording, RCA
    Records CD: 60752-2-RC; *Into the Woods*. 2002. Revival Cast
    Recording, Nonesuch CD: 79686-2.
"Perhaps" (cut from *Do I Hear a Waltz?*, 1964)
    Stephen Sondheim: The Story So Far.
"Pleasant Little Kingdom" (cut from *Follies*, 1971)
    Follies: The Complete Recording. 1998; *Sondheim: A Musical
    Tribute*.
"Pour Le Sport" (*The Last Resorts*, 1956)
    Sondheim Sings: Volume II; Marry Me a Little. 1981.
"Putting It Together" (rewrites)
    The Broadway Album, Barbra Streisand. 1985. Columbia
    Records LP: OC 40092 CD: CK 40092; *Putting It Together*.
"Prayer" (cut from *Pacific Overtures*, 1976)
    *Stephen Sondheim: The Story So Far; Pacific Overtures New
    Broadway Cast Recording*. 2005. PS Classics CD: PS-528.
"Rich And Happy" (*Merrily We Roll Along*, 1981)
    Original Broadway cast recording.
"Sand" (*Singing Out Loud*, 1992)
    Sondheim at the Movies.
"Second Midnight" (cut from *Into the Woods*, 1987)
    Stephen Sondheim: The Story So Far.

"Sheep Song" (*Candide*, 1974 revival)
  Candide. 1974. Revival cast recording; *Candide*. 1997. New Broadway cast.
"Silly People" (cut from *A Little Night Music*, 1973)
  Sondheim: A Musical Tribute; Chaffin, Philip. *Warm Spring Night*. 2005. [PS Classics 527]; *Marry Me a Little*.
"Smile, Girls" (cut from *Gypsy*, 1959)
  Sondheim on Sondheim; *Gypsy: 2008 Revival*.
"Soldiers and Girls" (aka "The One On the Left," cut from *Sunday in the Park with George*, 1984)
  Sunday in the Park with George. 2006. London cast recording PS Classics CD: PS-640; 2 disc set.
"Something Just Broke" (*Assassins*, U.K., 1992)
  Assassins. 2004. Broadway cast recording, PS Classics CD: PS-421.
"Sooner or Later" (*Dick Tracy*, 1990)
  Stephen Sondheim: The Story So Far; *Sondheim at the Movies*; *Putting It Together*. 1993.
"A Star Is Born" (1954)
  Sondheim Sings: Volume II.
"Take Me to the World" (*Evening Primrose*, 1966)
  Stephen Sondheim: The Story So Far; *The Frogs/Evening Primrose*; *Sondheim at the Movies*; Patinkin, Mandy. *Dress Casual*.
"Ten Years Old" (*The Fabulous Fifties*, 1960)
  Sondheim Sings: Volume II.
"That Frank" (*Merrily We Roll Along*, 1985 revised production)
  Merrily We Roll Along. 1994. Revival cast recording; *Merrily We Roll Along*. 1994. London cast recording.
"That Old Piano Roll" (cut from *Follies*, 1971)
  Follies, The Complete Recording. 1998; *Unsung Sondheim*.
"There's Always a Woman" (cut from *Anyone Can Whistle*, 1964)
  Unsung Sondheim; *Anyone Can Whistle Live at Carnegie Hall*. 1995. Columbia CD: CK 67224.
"There's Something About a War" (cut from *A Funny Thing Happened on the Way to the Forum*, 1962)
  A Stephen Sondheim Evening; *Stephen Sondheim: The Story So Far*.
"They Ask Me Why I Believe in You" (*I Believe in You*, 1956)
  Unsung Sondheim; Peters, Bernadette. *Sondheim, Etc. Live at Carnegie Hall*. 1997. Angel EMI, CD: 55870; *Stephen Sondheim: The Story So Far*.
"This World" (*Candide*, 1974 revival)
  Candide. 1974. Revival cast recording; *Candide*. 1997. New Broadway cast.
"Three Wishes for Christmas" (cut from *Gypsy*, 1959)
  Gypsy: 2008 Revival; Anderson, D. C., *All is Calm, All is Bright*. 2001. LML CD-136.

"Truly Content" (*The World of Jules Feiffer*, 1962)
  Unsung Sondheim; *Sondheim Sings: Volume I*; *Stephen Sondheim: The Story So Far*.
"Two by Two" (cut from *Do I Hear a Waltz?*, 1964)
  Bennett, Tony. *Songs for the Jet Set*. 1997. Columbia CS-9143, 1(965); CBS/Sony CD 25DP-5320.
"Two Fairy Tales" (cut from *A Little Night Music*, 1973)
  Sondheim: A Musical Tribute; *Marry Me a Little*.
"The Two of You" (*Kukla, Fran and Ollie*, 1952)
  Unsung Sondheim; *Stephen Sondheim: The Story So Far*.
"Uptown Downtown" (cut from *Follies*, 1971)
  Follies: The Complete Recording. 1998; *Side by Side by Sondheim*. *Marry Me a Little*.
"Water Under the Bridge" (*Singing Out Loud*, 1992)
  Unsung Sondheim; *Stephen Sondheim: The Story So Far*.
"The Wedding Is Off" (cut from *Company*, 1970)
  Sondheim on Sondheim.
"A Weekend in the Country" (1976 film version of *A Little Night Music*
  A Little Night Music. 1978. Original Soundtrack. LP: Columbia JS 35333.
"We're Gonna Be All Right" (original version from *Do I Hear a Waltz?*, 1964)
  Sondheim: A Musical Tribute; *Side by Side by Sondheim*.
"What Can You Lose?" (*Dick Tracy*, 1990)
  Stephen Sondheim: The Story So Far; *Sondheim at the Movies*.
"When" (*Evening Primrose*, 1966)
  Stephen Sondheim: The Story So Far; *The Frogs/Evening Primrose*; *Sondheim at the Movies*; Patinkin, Mandy. *Dress Casual*.
"Who Could Be Blue"/"Little White House" (cut from *Follies*, 1971)
  Follies: The Complete Recording. 1998; *Marry Me a Little*. 1981.
"Who Needs Him" (cut from *Gypsy*, 1959)
  Gypsy: 2008 Revival.
"With So Little to Be Sure Of" (1st version), (*Anyone Can Whistle*, 1964)
  Original Broadway cast recording (2003 reissue).
"The World's Full of Girls/Boys" (cut from *Follies*, 1971)
  Stavisky (soundtrack 1975. sung in French), RCA Records LP: ARL1-0952; CD: (fills out second disc of *Follies in Concert*, 1985) RCD2-7128.
"Your Eyes Are Blue" (cut from *A Funny Thing Happened on the Way to the Forum*, 1962)
  Marry Me a Little. 1981; *Sondheim: A Musical Tribute*.
"You're Only as Old as You Look" (1955)
  Sondheim Sings: Volume II.

Index of Songs

Subject Index

outdoor presentation of, 278
out of town tryouts of, 77, 85
revival of, 68, 278
reworking and tightening of, 77
songs cut from, 73, 90, 98–9, 100–1
unproduced film version of, 105–8
Invitation to a March (Laurents), 417*n*
irony, 243–4
Israel, 384

"Jack and the Beanstalk," 58
Jackson, Andrew, 112
James, Henry, 17
Jazz Age, 84
Jean, Gloria, 408
Jeter, Michael, 109
Johansson, Ingemar, 384
Johnny Sunstormer's Trip to Hell (Apel), 424
Johnson, Jack, 183
Johnson, Rita, 408
Johnston, Alva, 179, 181, 183
Jones, Allan, 408
Jones, Jack, 408
Jones, Peter, 416
Jones, Richard, 278
Jorgenson, Christine, 385
Jung, Carl, 3, 58

Kaiser-Frazer Corporation, 384
Kander, John, 244
Kaufman, George S., 84, 424
Kay, Ida, 408
Kaye, Nora, 339
Keaton, Diane, 402, 403*n*
Kefauver, Estes, 384
Kelly, Gene, 350
Kelly, George, 408
Kelly, Moira, 109
Kelly, Walt, 384
Kennedy, Jacqueline, 138
Kennedy, John F., 113, 137–8
Kennedy Center, 156*n*, 182, 273
Kern, Jerome, 303
Kernan, David, 46
Kernochan, Sarah, 17, 69, 72
Kerr, Jean, 293
Kerr, Walter, 40, 293
Ketchel, Stanley, 201–2, 257, 260
Khrushchev, Nikita, 384
Kind, Richard, 252
King and I, The, 41
Klondike gold fields, 179, 195, 217
Klotz, Florence, 412*n*
Kukla, Fran and Ollie, 377

Lady in the Dark, 415
"Lady or the Tiger, The" (Stockton), 298
Lahti, Christine, 109
Lake, Veronica, 408
Lamour, Dorothy, 181, 408
Lane, Nathan, 182, 199, 213–14, 218, 222–3, 234
Lansbury, Angela, 146
Lapine, James, 2–7, 117
collaboration of SS and, 3–6, 8–11, 17, 20, 21, 32, 55, 57–8, 69, 71, 77, 85, 92, 102, 105, 145–7, 171, 175, 177, 217, 278, 323, 331, 332

as a director, 4, 146, 177, 278
Hal Prince compared with, 4–5
plays of, 3, 4, 17, 58
reserved personality of, 5
teaching of, 4
writing style of, 9–11
Last of Sheila, The (film), 339
Last Resorts, The, 293–6, 319
book of, 293
notion of, 293
Last Resorts, The (Amory), 293
Latin language, 3, 43
La Touche, John, xii, 308, 319, 320
Laurents, Arthur, 3, 386
collaboration of SS and, 4, 41, 319, 339
eightieth birthday of, 416–17
Lavin, Linda, 301
Lawrence, D. H., 177
Lawrence, Richard, 112
League of Nations, 181
Lear, Norman, 57–8
Lee, Eugene, 244
Lee, Peggy, 30, 397
Legendary Mizners, The (Johnston), 179, 181
Legrand, Michel, 303
Lehrstücke (Brecht), 310–11
Leiber, Jerry, 311, 318
Leigh, Carolyn, xiii, 309
Lerner, Alan Jay, xi, 51
Lester, Richard, 350
Levine, Doug, 413–14
Lexicon of Musical Invective (Slonimsky), 41
Library of Congress, 379
librettists, 4–5, 303
librettos, 84, 150, 293, 319
lighting, 157
instruments of, 40
Lincoln Center, 150, 318
Library for the Performing Arts at, 156
Lindbergh, Charles, 183
Lindsay, John V., 398–9
Little Me, 309
Little Night Music, A, 30, 43, 154, 435
film version of, 340, 350
theme and variations format of, 4
Little Rock, Ark., 384
Lloyd, Jamie, 156, 278
Loesser, Frank, xi, 27, 379
Lolita (Nabokov), 384
London, 3, 310*n*
Regents Park, 278
SS shows in, 30, 46, 68, 142, 156–7, 217, 274, 278, 377, 433
West End of, 46, 157
Long, Huey, 112
Look, Ma, I'm Dancin'!, 308
Lorne, Marion, 408
Los Angeles, Calif., 179
Louis-Dreyfus, Julia, 109
Love Life, 181
Love Me Tonight (film), 350
Love Parade, The (film), 350
Lowe, Rob, 109
Lubitsch, Ernst, 350
Luck, Pluck and Virtue (Lapine), 4*n*
Luhrmann, Baz, 350

lyrics
anachronistic, 199
anodyne, 308
archness in, 303
changing of, 43, 92, 285, 318
couplets as, 303
dialect, 307
dialogue-like, 6, 8, 11, 17, 150, 254, 365
diction of, 199
discarding of, 55, 308
double entendres in, 340
ethnic, 307
flow of, 308
fragmentary, 6
funny, 319
glibness of, 43
heightened language in, 17
improvement of, 55
irony in, 309
jokes and puns in, 89, 92, 226, 227, 349, 407, 418, 419
movie, 308, 309
nonrhyming, 309
opposing adjectives in, 308
patter, 303
poetic, 17, 303, 308
pop, 30, 149, 308, 309
proto-feminist, 309
sentimental, 309
sexual content in, 407
spoken, 71
stream-of-consciousness, 11, 17, 30
witty, 303, 319
lyric writing
cardinal sins of, 226*n*
celebrated practitioners of, xi–xiii, 303, 308–9
conversational, 150, 365
female practitioners of, 308, 309
music writing vs., 319
organization in, 11, 17
principles of, xv, 52–5, 227
rewards of, 111
in service of character and story, 303
style in, xv, 303

Macbeth (Shakespeare), 278
MacGrath, Leueen, 84
Mackintosh, Cameron, 46, 417–18
MacLachlan, Kyle, 109
Madden, Mary Ann, 338
Mad magazine, 301
Madonna, 341
Mad Show, The, 301–2
Madwoman of Chaillot, The, 303
Mahagonny, 310–11
Make a Wish, 308
Maltby, Richard, Jr., 273
Mamoulian, Rouben, 350
Mandel, Babaloo, 105
Mansfield, Jane, 384
Manson, Charles, 130
Mantello, Joe, 278
Man Who Came to Dinner, The (Kaufman and Hart), 50
Marshall, Brenda, 408
Martin, Hugh, xii, 308–9
Martin, Millicent, 46
Martin, Steve, 109
Mary Poppins books, 422

Pirandello, Luigi, 129
"pizazz," 309
play doctors, 299–300, 301–2, 304–7
plays, 3–4, 57, 273
   one-act, 84, 274, 297
   preservation of, 156–7
   reinterpretation of, 278
   revival of, 156–7, 278
   television, 378
   three-act, 84
   two-act, 84
   "well-made," 4, 84
Playwrights Horizons, 5, 12, 48, 117,
   142
Pleasures and Palaces, 27
Poe, Edgar Allan, 145
Pogo, 384
Poiret, Jean, 373
Pollock, Lucille, 3
pop-rock, 327
popular culture, 303
popular music, 146, 307, 403, 427
   lyrics of, 30, 149, 308, 309, 345
Porgy and Bess (Gershwin/Heyward/
   Gershwin), 146, 223, 298, 303
Porter, Cole, xii, 117, 309, 340, 424n,
   425–7
Poseuses, Les (Seurat), 17
Pray by Blecht, A, 310–18, 320
   abandonment of, 318
   book of, 310
   notion of, 310
   problems with, 311, 318
Preisser, June, 408
Presley, Elvis, 363
Preston, Robert, 309
Prince, Hal, 40n, 146, 274, 278, 411–14
   collaboration of SS and, 5, 243–4,
     250, 260, 269, 270, 271, 319, 320,
     349
   fiftieth birthday of, 411–13
   James Lapine compared with, 4–5
   mercurial personality of, 5
   opera direction of, 5
   producing by, 219, 293, 308, 320
   sixty-fifth birthday of, 413–14
Prince, Judy, 412n
Princess Bride, The (film), 350
"Princess" shows of 1915–18, 303
Princess Theatre, 303
Princeton Triangle Club, 426
Princip, Gavrilo, 112
producers, 4, 50, 57–8, 223, 409n
   corporate, 278
production numbers, 84
Public Theater, 182, 273, 274
Puccini, Giacomo, 146
Pulitzer Prize, 50, 51
Putting It Together, 46–7

Quinn, Patrick, 182

Race to Urga, The, 318
radio, 409
   soap opera on, 378
Rainger, Ralph, 308
Rainmaker, The (Nash), 395
rap music, 309
Ratcliffe, Michael, 30
Ravel, Maurice, 41
Ray, James Earl, 112

Reagan, Ronald, 131
recitative, 6, 254
Reds (film), 341, 402–4
Reed, John "Jack," 403–4
Reiner, Rob, 350, 372
Reinhardt, Max, 5
Resnais, Alain, 403
revivals, 319–22
   creative casting of, 278
   drawbacks of, 278
   reevaluation of works in, 278
   of Shakespeare plays, 279
   of SS shows, 142, 156–7, 175, 217,
     278, 291
revues, 85, 111–13, 293, 303, 320,
   332–5, 377
   industrial, 380
rhymes, 111, 150, 162, 226n, 377
   false, 30, 43, 314n, 400
   lack of, 365
   of long words, 11
   "masculine," 308
   near-rhymes, 11
   pileup of, 309
   three-syllable, 308
   trick, 314n
rhythm, xv, 17, 120, 149, 162
   film editing and, 350
   square, 244
   train sounds in, 309
   waltz, 254
Rich, Frank, 293
Richard III (Shakespeare), 278
Rimbaud, Arthur, 145
"Road" movies, 181, 408
Road Show, 182, 223, 234, 241, 260,
   261, 272–91, 359
   absence of scene delineations in, 279,
     282, 285
   direction of, 273–4, 278, 279, 282,
     285, 291
   dismissive public and critical
     response to, 291
   elimination of leading lady in, 273
   Mizner brothers chronicle as basis of,
     273, 279, 281
   notion of, 273
   one-act format of, 274, 285
   problems with, 273–4
   Public Theater reading of, 273
   recording of, 117, 182n
   stage directions eliminated in, 274
Road to Bali (film), 181
Road to Morocco (film), 181
Road to Singapore (film), 181
Robbins, Jerome, 218–19, 310–11,
   318, 319
   choreography of, 339
   musical staging of, 4
Robin, Leo, xii, 308
Robinson, Hubbell, 387
Rockne, Knute, 183
rock 'n' roll, 146, 244
Rodgers, Mary, xii, 298, 299, 301,
   409–11, 421
Rodgers, Richard, xi, 41, 117, 297,
   386, 410
Rodgers and Hammerstein, 40, 65,
   77, 84
Rodgers and Hart, 297
Rogers, Elena, 156

Rogers, Ginger, 363
Ronde, La (Schnitzler), 58
Roosevelt, Franklin D., 120, 125
Roosevelt, Theodore, 112, 125, 183
Ross, Herbert, 339–40, 350
Roundabout Theatre Company, 142
Rubirosa, Porfirio Ariza, 384
Rudin, Scott, 234
Russell, Rosalind, 421
Russian Revolution, 341, 402–3

Sagan, Françoise, 384
Saint Joan (Shaw), 408
St. Louis Woman, 308
Saki, 387
Same Time Next Year (Mulligan), 409n
satire, 243, 297
Saturday Night, 293, 419, 433
Scapligliatura movement, 145
Schaeffer, Eric, 273–4, 291n
Schary, Dore, 408
Schnitzler, Arthur, 58
Schrank, John, 112, 125
Schwab's Pharmacy, 400n
Schwartz, Arthur, 303
Scola, Ettore, 145, 175, 177
Scott, Lizabeth, 408
Scrabble, 384
screenplays, 337, 350
Sea Around Us, The (Carson), 384
Segal, Vivienne, 387
Sentimental Guy, A, 181
Seurat, Georges, 3, 4, 11, 17, 21, 32,
   120, 217, 278
7 1/2 Cents (Bissell), 293
Seven Percent Solution, The (film),
   339–40
Seven Percent Solution, The (Meyer), 339
Shakespeare, William, 134, 278, 303
Sheader, Tim, 278
Sheen, Archbishop Fulton J., 384
Sheridan, Ann, 408
Sherrin, Ned, 46
Sherwood, Robert E., 84
Shevelove, Burt, xi, 146
   collaboration of SS and, 4, 58,
     380, 385
Shire, David, 273
Short, Martin, 109
Show Boat, 303
Sicilian underworld, 193
Side By Side By Sondheim
   Broadway production of, 377
   Chicago production of, 377
   London production of, 46, 377
   revue format of, 377
Sidney, Sylvia, 408
Siegel, Larry, 301
Signature Theatre, 273
Silvers, Phil, 308, 384
Sinatra, Frank, 30, 396
Singer, Paris, 207, 229–34, 239
Singing Out Loud (film), 199, 350–72
   derivation of, 350–1
   notion of, 350
   screenplay of, 350
Sirhan Sirhan, 112
Sirmay, Albert, 425
Sleuth (Shaffer), 409n
Slonimsky, Nicolas, 41
Smith College, 427

Illustration Credits

Catherine Ashmore: 67, 71, 94–95, 103, 290

Peter Cunningham: x, xvi

Barbara de Wilde: 272

Donmar Warehouse Theater: 143

Dover Publications ©1992 Donald W. Curl: 240–241

Gerry Goodstein: 6

Hal Leonard Publishing Corp.: 342

John Good Holbrook, LTD: 169, 170 (top)

James M. Kelly/Globe Photos: 332

Liz Lauren: 252, 255

Joan Marcus: 112, 129, 147, 150, 155, 161, 164, 275, 279, 286, 289

New York Times: 177

Paramount Pictures: 390 (top left), 398 (bottom)

Johan Persson: 170 (bottom)

Playbill, Inc. Used by permission. All rights reserved: vi

Stephen Sondheim: xiv, 2, 9, 10, 13, 14, 28–29, 53, 54, 56, 74, 78, 80, 93, 104, 110, 116, 118, 122–124, 126, 128, 132–133, 139–140, 144, 153, 159–160, 163, 168, 180, 188–189, 214, 216, 219, 224, 242, 246–247, 277, 280, 283, 295, 296, 298, 302, 305, 306, 313, 317, 318, 324–326, 334, 338, 340, 344, 346–348, 352, 355, 366, 371, 375, 379, 383, 384, 387, 389, 390 (top right; bottom left), 391, 393–397, 398 (top), 401, 406, 407, 411, 416–418, 421–425

Martha Swope: 5, 8, 20, 24, 34–35, 55, 60, 76, 83, 107, 108, 113, 119, 131, 137

Touchstone Pictures: 336 (top left), 345

Michael Le Poer Trench: 96

United Artists: 336 (bottom left), 373, 375

Universal Pictures: 336 (top right)

John Peter Weiss: 75

A Note About the Author

Stephen Sondheim wrote the music and lyrics for *A Funny Thing Happened on the Way to the Forum* (1962), *Anyone Can Whistle* (1964), *Company* (1970), *Follies* (1971), *A Little Night Music* (1973), *The Frogs* (1974), *Pacific Overtures* (1976), *Sweeney Todd, The Demon Barber of Fleet Street* (1979), *Merrily We Roll Along* (1981), *Sunday in the Park with George* (1984), *Into the Woods* (1987), *Assassins* (1991), *Passion* (1994), *Bounce* (2003) and *Road Show* (2008), as well as lyrics for *West Side Story* (1957), *Gypsy* (1959), *Do I Hear a Waltz?* (1964) and additional lyrics for *Candide* (1974). *Side by Side by Sondheim* (1976), *Marry Me a Little* (1980), *You're Gonna Love Tomorrow* (1983), *Putting It Together* (1993, 1999), *Moving On* (2000) and *Sondheim on Sondheim* (2010) are anthologies of his work as composer and lyricist. For films, he composed the scores of *Stavisky* (1974) and co-composed *Reds* (1981) as well as songs for *Dick Tracy* (1990). He also wrote the songs for the television production *Evening Primrose* (1966), co-authored the film *The Last of Sheila* (1973) and the play *Getting Away with Murder* (1996) and provided incidental music for the plays *The Girls of Summer* (1956), *Invitation to a March* (1960), *Twigs* (1971) and *The Enclave* (1973). *Saturday Night* (1954), his first professional musical, finally had its New York premiere in 1999. He has received the Tony Award for Best Original Score (Music/Lyrics) for *Company, Follies, A Little Night Music, Into the Woods* and *Passion,* all of which won the New York Drama Critics' Circle Award for Best Musical, as did *Pacific Overtures* and *Sunday in the Park with George.* In total, his works have accumulated more than sixty individual and collaborative Tony Awards. "Sooner or Later" from the film *Dick Tracy* won the Academy Award for Best Song. Mr. Sondheim received the Pulitzer Prize for Drama in 1985 for *Sunday in the Park with George.*

In 1983 he was elected to the American Academy of Arts and Letters, which awarded him the Gold Medal in Music in 2006. In 1990 he was appointed the first Visiting Professor of Contemporary Theatre at Oxford University and was the recipient of the Kennedy Center Honors in 1993. Mr. Sondheim is on the council of the Dramatists Guild of America, the national association of playwrights, composers and lyricists, having served as its president from 1973 to 1981. In 1981 he founded Young Playwrights, Inc., to develop and promote the work of American playwrights aged eighteen years and younger.

A Note on the Type

The text of this book was set in Berkeley Oldstyle, a typeface designed by Tony Stan based on a face originally developed by Frederick Goudy in 1938 for the University of California Press at Berkeley.

Composed by North Market Street Graphics, Lancaster, Pennylvania

Printed and bound by Quad/Graphics, Taunton, Massachusetts

Designed by Iris Weinstein